CARLYLE
TO THREESCORE-AND-TEN

MR. WILSON'S LIFE OF CARLYLE

VOL. I. CARLYLE TILL MARRIAGE (1795–1826)

VOL. II. CARLYLE TO "THE FRENCH REVOLUTION"
(1826–37)

VOL. III. CARLYLE ON CROMWELL AND OTHERS
(1837–48)

VOL. IV. CARLYLE AT HIS ZENITH (1848–53)

VOL. V. CARLYLE TO THREESCORE-AND-TEN
(1853–65)

Concluding Volume to follow.

Plate I

VOLTAIRE

(*From a painting by Largilliere*)

CARLYLE

TO THREESCORE-AND-TEN

(1853—1865)

BY

DAVID ALEC WILSON

LONDON
KEGAN PAUL, TRENCH, TRUBNER & CO., LTD.
NEW YORK: E. P. DUTTON & CO., INC.
1929

3989

Printed in Great Britain at
The Mayflower Press, Plymouth. William Brendon & Son, Ltd.

PREFACE

THIS is the fifth volume of a Life of Thomas Carlyle, and comes down to 1865. It is needless to repeat the acknowledgments and thanks in the Prefaces to preceding volumes : *Carlyle till Marriage,* 1923 ; *Carlyle to " The French Revolution,"* 1924 ; *Carlyle on Cromwell and Others,* 1925 ; and fourthly, *Carlyle at his Zenith,* 1927. This volume is *Carlyle to Threescore-and-ten ;* and the sixth and last is to be called *Carlyle in Old Age.*

There is an important addition to be now made to previous acknowledgments. After the publication of the fourth volume, the Marquess of Northampton supplied and allowed me to use all the letters written by Carlyle or Mrs. Carlyle to his grandfather, William Bingham Baring, the second Lord Ashburton, and to Harriet Baring, Lady Ashburton, the first wife of his grandfather, and to Louisa, Lady Ashburton, the second wife. These letters, unreserved and confidential, have been the pleasantest reading which any of this work has given me, and readers are sure to share my gratitude. It is a pity one cannot do more than say, thank you ; one feels so much more than these words usually mean.

For help in correcting the proofs, I am obliged to the same three old friends who did *Carlyle at his Zenith* : James Tennant, Samuel Scott, and Robert W. Carson ; and for the Index to my friend David E. Edward, the Librarian of Ayr town.

In December, 1928, Miss Carlyle Aitken of Dumfries presented to the National Library of Scotland in Edinburgh many hundreds of letters written by her uncle, Thomas

Carlyle, to his mother and others. Many of these had been already quoted or published by Messrs. J. A. Froude and A. Carlyle, and Prof. C. E. Norton, but all of them are interesting to a biographer ; and it is to be remembered that if Miss Carlyle Aitken had let them be sold by auction, she would have got many thousands of pounds. They are to be permanently kept for reference, and by the kindness of the Librarian, Dr. W. K. Dickson, I was enabled to read them all without delay. My best thanks are due to him and to his assistants, Dr. H. W. Meikle and Joseph Davidson. There is much quoted from these letters in the present volume, and there will be more in the next. Perhaps the day may come when copies of them, type-written or printed, will be in many public libraries, in many countries besides our own, for Carlyle was one of the right sort of great men who are without an effort Citizens of the World.

There seems to be something appropriate in the gift of his private letters to the National Library, when we recall the old name of the Library, " The Advocates' Library " : for Carlyle has gratefully told how, in his early years of difficulty, " The Advocates' Library was my principal or almost sole literary resource—lasting thanks to *it*, alone of Scottish institutions."

AYR, 1*st January*, 1929.

NOTICE.—*Free permission is given to publish translations of this book.*

CONTENTS

BOOK XXII

WRITING *FREDERICK*

CONTENTS

BOOK XXIV

THE PASSING SHOW

CONTENTS

BOOK XXV

FINISHING THE *FREDERICK*

LIST OF ILLUSTRATIONS

BOOK XXI
AT HISTORY AGAIN
1842-54

B

I

THE BARINGS AND MANY OTHERS
(1842–47)

IT seems to have been at the Sterling Club meetings in
1838 that Carlyle became acquainted with William
Bingham Baring, and perhaps it was in 1839 that he saw his
friend's wife for the first time, presiding at the dinner-table.
She was curious to hear the conversation of Carlyle, because
of what she had heard Charles Buller saying about him.
Baring himself was older than Buller, and only between
three and four years younger than Carlyle, and had long been
prominent in both business and politics,—one of " Peel's
men." By 1839 he had been sixteen years married to the
Lady Harriet,—a Montagu by birth, a daughter of Lord
Sandwich,—and they had lost their only child. She was
consoling herself by the social gaieties and glories that
were easily at her command,—a big and strong, good-
humoured woman, who could keep her sorrows to herself,
and continued to be, as she well deserved to be, the petted
wife of one of the richest men in England.[1]

By birth and marriage she was one of the leading ladies
of English society,—" on the whole," says Greville,[2] " the
most conspicuous woman in the Society of the present day."
Her husband's father, the first Lord Ashburton, was the
Baring who ' transacted the sale of Louisiana to the United
States,' and had a hand in ' the conclusion,' after Waterloo,
' of the long continental war ' ; and ' when, in the course
of events, she became the head of the family,' in 1848, ' she
was at once able,' according to " Dicky " Milnes, Lord
Houghton,[1] a reporter, sure to be right in such a case, ' not
only to sustain the social repute of the former generation,
but to stamp it with a special distinction . . .' by ' her

---

[1] *Monographs*, by R. M. Milnes, Lord Houghton, pp. 225–255.
[2] *The Greville Memoirs*, by C. C. F. Greville, 1896 Edition, Vol. VIII,
p. 109.

3

own singular talent . . . I do not know how I can better describe this faculty than as the fullest and freest exercise of an intellectual gaiety, that presented the most agreeable and amusing pictures in few and varied words ; making high comedy out of daily life, and relieving sound sense and serious observation with imaginative contrasts and delicate surprises.'

Milnes quotes with equal approval a French remark,— that "it was worth while to let yourself go to hear that woman chat," and the pathetic complaint of one of the merry lady's victims, " I do not mind being knocked down, but I can't stand being danced upon afterwards." ' It was in truth,' said Milnes, ' a joyous sincerity that no convention-alities, high or low, could restrain—a festive nature flowering through the artificial soil of elevated life. There could be no better guarantee of these qualities than the constant friendship between Lady Ashburton and Mr. Carlyle—on her part one of filial respect and duteous admiration. The frequent presence of the great moralist of itself gave to the life of Bath House and the Grange a reality that made the most ordinary worldly component parts of it more human and worthy than elsewhere. " Ask me to meet your printers," was the often-quoted speech of a lady of fashion.' An echo of the ripple of her laughter, one might say, can sometimes be heard, ' with the mind's ear,' in Carlyle's *Frederick*, which is one of the most amusing of our books, as well as one of the wisest.

Most of the letters she or her husband or her successor ever received from Carlyle were piously preserved. Here is the earliest remaining.—

' Chelsea, 9 *August*, 1842.

' MY DEAR MADAM,

    ' Tho I have not yet had the honour to receive your letter, which I shall be very proud of when it comes, yet knowing from Mr. Baring what its purport is, I make all haste to answer.

    ' Surely no visit whatever could give me greater pleasure than one to Addiscombe farm ; in company with the Taylors whom I like well,—or with, or without, whomso-ever *you* might please to like. Unluckily, however, I have just been voyaging with Mrs. Taylor's Brothers, to Belgium and back again,—with many sensations, enjoyments, and alas with *next to no sleep ;* and those jumbling Sea-waves, and those strange pepper-box Cathedrals, and other exotic phenomena are still keeping up such a Saturnalia in my head and heart that I am by no means equal to the enterprise at present ! I hope you pity me ; I do at least pity myself.

' Perhaps this first is not the last Note you will ever write to my poor address ? In that case, if you can so much as remember " Chelsea," the Penny Postman will at once do his duty.

' Will Mr. Baring please to accept my compliments and regrets.

> ' I remain always,
>> ' My dear Madam,
>>> ' Yours with great regard,
>>>> ' T. CARLYLE.'

This is the only " My dear Madam " among these letters. There are a few that start,—" Dear Lady Harriet," or " My dear Lady," &c., and a few more,—" Dear Lord Ashburton," but the commonest beginning is without any such formal words, as in this one of 11.7.1845.—

' I could not see you. They tell me you are not well too. The Housemaid said you were better ; but did not seem to know much about it. Why will you dine at 7 o'clock, and waste yourself with the frivolities of this generation ? Are you of no value to anyone, then !—I wish we were all safe at Alverstoke, reading German, or sitting silent ; far from all noise that had no meaning in it. I wish you were well again at least !—My wife returned in much satisfaction with Addiscombe and her visit . . . You will come and see us here when you come back,—will you not ? . . .

' Good night. The old Chelsea clock is striking midnight : the Sun is right under our feet, and wet winds are blustering,—and the quantity of insane confusion in this World is very great. Shall we ever have wings, think you ? *Ach Gott!*—I send you blessings as ever, and the best good night.

> ' *Ewig.*' (=Yours always)
>> ' T. C.'

On 4.11.1845 he explained the *Bayeux Tapestry.*— ' William the Conqueror's Wife, while her husband was conquering England, set about *sewing* the history of that affair ; and there it actually yet is, tho somewhat worn now ; laid carefully up in the Cathedral of Bayeux in Normandy ; an immense web of ancient sampler-work, divided into scenes and compartments, which used to go round the whole Nave of the Cathedral when exhibited on some Anniversary day. One of the strangest Historical Monuments in this world . . .'

On 16.12.1846 Carlyle was reporting how his wife had been confined to her room with a cold for three weeks, and he added : ' Yesterday and the day before I spent wholly in nailing down *listing*, in pasting up crevices ; in making a Summer temperature for the poor Patient ' to be her ' refuge while the cold lasts.'

Lady Harriet seems to have been advised by Carlyle to read Goethe, &c., and on 9.1.1847, he was writing to her : ' To-day I will leave a *Cicero's Letters and Life ;* which you are welcome to keep forever if you like it. The translation is English ; Middleton's ; by far the best, I believe, in any modern language. If you prefer a French one, tell me . . . I see hardly anybody this long while ; read nothing but *Acta Sanctorum,* (old Monk Legends and Chronicles) . . . their platitude, bottomless but *sincere,* is a little less disgusting to me than that of most modern Books.'

Carlyle was so afflicted by the contemporary famine in Ireland that he was intently studying the how and the why of it, and for that purpose he was trying to see all that books could show of Irish history from the beginning. Thus on 11.1.1847 he was writing to the Lady Harriet :

' I have nailed up a map of Ireland on the wall here ; and to-day am busy with St. Patrick's Purgatory and the Ancient Annals of that Country. Once a week also I have to read an Irish Newspaper. There never was, surely, under the Sun such a spectacle as that wretched Island now exhibits ! The Land, it seems to me inevitable, will all or nearly all be confiscated ; the whole frame of Society is not unlike tumbling to pieces. The Potato breaking down, all manner of Impostures tumble rapidly together ; and Nature, very audibly indeed, declares to that People,— " Wretched People, unless you can find more sense and faithfulness among you, you shall not any longer subsist on the Earth ! Your Impostor Aristocracy shall go and beg, your Impostor Populace shall starve to death : of *you* at last the World shall be quit ! " Is not this an awful Prophecy to terminate with ? '

Again on 24.3.1847, replying to her letter and a clipping

from a French newspaper she had sent him, he wrote to her without reserve : ' I feel disgusted with my trade (which has been a supreme blessing to me, too) ; disgusted with the whole pack of miserable rope-dancers who follow it in our day :—and the times also are getting too *swift* for Books ; I think often we are perhaps on the edge of great and terrible times.' (It may be needful to remind some readers that next year, 1848, was the year of many revolutions, when royalties went running from many places. They and their ministers had failed to read as Carlyle did the ' signs of the times,' and so were taken by surprise. Carlyle was impatient of official blindness at home, and the delay in relief measures and agrarian reform in Ireland, and went on.—) ' All Reform-Bills are a small matter to this of the Potato, if it continue dead ! And I would fain speak out the whole mind of me before I die. Shall I set up a Weekly Newspaper? Shall I squeeze into Parlt. itself, and there speak *Pamphlets*, hot, and hot, right from the heart,—and burn up the World-Humbug ? '

It was not possible. Members of Parliament were then unpaid and elections costly. The afflicted Irish people had to help themselves, and many deaths by starvation and countless confusions and strife were the consequence, and by and by the Irish Free State.

On 3.11.1847 Carlyle was describing in confidence to the Lady Harriet a man still interesting.—' Emerson went on Friday night last, but I was torn to pieces talking with him ; for his sad Yankee rule seemed to be, that talk should go on incessantly except when sleep interrupted it : a frightful rule . . . A pure-minded elevated man ; *elevated*, but without *breadth*, as a willow is, as a reed is ; no fruit at all to be gathered from him. A delicate, but thin pinched triangular face, no jaws nor lips, lean hook-nose ; face of a Cock : by none such was the Thames ever burnt ! A proud man too ; a certain sensitive fastidious *stickishness*, which reminded me of a miniature Washington's ; very exotic, tho Anglo-Saxon enough ; rather curious to think of. No getting into any intimacy with him, talk as you will. You have my leave to fall in love with him if you can ! . . . I wish him honestly well, do as I am bound, respect him honestly ; but *Friends*, it is clear, we can never in this World, to any real purpose, be.' This cannot be understood aright without realizing what Carlyle meant by friendship, as explained in Sartor, Book II, and near the end of Chapter III ; and the letters that continued to pass between Carlyle and Emerson seem to show more real friendship than Carlyle anticipated when writing now. In the common sense of the word, they were the best of friends.

On 6.11.1847 Carlyle was telling Lady Harriet about the best of her ancestors. ' I find, by indisputable traces, the first Earl of Sandwich was Captain in Oliver's *Ironsides*. Raised the " St. Neot's Troop " while hardly yet eighteen, and fought in it ; a brave young Ironside, beautiful to see ! And against his father's will too, I rather apprehend. There is a man for you,—before the Ages of Cant *began*. By God's blessing they shall end yet ; and Hudson and Albert, and the Bp. of Oxford, and Lord John, and the British Parliament and the Thirty-nine Articles, and whole troops of Phantasms shall go and not return ! ' In letters immediately following he calls her more than once " the Daughter of an Ironside," and once declares,—" Daughter of an Ironside, I am a kind of Ironside yet,—fallen also on base times ! "

II

THE SUBTERRANEAN LIFE OF CARLYLE
(1848)

FROM about the time when Carlyle by his book on the Letters and Speeches cleared the character of Cromwell, he began to receive many letters of thanks and appeals for sympathy or advice. This went on till the end of his life. His patience in responding was great, and his discretion perfect. He never spoke of such things at all; but the letters elicited from him were piously preserved, and here is one, a sample of many hundreds.

Julia Tosswill, whose ' pet name ' was May, had been born in 1827, and so she would be about twenty-one when she wrote to Carlyle in 1848. What made her do so, she afterwards explained,[1] was that she had for some time been ' devouring everything of Carlyle's that I could obtain, and at last I could no longer refrain from letting him know my gratitude for the new world of thought, which he had opened out to me.' So in short she made a ' bookmarker with the motto " Ernst ist das Leben," and sent it ' to him, ' pleading that as he had taught me Hero-worship, he would excuse my enthusiasm.

' Words can hardly describe my delight when I received the following most characteristic reply :

" Chelsea,

9th June, 1848.

" DEAR MISS MAY,

" You have sent me a beautiful Bookmarker, and a beautiful expression of your youthful regard : both of which I accept with thanks. Yours is the season of admiration, and generous young gratitude, wise and lasting, or transient and unwise. Much of it will die away in you as you grow older, but much also I hope will continue. For

---

[1] In an essay, ' Some Old Letters,' never published.

the quantity of wise admiration, that remains with us, measures accurately our wealth in this world.

" Be happy in your pleasant leafy Reigate,—which I once rode thro', on a summer morning, such as this may be, seven years ago, and shall remember now with new interest for your little innocent sake :—read my poor books till you have learned all I have to say to you, and continue to love me a little so long as you can.

" I remain,

" Yours with many kind wishes,

" T. CARLYLE." '

In 1851 May or Julia Tosswill became Mrs. Hodgson, but still continued the same " May." There are seven of her children still surviving.[2]

How well Carlyle assisted Sir C. Gavan Duffy socially by his steady support of him in those " distressful " times has been abundantly told by Sir Charles himself. Here is a bit of a letter to Lady Ashburton, dated 4.11.1848,—the Bingham Barings had become Lord and Lady Ashburton in that year.

' If you ever write to Lord Clarendon, will you sometime remind him that he must *not*, in any wise, send Duffy (were he once convicted) into the herd of common Felons ; that in fact nobody in the least believes the *Irish* rumour of his meaning to do so. I wrote to him, last week, a long letter on the subject ; but forbade any answer. Duffy's attempt at escape, they say, was grounded on this frightful surmise, which is currently rumoured in Dublin, tho I do not believe in it at all. A certain fact is, that Duffy is intrinsically no " felon," more than I am ; but on the contrary a good and even genial man, and, so far as I can judge, distinctly the best of that sad company he has got into. Here is the Note from him, which gave rise to that letter to Lord Cn. ;—but please do not shew that to any one except Lord Ashn., for it is of a shrill exasperated nature, and does the poor man no justice, exhibiting him in a mixed mood of panic and rage, *unjust* both of them, tho not inexcusable.'

Then follows something about William Maccall, which one hesitates to quote even now when all concerned have

---

[2] 1928. One of her children, Mrs. Hugh Verrall, Chalgrave, Harlequin Lane, Crowborough, deserves the thanks of readers for sending a copy of her mother's essay for our use.

been dead long ago. It is typical of the main subterranean side of Carlyle's life, which has been almost completely concealed.[3]

He lived according to the maxim,—' when thou doest alms, let not thy left hand know what thy right hand doeth.' Here is an instance of him begging money for a deserving man, and it may suffice to add that he begged successfully.

' The *Individuality of the Individual*, a book by Maccall, will not do much for you : nevertheless read it, that you may know the Man again on occasion. A poor Scotch Calvinist Preacher, who fled into Socinianism and England ; preached there, in various places, various ever *lighter* tones of that poor doctrine, till at length (as you see) it has flatly quitted him altogether ; and he is here now, these two years, trying, with the frightfullest prospects, to work out some independent basis for himself. A Man really of considerable faculty ; brave enough ; cheerful too, tho with a large fund of spleen in him : poor Soul, if I were a miniature *Providence* in this World, I would not quite see him strangled yet for a while ! Did *you* never think of that divine function ? It well beseems the powerful everywhere ; it is the summary of all that could beseem them at present ! Perhaps I shall speak to you of that some day ;—and you will listen, according to ability ? Soup-kitchens, charities, &c. &c., are not the way ; but there is and must be a way,— and it is worth finding, for the like of *you*.'

Lady Harriet and her husband were quick to meet Carlyle's suggestions about both Maccall and Gavan Duffy, and must have replied to him soon, for on 24.11.1848 he was writing to her again, sending her a translation of Seneca she wanted :—' A respectable grey old book, in legible print, with dim old yellow calf-binding ; has *prints* too, woodcuts of certain of the Virtues, &c., to assist the infant comprehension. Surely we shall get some seeds of morality sown in you at last ; and that strong soil will not always run to waste ! . . .

' Jane is quite well again ; I suppose she will answer your letter soon. Yesterday she went a second time to Lady Sandwich's ; to whom she seems to take, which I am very glad of. Her report was pretty good of the poor Patient, to whom company and cheerful conversation are, as you say, the chief remedies that avail. Jane found her quite lively, and very entertaining, especially after they had got

[3] See *Carlyle at His Zenith*, pp. 65–67, 372, 467–471.

under way a little, and brought the fuel into flame.' This Lady Sandwich was the mother of Lady Harriet, and Mrs. Carlyle and she were soon good friends for life.

'. . . *Individuality of the Individual*' (William Maccall), 'poor creature, has got some teaching (by Jane's good luck), to keep him alive . . .

' I found in *Sadi* a couplet which I must send you further-more, for your sins . . .

" Tell me, O wise man, how hast thou come to know so astonishingly much ? "

" By never being ashamed *to ask* of those that know ! " There ; what do you think of that ? If there is no tear in your eye, at reading of this and recollecting much sin that is past, I do not see the use of sending you *Seneca*.

' Duffy and his crimes you shall describe to me when we meet. I have myself noticed symptoms of a certain stratum of Irish *ambiguity* in some sections of his character ; different from what I ever observed in Mitchel ; but worse than the others, I cannot imagine him ; and at any rate the thing resolved upon respecting him seems *right*, and that is sufficient.' It is pleasant to add that juries refused to convict Gavan Duffy, so that Lord Clarendon had at last to let him go. The letter concludes :

' You are riding on Muff, enjoying the bright shore, I hope, at this moment. Adieu, dear Friend. To-day I cannot see you, but some other day (if it please God) I shall ; and good will betide us, after all, and not evil, if we be ourselves good ! Farewell, dear Lady.

' T. C.'

III

CHARLES BULLER, MACAULAY S HISTORY, &c.
(1848-50)

A FEW days later Carlyle was writing to Lady Ashburton about the death of Charles Buller:

'Chelsea, 29 Novr. 1848.

'Alas, alas, what sad tragedy is this,—the saddest, I think, that ever befell among friends of mine! "Five minutes to six"; about the very moment I awoke, this morning, with the thought of him painfully blazing in me. And it was all over. And we shall never see that blithe face more; for the rest of our pilgrimage, never more!

'That Monday you went away, the last time I saw him, he was unusually cheerful; spoke of his operation for the morrow as a thing of no significance, like the mere drawing of a tooth or less; and invited me to come and talk with him "next Wednesday."—I privately believe, it is the *chloroform* that has done it:—but, alas, of what moment is that now?

'To all of us his death is a sore loss; not to any living creature, I think, could it seem a *gain :* for his presence was cheering and beneficent to all, and hurtful and afflictive to none that lived. But to you, dear friend,—alas, it is a loss which I fear none of us can ever repair! In his own form he was by far the brightest Soul in your circle; or indeed in all the World, that I knew of . . . For himself it is perhaps happy . . . The Eternal Power has willed it *so*.

'I do not forbid you to weep. Nature will have its due . . . But . . . for us it is appointed still to *live*; and Destiny is striking us with an iron hammer on our hearts to say, "Remember to live well!" That is the one way of conquering grief. All pious thoughts be near you, dear Lady.

'It was soon after nine when our Messenger returned,

13

this morning ; my wife went off directly after to attend
poor Mrs. Buller. What in the World will become of that
poor bereaved old Mother, already at the point of death !
Her calmness yesterday, Jane said, was almost frightful.

'Lady Sandwich . . . I saw yesterday . . . I was to
" report her better " . . .

'God be merciful to us all. We ought to be *silent ;* and
accept, with pious submission,—with profitable thought,
unknown in these times,—whatever bitter cup is sent us.
May God bless you evermore, dear Lady, and make *all*
turn to *good* for you ! That is the prayer of those still left.

'T. C.'

Meanwhile from Mrs. Buller's house Mrs. Carlyle was
writing :—' Oh Lady Ashburton, what a horrible thing !
I can hardly yet believe it. I am here with his poor old
Mother, but what can mortal do or say ? She is still in the
fever of sleeplessness and excitement and looks *stronger*
than you ever saw her, but she is wishing every minute
that it may kill her, and I doubt not it will . . . She thinks
her Son knew her at the last, but Mrs. Richard is not sure
he was aware of her presence ; only (that) he said while
she was in the room,—" dear old Mother." '

Mrs. Buller did not live long afterwards.

The next letter is dated 29.1.1849, and reports that
Carlyle was ' revising *Oliver Cromwell* for a third edition . . .
It is an operation analogous to *darning of Stockings* on the
great scale ; with which kind of employment, if Conscience
would let one alone, I could do very well ;—but Conscience
will not ; Conscience barks and snarls unutterable things.—
A certain blockhead is for bringing Louis Blanc to me too !
" Le gamin philosophe." ' It does not appear who had so
described Louis Blanc. Carlyle liked him well.[1]

' Yesterday in the Park, Miss Farrar, with much difficulty
as she said (so unobservant was I), hailed me from a brougham ; it drove to the footpath, and I hurried up : Lady
Sandwich too was within ' (mother of Lady Ashburton) :
' " What in the World *were* you thinking about ? " said her
Ladyship ;—I would not have told for sixpence ; answered
in general, " The Universe and the Chaos under it," which
also was the truth so far. Lady S. very well . . .

' Macaulay is over, several nights ago,' i.e. I have finished
reading the first two volumes of his history just published.

[1] See *Carlyle at His Zenith*, p. 87.

' I was, if anything, a little disappointed ; little of the
Book, except that Chapter on the old state of England,
quite equal even to one's hopes of Macaulay. Pleasant
easy reading too ; clear, definite, every corner of it ; but
without concentration, modulation, a formless *flat*,—flat
like a Russian Steppe ; pleasant grass to gallop on, but
without stream, without mountain, without feature, grass,
grass to the uttermost horizon : in fine, *no story* to be told,
and nothing but a *Whig Evangelist* to tell it us ! I was not
sorry to end ; and shall not burn to begin again ! The true
" History of England," so far as England has a *History* in
those scandalous years, will turn out to be very brief (I
apprehend), and to lie leagues below all that,—where T. My.,
I perceive, will never find it or seek it.—Did man ever
look at such a series of empty *clockcases* as these " characters "
one and all are ? *This* is *not* their likeness, I say ; why
take their likeness at all ! ' . . .

It should be noted that this applies only to the first two
volumes of Macaulay's History, which was all that was
published then. In the three volumes still to come, there
is better reading than the chapter Carlyle liked in the first.
The siege of Londonderry is not only what Macaulay calls
it,—" the most memorable in the annals of the British Isles,"
—it is also one of the best described. The battle of the
Boyne, in Macaulay's History, needs only a few good maps,
such as Carlyle gives, to be as well told as any of the *Frederick*
battles ; and it is much more interesting to Englishmen.
Only it must be added that, if the fighting in the ' Frederick '
had been told at such length as the siege of Londonderry,
sixty volumes might not have sufficed for what Carlyle compressed into six.

In the next letter to Lord Ashburton, 6.2.1849, Carlyle
began by thanking him for a box of cigars, and dealt with the
cashing of a remittance from Emerson, and the Commission
on the British Museum Library. He sent for Ashburton's
amusement a letter from the man Squire, who was then
producing new letters of Oliver Cromwell. Carlyle had
decided to keep Squire at a safe distance,—' Oliver Cromwell's character remaining precisely what it was, whether
Squire be real or be imaginary . . . Alas, the *stupidity*
(want of *truth*, and therefore of the *sense* for truth) of human
creatures generally in England, at this time, fatally mani-
fests itself in all provinces of their existence,—from the
Poddle's drains,' (a sewer in Dublin), ' to the Bishop of

Dogbolt, Murphy's Almanac, Macaulay's History, and the Queen upon the Throne ! ' . . . Maybe it needs to be told that, like the illustrious Halifax of our Glorious Revolution, Carlyle was a republican in his private thoughts.

A letter of 18.1.1850 is to excuse himself from an immediate visit to the Grange, the Ashburtons' country house in Hampshire, as he was occupied with the proofs of the first of the Latter-day Pamphlets. But ' in the course of next week ' he hoped to ' have really done ' with it. He told Lady Ashburton that there were more to follow,—' sure to shock and enrage great quantities of people, for I really cannot manage to dress my talk at present, and besides there *is* no dressing of it on such a set of topics ! Pity me : at any rate the thing is now no secret, and you may speak of it as you like.'

When the first Pamphlet was finished, he might get away to the Grange,—' I fancy a week of your Park might do me good too. I will still hope and try my very best.

' We are nearly all frozen to death. Bitter tempest of North wind for two days . . . now wet snow and mud. I walked to Fulham one of these tempestuous days ; the Bishop's place looked very tattery ; the iron sky, and old Father Thames tumbling along with his ice-cargo, in the howl of the winds, were goodish company for a fellow like me.

' Oh Lady, dear Lady, adieu. And unless you are very strong keep out of this rude weather. Ever yours,

' T. CARLYLE.'

He went to the Grange, but only for a few days,[2] returning on 1.2.50 to resume writing his Pamphlets, which absorbed him till August. There is a letter of 14.5.50 excusing himself again. On 23.8.50 he wrote to tell where he was to rusticate and give his address for letters, ' Scotsbrig, Ecclefechan, N.B.' This letter unconsciously shows us how completely Mrs. Carlyle had conquered his hankering for a quiet life in the country. He seems to be forgetting that it was *her* doing that they were dwelling amid London soot and noises.—

' Dear Lady, I am in the agonies of packing ; and cannot go without a word (whh. might be a moan or howl, so sad is it !) of farewell to you,—of indication to you whither I am bound. I am in the vague a little as to your whereabouts in these current days : but I have to fancy it as at the

---

[2] See *Carlyle at His Zenith*, p. 244.

Grange ; I will hope it may be there. You will be better lodged there than you were this time twelvemonth, blowing, with bellows, a fire of wet peats at Glen Truin ! Why should one so wander in this World, which is itself such a wanderer ? It seems to me, if I had such a house as the Grange, I wd. try to get my implements about me, and steadfastly proceed with my trade there ; stationary as if I *were* chained like the old Ram,—in fact, constituting myself a " chained Ram " ; refusing to be like unto a wheel any more ! Alas, alas, we cannot manage it. Rest is not appointed to the Son of Adam ; we must go our journeys, we shall get to rest, and plenty of it, by and by. How often have I thot. here, were I in one of the Cottages of your Park (say a Gate-Keeper's Cottage, with some dumb and nearly deaf old Woman to look after me an hour each day), how much happier cd. I be among the Hampshire Trees ! And then the next thot. is, thou hast already a Cottage of thy own, two Cottages, a Town one at Chelsea (made very habitable by a dextrous hand), and a country one among the Nithsdale Moors ; and in neither of them canst *thou* abide,—O Censor of the World ! Well, well ; the World, it seems, is full of possibilities, which can never become actualities ; we see such every hour of the day : let us be peaceable then ; and go our rounds at least without kicking ! '

Let us pity the poor happy hen-pecked husband ! Maybe no man ever sacrificed more than Carlyle his own inclinations to the whims of his wife. But after all he was not peculiar,—like other men, only more so. In these monogamous days it is hopeless to expect from any woman the magnanimous complaisance of sweet Ruth, or of the blessed Rachel, the dearest of Jacob's wives.

IV

'HARMLESS READING'
(1850–51)

AFTER finishing the Latter-Day Pamphlets, writing on 14.9.1850 and dating from Scotsbrig, Carlyle was advising Lord Ashburton who had consulted him about a poor poet in need of help.—' A small gift of money, from such a place as The Grange, might properly enough be ventured on him ;—and if there were any delicate way of bestowing it (which I suppose there is not) *except* as pre-payment for a Copy of his Poems, it wd. be a second good deed to discourage him from farther attempts in that career. Poor Soul, he is a fellow creature, struggling, as we all do, in the midst of darkness, to better himself and get into clearer regions :—and so I will leave him to your tender mercies.'

Then followed congratulations on the success of ' her Ladyship's grand-to-do . . . For myself I am at present the weariest, or probably it should be the laziest, of all her Majesty's Subjects. Never in my life did I feel such a passion for lying still at any price . . . Nature herself perhaps prescribes this medicine to me. I sit, with some harmless reading or sometimes without any, plunged into convenient scraggy bushes, under shade of wild trees, " by melodious waterfalls," or at least clear-rushing Scotch *burns ;* and look out into the Universe in the truest way-worn manner. " To sit is better than to stand," say the red Indian Sages ; " to sleep is better than to wake ;—to be dead is best of all ! " It is to be hoped I shall rouse me by and by . . .

' My Lady sent me a bag of Hampshire thistle-down, the other day ;—intending probably that I should sow it here in Annandale ? Alas, alas, I find we have plenty here already ; no want of thistle-down in these parts either !

Tell her Ladyship that I will repay the compt. (perhaps in kind) before long.   And so Adieu for this evg.

' Yours ever truly,

' T. CARLYLE.'

On 2.11.1850 Carlyle wrote to Lady Ashburton and incidentally told what he had been doing.—

' All this while I have been doing literally *Nothing* : idle reading (chiefly in the *Annual Register*, old Nos. of it, which I recommend to you also, on occasion), idle musing, a vigorous " consumption of my own smoke," and for the rest *silence* as much as possible, have been my occupation since I left your Woods . . . I felt myself sometimes the most utterly lonely Man I ever read of in these ages.   The wild roar of Sophocles's *Philoctetes* (which also I have been reading) seems to me the dialect I could a little express myself in ; but it is better not.   On the whole perhaps I am not *quite* lonely either,—am I ?   " A stiff upper lip to it always," as the Yankees say.

' Kinglake came to us one night ; (Erasmus) Darwin also was there.   I like Kinglake . . . as compared with most . . . a hard Man, but always means something by what he says ;—a *feline* element in him too, I fear :—but even a genuine *felis* ' (or cat) ' is something ! '

Ten days later (12.11.1850), Carlyle was excusing himself from visiting them at Brighton, and sending a *Sophocles* by post, some French or English translation,—presumably his mention of the *Philoctetes* had made her curious.   As for his own occupations, he had to report :—' Of writing there is yet no definite outlook or project.   But I must *write ;* it is my one way of expressing all the imprisoned existence of me ; a miserable outlet and " way," as I often passionately reflect ; but it is and has been my sole one ; let me not spill that too, and go mad altogether.

' Well, here is the Note from Cobden, in reply to mine about his School Agitation.   Will neither you nor Lord A. join in that " Reform Movement," the one Reform conceivable to me now that Peel is gone ?   A certain " Mr. Lombe of Norfolk " has given £500.

' Adieu my noblest friend.   God bless you always.

' T. C.'

Two days later, 14.11.1850, he was explaining to Lady Ashburton the delay in arrival of the book (*Sophocles*) which he had sent.—' The clerks at St. Martin's ' (General Post-Office) ' have confiscated it,—found pencil-marks (annotations of mine), what they call " writing " in it ;—and now there is a negotiation going on,' which doubtless came to a satisfactory end.

Confessing he was ' *not well*,' he moralised :—' What fools are modern Moralists, compared to our rude Fathers. *Holy* in old days was *Healthy*, as you have heard me often say : *Gott der Heilige* equivalent to " God the *Healthy* " ;— fie upon this vile canting putrid era of the World ; over-loaded with such scandalous *Old Clothes*, pestiferous and choking, from the Hebrew and other quarters.

' T. C.'

Two days later, 16.11.1850, Carlyle was writing to Lord Ashburton about a " German Map " the Ashburtons wanted, and which he had left with their London housekeeper to be sent on with other books, and also about a Thomson's *Suetonius* which he was getting for them. On the same day he received a letter from Lord Ashburton announcing that the Lady was down with influenza, and enquiring how he was, and he replied at once, 16.11.1850.—' I am exceedingly concerned to hear of her Ladyship's sad condition :—not roaming along the downs, under the bright bracing air ; but lying imprisoned under Influenza and mere silent misery ! To-day too there is new frost, and of a vile damp character withal ; which I fear is no favourable circumstance in that complaint. Pray keep the doctor to his duty ;—and let us hear at least how matters go.

' I will straightway set about getting you a *Suetonius* in English or French ;—so that you may read the blackguard History of those ancient Blackguards : a *sin*, if it be one, to which human nature is prone ! Nay, by management, it is capable of being a virtue too. But the general rule is, " Poke not into carrion, for you will get mischief of it ; let all carrion, classical or other, get underground as soon as possible, and stay there ! "

' I am utterly alone here. I can yet work at nothing ;— only sit, like a Siberian Bear in Winter time, empty enough of pabulum or outlooks, and for the present contemplatively sucking his paws . . . But tell the lady to get well again, and not lie like a prisoner there : and keep well yourself,— and wish me well.'

In the next letter to Lady Ashburton, 21.11.1850, there is a glimpse of Carlyle reading '*Ménagiana at nights*, a curious old book (which) shews me extinct generations of Theologians, Savants, Beaux-Esprits, so many Nublés, Naudés, Benserades, Bois-Roberts,—once flowery leafy brilliancies and verdancies, gone all to black peat now : the universal lot of things, " As we are now, so you shall be," and only the soul of you and your work (if you or it had any Soul) can hope to endure.'

A letter of 26.4.1851 was to acknowledge invitations to two " At Homes " in May, and mentioned he might have a ten minutes' talk with the Duke of Argyll about ' Iona, the isle of St. Colm,' which belonged to the Duke. ' John Mill, did you see in the Times, is wedded to his widow Taylor ; a fact in biography : poor good Mill ! He has not announced it to anybody.' He told of a ' long pleasant walk in Kensington Gardens, walking like Adam under the Trees and the young budding Spring and azure old Eternities, —Oh Heaven,—avoiding carefully that monstrous Beehive of the Wind-dust-ry of all Nations ' being built for the Exhibition this year, the building transmuted now into the Crystal Palace.

A short letter of 19.6.1851 is merely to praise a ball Lady Ashburton had been giving, and to promise a short afternoon call, and two longer letters of 11 and 13.9.1851 are partly concerned about their impending visit to Paris and partly current news. That of 11.9.1851 begins thus quaintly, dating from Scotsbrig :—' Dear Lady, May I address a word to you from this beautiful Suburb of Creation, where, in the bright Autumn weather, in the great silence, I am often enough thinking of you.' He told of the visit to Malvern to try the water-cure for his dyspepsia. On 13.9.1851 he was reflecting on it thus :—' How strange since (as Dr. Gully says) we are made almost altogether of *water* (hardly a 20th part of us solid matter, and that mostly *lime, magnesia,* and the like) that human creatures should be so important to one another ! But, in all ways, whether of water or not, we are fearfully and wonderfully made. And some of us are very well made too ; and are inexpressibly beautiful and good,—and were made in Heaven, the essence of them, I do believe.'

As to whether he was the better of the treatment, it was too soon to say. ' Any way, I am glad to have this " Water-cure " *done,* since it was a thing to do. As poor Lord

Melbourne liked when a poet *died*, for then, said he, " You get all his books on your shelf and have finished with him . . ." '

' Pray give my real regards to Lady Sandwich ' at Paris,— she was the mother of Lady Ashburton, which explains what follows.—' Oh, be good to her ! You will find no other altogether like her in this World. And a day will come, a sad day, when all your tolerances will be great possessions to you.'

The next letter, 27.10.1851, was from Chelsea, and apparently to let her see she was *not* being forgotten,—as she seems to have said she feared that she was. ' My last Book was an old heavy *Life of Captain Cook*, by a Dr. Kippis ; rather an abridgt. of Cook's *Voyages* than any perceptible account of his life, which must however have been a remarkable one, could any glimpse of it be got. Clearly a braver Man than is made above four or five times in a generation. There is much in the Book about your great-grandfather,' then Lord of the Admiralty. ' I dare say there must be Letters of Cook, for one thing, still at Hinchinbrook ? . . . If you can remember when you go to Alverstoke, will you ask Croker if there is any descendant of Cook now alive that he knows of, and if so, what or where ? Let us turn the unfortunate Croker to this account (as even from Badgers one can make excellt. shaving brushes) ; and keep it in mind for me when we meet.'

V

ABOUT FREDERICK, &c.
(1851-52)

ON 14.11.1851 Carlyle was writing to Lady Ashburton, and after much fatherly advice and kind enquiries remarked :—' In late days I have taken to reading a most heavy but minute and accurate German History of Frederic the Great ; a task I have had before me these several years. Which, alas, does not hitherto profit according to hope. But I must finish the Five Volumes nevertheless. Frederic, the more I know of him, pleases me the better ; a Man and King whose love of *reality* was instinctive and supreme : that is his distinction among Men,—and truly it is one of the greatest and royallest, especially in days like ours. I find him the last of all our " Kings " ; and with some prophecy in him too of being the *first* of our coming Kings : the details poor Preuss (my dull Historian) gives me of his faithful incredible indefatigable toil in " governing " Prussia, and making it great and *free* (free of the Devil, I mean) are worthy of perpetual remembrance. I had long since some thot. of writing a Book about Frederic ; and if I were a Prussian I still should, as *my* poor homage due from me to such a Soul : but being English,—I had much rather have an English hero, if it pleased Panizzi and Company,— which, alas, it does not do, nor can do ! I find Panizzi '— the preposterous Panizzi mismanaging the British Museum library, and already known to us,—' the true representative of English dilettantism, Pedantry, Babblement, and hollow dining and drinking Nonsense of so-called " Literature " in this epoch ; and therefore I have forgiven, or endeavoured to forgive, the poor Man, fatal to me as he and the like of him have been and are.

' Kossuth still perorates . . . Senior with his young Woman came one day ; no refusing to go and dine, and so the other night it was fulfilled. Cameron there (Husband of the *Mrs.* Cn.), Painter Laurence, Crawford (of *Sterling's Life*) ; a passabler evening than was hoped. Cameron has snow-white hair, a sleek small red face, lively little black eyes, and no *chin* to speak of ; seems to be of Scotch breed or birth : may the Heavens be good to him, poor little fellow ! Senior, sage-dull tho he is, rather shines as a landlord . . .'

The same day when he wrote that letter of 14.11.1851, Lady Ashburton was writing, inviting the Carlyles to a long stay at their country house, and on 17.11.1851 he had to confess,—' Jane surprised me last night by saying she *had* written to you, accepting for us both ! I was obliged to *deny*, on the spur of the moment, that I wished to go, or could go,' and will write again ; but when he did write, five days later, 22.11.1851, it was to say he would go. Incidentally in that letter he praised Twisleton, and wished ' good luck ' to a book he was writing ' in aid of the Manchester Secular School people . . . Twisleton is the only Official Man in whom I find clear continual evidence of a human conscience being left. Falsity, injustice and contemptibility will actually kindle rage in him as in a human creature ! He may be useful yet, if Ld. John were fairly off for ever.

' I stand steadily by dull Preuss and *Frederick the Great :* one of the dullest Books of this era, and one of the greatest men.'

By the date of the next letter, 11.12.1851, Mrs. Carlyle was already at The Grange and Carlyle was to follow ' the day after to-morrow.' This letter seems to have been in reply to enquiries about a man soliciting help.—' The unfortunate creature seems to be very clearly, if not a swindler (which I do not think), a lazy vagabond lout who has got into the way of living by *beggary ;* in which course there is not the least reason why you should aid or confirm him : let him take her Majesty's bounty, and apply to the Drill-Serjeant since he cannot guide his own steps better ! Such " pathos," unattended by proper veritable exertion, on the part of a stout young fellow, a yard across the shoulders, and weighing sixteen stone avoirdupois, is not pretty but disgusting.

' I have had ten days of a *silence*—equal to that of Jonah in the Whale's Belly,' which may be a humourous reference to his wife's absence.

' Yours ever,

' T. C.'

The next letter to Lady Ashburton is dated 10.1.1852, and shows Carlyle at home and reading Jomini on War. A week later, 17.1.1852, he is returning to her (Nassau William) ' Senior's letter,' which had given details of Napoleon's *coup d'état* of 2.12.1851, with the remark :—' This poor Opera-King is in deadly earnest, it would seem . . . Weak, vain-glorious, somewhat despicable France finds itself suddenly caught as in a universal rat-trap ; which is a bad destiny indeed ; but I must say, the ratcatcher, the job, and the rats are all worthy of one another.'

On 10.2.1852 Carlyle was again thanking her for a letter, and in the course of chit-chat news he calls Lord John Russell, then leading the House of Commons, ' the ninth part of a tailor . . . No more despised " English Govt.," I do believe, ever darkened the light of the Sun.' That was a general opinion then. A letter of six days later, 16.2.1852, shows Carlyle embarked on his Frederick work. According to many good critics, the real hero of the *History of Frederick the Great* he was now to begin is Voltaire, and Frederick's performances are merely an illustration of the efficiency reached by applying Voltaire's matter-of-fact methods to business. Assuredly the reign of Frederick is little but a frame, so to speak, for the wonderful moving picture presented in the history, and Voltaire appears as the spiritual father of the hero. Meanwhile what Carlyle wrote on 16.2.1852 was :—' I continue reading about *Frédéric ;* ordering Maps, running after books, &c., to see what I am to order. The thing seems to myself very idle : what have I, here where I am, to say about the " lean drill-serjeant of the World " ? I do not even grow to love him better : a really mediocre intellect, a hard withered Soul ; great only in his invincible courage, in his constant unconscious loyalty to truth and fact : the last and only *King* I know of in Europe since Cromwell :—*should* we, or should we not, leave him to Mahon and Company ? On the whole, I will lay out a few pounds upon him ; and read a little further, so long as it continues amusing to me.'

VI

AT HOME AND ABROAD
(1852)

THE next letter of Carlyle to Lady Ashburton, 28.2.1852, shows him busy reading '*nine* volumes on the *Teutonic Knights*, which shd. and could easily have been distilled into half a volume.' By this time Lord John Russell had been supplanted in the leadership of the Commons by Disraeli, which seemed to Carlyle 'a terrible finger on the wall,' referring to the Book of Daniel.[1] 'To be governed by imbecile Lords is a fate long since appointed us by the wisdom of our Ancestors and the immortal Gods ; imbecile Lords fall on us from the sky like rain and influenza ; but here have we been raging and reforming, all the World battling and screaming since 1789 for some *new* era ; and the new era with its ballot boxes brings us—a pinchbeck Hebrew, almost professedly a son of Belial (skilled to make the worse appear the better reason, and to vend new-dyed old-clothes and varnished falsities in a profitable manner) . . .'

On 5.3.1852 he was acknowledging receipt of a 'Huc' she had sent him, presumably an excellent French book by E. R. Huc, a French missionary and traveller, who made his way over the desert of Gobi and China to Lhassa in Thibet. 'But I have not yet got a word of it read, I keep Huc for a holiday. *Frederick* still moves,—but only on its axis, I fear ; of *advance* in any direction there is no symptom hitherto ! And awful masses of reading and enquiring lie between me and any such result. And then what good is in it ? Holding my peace, I shall have a much quieter life, and might get tobacco and necessaries all the same ! Sometimes I think of going over to Germany for a year ; which truly if my enterprise continued might be very needful.'

Describing his rides near Addiscombe he defended himself

[1] Chapter V.

26

against her charge (in her letter under reply, it seems) of being *a misanthrope*. ' No, I am even a kind of *philanthrope*, but find it so dreadfully difficult to manage any real philanthropism. That is the secret of it, if you will believe me.'

The rest of the letter was full of kind fatherly admonitions about her health, warning her about the need of taking care in mounting a particular horse, with hopes that Lord Ashburton might come to town now that Parliament was to meet, and news of the weather.—' The weather here is venomously cold, night and morning ; but I hope and believe you have,' meaning at the Grange, ' less of that frozen fog in which the Sun so often drowns himself here : in the course of the day we too get bright skies, and the whole World promises to become young for us one other time. Singular old World : how it steadily swings round the Sun these many millions of years ; and what nonsense it often carries on the back of it,—making no complaint ; steadily keeping its time, whoever be behind ! '

A letter to Lord Ashburton of 26.5.1852 mentions his own health, and adjures him to ' take good care of yourself in the middle of the tumults ' of social entertainments, the Derby, &c., in bad weather, and concludes :—' There are now 250 Candidates for the London Library ! ' Meaning the Librarianship. ' A Sub-committee is to sift them down ; —and in the end, it is too plain, there must be at least 249 disappointments.'

On 21.7.1852 he was telling Lady Ashburton, ' We have got all your Notes.' She and Lord Ashburton were on the continent and Lord Ashburton had been ill. Carlyle was sympathetic and gave a favourable opinion of the doctor they seem to have named.

From Scotsbrig he was writing on 12.8.1852, just before his first trip to Germany, where the Ashburtons then were. His wife had bidden him go without her,—she preferred to superintend the workmen making alterations in their house in Cheyne Row. He confessed to being still uncertain,— ' Whether to go to Germany straightway ; or to give up *Frederick* and *it* (whh. really would not be difficult) for ever and a day ? That is the question.'

The next letter to Lady Ashburton was from Bonn, 6.9.1852.—' Your letter lay waiting me here . . . I have been, and still am, as you predicted, dreadfully off for sleep ; otherwise well, and the Country and River pleasant to me, and the people all good. Jane was to be with you yesterday at Addiscombe '—which shows the Ashburtons were now home. A letter from them to Carlyle was awaiting him at Frankfurt, and on 17.9.1852, ' Friday evg.,' he was writing from Cassel.—

' This day week at Coblentz we turned aside to Bad-Ems ; a beautiful drive up the Lahn, and a strange if not a beautiful place,—like a bit of the *Rue de Rivoli* or *Palais Royal* put into the throat of the Trossachs,—amusing to look at for three days. I tasted the water,—like *boiled* Selzer ;— listened to the music ; looked at the Nondescripts of Mankind there wrestling agt. ennui, dancing, gambling in *Kursaals*, and feeding sadly at *Tables-d'hôte :* I had some Books from Bonn Library to read withal, and finished most of them ; on Sunday Afternoon we drove to Nassau, and visited, not without interest, the Stammburg' (or ancestral castle) ' of the Orange Heroes, the birthplace of William the Silent . . . I was very glad to see it. We got to Frankfurt by rail on Monday night, a city I had often wished to see, and now did at last see when I could as well have dispensed with it. Alas, looking out next morning, a *known* face startled me among the trees of the Square : Goethe's face, I saw well, but it was *in stone,*—in *such* manner had my old wishes been fulfilled for me ! As is not quite unusual in this World.

' That same evening we got out to Homburg, and at Homburg I did stay 3 nights and 2 days ; left it this morning, and surely shall not soon forget it. A similar set of mortals, or of human occupations, I had hardly imagined to myself before. My only real pleasure (tho the *sight* of the place and its ways surpassed all Foote's Farces) was the hour last night with the Augustenburgs,' Duke and Duchess and family, ' who took me to their House and were extremely kind and human to me,—for *your* sake again as I reflected, whh. did not make the favour less agreeable to me. Poor old Wellington, I had heard that evg. he was dead ! Farewell to him, the farewell due to Heroes.—In the old Homburg Schloss (thanks to you for mentioning it) I had found, the day before, a great many things to interest me ; excellt. Portraits, Marlbro, Gustavus, " Great Elector " (Fr.'s Great Grandfather), Queen Christina, Czar Peter, &c. &c. The woods, as you predicted, offered excellent driving,— to walk I was too weak ; but a lean horse, drosky, and pony man with a leather soup plate on his head, supplied the defect ; and even told us about the War in Holstein, where *he* had served, witht. distinction . . .'

Dating Berlin, 1.10.52, where he was to stay a week, he mentioned ' I have been in the Wartburg, where Luther lived as *Junker Ganz*, and worked at translating the Bible : his old room is still there unchanged, his old oak table, the very floor he walked upon ; the window he looked out of (into sheer Abysses, over lonely Mountains, into uncertainties, immensities and eternities),—poor old fellow : I felt that there was not probably on the Earth a more truly *sacred* spot than that same ; and I did my worship (being in a *sleepless* excited condition) with great fervour there. We were next in Gotha ; and then—three days in Weimar itself. Schiller's old writing-table,' (of which there was a copy at the Grange), ' is still there ; his little poor harpsichord beside it, poor bed where he died, picture of his face when dead : that room also is rather memorable to me. Goethe's House was opened by favour ; nay the reigning powers (seeing us in the Newspapers) invited poor Neuberg and me to dinner ; and we went in spite of my " shocking bad hat " (a dusty wide-awake, whh. I hid dextrously below stairs). The " reigning Duchess," a sister of the Czar Emperor Nicholas, is a woman worth seeing,—highly polite and gracious, tho unluckily a little deaf, and cold as polished steel : poor female-soul, her Husband is a big gentlemanly-looking man, who does his parade-drawing-room duty with conscientious perfection, but is otherwise considered imbecile ; with him in this limited histrionic scene, has the Sister of Czar Nicholas had to lead her tragic fact of an existence, and make no complaint about it : she has small blue eyes, the *hardest* I ever looked into, a weak unmusical voice, a *circular* profile (receding chin and brow), a tall thin figure . . . At length we got away ; but on the whole, Weimar, with its silent stagnation from all real business, with its solemn inanities and dilettantisms, with its very Goethe threatening to become a bigger Lytton Bulwer,—O Heaven what a tragedy was that of Goethe to me, of such a Man driven thither for such a life ! Weimar, I say, is still a puzzle, and a kind of nightmare, in my imagination !—After Weimar came Leipzig Fair,' and then Dresden and " Saxon Switzerland " and Bohemia,—' the Ireland of Germany,' and Frankfurt on Oder, &c. &c.

Writing again on 7.10.1852, he praised as ' a handsome lively street ' the Berlin street where he was, " Under the

Lime-trees," saying that it 'resembles, tho afar off, *two* Edinburgh Princes Streets set to front one another'; but he joyfully added that this day's sight-seeing was the last he would have to do, so that he would soon be home. Prof. Magnus, '" the best portrait-painter in the World," say the Berliners,' was to show him that day Charlottenburg and Spandau; and thanks to Magnus and two other painters, Rauch and Cornelius, he was soon able to make sure of having seen all that German Art had done for Frederick's features.

To this time belongs a sample of Mrs. Carlyle's genius for making trifles interesting. In 1861 she was replying[2] to Lady Sandwich's questions about curtains, which they supposed that Carlyle would need for his bed. 'When I read your question to him the answer was, " Pooh! I can make myself curtains in two minutes, tell Lady Sandwich." " How? " I asked, thinking the secret worth any house-wife's knowing. " Why, easily, with a clothes-horse and my plaid. It was an expedient that suggested itself to me on my first visit to Germany, and I went all over Germany on the strength of it." . . . So the *curtains* need be no " worritting " thought,' concluded Mrs. Carlyle.

[2] One of the MSS. presented to the National Library of Scotland by Miss Carlyle Aitken, in 1928.

VII

THACKERAY'S "ESMOND," &c.
(1852–53)

THE next letter was dated Chelsea, 10.11.1852. He described his work at that time as ' " Annihilating Rubbish," . . . and with a New Assistant, a gentleman named Old Age, looking in upon me ; courteously informing me that *he* will help, for the future, more and more.'

Maybe in reply to curious questions about the new novel *Esmond*, he said :—' We have gone thro Thackeray's Novel ; my wife first, with great admiration " for the fine delineations of women " ; I next, with aversion and contempt mainly for his feline phantasms of " women," with many reflections on his singular fineness of sense and singular want of do.,—and on the whole with fairly more esteem for this Book than seemed likely at The Grange. I find the " style," both of painting and writing, worthy of peculiar recognition, in general quite excellt. for clearness, simplicity and grace,—and here and there with a fine *adagio* of affectionate sentimentality, which is almost beautiful, almost pious. Poor Thackeray, God help him, and us, after all ! Adieu, dear Lady, announce to us your advent to town, when you are coming . . .'

A letter of 21.12.1852 dealt with the topics of the day, and praised her for doing good.—' Be merry, be happy in your work of rural bounty ; and may many an old poor Soul, and many a hopeful simple young one, be filled with thanks and pleasure by your means. It is one of the opportunities these evil times do offer the like of you ; and it is well and beautiful that you make the most of it.'

On 30.12.1852 he was sending Lady Ashburton some information about the William Maccall he had been telling her about, and whom it seems the Ashburtons were helping. But what is best worth quoting is not apropos Maccall but things in general.—' Let us take all things with *piety ;* be impatient, be disloyal about nothing that *can* happen ! I always think there must be good lying in wait at the end of all actions and endeavours that are *good*, on the part of mortal creatures, and it is my fixed orthodox creed even, that we simply get out of all things the good (accurately measured, weighed in the *Eternal* balance, difft. very from our *temporary* one !) which we ourselves have put into it : this, in looking back upon my own old years, and general past life, is often solemnly made manifest to me. We will *despair* of nothing.'

On 19.1.1853 he was telling his sister Jean, Mrs. Aitken, that *Uncle Tom's Cabin* ' seemed a pretty perfect sample of Yankee-Governess Romance.' [1]

On 16.2.1853 he was describing to Lady Ashburton the editor of a British Quarterly he was getting for her. ' " Dr. Vaughan " is Lord Carlisle's favourite Dissenting Preacher ; was once a Playactor (and is so essentially still, under other conditions and in much fataller form), a windy unsound blockhead,—tho, I suppose, he sometimes stumbles on a man of talent to write for him, too. We have sunshine to-day ; after new snow, and new frost. Spring is struggling on, in spite of obstacles, as usual. My respects to Sambo, and to all the rooks with their faces to the sunset. Adieu, dear Lady ; good be ever with you.—T. C.'

On 28.2.1853 the Rev. W. H. Brookfield entered in his diary[2] that in coming away with the Carlyles from a ' rout' at the house of Monckton Milnes, he told them ' the schoolboy's fable :

' " There was once on a time a fox that fell into a well. A rabbit came and looked at him over the well side. Moral. This should teach us to beware of foxes." Carlyle laughed as much as I ever saw him do at anything, and said it was the profoundest piece of moral instruction he had ever heard.' The schoolboy was exhibiting as fine morals the lowest of all our animal instincts—to turn against anyone in misfortune.

On 3.3.1853 Carlyle was writing to Lord Ashburton, and assured him that the Austrians were not going to catch Mazzini at Milan, as they hoped to do. The immediate occasion of that letter, however, was to thank him for getting Carlyle elected a member of the Athenæum Club, with all the fees paid for life.—' I know not what to say. Certainly there are munificent Souls still extant in this World ; certainly here is one of the handsomest acts done in the handsomest manner ! You have really given me a very pretty Freehold for the rest of my life ; and in a way that cannot be refused,—that can only be accepted, with a feeling which is itself a real possession to one. I do return many thanks ; and will not speak another word. It is

---

[1] MSS. Letter.
[2] *Mrs. Brookfield and Her Circle*, by C. and F. Brookfield, II, p. 390.

Plate II

HARRIET, LADY ASHBURTON
(*From an engraving by F. Holl*)

[*face p. 32*

certain, except for this or some such miracle, I should
never have been a member of any Club.'

A letter of 18.5.1853 begins ' Dear Foreign Lady,' because
the Ashburtons were on the continent, Lord Ashburton
being ill and his wife attending him. ' Do you really mean
to snap your tether, then, and " go to the South " for good ?
You mustn't : " the effectual fervent prayers " of a few
righteous persons, or even of one, will plead for monstrous
England (poor luckless Caliban of an England that it is),
and prevail with the Powers and you.' He gave news about
his wife and many others, and reporting about himself he
said :—' Alas, it was on a bright Mayday like this (I reflected yesterday, the look of the sky suggesting it) that I
went trotting down by the side of my Father, to enter
Annan Academy, that balmy morning about forty years
ago. Said balmy morning, still present to me like *this*
morning, *whither is it gone ?* Said little boy, *where* is he ?
Neither of them are discoverable now ; their locality has grown
inscrutably *unknown ;*—and all romance is a poor froth or
flummery in comparison with the *fact* to each of us, if *we* were
not flummery ourselves, and incapable of thinking on facts.'

In a letter of 8.6.1853 he mentions how he had been
solicited ' to do a Life of Ld. Hastings (Moira) from " the
family papers " &c. Alas, it could not answer to me at all,
at all ! If the great Duke ' (of Wellington) ' were proposed,
I might pause, and ask what terms ? But the Lord Charles
Grandison Moira '—which hits off Moira to perfection. What
Carlyle was actually doing, at the time of writing, was
' *making an index* to the Fritz correspondence, &c., one
of the saddest drudgeries an African could be set to in such '
(hot) ' weather. What is ever to become of this *Fritz*, the
Gods only know.'

He mentions also ' our old friend (W. H.) Sleeman ; whom
you remember ? ' as sending him a pamphlet on Indian
children stolen by wolves. This is the same genial W. H.
Sleeman whose ' Rambles and Recollections of an Indian
Official ' is a readable and truthful description of India
just before the Mutiny. What a loss it has been to English
history that Wellington was not proposed to Carlyle !

He wrote again next day (9.6.1853), to send on a letter
from Clough, and one remark about Clough's young woman
may be quoted for the benefit of her sex :—' His little
Damsel, if she want a clever Man, must not insist on his
being a rich one too : she actually is not weight for that.

D

VIII

LAST LETTER TO REDWOOD
(1853)

THROUGH the summer and autumn of 1853 Carlyle
was minded to remain at home. Even when invited
by the " honest attorney " Charles Redwood, " more like
an angel than a Welshman," he answered :[1]—

'Chelsea, *5th August*, 1853.

'DEAR REDWOOD,

'I got your letter this morning and was very glad
to hear of you at first hand again, and very much obliged,
indeed, by your ever kind purpose towards me. Alas,
there is no Wales, no rural fields at all for me this year. I
got so thoroughly smashed to pieces last season by my
roaming up and down the world, that I privately resolved
to stay close at home . . . for at least one year. My wife
has been in Scotland ; returned four days ago ; we are now
to stay in the silent town, which really, when once the
quality is all out of it, becomes a very eligible place for
carrying on study in. So stands it. I shall still have to
build one other apartment in this place, a top storey extending over the whole house, with double walls (of a sort),
lighted from above, and with internal means of ventilation,
so we may be deaf to all conceivable street noises, and may
at least have the privilege of sleeping, and of reading,
thinking, living in absolute " divine silence " henceforth !
I have a plan for such a thing, and certainly it would be a
glorious conquest to me. My poor enterprise on Frederick
is the most impossible, of all I have ever buckled with in
this world, and cannot and will not come to the least success
with me. I have given up all thoughts of succeeding, my

---

[1] *Carlyle's Holidays in Wales*, by John Howells, in the ' *Red Dragon*,
the National Magazine of Wales,' Cardiff, April–June, 1884.

one trembling hope is that of some day finishing . . . and the writing part of it is still to begin !

' Adieu, dear Redwood. Do not forget me, nor will I you.

' T. CARLYLE.'

Before the time came for another invitation, Charles Redwood died.

A SOUVENIR OF FEATHER PENS
(1853)

ON 15.8.1853 Carlyle was writing to his sister Jean in Dumfries, Mrs. Aitken, what may remind us how recently steel pens came into fashion.—' A certain John Chorley (once a gentleman of mark in the Railway world and elsewhere ; at present, a retired philosopher, tho still young ; really a clever, learned man, and very fond of *me*) is the only person now known to me in the world who fairly possesses the faculty of *mending a pen* . . . This excellent Chorley complains that for a long time back he has been unable to find a really good penknife,—but finds all blades to be made of poor ill-tempered steel. I lately gave him my pen-knife to sharpen : he . . . observed that he had not seen such a bit of honest steel for ten years back. That pen-knife was got new-bladed by your James at Cutler Hinchcliff's. In consequence I have come to the resolution (and stated it to Chorley) of getting him a pen-knife from the same place, —the very *best* Hinchcliff can be persuaded to make. Chorley has obliged me hundreds of times. It would give me real pleasure to make him this little Gift. Here are the essential particulars :

' Double-bladed knife,—one blade a " cut-stick," the other for pens, sharp-pointed.' The only important ' particular is, that the steel be as good as mine is ! This will cause the grim heart of Chorley to rejoice when he sees it ; and he is a judge. Earnestly entreat James and the excellent Hinchcliff to do their very best.' If Hinchcliff does not make knives, ' he must knock the blades out of some useful buckhorn handle, and put in right ones of his own, *right* ones !

> ' Yours ever,
>   ' T. CARLYLE.'

THE SOUND-PROOF STUDY
(1853)

IT was mainly the fogs and noises of London that Carlyle disliked,[1]—the rest was all right. He said he saw in London ' " an epic grandeur " all its own,' and ' for comfort he knew no place like it.' " One great thing about London is that here no man is to bore another," said he. It was true, as Espinasse urged, that this was ignored in the case of Carlyle by inquirers after truth and especially Americans.[1]—' One American cleric, I remember, half-forced his way into the house to insist on Carlyle explaining to him difficulties which had occurred to him in studying " the moral character of Goorty,"—such was his pronunciation of Goethe's name. All he got was a recommendation to restudy the " moral character " of Goethe in Goethe's own writings.' But even the affliction of bores was likely to be less in London than in the country, and Mrs. Carlyle was now delighted by her husband's proposal to spend still more money on their house by building a new room on the top of it, such as he had just described to Redwood.

The recent enlargement of the first-floor public room, which was the drawing-room and library, had made it all the more receptive of their neighbours' noises. Now on one side they had a quiet neighbour ; but on the other side there was a dilapidated house which was rented this summer, 1853, by a laundryman Ronca, who heeded not Carlyle, and whose wife and daughters-in-law could hold their own in debate with the Carlyles' maid, " Irish Fanny," while screaming parrots reinforced his flock of " demon fowls." All which made Carlyle talk again of going " off into silence," meaning the country, and decide at last to take John Chorley's advice and build a sound-proof study.

Chorley had abundance of leisure, and great experience

---

[1] *Literary Recollections*, by F. Espinasse, pp. 265–6.

in business, and he was delighted to be of use. As soon as Carlyle consented Chorley ' went to Cubitt's, the chief builders ' thereabouts, and arranged everything, delivering Carlyle from all the bother of bargaining and superintending. On 11.8.53 a " right man " was setting up scaffolds and ladders from the street, and the work was fairly begun, to be finished in " six weeks."[2] Carlyle continued writing history, and as his wife reported to his brother,—" John Chorley has constituted himself the over-ruling Providence of the whole thing ; and is to be seen running up and down the long ladder in front of the house the first thing of a morning when one looks abroad. Neither Mr. C. nor I have set eyes on the silent apartment which is progressing so noisily overhead."

One of the Irish labourers, wrote Carlyle, ' had been ignorant that lath and plaster was not a floor ; he, from above, accordingly came plunging down into my bedroom, catching himself by the armpits, fast swinging, astonished in the vortex of old laths, lime and dust ! Perhaps it was with him,'—it was with one of the workmen anyhow,— ' that Irish Fanny, some time after, ran away into matrimony.' According to Mrs. Carlyle it happened five times that a workman fell through the lath and plaster,—' the last time within a yard of my head as I was stooping over a drawer.'

The builder seemed good at his work, however, and on 9.9.53 Carlyle told Emerson in a letter :—" My notion is, he will succeed ; in which case, it will be a great possession to me for the rest of my life. Alas, this is not the kind of *silence* I could have coveted, and could once get,—with green fields and clear skies to accompany it ! But one must take such as can be had,—and thank the gods . . . In fact I am already, by dint of mere obstinate quiescence in such circumstances as there are, intrinsically growing fairly sounder in nerves." Soon after this his wife made him get out of the way by going to Addiscombe, the beautiful vacant cottage the Ashburtons were offering them, and once there, he confessed he ' liked it much.' His work was never interrupted. He kept ' busy, reading, writing, riding,' while his wife came and went between there and Cheyne Row, and did not let him come home till Saturday, 1.10.53. Meanwhile there is something he wrote just before going there, which has not yet been printed and is worth reading now.

[2] Letter of T. C., dated 11.8.53, Illustrated Memorial Volume of the Carlyle's House Purchase Fund Committee, 1896, pp. 64–5.

XI

A NATIONAL PORTRAIT GALLERY, &c.
(1853)

WHILE the sound-proof study was being built, a large envelope was posted on 8.9.1853 to The Lady Ashburton, Achany, Bonar Bridge, Sutherlandshire. The contents included a MS. written by Carlyle and endorsed,—

> ' For Lord Ashburton
> (on a rainy day).'

It is an argument for a National Portrait Gallery, and tho we have such a Gallery to-day, it seems worth a glance, when compressed as much as possible.—

' The excellent uses of Paintings and Picture-Galleries are now so loudly acknowledged everywhere that there needs no recommendation, to Princes or Private Persons, to lay out money in that direction. But of all kinds of excellent Pictures, in Galleries or elsewhere, unspeakably the usefullest and most interesting to ingenuous souls are excellent Portraits of Historical Men. Perhaps in no class of Pictures, if we will consider well, can Pictorial genius better display itself ; the Portraits done by Raphael are equally supreme over other men's as his so-called ideal paintings are ;—nay perhaps it will one day be discovered that here is his and all men's veritable *ideal ;* here, in fitly (instead of unfitly) interpreting the real ; that, in Painting as in writing, and in Art everywhere, the only lasting Poetry is, after all, *History* . . . By Nature herself, the Painter is " appointed and equipped to give us likenesses of grand things and passages that are in his sight, and are not in ours . . ." If he cannot accomplish that feat in some measure, it appears he is lost, and informed by eternal Nature (whatever others may say and sing) that he has no right to exist under the title of Painter, and in fact does not *exist*, not in her domains. . . . What are " ideals " good for if Nature's grand truths

39

and performances remain uninterpreted and misinterpreted ? The births of Eternity,—and every flower in Spring is one, how much more every great event, every new heroic man : this, this and not the sickly cobwebs of his or other men's poor fancy is the real " ideal " of ideals ;—and will perhaps, one day again, be recognised for such by all wise souls.

' We shall then see changes in Painting, and in some other provinces ! The painting of Holy Families, rapes of Europa, &c., &c., will be a good deal abated, and that of swift-passing but long-memorable men and occurrences will, with an infinite increase of earnestness, begin.

' And I often say to myself,—Had any Painter caught up for me, 1800 years ago, an actual exact likeness of the Man Jesus, how gladly would I give for it the immense mammoth shipload of Holy Families, Flights to Egypt, Flayings of Bartholomew, &c., &c.! But the then Painters were not lucky enough to do that. And since they have irretrievably neglected that, what are all these " ideals " to me ? A kind of mockery ; really little better, even the Raphaels, in my deepest moods ! I advise any thoughtful Painters there may now be to lift up their eyes " being in torment " (too truly so, in the windy gulf of Dilettantism, beau-ideal, high-art, and so forth), and fix them piously on this glint of the better country beyond !—But to leave all that, and let the Painters settle their own interests as they can . . . let us assert at least that to us Non-Painters, and to the world at large, a *Gallery of true Historic Portraits* would be extremely beneficial and delightful.

' Consider it a little, under one or two of its many aspects . . . Whoever has attempted the serious study of Biography, the first want he feels is that of a faithful Portrait of his hero's physiognomy and outward figure. My experience is, there lies more elucidation of the hero's real character in such a Portrait than in half the written Lives you will read about him. In every way it is of all helps to the understanding of Historical Men the most indispensable and fundamental. Such Historical Men as have no credible Portraits left are, in many cases, themselves gone irretrievably inconceivable . . . and can only be reconstructed as distant shadowy figures, fit to inhabit and decorate the Imagination, but too uncertain to come home to the heart. . . . One seeks a Portrait, I say, as a first condition of success in all Biography ; and it is sad indeed, and testifies but ill for us in several respects, how seldom one can find one that is to be relied on, or find one at all.—And yet the commonest man,—what a pleasure has he in looking at the face belonging to a Name that has been familiar to him ! This is Martin Luther, then ; these brisk frank hazel eyes were his, with the wild silent depths, that are in them ; that solid yeoman countenance, frank as a hunter's, fit for a hearty jug of beer, as well as for a shot thro the Pope's fifth rib, when occasion called ? Well ! And this again is big Hal, that murdered all his wives ? This prosperous massive-looking bright-eyed squire, done in little by Holbein, here in the Hampton Court Gallery ? What, this ? Why, this seems a gallant royal-looking fellow ; and I am mistaken if there is not a jolly ringing laugh in him ; and on the whole a good deal of fire, insight, generosity, and other kingly strength and worth in the inner man of this one ;— and perhaps the great Dr. Dryasdust has a little misled me as to the record of this one ?—Perhaps !——

' And then to think of a National Series of such Portraits. —Portraits well painted, and with Historical notices (in some brief Catalogue, or fit Handbook) well decorated ; Portraits and Notices alike conscientiously containing the *truth*, or such approach as can be made to that :—Truly I could fancy few more profitable places for an ingenious human soul that wanted to instruct and nourish itself in things noble, patriotic and manful. A kind of real Pantheon it would in fact be : Pantheon, or Home of all the National Divinities, for these our Historic Heroes are,—where, unconsciously but very veritably, the better parts of the souls of all men might worship, which it is so difficult to do at present ! Worship, I say ; for they are silently looking there on the indisputable Divine Revelations of the past : " So did, of a truth, the Supreme Power manifest Himself in this land of ours ; these were the living texts He published abroad here in past times,—and they are very strange, and precious to us ! " Few things could be of a more *religious* nature ; salutary for all manner of men. Out of which, by degrees, such a benefit and series of benefits might arise, such a forwarding to the growth in all souls, of whatever best deserved to grow, as perhaps were not easily attainable at present in any other edifice or Establishment whatever, such as, in Sydenham Crystal-Palaces, commonplace Picture Galleries and the sublimest Showrooms, is not to be dreamed of as possible,—if, alas, even the *reverse* be not too possible in these latter !

'It seems to me to argue ill of the wisdom, especially of the sincerity of mankind in these ages, that . . . there is no such Gallery in any Nation whatsoever ;—and that the honour is still open to England of showing the example to all Nations in that respect, if it can and will. Last autumn at Berlin, which is full enough of pictures, and has Kaulbachs and Corneliuses covering acres of canvas with what can never profit any mortal, there did not seem to be within the circuit of the city (tho I knew Varnhagen, Preuss, &c., &c.,) any man who could direct me to a reasonable Portrait of Frederick the Great ;—and in fact I had, in a sense, to discover one for myself, those in the Royal Palaces, Public Galleries, Print and Picture shops, &c., &c., being in part quite unknown even to intelligent people, and in still greater part, of no worth when known ! So is it in all cities, or too nearly so.

'Edward Hyde the great Chancellor, first Earl of Clarendon, is the only Englishman I have ever heard of as attempting seriously to form a Gallery of English Portraits. He, in the sumptuous mansion he had built for himself in the then green and bushy Piccadilly regions, had formed such a Gallery, and was diligently making progress in the Collection, when his fall and exile overtook him ; and the great man, stripped of home and possessions, was sent into foreign parts, happily with pen and ink still left, there to write his *History ;*—or in fact to do his " Collection of English Portraits " to some extent, in another and still more lasting form : the Oil-Portraits were scattered again ; the House was pulled down . . . The Gallery of English Portraits went to the winds ; and no such enterprise of a real National Pantheon for England has since been undertaken by any Patriot. Yet a more patriotic enterprise could not well be proposed just now. For culture, instruction, spiritual improvement to the wise and instructible part of the Nation, I really see nothing executable that would be more indubitably advantageous ; and I have no hesitation in asserting that of all Galleries whatsoever the one that has in Nature the *best* right to exist on English Funds were a Gallery of Portraits of Historical English. If the Prince Consort would be pleased to take up this important and neglected Enterprise, I love to persuade myself he has the means both inward and outward of doing much to accomplish it ; and in the peaceable provinces of human endeavour, I really know few where more real benefit might be achieved

for England, and a more lasting meed of honour gained from
the wise both of England and of other countries. This is
actually my opinion,—tho the difficulties too are not
hidden from me ; and I perceive, success, here as elsewhere
is rigorously enough *conditional*.

MEANS

' There exist great quantities of Historical English Portraits in the Houses of the Nobility, in the Picture Market,
and fixed or floating over England ; part of which might
be acquired by money . . . Noble Houses which possessed
the Portrait of an Ancestor become Historical would
naturally at first be indisposed to part with it : in that case,
the evident resource would be to have a copy taken, of
rigorous sincere fidelity . . . Other Noble Houses might
possess Historical Portraits *not* of their own ancestral
lineage, and be willing for honour or advantage to part
with these into a National Gallery where the donors' or
vendors' names were kept on record.—In her Majesty's
Royal House, there are scattered many important Historical
Portraits, Royal and other ; these perhaps her Majesty
would generously consent to have collected into one Place,
where to herself they would not be lost, and to her people
they would first become accessible and useful. Majesty's
example would of course work on the Nobility, and render
donations or sales less and less unusual ;—and in fine if the
Gallery *succeeded*, i.e., could gain for itself among wise
men the character of a *real* National Pantheon, I see not
why patriotic Noblemen, or even merely vain ones, should
not in many cases be willing that Portraits of their Ancestors, such as the Nation had honoured by demanding them,
should go to the National Collection, and stand there (with
due label and *record*) in a safer prominent place and far more
conspicuous situation than they ever had before. By these
means the necessity of Copying would gradually diminish :
in fact a little real *success* would, here as elsewhere, tend
always to enlarge itself, to go on in geometrical progression :
were the Gallery really a faithful and worthy thing, all wise
men would gradually see it as such, and would loyally
foster and promote it so that its fortune then were certain.
Thus a truly wise and strenuous management, applied to it
during the life of one man, might secure its prosperity thro
a series of generations . . .

'Money naturally will be wanted ; but not excessively much money ; nor is that by any means the deepest primary want, or the one there would be real difficulty in supplying. A set of rooms . . . open, on stated days and under stated conditions, to the Public ; a few thousands annually,—e.g. from 5 to 10,000 pounds annually ;—this, in a few years, if well administered, might itself produce a valuable Gallery, and as it were secure it from the risk of failure.

'The great point I perceive, on which all turns, were this same " Well administered " : how to get it *well* administered ; there would the grand tug of difficulty be, on which hangs utility or inutility, success or want of success ! For there will two human qualities be required, neither of them common even among persons distinguished for their accomplishments at this epoch of the world ; and unless these two be vigilantly and continually in exercise in the establishment, it cannot become an excellent establishment. *First*, thorough knowledge, and sincerity of judgment, as to who *are* Heroes in English History ; whose Portraits, and with what degree of industry, are to be inquired after ; and how they are to be made intelligible and justly conspicuous to the visitors of the Gallery. For example, if the Mistresses of Charles II, and other such unclean creatures rumoured of in foolish *Books* of History, are to be admitted, *they* surely ought to be kept somewhat in the background ; and questions will arise, of difficult solution, as to the treatment, elucidation and location of such ; as to the purchase of such, when offered ;—in short, the question what Historical figures to select, and how best in the given circumstances to arrange and elucidate them, will be continually occurring ; can be wisely decided only by a wise and faithful judge of such matters ; and the *mis*decision of it, if too much persisted in, will be fatal. *Secondly*, there will be needed such a capacity of judging on the intrinsic worth of Portraits, as we by no means find to be common among great Pictorial Authorities, and persons habituated to the talk about Art, High Art, and the Correggiosity of Correggio ;—all which is quite beside the point of pursuit (namely, a probably-real *Likeness* of a given Historical Man), and is even very capable of leading one away from said real point of pursuit, and conducting you not to a *Likeness* but to an *Un*likeness by way of result.

'In such Books as *Lodge's Portraits, Houbraken's*, &c. (for I have not in my hand any large stock of Oil Portraits), nothing is so intolerable as the vague, characterless, and finally *incredible* result often brought out under the title of Portrait by a commonplace Dilettante Selector or Engraver : and I often feel that no Portrait at all were clearly usefuller to all creatures than *such* a Portrait.

' And indeed this leads us to the general conclusion, that Dilettantism, Ostentation, *Showmanship* in all forms, must be rigorously excluded from this Enterprise (banished to the Sydenham Crystal Palace, and to the &c., &c., where they *will* find entrance, and make temporary fortune), and that unless sincerity of mind, and what I could call the *pious* wish to instruct and cultivate oneself, preside in the Enterprise, it can never be a valuable or successful one. *With* that noble quality, however, I see nothing to hinder it from succeeding.   Choosing of Portraits ;   drawing up of Catalogues with succinct exact Historical Notices (lucid and illuminative) : in all this there is difficulty ; but no difficulty that cannot be overcome if wisely attacked.   In fine I perceive that sincerity and faithful human sense, in the Head or Directory President of this Enterprise, will be the basis of all things for it ; that with this everything is possible, and without it nothing.

' For which reason I confess to great doubts about applying to Parliament for money ; at least, if we are to have the money coupled with a Governing Committee, with Newspaper Reports, After-Dinner Oratory, and the other fatal *et ceteras ;* which lead infallibly to Ostentation instead of away from it.   That the Prince himself should be Sovereign of the thing,—the Prince, or somebody possessing the qualities of mind which I privately ascribe to the Prince ;— who should do the operation in much more *silence* than is common : this seems to me an essential condition.   From Committees and After-Dinner Oratory,—alas, what can we expect ?   We know these sad entities, some of us ; and all of us are beginning to know,—to our cost !   And if the Parliament would give no money on those terms, I believe, even in that worst case, the Prince might make more real progress with money he could spare of his own, than with Parliamentary money granted on the common terms.   And just as George the Third's modest, solid and excellent Library is *worth* far more than Panizzi's huge expensive unsound and ostentatious one, and calls forth a blessing yet on the faithful and really human soul of that simple King (instead of a *non-blessing* on certain other *in*human, pedant, and merely showman souls),—so might the Prince's Gallery of English Portraits, conducted even on his own resources if he could get no other on fair terms, be a blessing and a credit to this country ; and far better than any that a Parliament will ever be in a condition to produce. A fine and noble possibility, I do esteem it,—I from the distance ; but of course know little what unseen impediments there may be. I can only say *Faxit'* (may it be done !) ; 'and do so in a very hearty, and perhaps rather disinterested manner.'

It is curious to consider how general to-day are the opinions about National Portraits which Carlyle expressed in 1853, and how strange they seemed at the time. There has been a similar change about the views he used to express on the Classics and education. A young man in the Customs, William Allingham, had been applying to him for advice in reading, and while he had been told of the merits of Professor Newman in London, 'an excellent classicist,' he was now admonished, 27.9.1853 :[1]—' I perceive you greatly exaggerate the advantages derivable from College Lectures in these times, and do not value at anything like its real amount the solid privilege of being economically independent, and left free to attend the "lectures" you might give *yourself* (on far better than *Academical* subjects) on such tolerable terms ! No man can be *made* wise, except by his own virtuous efforts ; and, in these days of Books and Libraries, all the little help he can get from others is, as it were, brought to his own door, wherever he may live.' It is pleasant to add that, tho Allingham was a poet and left the Customs, and came to London next year and made a start in journalism, he ended by taking Carlyle's advice and returned in time to his work in the Customs. He is one of the best of the Boswells who let us hear yet with the mind's ear talk of Thomas Carlyle.[2]

[1] *Letters to William Allingham*, p. 134.
[2] *William Allingham : a Diary*, by H. Allingham and D. Radford, pp. 71–73.

XII

THE REAL BITTERNESS OF LIFE
(1853)

WRITING from Addiscombe on 15.9.53 to Neuberg then in Germany, Carlyle said,—" Western London " —the west end of London—" is like La Trappe." In short there was nothing to hinder his progress with *Frederick,* and yet,—" I have continued hovering about the edges of it, very unhappy on account of it." There was only one thing that could draw him away from it.—

' My dear old mother has, as you have heard, given us a good deal of alarm since you went. Alas, she is now past 82 ; and the inevitable cannot be supposed to be very distant ! For the last year or more she had been growing visibly feebler ; but in July last, matters seemed to come to a crisis : and after almost a miraculous escape, our poor patient seems ever since to be a degree better, and a hope that she may yet be spared to us for a while, is but too prone to rise in one. Ever since I have had consciousness in me, this thing has been my terror : alas, alas, it is the doom of all men, a merciful as well as stern one ;—and it is not for me to forget that it has been long delayed, and promises to fall as gently as it well could ! '

A fortnight later Carlyle was writing to comfort his friend John Forster, distressed by the death of his sister.— ' I am grateful for a word from your hand again, tho the news is very sad. Alas, the inexorable Years, that cut away from us, one after another, the true souls whom we loved, who loved us truly : that is *the real bitterness of life :* against which there is no remedy, and natural tears must fall ! But we ourselves, my friend, it is not long we have to stay behind ; we too shall find a shelter in the Silent King- doms ; and much Despicability that barked and snarled incessantly round us *here* shall there be without the walls forevermore. " Blessed are the Dead." I often silently say : " If we had done our work, it were good for us to be dead too,—and safe with all our loved ones round us, THERE !" " God is great," say the Moslems ; to which we add only, God is Good,—and have not any more to say.'

XIII

DEATH OF MRS. CARLYLE'S UNCLE
(1853)

OCTOBER saw the Carlyles at home again. The building of the Sound-Proof Study was finished, but painting and much else was needed before it would be fit for use. In the meantime, Carlyle went on with his work on *Frederick* in the enlarged drawing-room,—the new Study was not to be used till sometime in 1854.

In October dismal news from Liverpool came to Mrs. Carlyle. The house there of John Welsh, her mother's brother, had in July as often before been her half-way house in her journey between Scotland and London ; and now his daughter Helen, her favourite cousin, wrote to her describing the death of her father, when on a visit to Scotland. She wrote back at once, 12.10.1853.—

'Dearest Helen,—I know not what I am going to say. I am quite stupefied. I had somehow never taken alarm at my uncle's last illness. I had fixt my apprehensions on the journey home, and was kept from present anxiety by that far-off one. My beloved uncle, all that remained to me of my mother. A braver, more upright, more generous-hearted man never lived. When I took leave of him in Liverpool, and he said " God bless you, dear " (he had never called me dear before), I felt it was the last time we should be together, felt that distinctly for a few hours ; and then the impression wore off, and I thought I would go back soon, would go by the cheapest train (God help me), since it gave him pleasure to see me. That we have him no longer is all the grief ! It was well he should die thus, gently and beautifully, with all his loving kindness fresh as a young man's ; his enjoyment of life not wearied out ; all our love for him as warm as ever ; and well he should die in his own dear Scotland, amid quiet kindly things. We cannot, ought not to wish it had been other-

E   49

wise, to wish he had lived on till his loss should have been less felt.

'But what a change for you all, and for me too, little as I saw of him. To know that kind, good uncle was in the world for me, to care about me, however long absent, as nobody but one of one's own blood can, was a sweetness in my lonely life, which can be ill-spared.

'Poor dear little Maggie, I know how she will grieve . . . Kiss her for me. God support you all. Write to me when you can what you are going to do. Alas! that I should be so far away from your councils. I need to know precisely about your future in an economic sense; through all the dull grief that is weighing on me, comes a sharp anxiety lest you should be less independent than heretofore; to be relieved of that will be the best comfort you could give me at present. I never knew what money you had to live on, nor thought about it; now, it is the first question I ask. I am dreary and stupid, and can write no more just now.

'Your affectionate,

'J. C.'

'When I saw your handwriting again last night, my only thought was "how good of her to write another letter soon." I was long before I could understand it.'

XIV

MAZZINI, DELIA BACON, &c.
(1853)

PERHAPS the most exciting of the callers at Cheyne Row this fall was Mazzini. He had been trying to get up an insurrection in Milan against Austria this summer, and tho he had failed, he had got safe back to London. He was now alarming Mrs. Carlyle by saying he " might go off again within ten days." " I am out of all patience at his reckless folly," she wrote to Dr. Carlyle. " If one did not hear every day of new arrests and executions, one might let him scheme and talk, hoping it might all end in smoke ; but it ends in blood, and that is horrible.—Thirteen hundred arrests made in the Papal States within a week ! "

Far the most important of all who were resorting to their house was Joseph Neuberg, who had been ' worth ten couriers ' to Carlyle in Germany last year, and had now returned from Bonn, to spend the rest of his life in London and help Carlyle in his historical researches. He ' sat three months in the State-Paper Office ' in London, ' for example, *excerpting* there, with a skill and rapid felicity not to be rivalled,' as Carlyle has reported, and ' did all kinds of excerpting and abstracting, &c. &c., as if I myself had done it ;— and, in brief, was an *alter ego* ' (or another self), without whose help the *Frederick* with its ' horrible immensity of drudgery ' would have been ' impossible.'

On the other hand perhaps the least important caller in the fall of '53, and also the oddest, was Delia Bacon, an " American Gentlewoman " recommended by Emerson. *She* had not come across the Atlantic to *learn*,—she had come to *teach*. She had in fact done ordinary teaching in America, but what she came to teach us all now was that the *Man* Shakespeare was a *Myth*, and that the plays which bore his name had really been written by some " Secret Association," and not by him at all, but mainly by Francis Bacon. She was sure there would be evidence to prove that, in the British Museum or somewhere else ; and she wasted the time of many simple persons before she retired into a lunatic asylum. Carlyle saw and heard her, and said at once she was mad ; but he and his wife were both pitiful and tender with her, and she reported to Emerson " again and again," with " joyful fullness " in the next two years, their " cordial kindness " and " goodness " to her.

One Friday, 4.11.53, Neuberg found her at Carlyle's. But what he and Carlyle were considering that night was how to help poor Eckermann, the Boswell of Goethe. They had been corresponding with Marshall, the secretary of the Grand Duchess, and on hearing the facts from him, " I wrote Marshall instantly," said Carlyle to Neuberg, " that I could not *beg* for a man with £75 a year in so cheap a place as Weimar." He was sorry for him, however, and did what he could. He took the MS. of one of Goethe's dramas and tried to sell it to the British Museum for Eckermann's benefit, without success. Sir Frederick Madden, at the head of the manuscript department, was " courteous,"[1] but refused to buy.

Discussing with Espinasse the letter from Sir Walter Scott to Goethe in Eckermann's book,[2] and Goethe's talk about it, Carlyle 'made no remark' on the references to himself. Goethe had said that Carlyle was " a moral force of great significance, having in him much for the future," concerning whom " it was difficult to conceive all that he might produce or effect." In talking now to Espinasse, he merely laughed a little at Sir Walter's truly Scott-like mention to Goethe of " my friend Sir John Hope of Pinkie," and spoke in his usual depreciatory tone of " Wattie," saying, " He turned the history of his country into an opera."

---

[1] *Literary Recollections*, by F. Espinasse, pp. 174–6.
[2] Oxenford's Translation of the *Conversations of Goethe* with Eckermann, &c., pp. 274–7.

XV

GOETHE AND CHRIST, MAURICE AND DAMNATION
(1853)

CARLYLE gave Espinasse the book on Goethe by Eckermann to review ; and the excellent Espinasse, to whom Carlyle was far more interesting than Goethe, has told us[1] that in the passage where Goethe said of Christ, " Ich beuge mich vor Ihm," I bow down before Him, Carlyle had underlined the Ich or I, and pencilled opposite to it an emphatic note of exclamation.

Writing to Lady Ashburton on 3.11.53, Carlyle remarked, —' One evening Sir James Stephen came ; told us of Maurice what we already knew, that he was unanimously voted out.' Then the letter adds about Stephen what reveals the writer, —' talked abstrusely, not very coherently ; I see he is very deep still in Claphamism of a sort,' meaning Evangelicalism, ' fixed for life in the Jew element ; which much restricts the use of him to me.'

What had happened to the Rev. F. D. Maurice was that he had just been deprived of his chair of Theology at King's College, for publishing his ' Theological Essays.' As Carlyle confessed in his next letter of news to Lady Ashburton on 14.11.53, ' The Maurice question has no interest for me. Friedrich the Great said once to the orthodox of Neuchatel, —" If these people want to be damned for ever, why not ? " To Maurice himself, if they thrust him from the Church altogether, it might do good rather than harm. That is a *confiscated* affair altogether, and can in the long run yield only bankruptcy of spirit to the like of him. Alas, human stupidity is great ; I think sometimes it is the greatest ; and see, with wonder and awe, how (as Schiller says) the very Gods can never fight it down.'

---

[1] *Literary Recollections*, by F. Espinasse, pp. 174–6, and see Oxenford's translation of *Conversations of Goethe*, p. 567.

Next day he was writing to Arthur Helps,[2] to reässure him about their common friend.—' About Maurice and eternal damnation I hear a great deal, from the idle circles of mankind ; but to say truth, I have of myself almost no thought about it at all.   Like the Frenchman, tired with arguments about the being of God, I may *a fortiori* ' (with more reason) ' say, " *Monsr. je n'y prends aucun intérêt !* " ' (I take no interest in that.)   ' Perhaps it might do Maurice good if he were turned out of the Church altogether,—*which, it appears, is not likely at present.*[3]   That splitting of hairs, which he has long laboriously carried on, to prove that he belongs to her, *cannot* ultimately turn to good for any creature. As to the Church herself—well, I should say, so long as she talks about damnation at all, she must make it " eternal " ; there is no even *extinct* worth in any other kind.   God help her, poor old Church !   England *believes* now, and she herself at heart believes, *in no " damnation " except ruin at your bankers*[3] (such damnation as *has* now fallen on Hudson, they say) : and a poor church in these circumstances is ill off ! '

[2] *Correspondence of Sir Arthur Helps*, pp. 151–3.
[3] Italics added.

XVI

SIR JAMES STEPHEN, PRINCE ALBERT, &c.
(1853)

B Y the fifties James Stephen of the Colonial Office had retired and become Sir James and a Cambridge Professor. He was now resorting often to Carlyle's house. His son Leslie tells,[1]—' My father had thought it proper to explain, in a rather elaborate letter, that he did not sympathise with one of Carlyle's diatribes . . . in conversation . . . against the Church of England, tho he had not liked to protest at the moment. Carlyle responded very courteously and asked for further meetings,' which accordingly became more frequent.

Leslie Stephen explains a picturesque trifle Carlyle tells of his father.—" *He shuts his eyes on you, and talks as if he were dictating a Colonial Despatch,*" was what the elder Spring Rice, Lord Monteagle, had said about him to Carlyle, who thought it capital, and recalled it in connection with the phrase of Dickens,—" teaching you How *Not* to do it." The ' Colonial Office *being* an Impotency,' reflected Carlyle, ' what *could* an earnest and honest kind of man do, but try and teach you How *not* to do it ? Stephen seemed to me a master in that art.' This about shutting the eyes ' refers to a nervous trick of shyness,' wrote Leslie Stephen.[1] ' When talking his eyelids often had a tremulous motion which concealed the eyes themselves, and gave to at least one stranger the impression that he was being addressed by a blind man.'

The usual companion of James Stephen when he came to see Carlyle was one of his " long sons," and oftenest James FitzJames. The first time that James FitzJames called alone, according to his brother,[1] he was ' received by Mrs. Carlyle, who ordered him off the premises, on

---

[1] *Life of Sir James FitzJames Stephen,* by Leslie Stephen, pp. 201 and 53.

suspicion of being an American celebrity hunter. He submitted so peacefully that she relented ; called him back, and, discovering his name, apologised for her wrath.' Tho in time he became quite an intimate of Carlyle, and was much influenced by him, his brother and biographer Leslie quotes with praise an essay of his professing himself one of the humble ' pig-philosophers,'[2] and describes him as never in the least a ' mystic ' in the manner of Carlyle,[2] but at once a Puritan and a Utilitarian, in short a good Rationalist.[3]

Both the brothers reäppear in this history later. Carlyle enjoyed their father's talk in the fifties very much, ' serious ' talk, and ' able, tho always in that Colonial Office style.' About November, 1853, James Stephen told him that at the end of the session, Prince Albert had proposed Carlyle for a pension to Lord Aberdeen, the ' small-headed, sleek and feeble ' old fellow then playing the part of Prime Minister. Aberdeen said nothing about the Mazzini letters,[4] but refused the pension of course, pretending his objection was to Carlyle's " heterodoxy." In conversation once Carlyle had found him a simpering commonplace creature. Prime Ministers of his calibre cost us dear. In those weeks Aberdeen was holding on to office in desperation, and letting the country be dragged into the Crimean War,—as needless a war as any we ever waged. Before the year was out there was to be war with Russia.

Meanwhile Carlyle was comforting his mother and other relatives by telling them (18.11.53) :—' I am sure I should have had to refuse Lord Aberdeen's offer (in the *quantity* and in the style he would have offered) ; and that would not have been pleasant. I consider it likely enough there will yet a *better* offer of the kind be made, if I live some years ; and *that* we can deal with as shall then seem good. Few men, I suppose, ever *wanted* a pension less : and if it is thrown me as a bit of charity, I am bound not to take it ; if either it, or the way of giving it, is not quite to my mind, why should I dream of taking it ? " Having carried on my work thus far," as Johnson said,[5] " with so little

---

[2] *Life of Sir James FitzJames Stephen*, by Leslie Stephen, p. 202.
[3] *Ditto*, pp. 306–11.
[4] *Carlyle on Cromwell and Others*, pp. 263–6.
[5] On 7.2.1755 : *Letter to Lord Chesterfield.*—Napier's Edn. I, pp. 202–4. T. C. quoted from memory, the exact text being :—" Having carried on my work thus far with so little obligation to any favourer of learning, I shall not be disappointed tho I conclude it, if less be possible, with less . . ."

help from the powerful, I am content to finish it, if less be possible, with less ! "—And no Supreme Burgh Bailie (of the Aberdeen species), never so sleek or canny, " can do th' aither (thee either) ill or guid (good) " . . . It will be better not to mention it farther ; for really I should not like it to be known or talked of at all.'

By a curious coincidence Carlyle himself was now solicited by an old acquaintance, Mrs. Glen,[6] to support her application for a small pension on the Literary List, inasmuch as her husband, who had gone as a missionary to Astrakhan in 1818, had translated the Bible or part of it into Persian. The religious public generally, and Carlyle's own mother in particular, were zealous for a pension for the widow of the meritorious Mr. Glen, and Carlyle consented to take some trouble to explain the matter to the Duke of Argyll, and get him to persuade Aberdeen. So Mrs. Glen received her pension, £50,—Glen's was the kind of literary merit an Aberdeen could appreciate.

[6] See *Carlyle Till Marriage*, pp. 110–11, and 149–50.

XVII

BRACING COMPANY
(1853)

TOWARDS the end of 1853, when the Crimean war was impending, a familiar favourite of both Carlyle and his wife was spending the evening with them, Charlotte Williams Wynn, a lady famous for having refused a Duke, and reputed to have rejected three.[1] She tells us that Carlyle was " in great force, violently Russian in his feelings, assuring me our victories "—imaginary diplomatic " victories "—" were in truth so many defeats," which nobody now denies. " He was, however, very pleasant when he got off politics to history and the time of his Frederic," continued the despiser of Dukes, in a letter to Varnhagen von Ense.[2] " Nothing could be more interesting than his conversation then. He is such a picturesque talker that he transports one back to the period of when he is speaking. —I think his work is advancing and satisfying him better. He told me the more he studied Frederic the Great's character, the more he was struck by his thorough truth and earnestness of purpose, his sincerity and simplicity combined."

She leaves us guessing her own share in the talk. As she afterwards wrote[2] to a friend,—" Burning incense before your hero all day is so bad for him. Sooner or later it drags him down ; and when I was with Carlyle, I always felt it a matter of conscience, just because I did honestly love and admire him, to make a stand against what, in anyone else, one should have passed over."

Which was also Lady Ashburton's way of doing. She and Miss Wynn were in both mind and body two of the tall women of England, and must have been bracing company.

---

[1] *Mrs. Brookfield and her Circle*, by C. & F. Brookfield, II, p. 289.
[2] *Memorials of Charlotte Williams-Wynn*, by her sister, pp. 178 and 311.

XVIII

THE NEW ROOM
(1853)

IN spite of all the pains that Chorley had taken, the newly built room was far from satisfactory as a Sound-proof Study. There had been a strike while it was in progress, 'in consequence of which inferior men were engaged,' says the latest historian of the house,[1] whom it seems safe to believe about this, tho apparently Carlyle did not know it at the time. It was curiously like Carlyle to remain ignorant of a thing like that, which helped to explain the bad work that made him use strong language. He reminds one of the old divine in Scotland who left all temporal matters so entirely to others that, when once the maid rushed into his study crying that the house was on fire, he ordered her to go to his wife, declaring "That's not my business."

Another thing seems to have escaped notice, that the scandalous English way of allowing land to be let for a term of years for building, leaving the landowner still the owner of the land, had the natural effect of making people in England build as flimsily as possible. In Scotland the landowner got his "feu" or quit-rent, and had nothing more to do with the land. The builder or those who employed him or purchased from him enjoyed all the benefit of good work done, whereas in England, every shilling spent in making a building better than was needed for immediate purposes was for the benefit of the do-nothing landowner, a needless addition to what was paid him. Carlyle was aware of this defect in English law and custom, but did not always remember to allow for it and for the habits it produced.

When writing his Reminiscences by-and-by, Carlyle had

---

[1] Illustrated Memorial Volume of the Carlyle's House Purchase Fund Committee, 1896, pp. 65–6.

no praise for any of those who had worked upon the Study except one good young carpenter, and of course John Chorley. ' The work,' he wrote, ' of planning to begin with, and then of executing, in all its details, was mere work of Belial, i.e. of the Father of LIES ; such " work " as I had not conceived the possibility of among the sons of Adam till *then*. By degrees, I perceived it to be the ordinary English " work " of this epoch ; and endeavoured to be silent as to my own little failure . . . By many and long-continued efforts, I did get . . . my Study . . . patched together into supportability . . .

' The " architect " was one Parsons, really a clever creature, I could see, but swimming as for dear life in a mere " Mother of Dead Dogs," (ultimately did become bankrupt) ; his *men* of all types, Irish hodmen and upwards, for real *mendacity* of hand, for drunkenness, greediness, mutinous nomadism, and anarchic malfeasance throughout, excelled all experience or conception. Shut the *lid* on their " unexampled prosperity " and them, for evermore.' Or rather, let all take warning to beware of " scabs," and stop any building in progress when a strike is started.

The room was not dear. Including extras such as a big cupboard, it cost less than £200,[1] and was regularly used by Carlyle for a dozen years, till *Frederick* was finished. He said that while it excluded adjacent noises, it let in from far away the sounds of railway-whistles and bells and so on, that he never heard in the rooms below. It is an old proverb[2] that " The Almighty himself can do a great deal, but he cannot please everybody."

[2] Words painted on the inside of the wall of a German beer-garden at Lucerne, seen by D. A. W., on 23.8.1895.

XIX

LAST LETTER TO HIS MOTHER
(1853)

SUCH as it was, the new Study had to be cleaned and painted, and in order to be out of the way, the Carlyles agreed to spend some weeks in December at the Grange. The day before they departed was Carlyle's birthday, and the letter he wrote to his mother that day was the last she was ever to get from him.—

(Sunday) ' Chelsea, December 4, 1853.
' MY DEAR, GOOD MOTHER,

' I wrote to Jean the other day and have very little news to tell you ; but I cannot let this day pass without sending you some word or other, were it never so insignificant. We are going into the country to-morrow, to the Grange, for two weeks or perhaps a little more, partly to let the painters get done with that weary " room " of which you have heard so much ; partly because the Ashburtons, whose house ' at Addiscombe ' we visited lately without their own presence, would have it so, and Jane thought we were bound. She will go therefore : and I, having once landed her there, am to have liberty to leave again when I will. Meanwhile I have bargained to be private all day in their big house, to go on with my work just as if at home, &c. We will see how it answers. I confess I get no good of any company at present ; nor, except in stubbornly trying to work—alas ! too often in vain—is there any sure relief to me from thoughts which are very sad. But we must not " lose heart " ; lose faith—never, never !
' Dear old mother, weak and sick and dear to me, while I live in God's creation, what a day has this been in my solitary thought ; for, except a few words to Jane, I have not spoken to anyone, nor, indeed, hardly seen anyone, it being dusk and dark before I went out—a dim silent

Sabbath day, the sky foggy, dark with damp, and a universal stillness the consequence, and it is this day gone fifty-eight years that I was born. And my poor mother! Well! we are all in God's hands. Surely God is good. Surely we ought to trust in Him, or what trust is there for the sons of men? Oh, my dear mother! Let it ever be a comfort to you, however weak you are, that you did your part honourably and well while in strength, and were a noble mother to me and to us all. I am now myself grown old, and have had various things to do and suffer for so many years; but there is nothing I ever had to be so much thankful for as for the mother I had. That is a truth which I know well, and perhaps this day again it may be some comfort to you. Yes, surely, for if there has been any good in the things I have uttered in the world's hearing, it was *your* voice essentially that was speaking through me; essentially what you and my brave father meant and taught me to mean, this was the purport of all I spoke and wrote. And if in the few years that may remain to me, I am to get any more written for the world, the essence of it so far as it is worthy and good, will still be yours. May God reward you, dearest mother, for all you have done for me! I never can. Ah no! but will think of it with gratitude and pious love so long as I have the power of thinking. And I will pray God's blessing on you, now and always, and will write no more on that at present, for it is better for me to be silent.

'Perhaps a note from the doctor will arrive to-morrow; I am much obliged, as he knows, for his punctuality on that subject. He knows there is none so interesting to me, or can be. Alas! I know well he writes me the best view he can take; but I see too, how utterly frail my poor mother is, and how little he or any mortal can help. Nevertheless, it is a constant solace to me to think he is near you, and our good Jean. Certainly she does *me* a great service in assiduously watching over you; and it is a great blessing to us all that she is there to do such a duty.

'As to my own health, I am almost surprised to report it is so good. In spite of all these tumblings and agitations, I really feel almost better than I have done in late years; certainly not worse; and at this time within sight of sixty it is strange how little decay I feel; nothing but my eyesight gone a very little; and my hope, but also my fear or care at all, about this world, gone a great deal. Poor Jane is not at all strong, sleeps very ill, &c. Perhaps the fortnight

of fresh air and change of scene will do her some good.
But she is very tough, and a bit of good stuff too. I often
wonder how she holds out, and braves many things with
so thin a skin. She is sitting here reading. She sends her
affection to you and to them all. She speaks to me about
you almost daily, and answers many a question and speculation ever since she was at Scotsbrig. Give my love to
Jamie, to Isabella, and them all. May God's blessing be
on you all !

'T. CARLYLE.'

XX

AT THE GRANGE
(1853)

GOING to the Grange next day, 5.12.1853, the Carlyles had as fellow-passengers in the train the Henry Taylors and their children, and the Brookfields and theirs, and after leaving the railway-station in Hampshire, their journey was completed in ' a carriage for Ladies and Infants ; an open omnibus for gentlemen and maids, and a break for luggage,'[1] whereby they were all easily able to be in time for dinner.

' It was with no disregard of her sex that Lady Ashburton preferred the society of men,' wrote " Dicky " Milnes.[2] ' Having lost her only child, she shrank from the sympathies of family life, and avoided useless regrets. Nearly the whole of her female companions were ' childless, ' and yet to children generally she was kind and even affectionate.' So the young Taylors and Brookfields would be likely to share the feelings of the girl visitor, who once replied to a question about her stay, " I never count days at the Grange. I only know that it is morning when I come, and night when I go away."[2]

From Brookfield's Diary.[1]—' 6th. The Grange. Breakfast at 9.45. Carlyle at Breakfast today came out with,— " And upon the whole that is the great object to be attained by every son of Adam, to find a footing where he shall be able to snap his fingers in the face of men and devils."

' Lady Ashburton made all sorts of fun at this, at which he exclaimed with sham petulance,—" Why will you dig[3] harpoons into me and force such cries from me, and then laugh at me all day ? Let me be silent." . . .

---

[1] *Mrs. Brookfield and her Circle*, by C. & F. Brookfield, II, pp. 395–403, and 307 and 392.
[2] *Monographs*, by R. M. Milnes, Lord Houghton, p. 247.
[3] " Drin " in the text, a mistake, perhaps for drill or dig.

' Smoked with Carlyle in the Conservatory,'—which may remind us that smoking tobacco was then a vulgar habit, which one was supposed to hide. Brookfield goes on.— Talking about Sam Wilberforce ' (Bishop) ' I told Carlyle how old Hardman had said to old Kent : " Kent, you are cheating ! and you are right ;—you are right to get all you can in this world, for I'll be damned[4] if you get anything in the next."

' Carlyle spoke of the above Sam not without liking, but with thorough discrimination. " Oh, I can see well enough by the expression of his eye that he understands that I understand him well enough ; I look upon him as a supple, shifty, clever fellow, who holds his head up and always lights on his legs. I can see he likes me well enough, a good deal better than I like him ; and yet I like the fellow well enough too. He has got all he has by pure soapiness, suppleness, and sycophancy ; but as the Germans say, ' he does not hold his head down '." . . .

' At 12.15 I drove him to the Andover school, and Lord Ashburton arrived soon after. They both staid it out to the end, with much apparent interest. Carlyle put in a few questions of examination here and there in his odd way. " Queen Elizabeth—at what time was she alive in this world, and what did she do ? " It was amusing how he liked to put in his oar. He said they were the nicest children he had seen except at Glasnevin. . . .[5]

' Mr. Henry Taylor at dinner, speaking of Professor Owen, and praising him, said " what a pleasant smile he had."

' " No," said Carlyle, " that is just what I like least about him, an unreal smirk " (mimicking him), " altogether artificial, not the real man at all."

' Carlyle acquiesced in the idea set forth by Henry Taylor, that for the most part virtues are hereditary, and that it would be pretty safe to enquire not a servant's character but the character of his family.' The obvious limitation here implied should not be overlooked,—for the purposes of menial service. The absurdity of selecting ruling men or officials for hereditary reasons was derided by Carlyle.

Beginning about this time, Lord Ashburton and Mr. Brookfield endeavoured to practise a theory they shared with Carlyle, that early knowledge of common things should be a part of education. Lord Ashburton offered generous prizes for a synopsis of " the best pack of knowledge a man

---

[4] Left—in the original.　　[5] See *Carlyle at His Zenith*, pp. 108-9.

F

should take with him through life," and Mr. Brookfield tried to interest the teachers.

They had to face much ridicule, but they were not made to feel ridiculous, and did what they could in the right direction, ignoring quietly the " friends who wrote that inspired by such noble examples they were learning to black their own boots." The majority of every class is always timid and stolid, and in those reactionary years the wealthy classes in England were sincere obscurants. That indeed was their condemnation,—they ' loved darkness rather than light, because their deeds were evil.' Old ladies were known to refuse to engage a servant who could read, and Lady Jersey was true to her type when she scoffed at Lady Ashburton's " printers." When a soldier murdered a colonel, " This comes of Ragged Schools," cried Lady Jersey.

Her mockery did her betters no harm, tho she intended no good. " My ' printers,' as they call them, have become a sort of Order of the Garter," said Lady Ashburton. " I dare not talk to these knights as I could do to fine ladies and gentlemen."[6]

From Brookfield's Diary,[1] 7.12.53.—' 7th. Nobody at dinner today but the Carlyles, Taylors and Lushington. Lady Ashburton read part of a French Play well, and a bit of " In Memoriam " hurriedly, and rather as if it bored her.

' 8th. Mr. and Mrs. Robert Lowe and Lord Carnarvon came. Henry Taylor told at breakfast how some Americans called on Wordsworth at Rydal Mount and said : " I believe, Sir, that you are in *the poetic line.*" This was apropos a letter from the New York Library to Carlyle received this morning, offering him £500 if he would go over and deliver six lectures.

' 9th. The Bishop of Oxford ' (Wilberforce alias Soapy Sam) ' came to stay. . . . The Bishop's conversation is not really good, and after Carlyle's it is very thin and tinselly.

' A child at the school here, writing about a cart, said,— " A cart consists of several parts. Before making a cart, it is important to understand how to make it." This Carlyle seized upon, repeating it more than once with unction. I told him it reminded me of his advice to Tom Taylor, who once applied to him for some hints for some lectures he was giving,—" Just say what you think, but find out first just what you do think, if that be practicable." '

6 *Monographs*, by Lord Houghton, p. 254. Also *Mrs. Brookfield and Her Circle*, II, p. 436.

From the private journal of Bishop Wilberforce.[7]—
'December 10. Rode with Carlyle and Lowe; on horse
full of spirit round by Popham Lane. Well shaken. Carlyle
full of unconnected and inconsistent utterances. Full of
condemnation of the present day, of its honesty, &c. &c.,
praising the Georges I, II, & III for honesty and ability.'
The 'ability' is likely to be a mistaken episcopal para-
phrase of some other word. He goes on to describe the talk
of Carlyle.—' A heap of discordant ideas. Yet a good deal
of manhood, and of looking to some better state of being.
Poor man, a strange enigma! If he did but see the True
Man as his hope and deliverer, how were all his sighs
answered!'

The Bishop descended to dinner, and Mr. Brookfield tells
what followed.[1]—

'There was a spar after dinner between the Bishop of
Oxford and Carlyle. The Bishop treated some observation
of Carlyle's about the Guelphs (in which C. was rather
rescuing the Guelphs from obloquy—it arose out of talking
of Lord Hervey's Memoirs), with rather more laughter and
irreverence than was due from so flimsy to so genuine a
man; and contradicted him rather contemptuously as to
George II being a man of some worth. Carlyle was evidently angry—which rather destroyed his fluency and
presence of mind; but he maintained his point with some
vehemence—said he had searched such things diligently—
and if he—the Bishop—believed all the rubbishy carrion
that was left about such and such people " then you, my
Lord Bishop, have a great deal more credulity than I have,"
and such-like. The Bishop said " all history—all lives,
proved them to have been a low, sensual, etc." Carlyle
demanded " the name of *one* book." The Bishop talked on,
trying to declaim him down, but evidently had no authority,
(and) said,—" If you will give me time and opportunity
I will produce evidence," but I considered that he was
vanquished.'

The Gorham controversy then had its turn, and maybe
to chaff the Bishop, Carlyle did not disguise his opinions.
Mr. Gorham was a common " Evangelical " Church-of-
England parson, who had been made the victim of the test
case, in the attempt of the " Tractarians " or High-Church
party to monopolise the spoils of the Church by evicting the

---

[7] This is from the suppressed Vol. II of the *Life of Samuel Wilberforce,
Bishop*, &c., by Canon Ashwell and R. G. Wilberforce, p. 226.

Evangelicals. Mr. Gorham had got a "living," and the Bishop of Exeter had to "induct" him. Now that Bishop was "High Church," and insisted on "catechising" Mr. Gorham, and ended by refusing to induct him because he would not answer with a plain "Yes" the question,—"Do you believe that all the infants duly baptised are born again?"

Like the rest of the Evangelicals, Mr. Gorham hesitated to allege that Baptism alone regenerated every baby, so that any and every curate was doing a miracle of that sort, as often as he did a little sprinkling in the way of business. Mr. Gorham appealed to the Courts of Law, which decided in his favour, and the Archbishop gave him his "living"; and for doing so in obedience to the law, the Archbishop himself was excommunicated by the Bishop, which set the world laughing. Carlyle did not condescend to pretend to have any patience with "solemn Bishops and high Dignitaries" discussing "prevenient grace"; and according to Brookfield[1] he said :—

"That meeting of Solemn Augurs in the street and deliberating for days and weeks about the Chicken bowels was the saddest sight of this Century, and every lie they told was dotted down and will have to pay simple and compound interest before the world has done with it."

Here the English bishops, the best-paid set of bishops in the world, were compared to the humblest of all kinds of pagan soothsayers, the haruspices or gapers at the guts of chickens and other victims sacrificed,—whom it was almost excessively polite to call "augurs" at all. Cicero said he wondered one of them could keep from laughing when he saw another.

"Men are what they are, and the consequences will be what they will be," as a wise bishop said once. The Tractarians made a bold attempt to "win their trick" by a Bill, introduced by a bishop into the House of Lords, to make Convocation and not the Judicial Committee the sole judges of doctrine. But even the Lords distrusted Convocation as judges and flung their Bill out, in spite of the most plausible palaver of Soapy Sam.[8] It is interesting to know that Bishop Thirlwall had soon to confide to Sam that Wales was hopeless. The High Church party had completely failed there, and as for the "Low" or Evangelical,— "Dissenters out-preach them."[9]

[8] From the suppressed Vol. II of the *Life of Samuel Wilberforce*, pp. 41–2.
[9] *Ditto*, p. 249.

From Brookfield's Diary, 11.12.53, Sunday.[1]—' 11th. I
don't remember anything that occurred except that most
people went to church to hear the Bishop of Oxford preach,
but not I, nor Lady Ashburton, nor the Carlyles. As he
(Soapy Sam) sat between me and Mrs. Henry Taylor today
(at dinner), I overheard him pretending to be shy and
putting on the voice of an absolute lout. She said, " Why
don't you come out with us to the drawing-room as soon as
dinner is over ? " He replied in the voice of an innocent,
" I'm so ignorant of Society, it's just the thing I might do."
No joke intended,' concluded Mr. Brookfield, and if he was
right, then even Soapy Sam may have been feeling that he
needed the protection of the ladies when discussing prevenient grace and the mysteries of baptism in such company.

His safest plan was to taboo the dogmas of his trade there.
" When I am with High-Church people," Lady Ashburton
used to say, " my opposition to them makes me feel no
church at all—hardly bare walls with doors and windows."[10]
In a letter describing this party,[11] Henry Taylor praised
the Bishop's " tact " and " sociable cordiality . . . bright,
sharp and subtle, ready and graceful and full of resource in
conversation." For the nick-name " Soapy Sam," which
he knew was his, the Bishop had a witty explanation,—
" Quite natural,—I am always in hot water, and coming
out with clean hands."

By this time he and Carlyle were old acquaintances, and
Sam did not need to be told his hostess had said, " Coming
back to the society of Carlyle after the dons at Oxford, is
like returning from some conventional world to the human
race."[12] He may have had some such feeling himself, poor
fellow. Assuredly there was never an atom of personal
bitterness in any of their debates. Their friendship was so
well known that the Bishop's admirers could claim that he
was the model of the fine picture of an English bishop in
the seventh Latter-Day Pamphlet, where the " Bishop of
our Diocese " is humorously contrasted to his credit with
the wholesale " Sausage-Maker, Bobus of Houndsditch."

Venables indeed goes so far as to attribute Carlyle's
increasing tolerance for the Church of England to ' his personal liking for Bishop Wilberforce.[13] They suited one

---

[10] *Monographs*, by Lord Houghton, p. 250.
[11] *Autobiography of Henry Taylor*, II, p. 133.
[12] *Monographs*, by Lord Houghton, p. 251.
[13] G. S. Venables in *Fortnightly Review*, May, 1883, p. 633.

another well, whenever they met at the Grange or elsewhere. Once they were seen riding together up Portland Place on their way to an Islington dog-show, the Bishop in his proper costume, and Carlyle in his well-known slouched hat.'

After 11.12.53 we are without reporters, as Mr. Brookfield had to leave the Grange for about ten days, inspecting schools, and when he returned the Carlyles had gone. An entry in his diary for 23.12.53 gives a passing glimpse of the departed terrestrial paradise of the Grange.[1]—' The people that have come and (or) gone from Grange,' between 5 and 23.12.53.—' Lord and Lady Elcho, Lord and Lady Canning, Lord Carnarvon, Lord Mark Kerr, Bishop of Oxford ' (alias Soapy Sam), ' Mr. and Mrs. Carlyle, Rev. R. and Mrs. Trench, Mr. and Mrs. Marx, Mr. and Mrs. Salmon, James Spedding, F. Lushington, G. S. Venables, Clough, R. M. Milnes, Mr. Senior, A. W. Kinglake, Mr. Ellice (Bear Ellice), Mr. and Mrs. (Robert) Lowe, H. and Mrs. Taylor, Miss Salmon, Miss Baring, Geraldine Mildmay, Mr. and Mrs. Brookfield, Magdalene (Brookfield, now " rising four "), Arthur (Brookfield, 9 months old), Aubrey Taylor, Eleanor Taylor, Ida Taylor ' (juveniles also, but older than the Brookfields).

The owners of a great country-house who entertained at large in England had plainly a hotel-keeper's trouble but without the fees.

XXI

ADVICE ABOUT READING, &c.

(1853)

RECEIVING a letter from W. Latimer, a working cork-cutter at Carlisle, Carlyle replied in a letter which got into the newspapers and was often reprinted during the following years.—

'THE GRANGE,

'15 *Decr.*, 1853.

'SIR,—

'I myself hear nothing practical as yet about that cheap edition of my Books ; and am inclined to think it may still be a year or two before any such edition actually sees the light. This is all the intelligence I can send you on that subject.

'As you seem to be a studious enquiring man, I will recommend you to read *well* what good Books you have at command, and to reckon always that reading *well* is greatly more important than reading *much*. Not to say that the best wisdom, for every man, does not lie in books at all, but in what conclusions he himself can form, and what just insight arrive at, from all manner of suggestions and helps, whereof Books are but of one sort.

'With many kind wishes, I remain,

'Yours Sincerely,

'T. CARLYLE.'

One or two days later, Mrs. Carlyle received a long letter from her favourite cousin Helen, daughter of the uncle John Welsh who had died in October. Helen said she was herself unusually well.

On Sunday, 18.12.53, apparently, Mrs. Carlyle who had been worrying about the failure to make the new room a silent one, said to her husband,—" My dear, let us do as

71

you have sometimes been saying, fairly rent that Ronca's house, turn Ronca with his vermin out of it, and let it stand empty—empty and noiseless. What is £40 or £45 a year, to saving one's life and sanity? Neighbour Chalmers will help me ; the owner people are willing ; say you ' yes,' and I will go at once and have the whole bedlam swept away against your return." To which there could be no reply but a grateful,—" Yes, if you can." When Lady Ashburton and the others asked him why he sent his wife instead of going himself, he merely answered,—" Oh! I should only spoil the thing, she is sure to manage it," which she did. Neighbours and house-agents co-operating, it cost no more than £5 and the threat of a notice to quit to get Ronca to bind himself under a penalty never again to keep fowls or macaws or other nuisances.

Tho Mrs. Carlyle had been loath to quit the brilliant company at the Grange, she soon was glad she went,—for in a day or two a letter came from one of her cousins in Liverpool, announcing the unexpected sudden death of her favourite cousin Helen. She was " very thankful," she told Mrs. Russell of Thornhill, that she had not got the news " in a houseful of company. And the same day came Mr. Carlyle, who had suddenly taken the resolution to go to Scotsbrig, and see his mother once more, (Dr.) John's letter indicating that she was dying fast. I hurried him off all I could, for I was terrified he would arrive to find her dead, and he was just in time."

XXII

DEATH OF CARLYLE'S MOTHER
(1853)

FOR many weeks Carlyle's old mother (' about 82 ') had been visibly fading away, " like snowdrifts in thaw " as the song says, ' without any disease except old age.' Carlyle was in perplexity. If he went to Scotsbrig, he might ' be in the way.' His sisters, Jean (Mrs. Aitken from Dumfries) and Mary (Mrs. Austin from the Gill, a farm on Solway Shore, between Cummertrees and Ruthwell stations), had for months been staying by turns at Scotsbrig to assist the family there in attending their mother. They had long ago told her that " Tom " could be with her in a day if she wanted him, but she would not send for him. Why vex her son with bad news ? He came at last without being sent for, by the night express leaving London on Thursday, 22.12.1853.

From Kirtlebridge station on Friday morning, he was seen walking rapidly to Scotsbrig farm-house,[1] and without a word to anybody going in and up the staircase two steps at a time. He was half-way upstairs before he knew his mother was still alive. She had not long ago wakened from a sixteen hours' sleep, and now opened her eyes and said with joy,—" Thou's Tom."[1]

She had a restless weary day and slept a good deal ; but, as Carlyle reported to his brother in Canada, her mind to the end was ' clear, simple and composed : her spirit, her very form of character and humour—for she occasionally spoke with a faint touch of jocosity—continued *entire* to the very last.' Taking leave of " Tom " at midnight, she said as she used to do long ago,—" Tell us how thou sleeps ! "

[1] This and anything else in this chapter not taken from published letters and journals is from a long verbal statement by John Carlyle made in his own house, near Langholm, on 31.12.1895, to D. A. W. This John was nephew of T. C., the son of James, the farmer at Scotsbrig in 1853, and he was in immediate attendance.

On the next day, Saturday, she was weaker still, especially after the dusk on that short winter's day,—" struggling for breath," unable from sheer weakness to fill her lungs, as her son Dr. John explained to the others, yet wonderfully wide-awake. Hearing that Jean had gone to get coals in the dark from a shed in the yard, she made Dr. John hold the candle to the window for light to Jean.

Jean told how she used to overhear her mother " whispering her prayers " every night, forgetting none of her children, " going round by America too now," as she used to say, for now she had a son and a daughter there ; and omitting no public or private interest fit for prayer, herself and her own interests coming always last. " All the days of my appointed time will I wait till my change come,"— was a favourite text they had often heard her muttering. But on this her last night of all, tho her mind was unclouded, her pain was too great for prayer ; and at last her son Dr. John gave her a little laudanum about midnight to relieve her, which it did. She looked kindly on her Tom and kissed him " Good night," and said, as if remembering the long journey he had made to be with her,—" I'm muckle obleeged t' ye." Except a " Yes " and a " No," she spoke no other word. In a few minutes, she fell asleep, and in the morning, Sunday, Christmas, she did not awake, but lay sleeping deeper and deeper. For hours there was none in the room beside her but the doctor and " Uncle Tom," her grandson John[1] coming and going, his mother and aunts in adjoining rooms. Towards four o'clock her breathing grew fainter rather suddenly,—paused once or twice, and then ceased.

XXIII

HOLDING ON TO FREDERICK WORK
(1853-54)

WHILE Carlyle was waiting at Scotsbrig for the funeral, his wife was writing to him.—

' CHELSEA,
' *Tuesday, Dec. 27*, 1853.

' Oh, my dear ! never does one feel oneself so utterly helpless as in trying to speak comfort for great bereavement. I will not try it. Time is the only comforter for the loss of a mother. One does not believe in time while the grief is quite new. One feels as if it could never, never be less. And yet all griefs, when there is no bitterness in them, are soothed down by time. And your grief for your mother must be altogether sweet and soft. You must feel that you have always been a good son to her ; that you have always appreciated her as she deserved, and that she knew this, and loved you to the last moment. How thankful you may be that you went when you did. Oh ! what would I have given for last words ; but '—at Liverpool in 1842, when she was on her way to her mother, who was ill,—' the words that awaited me were, " Your mother is dead ! " And I deserved it should so end. I was not the dutiful child to my mother that you have been to yours.

' It is a great mercy you have had some sleep. It will surely be a comfortable reflection for you in coming home this time, that you will look out over a perfectly empty hencourt . . .'—so that you will not be bothered by the " demon fowls " when flinging yourself into the work on *Frederick*,' —which she knew it would be his intention to do.

Carlyle was writing copiously to her and others, incidentally mentioning that his farmer brother, James, ' comes and sits with me, or walks with me when I like, *goes* gently away when

75

he sees I had rather be alone.' He came home immediately
after the funeral, and by the first week in January
he was reading and praising a summary of some papers
done by Neuberg, while confessing to him that Frederick
was " far from cognate to my humour just now." Discussing a " chaotic mass " of papers to be burned, he made
a remark that reveals his method :—" There was next to
nothing but disquisition in it ; and *narrative* alone is the
permissible thing in my enterprise."

He had next to read a Life of General Bülow, which the
author, Varnhagen von Ense, had sent him. " I confess,"
he told Neuberg, (11.1.54), " to finding (it)—in parts—
extremely tiresome, and in fact ill-done,—being mere chaos
with a *skin* over it." He finished it three days later, and
then offered the book to Neuberg,—" if you care to take
it with you." " It is worth reading after all," he added,
" being very easily read ; and you can accept Dennewitz,
Grossbeeren and the other battles as Prussian Donnybrooks
at worst," referring to the war of 1813, when Bülow was
Prussia's best general.

On the same day, 11.1.54, he was telling Lady Ashburton
that he found *Frederick* ' totally alien to my humour at
present ! I foresee I shall have a furious wrestle with that
subject, if it ever come to anything ; wrestle at which I
could tremble in any humour. But there is no help ;—nor,
except in oneself, is there any hindrance possible : that too
should be a comfort ! '

Then he wrote to Varnhagen von Ense to acknowledge
his book,[1] (15.1.54), thanking him ' for so welcome and
friendly a Gift, which so many others, a long list now, have
preceded.' He mentioned his absence in Scotland and his
mother's death, to explain delay in acknowledgment, and
said,—' I have kept myself very silent, and as solitary as
possible, ever since my return. In the evenings of last week
I have read *Bülow*, as an agreeable halting-place for my
mind ; and was very sorry last night when it ended upon
me, as all things have to do.

' You have given us a flowing Narration, in your old clear
style ; painted out a stormy battling Life-Pilgrimage, with
many interesting particulars in it. Bülow was not much
other than a Name to me before ; but I possess him now
on much closer terms : the man and the scene he worked
in are very vividly brought out in this Book. Both in face

[1] *Last Words of Thomas Carlyle*, Pubr. Longmans, &c., pp. 274-8.

and in character, I find him an intensely Prussian Physiognomy ; really very interesting to me,—with his strange old Swedenborgian Father, his wild Brothers, and all his peculiar environments and personalities. Almost a type Prussian, as I said ; reminding me of much that I saw, and guessed, among your military people, while among you.'

Which was not intoxicating praise for either Bülow or his biographer, but enough to pass, and more than might have been expected. The letter ran on.—

'I have gone through great quantities of the dreariest Prussian reading since I saw you ; but cannot boast to myself that Prussia or Vater Fritz becomes in the least clearer to me by the process. Human stupidity (with the *pen*, or with other implements in its hand) is extremely potent in this Universe ! How I am to quit this Fritz after so much lost labour, is not clear to me ; still less how I am ever to manage any Picture of him on those terms. Mirabeau, so far as I can see, is the only man of real *genius*, that has ever spoken of him ; and he only in that cursory and offhand way.[2] In the end, I suppose I shall be reduced to Fritz's own letters and utterances, as my main resource. If I had been able to get any *sleep* in Germany, my own eyes might still have done a good deal for me ; but that also was not possible : the elements were too strong for so thin a skin ; I was driven half-distracted after five or six weeks of that sort,—to this hour the street of the *Linden*, and with it all Berlin, is incurably reversed to me ; and I cannot bring the North side out of a *southern* posture in my fancy, let me do what I will. I remember Lobositz, however ; I remember Kunersdorf too in a very impressive manner ; and wish I had gone to Reinsberg, to Prag, to Leuthen, &c. &c.'—as maybe Varnhagen had suggested. This prepares us for the second visit to Germany in 1858. After mention of Miss Wynn and another lady friend, the letter went on.—

'We are busy here, babbling about Turk wars, Palmerston resignation-reacceptances, Prince-Albert interferences, &c. &c.,—with very trifling degree of wisdom, and to me with no interest whatever. London (and) England everywhere are swelling higher and higher with golden wealth, and the opulencies which fools most prize ;—London in particular is stretching itself out on every side, at a rate which

[2] "Which you know" is implied. See T. C.'s *Frederick the Great*, Book I, Chapter I, &c., and Book XXI, Chapter IX.

to me is frightful and disgusting ; for we are already two
millions and more ; and our new populations are by no
means the beautifullest of the human species, but rather
the greediest and hungriest from all ends of the Earth that
are flocking towards us. We must take our destiny. " Unexampled prosperity," fools call it,—by no means I.

> ' Yours ever with thanks,
> ' T. CARLYLE.'

He worked on as well as he could, but was ' miserably
languid ' in spite of himself. In the end of January he confessed to his brother Dr. John :—' My soul is exceeding
sorrowful, all hung with *black* in general, thinking of what
is gone and what cannot return to me. I hold my peace in
general and accept the decrees of Heaven, still hoping that
some useful labour may be again possible for me here, which
is the one consolation I can conceive at present.'

Writing on Wednesday, 3.2.54, to tell Neuberg to come
on the Monday evening instead of the Sunday, as he and
his wife were to be at Bath House on the Sunday, he added
about the history in hand,—' I am again wandering in the
deeps, swallowed '—like Jonah by the great fish,—' in the
dark belly of the German Dryasdust (fatallest of created
Entities), and feel as if certainly preässured that Fritz will
never be attainable by me ; that, in fine, I ought, once for
all, to quit that horrible province of things ! ' In a few days
Neuberg received assurance he was still going on.—' In my
life I never got into such a Frisches Haff '—Fresh-water
Bay, the name of the big lagoon between Dantzig and
Königsberg,—' not half a fathom deep of brackish water,
anywhere, in endless square miles of superficies, and nothing
but sand round one to the world's end. If I ever do make
a readable little human Book out of *Frederick*, it will be a
kind of miracle in Literature. However, I do stick to it, by
mere *vis inertiæ*, and as if by a kind of sad enchantment
into the realms of sand and brackish Haffs. A new cargo
of German books arrived the other day.'

To relieve his feelings he varied his figures of speech. He
felt like a man smelting metal out of slag. At another time
he felt like one ploughing the barren wastes of Brandenburg
sand, or like a man driving a big waggon stuck fast in a
' sea of quagmires,' and rejoicing to see ' the heavy wheels
go round ' at all. This was a favourite figure of speech
Perhaps the humblest was when he told his brother,—" I

haggle along here in my old way ; much like a man doomed to *cobble shoes* (the dreariest of enterprises, hope nowhere in it, except the hope of getting done with it)." He went on,—" My progress is exceedingly below my intentions ; in fact, is exceedingly bad ; but I still persevere, tho falling on my nose so often. Gee-ho ! Chick-Chick ! "

XXIV

A WALK IN THE WEST END
(1854)

ON the west-end pavements one Sunday afternoon,
5.2.54, Carlyle might have been seen going about in
the company of " Father Prout," who was known as " Oliver
Yorke " to readers of *Fraser's Magazine*, and called Mahony
in the common world. Very conspicuous they both were
in the fashionable crowd, tho neither seemed to be aware
of it. Carlyle was in his everyday clothes and slouched hat,
and Father Prout, as a stranger, was more noticed.[1] He
was in a well-worn black suit, and was a. thickset figure,
but spare, not exactly stooping, but bending forward, both
arms behind his back, the left hand grasping the right arm,
and wore an ill-brushed hat " on the extreme back of his
head " : which had at least the advantage of revealing the
great bald forehead above his humorous smiling face, like
a cherub's, but mature. His piercing grey eyes were looking
at you over his spectacles ; and if you listened long enough
at a little distance, you might hear a sudden loud musical
laugh.[1] He was an ex-Jesuit, ex-priest, and " free-lance "
writer by trade, and used to describe himself as an " Irish
potato seasoned with Attic salt," for like Maginn he was a
Cork boy. He was a man of fifty now and usually lived
in Paris, for economy and other reasons,—Paris Correspondent for one thing ; but he was glad to come over to
London occasionally and talk of things in general with old
acquaintances. It was now nearly twenty years since he
and Carlyle were " Fraserians " together.

What they were talking about now is not reported and
cannot be guessed,—there was a wealth of topics. In the
contemporary world, Asia Minor and Egypt, Hungary and
Greece were known to " Father Prout." In the stirring

[1] *Works of Father Prout, Biog. Introduction*, pp. xvi to xxvii, &c., by
Charles Kent.

mes of 1848 he had been an English newspaper correspon-
ent at Rome, and maybe we owe to his letters or talk
me touches in the sketch of a " Reforming Pope " in the
st of the *Latter-Day Pamhplets*. Erasmus was a hero of
s,—which gives a clue to his character ; and it is said[2]
e was the parish priest who went to Rome to buy a Virgin
ary, and finding no other marble to his mind, bought a
iana, saying, " Those chaps of mine at Ardnagehy will
ever know the difference." As a young man in Ireland
e denounced the great Dan O'Connell in a large company
here he was in a minority of one. No wonder he and
arlyle were familiar friends.

They parted now, and Carlyle joined "mocking Hay-
vard," the fashionable wit and Peelite journalist, who had
ust been setting the world laughing at Disraeli, by disclosing
hat his official and yet eloquent eulogy of Wellington was
lagiarised from that of Thiers on St. Cyr.[3] Carlyle had
ately, in a letter to his brother Dr. John, praised a " scourg-
ng article " by Hayward in the *Edinburgh Review* on Dis-
aeli. " Diamond cut diamond," said he,—" Jew pull the
dirty ragged pate of Jew," a German proverb, which may
aave been quoted here because Hayward had the weakness
of being ashamed of the name of Abraham, which he had
nherited from a Jew, his grandfather.[4] " I agree with
Iayward, however," the letter continued. " There is hardly
any uglier phenomenon in these times than the political
aistory of that adventurer."

Meanwhile Lord Ashburton had been calling on Brook-
ield, " to discuss their educational projects," and as they
vere walking back together to Bath House they encountered
Carlyle with Hayward, who took his leave ; and as the
other three walked on together, Brookfield poked fun at
Carlyle for being seen with Hayward, saying,—" Tell me
vhat company a man keeps and I will tell you what he is."

Now it was known to Ashburton and Carlyle that late
nights with Thackeray were London's chief attraction to
the merry Mahony, " Father Prout " ; and also that Brookfield to his credit, altho a fashionable preacher as well as
a school inspector, and " in the running " for a bishopric,
found their company irresistibly attractive, in spite of Mrs.
Brookfield.—" Don't become a second Father Prout," she

[2] *Herself—Ireland*, by Mrs. T. P. O'Connor, p. 190.
[3] *The Correspondence of Abraham Hayward*, by H. E. Carlisle, I, p, 174.
[4] *Ditto*, I, pp. 88–9.

G

used to say.[5] So when he finished about Hayward, Carlyle replied,—" That's nothing,—I have just left a still worse man, Father Mahony," which seemed to Brookfield, when the laughing was over, to be hard on Mahony,—a mistake of Brookfield's, as the hit was rather at his wife's standard of values.

He might have seen this for himself if he had not soon had something more unusual to remember. It was this same afternoon, 5.2.54, that Lady Ashburton, in the course of confidential talk about these educational projects, burst into tears and said,—" I would do anything for those children." Mr. Brookfield explains that the " sorrow of her own life " was ever before her,—the loss of her only child in infancy.[5]

Perhaps it was at her instigation that her husband was now making a special study of popular education. At any rate on 9.2.54 Carlyle was writing to Lord Ashburton about a pamphlet Brookfield had sent him the day before, and which had turned on the pioneer efforts of Ashburton and Brookfield to promote the teaching of useful knowledge. Their fashionable friends were sarcastic, and told them that ' inspired by such noble examples they were at that moment "learning to black their own boots." ' Carlyle, on the contrary, was emphatic in his praise, declaring :

' I persuade myself you have here opened, in a really skilful, felicitous and compendious way,—by these Prizes and by what you have said of them,—a subject which will be found large enough, momentous enough one day ;—that, in fact, here is the wedge (one of the gentlest and best-ground wedges) fairly got into the wood of as ugly, huge and absurd a block as ever stopped the highway in this World ; and that henceforth there will be no rest till said wedge, and all manner of others like it, are hammered home, and the ugly enormous block (produce of mere Monkery and other extinct conditions and influences) is reduced to manageable pieces, and ultimately to splinters, to fuel and Euthanasia ! Heaven send it swiftly. There never was, I think, a more monstrous, pernicious delusion than this, which we find quietly established as a universal Nightmare over the " educated " part of the human species, that the end and aim of all learning, is that we may learn to wag our tongue ; write books, deliver bursts of Parliamentary eloquence, &c. &c. ! Which may the Devil fly away with, root and branch, the sooner the better ! Amen, amen.'

[5] *Mrs. Brookfield & Her Circle*, by C. & F. Brookfield, I, p. 172, and II, pp. 402-4.

XXV

A NOTE-BOOK SOLILOQUY, &c.
(1854)

CARLYLE was at his desk every morning and busy over his materials for his usual working hours. On evenings when there were no visitors, or after they had departed and his wife gone to bed, he used often to sit long after midnight reading, a habit common in Scotland.

Not long ago Mrs. Carlyle had been complaining to Erasmus Darwin ' of some man being grown disagreeable,'[1] and he made a reply which she remembered and quoted,— " The fact is I believe we are all getting rather old ! " The same sentiment appears in Carlyle's letters after his mother died, as when he wrote to St. Thomas (Erskine of Linlathen) :—' I must rally myself if I can for a new and sterner final epoch which I feel has now arrived for me.' On the last day of February, 1854, he was soliloquizing in his note-book.—

' Not quite idle ; always indeed professing to work ; but making, as it were, no way at all. Alas ! Alas ! In truth I am weak and forlorn to a degree ; have the profoundest feeling of utter loneliness in the world ; which the company, " when it comes," of my fellow creatures rather tends to aggravate than assuage. I have, however, or am getting, a kind of sad peace withal, " renunciation," more real superiority to vain wishes, worldly honours, advantages, &c., the peace that belongs to the *old*. My *Frederick* looks as if it never would take shape in me ; in fact the problem is to burn away the immense dungheap of the 18th century with its ghastly cants, foul, blind sensualities, cruelties and *inanity* now fallen *putrid*, rotting inevitably towards annihilation ; to destroy and extinguish all that, having got to know it, and to know that it must be rejected for evermore ; after which the perennial portion, pretty much Friedrich

[1] *J. W. Carlyle : Letters*, edited by L. Huxley, p. 364.

and Voltaire, so far as I can see, may remain conspicuous and capable of being delineated (very loosely expressed all this ; does not fit my thought like a skin ; but, like an Irish waistcoat, it does in some degree).

'Sunday morning last, there came into my mind a vision of the old Sunday mornings I had seen at Mainhill, &c. Poor old mother, father, and the rest of us bustling about to get dressed in time and down to the meeting-house at Ecclefechan. Inexpressibly sad to me, and full of meaning. They are gone now, vanished all ; their poor bits of thrifty clothes, more precious to me than Queen's or King's expensive trappings, their pious struggling effort, their " little life," it is all away. It has all melted into the still sea ; it was " rounded with a sleep." So with all things. Nature and this big universe in all corners of it show nothing else. Time ! Death ! All-devouring Time ! This thought, " *Exeunt omnes*," '—all go out, an old stage direction in plays,—clear the stage—' and how the generations are like crops of grass, *temporary*, very, and all *vanishes*, as it were an apparition and a ghost ; these things, though half a century old in me, possess my mind as they never did before.

'On the whole I have a strange interior *tomb* life, and dwell in secret among scenes and contemplations which I do not speak of to anybody. My mother ! my good heavy-laden dear and brave and now lost mother ! The thought that I shall never see her more with these eyes gives a strange painful flash in me many times when I look at that poor portrait I have of her. " Like Ulysses," as I say, I converse with the shade of my mother and sink out of all company and light common talk into that grand element of sorrow and eternal stillness. God is great. I will not ask or guess (*know* no man ever could or can) what He has appointed for His poor creatures of the earth ; a right and good and wise appointment, it full surely is. Let me look to it with pious manfulness, without either hope or fear that were excessive. Excessive ? Alas ! how very *small* it is in me ; really inconsiderable, beaten out of me by " many stripes," pretty continual for these fifty years, till I feel as if fairly broken and pounded in the mortar ; and have oftenest no prayer except Rest, rest ; let me sleep then if that must be my doom ! For as God lives, I am weary, very weary, and the way of this world does not suit me at all. Such changes grow upon the spirit of a man. When I look back thirty years and read my feelings, it is very strange.

' Oh pious mother ! kind, good, brave, and truthful soul as I have ever found, and more than I have ever elsewhere found in this world, your poor Tom, long out of his school-days now, has fallen very lonely, very lame and broken in this pilgrimage of his ; and you cannot help him or cheer him by a kind word any more. From your grave in Eccle-fechan kirkyard yonder you bid him trust in God, and that also he will try if he can understand, and *do*. The conquest of the world and of death and hell does verily yet lie in that, if one can understand and do it.'

On 4.3.1854 Carlyle was writing to Lady Ashburton, and after details about the weather and his wife reported :—

' One day Milnes gave me a visit ; very fat, and happy as ever ; full of amusement at Drummond's Pamphlet &c. &c. I read Drummond since you went ; really a most notable piece ; very *serious* withal, much more so than the *talk* of Henry (Drummond) almost ever is, and abounding in utter-ances and calculations that are enough to make the ears tingle,—if anybody *heard*, or listened, which the Bookseller tells me nobody does. " Bless you, Sir, 250 copies or so : I believe he has lost some 7 or 8 thousand pounds by his writings before this ! " For the rest, I in *substance* greatly agree with Henry in this Pamphlet ; deducting " Christ " &c., I find he has seen into many things in a really true and remarkable way. I sent off my copy of it (along with one of *Common Things*) to the good Thomas Erskine, who likes to see signs of the times. . . .

' I wish Lord Ashburton and you would interest yourselves about the Civil Service and Promotion by merit. The more I think of that, the more important it seems to me,—the crown and summary of all conceivable " reforms " ; and *immensely* wanted, if it could be well done ? And how can it ever be done, if the wise and distinguished do not help to say, " Try it ; let us *all* try it ! " It seems to me the real *Noah's Ark* for this perishing Epoch.'

XXVI

A LETTER ON EDUCATION
(1854)

ON 13.3.54 Carlyle was writing to Lord Ashburton a letter on Education, suggested by a pamphlet by Ashburton offering prizes for teaching common things, meaning the natural laws we follow in economics and in using fire and water and all sorts of common tools.[1]

There was nothing new in Ashburton's doctrine as he stated it, but it implied what was yet a novelty here in education, the advisability of teaching men to do things, and in short be practical. To a reader to-day the best of what he said are some sidelights on history, significant anecdotes. ' In the last naval war,' he said, referring to the wars that ended in 1815, ' there was one occasion I remember, on which, in order to spite their captain, the men refused to stand by their guns, and received each broadside that shattered their decks with cheers of savage exultation.' Which seemed to him like what strikers sometimes did. ' The mob of Petersburg thought the cholera the work of the physicians, and they murdered the physicians. The mob of Paris thought that the priests had poisoned the wells, and they murdered the priests.' And so on. Here now is Carlyle's letter.—

' DEAR LORD ASHBURTON,

' You have come upon a great truth,'—meaning that education should aim at teaching men to work,—' one of the deepest and most fertile, in reference to all provinces of human affairs ;—which has never, I suppose, been expressly *controverted* by anybody, but which has been forgotten profoundly on all hands,—as we may see everywhere, from Hugo Reid's "Ventilation"' (attempting to make air circulate

---

[1] Pamphlet on *Ashburton Prizes*, in London Library, pp. 15, 16.

y bellows-blasts) ' up to Oxford-University " Education,"
nd higher ! A truly fatal oblivion and ignoring on
he part of almost all men. To attempt " educating " in
gnorance of this principle produces—what we see among
he Educated : Education by *cram* ; really in many respects,
o feeding by *cram* (instead of *eating* with *appetite*) ; out of
which strange processes no body and no soul ever was, or
ver could be, increased in strength or in health, however
much it might be blown up in diameter !—I recommend
ou much to prosecute that idea ; which will lead to great
esults, in Education especially.

' As I said, there is nobody known to me who has *contra-
licted* the idea ; nor could anybody, at least since the notion
f *Original Sin* was, to all practical purposes, tacitly given
up ;—indeed it is in the notion of Man being originally
damned, and only likely to get his salvation by learning to
ead certain Greek and Hebrew Books, that Oxford University and the other *Cram* Establishments can make a good
excuse for themselves ; excuse partly valid while that notion
asted. But as to affirming, and expressly setting forth, of
his idea, I know nobody who has done so with any thing
like such faculty as Goethe in the Meister's *Wanderjahre ;*
which Book I again join my Lady in much recommending
o you, as worthy of perusal and re-perusal, till you have
completely got into the Author's point of view, which is not
easy for an English reader. You will find that no man was
ever more completely filled with your notion than Goethe,
who perhaps he says little of it in express terms ; and that
his whole scheme of Education is a beautiful (and truly un-
rivalled) symbolical preaching of the same.

' Richter also, whose *Levana* you know, has many good
hints on the subject ; and in particular, I can remember,
pleased me much by inculcating that nothing, no passion,
tendency, should be *rooted out* in a man, but only guided,
and the counter-tendency encouraged if necessary ; the
worth of the man being simply the *sum* of these and of his
wise management of these.

' In my own reading I can recollect no Book worth classing
in the same list with these, as respects this matter. But I
believe there is a good deal about it, under a very inferior
but more practical form, in the writings of Pestalozzi ; most
of which, I suppose, are to be had in French, if not in
English, out of the original German ; and the whole of
which are probably worth your attention while occupied in

this way.   Pestalozzi's *Life*, I believe, is biographicall
interesting as well ; and may be safely recommended, t
begin with : you will doubtless get there, best of all, indica
tion of what else he has written in the line that interest
you.

'Fellanberg's Books and Pamphlets might also be exam
ined with good hope : a Swiss Baron who set up a Schoc
of his own for Peasants, and practically hoed and ploughe
with them, for many a year ;—indeed you are, as it wer
bound to make due acquaintance with such a neighbour an
foregoer in this of "common things."   Of our English Work
on Education I know none even by name, except Locke'
Treatise on Education and Roger Ascham's *Schoolmaster*
both of which I, in like manner, hold you "bound" to reac
tho probably you will get little out of them for your presen
objects.   Pestalozzi's *Life* is the first new thing.   If in gettin
it, or getting, or enquiring after, anything else, or all thing
else, I can be of use, of course I shall be but too happy
And so, right good speed to your Lordship on this ne
career ; and may some of the things you are privileged t
see for truths get themselves a little realized into blesse
facts among us by the great help you can in various way
give them !   Amen.   And let us work while it is called T
day ; for the night cometh !—

'We are a little better in health here ; we, and all th
World, have made a mighty improvement in *weather* sinc
you went,—which is really an excellent thing, all othe
things remaining as they were.   I often think what utte
fools we are, with our Universe of Cant and Delusion, "pile
over us to the very Zenith, and reaching inwards to th
marrow of our bones,"—with our Doxologies, Theologie
39 Articles, Bishops of Exeter and Oxford, and Whewell'
Plurality of Worlds ;—and how I in particular (poor wretcl
the sorriest fool of all) am daily and hourly admonished c
that old *Teutonic* etymology "Gott der Heilige—God th
Healthy—God the Holy" (all one thing in very truth !)
and how inexpressibly it might have profited me, had mer
amid their Hebrew, Roman, Greek and other high ologie
and speculations, duly remembered that one small Germa
fact ;—or could I at this late date get it practically "remem
bered," for my own poor self ; which I cannot, and shal
die without being able to do !   I only meant to say tha
Health is the real basis of all morality and of all Religion
and that I, who am daily admonished of that fact, can a

little as another get it reduced to practice in any measure !
Alas, alas !—

' I send my homages to my Lady and Sambo ; may their
promenades be pleasant among the young primroses and
opening Woods. " Luck be on the House ! " as the Scotch
say.

' Yours ever truly,

' T. CARLYLE.'

XXVII

LETTERS TO AND FROM EMERSON
(1854)

THE correspondence between Carlyle and Emerson is the best memorial of their lifelong friendship. In telling Emerson of the sound-proof room, Carlyle had confided to him,—' In the course of about a year of that garret sanctuary, I hope to have swept away much litter from my existence.' After mention of sundry other persons, the letter had concluded :—' Thackeray has very rarely come athwart me since his return' from America : ' he is a big fellow, soul and body ; of many gifts and qualities (particularly in the Hogarth line, with a dash of Sterne super-added), of enormous *appetite* withal, and very uncertain and chaotic in all points except his *outer breeding*, which is fixed enough, and perfect according to the modern English style. I rather dread explosions in his history. A big, fierce, weeping, hungry man ; not a strong one. Ay de mi !—But I must end, I must end. Your Letter awakened in me, while reading it, one mad notion. I said to myself, " Well, if I live to finish this *Frédéric* impossibility, or even to fling it fairly into the fire, why should not I go, in my old days, and see Concord, Yankeeland, and that man again, after all ! " '

" Ay de mi ! "—the Spanish for Alas, poor me !—was a favourite exclamation of Carlyle on paper. Maybe it dated from 1828, when he and his wife were learning Spanish and reading Don Quixote together at Craigenputtock.[1]

Replying to this letter on 11.3.54, Emerson said *Jesuitism*, the last of the *Latter-Day Pamphlets*, had let him see—' why you like those papers so well. I think you have cleared your skirts ; it is a pretty good minority of one, enunciating with brilliant malice what shall be the universal opinion of the next edition of mankind. And the sanity was so manifest, that I felt that the over-gods had cleared their skirts

[1] See Carlyle to *The French Revolution*, pp. 77 and 81.

also to this generation, in not leaving themselves without witness, tho without this single voice perhaps I should not acquit them. Also I pardon the world that reads the book as tho it read it not, when I see your inveterate humours. It required courage . . . this writing Rabelais in 1850. . . .

' Then I learned that the newspapers had announced the death of your mother . . . I remembered what you had said of her to me, and your apprehensions of the event that has come. I can well believe you were grieved. The best son is not enough a son. My mother died in my house in November. . . . Age did not make that she should die without causing me pain. In my journeying lately, when I think of home the heart is taken out. . . .

' One good word closed your letter which ought to have had an instant reply, namely, that you might come westward when *Frédéric* was disposed of. Speed *Frédéric*, then, for all reasons and for this ! America is growing furiously, town and state ; new Kansas, new Nebraska looming up in these days, vicious politicians seething a wretched destiny for them at Washington. The politicians shall be sodden, the States escape, please God ! The fight of slave or freeman drawing nearer, the question is sharply, whether slavery or whether freedom shall be abolished. Come and see. Wealth is on a new scale.' The Kansas-Nebraska Act of this year, according to historians, began the civil war in fact, by making slavery there a question to be decided by the people. But nobody as yet foresaw that. Emerson went on.—' John Bull interests you. Come and see the Jonathanization of John. What, you scorn all this ? Well, then, come and see a few good people, impossible to be seen on any other shore, who heartily and always greet you. There is a very serious welcome for you here.'

This letter arrived at Cheyne Row about 1.4.54, and a week later Carlyle was replying :—' The Heavens will reward you ' for answering, he meant. ' It remains true, what I have often told you, that properly there is no voice in the world which is completely human to me, which fully understands all I say, and with clear sympathy and sense answers to me, but your voice only. That is a curious fact, and not quite a joyful one to me. The solitude, the silence of my poor soul, in the centre of this roaring whirlpool called Universe, is great always, and sometimes strange and almost awful. I have two million talking bipeds without feathers, close at my elbow, too ; and of these it is often hard for

me to say whether the so-called " wise " or the almost professedly foolish are the more inexpressibly unproductive to
me. " Silence, Silence ! " I often say to myself : " Be silent
thou poor fool ; and prepare for that Divine Silence which
is now not far ! "—On the whole, write to me whenever you
can ; and be not weary of well-doing. . . .'

Carlyle was humble in the abstract, when looking at his
ideals. He was slow to let his own work pass. But when
reading the works of other historians, he was under no
delusions and plain-spoken. So Emerson would not wonder
to see the present letter run on as it did.—' I make no way
in my Prussian History ; I bore and dig toilsomely through
the unutterablest mass of dead rubbish, which is not even
English, which is German and inhuman ; and hardly from
ten tons of learned inanity is there to be riddled one old rusty
nail. For I have been back as far as Pytheas ; and questioned all manner of extinct German shadows,—who answer
nothing but mumblings. And on the whole Fritz himself is
not sufficiently divine to me, far from it ; and I am getting
old, and heavy of heart ;—and in short, it oftenest seems to
me I shall never write any word about that matter ; and have
again fairly got into the element of the IMPOSSIBLE. Very
well : could I help it ?   I can at least be honestly silent
and " bear my indigence with dignity," as you once said.

' The insuperable difficulty of *Frédéric* is, that he, the
genuine little ray of Veritable and Eternal that was in him,
lay imbedded in the putrid Eighteenth Century, such an
Ocean of sordid nothingness, shams, and scandalous hypocrisies, as never weltered in the world before ; and that in
everything I can find yet written or recorded of him, he
still, to all intents and purposes, most tragically *lies* THERE
—and ought not to lie there, if any use is ever to be had
of him, or at least of *writing* about him ; for as to *him*, he
with his work is safe enough to us, far elsewhere.—Pity me,
pity me ; I know not on what hand to turn ; and have such
a Chaos filling all my earth and Heaven as was seldom seen
in British or Foreign Literature ! Add to which, the sacred
Entity, Literature itself, is not growing more venerable to
me, but less and ever less : good Heavens, I feel often as
if there were no madder set of bladders tumbling on the
billows of the general Bedlam at this moment than even the
Literary ones,—dear at twopence a gross, I should say, unless
one could *annihilate* them by purchase on those easy terms.
But do not tell this in Gath ; let it be a sad family secret.'

XXVIII

THE CRIMEAN WAR, &c.
(1854)

ANOTHER thing that was now diverting Carlyle's attention was the national crime of the Crimean war.
Dating vaguely ' Spring, 1854,' he was writing in his note-
book.—

' Russian war ; soldiers marching off, &c. Never such
enthusiasm seen among the population. Cold I as a very
stone to all that ; seems to me privately I have hardly seen
a madder business. 1696 was ' (the battle of) ' Zenta on
Theiss ' (river in Hungary) ; ' Eugene's task in this world
to break the backbone of Turk. A lazy, ugly, sensual, dark
fanatic, that Turk, whom we have now had for 400 years.'
—In conversation, it may be remarked, he found English
statesmen now knew nothing about all this. The note ran
on.—' I, for my own private part, would not buy the continuance of *him* there at the rate of sixpence a century. Let
him go whenever he can, stay no longer, with all *my* heart.
It will be a beautifuller, not an uglier, that will come in his
place ; uglier I should not know where to look for under
the sky at present. Then as to Russian increase of strength,
&c. Really, I would wait till Russia meddled with me before
I drew *sword* to stop his increase of strength. It is the idle
population of editors, &c., that have done all this to England.
One perceives clearly the ministers go forward in it against
their will. Indeed, I have seen no rational person who is
not privately very much inclined to be of my own opinion ;
all fools and loose-spoken inexperienced persons being of the
other.'

Indeed it is sad to remember how even Tennyson echoed
the popular nonsense, with his piffle about " the long, long
canker of peace," and schoolboy glorification of ignorance in
action by the Light Brigade.

Carlyle went on :—' It is very disgraceful for any " ministry " or government ; but such is the fate and curse of all
ministries here at present, inevitably. Poor souls ! What
could the ministry *do* after all ? To attend to their home
affairs, fortify their own coasts, encourage their own fisheries
(for new seamen), regulate their own population into or
towards proper manliness of spirit and position, and capa-
bility of self-defence, and so bid defiance to all the earth, as
England peculiarly might—to do this, or any portion of this,
is far from them ; therefore they must do the other thing.
Better speed to them.'

It was like Carlyle not to remark that " the editors " and
their employers are one of the few classes that profit by
war, so that when war or peace is in question, they can no
more be impartial advisers than the army contractors.

His concluding sentences refer to that " organization of
labour " which in the *Latter-Day Pamphlets* he had declared
to be " the universal vital Problem of the world." Even
yet there has nothing been done in that direction in England,
tho the folly of the Crimean war has long been admitted by
most of those who were implicated in the starting of it.
Our politicians were ignorant of the history of Eastern
Europe in recent centuries. One of them, Lord Salisbury,
afterwards said what betrayed their way of thinking,—
" We put our money on the wrong horse." But assuredly
the worst of the sinners who led us into the slaughter was
Napoleon III, a mere scoundrel. The Czar Nicholas was a
straightforward gentleman, sincere and even simple, and he
had done all he could to keep peace with the English. But
he had under-estimated the ignorance and mendacity of our
men in office, and supposed they had agreed to his proposals
for partitioning Turkey, if that became needful, in order to
protect the Christians living there, who were of the same
Greek communion as the Russians. The sympathy which
inspired the Russians for the victims of the outrageous Turks
was assuredly sincere, but our own " artful dodgers " never
suspected that.

So in 1854 Carlyle was helpless. Wisdom was not wanted,
and he had to turn to his history writing. He could not
hinder the war ; but he did what little he could to discredit
its promoters, and called our great ally, Napoleon III, a
" scandalous copper-captain." This way of describing a
sham-captain seems to date back to Henry VIII. It is said

that that King was called "old copper-nose," because he
minted bad silver coins, and the copper in them was palpable in the king's nose and some other projecting parts.
Be that as it may, a time shall surely come when men shall
understand, in spite of the evil-doing of political copper-
noses, that to love peace and mind our own business is not
only a Christian duty, but also worldly wisdom,—sheer
common-sense. Nothing for nothing and hideous damage
from fighting are Laws of Nature which no government can
alter ; and there is truth eternal in the words of Jesus,—
" Blessed are the peacemakers."

Dean Stanley was fond of telling how once in those days
he was walking in Hyde Park with Carlyle who was railing
as usual, and he asked :—" What is the advice which you
would give to a Canon of Canterbury ? "

The question had to be twice repeated—Carlyle must have
been unwilling to hear it ; but at last he answered :—
" Dearly beloved Roger, whatsoever thy hand findeth to do,
do it with all thy might."[1]—The anecdote of Dean Swift
these words recalled was that, when once there was no congregation and the clerk alone was present, then in place of,—
" Dearly belovëd brethren, the Scripture moveth us . . ."
he read :—" Dearly belovëd Roger, the Scripture moveth
you and me. . . ."

---

[1] *Life of Dean Stanley*, by R. E. Prothero and G. G. Bradley, I, p. 430.
See also Ecclesiastes ix, 10.

XXIX

AT THE CRYSTAL PALACE, &c.
(1854)

THE Carlyles spent some pleasant days with the Ashburtons at Addiscombe about the end of April,—" no *foreign* company but ourselves." His reading was a French *Life of Prince Henry*, a brother of King Frederick ; and he might have been seen reading it there on the grass, " on the sunny side of green bushes."

From Addiscombe one Sunday they ' made a pilgrimage to the Crystal Palace, which is but some two miles off, a monstrous mountain of glass building on the top of Sydenham Hill,' and a familiar sight to him, ' very conspicuous from Cheyne Walk. Innumerable objects of Art in it, whole acres of Egyptian monsters, and many really good copies of classical and modern sculpture, which well deserve examination one day. The living visitors, not so very numerous in so huge an edifice—probably not above 200—were almost all Jews. Outside were as many thousand of the Christian persuasion—or rather, Christian Cockney—unable to get in. The whole matter seemed to me to be Transcendental Cockneyism . . . " regardless of expense." '

Returning home in a day or so, he wrote in his journal.— ' No way made with my book, nor like to be made. I am in a heavy, stupefying state of health, too, and have no capacity of grasping the big chaos that lies around me, and reducing it to order. Order ! Reducing ! It is like compelling the grave to give up its dead, were it rightly done, and I am in no capacity for working such a miracle. Yet all things point to work—except in work there is simply no hope for me.

' I read old German books, dull as stupidity itself—nay, superannuated stupidity—gain with labour the dreariest glimpses of unimportant, extinct human things in that region of the world ; but when I begin operating, *how* to reduce that widespread black desert of Brandenburg sand

Plate III

FREDERICK
(*From a picture by Franke, Potsdam, 1770*)

[face p. 96

to a small human garden—alas! alas! But let me not spend time here making matters *worse*. Surely now I *am* at the bottom of the wheel.'

' I dream horribly,' Carlyle went on to write in his journal in April, 1854, ' —the fruit of incurable biliousness : waste scenes of solitary desolation, gathered from Craigenputtock, as I now perceive. . . . Every vision, I find, is the suitable representation of the mood of mind then possessing me. . . . But nearly all my dreams have come from bodily conditions of the nerves, I think ; and ninety-nine out of every hundred have been ugly and painful. . . . I find nothing sublime in the act of dreaming, nor even anything very strange. Shut your eyes at any time, there will be a phantasmagory of thoughts and images begin parading in unbroken series through your head. To sleep is but to shut your eyes and outer senses a little better. . . . The miracle of dreams was never much of a miracle to me, and now, this long while, none at all, beyond what everything is.'

H

XXX

JOHN WILSON AND LORD COCKBURN
(1854)

BY 29.4.1854 Carlyle had heard of the death of John
Wilson, and a few days later that of Lord Cockburn
the biographer of Jeffrey. Soliloquizing upon them in the
privacy of his journal, he decidedly preferred Cockburn,
saying that he, ' small, solid, and genuine, was by much the
wholesomer product ; a bright, cheery-voiced, hazel-eyed
man ; a Scotch dialect with plenty of good logic in it, and
of practical sagacity. Veracious, too. A gentleman, I should
say, and perfectly in the Scotch type, perhaps the very last
of that peculiar species.'

He recalled his first sight of big John Wilson,[1] the Tory
man of genius, and wrote of him :—' In London I seldom or
never heard any talk of him. I never read his blustering,
drunken *Noctes* after Gordon in Edinburgh ceased to bring
them to me. We lived apart, as in different centuries ; tho'
to say the truth, I always loved Wilson—really rather loved
him, and could have fancied a most strict and very profitable *friendship* between us in different, happier circumstances. . . .

' Wilson had much nobleness of heart, and many traits of
noble genius, but the central *tie-beam* seemed always wanting,
very long ago I perceived in him the most irreconcilable
contradictions, Toryism with *Sansculottism ;* Methodism of
a sort with total incredulity ; a noble, loyal, and religious
nature, not *strong* enough to vanquish the perverse element
it is born into. Hence a being all split into precipitous
chasms and the wildest volcanic tumults ; rocks overgrown, indeed, with tropical luxuriance of leaf and flower,
but knit together at the bottom—that was my old figure
of speech—only by an ocean of whisky punch. On these
terms nothing can be done. Wilson seemed to me always

[1] See *Carlyle Till Marriage*, pp. 90-1.

98

by far the most *gifted* of all our literary men, either then or till ; and yet intrinsically he has written nothing that can endure. The central gift was wanting. Adieu ! adieu ! Oh noble ill-starred brother ! Who shall say I am not myself *farther* wrong, and in a more hopeless course and case, tho' on the opposite side. . . . Wilson spoke always in a curious dialect, full of humour and ingenuity, but with an uncomfortable wavering between jest and earnest, as if it were his interest and unconscious purpose to *conceal* his real meaning in most things. . . . Adieu to him, good, grand, ruined soul, that never could be great, or, indeed, *be* anything. This present is a ruinous and ruining world.'

There are two things to remember in reading this.—It was a private note and meant to be read by no eyes but his own. He thought Wilson a " ruined soul," because Wilson had failed to make the best use of his great natural gifts,— " For unto whomsoever much is given, of him shall be much required."

XXXI

SCOTTISH HISTORICAL PORTRAITS
(1854)

IN May, 1854, a meeting of the Society of Antiquaries in
Edinburgh was enlivened by the most antiquarian of
their members, David Laing, Librarian.   He said he had
lately called upon Carlyle in London, and told him how the
latest project for an Exhibition of Scottish historical portraits had failed, like all the rest before it.   Carlyle admitted
—" I never see anyone from Edinburgh without suggesting
an Exhibition of that kind.   It would be of the greatest
interest."   Laing said the proposal might be revived when
the new buildings on the Mound were completed, and now
told his fellow-antiquaries,—" In order to call attention to
this, I suggested whether he might not write a letter expressing his views on the subject, as such a communication
might enable me at least to renew the proposal in a definite
form."   So Laing got a letter dated 3.5.1854, which he then
read to them.   How the project took root at last and grew
into a National Portrait Gallery belongs to local history.
In many respects the Gallery approximates to the require-
ments explained in the letter, and so does the National
Portrait Gallery in London ; but as the letter can be read
at full length in the *Essays of Carlyle*,[1] a few sentences may
here suffice.—

' It has always struck me that Historical Portrait-Galleries
far transcend in worth all other kinds of National Collections of Pictures ; that they ought to exist in every country ;
and that in no country is there at present such a thing to
be found.'   Then he mentioned Louis-Philippe's pictures
and   Chancellor   Clarendon's,   and   said   that   ' Historical

[1] In the last volume of most editions. See also *Proceedings of the
Society of Antiquaries of Scotland*, Vol. I, pp. 284–92.

Portraits abound in England ; but where they are, no man knows. . . . Nor is the English National Gallery poorer in this respect than others,—perhaps even much the reverse. . . .

' In the Dresden Gallery, for instance, you find Flayings of Bartholomew, Flayings of Marsyas, Rapes of the Sabines : but if you ask for a portrait of Martin Luther, of Friedrich the Wise, nay even of August the Big, of Marshal Saxe or poor Count Brühl, you will find no satisfactory answer. In Berlin itself, I found, not long ago, whole acres of mytho- logical smearing (Tower of Babel, and I know not what), by Kaulbach and others, still going on : but a *genuine Por- trait of Frederick the Great* was a thing I could nowhere hear of. That is strange, but that is true. I roamed through endless lines of Pictures ; inquired far and wide, even Sculptor Rauch could tell me of nothing : at last it was chiefly by good luck that the thing I was in quest of turned up.—This I find to be one of the saddest of those few defects in the world which are easily capable of remedy : I hope you in Scotland, in the " New National Museum " we hear talk of, will have a good eye to this, and remedy it in your own case ! Scotland at present is not worse than other countries in the point in question : but neither is it at all better ; and as Scotland, unlike some other countries, has a History of a very readable nature, and has never published even an *engraved* series of National Portraits, perhaps the evil is more sensible and patent there than elsewhere. It is an evil which should be everywhere remedied : and if Scotland be the first to set an example in that respect, Scotland will do honourably by herself, and achieve a benefit to all the world.' . . .

To this may be added the very first sentence in the rules he went on to suggest.—' That no living Scotchman's por- trait should be admitted, however " Historical " it promised to be. And I would further counsel,' he added, ' that you should be extremely chary about such " Historical men " as have died within the last twenty-five or thirty years ; it requires always the space of a generation to discriminate between popular monstrosities and Historical realities in the matter of Men,—to let mere dust-clouds settle into their natural place and bulk.' Which is all the more interesting because in 1862, when Carlyle was a Trustee of the National Portrait Gallery, he will be seen

taking the lead in enforcing this very rule against a
proposal to accept a portrait of Lord Brougham, then 8.
years of age but still busy.   Assuredly Carlyle was much
in earnest about this rule, 'since politicians might use
the Gallery to advance their fame.'   At any rate that is
how Moncure Conway puts the matter, and he seems to
be echoing Carlyle.[2]

[2] *Thomas Carlyle*, by Moncure D. Conway, pp. 113-14.

XXXII

MRS. CARLYLE AND MRS. MONTAGU
(1854)

FOR many years Mrs. Carlyle and old Mrs. Basil Montagu had seen little of each other, some female tiff about servants perhaps had chilled their friendship ; but on Saturday, 6.5.54, Mrs. Carlyle was at a party at the Procters' where Mrs. Montagu was living, Mrs. Procter being her daughter, and as the old lady was confined to her bedroom, she sent for Mrs. Carlyle, who went up to her room and reported the interview to her brother-in-law, Dr. John Carlyle, on 9.5.54. The " Noble Lady " was Mrs. Carlyle's private nickname for her old acquaintance.—

' I saw the " Noble Lady " ; and a strange tragic sight she was ! sitting all alone in a low-ceilinged confined room at the top of Procter's house ; a French bed in a corner, some relics of the grand Bedford-Square Drawing-room (small pictures and the like) scattered about. Herself stately, artistic as ever ; not a line of her figure, not a fold of her dress changed since we knew her first, 20 years ago and more !

' She made me sit on a low chair opposite to her, and began to speak of Edward Irving and long ago as if it were last year—last month ! There was something quite over-powering in the whole thing : the Pagan grandeur of the old woman, retired from the world, awaiting death, as erect and unyielding as ever, contrasted so strangely with the mean bedroom at the top of the house, and the uproar of company going on below. And the Past which she seemed to live and move in felt to gather round me too, till I fairly laid my head on her lap and burst into tears ! She stroked my hair very gently and said, " I think, Jane, your manner never changes any more than your hair, which is still black, I see." "But you too are not changed," I said. " You know," she said, " when I was still a young woman, I dressed and felt like an old one, and so age has not told so much on me as on most others."

' When I had staid with her an hour or so, she insisted on my going back to the company, and embraced me as she never did before. Her embrace used to be so freezing always to my youthful enthusiasm ; but this time she held me strongly to her heart, and kissed my cheeks many times heartily, like a mother. I was near going off into crying again. I felt that she was taking eternal farewell of me in her own mind. But I don't mean it to be so : I will go again to see her very soon. The great gentleness was indeed the chief change in her,—not a hard word did she say about anyone ; and her voice, tho' clear and strong as of old, had a *human* modulation in it. You may fancy the humour in which I went back to the Party, which was then at a white heat of excitement—about nothing ! '

It is pleasant to add that Mrs. Carlyle carried out her good resolution, and resumed calling on Mrs. Montagu, as friendly as ever. On her last recorded visit, more than two years hence, the very nickname sounds like praise in Mrs. Carlyle's private diary :—' Called for Mrs. Montagu, who is breaking up, they say ; but her figure is erect and her bearing indomitable as ever,—the " Noble Lady " to the last ! '

XXXIII

ALLINGHAM TAKES GOOD ADVICE
(1854)

IN 1854 William Allingham, then thirty years of age, had given up his post in the Customs and come to London to seek a career as a man of letters ; but decided in time to return to his regular work. On 6.6.1854 he was writing to his sister.[1]—

' MY DEAR CATHERINE,

' I would have written to you long ago, but for the way I was circumstanced. I still like London, and find I could make quite as large an income by writing as I expected. I had yesterday a letter from an editor who heard of my intention of going away, offering me £100 a year certain for doing something for him once a fortnight, and this is the *3rd regular* engagement that has been offered to me, with others in prospect ; so that if I would " take off my coat to it " (which is what Thackeray advised), I could make at the very outset £300 or £400 a year. But to do this I must give myself up entirely to desultory and ephemeral writing, truckle to editors and people, and undergo countless anxieties and annoyances, which would not at all suit me ; and therefore I think it much better, all things considered, to return into quiet exile and make the best of that. I believe all my friends here are sorry I am going—tho some, Carlyle in particular, think it a blessed escape for me out of the profession of literature.' . . .

As Mrs. Allingham wrote afterwards, Carlyle said he was " very glad to hear it," and added when saying good-bye,— " You'd have gone from bad to worse ; now you can do your day's work, and if you have anything to say or write, do so ; and if no man will have it, you can say,—'Well, thank God, I can do without selling it.' "

[1] *William Allingham : a Diary*, by H. Allingham and D. Radford, pp. 69–73. Letter dated 3.6.54, but written three days later.

XXXIV

IN THE WORKSHOP
(1854)

IN the slang of scholars, Carlyle had now " read himself
into " the eighteenth century. Which means that he
knew the people who lived then and who could still be
known to a reader as well as they knew each other, and
maybe better. By this time it was plain that there was no
other work for him except to show again the people of the
eighteenth century as they appeared to him. But how ?
That was the question. He tried writing on *The Hohen-
zollerns*, and after giving up that he tried *Sketches of German
History*,—also without success. He was now about to begin
his longest work, *The History of Friedrich II of Prussia,
called Frederick the Great*, but he was still awhile in the
nervous condition known to artists of every kind, not
writers only, or painters, but also to real workers of any
sort, who are groping around any big job that has to be
done, and trying with all their might to find out the very best
way to do it.

Here is what he was writing in his journal on 15.6.54.—
' Being to all appearance just about the *nadir* in my affairs
at present, solitary, without any human being to whom I
can with profit communicate myself, and totally unable
from illness, &c., to get any hold of the ugly chaos, wide as
the world, which I am called to subdue into the form of
work done, I rushed out yesterday and took a violent, long
fatiguing walk in the Surrey precincts, Tooting, &c., that
at least I might be quite alone with my unbeautiful self and
my ditto affairs. A beautiful, soft, bright day ; the sky
unusually clear, moist clouds floating about upon the wind
far enough aloft, and the sun shining out from time to time.
Sitting silent on Wandsworth Common, remote amid the
furze bushes, I said, " Suppose we write a *journal of a week i*
the time of *acti labores* " (work done) " may once again

come, in spite of all appearances to the contrary, and then it will be pleasant to look back." I did not much entertain the project, nor at this time am I clear to do it. Here, however, is yesterday :—Wrote some business notes *invitissimâ Minervâ*' (very much against the grain) ' after breakfast ; had lost the little dog, &c., who, however, was found about noon. Then examined the scribble I had been doing about Jülich and Berg ; Preussen, &c. Totally without worth ! Decided to run out, as above said. Out at half-past one p.m. ; return towards five. Asleep on the sofa before dinner at half-past five ; take my *Schlosser*, vol. 4 ; can do little at it till tea. Not a bad book, though very crabbed and lean. Brother John enters at eight ; gossip with him till nine ; then out to escort him home, getting three-quarters of an hour of walking to myself withal. Had refused the Lowe *soirée* before. Jane poorly ; in a low way for some days back. Read till one a.m., she soon leaving me. To bed then, having learned little ; how little ! To-day I am at my desk again ; intend to try Liegnitz and Silesian matters. Small hope there. My eyes are very dim ; bad light (from sky direct), though abundant. Chiefly the state of liver, I suppose, which indeed in itself and its effects is beyond description. Have taken to iron pens ; compelled to it by the ever-fluctuating "cheap and nasty" system which may the Devil confound, as indeed he does. Basta ! Basta !' (Enough, enough.) ' Liegnitz itself will be better than that.'

Charles Gavan Duffy had been in Parliament since 1852, and was in London this year, 1854, but he was too busy to make notes for us, tho calling ' continually ' on the Carlyles. He was serving with Bright, Palmerston and Co. on a Select Committee on the Irish Land Question, and keeping late hours in attending the Commons' Palaver. One day he had brought Mrs. Carlyle and Miss Jewsbury to ' luncheon at the House of Commons, where Mrs. Carlyle met some old friends, and her lively fancy played about the subject so habitually afterwards that Carlyle was incited to take a little interest in it,' declares Duffy,[1] so that ' he asked my opinion from time to time of the notable men in Parliament, and uttered trenchant comments on them.'

[1] *Conversations with Carlyle*, by Sir Charles Gavan Duffy, pp. 187 and 190–2.

As for Mrs. Carlyle, Duffy tells us that ' her appearance at that time was peculiarly interesting. Her face was colourless but most expressive, answering promptly to every emotion ; her eyes were frank and pleasant, and her smile, which was gracious, passed easily into banter or mockery. Ill-health repressed the activity of her body, but not of her spirit, which was as vivacious as of old.'

The late hours in the Commons made Duffy himself ill in June, and he went to Malvern. Writing to enquire about him, Carlyle said that there ' the fresh hill breezes may do you good, tho the medical " sheetings " &c. not very much,' and added, 22.6.54,—' I am myself in rather poor case this long while ; decidedly below par in bodily health, and with a very fair proportion of other things to keep my spirits from rising above their due level ! My work, too, which ought to be the consolation for all sorrows, and is really the only conquest one can make in this world, sticks obstinately in the slough,' (or bog, like Christian in the *Pilgrim's Progress*), ' these many long months, let me try and wriggle as I will : in fact, it is the most ungainly job I ever had ; and *fire* enough to burn up such a mass of sordid litter, and extract the thread of gold out of it (if there be any in it), is actually not at my disposal in my present mood. Let us hope, let us hope, nevertheless ! National Palaver and its affairs are without interest to me altogether of late ; and, in fact, lie below the horizon as a thing I have no interest in. Crystal Palace, Turk War, Policy of Lord John, do., do. Not an *ideal* heroic world this ; no, not by any means.—

' Yours ever truly,

' T. CARLYLE.'

There was a serious epidemic of Asiatic cholera in England this summer, and funerals in Chelsea were unusually frequent. Both Mrs. Carlyle and her husband remained at home. His work never stopped.

In the first week of July a London wine merchant, Charles Augustus Ward, aged 26, sent MSS. to Carlyle and obtained an interview.[2] According to Mr. Ward's diary, Carlyle listened attentively for three hours and a half, while Mr. Ward read the MS. of one of his books, and then Carlyle explained to him frankly that publication was impossible.

[2] *Times*, Monday, 22.6.1914, p. 5, and Monday, 29.6.1914, p. 6, and *Daily Mail Over-Seas Edition*, July 4, 1914, p. 400.

The MS. was left behind for further examination, and in a letter dated 6.7.54 Carlyle wrote.—

' I have looked a little into your manuscript; and am sorry to report that I do not see any likelihood of its ever, in its present form, being successful as a literary production.

' If you resolve to devote yourself to literature, and the questionable enterprise of unfolding whatever gifts may be in you in the shape of mere spoken or written *words*,— which, for a young man in earnest with his life, and possessed of real capabilities and opportunities for *work* in this world, I consider a very questionable enterprise indeed,—it is clearly necessary, in the first place, that you instruct *yourself*, acquire knowledge far and wide, amass experiences, and digest the same into definite results,—in short, that you should have attained to some conquest of what at least seems to yourself Wisdom and beautiful insight before you attempt uttering yourself with the whole world for audience. You are otherwise (I mean to say, *every man* is otherwise) in the condition of a man " speaking " without having anything to say.'

On the day following Carlyle was adding to that letter as if remorseful :—' I should be sorry indeed if my hard word went farther than I intended, and were to discourage you from any noble impulse you may trace in yourself ! I did not, and do not, deny your talent, even for writing Books one day; I only sought to make you aware of the inexorable conditions that determine whether *possibility* shall become *reality* in such cases, or shall remain always futile.

' By all means, employ your spare time in seeking knowledge ; redeem, if you can, a few hours of every day ; read Books, and try to make sure that they are wise Books ; consort with wise men, avoid the company of fools ; think, reflect, enquire ; study earnestly to find some true and noble thing in this world to which you can swear fealty : the day may come when you are really called to *speak* to your fellow-creatures ;—but I can tell you, it will be happier for you if it never come ; if whatever nobleness and wisdom are in you can come out in the way of silent work and successful conduct,—appealing to the Eternal Powers (who are good judges and *can* reward), not the Ephemeral

Reviewers who have no power except in the circulating
libraries, and no judgment that is infallible for the
guidance of man.'

Mr. Ward became a life-member of the London Library
this year, and sixty years afterwards, when he died at
Walthamstow in 1914, his executors gave to the Library
3000 volumes of his, which are thus described.[2]—' Nearly
every volume is annotated by him. The basis is theological
and philosophical. It is especially rich in old dictionaries
of language, (and) editions of Milton and Coleridge, Bacon,
Rousseau and Montaigne.'

Mr. Ward had remained in business till the eighties, and
published three books and many articles. He used to send
to Carlyle presents of fruit and vegetables, and among the
letters he received there is another still worth reading,
awaiting us in 1862.

An addition to the Cheyne Row circle was announced by
Mrs. Carlyle to Mrs. Russell in a letter of 17.7.54 :—' I am
hoping for a considerable acquisition before long : Miss
Jewsbury, the authoress of *The Half Sisters*, &c., the most
intimate friend I have in the world, and who has lived
generally at Manchester since we first knew each other, has
decided to come and live near me for good. Her brother
married eighteen months ago, and has realised a baby, and
a wife's mother in the house besides. So Geraldine felt it
getting too hot for her there. It will be a real gain to have
a woman I like, so near as the street in which I have decided
on an apartment for her. All my acquaintances live so far
off that it is mechanically impossible to be intimate with
them.'

It may be remembered that Carlyle had stopped his wife
correcting the proofs of Geraldine Jewsbury's *Half Sisters*,
because of its indecency[3] ; and doubtless she blamed him
also for his wife's refusal to accept the dedication of it,—
which seems to explain why in writing to Mrs. Carlyle after
then poor Geraldine ejaculated, " Of course, one would
never have the wild expectation that Mr. Carlyle will ever
approve or admire any human effort."[4]

Here now is a sample letter, brief enough to print, which

[3] See *Carlyle on Cromwell and Others*, pp. 408–9.
[4] Selections from the Letters of *G. E. Jewsbury to J. W. Carlyle*, by
Mrs. Ireland, p. 429 and Preface, p. x.

shows the kind of help that Neuberg was giving during the years that *Frederick* occupied him and Carlyle.—

' CHELSEA,
　　　　　　　　　　　' 17 *july*, 1854.
' DEAR NEUBERG,

　' I.—Walpole's forged " Letter of Frederic " to Rousseau (about jany. 1766) I have got the words of, in Burton's *Life of Hume* (Edin.h 1846) II, 321 ;—but there is no date to it, nor can I learn *when* it was first sent to R. or circulated in Paris,—nor whether Rousseau ever believed in it.　More particulars you will probably find (and could *collate* the " Burton " Copy of the Letter at the same time, and see whether it is all exact) in Musset de Pathay (*Vie* de J. J. Rousseau, Paris, 1821) apropos of that year 1766, and of R.'s flight to England.　If Musset cannot be had, there is a *Narrative* by Hume, and another by Walpole, which will probably clear the matter ;—and at any rate, it is really of no *vital* moment.　So don't bother *too* much.　However, when your hand is in, you might look further in the old Newspaper " St. James's Chronicle for 7 April 1766," where is a Letter of Rousseau's own about it (rather maddish, I believe), wh refers to a shortly prior No. where the forged Letter itself has been given.　No more of that.

　' The " Müller " you spoke of is not in the London Library : he too and Söltl may stand over, since they are so hard of access.'

　(Note.—The reference is to a previous letter of enquiry about a " modern Book . . . by one *Söltl*, a Munich man—on the Thirty Years' War.")

　' 2.—There is a good Letter by *Rabener*, who was in Dresden when F.c besieged it in 1760, which gives an account of that phenomenon ;　I think I have *got* nearly all the Letter in *Jorden's Lexicon Deutscher Dichter* &c. VI, 237 ; but it has no *date ;*—nor have we a copy of Rabener's *Familiar Letters* (some equivalent *German* Title) which were edited as part of his *Werke*, by Herr *Weisse*, about 1772, & 3, to whom this Letter is addressed.　Pray look out that Book, also Jorden (place above quoted, VI, 237), and add what of the Letter is *wanting* in *Jorden* (very little, I guess)—the date at any rate.

　' I have nothing more to trouble you with at this hour ; nor is ' (there) ' the least *haste*, &c. about the matter now on hand.

' We are out tonight ; and *possibly* (not very probably I)
may be on Wednesday evening. Otherwise at home steadily
and glad of your advent any night.

' Yours always,

' T. CARLYLE.'

In the last paragraph—' *possibly* (not very probably
I) '—needed no explanation to Neuberg, who was well aware
that Mrs. Carlyle desired her husband to dine out and move
about in Society more than he did. He seldom, if ever
displeased her by an absolute refusal, but developed great
ingenuity in escaping at the last moment. His forgetfulness
at times seemed to border on the miraculous.

The correspondence with Preuss in Berlin was done by
Neuberg, who put into letters the conundrums Carlyle
supplied. When Neuberg revisited Germany this fall, he
took with him queries for savants, and one beyond the power
of any savant to answer without a knowledge of current
business.—' I wish you knew of anybody that could give
me a sound opinion about the *present* practice of Prussian
law ; and the real result Fred^k had upon it by his strenuous
exertions on that behalf.'

Neuberg was invaluable in dating events, a matter always
of great importance to Carlyle, and complicated by the
change from old style to new in 1752 ; but perhaps his most
important contribution to the great history was in the
summaries he made of the newspapers. One of Carlyle's best
strokes of genius was to quote the current press as a comic
chorus to the true story ; and nobody could have assisted
him better than Neuberg did in gathering the material
required : for Neuberg shared his sentiments, and felt with
him that facts were sacred, and so was superior to the
besetting sin of common men, who are prone to invent whenever they feel safe from contradiction.

One of the episodes in German history, which Carlyle
sifted clear but found useless for *Frederick*, was saved from
the waste-paper basket in July, 1854. " Patching it out
into printable form " occupied him for " 4 or 5 days." Then
as he said, it was copied by Neuberg " in a most faithful,
charitable, ingenious and excellent manner," and the readers
of the *Westminster Review*[5] soon had it before them as " The
Prinzenraub," or the " Kidnapping of the Princes." These
" Princes " were two boys of fourteen and twelve, sons of

[5] January, 1855. Reprinted in the *Miscellaneous Essays* of T. C.

Elector Frederick of Saxony, and in 1455 they had been kidnapped, but were recovered soon. The elder of them succeeded his father in due course, and became the father of Frederick the Wise, the protector of Luther. He was also the ancestor of Prince Albert, husband of Queen Victoria. The noteworthy thing about the essay is that it shows how the historian gloated on genealogy. He took to it like a duck to water, which was natural enough, for their own genealogy was as much a matter of talk among the peasants and farmers of Dumfriesshire when he was young as among the German Royalties.

I

BOOK XXII

WRITING "FREDERICK"

1854–56

I

MRS. RUSKIN AND SEXUAL MYSTERIES, &c.
(1854)

WRITING to Mrs. Russell early this summer, Mrs. Carlyle favoured her with the latest gossip.—' There is a great deal of talking about the Ruskins here at present. Mrs. Ruskin has been taken to Scotland by *her* Parents ; and Ruskin is gone to Switzerland with *his ;* and the separation is understood to be permanent. There is even a rumour that *Mrs.* Ruskin is to sue for a divorce. I know nothing about it, except that I have always pitied Mrs. Ruskin, while people generally blame her,—for love of dress and company and flirtation. She was too young and pretty to be so left to her own devices as she was by her Husband, who seemed to wish nothing more of her but the credit of having a pretty, well-dressed wife.'

The " rumour " was not far wrong. The marriage of Ruskin and his wife was soon annulled, at the suit of Mrs. Ruskin, acting by her father's advice,[1] and suing on the ground that the marriage had not been consummated ; and Ruskin remained a butt for indecent innuendo for the rest of his life. Which deserves mention here because it seems to have suggested to Geraldine Jewsbury an explanation why Carlyle had never responded to her advances, even when she laid herself at his feet, as she once did. " He must be another like Ruskin," Geraldine Jewsbury would think, and by-and-by she confided her vain imagination as a fact to Froude, and Froude was foolish enough to believe it.[2] At least he said so.[3] In fairness to Geraldine we should

[1] This was certified to D. A. W. by an old gentleman who knew it at first hand before the public knew anything.
[2] The most conclusive document on this matter is " Froude and Carlyle, the Imputation Considered Medically," by Sir James Crichton-Browne, M.D., &c. *British Medical Journal*, 27.6.1903, pp. 1498–1502.
[3] *My Relations with Carlyle*, by J. A. Froude, pp. 21–2.

never forget that there is no corroboration of Froude's story and that nobody of sense can feel sure of anything he said especially anything of that sort, without corroboration.

Perhaps the likeliest guess is that Froude may have merely enquired of the unfortunate lady whether she had heard the story, and she may have said something in reply which he took for corroboration. The Ruskin case this year was the delight of all the smutty-story-tellers in the town. In the smoking-room of the House of Commons, Gavan Duffy was expectorating his nausea when the impotence of his own hero, Carlyle, was flung in his face. Whereupon within a week, he quoted that to Carlyle and was told that it was untrue.

By-and-by this report to Carlyle of the current gossip seemed to Gavan Duffy, and to David Masson also and others, to explain some of the invectives against sexual depravity in the *Frederick*.[4] Enough, enough !

Not long ago Dr. John Carlyle had married a rich widow and now his wife and he had decided to leave Moffat, where they were living, and take a house within reach of London. So they were house-hunting this August, and when they were returning to town from Harrow, their train was derailed in a collision. The shock caused a premature confinement, and ' after a week of grievous suffering,'[5] mother and child died.[6] Carlyle and Neuberg were both at the funeral 30.8.1854, and after then Dr. John lived mainly at Edinburgh and Dumfries.

In letters not dated, but written soon after the accident Mrs. Carlyle told Mrs. Russell about ' Mrs. John Carlyle's death. That was a horrid business. It looked such a *waste* of a woman and child. Of course she was to die ; yet humanly viewed, one could not help believing that if she had staid at home and taken the ordinary care of herself that her situation required, she might have borne a living child and done well. But her constant excursions on railways, and sightseeing and house-hunting, seemed to us often, even before the accident which brought on her mortal illness, a sheer tempting of Providence.

' I heard from my aunt Elizabeth the other day, and she sent with her Letter a small Book on *Grace*. They are

[4] *The Truth About Carlyle*, by D. A. W., with a Preface by Sir James Crichton-Browne, pp. 103–4.

[5] *Cornhill Magazine*, November, 1926, p. 633.

[6] Told D. A. W. by Alexander Carlyle, and also by the Rev. William Watts, a grandson of the lady.

indefatigable in their efforts at conversion. Except " to convert " me, they seem to have no interest in me whatever. Mrs. George Welsh is coming to stay at Richmond with her Son, through the Winter, at least. He is a good and clever lad, and a kind son as ever was.'

To her cousin John Welsh, Mrs. Carlyle wrote about the accident.[5] ' As for Dr. Carlyle he has not seemed to know what he was doing—and is now in an apathetic state that I do not feel much interest in. My Husband positively looks more heart-sore than *he* does.'—She may easily have been quite mistaken.

In a few weeks John Carlyle went to Moffat, to wind up his household there, and Carlyle was writing to him.— ' Alas, Moffat is a changed place to you ; a sadly changed place even to me when I think of it ! But we must not look too much behind ; we must do what is at hand and ahead ; our Life, and what we have to *do*, is still ahead. It will give me great comfort indeed to hear that you have gathered yourself together, and made a wise arrangement for still profiting by your future years.' John busied himself about his stepsons, and did all he could to supply the place of the mother they had lost.

Writing from the Highlands, Lord Ashburton described to Carlyle their sport, and ' Stanley's waiting in vain for five hours to have a shot ; and going, like the Primeval Serpent, on his belly,' as Carlyle humorously summed the matter up, enquiring, ' would he take so much trouble, or the half of it, to pay the whole National Debt, for instance, or to reduce the Czar of Russia to a Pillar of Salt, and make all friends of progress happy for evermore ? Not a bit of it.'

' I am shocked to find my lady fishes *with an otter*,' Carlyle continued. ' I imagined she went out with rod and fly, in a Christian manner, and disdained such associates ! I myself have no game here of any kind, except it be spiders in the garden, where I go to smoke ; of which, being disgusted at last,'—by their wholesale murdering of the flies, as he told another,—' I have killed near upon 50 brace, I should think. A sad operation, but an indispensable one. What an opulence of life there is in this Universe, especially among the more contemptible branches of its population ! " You cannot kill a fly," they say, " but there will come forty to its funeral." '

In this letter he also said that he would stand by his old promise, as 'even my wife assents,'—that if Lord Ashburton preserved in London the 'noble free-flowing beard' he now could boast, his own 'razors shall be thrown away, and a second beard appear on the streets.' But what he was now considering was how it would be best to begin the history. In a letter of 18.7.1854 he was confiding to his friend John Forster,[7] 'I do not mean to go out of town this Autumn at all, but to stay at home, and if I can do no work, be at least very miserable for doing none.'

[7] John Forster Letters in South Kensington Museum.

II

CATCHING SIGHT OF FREDERICK WILLIAM
(1854)

IN September, 1854, Carlyle got access to " a mass of old German-Ambassador papers " at the house of Lord de Grey, a grandson of the Sir Thomas Robinson who had been the English ambassador at Vienna, &c., in the time of Frederick and his father. By the beginning of October he was admitted to the State Paper Office by Lord Clarendon, with liberty " to examine for historical purposes the correspondence of the British Ministers at the Court of Vienna during the years 1720 to 1745, and at the Court of Berlin during the years 1720 to 1756." Writing to Neuberg, who was then in Germany, on the first Sunday after admission, 8.10.1854, Carlyle declared,—" I never saw Friedrich William nearly so well, nor indeed saw him at all before." He had discovered the amusing " Double Marriage " project of Frederick William's wife, the mother of Frederick, and begun to see through the sordid intrigues, which explained the hatred of Vienna felt by Frederick, and focussed the folly of hereditary kingship. The Prussian pedants had missed the point of the story, and so had Macaulay.

' Frederick's Century,' wrote Carlyle to Neuberg, ' did nothing I approve except *cut its own throat*, and *so* end its dishonest nonsenses, in the French Revolution ! Alas, and I begin to see that even that process was a much more lengthy, miscellaneous and dismal one than I had in former times imagined. A long ugly Slough of Despond indeed ; and in the outlook beyond (which I still privately believe in), it is as if almost nobody would go along with me ; and the whole world, rejoicing in its Crystal Palaces, its Turk wars, &c. &c., requested me to be so kind as to hold my tongue. How even to speak to the " fit audience tho' few," I do not see. However, we will try. I only stick to the speaking function, Literature, because Fate has allowed me no other. I do begin to see into the chaos of German History, like a boundless dim land of *spectral* realities, vanished ghosts that once inhabited this earth. The State Paper Office gives me daily a headache. I often think to myself, " Would that Neuberg were returned ! " '

He was now getting sight of the huge task he had undertaken,—to reveal Eighteenth Century Europe as Tacitus revealed Imperial Rome, and show how wars that extended to America and India had been caused by a few commonplace men, and women whom it would be flattery to call commonplace. Consider the Pompadour in France and the Czarina Elizabeth in Russia, Peter the Great's daughter, better known as the ' *infâme Catin du Nord*,' (notorious whore of the North), to say nothing of the 'Termagant Elizabeth,' Queen of Spain, and Maria Theresa, who was the most 'respectable' among the women then ruling the world, but also sanguinary and selfish. It may well be a common opinion on the continent, where those days are better remembered than in England, that Carlyle's History of Frederick, disclosing the old-fashioned ways of doing as both repulsive and ridiculous, contributed to the happy conclusion of 1918. What is plain to everybody now is how well it makes a trilogy with his Cromwell in the Seventeenth Century, and his French Revolution at the end of the Eighteenth ; and the lesson of the three great histories is the same,— that in moral as in material things the Laws of Nature are inevitable and eternal.

III

CEASING TO SHAVE
(1854)

NEXT morning, 9.10.54, Lord Ashburton entered unexpectedly, 'hot from the Highlands.' What had
brought him to town was money-market business, and he
was to return in 48 hours ; but what brought him to Cheyne
Row was to show off his 'really handsome beard,' and
remind Carlyle that he had said last year,—" If *you* adopt
a beard, *I will follow.*" So now he claimed performance of
the promise, and was supported by Mrs. Carlyle.

Their victim admitted the promise, and even the desir-
ability of a beard, but begged for time.—On a sudden,
Ashburton called Mrs. Carlyle to him—to get her permission, no doubt, and discover where the razors were. Then
he went up to Carlyle's bedroom and took them all away.
Four days later Carlyle admitted to his brother John,—" I
save half an hour daily " by not shaving, and saw " no way
out " except to let the hair grow.

It became the fashion to do so, and even handsome
Venables made his " pair of Moustachios for three months
his pride, and pleasure, and principal occupation "[1] ; and
then he removed them, in deference perhaps to the custom
of the bar. But Ashburton and Carlyle were free to please
themselves, or rather, their wives ; and as Lady Ashburton
was proud of her husband's " magnificent " beard,[1] he kept
it. If Mrs. Carlyle regretted making her husband grow a
beard, she never admitted it, tho she told him it made him
like an " escaped maniac " when he went out for his evening
walk. As for the saving of time he was talking about, she
told Thackeray's daughters[2] and other such familiars that
there was no time saved,—" All the time he has saved by
ceasing to shave, he spends wandering about the house,

---

[1] *Mrs. Brookfield and Her Circle*, by C. & F. Brookfield, II, p. 424.
[2] Chapters from some Memoirs, by Anne Thackeray Ritchie, p. 136, &c.

bemoaning what's amiss in the Universe." In a letter of 4.11.54 he himself told Lady Ashburton that he felt ' as if I had got a dirty gorse Common on my chin,' and bade her tell Lord Ashburton that ' had he not carried off my razors, it had *gone* before now,—it grows daily more ugly.'

IV

WINDSOR CASTLE, PRINCE ALBERT, &c.
(1854)

NEUBERG lost no time in returning to London, and was soon installed in the State Paper Office, and making copies and summaries of documents for " the Master," as he used to call Carlyle. Perhaps it was in imitation of Neuberg that John Ruskin began to do likewise. " The Master " said nothing. He had a rare talent for silence, tho he often found brevity difficult. Delivered now by Neuberg from State-Paper-Office headaches, he was soon making steady progress.

In the undated letter of this autumn already quoted,[1] Mrs. Carlyle wrote to Mrs. Russell :—' We have staid generally here this whole year, in spite of the cholera. But, indeed, what use is there flying from cholera in a town, when it finds its way into such fresh green places as about Ecclefechan ? It was very sad to walk out here for many weeks : in a single half mile of street, I often met as many as six funerals.'

Both Mrs. Carlyle and her husband were at home the whole of this year. ' She was in poor fluctuating health,' he wrote long afterwards, ' I in dismal continual wrestle with *Friedrich*, the *unexecutable* book, the second of my twelve years' " wrestle " in that element ! My days were black and spiritually muddy ; hers, too, very weak and dreamy, tho' *un*complaining ; never did complain once of *her un*chosen sufferings and miserable eclipse under the writing of that sad book.' That was how things appeared to Carlyle in looking back, when the *Frederick* work was done and his wife had lately died ; but at the time he did not altogether feel like that. When Carlyle was at work, he was not thinking of his feelings, but of what he was doing, and too busy to notice whether he was happy or not.

---

[1] Book XXII, Chapter I.

On Wednesday, 8.11.1854, he went to see portraits of many kinds in the Library at Windsor Castle, ' introduced by Lady Ashburton and her high people ' ; and on Friday he described the visit to his sister Jean.—

' It is some twenty and odd miles off : one of the beautifullest Palaces,—for situation, etc., much the beautifullest I ever saw. Built on a short steep hill (high for those parts, and beautifully *clothed* ' with trees) ; ' commanding an immense plain, the richest in the Island ; with oak forests, with the River, with etc., etc., to all lengths. I regarded little or nothing of that ; but proceeded straight to my Print rooms, where a Mr. Glover, the " Librarian " of the place, was extremely kind to me, and I saw really a great many things that may be useful in my operations ; and had four diligent and goodish hours out of a day. I mean to go back when the weather is brighter (for Pictures and old eyes), and when the " Court " is not there.

' Towards four o'clock, while I was busy with a hundred Prints of Frederick, there came a soft step to the door ; I did not look up till Glover said, " Prince Albert ! "—and there in truth was the handsome young gentleman, very jolly and handsome in his loose greyish clothes, standing in the door ; not advancing till I bowed. His figure and general face were well known to me, well-built figure of near my own height, florid *blond* face (with fair hair) ; but the *eyes* were much better than I had fancied ; a pair of strong steady eyes, with a good healthy briskness in them. He was civility itself, and in a fine simple fashion : a sensible man withal. We talked first of Frederick's Portraits ; then went, by a step or two, into the Saxon genealogy line, into the Wartburg, Coburg, Luther, Frederick the Wise (that is the Prince who caught up Luther, put him safe into the Wartburg ; he is ancestor of Albert).' This must be understood to mean—in the same line of descent. Frederick the Wise was never married and was succeeded by his brother.[2] The interview lasted ' about an hour,' and so they doubtless were seated most of the time. Carlyle's report runs on.—

' We had there sufficient scope of talk, and went on very well, the Prince showing me a Portrait he had copied of " Frederick the Wise " (not ill done), telling of a Luther autograph he had (from Coburg, and a joke appended to the getting of it there),—when a *domestic* glided in upon us,

[2] See *The Prinzenraub*, in the *Miscellaneous Essays* of T. C.

murmured something, of which I heard, " gone out to the Terrace." (Queen out, wants you,—he had been in Town all morning)—whereupon, in a minute or two, our Dialogue winding itself up in some tolerable way, Prince Albert (prince of courtesy) bowed himself out, back foremost and with some indistinct mention of " your *Works*," which did not much affect me ; and so ended our interview.'

His report to Lady Ashburton is to the same effect. He praised Glover as a librarian, and declared the Windsor collection of engraved Portraits, Miniatures, &c. was the best he had ever seen, and beyond his expectation.

It may illustrate the continuity that was one of Carlyle's characteristics to mention that 4.11.1854 was the date of his last letter to David Hope,[3] the Glasgow merchant, whose acquaintance he had made in 1820. They had never lost touch with each other, and Hope had just sent him a friend's book of poetry, suggesting a review. Carlyle excused himself because " so busy with an abstruse mass of *prose* matter," and explained he was held in London by work, and among other common friends referred to the John Johnson who had given him lessons in his early years[4] and had come home now from America.—" I am glad to think of my old friend and benefactor, Mr. Johnson, as returned to his native region, after so many wanderings. May all good that can be yet possible wait on him there. It is a long time now since he drilled me in the *syntaxes ;* and with beneficent mockery and otherwise, brought me to understand that I as yet understood nothing."[3]

---

[3] *Scribners' Magazine*, 1893, p. 425.   [4] *Carlyle Till Marriage*, p. 25.

V

A LETTER TO HIS YOUNGEST SISTER
(1854)

BY this time Mrs. Hanning, Carlyle's youngest sister "Jenny," had been three years beside her husband in Hamilton, Canada, and as she said in her old age,[1] was glad she had heeded her own feelings only and rejoined him against the advice of her relatives. In the letters from "Tom" which she carefully preserved there was one she thought confidential and may have afterwards destroyed. At any rate it is not in the volume of such letters published but she had allowed a copy to be made of it for our benefit here. To explain the reference to newspapers in the opening sentence, it should be said that Carlyle and his brother and sisters continued a custom, which was common where postage was dear, of sending to each other, instead of letter, a newspaper bearing a mark to show that all was well with the sender.

'CHELSEA,
                                    ' 13 dec.ʳ 1854.

' MY DEAR SISTER,
        ' I got a little newspaper from you yesterday ; I had a short letter from you not long before ; and newspapers come now and then, testifying that you go on without bad accident, which it is always a pleasure to us to know. I am kept very busy here, hunted about by confusions of which you can have little idea ! However, I determine to write a word to you today, the *first thing* in the morning, let the rest of the day's work go as it will. Tho' I absolutely write no letter that *can* be avoided, this seems to me to be one that ought to be written.

[1] To D. A. W. who stayed some days in 1895 in the house of her daughter and son-in-law, Mrs. and Mr. Leslie, near Toronto, with whom Mrs. Hanning then was living. D. A. W. read aloud to her all the letters at the earnest request of the Leslies, as the old lady had said she would take his advice about publishing. See *Carlyle at his Zenith*, Book XVII, Chapter XXXIII, pp. 312–6.

' I have not been in Annandale, nor anywhere away from home even for a day, since the last sad journey I made about a year ago ' . . . (to Scotsbrig, on the occasion of their mother's illness and death.) ' I have been in poorish health, rather worse than you used to witness in me, (but) not very *much* worse,—in fact the chief origin of it is, confusions of many kinds that have long been going on with " repairing of the house " here, (a very sad and almost endless business, as I find, *not* suitable to a thin skinned man), this with *sorrows* which you may judge of in part (irreparable *losses* in which you also have shared), and as the result of all, little or no visible progress possible for me in the work I have on hand, is the chief cause of my sicklier condition of late. Besides, it is certain enough I am getting *old ;* nor do I forget that most serious fact : however, it is really wonderful how softly I am handled in that respect hitherto ; only *one* of my eyes has yet given symptoms of failing ; and except the dispiritment, and indeed the *indifference*, about most earthly things, I trace wonderfully little effect of age on me yet.' (He was now fifty-nine.) ' I hope too, by obstinate persistence, to get on a little better with my tasks ; and on the whole to improve a little by-and-by. Jane too continues much as you knew her ; is subject to colds, &c., in winter time ; but has generally better health,— I should say certainly not worse,—than she has been used to these thirty years now.'

(Then he goes into details of deaths and other events, among their brothers and sisters and other relatives and friends and neighbours she knew, and coming round to her affairs and her husband, Robert Hanning, he says :—) ' You need not doubt we are right glad to hear of Robert's steady industrious behaviour, and of your content with one another. The little lasses too ' (her two daughters) ' will be growing apace. Try always to *help* him and them in all good things, dear Jenny : that you will find to be a great gain in the end. And take care of your health.'

(Then he gives news about the weather of late, and, says :—) ' That and the Turk War are what we mainly talk of. Give my ever-affectionate regards to Alick ' (his brother, who was now also living not far from Mrs. Hanning in Canada), ' whom I have loved for near sixty years now ! My blessings on you and your household, dear sister.

'   Yours ever,
'   T. CARLYLE.'

K

VI

AN ELECTION AT GLASGOW
(1854)

A CURIOUS thing had happened at Glasgow University
this November, (1854). The students there were
electing a "Lord Rector," whose function is mainly to
make a speech to them about anything he likes, at any time
during his term of office. The Tories among the students
put up Benjamin Disraeli, and the Liberals Thomas Carlyle.

If the students had been left to themselves, Carlyle would
have been elected and little said about the matter anywhere.
But Scotland was then fanatical, and still heated by the
religious fever that issued in the "Disruption" of the
Church of Scotland, and the newspapers gave space to
scribblers telling what the "orthodox" were thinking of
Carlyle.[1]—

'Carlyle's philanthropy is not that of Howard, his cure
for national distress is to bury our paupers in peat bogs,
driving wooden boards on the top of them. His entire
works may be described as reiterating the doctrine that
"Whatever is is wrong." He has thrown off every form of
religious belief and settled down into the conviction that the
Christian profession of Englishmen is a sham. . . .

'Elect him and you bid Godspeed to Pantheism and
Spiritualism,' meaning trickery by ghosts. 'Mr. Carlyle
neither possesses the talent nor the distinction, nor does he
occupy the position, which entitle a man to such an honour
as the Rectorial Chair. . . .

'The *Scotch Guardian* writes :—But for the folly exhibited
in bringing forward Mr. Disraeli, scarcely any party within
the College or out of it would have ventured to nominate
a still more obnoxious personage. This is the first instance
we have been able to discover, in which the suffrages of

[1] *Thomas Carlyle*, by John Nichol, Prof. of English Lit., pp. 123–6.

the youth of the University have been sought for a candidate who denied in his writings that the revealed Word of God is " the way, the truth, the life." It is impossible to separate Mr. Carlyle from that obtrusive feature of his works in which the solemn verities of our holy religion are sneered at as worn-out " biblicalities," " unbelievabilities," and religious profession is denounced as " dead putrescent cant."

' The reader of the *Life of John Sterling* is not left to doubt for a moment the author's malignant hostility to the religion of the Bible. In that work— saving faith is described as " stealing into heaven by the modern method of sticking ostrich-like your head into fallacies on earth," that is to say, by believing in the doctrines of the Gospels. How, after this, could the Principal and Professors of the University, the guardians of the faiths and morals of its inexperienced youth, accompany to the Common Hall, and allow to address the students a man who has degraded his powers to the life-labour of sapping and mining the foundations of the truth, and opened the fire of his fiendish raillery against the citadel of our best aspirations and dearest hopes ? '

The benches of the rooms where Carlyle's supporters met were riotously broken ; and in the end his name had to be withdrawn, and an orthodox ' nobleman ' became the successful Liberal candidate. A letter from Carlyle dated 16.12.1854 to the spokesman of his supporters was printed in 1892,[1] and it is only needful to add to it that at that time " men of eminence were not consulted as to their nomination,"[2] and that the addressee of the letter would be a young man of 21, afterwards better known as the Glasgow Professor of English Literature, John Nichol.[2]

' I have received your Pamphlet ; and return many thanks for all your kindness to me. I am sorry to learn, as I do for the first time from this narrative, what angry nonsense some of my countrymen see good to write of me. Not being much a reader of Newspapers, I had hardly heard of the Election till after it was finished ; and I did not know that anything of this melancholy element of Heterodoxy, " Pantheism," etc. etc., had been introduced into the matter. It is an evil after its sort, this of being hated and denounced by fools and ignorant persons ; but it cannot be mended for the present, and so must be left standing there.

[2] *Memoir of John Nichol*, by Prof. W. Knight, pp. 114, 118–24, and the private talk of Prof. Nichol to D. A. W., in 1884.

' That another wiser class think differently, nay, that they alone have any real knowledge of the question, or any real right to vote upon it, is surely an abundant compensation. If that be so, then all is still right ; and probably there is no harm done at all !—To you, and the other young gentlemen who have gone with you on this occasion, I can only say that I feel you have loyally meant to do me a great honour and kindness ; that I am deeply sensible of your genial recognition, of your noble enthusiasm (which reminds me of my own young years) ; and that in fine there is no loss or gain of an Election which can in the least alter these valuable facts, or which is not wholly insignificant to me in comparison with them. " Elections " are not a thing transacted by the gods, in general ; and I have known very unbeautiful creatures " elected " to be kings, chief-priests, railway kings, etc., by the " most sweet voices," and the spiritual virtue that inspires these, in our time !

' Leaving all that, I will beg you all to retain your honourable good feelings towards me ; and to think that if anything I have done or written can help any one of you in the noble problem of living like a wise man in these foolish times, it will be more valuable to me than ever so many Elections or Non-elections.

' With many good wishes and regards, I heartily thank you all, and remain—

' Yours very sincerely,

' T. CARLYLE.'

VII

CHIT-CHAT
(1854–55, &c.)

IN November, 1854, Carlyle had been telling Mr. Brookfield of a letter from Lady Ashburton, saying she would ' be in London on such a day,'—" D.V." ; and he added,— " D." meaning God, " never is willing ; entirely declines co-operation on any terms whatever."[1]

By December Carlyle was fairly under weigh with *Frederick*, and unwilling to ' waste a month at present,' said his wife. So she engaged to go to the Grange alone on 19.12.54 ; but when the time came, she found herself ' shut up in the house with one of her long colds,' and had to be excused.

On New Year's Day, Mr. Brookfield at the Grange was writing in his Diary :—' At lunch I spoke of missing Carlyle less than I had supposed ' that I would, and Lady Ashburton ' broke in,—" *Oh, nobody is ever missed.*" ' Next day she ' read a letter at breakfast from somebody who said everything needful had now gone to the Crimea except common sense and foresight. Lord Elcho asked her,—" Is that from Clarendon ? " " No, sir," she replied instantly, " it is from John Smith, Esquire, Bayswater, Middlesex." '[1]

Meanwhile at Cheyne Row the work in hand was making progress. Carlyle was writing (22.1.55) to Neuberg, whom snowy roads seem to have detained at home the night before, —' My glass roof is covered with *snow* ' ; (but) ' there is light to work by, and silence.' The *Frederick* was going on so fast that if certain extracts did not come soon,—' I shall have to struggle through the period without them, or with what I can remember of them by looking at them. Pray think over in your own mind what it is that looks most *vivid* to you. . . . That *last* Dispatch of Hyndford's ought certainly to come. Then there was the Grumkow letter . . .' and so on. A little later he reports, ' The wind is howling over

---

[1] *Mrs. Brookfield and Her Circle*, by C. & F. Brookfield, II, pp. 411–12.

my glass roof, but cannot get in,' and even the cold is kept out.

In those years, the forties and fifties, one of the commonest callers on the Carlyles in the evenings was Prof. Masson. He was a favourite of both, and a loyal admirer of both to the end of his life. He used to say :[2]—' The mere fact that Froude imagined that Carlyle could ever have used strong language to his wife, is alone enough to show he was never on an intimate footing in their house as long as she was alive,' which is a fact that can otherwise be proved by direct evidence. ' It was simply inconceivable,' said Masson. ' She used to tell stories at her husband's expense, whereat he used to laugh as heartily as the rest of us.'

Bozzy Espinasse is explicit to the same effect,[3] corroborating the Mitfords also by telling how he once heard Mrs. Carlyle say, " I can't bear to be thought of as only Mr. Carlyle's wife " ; and how she delighted to tell ' before company ' anecdotes that made him ridiculous. But it was always the fun that was uppermost, and what Masson remembered as one of her best stories, and one she repeatedly told with enjoyment, was unlike the rest in being an occasion ' when I did not get the last word,'—which she seemed to consider a wife's perquisite. ' We needed a garden roller,' she would say, ' and a neighbour had one to sell. So I sent Carlyle to buy it ; and he went and bought it, and reporting to me what he had done, concluded,—" The lady of that house is a handsome woman." " O, Carlyle ! " I cried, " she isn't." And I explained to him how very absurd it was to suppose a woman like her handsome. He only replied to me,—" She *is* a *most* handsome woman." " Carlyle, Carlyle ! " I cried again, " she isn't, I tell you," and I copiously explained to him how he was talking nonsense. He listened patiently to a long rigmarole, and I believed I had convinced him,—till I ended. Then he dumbfounded me by his final delivery,—" She *is* the most handsome woman I ever set eyes on." '

One night in the fifties David Masson was walking in Hyde Park with Carlyle, and remembered it as the only time he ever saw " the Master " shrug his shoulders. The sky was clear and glittering with stars, brighter and brighter

[2] To D. A. W. My notes of his talk, intended with his knowledge for this book, extend over many years. The last quoted in this chapter was on 6.11.1902.

[3] *Literary Recollections*, by F. Espinasse, p. 268, and see next chapter.

as the daylight faded, and Carlyle was watching them a long time in silence as they walked, and then he began to speak as if in soliloquy of the infinite beauty and harmony of the Universe, and went on to talk with loathing about the prevailing fashion of " sniggering at things." He paused and added slowly, " Maybe I have given way too much to it myself," and as he said so he gave a shrug of disgust, and became silent again, contemplating the stars.

VIII

MR. MITFORD, LORD REDESDALE'S REPORT

NEITHER of the Carlyles was at the Grange this year, but among the acquaintances they had made there was a family of Mitfords, and Mr. A. B. F. Mitford, (Lord Redesdale,) made an interesting report in his old age of what the Mitfords thought of them.[1]—

' Lady Ashburton's mother, Lady Sandwich, was a Corry,' (and Irish in short). ' I knew her from childhood. At the Grange my father and aunt made the acquaintance of the Carlyles, Thackeray, Charles Buller, Monckton Milnes, Dickie Doyle, and a host of others, all of whom were like the Ashburtons, hearty admirers of Carlyle's genius. Mrs. Carlyle was always welcome, either at the Grange or at Addiscombe, but he was the sun, she the moon—the satellite.

' The Carlyles were an ill-assorted couple. But he loved her and was happy in his love. Not so she ! Jealous of him she was—furiously jealous—not as a lover, for there she knew she was safe. But she could not bear to think that if she was famous it was as his wife, whereas she would fain have had him to be known as the husband of that wonderful Mrs. Carlyle. It was his success that she resented ; it irked her to be in the second place, and she could not forgive it. That she entertained any sentimental feeling about Carlyle's intimacy with Lady Ashburton is an absurd supposition.' (But in short) ' there was something else of which the lady was jealous, and that was the agony of concentration which her husband's work meant for him. At moments her *saeva indignatio*' (savage wrath) ' against " that Carlyle," as she would sometimes contemptuously call him, passed all bounds.' *Car*lyle, with emphasis on the first syllable, was the old Dumfriesshire pronunciation, it should be explained. Mr. Mitford goes on.—

---

[1] *Memories*, by A. B. F. Mitford, Lord Redesdale, II, pp. 649–54.

'One day my aunt went to call upon her and found her
n one of her tantrums.—What was the matter, she asked :
'Oh ! my dear, it's just that Carlyle ! Would you believe
t, I have had a headache for three days, and he's only
just found it out. 'I'm afraid you're not quite well, my
dear,' he said—and all the time he was working, working !
I just threw a tea-cup at his head."' Which may mean
no more than that she said she'd like to throw a tea-cup.
She was not likely to break a tea-cup in a temper !

'Another time "that Carlyle" was in great disgrace and
Mrs. Carlyle in tears, because the poor man had resented
the presence of a dead mouse embalmed in his porridge at
breakfast.

'Poor Mrs. Carlyle was much to be pitied, not for any
wrong that he did her, but because she was one of those
people who make themselves wretched, and pass on their
misery to those near them. My aunt was one of those
sympathetic people to whom others carry their troubles,
and Mrs. Carlyle spared her not a moan. Carlyle's self-
reproaches after her death were a delusion, born of her own
shrewish complaints, which in his sorrow he schooled himself into believing to be well-founded. . . . She was not an
easy woman to live with. . . .

'In society Mrs. Carlyle was bright, witty and stimulating,
but she was in her inmost heart a discontented woman, in
whom the milk of human kindness had been turned sour.

'Much is said in Froude's volumes about her beauty.
When I knew her she was an elderly, even an old woman,
but I could see no trace of good looks—and people who had
known her when she was young laughed at the idea. However, love is blind, and in Carlyle's eyes she was all that is
beautiful.'

"Saeva indignatio."—The quotation is from Swift's epitaph on himself, which may still be read upon his grave in
St. Patrick's Cathedral, Dublin :—

'Ubi saeva indignatio
Cor ulterius lacerare nequit' :—

'where savage wrath can tear his heart no more.'
Mrs. Carlyle was not aware of what Mr. Mitford was
thinking of her ; which was lucky for her, and perhaps also
for Mr. Mitford.

IX

THE "BACK-CHAT" OF MRS. CARLYLE
(1855)

THE servants of the Carlyles seem to have agreed that tho Mrs. Carlyle did little house-work with her hands, she watched expenses well. Their evidence is confirmed by a document still worth reading. It shows as well as the best of her letters her faculty for animating the details of business.—

Note by Carlyle, dated February 12, 1855.—' The enclosed was read with great laughter ; had been found lying on my table as I returned out of the frosty garden from smoking. Debt is already paid off. Quarterly income to be £58 henceforth, and all is settled to poor Goody's heart's content. The piece is so clever that I cannot just yet find in my heart to burn it, as perhaps I ought to do.'

' Budget of a *Femme Incomprise* ' (a woman not appreciated).

' I don't choose to *speak* again on the *money question !* The " replies " from the Noble Lord are unfair and unkind, and little to the purpose. When you tell me " I pester your life out about money," that " your soul is sick with hearing about it," that " I had better make the money I have serve," " at all rates, hang it, let you alone of it,"—all that I call perfectly unfair, the reverse of kind, and tending to nothing but disagreement. If I were greedy or extravagant or a bad manager, you would be justified in " staving me off " with loud words ; but you cannot say *that* of me (whatever else)—cannot *think* it of me. At least, I am sure that I never " asked for more " to myself from you or anyone, not even from my own mother, in all my life, and that through six and twenty years I have kept house for you at more or less cost according to given circumstances, but always on less than it costs the generality of people living in the same style.

' What I should have expected you to say rather would ave been : " My dear, you *must* be dreadfully hampered ı your finances, and dreadfully anxious and unhappy about t, and quite desperate of *making it do*, since *you* are ' asking or more.' Make me understand the case, then. I can and ıill help you out of that *sordid* suffering at least, either by iving you more, if that be found prudent to do, or by educing our wants to within the present means." That is he sort of thing you would have said had you been a perfect ıan ; so I suppose you are not a perfect man. Then, ıstead of crying in my bed half the night after, I would ave explained my budget to you in peace and confidence. 3ut now I am driven to explain it on paper " in a state of ıind " ; *driven*, for I cannot, it is not in my nature to, live ' entangled in the details," and I *will not*. I would sooner ang myself, tho " pestering you about money " is also ıore repugnant to me than you dream of.

' You don't understand why the allowance which sufficed ı former years no longer suffices. That is what I would xplain to the Noble Lord if he would but—what shall I ay ?—*keep his temper*.

' The beginning of my embarrassments, it will not surprise he Noble Lord to learn, since it has also been " the begin- ıing of " almost every human ill to himself, was *the repairing f the house*. There was a destruction, an *irregularity*, an ıcessant recurrence of small incidental expenses, during all hat period, or *two* periods, through which I found myself ı September gone a year, *ten* pounds behind, instead of aving some pounds saved up towards the winter's coals. could have worked round " out of that," however, in ourse of time, if habits of *unpinched* housekeeping had not ıeen long taken to by *you* as well as myself, and if new ınavoidable or not to be avoided *current* expenses had not ollowed close on those incidental ones. I will show the ʋoble Lord, with his permission, what the new current xpenses *are*, and to what they amount per annum. (Hear ıear ! and cries of " Be brief ! ")

' 1. We have a servant of " higher grade " than we ever entured on before ; more expensive in money. Anne's ʋages are 16 pounds a year ; Fanny's were 13. Most of he others had 12 ; and Anne never dreams of being other han *well fed*. The others *scrambled* for their living out of urs. Her regular meat dinner at one o'clock, regular llowance of butter, &c., adds at least three pounds a year

to the *year's* bills. But she plagues us with no fits of illness
nor of *drunkenness*, no *warnings* nor complainings. She
does perfectly what she is *paid* and *fed* to do. I see house
not so well kept with " cook," " housemaid," and " man
servant." (Question !). Anne is the last item I should vote
for retrenching in. I may set her down, however, at six
additional pounds.

' 2. We have now gas and water " laid on," both producing
an admirable result. But between " water laid on " at one
pound sixteen shillings per annum, with *shilling* to turn
cock, and water carried at fourpence a week there is a
yearly difference of 19 shillings and four pence ; and betwixt *gas* all the year round and a few sixpenny boxes of
lights in the winter the difference may be computed at
fifteen shillings. These two excellent innovations, then
increase the yearly expenditure by one pound fourteen
shillings and four pence—a trifle to speak of ; but you
my Lord, born and bred in thrifty Scotland, must know
well the proverb, " Every little mak's a mickle."

' 3. We are higher *taxed*. Within the last eighteen months
there has been added to the Lighting, Pavement, and Improvement Rate ten shillings yearly, to the Poor Rate one
pound, to the sewer rate ten shillings ; and now the double
Income Tax makes a difference of £5. 16s. 8d. yearly, which
sums, added together, amount to a difference of £7. 16s. 8d
yearly, on taxes which already amounted to £17. 12s. 8d
There need be no reflections for want of taxes.

' 4. Provisions of all sorts are higher priced than in former
years. Four shillings a week for bread, instead of two
shillings and sixpence, makes at the year's end a difference
of £3. 18s. Butter has kept all the year round 2d. a pound
dearer than I ever knew it. On the quantity we use—two
pounds and a half per week " quite reg'lar "—there is a
difference of 21s. 8d. by the year. Butcher's meat is a
penny a pound dearer. At the rate of a pound and a half
a day, *bones* included—no exorbitant allowance for three
people—the difference on that at the year's end would be
£2. 5s. 6d. Coals, which had been for some years at 21s.
per ton, cost this year 26s., last year 29s. bought judiciously
too. If I had had to pay 50s. a ton for them, as some
housewives had to, God knows what would have become of
me. (Passionate cries of " Question ! question ! ") We
burn, or used to burn—I am afraid they are going faster
this winter—twelve tons, one year with another. Candles

re *viz :* composites a shilling a pound, instead of 10d. ;
dips 8 pence, instead of 5d. or 6d. Of the former we burn
three pounds in nine days—the greater part of the year
you sit so late—and of dips two pounds a fortnight on the
average of the whole year. Bacon is 2d. a pound dearer ;
soap ditto ; potatoes, at the cheapest, a penny a pound,
instead of three pounds for 2d. We use three pounds of
potatoes in two days' meals. Who could imagine that at
the year's end that makes a difference of 15s. 2d. on one's
mere potatoes ? Compute all this, and you will find that
the difference on *provisions* cannot be under twelve pounds
a the year.

' 5. What I should blush to state if I were not *at bay*, so
to speak : ever since we have been in London *you* have, in
the handsomest manner, paid the winter's butter with *your
own money*, though it was not in the bond. And this gentle-
manlike proceeding on your part, till the butter became
meatable, was a good two pounds saved me.

' Add up these differences :—

					£		
1.	Rise on servant	.	.	.	£6	0	0
2.	Rise on light and water		.	.	1	14	4
3.	On Taxes	.	.	.	7	16	8
4.	On provisions	.	.	.	12	0	0
5.	Cessation of Butter	.	.	.	2	0	0

You will find a total of   .   .   . £29 11 0

' My calculation will be found quite correct, though I am
not strong in arithmetic. I have *thochtered* all this well in
my head, and *indignation* makes a sort of arithmetic, as
well as verses. Do you finally understand why the allowance which sufficed formerly no longer suffices, and pity
my difficulties instead of being angry at them ?

' The only thing you can reproach me with, *if you like*, is
that fifteen months ago, when I found myself already in
debt, and everything *rising* on me, I did not fall at once
to *pinching* and *muddling*, as when we didn't know where
the next money was to come from, instead of " lashing
down " at the accustomed rate : nay, expanding into a
regular servant." But you are to recollect that when I
first complained to you of the *prices*, you said, quite good-
naturedly, " Then you are coming to bankruptcy, are you ?
Not going to be able *to go on*, you think ? Well, then, we
must come to your assistance, poor *crittur*. You mustn't

be made a bankrupt of." So I kept my mind easy, a
retrenched in nothing, relying on the promised " assistance
But when " Oh ! it was lang o' coming, lang o' coming
my arrears taking every quarter a more alarming cif
what could I do but put you in mind ? Once, twice,
the third speaking, what you were pleasantly calling "
great heap of money "—£15—was—what shall I say ?
flung to me. Far from *leaving anything* to meet the increase
demand of another nine months, this sum did not clear n
of debt, not by five pounds. But from time to time e
couraging *words* fell from the Noble Lord. " No, yo
cannot pay the double Income Tax ; clearly, I must pa
that for you." And again : " I will burn as many coa
as I like ; if you can't pay for them somebody must !
All resulting, however, thus far in " *Don't you wish you m*
get it ? " Decidedly I should have needed to be more tha
mortal, or else " a born daughter of Chaos," to have go
on without attempt made at ascertaining what *coming*
my assistance meant : whether it meant £15 without
blessing once for all ; and, if so, what retrenchments were
be permitted.

' You asked me at last money row, with withering sa
casm, " had I the slightest idea what amount of mone
would *satisfy me*. Was I wanting £50 more ; or forty,
thirty ? Was there any conceivable sum of money tha
could put an end to my eternal botheration ? " I wi
answer the question as if it had been asked practically an
kindly.

' Yes. I have the strongest idea what amount of mone
would " *satisfy* " me. I have computed it often enough
I lay awake at nights, and didn't I wish I might get it
Indeed, when I can't sleep now it is my " difficulties "
think about more than my sins, till they become " a re
mental awgony in my own inside." The above-named sun
£29 divided into quarterly payments, would *satisfy* me (wit
a certain parsimony about little things somewhat less migl
do), I engaging my word of a gentlewoman to *give back*
the year's end whatever portion thereof any diminution o
the demand on me might enable me to save.

' I am not so unpractical, however, as to ask for the whol
£29 without thought or care where it is to come from.
have settled all that (derisive laughter, and Hear, hear !
so that nine pounds only will have to be disbursed b
you over and above your long-accustomed disbursement

Hear, hear !) You anticipate, perhaps, some draft on your waste-paper basket. No, my Lord, it has never been my habit to interfere with your ways of making money, or the rate which you make it at ; and if I never did it in early years, most unlikely that I should do it *now*. My bill of ways and means has nothing to do with making money, only with disposing of the money made. (Bravo ! hear !)

' 1. Ever since my mother's death you have allowed me for old Mary Mills £3 yearly. She needs them no more. *Continue these three pounds for the house.*

' 2. Through the same long term of years you have made me the handsomest Christmas and birthday presents ; and when I had purposely disgusted you from *buying me things*, you gave me at the New Year £5. Oh I know the meaning of that £5 quite well. *Give me nothing ;* neither money nor money's worth. I would have it so anyhow, and continue the £5 for the house.

' 3. Ever since we came to London you have paid some £2 I guess, for *butter*, now become uneatable. Continue that £2 for the house ; and we have already *ten* pounds which you can't miss, not having been used to them.

' 4. My allowance of £25 is a very liberal one ; has enabled me to spend freely for myself ; and I don't deny there is a pleasure in that when there is no household crisis ; but with an appalling deficit in the house exchequer, it is not only no pleasure but an impossibility. I can keep up my dignity and my wardrobe on a less sum—on £15. a year. A silk dress, " a splendid dressing-gown," " a milliner's bonnet " the less ; what signifies that at my age ? Nothing. Besides, I have had so many " gowns " given me that they may serve for two or three years. By then God knows if I shall be needing *gowns* at all. So deduct £10 from my personal allowance ; and continue that for the house.

' But why not transfer it *privately* from my own purse to the house one, and ask only for £19 ? It would have sounded more modest—*figured* better. Just because " that sort of thing " don't please me. I have tried it and found it a bad *go :* a virtue *not* its own reward ! I am for every herring to hang by its own head, every purse to stand on its own bottom. It would worry me to be thought rolling in the wealth of £25, when I was cleverly making £15 do, and investing £10 in coals and taxes. Mrs. X is up to that sort of self-sacrifice thing, and to finding compensation in

the sympathy of many friends, and in smouldering discon
tent with X for having no intuition of her magnanimity
I am up to neither the magnanimity nor the compensation
but I am quite up to laying down £10 of my allowance in
a straightforward recognised way, without standing on my
toes to it either. And what is more, I am determined
upon it, *will not* accept more than £15 in the present state
of affairs.

'There only remains to disclose the actual state of the
exchequer. It is empty as a drum. (Sensation.) If I consider twenty-nine more pounds indispensable—things re
maining as they are—for the coming year, beginning the
22nd of March, it is just because I have found it so in the
year that is gone ; and I commenced that, as I have already
stated, with £10 of arrears. You assisted me with £15, and
I have assisted myself with £10, five last August, which I
took from the Savings Bank, and the five you gave me at
New Year, which I threw into the coal account. Don't
suppose—" if thou's i' the habit of supposing "—that I tell
you this in the *un*devout imagination of being *repaid*. By
all that's sacred for me—*the memory of my father and mother*
—what else can an irreligious creature like me swear by ?
I would not take back that money if you *offered* it with the
best grace, and had picked it up in the street. I tell it you
simply that you may see I am not so dreadfully greedy as
you have appeared to think me latterly. Setting *my £10*
then against the original arrears, with £15 in assistance from
you, it would follow, from my own computation, that I
should need £14 more to clear off arrears on the weekly
bills and carry me on paying my way until 22nd of March
next quarter-day. (Cries of Shame ! and Turn her out !
I say only " *should need*." Your money is of course yours
to do as you will with, and I *would like* to again " walk the
causeway " carrying my head as high—as—Mr. A., the
upholsterer, owing no man anything, and *dearly I would*
like to " at all rates let YOU alone of it," if I knew who
else had any business with my housekeeping, or to whom
else I could properly address myself for that moment; a
what with that expensive, most ill-timed dressing-gown
and my cheap ill-timed chiffonnier, and my half-year's bill
to Rhind and Catchpole, I have only what will serve me til
June comes round.

'If I was a man, I might fling the gauntlet to Society
join with a few brave fellows, and " rob a diligence." Bu

Plate IV

MRS. CARLYLE
(*From a photograph by R. Tait, 1857*)

[face p. *144*

ny sex " kind o' debars from that." Mercy ! to think
here are women—your friend Lady A., for example (" *Ru-
neurs !* " Sensation)—I say for *example ;* who spend not
merely the additional pounds I must make such pother
bout, but *four times my whole income* in the *ball* of one
night, and none the worse for it, nor anyone the better. It
s—what shall I say ?—" curious," upon my honour. But
ust in the same manner Mrs. Freeman might say : " To
hink there are women—Mrs. Carlyle, for example—who
pend £3. 14s. 6d. on one dressing-gown, and I with just
wo loaves and eighteen pence from the parish, to live on by
he week." There is no bottom to such reflections. The
only thing one is perfectly sure of is " it will come all to the
same ultimately," and I can't say I'll regret the loss of
myself, for one.—I add no more, but remain, dear Sir,

' Your obedient humble servant,
' JANE WELSH CARLYLE.'

X

IN TIME OF WAR
(1855)

OWING to the Crimean War the London season was one
of little dinners this year, and Brookfield[1] tells us
' there were many such at Bath House,' where ' Venables
Poodle Byng, G. Bunsen, both the Carlyles and ourselve
would stay till late,' and ' very pleasant they were.'

While Carlyle was cursing the war and those that made
it, and steadily working at his *Frederick*, Tennyson was
doing his *Maud*, which Carlyle called a " cobweb,"[2] in talking
to Fitzgerald. Of course what keeps Tennyson in mind is
' The Charge of the Light Brigade,'—his fantasy upon the
words in the *Times* that—" Some one had blundered."
As the French general said, " It was magnificent, but it
was not war." In short, as Leslie Stephen remarked,[3] the
poet was falling in too easily with the current delusion of
the time (embodied also in Kingsley's *Two Years Ago*) that
the Crimean War implied the moral regeneration of the
country . . . ' I don't think that the war can now be credited
with that effect,' added Leslie Stephen ; and we can all
agree with him, tho in 1914 we made the same mistake.
What Mrs. Carlyle was writing to Mrs. Russell is worth
reading :—' Oh, aren't you miserable about this war ?
am haunted day and night with the thought of all the
women of England, Scotland, and Ireland, who must be
in agonies of suspense about their nearest and dearest
Thank God I have no husband, or father, or son, in that
horrible war. I have some few acquaintances, however
and one intimate friend—Colonel Sterling ; and I read the
list of killed and wounded always with a sick dread of
finding his name.'

[1] *Mrs. Brookfield and Her Circle*, by C. & F. Brookfield, II, p. 416.
[2] *Letters of Edward Fitzgerald*, I, p. 305.
[3] *Studies of a Biographer*, by Leslie Stephen, II, p. 237.

There is a flash as of X-rays in what Mrs. Carlyle wrote to the same lady many months later : [4]—' My own only two friends in the Crimean army, Sir Colin Campbell and Colonel Sterling, make no doubt but that Autumn ' (1856) ' will see them all home. *The people in the City, a Cabinet minister told me yesterday, are getting as wild for war with America as they were for war with Russia*[5] *;* but there will be more words to *that ! '*

Which may be easily explained. Whoever loses by war, the ' City ' always wins. Consider the rates of interest on good security in 1920 compared with 1913. So it has been suggested that in time of war the money required by Government should be raised by compulsory loans without interest, assessed in proportion to means, like the Income-tax.

Besides, a war should be the signal for at least the temporary disappearance from public life of every man connected with the starting of it. Why not ? Any war is a kind of political shipwreck. In civilised countries, every captain has to stand an enquiry when his ship is wrecked, and so should our political leaders, of every sort. In the ' good time coming,' even they and the ' City-men,' almighty for mischief to-day, may thus be made to realise how ' Blessed are the Peace-makers.''

[4] Dated only Friday, but assigned by the editor to 8.2.1856.
[5] Italics added.

XI

ON NAPOLEON THE LITTLE AND EXHIBITION:
(1855)

OUR International Exhibition of 1851 was being imi
tated in Paris this year, and the Ashburtons wer
going over to see the show. On 13.4.55 Carlyle remarked
in a letter to Lady Ashburton :—' If it was Louis Napoleon
so-called Emperor, that made this " French Exhibition,"
it shall be another of my griefs against him ; which alread
make a heavy score,—taking in Sebastopol, the Thief
Acrobat General-in-Chief ; the Charlatan that went to pu
stars in the Holy Places, and gather votes from dirty French
Priests.—Pah ! I find that a very damnatory symptom i
the man. My poor Fritz, scraggy as he was, would hav
much scorned any such adventure, at his worst pinch. H
(Napoleon) will never " fix " himself, except in Chaos, b
these methods. He will go to the Devil, I doubt ;—an
this " Glass Box of never-imagined size," (equivalent t
the *Millennium* in the minds of simple persons), which
whirls you away to Paris again, this also will be charge
to his account.—My notion really is, there has been a tripl
portion of folly in the English nation ever since that yea
of loud Inanity, (1851), when it was said to all manner o
Paxtons, Coles and flabby windy creatures, " Jubilate ! '
and to all manner of serious thinking persons, " Hold you
peace, under penalties ! " '

There is a proverb that the greatest pleasure in pros
perity is to see again the scenes familiar in poorer days
and that may be why Napoleon the Little now brought hi
wife to see London and visit Queen Victoria. She receive
him as her " great ally " in the war going on, to say nothin
of his having had the chief share in starting it,—to pro
the throne which he had got by murdering and evil-doin
like Nero's. It has to be added that the " enthusiasti
public welcome " appears to have been exaggerated. A

148

ny rate, here is what Carlyle was writing to his brother
ohn.—

> ' CHELSEA,
>
> ' *April* 20, 1855 (*Friday*).
>
> ' Louis Napoleon has not been shot hitherto. That is the
> est that can be said. He gathers, they say, great crowds
> bout him, but his reception from the hip-hip-hurrahing
> lasses is not warm at all. On Monday, just before they
> rrived, I came (in omnibus) down Piccadilly. Two thin
> nd thinnest rows of the most abject-looking human
> retches I had ever seen or dreamt of—lame, crook-backed,
> warfish, dirty-shirted, with the air of pickpockets and
> ity jackals, not a *gent* hardly among them, much less any
> estige of a gentleman—were drawn up from St. James's
> treet to Hyde Park Corner to receive the august pair. I
> oked at them with a shuddering thankfulness that they
> ere not drawn up to receive *me*.
>
> ' April 23. We have got done with our Emperor. Thank
> [eaven he took himself away before the week ended. Never
> as such a blaze of enthusiastic reception, &c., says rumour,
> hich I for my own share cannot confirm or decisively con-
> adict. Royal children all weeping when the *soi-disant* '
> elf-styled) ' august pair took themselves away again—*à la
> mne heure !* ' (So be it !)

Meanwhile C. C. F. Greville, Privy Council Clerk, was
riting what is in curious contrast to this.[1] ' April 20th.—
he visit of the Emperor has been one continued ovation,
ad the success of it complete. None of the sovereigns who
ave been here before have ever been received with such
agnificence by the Court or by such curiosity and delight
y the people. Wherever and whenever they have appeared,
ey have been greeted by enormous multitudes and pro-
gious acclamations. The Queen is exceedingly pleased
ith both of them ; she thinks the Emperor frank, cordial,
ad true. He has done his best to please her, talked to her
great deal, amused her, and has completely succeeded.
verybody is struck with his mean and diminutive figure
ad vulgar appearance, but his manners are good and not
adignified.'
Poor Greville was naturally biased in favour of Napoleon,

---

[1] *The Greville Memoirs*, by C. C. F. Greville, VII, pp. 261–2, 270,
5–6.

who was very good to him, so that what he says about the
Emperor's poor appearance is a kind of admission and
credible all the more.   When dining this summer with the
Emperor at St. Cloud, where Lord and Lady Ashburton
were of the party, Greville is full of praise for the Emperor
demeanour, but, he confesses, ' I was struck with his appearance being so very *mesquin* (or shabby), more than I thought
at first.'   Being honoured with a confidential talk with the
Emperor this summer, Greville heard him talk of the war
and ' the generals engaged, comparing them, much to the
disadvantage, with the generals of the Empire.'   Among
other things the Emperor talked ' of the Exhibition here
and with some appearance of disappointment that the people
will not go to it.'

It is quite plain from Greville that not only he himself
and our Chancellor of the Exchequer, Sir G. C. Lewis, and
many others, but most of the men of sense in France also
were of the same sentiments as Carlyle, namely, in the
words of Greville, they ' had been all along against the
war, and thought it ought to have been prevented and
might have been,' and, in short, that it should be stopped
as soon as possible.

XII

MAJOR DAVIDSON'S REPORT
(1855)

IN 1855 the Crimean War brought up to London a Major
Davidson, who had been a boy in Haddington long ago,
and a patient of Dr. Welsh, and well known to Dr. Welsh's
daughter, now Mrs. Carlyle. He had gone east at sixteen,
as an East India Company's cadet, and returned on pension
after twenty years, a tall and handsome man, still under
forty, with peculiar skill in bullets and cannon balls. In
1855 he was only forty-four and eager " to do his bit,"
kindling like an old war-horse at the sound of battle. He
was an earnest Christian of a kind now rare, without any
misgivings about the inspiration of the Bible, or the pleasure
of killing at the proper season. " The Lord showed him "
something now to do.

As he afterwards explained,[1] ' it was the constant practice of the Russians to restore during the night the batteries
we had silenced during the day ; so that in the morning
the assaulting party, instead of a practical breach, found
the work repaired and furnished with fresh guns.' This
reminded Davidson of a thing he had thought of long ago
' during the practice of the artillery at Ahmednuggar ' ; and
now, with the willing help of the Astronomer Royal at
Edinburgh, he devised a ' collimating telescope ' that would
have enabled artillery men to work the guns upon such
objects with as much precision during the night as during
the day.

The Astronomer Royal at Greenwich gave it his blessing,
but our officers did not get it in time for this war. Something like it came into general use afterwards, and of course
somebody else got the credit and reward. But that was no
fault of Major Davidson, who did all he could in 1855 ; and

---

[1] *Memoirs of a Long Life*, by Col. Davidson, especially pp. 299–309.

151

being in London, he went to see Mrs. Carlyle, and was blithely welcomed.

She discovered he was a poet as well as an artillery-man. So when he returned to town the second time this year, she invited him to a ' family dinner here at six o'clock to meet Alfred Tennyson.' He came rejoicing, and here is his report.—

*Repeated
in
p 177*

' The only other guests were Mr. Carlyle's brother and a young man. Mr. Tennyson came in a morning suit, a tall strongly-built man, with a handsome clear-cut face, close shaved, the features large and powerful. During dinner, Carlyle said, speaking of some distinguished man,—I cannot recall whom,—" He had a face like yours, Tennyson." There was a mask of Dante, which I think the young man had brought, at that moment on the table,' but no suggestion of any likeness to it.

' They spoke about the difficulty of making speeches. Tennyson said if allowed to sit he might manage it, but it was severe upon the nerves to stand up when everyone else was sitting.

' The question was discussed as to whether they would accept titles if offered. Tennyson was disposed to decline such honours for himself, and said no title could equal the simple name of " Thomas Carlyle."

' After dinner long clay pipes were laid on the table, and a smoking parliament commenced. We went upstairs. It was most interesting to hear these two men talk, and I noticed that when Carlyle was at a loss for a poetical quotation, Tennyson promptly supplied it.

' Referring to the *Life of Frederick*, Tennyson said, " At this crisis, Peter the Great would have been a better subject." Carlyle agreed, and added, " And it would have been *better for me*."

' Alluding to the state of Europe, the war in the Crimea being at its height, Tennyson said, " The world is looking for the coming man." I said, " The coming Man has already come, and they crucified Him." Carlyle said emphatically, " I quite agree with you."

' Speaking of modes of government, Carlyle said, " If I had to govern a country, I would take the Bible as my rule, and if it involved the occasional cutting off of a head, I should not mind."

' He told Mr. Tennyson about my plan for night firing,

and his knowledge of mathematics enabled him to describe
it correctly.'

Major Davidson promised Mrs. Carlyle to call upon Mrs.
Welsh's old servant " Betty," whom he used to know.
She was now Mrs. Braid, and living in Edinburgh.   It was
a promise he kept with pleasure.—Mrs. Carlyle was a true
prophet when she wrote to him in sending the address,—
'Dear darling old Betty will be delighted to see you !   It
will be next best to seeing myself, and I should say *you* will
enjoy seeing *her*, and hearing her ; and so the doctrine of
" virtue ever its own reward " will for once at least hold
good ! '

'At the request of Mrs. Carlyle,' Major Davidson adds,[2]
Mr. Thomas Erskine called on me ' in Edinburgh.   No
doubt he had told her how Erskine's writings had helped
him to become a Christian, and he assures us that ' there
was that about ' Erskine ' which could not fail to make one
love and respect him.   But I must confess I was disappointed
at the way he pressed his latterly acquired views, which I
felt were contrary to Scripture, and calculated to imperil
the faith of his followers.'

As for Carlyle himself, Major Davidson tells us, but without a date, and it may have been years after the first
meeting, for the friendship lasted :—' One evening after tea
at Cheyne Row, Mr. Carlyle put on his slouch hat, and, taking
his heavy walking-stick, he volunteered to walk with me
to my hotel in Trafalgar Square, a pretty long stretch.
Having him thus all to myself, I tried, but with little
success, to get some distinct expression of his views on
personal religion, and his own position in regard to it.   He
remarked, however, that he thought Thomas Erskine about
the best specimen he knew of what a Christian ought to be.
I said it was impossible not to be struck with the deep and
living piety of Mr. Erskine, and that long ago I had sat at
his feet a willing learner, but that I took exception to the
views he had more recently adopted.   What he said in reply
I do not now remember.'—It was sure to be—nothing,
politely put.

[2] *Memoirs of a Long Life*, by Col. Davidson, p. 328.

XIII

COOPER, FORSTER, LANDOR, &c.
(1855)

LECTURING and writing for a living, Thomas Cooper
the Chartist, a man of fifty now, continued poor. The
publisher Chapman, in talking about Kingsley's *Alton Locke*
suggested to him to write a Chartist novel.—" You ought
to know a deal more about Chartism than he possibly can,'
said Chapman to Cooper.

But when Cooper had done it, Chapman was advised
against publishing by his reader John Forster, who said,—
" evidently prose fiction is not Mr. Cooper's *forte*."

Routledge became his publisher, and in the beginning of
1855 was bringing out as his second novel a book which
contained much of the very stuff John Forster had con
demned, and about that time Thomas Cooper reports he
' went to 5 Cheyne Row, Chelsea,' to spend ' a couple of
hours ' in Carlyle's company ; but ' had not been with him
more than half an hour when Mr. John Forster was an
nounced.' Cooper confesses, ' I felt inclined to " cut my
stick." ' He was about to ' decamp hastily ' when ' a
loaded truck stopped at the street door—there was a loud
knock—and the maid-servant came in, breathless with
running upstairs, and said " A huge parcel has been brought.'

' Mr. Carlyle seemed all wonder, and muttered, " A huge
parcel ! *What* huge parcel ?—But I'll come down and see.'
And, somehow or other, we all went down to see—for there
was a large wooden case, evidently containing a picture
A hammer and chisel were soon brought.' . . .

Then Cooper offered to handle the tools, but Carlyle did
that himself, remarking as he worked, " It's doubtless the
picture from old Landor " ; and so it was, ' a very noble
picture ' in a ' fine gilded frame. It was a portrait of David
Hume, in full dress—the dress he is said always to have
worn when he sat down to write.' . . .

' " Only think of that old Landor sending me this ! " broke out Carlyle again and again, as we all stood admiring the picture.'

When it was put aside, the three men sat talking pleasantly together awhile. Carlyle went out of the room to fetch a book and Forster said to Cooper significantly,—" You have just had a novel published by Routledge. Do you happen to know whether a copy has been sent to the *Examiner ?* "

" I do not know, but will inquire."

" Take care that it is addressed to me, will you ? " said Mr. Forster. " You understand what I mean ? Take care that it is addressed to me, personally."

' And he nodded and smiled,' adds Cooper. ' I thought I did understand what he meant,' and answered at once,— " Thank you, sir, I will address a copy to you myself."

' I rose to go soon after,' he continues, and as usual Carlyle ' *would* go with me to the street door to say " Good night." So I whispered to him, in the passage, and requested him to strengthen the good intent there seemed to lie in John Forster's mind towards me. Carlyle gave me one of his humorous smiles, and squeezed my hand, as an assurance that I might depend upon him. And so the favourable critique appeared in the *Examiner*.'

Routledge paid him £100 for each of his novels, and he then returned to what suited him better than novel writing.[1]

---

[1] *The Life of Thomas Cooper written by himself,* pp. 334–50.

XIV

INTERNATIONAL COPYRIGHT LAW
(1855)

O N 8.5.55[1] Carlyle complied with a request from Philadelphia for " a letter which may be published " on " International Copy-Right Law." An " extensive publisher " named Carey had been arguing against it, and the gist of what was now sent was to demolish Carey. After mentioning the importance of Literature, ' becoming Church and Parliament and Government and Opera-House all united,' Carlyle went on to say that the denial of International Copyright was ' incapable of being supported by any argument which is not lamentable to behold.' It meant ' to forbid the writer of a book the liberty of selling his manufactures unplundered in the public market at what he can get.

' No one has such property in any object as the writer of a book has in said book. That book belongs to him as nothing else does. Belongs to him as the universe does to the Maker, not as field A or field B does to Jack or Tom, who did not call into existence said fields at all, but have merely obtained possession of them by the consent of neighbours.

' Mr. Carey's similitude of the big " flower-garden " from which the author makes a bouquet, big " store of bricks " from which the author builds a house, halts fatally in one leg and collapses altogether if examined. The fatal halt is this. No author *takes away* the least " flower " or fraction of a " brick," by making his bouquet (well or ill) from Mr. Carey's flower garden, or his house from Mr. Carey's brick-store.—Supposing him to have added nothing whatever, is there not precisely the same stock left, for others to do

---

[1] This is the date of the letter to Neuberg sending the draft ready for copying. The printed date was the date of sending off the fair copy, 14th May.

better with, as before he appeared there ? Precisely the same ; by hypothesis (his work being Zero), no change whatever.

' As to the other leg of the similitude, I should like to ask Mr. Carey where he supposes these flowers, bricks &c. all came from ; and whether it has not fallen within his experience as an extensive Publisher to see such a thing as a " brick " that was *not* there before ? In the interest of human fairplay, sophisms of a conspicuously untenable character and similitudes that fall flat,' should be ' wheeled out of the ring.'

XV

ARTHUR HELPS, JOHN CAMPBELL, &c.
(1855)

CARLYLE had been wearying for news of Helps, and wondering,—" What has come over him ? " when Helps invited him to come and stay with him awhile, and sent the second volume of his *Conquerors of the New World*, announcing that his work was within two months of completion. This was the very volume he had long ago suggested Carlyle might write, if he did not himself survive to do it.

The reply was dated 17.5.1855 ;[1] and after a hint to avoid confusing two Peter Martyrs, ran on.—' Charles V remains entirely invisible in Robertson and all English histories hitherto ; I know only, for absolutely certain, that he has the Austrian chin, a pair of lazy deep eyes,—and shows here and there a long-headed *Flemish Mercantile* character to me, of much obstinacy and occasional arrogance and wrath ; dead to the higher considerations, or pretty nearly so. Good speed to you, good speed ! Happy man that are within " two months " of the shore ; not bound in dreary Polar seas, like some others of us ; nothing on any azimuth but icebergs and walruses, the very stars for most part gone out !

' It would do me real good, I am certain, to get down for a whole week, but. . . .' In short, he could not quit his work at present, but would come by-and-by. ' We cannot help it, we must toil along with the general " Balaklava " round us, the Supreme Charlatan on the top of it ; and Roebuck's Committee publishing daily reports by way of remedy. God is great.' Balaklava battle was then recent enough to be a by-word for a muddle.

In returning to Helps on 2.6.55 some of the history Helps

---

[1] *Correspondence of Sir Arthur Helps* (1917), pp. 171–3, 178–9, 191, 241, 267–8.

had sent for criticism, Carlyle said it was an ' easily re-membered ' book, and praised the author's ' rare determina-tion everywhere to spare no cost in getting to the actual truth.'

It was this summer that Carlyle attended one or more of the performances of ' the Guild farce of *Mr. Nightingale's Diary,'* at the ' smallest theatre in the world,' namely, the Tavistock House Theatre which Charles Dickens now ' threw open to many friends,' its ' lessee and manager, Mr. Crummles ' being Dickens himself. ' The success was wonderful,' says Forster,[2] ' and in the three delighted audiences were not a few of the notabilities of London. Mr. Carlyle compared Dickens's wild picturesqueness as the old lighthouse keeper to the famous figure in Nicholas Poussin's bacchanalian dance in the National Gallery ; and at one of the joyous suppers that followed on each night of the play, Lord Campbell told the company that he had much rather have written *Pickwick* than be ' what he was then himself,—' Chief Justice of England and a Peer of Parliament.'

Which shows what a boy *John* Campbell was in brain, tho now far over 70,—supposing still in his simplicity that being a Chief Justice or a Peer made a man great ! He was fated to be a Lord Chancellor himself yet, and is surely the most remarkable of all, were it only because he became Biographer-in-Chief to all the Chief Justices and Lord Chancellors of England. He was a *faithful* flunkey too, poor fellow, whatever the critics might say, *sincere* in soul. How could he make Chief Justices and Lord Chancellors interesting *without* inventing something ? He made the best of his bad briefs.

---

[2] *Charles Dickens*, by John Forster, III, pp. 50–1. Compare *Edmund Yates : His Recollections and Experiences*, I, pp. 279–80.

XVI

THE TWO MISSES LOWE
(1855)

IN Dr. Johnson's will he had bequeathed £100 of Stock in the Three per Cents to each of his godchildren, the son and daughter of Mauritius Lowe, a painter. Mauritius Lowe died ten years after Johnson, and by 1855 his son was also dead, but the goddaughter was in her 78th year and living at Deptford, with her younger sister, aged 72. They had lived there for many years ' in rigorous tho not undignified poverty,' but now some unforeseen occurrences threatened to reduce them to absolute indigence.[1]   So in May this year a Memorial was presented to the Prime Minister, Lord Palmerston, soliciting ' from the Government some small public subvention, to screen their last years from the worst misery.'   This was asked for the sake of Dr. Johnson, and his English Dictionary.

' Samuel Johnson himself is far beyond the reach of our gratitude. He left no child or representative of any kind to claim pensions or distinctions from us ; and here, by accident, thrown upon the waste seabeach, is something venerably human with Johnson's mark still legible upon it ; Johnson, as it were, mutely bequeathing it to us. . . .'

The memorial was signed by these nineteen.—

> Henry Hallam, Wilton Crescent.
> James Stephen, Trinity Hall, Cambridge.
> S. Oxon, Cuddesdon Palace (Samuel, Bishop
>   Wilberforce).
> Thomas Carlyle, 5, Cheyne Row, Chelsea.
> Alexander Dyce, 9, Gray's Inn Square.
> B. W. Procter, 32, Weymouth Street, Portland
>   Place.

[1] Letter to the *Times*, printed 1.11.55 ; and Appendix IX, Napier's edition of Boswell's *Dr. Johnson*, IV, pp. 385–93.

C. L. Eastlake, 7, Fitzroy Square.
John Forster, 58, Lincoln's Inn Fields.
T. B. Macaulay, Albany.
W. M. Thackeray, 36, Onslow Square.
Alfred Tennyson, Freshwater, Isle of Wight.
A. W. Fonblanque, Board of Trade.
Charles Dickens, Tavistock House.
E. Bulwer Lytton, 1, Park Lane.
G. R. Gleig, Warwick Square.
Richard Owen, Royal College of Surgeons.
Rod. E. Murchison, Belgrave Square.
B. Disraeli, Grosvenor Gate.
H. H. Milman, Deanery, St. Paul's.

On 30.6.55 Carlyle was writing to Lady Ashburton in Paris, remonstrating against her staying there so long.— Dear Lady, Have you no thought of coming home, then ? You are much wanted here. . . . Is it not a shame to think of the Grange and its green Woods, in these parching brick wildernesses ; or of poor Addiscombe ?

' The Johnson's God-daughter affair has not gone a good road, chiefly perhaps for want of you on the scene. A sublime little Memorial was drawn up (and) presented to Palmerston by Ld. Granville, then urged upon him by Lord Stanley : Palmerston, in about a month, gave £100 " Donation," and there rested. . . . Dickens is certain " Miss Coutts will give the annual £20 still wanted " ; and I too know a Better who was equally munificent at an earlier stage,—to whom I will still apply in extremity. But I wish you had been here ; I wish you were here.'

At last on 1.11.55 a remarkable letter appeared in the *Times*, signed by Thomas Carlyle, Charles Dickens, and John Forster. It told the whole story and appealed for subscriptions, which soon came in, and enough was raised to buy an annuity of £38 on the joint lives of the two sisters ; and someone, John Ruskin apparently, added £5 a year more to that. The elder sister lived to 1860, the younger to 1866,— both well above fourscore.

M

XVII

GAVAN DUFFY AND THACKERAY, &c.
(1855)

CHARLES GAVAN DUFFY was now in London
attending the House of Commons as a member. D
Cullen, the Roman Catholic Archbishop of Dublin, abhorre
him as " an Irish Mazzini," and was busily contrivin
the biggest stroke his Church had yet given Ireland, b
paralysing the Irish members and helping the Governmen
to buy them off.[1] While this was happening, Gavan Duff
tells us how he was employed.—

' The business in which I was determined, if possible, t
succeed swallowed up my whole life. I breakfasted on Blu
Books and lunched on Irish correspondence, and I neve
had leisure to go to a theatre or exhibition, and if I dine
out once or twice a week it was apt to be with men immerse
in the same pursuit, where nothing had changed but th
venue. When a bore of vigorous lungs was on his legs,
sometimes escaped to Westminster Abbey for an hour, o
if a debate arose in which I took no interest I made for th
National Gallery, but these were rare chances. One pleasur
only I allowed nothing to interfere with. I spent a coupl
of hours every Sunday with Thomas Carlyle in Hyde Parl
or Battersea Park, with an occasional détour to Joh
Forster's at Palace Gate.'

Unfortunately he has to report[2] that he ' had no leisur
for notes,' but happily he found ' one pleasant day full
recorded in my diary.'—

' July 28, (1855). " Il Vero Tommaso ",' or True Thoma.
as Duffy and his friends named Carlyle among themselve
' brought me to-day to see Thackeray. He is a large, robus

---

[1] *My Life in Two Hemispheres*, by Sir Charles Gavan Duffy, I
pp. 83, 95, &c.
[2] *Conversations with Carlyle*, by Sir Charles Gavan Duffy, pp. 192–20

fresh-looking man, with hair turning grey. The expression of his face disappointed me ; the damaged nose and bad teeth mar its otherwise benign effect, and were imperfectly relieved by a smile which was warm but hardly genial. He is near-sighted, and said, " I must put on my glasses to have a good look at you." ' In telling Gavan Duffy how he had liked his friends in America, Thackeray mentioned John Dillon as ' a modest fellow, and Meagher pleased him by laughing at the popular ovations offered to him. They both said whatever they thought, frankly ; rather a surprise to him, as in Ireland he had only met three men who spoke the truth ; but then, he added, smiling, he had not made the acquaintance of the Young Irelanders.'

Duffy : " May one inquire the names of these three exceptional Irishmen ? " " That would not be fair," replied Thackeray, " to the remainder of my acquaintances ; but I do not mind saying that Deasy was one of them,"— Richard Deasy, then an Irish member, afterwards Attorney-General, and finally Baron of the Exchequer in Ireland.

Talking of the lectures on ' The Four Georges ' which he was then preparing, Thackeray remarked,—" I sometimes ponder the question whether every soul of these people I have to speak of was not damned in the end. The Marquis of Hertford receiving London Society in an attitude seen elsewhere only in hospitals, surrounded by smiling crowds, who ate his dinners and congratulated him on his good looks, is a story from which I shrink,—it could be told indeed nakedly only by Swift." This would be the Hertford who was nephew to Sir Robert Walpole and the original of Thackeray's Marquis of Steyne.

Then Duffy enquired about an agitation in which Thackeray had recently taken part, and was told :—" They have ruined an excellent cause among them. Lindsay had certainly made some remarkable statements, but they did not bear investigation. Sir Charles Wood made pie of them. Layard was a good, simple soul, altogether unfit for the task he took in hand. He set himself to overthrow the aristocratic scheme of patronage, and quite recently complained to me that the aristocracy had ceased to ask him to dinner ! The constitutional system is getting frightfully damaged in England, and we cannot count on a long life for it in its present relations."

Duffy :—" How are we to get on in Ireland, where we have only the seamy side of the Constitution ? "

Thackeray :—" I have never doubted your right to rebel against it, if you only make sure of success ; but in the name of social tranquillity and common sense I deny the right of unsuccessful rebellion."

Duffy :—" It is no more possible to make sure before-hand that you are going to win in an insurrection than in a game of roulette. You have to take your chance in both cases. So far as my reading carries me, I find that a success-ful rebellion is often preceded by an unsuccessful one, which had the same identical provocation and justification as its more fortunate successor." Then Duffy went on to relate the horrors of the Irish famine, ' the exportation of the natural food of the people to pay inordinate rents, the hopeless feebleness and fatuity of Lord John Russell's government,' and the multitudinous deaths from starvation resulting from it, and he demanded of Thackeray,—" Tell me, if you were an Irishman, what would you have done under the circumstances ? " ' He paused a moment, and replied : " I would perhaps have done as you did." '

' Then they all three walked out together, going in the direction of Hyde Park, and discussed the impudent words ' of Prince Albert,—" Constitutional Government is on its trial,"—as if the domination of mankind by the German Royal Caste were a law of Nature ! " John Lemoine told me," said Thackeray, " he was reprimanded for reflecting on it in the *Journal des Débats*, and that he believed the inspiration came from Windsor."

An Italian boy passed them carrying busts on a tray on his head. Napoleon the Little was among them, and Thackeray took off his hat and saluted that one, ' half, but only half, mockingly, and murmured something about a man who understood his business and mastered the art of government.' Whereupon Duffy cried :—" Carlyle's theory of governing by the best man would be very satisfactory, if we could always contrive to catch the best man, but I object under any pretence to be governed by the worst, however carefully he has studied the art."

Their talk then turned on books, and Duffy said,—" I have noted with wonder the fitness of the Irish names of men and places in *Barry Lyndon*, that being the point where a stranger usually blunders or breaks down." And Thack-eray in taking leave, as he then did, modestly said to explain his accuracy that he ' had lived a good deal among Irish people in London and elsewhere.'

Duffy observed how ' graciously Carlyle had refrained from taking any part in the conversation, which struck me as a fine piece of courtesy.' But as they two walked on together towards Chelsea, Carlyle said :—" All this talk about administrative reforms is very idle and worthless. The people of England live by steadfast industry, and take no heed at all of patronage and promotion. The public service in England is notoriously the honestest in Europe, the least liable to be diverted from its duty by any temptation, and that was nearly all one wanted to know about it. If there was any possibility of getting honest work done just now, there was much need of quite other work than those people had in hand. Think of the inorganic mass of men in the disjointed districts called London, with a population equal to that of half-a-dozen Greek States of old, bestridden by Aldermen and Vestrymen, with all their haranguing and debating apparatus, whom we are ordered to obey, if it were possible, as the guardians of our interests, but who cannot supply us from year's end to year's end with a wholesome glass of clean water."

Duffy replied :—" It may be of slight importance to prosperous people how the service is filled, but it is not a matter of indifference to the considerable class who find the public service their only road to employment that is not servile. It seems to me a serious and dangerous injustice in the English system that all the great prizes of public life are reserved for the aristocracy, and all the petty prizes for their nominees."

" This assumption," answered Carlyle, " does not represent the actual fact as one finds it in operation. The higher classes, having more leisure and easier access to Parliament, naturally come in for more of the guerdons which are distributed in that region, but probably no one is denied the share he is fairly entitled to, especially in the highest offices."

" Edmund Burke," said Duffy, " was a conspicuous example of one who had been denied his share."

" I do not know what Edmund Burke had to complain of," replied Carlyle. " He came to London having nothing, and people there, the aristocracy chiefly, made him a leading man in the business he worked in ; he became a Privy Councillor and a Minister of the Crown, and died, leaving a good estate. This was not an inconsiderable payment for the strange industry he was engaged in. What is to be desired more ? "

" Why," said Duffy, " it is to be desired that he had been recognised for what he undoubtedly was—the brain and soul of his party. He was never admitted to the Cabinet, of which he framed the policy, and which he defended in the House of Commons with supreme ability. It seems to me a public scandal that Charles Fox was set over the head of a man who taught him his business, only because Fox was one of the aristocracy, that is to say, was the son of a disreputable and unprincipled politician, who had grown rich by nefarious jobbing, and who was made a peer only because he had become intolerable to the House of Commons."

" The Cabinet," Carlyle replied, " was in those days composed for the most part of great peers, and Burke, or any one on his behalf, might as reasonably complain that he was not made a marquis as that he was not made a member of the Cabinet. There is perpetually something above a man which he does not attain, and it is good sense of a very essential sort to be content without it. Burke's achievements, which might have been conveniently abridged, had obtained in substance the reward he sought and expected." Carlyle was likely to be familiar with what Fitzgerald used to say,—" We Irish folks can see the Irishman in Burke."[3]

Then Duffy enquired about a lively little book, written by one of the Lindsay-Layard party, in a dialect which was then called Carlylese.—" Have you read it ? " he asked. " Yes," was the reply. " I have looked into it, and noted the resemblance you speak of. It is like my style,—if I may be supposed to be a judge of the matter,—as like perhaps as the reflection of my face in a dish-cover."

Then Carlyle had a question.—" Did the address of Malvern, which I read in a letter of yours, indicate you have been at the water cure ? " " It did," said Duffy. " I read a pamphlet of Bulwer Lytton's, entitled ' *The Confessions of a Water Patient*,' describing the water cure as a magical remedy for the exhaustion of literary or political work, and I gave it a trial. The early hours, simple meals, and absolute rest, were balsamic ; but I have slight faith in the system, which is kept alive largely by fables. We were told how patients were carried into the establishment, and after a few weeks walked out, but nothing was said of cases where the patients walked in, and were carried out in an oak box. The fanaticism of some of the patients passed

[3] *More Letters of Edward Fitzgerald* (1901), p. 95.

elief. One poor fellow, who was visibly fading away, told
me that his relapses were part of the cure : the doctor
must break him down before he could build him up !
Crowds of new patients arrived every week, and nobody
asked what became of those who disappeared. My time
passed pleasantly enough, as there were intelligent people
to talk to—Indian Officers, Oxford Professors, Californian
diggers, and London men and women of letters."

Carlyle said,—" I have marvelled to note during the
summer months what a steady stream of simpletons sets
from London to Worcestershire." " Yes," said Duffy,
' simpletons tempered by sages. My bathman told me, and
everyone who would listen to him, of his attendance on Mr.
Carlyle, and of that great man's behaviour under the douche,
or wrapped in wet sheets like an Egyptian mummy swathed
in its cerements. The bathman was a living witness that a
man may still occasionally be a hero to his *valet de chambre*."

Carlyle laughed and said,—" It is very proper that I
should be found out. A number of friendly people, John
Forster principally, induced me to go to Malvern on the
evidence of Bulwer Lytton that it is a panacea for dyspepsia
and all its kin, and I fared as a man deserves to fare who
puts faith in such testimony. I am somewhat ashamed of
the adventure. Dr. Gully is not without insight, but somebody—it was probably Thackeray—said of the other practitioners, that the system had been discovered in Germany
by an inspired peasant, and is administered in England by
peasants who are not inspired."

Then Duffy praised Arthur Helps, declaring that the Elles-
mere of his dialogues was " as dramatically conceived, and
as consistently drawn, as Sir Roger de Coverley " by Addison.
What did Carlyle know about him ? " Mr. Helps," said
Carlyle, " had been over in Ireland in an official situation,
private secretary to the Lord-Lieutenant or other eminent
personage, but he left this place to retire on literature
exclusively. He had been a rich man, but latterly has lost
some of his fortune somehow, and now lives near South-
ampton and writes books. He is not at all a considerable
man, but he has some truth in him, and pretty bits of
fancy too. One of his little books reduces him to death's
door in producing it, and there is a long convalescence in
each case.

" He is writing now on the slave trade from the far-off
beginning of it. He is rather wearisome from the little bits

of theories and speculations he keeps talking and talkin
about, and he has a bad fashion, which he learned up i
London, of making a joke of everything that turns up, eve
when one can perceive he is serious and anxious at bottom
When Emerson was in England, Helps met him and m
down at Stonehenge, and brought us home with him, whic
I remember because Emerson there broached some amazin
theories about war altogether ceasing in the world ; bu
when he was being closely pressed on the method of th
prodigious change, luckily for him, luncheon was announce
and he would not say another word about it."—It was th
most interesting of all subjects to Carlyle.

By July, 1855, Gavan Duffy was convinced that no mor
good could be done for his country in the present Parli
ment, because with the help of Dr. Cullen, the Italianise
archbishop, and his assistants, the English politicians ha
once more prevailed,—by their traditional method of buyin
enough of the Irish members to enable them to continu
bleeding Ireland white. So Duffy was now preparing to d
as he had announced at his election he would do in tha
event,—resign his seat. He decided to emigrate to Australi
and said good-bye to the Carlyles about the date of thi
very talk. Maybe it was recorded so completely because i
seemed likely to be the last for a long time. He was goin
away ' for years, and it might be for ever.' One of th
things that Duffy said in these days may be an echo of thei
confidential talk,—" There is no more hope for Ireland tha
for a corpse on the dissecting table."[4] If ever he said so t
Carlyle, he would be told there was life in " ould Ireland '
yet. Assuredly he took much counsel with Carlyle, and the
continued always the best of friends.

[4] *New Ireland*, by A. M. Sullivan, p. 177.

XVIII

A VISIT TO FITZGERALD
(1855)

BY this time Edward Fitzgerald was one of Carlyle's 'oldest acquaintances' in England. He was now reminding him of an old promise to visit him in Suffolk, and offering him the choice of a farm-house called Farlingay, near Woodbridge, where Fitzgerald had such rooms that in them, he told him, " even you could sleep composedly," or Bredfield Rectory, two miles farther away, where Fitzgerald was as much at home as at Farlingay. The Rector was the Rev. George Crabbe, the son and biographer of the poet, an excellent man, devoted to tobacco and practical Christianity. He was a widower, and his eldest daughter with fair golden ringlets was the angel of the house, and ministered to her father and brothers and sisters, and to Fitzgerald too,—tho she had refused to marry him sixteen years ago. Fitzgerald was content to be a " friend for life," —which may have been hard on the girl,[1]—she should have got another chance or two. She may have *repented* the refusal.

Carlyle chose Farlingay, and Fitzgerald, " the best of landlords," met him at Ipswich Railway Station and drove him there on 8.8.55. The letters Carlyle sent his wife show that he much enjoyed the ten days he spent in Suffolk. For one thing, the sky was bright, and the ' sunny autumn days ' as beautiful as ' could be desired,' through all the time the visit lasted. During the morning hours which were more or less sacred to *Frederick*, Carlyle was reading the works of Voltaire, and sitting under an elm-tree beside the house. On the second morning, 10.8.55, ' as nice a morning as I remember to have seen,' he found ' good Fitz ' awaiting him, sitting on a huge stump of a tree root, on which grew

---

[1] *Life of Edward Fitzgerald*, by Thomas Wright, I, pp. 138–9, 146, 163, 270–5. *Letters of Edward Fitzgerald*, I, pp. 293–304.

mignonette. They went driving in the gig, and afterwards, as he reported,—' I walked lustily through pleasant lanes and quiet country roads, all of hard smooth sand. I already seem to feel twice as strong for walking : (and) step along at a great rate in spite of the windless heat.'

He was sleeping well. The quiet was perfect every night but one, when the cows serenaded the household and kept it all awake from 2 a.m. till 6. Instead of going to Scotland this summer, he wrote to one of his sisters there a description of what he saw around him.—' The country is now all golden with excellent wheat ; plenty of green lanes too, endless country roads and paths, with trees everywhere framing the gold picture in luxuriant green : a country not unlike Scotland in its fruitfullest places, except that there are never mountains in the distance, and that the streams are few, and all sedgy, silent, and we must say, rather ugly.'

He walked about a great deal and often had a bathe in salt water. Fitzgerald took him in the gig to see Aldeburgh and Orford and other places, while in the evenings, as Farmer Smith and his son Alfred sat smoking with them, Fitzgerald heard with wonder Carlyle plying them with questions about soils and crops. ' The farmer was astonished to find that he was as conversant with soils and crops as if he had been all his life tilling the land.'[2] With Fitzgerald his talk was literary enough, or turned on Naseby battle-field, in which ' good Fitz ' had a special interest ; but it is an easy guess that one of the remarks intended for them all was this,—" Burns ought to have been the King of England, and George III an exciseman."

What most of us delight to dwell upon Carlyle habitually tabooed,—oneself and one's private affairs. " Carlyle never spoke of himself in that way," remarked Fitzgerald, who could only recall in many years a single reference to himself in his talk, when ' one day he happened to mention,—" About the time when men began to talk of me." ' But that cannot be dated. A saying assigned to this visit and treasured by those who heard it is this :—" Piety does not mean that a man should make a sour face about things, and refuse to enjoy in moderation what his Maker has given."

' There were drives to Dunwich and the ruin of Framling ham Castle '[1]; but perhaps their pleasantest was on Sunday

[2] *Letters of Edward Fitzgerald*, II, p. 334.
[3] *Life of Edward Fitzgerald*, by John Glyde, pp. 225-6.

2.8.55, to Aldeburgh. They started in the morning, ' and
the pony and trap with the strange, uncouth pair—Fitzgerald in his scare-crow clothes, and Carlyle with the usual
long clay pipe in his mouth—passed the Church just as the
worshippers were leaving it after morning service. The
shocked look on the face of conventionality and "gigmanity"
was entirely to their taste,' and made them laugh.

It was ' a very pleasant drive,' Carlyle assured his wife
next day, and he did his best in writing to coax her to
come there for summer quarters. " There is no sea like the
Aldeburgh sea," Fitzgerald used to say ; and Carlyle told
his wife that it was ' a beautiful little sea town, one of the
best bathing places I have seen. Nothing can excel the
sea—a mile of fine shingly beach, with patches of smooth
sand every here and there ; clear water shelving rapidly,
deep at all hours ; beach solitary. My notion is, if you have
yet gone nowhere, you should think of Aldeburgh. I could
like very well a fortnight or so of it. Never saw a place
more promising. Adieu, dearest ! Drown Nero, and be
reasonable.

' Yours ever,

' T. C.'

On the very day he was writing this, 13.8.55, his wife
was exploring the coast near Brighton. A ' solitary beach '
had not the attraction for her that it had for him, and her
way of saying No about Aldeburgh was to take a fancy to
a vacant hut at Rottingdean near Brighton, and make
plans to rent and furnish it, so as to have a place ' all to
oneself.'

The last three days of the visit were spent at the Rectory
with Crabbe, ' a very excellent old Parson of those parts,
who took much to me,'—and then on Saturday, 18.8.55,
he came home by the Ipswich steamer, in preference to
being shut up in the railway carriage ' like a great cod-fish
in a hamper ' ; and that night Mrs. Carlyle walked round
in the evening to Cadogan Place to chat with Mrs. Brookfield
about the unreasonableness of husbands in general and her
own in particular, because he objected to the unfurnished
hut for summer quarters,—" Often as he has wished for a
little place to reach easily in the country, and tho this was
very pretty as well as very cheap."[4] On Monday morning,
20.8.55, Mrs. Carlyle made her husband come with her, and

---

[4] *Mrs. Brookfield and Her Circle*, by C. & F. Brookfield, II, p. 418.

they reached London Bridge on the way to Brighton. Bu the morning was very wet," and they went no farther.[5]

A few days later Fitzgerald and he were writing to eac other about the new pillar they projected setting up a Naseby, and drafting the inscription.[6] Carlyle sent photograph to Alfred Smith, who remarked,—" Carlyle a big man, no doubt, tho I don't know much about him So I'll put him in a frame," which he did. It was surprise to Fitzgerald to see what an impression Carlyle had made on Smith.

Another thing Fitzgerald discovered now was that Car lyle's tastes in boating were like his own. So in a few week ' good Fitz ' was making trial of Spring Rice's Governmen Cutter, touching at Boulogne and Brighton, ' delighted t sail the salt seas once more before a Breeze unpolluted b Smoke and Grease.'[6]

[5] Unpublished letter of T. C. to Joseph Neuberg.
[6] *More Letters of Edward Fitzgerald*, 1901, pp. 37–40.

XIX

AT ADDISCOMBE WITH VOLTAIRE
(1855)

CARLYLE had more in common with Voltaire than with Goethe or any other man of letters. Frederick was as much a disciple of Voltaire as Cromwell had been of Christ. Of all the reading Carlyle did during the dozen years of drudgery which the history of Frederick took, perhaps the most enjoyable was the writings of Voltaire,—whose figure seems occasionally to predominate in the history, like Falstaff in some of Shakespeare's plays.

Carlyle and Neuberg were giving each other medical advice this fall. Whether Neuberg was any the better of the blue pill Carlyle advised, their letters do not show. Assuredly Carlyle took his advice and the loan of his idle horse with great benefit. He rode far and wide about the suburbs of London. On Sunday, 26.8.55, he rode to Addiscombe, and while the horse was being refreshed there, he spent ' a perfectly silent four hours among the silent leafy shades, Beuchot Voltaire volumes (the only useful edition of Voltaire) and other beautiful conveniences of that place.'

He slept so much better than usual that night that his wife decided to accept the kind suggestion of the Ashburtons and use their vacant house there. So the next Thursday while he ' trotted out in the breezy twilight,' his wife went out by train and made the commissariat arrangements needful in an empty house, and left him to stay there for some weeks. She returned from time to time as might be needful, but for her own part, preferred to stay at home.

' In general,' he wrote to Neuberg, ' I am as lonely as La Trappe, or even more so, for there is but *one* La Trappist here, and the very eyes are kept incommunicative ; on the other hand, I have plenty of Voltaire literature . . . pleasant, most clear, ingenious and by no means unveracious reading. All my leisure is taken up with Voltaire, and nearly every day I have one of the finest rides, through these green lanes,

over these green commons, still as beautiful as in Summe
green as an emerald. The old country roads, old as Hengi
many of them, are very pretty.'

To his delight he discovered in the library of the hous
an edition of Voltaire later and better than even Beuchot'
—Renouard's, in above sixty volumes. But he never any
where discovered a good biography of Voltaire. ' Frenc
editors,' he declared, ' tho they *have* Indexes always (
some sort, are still more intolerable than Prussian, for the
have not the least conscience about being accurate,—sorro
on them ! There is no darker mass anywhere, with a varnis
of regularity on the surface of it, than these Lives, Letter
&c., &c., of Voltaire. What will become of me with th
double chaos, of Fritz and him ? They are prettyish me
both, if I could get them extricated ; but alas, alas ! '

Writing to Fitzgerald on Saturday, 15.9.55,[1] he gave h
news and told of his reading. ' I find Voltaire a " gentl
man," living in a world partly furnished with such ; an
that there are now no " gentlemen " (not quite none). . .
' Today I ride back to Chelsea, but mean to return hith
on Monday. There is a great circle of yellow light all th
way from Shooter's Hill to Primrose Hill, spread round m
horizon every night, I see it while smoking my pipe befo
bed (so bright, last night, it cast a visible shadow of n
against the white window shutters) ; and this is all I hav
to do with London and its gases for a fortnight or mor
My wife writes to me, there was an awful jangle of bel
last day she went home from this ; a Quaker asked in th
railway, of some porter, " Can thou tell me what those bel
mean ? "—" Well I suppose something is up. They sa
Sebastopol is took, and the Rushans run away." '

His wife was making him return for a week-end becaus
Clough and his wife and Browning and Neuberg were dinin
at Cheyne Row on the Sunday. Riding back to Addiscoml
' in the damp dusk of Monday,' 17.9.55, to be again ' a
solitary as St. Antony,' he wrote to Neuberg :—' A grea
relief to get rid of the babblement of the world altogethe
for a few hours ; and let the sombrest voices of Fact spea
to us a little, which at least do mean what they say !—Th
Life of Frederick, I must own, takes a very formidab
aspect in some of these abstruse " Dialogues with th
Silences " ; a work as good as " impossible," &c. &c.,—tha

[1] *Letters of Edward Fitzgerald*, I pp. 302–3.

is still my private opinion about it ;—nevertheless, I do not mean to give in ; nor do I doubt that some good (whether in that form or another) will come to me from whatever *honest* labour I have put into that affair. *Vorwärts* (Forward), therefore. . . . " Sebastopol " does not concern me much : if " taken," what good could be in it, except that people would give up speaking of it ? '

He came home next day, Sunday, 23.9.55, the last thing he did at Addiscombe being to write this letter to its owner, his absent hostess.—

' ADDISCOMBE FARM,

' 23 *Septr.*, 1855.

' DEAR LADY,

' The Sun has gone across the Line, under happy enough auspices ; and now the time has come when I too must take my road into other latitudes of a dimmer description. The last act I do in your Mansion here is to take farewell of you : it seems as if I were parting far away and for a long time,—tho the historical fact I believe is, I am coming 10 miles nearer you, and we may hope, within another three weeks, to see the Lady of this little Surrey *Monbijou* in person. . . . So it is in fact ; but a certain cloud of sadness hangs over this bright region, in spite of the lively Sunshine, as I take leave of it ; and the *end*, like the end of all things, makes the heart *wae :* Do you know that Scotch word ? There is none in English that so expresses the thing. *Ay de mi, Ay de mi !*

' I have had 24 of the strangest beneficent Days, here in your domain, shut out from all the World ; eight-and-forty times (only think of that) I must have made tea for myself in your little fairy teapot (the red tile-china saucy little teapot),—and I often thought to myself there was perhaps nobody in Surrey who got as *good ;* being done by an artist in tea, and all under his own hand ! With the window-screens half down, warm Sun and fresh air streaming in, and the Day all ahead of one and belonging to one's-self, those were singular mornings, and a curious manna all that, falling out of the sky upon a poor pilgrim in this modern World. I have had such rides too, most memorable and beneficial ; yesterday, my last, was one of my longest and finest ; over the heights behind Addington ; far round to Northeastward, by I know not what solitary footpaths, hills, lanes and dells ; ending on Hayes Common, as has often been the case. My thoughts have often been very sombre,—as what solitary creature's are not, with so many years behind him, especially if he have *liver* too, and a history of Fritz which no Man *can* write, even if Vulture Panizzi were to offer pens from his own ugly person. Alas, alas! But I do believe in the absolute necessity of encountering such moods, were they even much painfuller than they are : and, on the whole, it is evident to me, I am in fact rather *better*, both in body and mind for my Quasi-Moslem *Ramadhan* out here ; and shall hope to do a little better amid my insoluble imbroglios than has lately been the doom of me, when I get back. Take thanks therefore, O Royal Lady ; and reckon, if you like, that this is one of the good things you have done with your bounties in the year now running downwards : —truly it is but a poor item, you will say ; yes, but I answer, it is really one. That is to say, Provided I am not entirely a Son of Chaos and Satanas ; for in that sad case, it will be a *maleficence*, and reckoned against you as such, you unfortunate mistaken Woman! " But we hope better things, tho we thus speak,"—as the Scotch Preachers say. . . .

'Jane came out to me on Thursday evg. ; staid two days this time, settling my affairs for me : Friday we went to the Crystal Palace in compliment to her, *walking* to and from ;—saw no Wagner there, tho curious-looking beings, bearded Germans &c., were in great plenty. This is the second time I have been there besides the visit with Poodle and Lord An. : my experience still is, that except the copies of Sculptures there is nothing in the place that can in reality *interest* anything but children. It is the Apotheosis of Mercantile Cockneyism, however, and worth seeing as the *Ne-plus-ultra* of what that can amount to. " A glass Box of never-imagined size," whereby at length the Millennium *is* realized (to Mankind of the Cockney species) —Shares steadily going down.

' Assiduous Mortals have been clipping, mowing, trimming all round here,—yesterday a Man shaved the beard (as it were) of all the trellises, pillars &c. about these windows which has had a good effect. Everything is still green as emeralds, the Sun burningly bright by day, but frosts at night, and heavy mist till 9 a.m. ;—such of the trees as have any fruit to show for themselves are now showing it sprinklings of yellow leaves are traceable in unfavourable localities ; changed fractions of tint here and there indicate that in that province also old age is coming. All says

' Oh my Lady, come and see us then ; before we die ! "
When *are* you coming ? Surely soon now.

' Yours   ' T. C.'

see on p152

Soon after Carlyle came home, there was what his wife
called ' a (strictly) family dinner ' at his house,[1] reported
to us by a ' tall grave stranger,' Col. Davidson, who had
been a playmate of Mrs. Carlyle when both were young
at Haddington. The hour was six o'clock.—

' The other guests were the Poet-Laureate, Mr. Carlyle's
brother and a young man. Mr. Tennyson came in a
morning suit, a tall, strongly-built man, with a handsome
clear-cut face, close-shaved. During dinner, speaking of
some distinguished man, Carlyle said,—" He had a face
like yours, Tennyson." There was a mask of Dante at
that moment on the table.

' They spoke about the difficulty of making speeches.
Tennyson said if allowed to sit he might manage it, but
it was severe upon the nerves to stand up when every one
else was sitting. The question was discussed as to whether
they would accept titles if offered. Tennyson was disposed
to decline such honours for himself, and said no title
could excel the simple name of " Thomas Carlyle." After
dinner long clay pipes were laid on the table and smoking
commenced.' And then ' we went upstairs.

' I noticed that when Carlyle was at a loss for a poetical
quotation, Tennyson promptly supplied it. Referring to
the Life of Frederick, Tennyson said,—" At this crisis,
Peter the Great would have been a better subject." Carlyle
agreed, and added, " And it would have been *better for me.*"

' Alluding to the state of Europe, the war in the Crimea
being at its height, Tennyson remarked,—" The world is
looking for the coming man." I said,—" The coming Man
has already come, and they crucified Him." Carlyle said
emphatically,—" I quite agree with you."

' Speaking of modes of government, Carlyle said,—" If I
had to govern a country, I would take the Bible as my
rule, and if it involved the occasional cutting off of a head,
I should not mind."

' He told Mr. Tennyson about my plan for night firing,'
—which was what had brought the Colonel to London,—
and his knowledge of mathematics enabled him to
describe it correctly.'

---

[1] *Memories of a Long Life*, by Col. Davidson, C.B., pp. 307-9.

N

XX

AT WORK AT HOME ON HISTORY
(1855)

CARLYLE would be at his desk as usual at Cheyne Row on Monday morning, 24.9.55. Perhaps his habits of work should be explained. No man of business making money in the city was more methodical. When he noted in his diary or said that he was doing nothing, he often merely meant that he was not successful in doing what he could leave standing, or that he could not satisfy his literary or artistic conscience, so to speak. His habits at home varied little. What has been told of his *Frederick* years was true of most of his life.

He rose early, and began the day with a sponge bath in his bedroom. Then he usually went out for a walk and was home in time for eight o'clock breakfast. He began work as soon as his after-breakfast smoke was finished, and was not interrupted. He did not smoke at work ; but occasionally paused in the middle of his work and took a few spoonfuls of strong beef-soup or milk pudding, and that would be followed by a whiff of tobacco. The custom was for the maid to put the soup or pudding within his reach without a word to him, and leave it to be taken when he felt inclined.

After 2 o'clock came exercise out of doors and dinner about 5 or 6, followed by a nap and tea, and social intercourse or reading for pleasure, which sometimes made him sit up late. It was in these afternoon or evening hours of relaxation that he did such duties as attending a Committee meeting of the London Library, or assisting the Librarian in getting German books, as he and Neuberg were doing this October. But that sort of thing was never allowed to interfere with the regular day's work.

One of the first things he read for pleasure after returning from Addiscombe was Lewes's *Life of Goethe*. "Decidedly good," he called it, and the sagacious Charlotte

Williams Wynn, who was one of the first to whom he lent it, agreed with him.[1] That was in October. In the same month Charles Gavan Duffy came to London again and called and took leave of the Carlyles before departing for Australia.[2]

The *Frederick* was now making steady progress. On 10.10.55 Carlyle was writing to his faithful Neuberg :— ' I know not whether you have yet made any way into that last mass of Fk. Papers. I wish you would now cut a passage thro them, as soon as you handily can,—above all things, annihilate about ¾ of them, and let me have the remaining ¼. I long infinitely to settle some resolution as to those winged masses ; and the first step is to *see* what I have. Often it comes into my head that *fire* (to the whole) w'd be the readiest way. Which probably *is* their just fate ; and may overtake them yet. . . . I can remember little except Gundling, the Tobacco Parliament, and Kaiser Karl VI and the Pragmatic Sanction. I think there was a thought in me as to that latter business ; but it is nowhere expressed well, and is 4 or 5 times expressed ill : to annihilate all of these except the one best, and extricate that into legibility, would be a great service done.'

The first two volumes to which he was now giving finishing touches extended to the end of Book X ; and readers not yet familiar with his *Frederick*, a masterpiece of history, should look at Chapter VII of Book V, ' Tobacco-Parliament.' It is as delightful as the best chapter in *Don Quixote*, and yet as true as writing can be, surpassing blue books or even histories as diamonds surpass common coal.

A passage assigned to Smelfungus, which meant Carlyle of course, contains one of the few expressions of opinion he allowed himself :—' Tobacco-smoke is the one element in which, by our European manners, men can sit silent together without embarrassment, and where no man is bound to speak one word more than he has actually and veritably got to say.' As it is easier to be silent than to speak when smoking, he seriously suggests the use of it in ' Constitutional Parliaments. The results might evidently be incalculable. The essence of what little intellect and insight there is in that room we shall or can get nothing more out of any Parliament ; and sedative, gently-soothing,

---

[1] *Memorials of Charlotte Williams Wynn*, by her Sister, pp. 223–5.
[2] *My Life in Two Hemispheres*, by Sir Charles Gavan Duffy, II, p. 124.

gently clarifying tobacco-smoke (if the room were well
ventilated, open atop, and the air kept good), with the
obligation to a minimum of speech, surely gives human
intellect and insight the best chance they can have. Best
chance, instead of the worst chance as at present : ah me,
ah me, who will reduce fools to silence again in any measure ?
Who will deliver men from the hideous nightmare of
Stump-Oratory, under which the grandest Nations are
choking to a nameless death, bleeding (too truly) from
mouth and nose and ears, in our sad days ? '

With charming candour, however, considering how
much he loved tobacco, Carlyle admits it had done the
Germans more harm than good, its ' influences ' being
' generally bad ; pacificatory but bad, engaging you in
idle cloudy dreams ;—still worse, promoting composure
among the palpably chaotic and discomposed ; soothing
all things into lazy peace ; that all things may be left to
themselves very much, and to the laws of gravity and
decomposition. Whereby German affairs are come to be
greatly overgrown with funguses in our Time ; and give
symptoms of dry and of wet rot, wherever handled.' Which
shows that the events of 1914 to 1919 would not have
surprised Carlyle. Here is another paragraph that sends
X-rays into the very inside of English history.

' This Smoking Parliament or *Tabaks-Collegium* of his
Prussian Majesty '—Frederick William, the father of
Frederick the Great—' was a thing much talked of in the
world ; but till Seckendorf and Grumkow started their
grand operations there, its proceedings are not on record ;
nor indeed till then had its political or parliamentary
function become so decidedly evident. It was originally a
simple Smoking-Club ; got together on hest of Nature,
without ulterior intentions :—thus English *Parliamenta*
themselves are understood to have been, in the old Norman
time, mere royal Christmas-Festivities, with natural colloquy
or *parley*ing between King and Nobles ensuing thereupon,
and what wisest consultation concerning the arduous things
of the realm the circumstances gave rise to. Such parleyings
or consultations,—always two in number in regard to
every matter, it would seem, or even three ; one sober, one
drunk, and one just after being drunk,—proving of extreme
service in practice, grew to be Parliament, with its three
readings, and what not.'

XXI

PRAGMATIC SANCTION AND DOUBLE MARRIAGE
(1855)

HERE is a more spacious extract from the second
chapter of Book V to reveal what the Pragmatic
Sanction was, which stalks like a nightmare through our
old books, and maybe more than anything else in politics
led to the wars that desolated Europe in the eighteenth
century.—

' *Imperial Majesty's Pragmatic Sanction.*

' Kaiser Karl meanwhile was rather short of heirs ;
which formed another of his real troubles, and involved
him in much Shadow-hunting. His wife . . . did at
length bring him children, brought him a boy even ; but
the boy died within the year ; and, on the whole, there
remained nothing but two Daughters ; Maria Theresa the
elder of them, born 1717,—the prettiest little maiden in
the world ;—no son to inherit Kaiser Karl. Under which
circumstances Kaiser Karl produced now, in the year
1724, a document which he had executed privately as
long ago as 1713, . . . and solemnly publishes it to the
world, as a thing all men are to take notice of. All men
had notice enough of this Imperial bit of Sheepskin, before
they got done with it, five-and-twenty years hence. A
very famous Pragmatic Sanction ; now published for the
world's comfort !

' By which Document, Kaiser Karl had formally settled,
and fixed according to the power he has, in the shape of
what they call a Pragmatic Sanction, or unalterable
Ordinance in his Imperial House, " That, failing Heirs-
male, his Daughters, his Eldest Daughter, should succeed
him ; failing Daughters, his nieces ; and in short, that
Heirs-female ranking from their kinship to Kaiser Karl,
and not to any prior Kaiser, should be as good as Heirs-
male of Karl's body would have been." A Pragmatic

181

Sanction is the high name he gives this document, or the Act it represents ; " Pragmatic Sanction " being . . . the received title for Ordinances of a very irrevocable nature, which a sovereign makes, in affairs that belong wholly to himself. . . .

' This Pragmatic Sanction of Kaiser Karl's . . . was transmitted ' in 1724 ' to all Courts and Sovereignities, as an unalterable law of Things Imperial. Thereby the good man hopes his beautiful little Theresa, now seven years old, may succeed him, all as a son would have done, in the Austrian States and Dignities ; and incalculable damages, wars, and chances of war, be prevented, for his House and for all the world.

' The world, incredulous of to-morrow, in its lazy way, was not sufficiently attentive to this new law of things. Some who were personally interested, as the Saxon Sovereignity, and the Bavarian, denied that it was just : reminded Kaiser Karl that he was not the Noah or Adam of Kaisers ; and that the case of Heirs-female was not quite a new idea on sheepskin. No ; there are older Pragmatic Sanctions and settlements, by Prior Kaisers of blessed memory ; under which, if Daughters are to come in, we, descended from Imperial Daughters of older standing shall have a word to say !—To this Kaiser Karl answers steadily, with endless argument, That every Kaiser is a Patriarch, and First Man, in such matters ; and that so it has been pragmatically sanctioned by him, and that so it shall and must irrevocably be. . . . To procure adherences and assurances to this dear Pragmatic Sanction was . . . the one grand business of his life henceforth. With which he kept all Europe in perpetual travail and diplomacy ; raying-out ambassadors, and less ostensible agents, with bribes, and with entreaties and proposals, into every high Sovereign Court and every low ; negotiating unweariedly by all methods, with all men. For it was his evening-song and his morning-prayer ; the grand meaning of Life to him, till Life ended. You would have said, the first question he asks of every creature is, " Will you covenant for my Pragmatic Sanction with me ? O, agree to it ; accept that new Law of Nature : when the morrow comes, it will be salutary for you ! " . . .

' Bright little Prince Eugene, who dictated square miles of Letters and Diplomacies on the subject (Letters of a steady depth of dulness, which at last grows almost sublime),

was wont to tell his Majesty: " Treating, your Majesty ?
A well-trained Army and a full Treasury ; that is the only
Treaty that will make this Pragmatic Sanction valid ! "
But his Majesty never would believe. So the bright old
Eugene dictated,—or, we hope and guess, he only gave
his clerks some key-word, and signed his name (in three
languages, " Eugenio von Savoye ") to these square miles
of dull epistolary matter,—probably taking Spanish snuff
when he had done. For he wears it in both waistcoat-
pockets ;—has (as his Portraits still tell us) given up
breathing by the nose. The bright little soul, with a flash
in him as of Heaven's own lightning ; but now growing
very old and snuffy. . . .

'It was this of the Pragmatic Sanction most of all,
that thwarted our Prussian Double-Marriage, which lay
so far away from it. This it was that pretty nearly broke
the hearts of Friedrich, Wilhelmina, and their Mother
and Father. For there was never such negotiating ; not
for admittance to the Kingdom of Heaven, in the pious
times. And the open goings-forth of it were into all places.
Above ground and below, no Sovereign mortal could say he
was safe from it, let him agree or not. Friedrich Wilhelm
had cheerfully, and with all his heart, agreed to the Pragmatic
Sanction ; this above ground, in sight of the sun ; and
rashly fancied he had then done with it. Till, to his horror,
he found the Imperial moles, by way of keeping assurance
doubly sure, had been under the foundations of his very
house for long years past, and had all but brought it down
upon him in the most hideous manner ! '

The ' Double Marriage ' was the project started by the
Queen of Prussia when her children were yet young. It
was that her eldest son, by-and-by Frederick the Great,
and her eldest daughter, Wilhelmina, were both to marry
their first cousins, the daughter Amelia and the eldest son
of her brother, George II. This eldest son was the Prince
Fred who died in 1751, before his father, George II, and who
lives in English history partly because of his quarrels with
his father, but mainly because of the memorial poem
embalmed in Carlyle's history, Book XVI, Chapter VIII.—

' And so poor Fred is ended ;—and sulky people ask in
their cruel way, " Why Not ? " A poor dissolute flabby
fellow-creature ; with a sad destiny, and a sadly conspicuous too. Could write Madrigals ; be set to make
Opposition cabals. Read this sudden Epitaph in doggerel ;

an uncommonly successful Piece of its kind ; which is now
his main monument with posterity. The " Brother " (here
of Culloden), and the " Sister " (Amelia, our Friedrich'
first love, now growing gossipy and spiteful, poor Princess)
are old friends :

> " Here lies Prince Fred,
> Who was alive and is dead :
> Had it been his Father,
> I had much rather ;
> Had it been his Brother,
> Sooner than any other ;
> Had it been his Sister,
> There's no one would have missed her;
> Had it been his whole generation,
> Best of all for the Nation :
> But since it's only Fred,
> There's no more to be said." '

The Double Marriage was prevented by the contrivances
of the Kaiser Karl VI, who imagined it might endanger
his own dear Pragmatic Sanction. Carlyle's way of holding
up the mirror to Nature as revealed in the history of
Europe then is full of the humour and the tragedy of real
life. It reads like the Notes of the Recording Angel. The
history as he tells it must have been as enjoyable to write
as it is to read ; but of course he would not be thinking
of that.

He made such rapid progress that by 29.11.55 he was
' busy ending the first Silesian War in the rough,' Book
XIII ; and as that was to be in the third volume, he was
hoping that the printing of the first two would begin before
long, and the whole work be finished in two more. One of
his most characteristic expressions is in Book XII, Chapter
IX, where he concludes some speculations on the might-
have-beens of history and the Pragmatic Sanction Wars
by saying,—" Heaven makes use of Shadow-hunting
Kaisers too : and its ways in this mad world are through
the great Deep." His faith in the justice of Heaven was
never shaken. He never forgot as we are prone to do the
infinite background of the unknown.

XXII

DIARY OF MRS. CARLYLE
(1855)

MRS. CARLYLE had now taken to writing a kind of diary in a little note-book which her husband never saw or suspected till long after her death. ' It bears a label in his hand,' his nephew says,[1] ' on the outer cover, "Diary of Hers, 21 October, 1855—14 April, 1856"; but he has not annotated it or prepared it in any way for publication; and the natural inference is that he did not wish it to be published.' Which did not hinder Mr. Froude from filling many pages of the ' Letters and Memorials' with it and some foolish notes of his own. Poor Froude! Let us read some of it now since it is printed, and forgive Froude if we can. It is like peeping into a lady's room when she is tittivating her face, or hiding oneself in a corner to overhear her private prayers.—

' October 21, 1855.—I remember Charles Buller saying of the Duchess de Praslin's murder, "What could a poor fellow do with a wife who kept a journal but murder her?" There was a certain truth hidden in this light remark. Your journal all about feelings aggravates whatever is factitious and morbid in you; that I have made experience of. And now the only sort of journal I would keep should have to do with what Mr. Carlyle calls "the fact of things." It is very bleak and barren, this fact of things, as I now see it—very; and what good is to result from writing of it in a paper book is more than I can tell. But I have taken a notion to, and perhaps I shall blacken more paper this time, when I begin promiscuously without any moral end

---

[1] *New Letters and Memorials of J. W. Carlyle*, edited by A. Carlyle, II, pp. 84-8.

in view ; but just as the Scotch professor drank whisky because I like it, and because it's cheap.

'October 22.—I was cut short in my introduction las night by Mr. C.'s return from Bath House. That eterna Bath House. I wonder how many thousand miles Mr. C has walked between there and here, putting it all together setting up always another milestone and another betwix himself and me. Oh, good gracious ! when I first notice that heavy yellow house without knowing, or caring t know, who it belonged to, how far was I from dreamin, that through years and years I should carry every stone's weight of it on my heart. About feelings already Well, I will not proceed, tho . . . as George Sand ha shrewdly remarked, " *rien ne soulage comme la rhétorique*," nothing is so comforting as a flow of words.

Here may be intercalated an undated letter to he friend Mrs. Russell of Thornhill, which the editor date this autumn.[1]—It shows the real relations of Mrs. Carlyl and the first Lady Ashburton, and how Mrs. Carlyle spen her time. Her peevishness about Bath House seems lik the sick whim of a nervous invalid.—

' MY DEAR MRS. RUSSELL,

' I was unusually busy, or perhaps I should say unusually *idle* all last week,—a succession of *callers* ever day, and Plays and Parties in the evenings. . . . Las week I was at *two* Plays besides a Conjurer,—gaieties neve coming single any more than misfortunes !

' Did I ever tell you that I have a beautiful view o Drumlanrig ' Castle near Thornhill, ' hanging in this room It was done by Lady Ashburton, who showed it to me on day, as a mere sketch, and I wouldn't give it her again I wish some one would do me a sketch of Templand. D you know any *accomplished* young lady up to such thing ?

' And now good-bye. I have a sewing-woman in th house to-day, and must seek her work. . . .

' Affectionately yours,

' JANE CARLYLE.'

Diary, ' October 31.—Rain ! rain ! rain ! " Oh, Lord this is too ridiculous," as the Annandale farmer exclaimed starting to his feet when it began pouring, in the midst o his prayer for a dry hay time. To-day's post brought th

indest of letters from Geraldine, inclosing a note from
ady de Capel Broke she is staying with, inviting me to
Oakley Hall. This lady's " faith in things unseen " excited
imilar faith on my part, and I would go, had I nothing to
onsider but how I should like it when there. I had to
rite a refusal, however. Mr. C. is " neither to hold nor
ind " when I make new visiting acquaintances on my own
asis, however unexceptionable the person may be ; and
here were other reasons, " which it may be interesting not
o state." '

Mr. Alexander Carlyle distinctly scores against Mr.
Froude by pointing out his unfairness in quoting this and
mitting the final clause about ' other reasons.'[2]   It may
lso be remarked that on ' 6th June ' following, Mrs.
Carlyle wrote in her note-book,—' Lunched at Darwin's,
who drove me to call at Mrs. Rennie's and Lady Broke's,'
nd that Carlyle's note in that place showed that he did
ot know that lady at all.[2]   The diary for October 31
oncludes.—

' The evening devoted to mending Mr. C.'s trowsers
mong other things ! " Being an only child," I never
" wished " to sew men's trowsers—no, never ! '—which
ecalls how it is said that she was once surprised by visitors
when so engaged, and calmly continuing her work was
egged to show something of her husband's, and at once
eld up the garment she was mending and said, " There
re his trowsers if you want to look at them." It may be
a story told by herself and well invented, if it is not true.
    ' November 1.—At last a fair morning to rise to, thanks
God ! Mazzini never says " Thank God " by any chance,
ut always " Thanks God " ; and I find it sounds more
grateful. . . .
    ' November 5.—Alone this evening. Lady A. in town
gain ; and Mr. C. of course at Bath House.

> ' When I think of what I is
>   And what I used to was,
> I gin to think I've sold myself
>   For very little cause.

    ' November 6.—Mended Mr. C's dressing-gown. Much
movement under the free sky is needful for me to keep my

[2] *New Letters and Memorials of J. W. Carlyle*, edited by A. Carlyle,
I, p. 103 and footnote.

heart from throbbing up into my head and maddening i
They must be comfortable people who have leisure to thin
about going to Heaven ! My most constant and pressin
anxiety is to keep out of Bedlam ! that's all. Ach !
there were no feelings " what steady sailing craft we shoul
be," as the nautical gentleman of some novel says.

' November 7—Dear, dear ! what a sick day this ha
been with me. Oh, my mother ! Nobody sees when I ar
suffering now ; and I have learnt to suffer " all to myself.
From " only childness " to that, is a far and a rough roa
to travel.

> ' Oh, little did my mother think,
> The day she cradled me,
> The lands I was to travel in,
> The death I was to dee.

' November 13.—Taken to Lord John ' Russell's ' lectur
at Exeter Hall. The crowd was immense, and the applaus
terrific ; the lecture " water bewitched."   One thin
rather puzzled me : at every ·mention of the nam
Christ (and there was far too much of it) the clapping an
stamping rose to such a pitch that one expected always i
must end in " Hip, hip, hurrah ! " Did the Young Men'
Christian Association take his Lordship's recognition o
Christ as a personal compliment, or did it strike them witl
admiration that a Lord should know about Christ ? '

On this same day, 13.11.55, Carlyle was writing to Lad
Ashburton about her invitation to his wife and himself t
spend the Christmas holidays at the Grange.—

' DEAR LADY, . . .

' You do not *doubt* but we are willing, and some o
us thrice willing, to come to The Grange ? No that i
beyond " doubt," now and at all times. But the question
How ? What can I say ? I hate loud large meetings
especially of the kind called literary. Oh Heaven, Ton
Taylor & Co. (a most extensive firm at this epoch) furnishe
richly with the talent of utterance, and with nothing i
them but the *absence* of knowledge or of wisdom to utter
—careering with outspread wings (in *Punch* and elsewhere
on the top of popular delirium, discharging *that* sad functio
of giving dumb stupidity a voice. These are not lovely t
me in the humour I am in ! Well, some other sort tha
those might be lovelier. I remember one evening witl

Milnes and you too, Ld. A. and you, as among the pleasantest or 20 years ;—but perhaps nothing of that kind is possible ; the case being indeed very intricate ! In all cases there is One always at The Grange, the sight of whom is of the nature of happiness to me ; pleasant in all moods and situations hitherto : for the sake of that one, *I* will encounter anything, even Tom Taylor & Co. . . . And this is all I can say ;—and inexorable time (I perceive) cuts me short for the present ; the " Miss Lowe Subscription " (blessings on it !) calling me to the Athenæum as fast as I can now run.

' Adieu, best of Women, best of friends. I hope to write again before Wednesday ; and at worst shall see you then. Adieu.

' T. C.'

Needless to say, Mrs. Carlyle also was willing to go to the Grange. Meanwhile she continued her journal.

' November 20.—I have been fretting inwardly all this day at the prospect of having to go and appeal before the Tax Commissioners at Kensington to-morrow morning. Still, it must be done. If Mr. C. should go himself he would run his head against some post in his impatience ; and besides, for me, when it is over it will be over, whereas he would not get the better of it for twelve months—if ever at all.

' November 21.—O me miseram ! Not one wink of sleep the whole night through ! so great the " rale mental agony in my own inside " at the thought of that horrid appealing. It was with a feeling like the ghost of a dead dog, that I rose and dressed and drank my coffee, and then started for Kensington. Mr. C. said,—" The voice of honour seemed to call on him to go himself." But either it did not call loud enough, or he would not listen to that charmer.' Or, most likely of all, his wife would not let him.

' I went in a cab to save all my breath for appealing. Set down at 30 Hornton Street, I found a dirty private-like house, only with Tax Office painted on the door. A dirty woman-servant opened the door, and told me the Commissioners would not be there for half-an-hour, but I might walk up. There were already some half-score of men assembled in the waiting-room, among whom I saw the man who cleans our clocks, and a young apothecary of Cheyne Walk. All the others, to look at them, could not have been suspected for an instant, I should have said, of making a hundred a year. Feeling in a false position, I stood by myself at a window and " thought shame " (as children say). Men trooped in by twos and threes, till the small room was pretty well filled ; at last a woman showed herself. O my ! did I ever know the full value of any sort of woman—as woman—before ! By this time some benches had been brought in, and I was sitting nearest the door. The woman sat down on the same bench with me, and, misery acquainting one with strange bedfellows, we entered into conversation without having been introduced, and I had " the happiness," as Allan termed it, " of seeing a woman more miserable than myself."

' Two more women arrived at intervals, one a young girl of Dundee, " sent by my uncle that's ill " ; who looked to be always recapitulating inwardly what she had been told to say to the Commissioners. The other, a widow, and such a goose, poor thing ; she was bringing an appeal against no overcharge in her individual paper, but against the doubling of the Income-Tax. She had paid the double tax once, she said, because she was told they would take her goods for it if she didn't—and it was so disgraceful for one in a small business to have her goods taken ; besides it was disadvantageous ; but now that it was come round again she would give up. She seemed to attach an irresistible pathos to the title of *widow*, this woman. " And me a widow, ma'am," was the winding up of her every paragraph. The men seemed as worried as the woman, tho they put a better face on it, even carrying on a sort of sickly laughing and bantering with one another.

' " First-come lady," called the clerk, opening a small side-door, and I stept forward into a *grand peut-être*.'

" A great perhaps."—The quotation is from the traditional report of the last words of Rabelais on his death-bed,—" I am going to seek a *great perhaps*. Draw the curtain, the farce is finished." Which is like Shakespeare's " All the world's a stage, and all the men and women merely players." The " great perhaps " had long been a proverb for any uncertain adventure. Mrs. Carlyle's Diary runs on.—

' There was an instant of darkness while the one door was shut behind and the other opened in front ; and there stood in a dim room where three men sat round a large table spread with papers. One held a pen ready over an open ledger; another was taking snuff, and had taken still worse in his time, to judge by his shaky, clayed appearance. The third, who was plainly the cock of that dungheap, was sitting for Rhadamanthus—a Rhadamanthus without the justice.

'" Name," said the horned-owl-looking individual holding the pen. " Carlyle." " What ? " " Car-lyle." Seeing he still looked dubious, I spelt it for him. " Ha ! " cried Rhadamanthus, a big, bloodless-faced, insolent-looking fellow. " What is this ? Why is Mr. Carlyle not come himself ? Didn't he get a letter ordering him to appear ? Mr. Carlyle wrote some nonsense about being exempt from coming, and I desired an answer to be sent that he must come, must do as other people." " Then, sir," I said, " your desire has been neglected, it would seem, my husband having received no such letter ; and I was told by one of your fellow Commissioners that Mr. Carlyle's personal appearance was not indispensable." " Huffgh ! Huffgh ! What does Mr. Carlyle mean by saying he has no income from his writings, when he himself fixed it in the beginning at a hundred and fifty ? " " It means, sir, that, in ceasing to write, one ceases to be paid for writing, and Mr. Carlyle has published nothing for several years." " Huffgh ! Huffgh ! I understand nothing about that." " I do," whispered the snuff-taking Commissioner at my ear. " I can quite understand a literary man does not always make money. I would take it off, for my share, but " (sinking his voice still lower), " I am only one voice here and not the most important."

'" There," said I, handing to Rhadamanthus Chapman and Hall's account ; " that will prove Mr. Carlyle's statement." " What am I to make of that ? Huffgh ! We should have Mr. Carlyle here to swear to this before we believe it." " If a gentleman's word of honour written at the bottom of that paper is not enough, you can put me on my oath : I am ready to swear to it." " You ! You, indeed ! No, no ! We can do nothing with your oath." " But, sir, I understand my husband's affairs fully,—better than he does himself." " That I can well believe ; but we can make nothing of this," flinging my document contemptuously on the table.

' The Horned Owl picked it up, glanced over it when

Rhadamanthus was tossing papers about and grumblin
about " people that wouldn't conform to rules " ; then
the Horned Owl ' handed it back to him, saying depreca
tingly : " But, sir, this is a very plain statement." " The
what has Mr. Carlyle to live upon ? You don't mean t
tell me he lives on that ? " ' said Rhadamanthus, ' pointin
to the document. " Heaven forbid, sir," ' said Mrs. Carlyl
' " But I am not here to explain what Mr. Carlyle has t
live on, only to declare his income from literature durin
the last three years." " True, true ! " mumbled the no
most-important voice at my elbow. " Mr. Carlyle, I believe
has landed income ? " " Of which," said I haughtily, fo
my spirit was up, " I have fortunately no account t
render in this kingdom and to this board." " Take of
fifty pounds, say a hundred—take off a hundred pounds,"
said Rhadamanthus to the Horned Owl. " If we writ
Mr. Carlyle down a hundred and fifty he has no reason t
complain, I think. There, you may go. Mr. Carlyle ha
no reason to complain."

' Second-come woman was already introduced, and
was motioned to the door ; but I could not depar
without saying that " at all events there was no use i
complaining since they had the power to enforce thei
decision."

' On stepping out, my first thought was, what a merc
Carlyle did not come himself ! For the rest, tho it migh
have gone better, I was thankful that it had not gon
worse. When one has been threatened with a grea
injustice, one accepts a smaller as a favour.

' Went back to spend the evening with Geraldine whe
Mr. C. set forth for Bath House. Her ladyship in tow
for two days.

' December 4.—I hardly ever begin to write here that
am not tempted to break out into Jobisms about my ba
nights. How I keep on my legs and in my senses with suc
little snatches of sleep is a wonder to myself. Oh, to cur
anyone of a terror of annihilation, just put him on m
allowance of sleep, and see if he don't get to long for sleep
sleep, unfathomable and everlasting sleep as the onl
conceivable Heaven.

' December 11.—Oh dear ! I wish this Grange busines
were well over. It occupies me (the mere preparation fo
it) to the exclusion of all quiet thought and placid occupation
To have to care for my dress at this time of day more tha

er I did when young and pretty and happy (God bless me,
 think that I was once all that!) on penalty of being
garded as a blot on the Grange gold and azure, is really
o bad. *Ach Gott!* If we had been left in the sphere we
long to, how much better it would have been for us in
any ways!'

This is the sixteenth entry in this little note-book or
diary," and the next is dated 'March 27, 1856.' We
ust see what was happening during that interval.

O

XXIII

ALEXANDER GILCHRIST HAS AN INTERVIEW
(1855)

ALEXANDER GILCHRIST was a man of 27 years
age in 1855. The son of a clergyman who for reaso
of conscience had quitted the pulpit, young Gilchrist h
qualified for the bar and married the daughter of a prospero
solicitor. Supporting himself by journalism as an a
critic, he had published a life of Etty the painter in 18
and had sent it to Carlyle and received an appreciative let
of acknowledgment. Then Gilchrist supplied some prints
old costumes and portraits, and also pamphlets useful i
the work on Frederick, and was invited to Cheyne Row,
" to meet Ruskin," it appears.[1]

' Of the Frederick books,' Carlyle wrote to him
28.11.1855, ' I have read three ; all of them worth looki
at ; one of them a conspicuously excellent Piece, which
had never seen before, his *Instructions Militaires*, extreme
physiognomic of the man, and in all ways demanding
be read. I think the Prussians must still keep it secret. .
No trace of it hitherto in any of the collections of his book
nor did I know it had ever been translated into Englis
Were I Commander-in-Chief I would study that book
the last fibre of meaning in it ; and make all my office
down to the lowest corporal who had sense in his head, re
it and again read it.—Alas, I fear if *our* " Commander-i
Chief " so-called, did read it till he really *understood* it,
the first effect would be, said Commander-in-chief wou
go distracted, and do himself a mischief, with rope
otherwise ! It is certain our highest War-Secretary, Du
of Newcastle or whoever he might be, if he applied
Frederick to be made a Drummer, would not even

[1] *Anne Gilchrist, Her Life and Writings*, by H. H. Gilchrist, pp. 44
&c.

194

allowed to drum : " Go first and learn it, then apply to me ! " . . . Ruskin took my copy of *Etty* with him ; hopes to make your acquaintance before long. . . .'

Gilchrist came to Cheyne Row next evening and here is his report of it.[2]—

'*November 29th*, 1855.

' At half-past seven on Friday evening last, an omnibus set me down in Great Cheyne Row. Shown up into the large, comfortable drawing-room, I found Mrs. Carlyle alone (Carlyle downstairs fetching,' i.e. making up for, ' a short allowance of sleep over night), and was more favourably impressed by her than I had expected. After exchanging a few words, as she was making the tea, Carlyle appeared in his long brown indoors coat, and shook me cordially by the hand ; was from that moment to the last *very* kind. " I have brought you here on false pretences." Ruskin was coming the *following* night ; Mrs. Carlyle was engaged out to a party. " You must not suppose," she had before said, " the wife of a philosopher sits at home over the fire in white satin shoes."

' Carlyle was very pleased with all I had brought him ; was " like a wild man," said Mrs. Carlyle, the night before, over the pamphlets. These were nearly all new to him, and nearly all more or less worth seeing.

' After tea, Mrs. Carlyle left. And for the rest of the evening (till twelve) I sat with him alone, he pouring himself out as is his wont ; sitting the latter part of the time on a footstool by the fire, smoking, and looking in his old long brown kind of great-coat, as he was bewailing the pass men and things had come to, and as he thought of it hardly caring to live,—looking like a veritable Prophet, mourning in sackcloth and ashes the sins of the world.

' Carlyle gave me a new and heroic view of Marlborough and his Duchess, among other things. Which led to Macaulay and his blackening of Marlborough's face, and to a long imaginary address to Macaulay for flying at great men—as the *canaille* of themselves are ever prone to do. "' Come out of that, I tell you, you big blockhead—big as you look, you low miserable creature, you ! "

' (At another time Carlyle, after reading in Macaulay's *History of England*, laid down the book and said, " Flow on, thou shining river ! ")

[2] *Ditto*, pp. 41–3.

' Carlyle took me up into his study, showed his daguerreo type from Cooper's " Cromwell," for which he has a great fondness ; his screen covered with small prints relative to Frederick ; a (framed) Albert Dürer, that had once belonged to the Elector of Saxony who saved Luther. *Gave* me also a plaster mask of Dante's face which he has had many years.

' Carlyle spoke affectionately of Hollar '—an engraver— ' despondingly of literature. " If he were on his death bed," (Carlyle spoke this with intense sincerity), " the only thing he had done would give him any pleasure was the ' Cromwell ' ; some little pleasure to have done that—to have dispersed the lies, and shown him as some day all men would see him to have been ! " " One might as well go on the stage and be a mountebank as take to literature "— with other " splenetic words," as on my interposing he confessed them to be. Carlyle showed himself truly lovable as well as grand, throughout.'

Here ends the report of Mr. Gilchrist. In a letter from Carlyle to Lady Ashburton dated 15.12.55, announcing that his wife and he were coming to the Grange on the Monday following, there are remarks which show how he had discovered the condition of the British army.—

' Yesterday Anthony Sterling called on me ; just home from the Crimea as Lieutenant to Sir Colin ; and, somewhat to his provocation, just about returning again with the said Sir C. His account of the Crimean Affairs is surly and miserable : Russian Officers alone know anything about War ; British Infantry (such the *Berserkir* fury lodged in the heart of them) could probably beat still in open fight but Russians able to scheme and manœuvre, British or French not, it will hardly be allowed to come to that Anthony has a beard as big as a moderate corn-sheaf ; a grim military stoic, impressive after his sort ;—no such Fighting Apparatus as the British, I believe with him, ever took the field in this World before !—

' T. C.'

On Monday, 17.12.55, Mrs. Carlyle went to the Grange taking her husband, who felt the need of a rest and change and told Neuberg :—" There has a good deal of MSS accumulated to keep your hand in use during my absence " ; and, in short, we must try to begin to print in the spring.

XXIV

HARRIET, LADY ASHBURTON'S LAST CHRISTMAS AT THE GRANGE
(1855-56)

BOTH Carlyle and Lord Ashburton were now 'magnificently' bearded, to the satisfaction of their wives, and Lady Harriet's gaiety and wit were at their brightest. It was the last of the great " Gatherings of the Clans," as he used to call these festivities, which she was ever to see, and it lingered long in the memories of her ' printers ' as the best of all.[1] " She is very loyal to her *printers*," said Brookfield to Tennyson on this occasion.[2] She had sent Jowett to make Tennyson come.

Besides the Carlyles and the Brookfields and their children and Alfred Tennyson, there were among the guests on this occasion nearly all the habituals except Thackeray, who had gone to lecture in America.[3] Venables was there, and James Spedding, Goldwin Smith and Jowett, Lord Clarendon and his wife and many others, and the old Judge Sir James Parke came gladly, ' for breathing time in the midst of assize business.'

Perhaps the most interesting sight to Mrs. Carlyle was old Henry Drummond, once the associate of Edward Irving, who used to be himself the owner of the Grange, and was now again prominent in public life, M.P. and so on. This reminder of Irving may have been what made Mrs. Carlyle speak plainly to Brookfield. The fine ladies in London had all been running after him, declaring " he preaches more beautifully than anybody ever did before "; and Lady Ashburton and Mrs. Carlyle agreed in fearing for him that he might let something drop which the jealous fanatics might use to deprive him of his job as an Inspector of

[1] *Mrs. Brookfield and Her Circle*, by C. & F. Brookfield, II pp. 425-39 and 455.
[2] *Alfred Lord Tennyson*, by his Son, I. p. 413.
[3] *Life of W. M. Thackeray*, by H. Merivale and F. T. Marzials, p. 184.

Schools. Lady Ashburton was tactful, and warned him
through his wife. Mrs. Carlyle, remembering Edward Irving,
dealt with him directly. He was comforted by a letter from
Miss Wynn, who wrote to him :—Mrs. Carlyle " has certainly had experience sufficient of the utter ruin that follows
the trade of a Popular Preacher . . . to induce her to preserve her friends from entering on that career, but in your
case I am quite convinced that it was merely annoyance
that one to whom she looks up should openly profess a
belief which is denied to her. . . . *No one cares to answer
her sweeping declamation against Christianity and the Church,
and so she thinks one agrees with her. . . . If you had a fitting
opportunity, a long walk or so, I wish earnestly you could get
her to talk, and do so yourself. I am well aware that any
effect on her must be made at the cost of being scalped yourself,
but a thorough bit of self-sacrifice would, I know, not be
unpleasant to you.*"[4]—He never risked it.

Soon after the Carlyles arrived, an incident happened
which illuminates a controversy. Did Lady Ashburton
make Mrs. Carlyle uncomfortable in many little ways invisible to others ? That is what Miss Jewsbury said, who
never saw her, and Mr. Froude believed. Or is Mr. Venables,
corroborated by other friends of both, more credible in
declaring that Lady Harriet had *no* " little ways," and that
' in her house, if in no other, the wives of her friends took
the social rank of their husbands, and of some of them '
can say from my own knowledge that they became warmly
attached to Lady Ashburton.'[5]

The Brookfields testify,[1] impartial and clear-seeing friends
of both :—' Lady Ashburton this Xmas consulted Mrs.
Brookfield as to what would be most useful to give to Mrs.
Carlyle as a gift from the Xmas tree, and a silk dress was
finally decided upon ; but this present seems to have a
little angered that lady. She would not take it ; she vowed
she was being insulted, and Lady Ashburton at last was
forced to seek her in her room, and assure her with tears in
her eyes she had not meant to offend. But that slight
breeze was the only storm that arose in those days, which
says a good deal for Lady Ashburton's cleverness and tact
in managing so many warring and diversified temperaments.

Mrs. Brookfield described Mrs. Carlyle as ' very slight,

[4] Italics added.
[5] *Carlyle in Society and at Home*, by G. S. Venables, *Fortnightly
Review*, May, 1883, p. 624.

at, erect in figure, animated in expression, with very good
es and teeth, but with no pretension to beauty. . . . She
ed to remain in her own room during the early part of
e day, while her husband took his walks accompanied
by his admirers ' (or friends). ' When she did appear she
as always especially taken care of by Lady Ashburton,
d she expected and was conceded a certain prominence
nong the many other visitors of more or less distinction. . . .
rs. Carlyle's instinct was always to take the lead. At the
range this was not easy, for our hostess . . . scattered
pearls and diamonds whenever she spoke " and was " the
st attraction and interest to all around her. No wonder!"
ere are some of Lady Ashburton's sayings reported by
ilnes.[6]—

" The most dreadful thing against women is the character
   the men that praise them."
" *She* never speaks to anyone, which of course is a great
   dvantage to anyone."
" There is no *rebound* about her : it is like talking into
   soft surface."
" I like men to be men ; you cannot get round them
   ithout."
" X has nothing truly human about him ; he cannot even
   yawn like a man."
" You seem to think that married people always want
   vents to talk about : I wonder what news Adam used to
   ring to Eve of an afternoon."
" Your notion of a wife is evidently a Strasbourg goose,
   hom you will always find by the fireside when you come
   ome from amusing yourself."
" Of course there will be slavery in the world as long as
   here is a black and a white—a man and a woman."
" I am strongly in favour of Polygamy. I should like to go
   ut, and the other wife to stay at home and take care of things,
   nd hear all I had to tell her when I came back."
" When I passed by Bennett's church in the morning, all
   ressed in my diamonds and flowers, to be drawn by
   winton, the beadle in full costume bowed low to me, taking
   ne for an altar-piece or something to be reverenced."
" In one's youth one doubts whether one has a body, and
   hen one gets old whether one has a soul ; but the body
   sserts itself so much the stronger of the two."

[6] *Monographs*, by R. M. Milnes, Lord Houghton, pp. 249–254.

The Brookfields say that Mrs. Carlyle was ' clever an amusing' in conversation, altho she ' had the fatal pr pensity of telling her stories at extraordinary length ' ; b that would be mostly in quiet circles. Nobody ever thougl her self-assertive while she lived. On the contrary, Goldw Smith, who was present observing her on this visit, ha described her as ' a modest personage,' who remained ' i the background.' He added,—' Nobody knew that she wa so clever as her letters prove her to have been.'[7]

What the Brookfields tell us about Lady Ashburton abundantly confirmed. She ' was an ideal hostess,' the say, ' for she knew how to make each of her guests happy i his own way. She knew how and when to use the best, th most appreciative or the most encouraging word. She neve intruded herself, in fact she cleverly made herself missec She would dine in her own apartments. Her assemblie were models of good management. This last great one ha something more ; there was a wistful affection mixed i with her attention to her friends which everybody felt, thoug few of them recognised the cause ' at the time—for she seem to have confided to nobody her fears about her failing healtl

The assemblies at the Grange at no time partook of th Sévigné-de Staël type, were never conferences of hig wisdom nor even tournaments of wit ; on the contrary, the might rather have been called the relaxations of Giants for the Literati there were expected to recreate themselves and everybody was at ease.[5] Lady Ashburton never ' vie with ' her guests, and gave to many and especially t Carlyle ' a filial respect and a duteous admiration.'[1]

Mr. Venables,[5] R. M. Milnes (Lord Houghton),[8] and th other witnesses confirm the Brookfields, and what Mrs Carlyle wrote and said can be reconciled with what the say. There never need have been any controversy. Mrs Carlyle's health was now indifferent and Lady Ashburton' was failing altogether. Mrs. Brookfield's advice about givin a dress was a bad mistake, and the tiff it caused would no have blown quickly by if it had not been true, as Milne wrote to his daughter afterwards,[8] that Mrs. Carlyle ' wa really very fond of Lady Ashburton, and certainly no jealous in the vulgar sense of the word. She strongly enjoye

---

[7] *Reminiscences*, by Goldwin Smith, p. 142.
[8] Lord Houghton's *Monographs*, pp. 246-7 ; and T. Wemyss Reid' Richard Monckton Milnes (Lord Houghton), II, pp. 423-5. Compar the *Reminiscences*, by Goldwin Smith, pp. 140-3.

being at the Grange, though perhaps *froissée*' (bothered) 'by the indifferent formality and the fine ladies, whom Carlyle rather liked and admired. She was really attached to me and I to her,' he concluded. There is no doubt that he was right in thinking she liked Lady Ashburton and the Grange.

The smoking-room at the Grange was the Conservatory, and on Christmas night there, 25.12.55, Mr. Brookfield heard someone say,—" Fine moon to-night, Mr. Carlyle ! " He entered in his diary the reply. " Ay, poor old girl. She's been hanging about this planet off and on for a good number of months now." Talking of Thurlow, someone said or quoted,—" No man ever was so wise as he looked."

A copy of *Maud* was forwarded to Tennyson while he was there, and Mrs. Brookfield described what followed. 2nd January, 1856. ' We were, all of us, of course, eager to hear his new Poem read aloud by himself, and he most kindly agreed to gratify us. But there were difficulties to be got over. The Carlyles were among the guests, and Carlyle could not endure to listen to anyone reading aloud—not even to Alfred Tennyson. Carlyle was accustomed to take an early walk daily, and to be accompanied. What was to be done ? All the visitors were presumably anxious to listen to Tennyson. Lord and Lady Ashburton were kept waiting ; chairs had been arranged in a quiet sitting room ; the visitors (ourselves among the number) were taking their places. Alfred was ready. So was Carlyle—in the Hall—waiting for a companion. It was quite an anxious moment. Each probably wondered which would volunteer like Quintus Curtius of old. At length Mr. Goldwin Smith generously stepped forward, and Brookfield joined them while the rest remained.'

In the walk outside, Goldwin Smith did most of the talking. Upon Gladstone's Church and State ideas he seemed " very instructive " to Brookfield. Carlyle said little or nothing.[9]

Mrs. Carlyle was listening in the meantime to the Laureate's recitation, and wrote a few days later to Allingham, a common friend, and as customs-officer at Lymington, a quasi-neighbour of Tennyson across the Solent.—

' Alfred Tennyson read *Maud* and other poems aloud to us, and was much made of by all the large party assembled

---

[9] Compare *Reminiscences*, by Goldwin Smith, p. 142.

there. He seemed strangely excited about *Maud*—as sensitive to criticisms as if they were imputations on his honour : and all his friends are excited about *Maud* for him ! . . .

'Dear Mr. Allingham, be a poet by all means, for you have a *real gift* that way ; but for God's sake beware of becoming too caring about whether your gift is *appreciated* by the million of Jackasses. The nightingale doesn't trouble itself about *appreciation*, and sings none the worse for that.'[10]

A few weeks later Allingham was visiting Tennyson and remarking of Byron,—" He was a Lord, and talked about, and he wrote vulgarly, therefore he was popular."

Tennyson :—" Why am I popular ? I don't write very vulgarly."

Allingham :—" I have often wondered that you are, and Browning wonders."

Tennyson :—" I believe it's because I'm Poet-Laureate. It's something like being a Lord."[11]

Which was creditable to his modesty and sense, but by no means a complete explanation of the mystery, as most of the other laureates could have told him.

None of Tennyson's friends had done more to drag him into notice than Brookfield and Carlyle ; and the extravagance of the worship he was receiving at the Grange tickled them both ; and when they were smoking together in the Conservatory next night after dinner, the stupid adorers all at a safe distance, they laughed with much good humour.

" It reminds me of your old friend Slush," said Carlyle, alluding to a story Brookfield was fond of telling. He and a friend were once at Harewood, near Harrogate, and asked the landlord of an inn where they could see " the Airedale poet." " I think they'd be able to tell you round at the stables," he answered. They went and asked the stable-boy, who put his hands to his mouth and shouted, " Slush ! " " Aye, aye, sir." " Here's a gentleman wants you." A " slovenly, unkempt " individual, or what seemed such to them, appeared and accepted a pot of ale. Poor Slush ! We can never tell each other's feelings. He may have taken their ale in the spirit of a slave, who grabs whatever he can get, or he may have been like the gloriously independent minstrel in Goethe's poem, who flung back the chain of gold to the King, and would take no more than a drink. Be

[10] *Letters to William Allingham*, pp. 143-4.
[11] *William Allingham, A Diary*, p. 132.

hat as it may, the contrast was ludicrous between Slush
nd his admirers, two superfine young gentlemen,—for it
as to be confessed that ' Brooks ' had been a bit of a dandy
1 those early days, ' shirt collars up, velvet waistcoat, gold
uttons, blue satin cravat, boots and straps,'—and Carlyle
sed to laugh violently whenever he repeated the story.[12]

Tennyson had been Laureate since 1850, but was still
egardless of trifles in his appearance, and the likeness to
lush was worth recalling. Meanwhile here is Tennyson's
npression of his hostess in January, 1856.[2]—' It seems a
ouse not uneasy to live in, only I regret my little fumitory
t Farringford. Here they smoke among the oranges,
emons, and camellias. . . . I cannot see in Lady Ashburton
touch of the haughtiness which fame attributes to her. She
s most perfectly natural, tho like enough she sometimes
nubs her own grade now and then, when she sees presump-
ion and folly.'

' One of these mornings Tennyson came into breakfast
ather late,' wrote Mrs. Brookfield,[1] ' with a perturbed
xpression of face, his watch in his hand, saying with great
ravity : " My watch has stopped ; what am I to do ? "
Ve all felt concerned for a moment. Then Mr. Fairbairn,
vith equal gravity, rose from his chair, took the watch from
lfred's hand, asked for his key, *wound it up*, and silently
eturned it to its owner.'

The hero of this episode had on arrival been mistaken for
n analytical chemist, Taylor, and idle noses discovered " an
offensive enteric odour " from his portmanteau and dis-
nterred stomach in his hatbox. He was really a William
Fairbairn of Manchester, famous then for his Conway and
Britannia tubular bridges[13] ; and probably the subject of
he laudatory conversation mentioned by Venables,[5] which
vas summed up by Carlyle,—" He seemed to be a clean,
veracious smith."

Carlyle was more in evidence on this visit than usual.
Frederick had been moving. He felt free to relax, and in a
etter to Neuberg, after mentioning the weather, ' rigorous
rost, cold but *clean*, and even brightly sunny,' he added :
—' I have been totally *idle ;* finding indeed there is nothing
o good I can do here as be out of doors, on foot or on
iorseback, and get the *maximum* of fresh air and exercise

[12] See footnote [1] and also *Random Reminiscences* by C. H. E. Brook-
eld, Chapter I, p. 18.
[13] *Home Life of Sir David Brewster*, by Mrs. Gordon, p. 225-6.

while here. *Work* I never could do in this element at all
and it seems the handsomest way to give over even trying.'

After dinner on 4th January Mrs. Tom Taylor sang a
good deal, and her " Coulin " was a treat to Carlyle, who
was particularly fond of that beautiful old Irish melody.
Moore's words to it begin,—

> ' Tho the last glimpse of Erin with sorrow I see,
> Yet wherever thou art shall seem Erin to me ;
> In exile thy bosom shall still be my home,
> And thine eyes make my climate wherever I roam.'

' As people were bidding good-night to one another,
wrote Brookfield in his Diary, ' Carlyle whispered rather
loud to me with regard to one,—" Who is he at all ? " I
whispered in reply,—" His name is Zincke." " Oh, Zincke's
the name of him. Well, God give Zinke a good night, and
may the like of him never cross my path on this planet
again for evermore.—Zincke ? " ' This was a Rev. F. B.
Zincke, Vicar of Wherstead near Ipswich, who had written
in what Fitzgerald called ' a light dashing way '[14] a book
upon ' Egypt of the Pharaohs.'

In the Conservatory next day, 5.1.56, Spedding quoted
poetry about the Cuckoo, and Carlyle gave an account of
a funny sight he had seen in early days,—a young cuckoo,
" a great big uncouth lump of meat and feathers," followed
by a titlark step-mother, " proud of the mere size " of the
new nestling, and " anxious as if it were the ' apple of its
eye,' a similitude of many things."

Mr. Brookfield had forgotten a promise to dine with the
Proctors and written to excuse himself. Mrs. Proctor
replied :—' What a greedy man you are—not content with
the land flowing with milk and honey, you envy us our little
dinner of pork chops. . . . How merry you must be. Carlyle's
laugh alone would be sufficient. It appears to me that he
would be better employed in finishing the life of Frederick
of Prussia, and you in the pulpit in Berkeley Chapel.'

On 6.1.1856 Brookfield was writing in his Diary at the
Grange.—' Doing History ' examination ' papers mostly all
this visit. Walked with Venables, Spedding, Mr. and Mrs.
Carlyle.

' We played at night the game of Earth, Air, and Water,
in which each person has to assume the name of one inhabi-
tant of Earth. Lady Ashburton very characteristically

---

[14] *Letters of Edward Fitzgerald*, II, pp. 149, 150, 231.

hose (with suitable intonation as she announced her reply
o " what fish will you be ?   What quadruped ?   What
ird ? ") " A dab, a lamb, a dove."   Carlyle being called
upon replied with inexpressible humour,—" I am an ass."
The zeal with which he afterwards played at it, hurling the
handkerchief at J.O.B. (Mrs. Brookfield), and rapidly
ounting to ten, was very humorous.

' One of these days Carlyle sate in an ante-room between
he Hall and Drawing room with only Lady Ashburton and
himself, his wife and myself present.   From the pitiless
inclemency of the day he took occasion to relate, a story
already told, [15] about an old man who came to his father's
door on a wet and stormy day ; and then the talk turned
upon the authorship of Eikon Basilike, the literary fraud
concocted by the clergyman Gauden, and put out in the
name of Charles I after his execution—as if written by him.
Carlyle declared that the author " was the most portentously
self-righteous mortal ever extant in this planet " ; and per-
sonating Charles " seemed to say to the Almighty, in place
of asking for His grace and mercy,—' Oh, Lord, I have
attained to such a pitch of Heavenly perfection that I fear
it is not even in Thy power to make me any better than I
am ; but if at any time Thou shouldst find an opportunity
for adding a little finish and perfectness to my many excel-
lencies I should feel obliged to thee.' "

The forger was made a bishop and his work appeared a
" supplementary revelation " to Church-of-England divines
for some generations—Macaulay is almost humorous in
discussing it and them.[16]

' In a ride near the Grange with Carlyle and Twistleton,'
reports Venables,[17] ' one of us asked him whether Frederick
the Great had, according to the law of the Empire, a valid
title to some petty territory.   He replied in a narrative
which may have lasted for an hour, including an account
of all the pedigrees, the imperial grants, the family compacts,
and the other elements of the controversy ; and altho the
question was one of secondary interest, neither of his hearers
was impatient or weary.   The statement resembled the
summing up of a complicated litigation by Austin, Thesiger
or Cockburn, or some other great master.   The historical

[15] *Carlyle Till Marriage*, Book I, Chapter IV, pp. 22-3.
[16] *History of England*, Chapter XIX, apropos the Liberty of the
Press. Undated.
[17] *Fortnightly Review*, May, 1883, p. 634.

episode was itself so unimportant that it is not mentioned
in *Frederick*.'

It may have been on the occasion of this visit that John
Tyndall, a clever Irishman of about 35, who had for the
last two years been Professor of Natural History in the
Royal Institution in London, became ' really acquainted '
with Carlyle at the Grange. He had previously seen him
in the picture gallery of Bath House, and noticed ' the
Scotch accent, rich and pleasant.' But at the Grange, as
Tyndall tells us,[18] ' sitting beside him at luncheon, I spoke
to him. I asked Carlyle in a low voice whether the gentleman opposite was not Spedding ? " Yes," he replied aloud
" that's Spedding." He had no notion of tolerating a confidential whisper,' at table. Tyndall goes on.—

' The subject of Homeopathy was introduced. Carlyle'
appreciation of the relation of cause and effect was as sharp
and clear as that of any physicist ; and he thought homeopathy an outrageous defiance of the proportion which must
subsist between them. I sought to offer an explanation of
the alleged effects of " infinitesimals," by reference to the
asserted power of the Alpine muleteer's bell to bring down
an avalanche. If the snow could be loosened by a force so
small, it was because it was already on the verge of slipping
And if homeopathic globules had any sensible effect, it
must be because the patient was on the brink of a change
which they merely precipitated. Carlyle, however, would
listen to neither defence nor explanation. He deemed
homeopathy a delusion, and those who practised it pro-
fessionally impostors. He raised his voice so as to drown
remonstrance ; while a " tsh ! " with which Mrs. Carlyle
sometimes sought to quiet him, was here interposed,'—
successfully, for he said no more about it.

In those days the homeopathic medicines were make-
believes that operated spiritually. The common homeo-
paths were working on the imagination, like later Christian
Scientists ; and made what cures they did otherwise by
judiciously withholding medicine and leaving recovery to
nature unassisted.[19] They were not all quacks tho' their
ways of thinking were often confused. David Masson
listened once while one of them said all he could to conver

[18] Tyndall's *New Fragments*, pp. 352–4.
[19] Verbal statements to D. A. W. of old Dr. George Keith of Edin
burgh, famous as author of *Plea for a Simpler Life*, &c.

Carlyle, and was rewarded by a compendious summary of his argument, concluding :—" On your own showing, if all the generations of men since Adam's time had taken your physic, the whole lot swallowed would not have been equal to one good dose of Glauber's Salts."[20]

Returning to Tyndall's report of his talk at the Grange,—after homeopathy, Carlyle discussed George III appreciatively. The capacity of the King was small, but he paid out conscientiously the modicum of knowledge he possessed. This was illustrated by the way in which he collected his library, always seeking the best advice and purchasing the best books.

' In the evening, while we stood before the drawing-room fire, I spoke to him of Emerson. There was something lofty in the tone of Carlyle's own voice as he spoke of the " loftiness " of his great American friend. I mentioned Lewes's *Life of Goethe*, which I had just been reading, and ventured to express a doubt whether Lewes, as a man, was strong enough to grapple with his subject. He was disposed to commend the *Life* as the best we had, but he was far from regarding it as adequate.

' Carlyle was a bold rider, and during this visit to the Grange he indulged in some wild galloping. Professor Hofmann was his companion, and humorously described their motion as tantamount to being shot like a projectile through space. Brookfield was one of the guests, a clergyman of grace and culture, who might have been a great actor, and who entertained a high notion of the actor's vocation. One evening he gave us an illustration of his dramatic gifts—extemporising, and drawing by oblique references, the principal personages round him into his performance. It was then I first heard the resonant laugh of Carlyle. Himself a humourist on a high plane, he keenly enjoyed humour in others. Lady Ashburton, with fine voice and expression, read for us one of Browning's poems. It was obvious from his ejaculatory remarks that Carlyle enjoyed and admired Browning.'

On Monday, 14.1.56, the Carlyles came home. Soon after then is the likeliest date for what Fitzgerald mentions only as in January.[21] Carlyle called Tennyson's *Maud* " a cobweb."

[20] Verbal statement to D. A. W. of David Masson in 1902.
[21] *Letters of Edward Fitzgerald*, I, p. 305.

XXV

NAPOLEON AND FREDERICK COMPARED
(1856)

A FEW days later Carlyle was writing to Lord Ashburton on a matter of great historical interest.—

' CHELSEA,
' 18 *Jany.*, 1856.

' DEAR LORD ASHBURTON,
 ' Many thanks for your active remembrance of my wants and me ; to you, and to another high Personage, I am surely much indebted in these days ! ' (The reference was not to Lady Ashburton, but to H.R.H. the Prince Consort, as will appear.)
 ' It is the opinion, then, that some important, not superficial but essential, improvement in military *tactics* has been introduced, in the Prussian and all Armies, since Frederick had done with them ? I wish much to know accurately *what*, who did it, and at least who says it was done. I used to hear the same assertion about Frederick's *Strategies* (this of *tactics* is quite new to me) ; but I find after long examination, that such does not appear ; that Napoleon did not " improve " upon Frederick in this respect, but perhaps considerably the *reverse*, that in fact he did not differ from Fredk. except as a blazing Corsican Pirate, of wondrous gifts, and commanding a Nation gone wholly mad, must differ from a veritable Sovereign Man, also of wondrous gifts, whose poor Nation has not gone mad at all, but has to depend on the sober truth of things for any success it may have. Fredk. could not spend " 10,000 men a week," nor blaze away gunpowder and resources at that rate :—what a dreadful expense was that in *mendacities* alone (the account of it not *yet* settled in France by any means) ! Fredk. never wrote a *bulletin ;* nor *thought* one. I believe it will turn out that his feats of soldiership were far ahead of Napoleon's, so soon as men recover their eyesight, and learn to discriminate greatness from bulk. Wellington, in his way,

as a soldier of the Frederick kind. Anybody that tries
the Napoleon line, *without* a " mad " Nation to depend on,
will certainly run his head against stone walls,—of which
there have been instances in our day !

' All this however has nothing to do with special improve-
ments in tactics, drilling of Men, &c., &c., and I am very
anxious to get to the bottom of what you assert on that head.

' I read *Jomini*, for many painful weeks, with great diligence, some years ago, all that he had to say about Fredk.
and his campaigns ; but gained absolutely nothing from
Jomini, except the growing suspicion (now become a private
conviction with me) that nothing could be gained from him ;
that he had not even studied this matter well ; that he had,
with very much to say for himself, a most feeble unfurnished
intellect, was not to be depended on for common honesty
(steals Tempelhof's Plates, &c.) ; and in short would avail a
sincere enquirer almost nothing, in spite of the big name. He
is continually adoring Buonaparte at the expense of Fredk.,
and others, and had *bow-wowed* me into that opinion, till I saw
better into some things. That is my experience of Jomini.

' Clausewitz I had heard of lately, as a truly superior man
and writer : I must decidely look into Clausewitz for this
new opinion. Col. Sterling (who knows nothing about the
" opinion ") has a copy of Clausewitz, which he promises
to search out for me tonight,—if he can ; for he is off to
the Crimea again tomorrow morning, and may fail in the
Clausewitz ! If he do, I will (with thankful surprise) apply to
the High Quarter you indicate,—will ask you to apply, that
is. I suppose it is not seemly for the like of me to thank
H.R.H. the Prince Consort in word or message of any kind ;
but I hope you will, on some good occasion, indicate for me
how sensible I am to this mark of humanity in high places.

' Not having any chance to see you tonight, I have
scribbled all this,—which, unless you like, you need not read !
I should have desired much to hear how the gout is,—all
this while. I have been utterly weak, and incapable of work,
ever since I returned ; but feel as if beginning to improve.

' Ever sincerely yours,
' T. CARLYLE.'

That H.R.H. the Prince Consort had offered to lend Carlyle
his Clausewitz, i.e. Clausewitz's great book " on War," is to
be remembered to his credit, and may be perhaps explained
by their talk at Windsor Castle in 1854.[1]

[1] Book XXII, Chapter IV.

P

Five days later, on 23.1.56, he returned to the subject of Clausewitz, which Col. Sterling had been able to supply.

'CHELSEA,

'23 *Jany.*, 1856.

'DEAR LORD ASHBURTON, . . .

'Every night, since Saturday, I have been in *Clause witz ;* who is a truly able man, of strong judgement, clear utterance,—tho' highly *metaphysical* (lost frequently in definitions, theoretical hair-splittings) ; a visible contemporary of Kant. Except Lloyd ; much more, except Napoleon, and Fredk. himself in the best moments, he is the cleverest man I have heard speak of War ;—and I am much obliged to your Lordship and the Prince for having (as if by accident) pushed me into him.

'What will surprise you, however, he does not in the least confirm the assertion made, but precisely the reverse ;— strengthens and clears up, so far as he touches on that matter, the notion I had already groped out about it. Frederick's *velocity* does not appear to have been surpassed hitherto by anybody, but only to have been imitated and now rivalled by everybody ; and the intrinsic differences of method (which in *strategy* are manifold, and in *tactics*, at least *minor tactics*, i.e. drill matters and the like, inconsiderable) between Napoln. and Fk. are, as I still find, what were shadowed out in my last note. Clausewitz admires Napoleon beyond measure ; and does not say or intimate anywhere what I there said of Napoleon ; but he wrote from 25 to 45 years ago ; and had he been fairly *out* of the comet's tail, I believe he would have seen the *Stars* again more clearly, and spoken perhaps with emphasis of their superior method of motion !—This is what I hitherto get out of the man ; but I intend to read to the end, and lie *open* to light, were there any extant in this Country. For the rest, not being Commander in the Crimea, nor Chief at the Horseguards, a very distant outline (provided it be a real one) will suffice me, and errors will not be immediately fatal.—Perhaps we shall hear something of *Muffling* by and by ? No haste at all. I wish we had a Russian Peace first !

'May good weather, and all bright and good things, be about The Grange, till we see you again.

'Yours always,

'T. CARLYLE.'

XXVI

AT HOME AGAIN
(1856)

IN December, 1855, the serial publication of *Little Dorrit* had started, and the sales delighted the author, Charles Dickens. On 30.1.1856 he was telling John Forster,[1] "I have a grim pleasure upon me to-night in thinking that the Circumlocution Office sees the light, and in wondering what effect it will make." In *Little Dorrit* a typical public office was derided under that name, which was a permanent addition to English Phrases. Perhaps the first to appreciate it was Carlyle, who wrote to John Forster about them:—[2] '. . . Long life to you dear F. and recommend me to Dickens; and thank him a hundred times for "the Circumlocution Office"; which is priceless after its sort! We have laughed loud and long over it here; and *laughter* is by no means the supreme result in it. Oh, Heavens!'

With *Frederick* Carlyle was making such progress that by Saturday, 23.2.1856, he was doing the first draft of the battle of Hohenfriedberg in the second Silesian war, Book XV, Chapter X,—the first book in Volume IV of the first edition in six volumes; but it was May before he could pause in his progress and overhaul for the printers the MSS. of the first two volumes.

In Arts and crafts there is a plain distinction between ' mechanical work,' such as sewing or carpentry or masonry, and ' process work,' such as cooking or cultivating or metal-melting, wherein one deals direct with moving or living Nature, and must wait upon natural movements. Carlyle's way of writing was remarkably like process-work, and much surprised he would have been if he had been told, when beginning the fifteenth book, that he had only half-finished his history. It was growing under his hands more than he yet suspected.

---

[1] *Life of Charles Dickens*, by John Forster, Vol. III, pp. 135–136.
[2] John Forster Papers in South Kensington Museum.

Meanwhile his wife had resumed writing in her diary on 24.3.56.—'We are now at the 24th of March, 1856, and from this point of time, my journal, let us renew our daily intercourse without looking back.' Like many another 'good resolution' to keep a diary, this one did not last long; but let us read on.—' Looking back was not intended by Nature, evidently, from the fact that our eyes are in our faces and not in our hind heads. Look straight before you then, Jane Carlyle, above all, at the duty nearest hand, and what's more, do it. Ah, the spirit is willing, but the flesh is weak, and four weeks of illness have made mine weak as water. No galloping over London as in seven-leagued boots for me at present. To-day I walked with effort one little mile, and thought it a great feat. Sleep has come to look to me the highest virtue and the greatest happiness; that is, good sleep, untroubled, beautiful, like a child's. Ah me

'March 26. To-day it has blown knives and files; a cold, rasping, savage day; excruciating for sick nerves Dear Geraldine (Jewsbury), as if she would contend with the very elements on my behalf, brought me a bunch of violets and a bouquet. Talking with her all I have done or could do. "Have mercy upon me, O Lord; for I am weak: O Lord, heal me, for my bones are vexed. My soul also is sore vexed: but thou, O Lord, how long? Return O Lord, deliver my soul: O save me for thy mercy's sake."

'March 27.—Mr. C. took Nero out with him to-night, and half an hour after he opened the door with his latch-key and called in, "is that vermin come back?" Having received my horrified "No!" he hurried off again, and for twenty minutes I was in the agonies of one's dog lost, my heart beating up into my ears. At last I heard Mr. C.'s feet in the street; and, oh, joy! heard him gollaring at something, and one knew what the little bad something was Ach! We could have better spared a better dog.

'March 30.—Plattnauer told me how the " grande passion " between —— and —— had gone to the dogs utterly —the general recipients of " grandes passions."

> " Oh waly, waly, love is bonnie
> A little while when it is new;
>   But when it's auld
>   It waxeth cauld,
> And melts away like morning dew."

'Beautiful verse, sweet and sad, like barley sugar dissolved in tears. About the morning dew, however! I should

ather say, " Goes out like candle-snuff " would be a truer
imile ; only that would not suit the rhyme.

' April 11.—To-day I called on " My Lady " come to
own for the season. She was perfectly civil, for a wonder.

' To-day also I lighted upon an interesting man. It was
n our baker's shop. While the baker was making out my
bill he addressed some counsel to a dark little man with a
wooden leg and a basket of small wares. That made me
ook at the man to watch its effect upon him. " I'll tell
you what to do," said this Jesuit of a baker. " Go and
oin some Methodists' chapel for six months ; make your-
elf agreeable to them, and you'll soon have friends that
will help you in your object." The man of the wooden leg
aid not a word, but looked hard in the baker's face with
half-perplexed, half-amused, and wholly disagreeing
xpression. " Nothing like religion," went on the tempter,
" for gaining a man friends. Don't you think so, ma'am ? "
catching my eye on him). " I think," said I, " that what-
ver this man's object may be, he is not likely to be bene-
ted in the long run by constituting himself a hypocrite."
The man's black eye flashed on me a look of thanks. " Oh,"
aid the baker, " I don't mean him to be a hypocrite, but
ruly religious, you know." " If this man will be advised
y me," I said, " he will keep himself clear of the *true religion*
hat is purposely put on some morning to make himself
riends." " Yes," said the poor man pithily, " not that at
o price ! " Which pleased Mrs. Carlyle so much that she
erself took pains to help the poor fellow, and got a friendly
awyer to read his papers for him for nothing. He had
rroneously supposed he had a valid claim to some property
ft by a grandfather.

' 14th April.—Lay on the sofa most of the day, feeling
too ill for anything." Nevertheless, towards seven o'clock,
ook myself upstairs and dressed myself very fine, and was
riven to Bath House to a dinner-party. The Twistletons,
ilnes, " the Bear " (Ellice), Goldwin Smith and Delane.
ame home with virtue's own reward in the shape of a sore
roat. My throat fairly made sore by telling Lord Ash-
urton French Criminal Trials, all the evening, out of a
ook he hadn't seen. He was so unwell ! And since he
as there, instead of where he should have been, viz., in
s bed, I " felt it my duty " to amuse him without letting
m talk.'

XXVII

MORE OF THE DIARY OF MRS. CARLYLE
(1856)

HAVING finished her diary in note-book 'No. 1' on 14.4.56, Mrs. Carlyle began writing in 'No. 2' next day, and made daily entries till the end of the month But in May there were only 8 entries, and in a few more weeks it stopped, which was a good symptom. Her hus band who read it after her death described the note-book 'No. 2' as a 'sad record,' and said it showed 'the deepe downbreak of her own poor health, which from this time as I *now* see better, continued to advance upon the *citade* or *nervous-system*.'

In truth, as lady-doctors discussing all her symptom seem to agree, she had nothing to complain about but th inevitable result of time. Old age is earlier in some case than in others. She had been an only child, and delicat all her life, and was now older at fifty-five than some ar at sixty-five or even seventy-five ; but she was a well coddled wife and had long had nothing to do but take car of herself. So she was able to eke out her life's tape wonderfully well, to the surprise of her doctors, for te years more.

' 15th April, 1856.—I am very feeble and ailing at pre sent, and my ailment is of a sort that I understand neithe the ways nor outlooks of ; so that the positive suffering i complicated with dark apprehensions. Alas, alas, and ther is nobody I care to tell about it,—not one,—poor ex-spoil child that I am.'—It is likely she told her husband, but sh would not count him " one." She went on.—

' To keep up the appearance of being alive is just as muc as I can manage. Every day I get up with the *wish* to d ever so many things ; but my wishes are no longer " pre sentiments of my powers," if they ever were so. At th day's end I find I have merely *got thro' it*, better or worse, not *employed* it ; all strength for *work* of any sort being used up in bearing the bodily pressure without crying out. I am in arrears with even " the needle-work of the Family." In fact, look at it which way I will, I don't see why, if I *did* die, I should " regret the loss of myself " (as Mr. Davis's beggar-man said).

' 17th April.—Went with Geraldine to look at the Marlborough House pictures ; but was too tired and sick to do anything but sit *about* on chairs. Came home half-dead and lay on the sofa till Miss Williams Wynn came to tea.

' 18th April.—Baked. Went to see the Chelsea Commission at work on Lord Lucan. How sick I have been all this day ! " Be thankful you are not in Purgatory ! " as the Annandale man told his complaining friend.

' 19th April.—Wrote a business letter. Dragged myself to Sloane Street, to see Mrs. Hawkes. She looked more suffering than myself ; and, as usual, made melancholy *fun* of her sufferings. She told me that Mrs. Hooper, the authoress of *The House of Raby*, is going blind. Poor creature ! *all* her faculties needed to make ends meet ; and going blind !

' 20th April (Sunday).—Plattnauer in the morning. I was too poorly for walking with him, so we talked *intimately* over the fire. Except Geraldine no other callers. I fell asleep while Geraldine was here, and again after she had gone ! This weakness is incomprehensible ; if I had any person or thing to take hold of and lean my weight on !

' 21st April.—I feel weaklier every day ; and my soul is also sore vexed. Oh how long ? I put myself in an omnibus, being unable to walk, and was carried to Islington and back again. What a good shilling's worth of exercise !

' 22nd April.—Not up to even a ride in an omnibus to-day.

' 23rd April.—The Countess ' (Pepoli, an old friend, once Elizabeth Fergus of Kirkcaldy), ' sat an hour with me in the morning. She is sure I " don't eat enough." I could not walk further than half way to Sloane Square ! Oh dear, Oh dear ! This living merely to live is weary work !

' 24th April.—Soon after breakfast I went by two omnibuses to Hampstead, with Nero and a Book ; and spent several hours sitting on the Heath, and riding in a donkey-chair. The pleasantest thing I have tried for some time ; and the fresh wind up there has revived me a little.' But apparently she said nothing of that to her husband for a reason worth telling. He was repeatedly trying to persuade her to leave London altogether, which was assuredly the thing she should have done in order to recover her health. But she liked London too much, and would not be persuaded, and was careful not to let him know anything that might help his arguments.

The improvement noted on 24.4.56 continued. She began to dine out and go to festivities, with or without her husband.

' 29th April.—Walked a good spell to-day. Called at Bath House.

' 30th April.—Walked to Alabaster's and bought a bonnet ; and took some things to be framed. Dined at the Wedgwood's. Such a large party : " Distinguished females " not a few ! Mrs. G. said : " Mrs. Carlyle ! I am astonished to meet you here. Miss Jewsbury told me last week she thought you were dying." " She was right," I said.

' 1st May.—Such a first of May for bitter cold ! All day in the house, shivering. Lady Stanley and her mother came ; and we engaged to go to Lady Stanley's Party on Saturday night. When I had sent off for Mrs. Strachan to consult about new trimming my white silk gown, I reminded myself of the " Bairns " of the " wee Wifie that lived in a shoe."

> " She went to the butcher to buy a sheep's head,
> When she came back they were all lying dead !
> She went to the wright's to order a coffin,
> When she came back they were all sitting laughing ! "

Last week I was all for dying ; this week all for Ball dresses.

' 15th May.—Alack ! *hiatus* of a whole fortnight ! for no particular reason ; only a general indisposition to do anything to-day that could possibly be put off till to-morrow. Perhaps it is a symptom of returning health this almighty indolence ; or is it a premonitory symptom of apoplexy ? I'm sure I don't know ; and sometimes don't care.'

The first guess was right,—she was *beginning* to get better. Thus on the same 15.5.56, she went on to describe a dinner-party at the house of George Rennie, a Haddington man, who had once been her " fiancé " there. Rennie had got out of a carriage to speak to Carlyle in Piccadilly on 24.4.56, and announce his return from the Falkland Islands where he had been Governor. He had been an M.P. and was described by Carlyle as a man of sense and veracity, who ' had swallowed manfully his many disappointments ' and

ccepted that job, apparently, as a kind of political conso-
ation prize. After meeting Carlyle he had called at Cheyne
Row and presented his ' tall son,' and persuaded the Car-
yles to come and dine at his house. Ruskin called for them
ifter dinner and took them ' to a great soirée at Bath House.'

Then Mrs. Carlyle's diary of 15.5.56 went on to tell of a
ittle tea-party at Geraldine Jewsbury's, and of bad news
rom an old servant now living in Edinburgh,—' another
eason why I should make an effort to go to Scotland this
Autumn.' The entries for that day conclude with a fine
inecdote of Sir Charles Napier.—' Mr. Knighton told us
ast night that when Sir Charles Napier was about going to
ndia, a person was dispatched to his house late one evening
o tell him it was of the greatest importance he should start
oon. " When did he think he could be ready ? " " Let
ne see," said Sir Charles, taking out his watch, " what
ime is it now ? Well, I can be ready in half an hour. Will
hat do ? " And he spoke in perfect good faith. The
nessenger smiled and told him he believed a fortnight hence
vas as soon as he was expected to go. What a capital man !
t reminded me of my father, who was just as prompt.'

This was the same William Knighton whose notes are
waiting us soon.

XXVIII

THE DEVIL UP TO DATE AND MANY OTHERS
(1856)

IN the drawing-room on the first floor Mrs. Carlyle received callers, and more than once in these month she brought her husband down from his garret work-shop Thus in the spring or early summer the Rev. Thoma Guthrie of Edinburgh, ' the apostle of ragged schools,' wa in London, and writing home to his wife :—[1]' I did not wish to disturb Carlyle, but he came, and an uncommon looking man he is ; an eagle-like look in his great glaring eyes, hai half-gray, and a strong Dumfriesshire tongue. He was i a *robe de chambre*, most kind and courteous. I got him upon the neglect of the uneducated and lapsed classes ; h and I were quite at one. He uttered a number of grea thoughts in magnificent language ; lightning'd and thundered away in sublime style, at the heads of governors, ladie and gentlemen, and this selfish world ; and looked to m very much, as he swung his arm, clenched his fist, and glared round him with his black beard and shining eye and grizzly hair, like an incarnation of Thor or Woden, o some other Scandinavian divinity.'

As often as Peter Swan of Kirkcaldy came to London, h used to call on his old teacher, but the accounts of what wa said are not dated. A witness of ' more than one of thes interviews '[2] reports their talk began with enquiries abou common friends, and adds :—' Carlyle was very beautifu on these occasions. The rugged face would melt in tende regret, and he would pour out, in the most exquisite lan guage, a kind of tuneful dirge over some deceased acquaint ance. By degrees ' . . . they passed to things in genera.

---

[1] Thomas Guthrie, *Autobiography & Letters*, pp. 636–7.
[2] Credible but anonymous reporter in the *British Weekly*, cuttin supplied by Robert Cochrane, for many years editing *Chambers' Journa* Edinburgh.

and talk was mingled with 'great explosions of laughter.'
When Swan once returning from Germany told of having
seen Luther's room in the Wartburg at Eisenach,—" Ay,"
said Carlyle, " were you there ? When I was standing in
that room, I felt it was the holiest spot I had ever seen in
his world, and I think so still."

Meanwhile his old friend, Walter Savage Landor, had
passed 81 this year, which was the date of his *Anthony and
Cleopatra*. Carlyle wrote to thank him for Anthony's
speech,—

> ' I have been sitting longer at life's feast
> Than does me good ; I will arise and go.'

' You look,' wrote Carlyle,[3] ' into the eyes of Death withal,
as the brave all do habitually from an early period of their
course ; and certainly one's heart answers to you. Yea,
valiant brother, yea, even so ! There is a tone as of the old
Roman in these things which does me good, and is very sad
to me, and very noble.' Which recalls the lines that Landor
had written not long ago,—the best he ever wrote :—

> ' I strove with none, for none was worth my strife,
>   Nature I loved, and, next to Nature, Art ;
> I warmed both hands before the fire of life ;
>   It sinks, and I am ready to depart.'

About this time Carlyle wrote a letter to John Forster[3]
referring to a ' Conversation between Alfieri and Metastasio
published in Fraser's Magazine,' and saying one of these
pieces was ' as good as anything I ever saw from Landor.
Do you think the grand old Pagan wrote that piece just
now ? The sound of it is like the ring of Roman swords
on the helmets of Barbarians. An unsubduable old Roman !
Make my loyal respects to him the first time you write.'

Carlyle to Lady Ashburton

' CHELSEA,
' 15 *March*, 1856.

' The *Bourbier* came ; some faithful hand left it here last
Saturday night ; and I am likely to derive more help from
it than I expected : this is really all the news ; and I ought
to end here,—and pay my obeisance *silently*, to a Daughter
of the Sun, in this black sunless weather and grim condition of things. We have the fiercest cold, with grey dusty

---

[3] *W. S. Landor, a Biography*, by John Forster, II, pp. 513 and 66.

winds : my poor Wife has been prisoner the last fortnight
with some influenza she caught ; no likelihood for her till
the wind turn west : everybody seems to be suffering, but
thou of thick skin : I could not see Lady Sandwich in
her new House when I called ; nor get the slightest assurance that you were not suffering like the others. Who
knows ? My own mind is all a grey whirl of dusty dreary
un——

'At this point, Saturday 4 p.m., there rushed in, the *close*
time having expired, two figures, little Ld. Goderich and a
bigger Mr. Bruce Welsh, M.P. for something ; who sat and
sat till the Post hour was gone ; and ever since, there has
been one confusion on the back of another ; a poor man
hunted by several demons, from without and from within :
so that the actual date (to whh. by way of melancholy
memorial, I let the other stand prefixed) is Wedy. 18
March.

'There has Spring come, March the Lion is becoming
March the Lamb ; copious rains, and today a grey atmosphere
altogether genial for the plant creation. But your poor
servant is still dark, Oh good Lady ; in fact, an incurable
mortal, whose task in the world prospers ill and that only ;
who has no *wheel*-vehicle (in any sense of that big word) for
travelling in this world ; who goes *barefoot* (if you will
observe), or worse, in torn boots that do not fit ; and whose
way, once for all, will never be smooth ! Pity the poor
white man ; yes you actually should, in your noble heart :
the poor soul is truly ill off in this generation of evil-doers
(and diners-out), and has little comfort except in *thinking*
of one or two things, which are mostly hidden from his
bodily eyes !'—The words—pity the poor white man—are
a quotation from the song of the negress who succoured
Mungo Park, see *Past and Present*, Book III, Chapter XIII.

'I have had a couple of Dinners ; inevitable :—that,
after all, is perhaps the main fountain of darkness just at
this time ; but there is never wanting some fountain, nor
will be. Let me speak no more of it.

'At the second dinner (Darwin's, Monday night, where a
certain Pertz from Berlin with the Lyells, &c., were the
heroes), this was the news about those Berlin suicides, if
you care anything for them : 1st. Kaumer is *not* the
babbling ever-publishing Historian von Kaumer, but a
Cousin of his ; Keeper (or something like that) of the
King's Private Library ; and is understood to have been

nsane, there being a touch of that kind in the blood of
im. 2nd. The von Canitz was Secretary or Under-do.
n some Public Office, a stout *Junker* partisan,—and had all
he while been betraying the Royal secrets to the *Junker*
'arty (Derbyites or worse, of that climate),—in fact, com-
nunicating all the Russian Despatches to said Party.
Seeing himself found out, he had nothing left but to take
i pistol. The Police Official, who is killed in duel, Pertz
lid not know; a man said to be of perfect exactitude,
strenuous industry in his business; conduct unblameable
here or elsewhere: and the pestilent Junker Aristocracy,
young Soldiers, gambling high-sniffing fellows (at deadly
feud with the Liberals ever since that 1848), had provoked
iim to duel and be shot in that manner. Enough to breed
tumult and almost Civil-war (for a day or two), thot. young
Pertz; who however is youthfully simple perhaps, and has
. small elementary moustache over his grave mouth. He
xpected tumult some day soon, perhaps this very day
anniversary of something in 1848), but I had faith in the
moustache.—More I did not learn at this dinner; or hardly
nore: Clough is in Berlin, Secretary to something that is
investigating Foreign *Military* Schools, it appears, (more
power to them). The Lyells &c., were very dull people :—
nd indeed men generally, and even women generally, are
getting dreadfully dull to me.—The first dinner, inevitable
oo, was at the great Lord Stanhope's :—yes, well do I
remember the first time I ever saw that little man; the
irst time I saw *you*, and long before I could make any
nore acquaintance in your house :—the very voice of that
nan, bad as it is, has had a meaning to me ever since.
Young Stanley, old Lyndhurst, Gladstone, Elgin, &c., &c.,
had Lyndhurst mainly, toughest of old men and Attor-
neys; eyes hard as a Scotch pebble, long nostrils as if
growing into the upper lip, mean head, but full of wrinkled
vivacity, and fond of talking: *I have seen few faces more
like my notion of the Devil's.*[4]

'Yours, T. C.'

Mrs. Carlyle was fond of telling a story, which may
have been in her husband's mind when writing this. As
he put it once in a letter :—[5]' When Lord Lyndhurst's
first wife died, old Croker put on a long face and a black

[4] Italics added.
[5] Our thanks for this are due to Prof. W. H. Woodward.

coat and went to condole with his Lordship. His Lord
ship received his condolence with due solemnity, and sai
in a heart-struck tone :—" My dear Croker, be kind t
your wife while she is with you ! Oh, my dear fellow, lov
her and cherish her while she lives ; but—when she dies-
don't bury her *in the country*—it has cost me fifty pound
for turnpikes, by God ! " ' '

A month later, 16.5.56, Carlyle was writing to Lor
Ashburton about a man who was afterwards very con
spicuous, John Ruskin.—

' This morning Ruskin, from Dover, sent me the enclose
Note, with an old Newspaper from which I have cut ou
what was of use to you,—Ruskin's *Speech* at Oxford to hi
assembled Mechanics. I have not read it, being extremel
busy all morning : please do not burn it till I come; per
haps to-morrow or next day (if the Fates are so beneficen
I may find a chance of looking into it. Ruskin I hav
found in all things to mean well, and aim high with th
very highest ; but he strikes me always as infinitely to
hopeful of men and things, in fact as having soared alo
out of all contact with rugged *facts ;* which class of object
accordingly he contemplates, as with outspread level wing
very much at his ease, far up in the azure æther.—It
certain, however, he does teach various working young me
to *draw,* and has a boundless zeal to continue teaching mor
and more. His Fourth Volume (which I have not time t
read) is full of the finest " eloquence," Swiss descriptior
&c.,—the like of which I have hardly ever seen ;—bu
tending nowhither, except towards the impracticable, th
impossible, so far as I could surmise. It is one of th
strangest Books, for gift and want of gift, I have ever me
with. The man himself I find exceedingly amiable, in spit
of all that is said. But he flies out like a soda-water bottle
gets into the *eyes* of various people (being incautiousl
drawn), and these of course complain dreadfully !

' T. CARLYLE.'

XXIX

AT WORK
(1856)

ON Thursday, 3.4.56, Carlyle was writing to Lady Ashburton, and remarked :—' On Sunday night late the
voice of cannon was heard ; then soon afterwards the voice
of bells. Peace come, ah yes *their* Peace,—with my blessing
on it. We were threatened with an illumination ; but that
blew over. I should have grudged much to spend any
tallow or composition candle on such an affair. Frederick's
old Applewoman came to my mind : an old Applewoman
whom the King had been used to fling a coin to, or exchange
a word with at the gate of Potsdam, on his rides,—she,
after the 7 years war, seeing him again, remarked " where
has your Majesty been ? I have not seen you this long,
long while ! "—" What, Lieschen, did you never hear of
the big war we were in ? "—" War, yes they talked about
war, this and that ; but what knew I of it ? *Pack schlagt
sich, Pack verträgt sich* (Doggery has its battlings, Doggery
has its settlings) "—not worth the notice of a poor diligent
body selling apples here ! '

Then, apropos the Prince Imperial of France, born 16.3.56,
he continued : ' Or what are we to say to the " Child of
France," and its amazing Messiah-ship ? I declare that to
be the highest flight of Playactorism yet recorded in secular
affairs : a cool strength (almost unconscious strength) of
human Impudence, which strikes the observer dumb.
Apparently this Universe is made of nothing but painted
pasteboards, newspaper paragraphs, theatrical draperies
well adjusted and the Infinite of human Gullibility applied
with a brow of brass ? By working late and early for a
long time, men do pretty much get " Barabbas the Robber "
shuffled up for them, by authentic " Universal Suffrage " ;
and great Nations (one great, and still big), are found to
have attained that tragical topgallant,—preparatory to

plunging, we may guess, since they can *soar* no farther
It often strikes me the Jews were quite correct on tha
memorable occasion : " Barabbas is our man " ; we are fo
Barabbas : who so like us as he ?—England too, I am per
petually grieved to believe, is travelling rapidly on th
same road : but I always hope it will pause, and institut
alarming, thrice-alarming, unexpected reflexions, while tim
yet is.—Any way I mean to write the history of Fredk., I
and that ought to be the one concern for me, amid suc
phenomena.

'Doubtless they are babbling away in their Houses o
Parlt., but I hear not the least whisper of them ; I in fac
speak to nobody, hardly somebody once a week : the ver
letters I get are fewer and fewer,—and *all* of them rathe
a sorrow than otherwise, except only one sort (really so) o
which *you* know the uncommon frequency of late. *Alla
Kereem* (" God is bountiful,"—an Arabian proverb). '
think always cheerier days are coming. On, on, any way
—Oh my noble Lady, may all the Gods bless *you*. I en
as I began. You will say when you come ?

'T. C.'

The publisher Chapman called this month, May, 185
and settled with Carlyle for a 'Collective Edition' of h
works. It was to be in 16 volumes at 6/– each, and to con
out a volume a month, beginning in September. Carly
saw plainly that the publisher's real object was to get th
Frederick, and decided to let him have it. As he wrote t
his sister, he thought Chapman 'so far as I know exact t
his bargain,' and he added, 'I shall probably continu
with him after all, " keeping an eye on my partner," a
the Irish gentleman did, when dancing with a bear.'

Alexander Gilchrist and Joseph Neuberg divided betwee
them the supervision of the 16 volumes, so as to leave hi
" at leisure to go on with *Frederick* " as if there we
" nothing else to mind." But Carlyle desired to put index
in the new edition, and summaries also in many of th
volumes. So in May he wrote to Neuberg to help him
discover some fit and 'hireable' person, because '
grieves me often to think what slavery you have ha
without return or result, except an inward one, so to speak

As for the MSS. which he was now rereading in the ho
of making the opening volumes of the new book ready f
printing this autumn, he had to write,—'There is gre

misery and travail here about getting some beginning for Volume I actually ready for Printers : I spent yesterday looking over some of these unutterable Paper-masses. Not one word would suit, and I was not far from clearing my drawers, and delivering the whole abomination to the fire. However, I must have more patience, the thing requires to be done ' ; and he decided to allow himself the luxury of a horse, which Neuberg seems to have been advising, as a means of making Chelsea tolerable.

XXX

NEWS OF THE DAY
(1856)

O N 29.5.56 Mrs. Carlyle wrote in her diary :—' Palmer (a man who had poisoned his wife to get the insurance money), ' is convicted after a horridly interesting trial lasting twelve days. From first to last he has preserved the most wonderful coolness, forcing a certain admiration from one, murderer tho he be ! Mr. Barlow says,—" Nine-tenths of the misery of human life proceeds, according to *my* observation, from the Institution of Marriage ! " He should say from the demoralization, the desecration, of the Institution of marriage, and then I should cordially agree with him.'

On the same day there were fireworks in London to celebrate the peace with Russia ; and so Mrs. Carlyle ' Went, well muffled up, in a cab, to Bath House to see ' them ; and of course she took her husband and they spent the evening there with other habituals, such as the Taylors and the Brookfields. The women liked the show. The men did not. Carlyle compared it to " Parliamentary Eloquence," and agreed with Francis Baring who said, " Every rocket that goes up I think to myself,—' There goes half a crown.' " When Brookfield and he were looking on from the roof together, Carlyle remarked that it was ' all " Hell and Tommy." ' That had been Charles Buller's name for a picture on Macready's staircase, showing a funny figure " Tommy " in delirious surroundings.[1]

It may have been about the Crimean War that Carlyle was thinking when he said,—what might have been said in 1914,—" The British Public with its contagious enthusiasms reminds me of nothing so much as the Gadarene swine. There they are, quietly grubbing aud grunting in

[1] *Mrs. Brookfield and Her Circle*, by C. & F. Brookfield, II, p. 443, &c.

search of pignuts or other aliments, when suddenly the Devil enters into them, up go their tails into the sky, and away they go, plunging into bottomless abysses of delirium and confusion and nameless distraction."

It seems to have been in the early summer of 1856 that Alexander Gilchrist, a new next-door neighbour of the Carlyles, ' Called' on Carlyle about half-past three p.m.,' and found fashionable visitors there. His report of the talk is one of the best things he ever wrote.[2]

' Lady Stanley and her friend Miss Brown were there. They talked the usual small talk: about the Peace, the Naval Review, and so forth. Carlyle agreed with them in being glad of peace " on any terms." We couldn't fight. We were the handiest nation for others to fight with, except the Yankees. When he read of their blustering (Carlyle) thought to himself, " Well, I think you, at all events, are the handiest nation to fight with I know of; you, at all events, we can tackle." Opposition from the ladies, who thought the Americans had always beaten us; to which Carlyle dissented.

' Lady Stanley mentioned Montalembert, and his new book on England, as so good; and that he was fond of the English. What did Carlyle think?

' " Oh! I think him a very stupid fellow: I believe, too, there is a great deal of abuse of me: I have not read it."

' Reverting to the subject of the Naval Review, and what a muddle it had been, Lady Stanley said it was " not to be talked about except under the breath, but the Queen was the cause of the confusion, in not having chosen some other day—the previous day—and slept at the Isle of Wight."

' Carlyle: " Well, I suppose the Queen thought it was hard if she, of all her subjects, must choose a day which was inconvenient to her."

' Lady Stanley: " Oh! but the line was shut up by her going; and the greedy railway people took more passengers than they could accommodate."

' Carlyle: " I heard, drunken peers were seen about."

' Lady Stanley: " No; drunken stokers."

' Carlyle: " Ah! there was a good deal of spirituous liquor going."

[2] *Anne Gilchrist, Her Life and Writings*, by H. H. Gilchrist, pp. 55 and 59–62.

' Carlyle asked Miss Brown whether she was related by her ancestors to a Marshal Brown, an Irish Jacobite, and distinguished General in the Austrian service ? Carlyle mentioned that there were two Browns, Austrian Generals ; Marshal Brown the more celebrated. " A Life of him (French) in existence, which I have never seen. Cannot find out anything about him."

' Miss Brown didn't know ; he probably was related. One Brown (an ancestor) had offered the crown of Ireland ' to (another) ' family ; Miss Brown thinks he had been hung.

' " It was a hanging business, that." Carlyle ended by asking her to inquire into the history of the Browns ; it would oblige him much.

' When I first went in, the ladies were commending Carlyle's beard. " There is much to be said in favour of a beard,—I see them gradually appearing up and down the world," ' said Carlyle, and he ' admitted upright collars did not go well with them,—flat linen ones, which used to be worn with beards, were necessary.

' The pretty lady (Stanley) talked much with Mrs. Carlyle, next whom she sat ; Miss Brown with Carlyle.

' On leaving, the pretty lady coaxingly said to Carlyle,— " You will come to my Saturday evening ? Now don't screw up your mouth so ; you must say yes." (Lady Stanley speaking imperatively,)—" Say yes now ! " " Yes," (round and full), says Carlyle ; who then conducted them to the street door. " These illustrious people ! " he mutters, after they had left.'

It may have been not long afterwards that Alexander Gilchrist heard another memorable talk ' one evening at Cheyne Row.[2] We talked of rising from the ranks. Carlyle spoke of an old British officer, Colonel ' Smith, let us call him, instead of a ——, for Mr. Gilchrist concealed the name. This Colonel Smith ' had saved Head against his will from causing a rebellion in Canada.' That would be Sir Francis B. Head, Governor of Upper Canada, 1835–37. Colonel Smith ' had been promised rewards, but received none, except a small sum of money, and the being made a poor knight of Windsor. Buller was to have taken up the case, but died.

' Colonel Smith had been in debt ever since he held a commission, (and) fought in thirty battles ; a wonderful man ; simple-minded and good. Wrote a book on the teaching of children under ten ; those he considered the most important years of education. This soldier was cured of all doubts of immortality by a vision of Heaven he once had. All the colonel could remember was a high brass pillar, on which he saw his own face ! Looked down on earth and saw his wife weeping ; but it affected him not : life seemed too short to be considered. The Colonel had had eighteen children—nearly all died.'

" Is his wife living ? " was the natural query from Mr. Gilchrist or some other person present, and the answer was " No, she long was gone to look on the brass column." Mr. Gilchrist concludes,—' Carlyle laughed heartily ' at the brass column ' when telling this story.'

The first two volumes of Froude's *History of England* were published this year, and Espinasse reports that Carlyle said of it,[3]—" Meritorious, but too much raw material." The same reporter adds some things which may fall about this time.—John Stuart Mill presented to Carlyle his *Elements of Political Economy*, and tho contemptuous of the dismal science, Carlyle called it " a very clever book," and said that its complex treatment of the subject was like " extracting the cube root in Roman numerals. It could be done, but was not worth doing." He told Espinasse that formerly Mill used to come to him every Sunday for a walk. In conversation he used to insist on " having everything demonstrated." They were " agreed on one point, that if the Bible could be buried for a generation and then dug up again, it would in that case be rightly enjoyed." ' In those days,' says Espinasse,[3] ' Carlyle always spoke of Mill with a certain regard,' as if regretting ' that their active friendship had come to an end.'

The work continued " boiling," so to speak. Here is how he accepted an invitation to dinner on 7.6.1856, writing to Sir John Richardson.[4] . . . " It is needless to say what a wretchedly *dyspeptic* soul I am, bewildered too, and indeed quite *confiscated*, and buried among historical marine stores, and in fact called upon by the voice of reason to eschew and refuse all manner of Dinners ! The plain fact nevertheless is, we mean to *come* upon your summons. The voice of reason says one thing ; and that of Richardson, saying another, is the stronger," to say nothing of Mrs. Carlyle.

[3] *Literary Recollections,* by F. Espinasse, p. 218.
[4] From a Catalogue of Henry Sotheran & Co., Strand, &c., 1923, p. 43. "Autograph Letters." Sir John R., the famous Arctic explorer, lived near Alverstoke.

XXXI

IN SUMMER QUARTERS
(1856)

MRS. CARLYLE'S nervous weakness was at its worst this summer,—it was the time her husband called the *nadir* of her sufferings; and her temper was showing signs of wear and tear. Thus the beautiful and sensible Charlotte Williams Wynn appeared to her one day 'a dingle-doosie' or gadabout, literally, a bit of burning wood with which a nurse or a child makes circles in the air for amusement.

Even the Crimean warrior, Sir Colin Campbell, an old favourite and illustrious, could not please her now. He 'left me cold,' she confided to her journal one evening, 4th July. '"Simple" they call him. I don't believe it. He is (as) full of soft souder as an egg is full of meat.' Soft souder (pronounced sowder) used to mean in Scotch insincere and flattering patter. Souder means solder. Applied to speech, it means peace-making talk, but insincerity is always implied and so it is used contemptuously, and Campbell would have shuddered if he had known it was applied to him.

She went to "the most magnificent ball of the season," and told Mrs. Russell that when there she was thinking how much better she would have liked to see people making hay than all these ladies waltzing with bare shoulders 'in laces and diamonds.' When Lady Ashburton called to tell about how she and her husband were going to shooting-quarters in the Highlands this month, July, Mrs. Carlyle was sure to say to her what she was saying to others,— "Carlyle is hithering and thithering as usual. I cannot make any plans. I feel drawn to Scotland, but he cannot make up his mind,—no hope of his leaving London till August, the more's the pity."

On 19.7.56 Carlyle was writing to Lord Ashburton on the

theory of education, something worth consideration yet, and incidentally suggesting to him and Lady Ashburton to read what he would bring to them next day when he walked out to Addiscombe, a narrative of recent events in India, in the Deccan, and injustice done to a Brigadier Mackenzie there. About education Carlyle had learned from Goethe and his own experience a great deal still little understood among us, about the absurdity of Latin and Greek and the uses of practical education. Here is the first part of what he was writing to Ashburton.—

' In regard to Education, you have often heard me say (and yet perhaps you know not how serious I am) that the essence of all doctrine on the matter, the real summary of whatever I believe to be wisest on the subject, is set forth, symbolically, *not* unintelligibly, in Goethe's *Wilhelm Meister*. This is deeply my opinion, and has become ever more so, for the last five-and-twenty years or more. And continues to deepen, tho I cannot fairly get one human creature to share it ; in fact I believe it to be the very Gospel of the matter :—and in you, I must say, I find very many affinities to it, far more than I have done in any other person. The vain preaching I have had, and fruitless recommending of that doctrine to this and the other man of likelihood, is almost surprising to me ! Nobody *will* understand it ; for the sad reason, I believe, that nobody will give due meditation to it,—or has any *clear sky* in his mind for a quite new idea to print itself upon : *London Fog* is a far commoner material for minds ! Of whom there is no hope.'

Apparently Carlyle did not want to leave London this year. His work was moving forward rapidly, and by taking Neuberg's advice and buying a horse, he was able to get country air enough every day. But his wife was needing a change ; and Lady Ashburton, who was ill herself at the time, had never done a kindness more in season than now when she suggested,—" Come, both of you, with us to Edinburgh—there's abundance of room, no extra cost or trouble."

So after breakfast one morning about the last week of July they departed together from London in the Edinburgh express, in the ' great Railway-carriage called " the Queen's Saloon ",' which Ashburton had hired for his delicate wife.

" Here is Hinchinbrook," cried Lady Ashburton cheerily opening a door to tell the Carlyles as the train flew by the place,—the Hinchinbrook of the Cromwells and the Montagus. She was a Montagu herself.

They had to change carriages at Newcastle, but were " up to time " at Edinburgh. As Mrs. Carlyle wrote to Mrs. Russell of Thornhill a few days later, ' We staid (stayed) over night at a hotel (in Edinburgh) with the Ashburtons ; and then they went north, and I came over the water to Auchtertool,—Mr. Carlyle accompanying me, for a twenty-four hours' stay.

' Oh, mercy ! into what freshness and cleanness and kindness I have plumped here ! Out of the smoulder and din and artificiality of London. It has been like plumping down into a bed of rose-leaves with the dew on them. My cousins are so kind ! And the only thought that comes to spoil my enjoyment is, that I must go back to London some time,—cannot get staid (stayed) here for ever.' Leaving her happy there, Carlyle went ' after some days ' to live at " the Gill," his sister's farm on the Solway.

In spite of fictioneers and later peevish letters, there is proof that Mrs. Carlyle was at the time as grateful as she should have been to the " beneficent "[1] lady, who so well interposed to make a stay-at-home husband do what his wife wanted.[2]

At the Gill Carlyle was working steadily at *Frederick*, giving finishing touches to the first three volumes for the most part. In a letter to Neuberg, 13.8.56, he remarked :— ' You seem to have all the World and his Wife about you in those Pump-rooms at Kissingen : it ' i.e. reading your letters, ' is like reading the Gazette of a big sea-fight, while sitting far inland amid solitary bushes by a tinkling little brook.'

He can be seen through eyes that then were young,— those of the daughters of his sister Mrs. Austin, who by-and-by reported.[3]—

' He sauntered outside in the morning before breakfast, generally in the " loaning," a grassy path from the house into the fields. After breakfast at eight, he used to work in the sitting-room which was reserved for him till two o'clock. Then he went out either riding or walking for hours and returned to dinner about six. After dinner he

---

[1] Quoted from an unpublished letter from T. C. to J. Neuberg.
[2] *New Letters and Memorials of J. W. Carlyle*, by A. Carlyle, II, pp. 116-7 and footnote there.
[3] Statements of the Misses Austin at the Gill to D. A. W. on 15.8.1902.

took a nap, and then came tea and then another walk,
generally on the Priest-side sands, returning to supper.
Then came talking or reading aloud till bed-time.

' He avoided strangers calling in the afternoons. A
letter came from Mrs. Carlyle every day ; and once or
twice it failed to come and he was uneasy all the rest of
the day.'

He bathed whenever the tide suited, and was a familiar
figure in adjacent Cummertrees, where a boy who watched
him[4] remarked that when walking about he carried a
' heavy yellow stick.' He was ' quite erect and moved
about rapidly with an air of great decision. He stepped high
and had a faraway look, which was just like many of the
farmers, and so was his way of opening his mouth at times
to breathe ; but what was odd was that he seemed the
embodiment of will.'

At the Gill on this occasion, his evening reading for
pleasure when the rest were in bed was mainly Plato. As
he wrote to a brother, he found Plato ' nearly insupportable,
with definitioning and hair-splitting, tho there is a fine
high vein too in him, of magnanimous perception, humour,
godlike indignation veiled in silence, and other rare gifts.'
During three days he spent at Scotsbrig he re-read Suetonius,
a book which he had not seen for thirty years. On the
Sunday there, his brother James and he went to the grave-
yard at Ecclefechan, and stood with ' bared heads ' some
moments by the graves of their parents,—eyes wet but
nothing said. From the Gill he sometimes rode as far as
Dumfries, to see his sister Jean, Mrs. Aitken.

---

[4] Afterwards the Rev. Christopher Mc.Kune, parish minister of
Crawford, Lanarkshire, who in August, 1902, in the course of many talks,
told D. A. W. all he could remember.

XXXII

COMFORTING COVENTRY PATMORE
(1856)

FROM ' The Gill, Cummertrees, Annan ' Carlyle wrote twice this year to Coventry Patmore,[1] the British Museum Assistant Librarian, who was becoming distinguished for poetry, and had sent him what proved to be his most successful piece, " The Angel in the House." First on 31.7.56 :—' Last night I gave myself the pleasure of a deliberate perusal. Upon which, so favourable was the issue, I now give you the superfluous trouble of my verdict —prior to getting into the Solway for a little swim, the *sound* of which I also hear approaching.

' Certainly it is a beautiful little piece, nearly perfect in its kind,' and so on,—a very favourable verdict, but after much praise adding,—' The whole matter is an " ideal " soars high above reality, and leaves the mud of fact lying far under its feet. But this you will say is a merit, its poetic certificate—well, well.' The letter ends.—

' I am here in a kind of retreat for four or three weeks in the most silent country I could get, near my native Solway, and apart from all mankind,—really, a kind of Catholic " retreat " *minus* the invocations to the virgin &c. I am about 10 miles from my Birthplace, know all the mountain tops 50 miles round since my eyes first opened ; and I do not want for objects of a sufficiently *devotional* nature, sad and otherwise. But the " tide is in " : time and tide will wait on no man.'

A few days later (9.8.56) he wrote again, perhaps in reply to some desponding complaint about reviewers.— ' The Public of readers, now that everybody has taken to read, and whosoever has twopence in his pocket to pay into a circulating library, whether he have any fraction of

---

[1] Letters printed in the *Athenæum*, 17.7.86.

234

wit in his head or not, is a sovereign Rhadamanthus of Books for the time being, has become more astonishing than ever ! Probably there never was such a *Plebs* before, entitled to hold up its thumb with *vivat* or *pereat* to the poor fencers in the literary ring.—The only remedy is, not to mind them ; to set one's face against them like a flint : for they cannot kill one, after all, tho they think they do it ; one has to say, " Dull, impious *canaille*, it was not for you that I wrote ; not to please *you* that I was brandishing what weapons the gods gave me ! " Patience, too, in this world, is a very necessary element of victory. It is certain, if there is any perennial running Brook, were it the smallest rill coming from the eternal fountains, whole Atlantic Oceans of froth will not be able to cover it up for ever ; said rill will, one day, be *seen* running under the light of the sun, said froth having altogether vanished no man knows whither. That is the hand of Nature, in spite of all blusterings of any Plebs or Devil, and we must silently trust to that.

'Unhappily the reviewer too is generally in the exact ratio of the readers ; a dark blockhead with braggartism superadded, being a vocal one withal, and conscious of being *wise*. Him also we must leave to his fate : an inevitable phenomenon (" Like people like priest "), yet a transitory one too. . . . Recommending perseverance in the meantime and at all times ; and what the Scotch call " a stout heart to a steep hill," I remain always,

'Yours very sincerely,

'T. CARLYLE.'

XXXIII

ON CHASING THE DEER, &c.
(1856)

IN September Carlyle left for Kirkcaldy to meet his
wife; and on the way becomes visible to us through
the eyes of Sydney Dobell, a poet of the day, who was in
lodgings with his wife at Portobello, and wrote home :[1]—

'We spent some hours with Carlyle as he passed through
Edinburgh, and went as far as Granton with him on his
way to Fife. He declared he had been spending " the most
altogether blessed days he could remember, covered in
with solitude and silence." *All of his face that his moustache
and thick beard left bare had a ruddy health upon it which
contrasted pleasantly with his morbid London looks.*[2] You
should have seen the looks of the people in the train as he
rolled forth (swaying to and fro the while, with the restless-
ness of some wild creature), denunciations of railways,
nineteenth centuries, steam-engines, cheap literature,
" clever " people, and civilization generally. Tho of
course they had no notion of who he was, he gradually got
them into a sort of mesmeric possession that stilled every
voice but his own and stretched every eye. In the midst
of all this thunderous lava he was very kind and sweet to
us, and his last words to E ' (Emily, Mrs. Dobell) ' were
a spontaneous assurance that he should seek us out when
he returned from the north.'

From Kirkcaldy he went for a fortnight to Kinloch
Luichart, beyond Strathpeffer, where the Ashburtons had
a " hunting-seat," and Ashburton was glad to have his
company, and willing to listen patiently to a demonstration

---

[1] *Life and Letters of Sydney Dobell*, II, p. 33–4 : edited into accuracy
by omission, Mr. Dobell, apparently supposing in error that T. C. had
been born near "the moorlands" and had just come from living there
alone.   [2] Italics added.

hat he and the other English Grandees " a-chasing
he deer " were absurd. " The rat-catcher," said Carlyle,
" is the only real hunter in England."

By this time plentiful walking in all weathers had done
Carlyle much good. Tho the ' surly black mountains '
and lonely ' crags and bogs ' appeared to him ' not beautiful
at all,' the fertile parts of Scotland seemed more attractive
han ever in contrast with his home in Chelsea, on which
he smoke and noise of London were closing more and
more every year. The swift improvement in health on
coming north this summer, which his wife admitted she
felt herself, made him hope she might reconsider her
esolution to remain in London. In August he had been
writing to her about it :—

' I seem to be doing really excellently in regard to health.
What a change (*mostly* for the better) has been brought
about, since I escaped from that Devil's oven with its dirts
and noises.—The disgusting *dearth*[3] of London, the noise,
unwholesomeness, dirt, and fret of one's whole existence
here has often forced itself upon me when I look at this
frugality and these results. If I had done with those books
what more have I to do with that healthless, profitless, mad,
and heavy-laden place ? *I will really put it to you once more
to consider if it were not better we returned to poor old Scotland,*[2]
here to adjust ourselves a little, there to lay our bones, I
care not much in what part. Annandale is very sad to me,
and has no charm almost, except that Jamie would be here.
It is certain we might live here in opulence, keep brougham,
cow, minister's man, &c., and give our poor selves and
Nero a much wholesomer life, were those printing enterprises
once ended.'

Which he would hope to mean next year or the next
again at the farthest. The reference to Nero was Carlylean.
Indeed it is only in the country that a dog can have a
dog's life ; and if " Agrippina," as Lady Ashburton named
Nero's mistress, had heeded the needs of the four-footed
member of the family, she would have quitted London,
which she never once thought of doing. Her preference
was as fixed as Dr. Johnson's. What mattered the choice
he gave her ? Ayrshire or Fifeshire or the Lothians would
have been as dull as Dumfriesshire to Nero's mistress, and

---

[3] Meaning dearness or high prices,—a north country use of the word.

both he and her husband had to accept her will on th
matter. The new suggestion merely caused a little peevish
ness, which might perplex biographers and other outsiders
But that was all.

Before the end of August Mrs. Carlyle was reporting t
her husband how the noise of sundry cousins' babies ha
made Auchtertool cease to be ' like Paradise, as it was i
my first two weeks.' So she moved about on visits t
friends at Kirkcaldy and Haddington, Scotsbrig an
Thornhill, as well as Edinburgh, where she heard th
preaching of Dr. Guthrie,—' the very most eloquen
preacher I ever heard. Never was there such exquisit
artistic simplicity ! Never such gushing affluence of imagery
It reminded me of those god-daughters of good fairies i
my nursery tales, who every time they opened their blesse
mouths, '' pearls and rubies rolled out.'' But alas ! the
were the pearls and rubies of a dream ! One brought awa
none of them in one's pocket to buy a meal of meat with
if one happened to need one.' Besides, the church itsel
she declared to be ' overheated ' and ' just like one o
Soyer's patent stew-pans,' so that she caught a ' horri
cold ' there, and in short she ' never looked at eloquen
Guthrie again.' But, as she afterwards told Mrs. Russell
the cold she caught was merely ' a common cold ' and di
not last long, and except for it ' all the time I was in Scotlan
nothing ailed my health.' Her old friends and relative
welcomed her warmly, and made her promise to come bac
again soon.

XXXIV

OLD BETTY AND THE RELIGIOUS AUNTS
(1856)

NOBODY in Edinburgh, or almost anywhere else, was dearer to Mrs. Carlyle than " old Betty," alias Elizabeth Pringle,[1] Mrs. Braid, an old woman of 66, who now kept a little shop there to supplement the earnings of her husband, a mason. Their only son was now a helpless paralytic and a burden. In 1815 Betty had gone as a young woman of 25[1] to be a general servant to Mrs. Carlyle's parents, Dr. and Mrs. Welsh, when their daughter Jeannie was a girl of 14. Jeannie grew up beside Betty, and never lost touch with her. She married Braid as Jeannie married Carlyle, but they were always Jeannie and Betty to each other. Mrs. Carlyle clung to her all the more when her mother died, and not only visited Betty often when in Edinburgh, but also made her husband visit her, and such friends as the good St. Thomas (Erskine, of Linlathen), who used to call upon Betty and report to Cheyne Row how she was, to save Betty the trouble of writing.

So Betty was the first to be told the funny story of the graceless breakfast. It was on the morning of Friday, 22.8.56, at the house (" Craigenvilla," in Morningside, Edinburgh) of three old maiden aunts, sisters of Dr. Welsh, where Mrs. Carlyle was staying,—the same three old aunts who were always sending her tracts. " Two of them were members of Dr. Candlish's congregation," reports Major Davidson who called at Cheyne Row in 1855,[2] " and, being their elder, I had frequent and pleasant intercourse with all

---

[1] Notes of the late R. H. Shepherd, author of a good book, *Memoirs of Thomas Carlyle*, 2 vols., 1881. These Notes are in MS. and in bound volumes containing cuttings from newspapers and magazines and copies of unpublished letters, &c., relating to Thomas Carlyle, prepared by Mr. Shepherd for C. Oscar Gridley, a Trustee of the Carlyle House Trust, who kindly lent them to D. A. W.

[2] *Memories of a Long Life*, by Col. Davidson, p. 334.

three. They kept up a correspondence with Mrs. Carlyle, and she occasionally visited them, but she did not fall in readily with their religious views and habits."

Assuredly she did not ! Some years before that they had received her with unexpected warmth and she wrote to her husband :—' My heart was opened by their kindness to tell them that it was nothing but apprehension of their bothering me about my soul, which had estranged me from them so entirely. Anne's reply, given with an arch look and tone, was very nice,—" Indeed, Jeannie, you need not have been afraid of our setting ourselves to reform you it is plain enough that nothing short of God's own grace can do that, but I won't despair that a time may come tho I am not such a fool as to think that I can hasten it."

On this memorable morning of the graceless breakfast Mrs. Carlyle received a letter from Cheyne Row as she was coming downstairs, and began to read it at table. Now Aunt Anne was in Dumfriesshire, and a letter from her was handed to Aunt Grace, who began to read it too, and Aunt Elizabeth was also interested, perhaps listening to news ; and Mrs. Carlyle absent-mindedly sipped her tea and took a bite from her soda-scone as she read, when suddenly Grace shrieked out like a madwoman,—" Mercy We have forgotten the blessing ! " Mrs. Carlyle told her husband that ' I started on my chair, and dropped the morsel out of my mouth, into my hand, till I should see what steps were to be taken for making our peace. But the case was judged past remedy, and the breakfast allowed to proceed unblessed.'

When she was talking to Betty ' regretting that my aunts should live in such a fuss of religion,' " My dear," said Betty, " they are idle, plenty to live on, and noch (nothing) to do for't ; *they micht ha'e ta'en to waur* " (*they might have taken to worse*) ; " so we maun thole them an no' compleen," (we must endure them and not complain) Whereon Carlyle commented :—' " They might have taken to waur," wise Betty ! This was never forgotten.' It well deserved to be remembered,—it gives Betty a place in literature.

Mrs. Carlyle and her husband returned home together on 4.10.56.

BOOK XXIII
PORTRAYING EUROPE
1856–59

I

THE PLAGUE OF BUGS
(1856)

ONE of the best of Mrs. Carlyle's maids, a clever woman
who afterwards managed successfully for many years
a country hotel,[1] declared that Mrs. Carlyle exaggerated
everything in talking or writing for the fun of the thing,
and was like a petted and spoiled child all her life. Bearing
this in mind, let us look into a letter she wrote to Mrs.
Russell on 10.10.56, a few days after reaching home.

She had enjoyed her visit to Scotland. ' A doctor's
prescription for me long ago, that I " should be kept always
happy and tranquil," had got itself carried into effect for
ten whole weeks, and was found an efficacy. But I arrived
here with a furious face-ache, Mr. C. having insisted on my
sitting in a violent draught all the journey,'—which may
mean only that he had kept a window slightly open for
ventilation,—' and so I began to be ill at once,' and have
been growing worse. ' Figure this : (Scene—a room where
everything is enveloped in dark-yellow London fog ! For
air to breathe, a sort of liquid soot ! Breakfast on the
table—" adulterated coffee," " adulterated bread," " adulterated cream," and " adulterated water ! ") Mr. C. at one
end of the table, looking remarkably bilious ; Mrs. C. at the
other, looking half dead ! Mr. C. : " My dear, I have to inform
you that my bed is full of bugs, or fleas, or some sort of
animals that crawl over me all night ! " Now I must tell
you, Mr. C. had written to me, at Auchtertool, to " write
emphatically to Anne about keeping all the windows open ;
for with her horror of fresh air, she was quite capable of
having the house full of bugs when we returned " ; and so
I imputed this announcement to one of those fixed ideas that

---

[1] Jessie Hiddlestone, afterwards Mrs. Broadfoot of Thornhill. She
was in the house in 1865–66, and D. A. W. was acquainted with her in
her old age.

men, and especially husbands, are apt to take up, just out of sheer love of worrying ! Living in a universe of bugs outside, I had entirely ceased to fear them in my own house, having kept it so many years perfectly clean from all such abominations.' She clearly implies she had not written to Anne as requested, and goes on :—' I answered (him) with merely a sarcastic shrug, that was no doubt very ill-timed under the circumstances, and which drew on me no end of what the Germans call *Kraftspruche !* ' Or plain language enough to show he would not take her word for the absence of bugs. 'But,' she wrote, 'clearly the practical thing to be done was to go and examine his bed—and I am practical, *moi !* So, instead of getting into a controversy that had no basis, I proceeded to toss over his blankets and pillows, with a certain sense of injury !' She soon found bugs 'enough,' she wrote, ' to make me put on my bonnet and rush out wildly, in the black rain, to hunt up a certain trustworthy carpenter to come and take down the bed. The next three days I seemed to be in the thick of a domestic Balaklava,' and Anne for her part, instead of repenting her carelessness, was 'indignant that the house should be turned up after she had " settled it," and that " such a fuss should be made about bugs, which are inevitable in London ! " ' " It is to be hoped," said she, " you will get a person to keep your house cleaner than I have done, as I mean to leave this day month." " Very good," replied Mrs. Carlyle ; but when the bugs had been abolished, Anne did not go, tho for some days she had let her mistress suppose she would. To return to the letter.—

' Oh, my darling,' Mrs. Russell is told, ' I wish you were here to give me a kiss, and cheer me up a bit with your soft voice ! In cases of this sort, Geraldine (Jewsbury) with the best intentions is no help. She is unpractical, like all women of genius ! She was so pleased with your letter ! " My dear," she said to me, " how is it that women who don't write books write always so much nicer letters than those who do ? " I told her it was, I supposed, because they did not write in the " Valley of the shadow " of their future biographer, but wrote what they had to say frankly and naturally.' Which is the charm of Mrs. Carlyle's own letters.

II

WILLIAM KNIGHTON'S NOTES
(1856)

WILLIAM KNIGHTON was a notable Anglo-Indian in his day, one of the handful of good men who make the conquest of India by the English less of a horror than the other conquests once familiar there. In 1856 he was at home on furlough, and ' for many months,'[1] he said, spent an evening every week with Carlyle. ' Our wives too became great friends.'

In 1854 he had published *Forest Life in Ceylon*,—an excellent book about the island ; and in 1855 his *Private Life of an Eastern King* showed what could be seen by a quick-sighted courtier at Lucknow, attending his Majesty Nasir-ud-Deen, the King of Oude. The presence of the Resident and the Company's troops made Knighton and other Englishmen there secure from sudden death, and so able to observe with coolness. His book is not one of the official documents, which are of many colours but all shady, and for that very reason it is all the better evidence.

He was now a genial and sensible man in the prime of life, full of knowledge of faraway men and manners, and always welcome at Cheyne Row. The notes he gives us are jottings made at the time for remembrance, and naturally omit his own good stories, such as curious readers may guess from his books.[1] It was a happy inspiration to print his notes in 1881 unaltered. Perhaps nothing published then was a more undeniable addition to permanent literature. With thanks to him and to the editors of the *Contemporary Review*, let us read and try to see inside the house in Cheyne Row.—

' 22.10.1856. My wife and I spent the evening, 8 to 11, with Mr. and Mrs. Carlyle. Miss Jewsbury there, and an

[1] *Conversations with Carlyle*, by William Knighton, *Contemporary Review*, June, 1881. See also the same author's *Struggles for Life*, (1886), p. 286, note.

Oxford Commissioner and his wife—" intelligent people,"
as Carlyle called them. We had tea. The Commissioner
handed the kettle for Mrs. Carlyle.'

C.—" I had some men to make a room for me on the top
of my house. They used bad timber—did not know their
work—came tumbling through the roof often into the other
rooms at the top—workmen complained of the master—
the master of the workmen—everything done in the same
way nowadays—an age of shams—shams in religion, in
social life, in politics. It was the same two hundred years
ago, it was all sham, and the people that would not have
shams, the earnest thinking men, rose and swore it should
not be so any longer—they would cut each other's throats
for it, if need were, but the shams they would not endure."

K—" If everyone thought so now, we should have another
revolution."

C.—" *That's exactly what we do want*—a thorough revolution ;
but not a revolution after the French model—a quiet, peaceful,
sensible revolution. But I see no help for these times—they
must just go to perdition their own way, and then——"

K.—" And then ? "

C.—" And then revolutions and misgovernment in
cycles—in eternal cycles, so far as I can see."

The subject changed to literary men :—

C.—" The most contemptible man of the day is the
literary man—the honest shoe-black is a more respectable
and useful citizen. If I knew of any young man going to
devote himself entirely to literature as a profession, I should
say ' For God's sake, sir, stop, don't ; be an honest, useful
man any other way. You never will be *that* way.' Men
write without thinking nowadays. Everyone thinks he can
write—that's all the thinking many do. Even history is
written without research."

' The subject changed. The Oxford Commissioner spoke
of the dogs of Constantinople ' :—

C.—" Strange the bad name the dog has got ; yet he is
the most respectable of all the animal creation we come in
contact with——"

K.—" Except the horse——"

C.—" No, not even excepting the horse. ' Is thy servant
a dead dog that he should do this thing ? ' "

Mrs. C.—" Not a *dead* dog, Carlyle—' Is thy servant a
dog ? ' "

C.—" Dead dog occurs somewhere as the vilest of things

—very odd—perhaps because they are scavengers in the East ; in some cases, the only scavengers."

' The quotation introduced the subject of the Hebrew Scriptures. C. spoke warmly in praise of their sublimity and beauty. " Homer comes next—the next book to the Bible for everything grand and great ; and yet how tiresome parts of both are. Take the combats in Homer—one man gets a spear run through him one way, another another way. Men we heard nothing of before, and never shall hear of again—very tiresome. The Odyssey, written by a different hand, a younger man, in a more artificial age—a finer poem in many respects than the Iliad. Nothing finer than Ulysses bending his bow on those who were eating his substance, and shouting out, stentor-like, ' Ye dogs '—the dog again, poor fellow ! The Iliad, evidently a collection of ballads by one hand, with interpolations, etc., of a later age. ' Robin Hood's Garland ' similar. The simplicity—the grand simplicity of it ! The epithets applied to different men very strange. One fellow has nothing to distinguish him but well-fitting boots. Only think of calling a man ' the well-booted '—' the well-booted Knighton,' for instance, ha ! ha ! ha ! "

' Spoke of Thirlwall's *Greece*.

C.—" Thirlwall so hedges himself in with qualifications and *ifs* and *buts*. He takes you a little one way, and then says, ' Stop, turn back with me so far ; perhaps that's the way, but So-and-so thinks differently ' ; and so on. *It spoils a man to make a bishop of him*." ' Indeed it used to be said of Thirlwall that he was like Lord Eldon, he exercised his ingenuity to evade a decision of the question. Mr. Knighton goes on.—

' The Commissioner mentioned a Dean who would probably have been a bishop had he not spoken of the " extraordinary conduct of Judas Iscariot."

' Carlyle laughed long and loudly. " The extraordinary conduct ! Very good ! ' Conduct not to be expected from any gentleman,' he might have added. Was it the same man who always spoke of the crucifixion as ' the execution of Jesus Christ ' ? But the ' extraordinary conduct of Judas Iscariot ' was far better."

' Got back to Greece :—

C.—" Plato is too inconclusive for me ; his fancy is wonderful and his language polished, but he is the most inconclusive of great writers. I have no patience with him.

His *Republic* is the best of his works by far. With what
disdain he speaks of the great unwashed and their blatant
democracies ! It is a pity we have no readable literal translations of Sophocles and Æschylus. I was looking at an
English translation of Æschylus the other day, and I had
to turn to the Greek to see what the man meant."

K.—" Why not have the works turned neatly into blank
verse, without sacrificing the original ? "

C.—" No, no—no blank verse. I would say to the trans-
lator—' Give me Sophocles, give me Æschylus ; I don't
want your silly poesy. I want to know what those men,
in their wisdom, thought and wrote ; not what you, in your
folly, think and write.' Such works, properly done, ought
to be very popular, for England sympathises with ancient
Greece, and the great men of ancient Greece." '

(Hereabout may be placed a note of Mr. Knighton's not
dated :—)

' It was amusing to see how impatient he was of correction from his wife, and yet he would take correction from
mine like a lamb. He was talking on one occasion with a
distinguished nobleman about Herat. He pronounced it
wrongly, Hĕrat. My wife was an attentive listener. I was
conversing with Mrs. Carlyle about a paper of mine that
had recently appeared in *Household Words*, on " The Buried
City of Ceylon," when I heard Carlyle say to my wife,
" You seem interested in our conversation."

' " I cannot quite make out what city you are talking
about," said she.

' " Why, do you not know Hĕrat, on the western confines
of Afghanistan and the eastern of Persia, that diplomatists
are so much interested in just now ? "

' " Oh, you mean Herāt," said she, " that's quite a
different thing. Nobody calls it Hĕrat."

' He accepted the correction without a murmur, and for
the rest of the evening spoke of the city as Herāt.

' On another occasion he quoted wrongly from the Bible :
" Is thy servant a dead dog to do this thing ? " " It is
not a *dead* dog, Carlyle," said his wife—she spoke with a
burr on the r, *Car*lyle ; " it is not a dead dog, Carlyle, but
a dog,—' Is thy servant a dog to do this thing ? ' " Carlyle
heard her patiently to the end, and a little after took occasion to repeat his misquotation quite gravely : " Is thy
servant a dead dog to do this thing ? " His wife, like a
prudent woman, did not hear it.'

III

A THIEF IN THE HOUSE
(1856)

FOR the next seven months Carlyle was to be working steadily,—' like to a star, that maketh not haste and taketh not rest,'—he was shaping for the printer the MSS. of the first two volumes of *Frederick ;* and then for 13 months longer, he was reshaping proofs.   His life till June, 1858, is in these two volumes, as the Spaniard's soul was in the bag of doubloons.

In October, 1856, the Ashburtons left for Nice, anticipating nothing but a pleasant winter, and about the same time Carlyle bought a bay horse, Fritz, which was to be his almost daily companion, in all weathers and seasons, for many a year.   To buy a horse in England without being cheated is a rare feat, and in doing it he was assisted by Neuberg and Robert Farie.[1]   This Farie was a Scottish gentleman ' of means ' who was idle in London, and much about their house, ' a great admirer of Mrs. Carlyle,' says Espinasse.   He translated Goethe's *Campaign in France ;* and renewing acquaintance with the book for his sake, Carlyle laughed heartily at Goethe for " peering into nature,"—when fascinated in crossing a stream by a piece of crockery in the water glittering in the sunbeams.

Carlyle was making a sadder mistake himself this October, esteeming " almost like monitions of Providence " his success in getting a horse and a good clerk.   The horse was all right, but the clerk was the would-be Judas of this history.

He called himself Frederick Martin ; and had been bred in Berlin, a blend of Jew and Slav by blood.   Being a teacher in a provincial town in England, serving under one he called a " vulgar-minded usher," he wrote without any introduction to Carlyle to beg advice as a stranger.   He

---

[1] Named in an unpublished Neuberg letter ; and see also *Literary Recollections*, by F. Espinasse, pp. 235–7.

wanted to come to London ; but was exhorted to stay where he was, and " rather . . . carry on his provincial engagements . . . under all disadvantages." He presented himself in person nevertheless ; and seemed a " cultivated " man of " gentlemanly " manners. When advised to go back, he went or pretended to do so, but soon was again in London, declaring it " impossible " to continue where he had been. A wife and one or two children were depending on him.

Many an exile had Carlyle befriended ; and since 1853 he had been saving for some such emergency some quasi-mechanical research work, and copying of French and German extracts in the British Museum. He grudged to see Neuberg doing mechanical work, and preferred to pay for it, especially when he could help a deserving scholar in difficulties. Martin was excellent at French and German. Besides the Museum work, there was now a great deal of copying to be done for the printers ; and so Martin was tried at English, but " made nonsense " of it. " Wagner " was Carlyle's name for him in Letters to Neuberg, which gives readers of Faust a clue to what he thought of him ; and once there was an express reference to him as " my imbecile clerk."[2]

" Your words and style are so peculiar," said " Wagner," defending himself to Carlyle. He was a small man ' of peculiarly servile demeanour,' say those who knew him then, ' continually bewailing his lot,' so that Espinasse heard Carlyle allude to him as the " peesweep " or lapwing. He snivelled a good deal, a frequent drop depending from his nose, which made him unpleasant close at hand to Carlyle, whose senses were acute. So " Wagner " was readily allowed to take papers home to copy ; which gave him access to where papers were kept and possession of MSS. in his own house, whereby he was gradually able to steal a great many, becoming cunning in choosing what would not be missed. He stole a great deal of the *Frederick* MSS. by merely omitting to return it. He also abstracted from drawers hundreds of old letters and other papers. Many have not yet been published ; some have, such as *The Reminiscences of My Irish Journey* in 1849, *Last Words of Thomas Carlyle, including Wotton Reinfred* (Longmans, 1892), and many letters. What made stealing easy was

² *New Letters and Memorials of J. W. Carlyle*, by A. Carlyle and Sir James Crichton-Browne, II. p. 143.

hat Carlyle in his modesty little suspected that there was
any money value in these things. " Wagner " had the eye
of the hereditary old clothesman for unconsidered trifles ;
and Neuberg was busy this winter with his sister's affairs.
She had lost her husband, and he made a home for her and
her children.

Carlyle was anxious to trouble him as little as possible,
and told him merely to mark with pencil for " Wagner " to
copy whatever he thought fit. The fellow's opportunity
was brief, but he made the most of it.[3] We will see him
again.

[3] Francis Espinasse and J. T. Wells, who was for many years a missionary in Edinburgh, described F. Martin to D. A. W. from personal know-
edge ; and see Espinasse's *Literary Recollections*, pp. 260–3, and the
Autobiography of Moncure D. Conway, II, Chapter L, pp. 370–5. In
895 an honest bookseller in Edinburgh showed D. A. W. a collection of
C. C. letters he had bought and wished to sell for £70. He allowed them
all to be read and shown to David Masson and others, on receiving a
promise to do nothing to lessen the selling value. We all agreed that
these were documents probably stolen by Frederick Martin. Neither
Ballantyne nor Neuberg nor Larkin had anything to do with the stolen
MSS.

IV

MORE OF KNIGHTON'S NOTES, &c.
(1856)

IN November the notes of William Knighton give us another look inside the busy house in Cheyne Row.[1]—

'Nov. 28, 1856.—Spent the evening with Mr. and Mrs. Carlyle at 5, Cheyne Row, Chelsea. Had tea when we went in. Mrs. C. in cap and shawl—an invalid. C. in dressing-gown.'

K.—" The magazines and reviews have been very busy with you lately, sir."

C.—" Ay, have they? I never read them. I have the most utter contempt and abhorrence for the literary *canaille* of the day, with their Reviews, and Magazines, and *Times* newspaper. They should try and understand me—that would be more sensible. And what have they been saying? '

K.—" The *North British Review* had an excellent article as I thought it, on ' The Religious Tendencies of the Day —Newman, Coleridge, and Carlyle,' endeavouring to point out what they believe to be your influence on religious questions in the world. One of Ainsworth's Magazines— *Bentley* or the *New Monthly*—has an article this month too about you, but solely as a literary man—a poor article—all about your style, which is not to their liking."

C.—" Blind leaders of the blind! How shall they understand me with their devotion to the devil? Give me a God-fearing man and a God-believing man, and that man will understand me; but your Ainsworth's Magazines are only a part of that awful system of cant and lying that sweeps England to perdition in these days. Where there is no truth, there can be no utterances worth listening to. Some of these reviewers remind me of men accumulating first laboriously a heap of refuse, and then proceeding diligently

[1] See Note [1], Chapter II.

o examine it and grope in it for novelties. That's the
work that befits them, believe me. I care nothing what
hey say of me or to me."

Mrs. C.—" Some time ago a clergyman sent him an essay
—a voluminous essay in MS. We were sitting together
when he got it, and he read the first sentence, something
after this manner : ' Sir, I have a great respect for you.
You are drawing on towards the brink of the grave. Age
is creeping over you. It behoves you to think of another
world and of religion.' He read no more, but, getting up,
put the whole mass of writing into the fire there, and
watched it consume. I pitied the poor man who had taken
so much trouble in vain—to say that his laborious composition should not even be read ! "

C.—" Ha, ha, ha !—ha, ha, ha, ! O yes, they will send
me such things ; but they cannot make me read them.
Ha, ha, ha ! "

Mrs. C.—" We have been greatly amused with a book of
Mr. Charles Reade's, *It is Never Too Late to Mend*. Mr.
Reade has evidently adopted, unconsciously I suppose,
Carlyle's style and mannerism—completely so—and yet the
views of the two men are so widely dissimilar—as opposite
as possible to each other, in fact. It is a stupid book—a
very stupid book : the author sympathises with criminals
and such-like, all which Mr. Carlyle and I hold in abhorrence."

C.—" That sympathy with criminals, and convicts, and
ticket-of-leave men is just one of the worst symptoms of the
age in which we live. But it is not to be wondered at that
men, with no sincerity about themselves, should do their
best for their brethren, the children of the Devil. If they
had any real abhorrence of the crime, they would fling their
mawkish sympathy to the winds. They don't see, they
never will see, that men who act so are like unto those they
succour. The one is the liar, with dirty linen, living in a
prison—the other is the liar, with clean linen, living in his
own house."

K.—" The ticket-of-leave system sometimes leads to
crimes in our very streets. What is the use of prisons, one
may ask, if the people that ought to be in them are jostling
us at every corner ? "

C.—" The people that ought to be in them ! Ha, ha,
ha ! "—(a loud, hearty, honest laugh)—" they would be large
prisons that would hold all that ought to be in them. Had
these sympathisers any conscientious abhorrence of crime,

they would say to the criminal, ' Out of my sight, villain
Go away with you to your father, the devil.' They do no
see that their sympathy with these wretches only prove
they are convinced of the fact that it is accident, as we ca
it, that prevents them taking the other's place. The resul
of all this, and of all our hollowness and deceit, and want o
faith and godliness, is that we are rushing on to ruin—al
our English and American agitations and democracies not
withstanding. I have no faith in these democracies, or i
(such) republics at all. Things may last so for fifty years
perhaps, not longer, certainly."

K.—" Is there no native energy in the English race t
prevent this ? Have we not men of genius to lead us in a
great abundance as ever ? "

C.—" Yes, I think we have as many men of genius, a
much talent ; but that will not save us, as things go. Ou
talent is all directed to talking and writing, instead o
doing."

K.—" The age of Elizabeth was a heroic age : yet ther
was much writing then, too, although not quite so mucl
talking."

C.—" No nation was ever saved by writing and talking
only by acting. It was the great ages before Elizabeth
and the great men in those ages, who prepared the way fo
the achievements of the reign of Elizabeth. England ha
been held ever since the Norman Conquest, and long before
by a superior race ; but for a thousand years they wer
doers simply, not talkers and writers. Compare Domesday
Book with our modern Blue-Books and Parliamentary Com
mittee's Reports and such-like, that nobody reads or ca
read. This very Chelsea is described in that Domesday
Book as a *sylva sexaginta porcorum* (a wood of sixty swine)
It could feed just sixty swine, and a fellow in a leathe
jerkin, with a horn to look after them, and make pudding
of them. Two lines of such a book teach us more than whol
volumes of frothy Blue-Books."

K.—" Yet our Parliament contains some of the cleveres
men, and our aristocracy, as a class, is a noble and superio
race."

C.—" So far as my experience goes, the best of actua
men in England—infinitely better that aristocracy, tha
the talking and writing lawyers and editors, and unbelievin
divines."

K.—" And yet no hope for England ? "

C.—" None ; *for a hundred years we have been going down-hill fast,* losing faith and hope. *What kind of a boy is this that is to be our King of England next ? The German race we have imported from the Continent has been a heavy, stupid race. Prince Albert is an exception.* He looks forward, I think, and is preparing for what he foresees—that those boys of his will live in troublesome times ; but he cannot say so, of course."

' There was a pause, and we talked afterwards of Ceylon and Buddhism. He said there was doubtless much in that old creed if we could get at it ; but the men who had translated hitherto were utterly incompetent for their task, giving us, for the most part, words and not ideas. Sir Arthur Buller, one of his old pupils, had told him the Singhalese '—the natives of Ceylon,—' were incorrigible liars.

' I mentioned their belief in transmigration and its effects. One man committed suicide to escape the pain of a tooth-ache, another to get rid of a whitlow, concluding, " all over the East man seems more earnest in religion than in the West." '

An anecdote may here be intercalated to confirm Mr. Knighton.[2] A judge at Colombo had sentenced a native Singhalese to death, and was immediately answered by the man condemned, breaking the solemn silence in a clear and composed voice :—" Hanged I suppose I will be, as you order it, but this I promise you,—I'll be a dog in the next life, and I'll go mad, and the first person I'll bite shall be you, assuredly." The words were duly translated into English before the prisoner was removed.

Carlyle agreed with Knighton at once and said :—" True, very true. The only great outburst we have had of true faith within the last two centuries in Europe was Methodism ; but, in our own time, it is like the rest, hollow and false—utterly untrue."

K.—" I have seen some, sir, that were as devoted to their creed—some Methodists—as any devotees of the East."

C.—" Exceptions. I heard one of the best of them at Derby once. He had been a joiner, I believe, and he spoke earnestly. That man saw before him, in the other world, two states of existence—the one that in which he would be roasted everlastingly, the other that in which he would

[2] Told to D. A. W. in the nineties by a retired magistrate who had served long in Colombo and probably heard it from the judge, and was sure to be accurate.

float everlastingly in bliss of some kind. ' It is of infinite importance to me,' said he to himself, ' that I should not roast everlastingly ' ; and hence his speeches and his rantings, his violent sayings, and his Methodistical cant. But truly, anything more despicable, anything more un-worthy of an honest, noble soul, we could not easily find anywhere than that. It is the rankest flunkeyism, yet that is enthusiastic Methodism in these days."

K.—" I believe it is ; I never heard it so put before ; but, honestly and candidly, I think it is, and I have seen much of Methodism. I startled one of their preachers once, in Ceylon, by showing him the word Methodeia, a trick or imposture, in the Greek lexicon, as the derivation of the word ' methodism.' "

C.—" Good, very good. He was dumbfounded at that, I should think. Ha, ha, ha ! But the word doesn't come from that, does it ? It *looks* like it."

K.—" No, I believe now that it comes from our own word method. Wesley, at Oxford, originated both the appellation and the schism with his prayer-meetings."

C.—" I was going to tell you about an Indian poem some-one sent me translated, when you led me off to Methodism. I think it is called the Mahabharata. It describes seven sons as setting off to seek their fortunes. They all go different ways, and six of them land in Hell, after many adventures. The seventh is of nobler seed. He perseveres, fights his way manfully through great trials. His faithful dog, an ugly little monster, but very faithful, dies at last. He himself, fainting and wellnigh despairing, meets an old man, Indra disguised, who offers to open for him the gates of Heaven. ' But where are my brothers ? ' he asks ; ' are they there ? ' ' No ; they are all in Hell.' ' Then I will go to Hell, too, and stop with them, unless you get them out.' So saying, he turns off and trudges away. Indra pities him, and gets his brethren out of Hell. The six enter Heaven first. The seventh stops. ' My poor faithful dog,' says he, ' I will not leave him.' Indra remonstrates, but it is useless ; the faithful dog, ugly as he was, is too well remembered, and he will not have Paradise without it. He succeeds finally. Indra relents, and lets even the dog in ; but, sir, there is more pathos about that dog than in a thousand of our modern novels—pathos enough to make a man sit down and cry almost."

K.—" The whole story must have been intended to

lustrate the efficacy of prayer.   It reminds one faintly of
Abraham's intercession for Sodom and Gomorrah—a grand
ld picture, not inferior on the whole, I should think, to
ours of the Mahabharata."

C.—" Lot's intercession, you mean."

K.—" No, Abraham's.   Lot was living in the vale at the
ime, in Sodom."[3]

C.—" Lot certainly interceded for some one.[4]   However,
t is a point of little consequence.   As I said, sir, there is
rue pathos about that dog.   I have seldom read anything
vith more."

Knighton was right.   Abraham it was who interceded for
Sodom and Gomorrah, and Lot only for a convenient place
of refuge for himself, saying, " This city, is it not a *little*
one ? "   So it was spared and called " the little one," i.e.
Zoar.

It might be after Knighton's departure, at any rate it was
on 28.11.1856, that Carlyle wrote this reply to a young woman
who had asked him where she could find materials for the
tudy of Mirabeau and Napoleon.[5]

' You will find done by me somewhere a short essay on
Mirabeau and his life, but I never wrote anything specially
on Napoleon.

' On the whole I do not much advise at this stage of your
culture an extensive prosecution of your inquiries into either
of these personages.   The first, with all his great gifts, is
airly definable from the other side as a mutinous, dissolute
Blackguard, set on a high place.

' The second has a great deal of the Play-actor-turned-
Pirate in his character and history, an immense Gambler à
a Dick Turpin ;   who, after all his huge reckless bettings,
and enormous temporary successes (more astonishing to the
oolish than to the wise), ended by losing his last guinea,
and by being flung out of the room head foremost.

' There is another kind of heroes to be heard tell of in
history, whom I would much rather recommend to an ingenuous young soul seeking after what is great and noble.'

[3] Genesis xviii. 16–33.   [4] Genesis xix. 15-22.
[5] London morning and evening papers, 29.4.1922, the original being
advertised for sale by auction on May 12.

S

V

HENRY LARKIN BEGINS MAKING INDEXES, &c
(1856–57)

IN December, 1856, Henry Larkin was in London, a
collector or cashier on the Chelsea steamers, with hi
evenings free ; and heard that while Carlyle was busy o
Frederick, the new collected edition of his works was needin
indexes. He volunteered to do them and was asked to te
one Tuesday (16.12.56),—" at 7½ o'clock : if I hear nothin
from you, let us expect you then for an hour and a half."

' In the drawing-room,' Larkin reports,[1] ' Mrs. Carlyle
sitting at needlework by a small table, rose to receive me
She was very kind, but reserved, and looked sorrowful
and in short both ill and depressed.

" Mr. Carlyle will be down presently," said she, " bu
has not yet finished his afternoon sleep. He always take
a long sleep before tea, and then complains that he ca
get no sleep at night."

While Larkin was ' still wondering at this strange recep
tion,' Carlyle entered and ' bowed ceremoniously ' an
' shook hands.' The tea went on, but never a word wa
said about indexes. Nine o'clock arrived and Larkin ros
to go. Carlyle bade him be seated,—" There is no need t
hurry away. I always go out for a walk before bed, an
will walk out with you." Mrs. Carlyle joining in thi
Larkin resumed his seat, ' considerably more at ease,' an
the talk dribbled on, with occasional remarks from her bu
nothing to report, till Carlyle mentioned indexes, which th
visitor ' had been waiting for him to refer to,' and now h
declares, ' for the first time I felt that I saw Carlyle himself

On Larkin saying, " I prefer serving you in silence t
any writing I can do," Carlyle told him the lives of Sterlin
and Schiller were the first requiring attention ;—" a sum
mary of each chapter and an index of both."

" If you find yourself fit for the work and the work fi
for you," said Carlyle, " I can at least promise you enoug
of it. But one absolute condition is that I myself am no
to be worried about it, my thoughts being entirely absorbe
in other work. In short, superfluous talk, including writin
is on all occasions, the one thing to be avoided."

So saying, ' he handed me the books,' reports Larki

---

[1] *Carlyle and Mrs. Carlyle,* by Henry Larkin, *British Quarterly Revie*
July, 1881, No. 147, pp. 32–9.

' and at eleven o'clock instead of nine we went out together. He walked with me a mile or more on my road, talking in a kind, fatherly way, which sent me home gratefully triumphant.'

Three days later, 19.12.56, Carlyle received a letter from Lord Ashburton at Nice, reporting news of Lady Ashburton more ominous than either the writer or addressee then supposed. She was ' on the invalid list,' and alluding to that Carlyle wrote to him on 20.12.56,—' I suppose I need not say how glad I shall be to hear your favourable report on that evil matter confirm itself into the certainty you now seem to anticipate! It was of you always that one was in dread; and now it appears you go scot-free, and a thinner-skinned party pays the penalty. Let us hope that that too is on the way to " all well." . . . On the whole, I cannot think, somehow, you have *lost* much by Nice, *tel quel*. We have hardly seen the sun physical once a fort-night; Sun moral I, for my own poor share, have not seen or heard of at all.' . . .

The news he had to give in reply included his purchase of a horse, ' an excellent little Nag.'—' I am confident you bought Kinloch Luichart Estate with about the tithe of the haggling, trying, corresponding, &c. I had on that small matter.' Then he had got a copyist,—meaning Frederick Martin, whom he describes but does not name :—' a desolate little German with a good hand of writing, who has cost me endless trouble ;—a weak helpless creature, tho a willing. His last Clerk function was with Heyne, the black-guard Paris Jew. I often wonder what the poor creature thinks of being *Wagner* to such a pair of *Fausts!* ' (referring to Goethe's play). . . .

' " Christmas dinner " this time will consist of mutton-chop eaten with the maximum of quietude. For by way of consummation to everything, my poor wife has fallen prisoner to cold, &c.; did not get out at all for about two months; and is still very feeble, tho evidently recovering for some weeks past. Lady Sandwich too, as you doubtless know, has been unwell. . . . She left a card lately, but would not quit her carriage here.'

Meanwhile Larkin was busy, and before the end of January he had finished and sent in for approval the index for *John*

Sterling. In acknowledging it on 30.1.1857, Carlyle remarked about indexes in general :—' Nothing important to be omitted, nor anything insignificant let in ; that is the clear Theory ;—but as to Practice, in that, as in all things, we require (as the Hindoo Algebraist says of Quadratic Equations in complex cases) " a clear judgment and the blessing of God." '

The summaries required in addition were a pure joy to Larkin, who was disappointed when none was wanted for *Cromwell.* Discovering no errors of the press in the text, he was ready with other corrections ; but he was told (4.2.57) : —" Breaking in upon the Text,—of course it must be done if there is an absolute *mistake ;* but otherwise I always avoid it with a kind of shudder ! The thing has congealed itself *so ;* cold and hard now, burning hot as it once was ; so let it lie in God's name !—I will alter ' long clothes,' for that seems to be a real error ; and I am glad to know it, there and for the future."

" The first clothes worn by an infant, extending below the feet " is the dictionary definition of " long clothes," a phrase which Carlyle had applied to the loose dress of little boys.

In February, 1857, Henry Larkin had a cheerier reception at Cheyne Row than his first had been and tells us,— ' I was especially surprised and delighted at the change in Mrs. Carlyle. She had been very kind before, with a patiently hopeless look. But all this had now passed away. All the blinds were drawn up, and her face was illuminated with the brightest of welcomes. She expressed a good deal of bantering astonishment at what she called my " accurate knowledge of baby-linen," and was altogether cheerful and congratulatory.

' After this my visits were less formal, and were entirely pleasant. Mrs. Carlyle and I seemed to get on very happily together. She said she didn't see why Carlyle (she always called him Carlyle when in her best moods) '—Cār'-lyle, the old Dumfriesshire pronunciation,—' should have me all to himself ; and enlisted my services ' with mutual satisfaction.

The enthusiastic thoroughness of Larkin's work on the indexes can still be seen. A reader who has dipped into them for thirty years cannot remember that he ever found there anything amiss or wanting, so that the *Quarterly Reviewer* who declared " the index to be the only intelligible part "[2] of the first two volumes of *Frederick* may have been sincere, however absurd.

' I tried,' says Larkin, ' to make the index not merely a verbal reference, which was all Carlyle asked for or expected, but an approximately complete key to the intellectual contents of the book. And I will venture to say that anyone, desiring to get Carlyle's whole meaning as to any person or leading thought, would find himself considerably aided by referring to the index.'

So Mrs. Carlyle may have been more accurate than usual when ' in those early days ' she said to him ' in her pleasant half-flattering, half-bantering way,'—

" You are the only one I have ever heard Carlyle speak of without what Sir Robert Peel would call ' mitigating circumstances.' "

It seems only fair to Larkin to add what Carlyle wrote about him in the Letters and Memorials of his wife which occupied him after her death, when *Frederick* was finished.— ' Henry Larkin (young Londoner, then collector or cashier on the Chelsea steamers, now partner in some prosperous business) had come to me some three years before this ' (July, 1858), ' in a loyally volunteer and interesting manner —a helper sent me by favour of Heaven, as I often said and felt in the years coming. He did for me all manner of maps, indexes, summaries, copyings, sortings, miscellanea of every kind, in a way not to be surpassed for completeness, ingenuity, patience, exactitude, and total and continual absence of fuss. Never had I loyaller or more effective help ; nowhere was there a more honest-minded man ; really of fine talent, too ; clear, swift discernment, delicate sense of humour, &c. ; but he preferred serving me in silence to any writing he could do (that was his own account on volunteering himself). Till *Frederick* ended he was my factotum, always at hand ; and still from the distance is prompt and eager to help me ; actually a man to thank Heaven for, as I still gratefully acknowledge. T. C.'

After the death of Carlyle, he remained in England long enough to do all he could to minimize the mischief made by the fanciful Froude and others,[3] and then departed with his family for New Zealand, where at last he died.

---

[2] *Carlyle and Mrs. Carlyle*, by Henry Larkin, *British Quarterly Review*, July, 1881, No. 147, pp. 32–9.
[3] *Carlyle and Mrs. Carlyle: a Ten Years' Reminiscence*, by Henry Larkin, *Quarterly Review*, July, 1881, and *Carlyle and the Open Secret of his Life*, by Henry Larkin, 1886.

VI

PROPHECIES NOW FULFILLED
(1857)

ON 18.2.57 William Knighton listened to Carlyle's denunciations of his contemporaries in general and the French in particular, and was happily inspired again to make as good a record as Boswell himself could have done. One has to recollect that in those years the little Napoleon was planning to become the Boss of Europe, as the only sure way of keeping his place at the top of the French. Here is Mr. Knighton's report.—

' 18th Feb. 1857.—Spent the evening with C. at his house. We were alone. Mrs. C. is ill.

' I mentioned that I had seen some verses of his written in Sir J. E. Tennent's Album, dated Paris, 1824.'

K.—" Were you much interested in Paris ? "

C.—" I was, at *that* time, very much. I was young, and my mind was open to fresh impressions ; but I was there since, a year or two before this man made himself Emperor, and I found them all empty, grimacing, going on all day with foolish empty grimacings. There is no hope for Paris. They are on the high-road that is so easily travelled downwards, but the ascending of which is the difficulty. Alas ! it is not Paris only that is thus."

' After a pause he resumed :—

" I sat one evening at the foot of the column in the Place Vendôme and smoked my cigar there, watching their grimacing, and superficial, empty, nonsensical mimicry, and hollowness, when a party of soldiers came, with two or three drummers beating away in earnest ahead of them— rat-at-tat-ta, rat-at-tat-ta they went—and the Parisians were delighted with them. They could understand that, but anything better they could not. Rat-at-tat-ta, rat-at-tat-ta they went along, waking the echoes, the drummers seemingly delighted with their own performance, the people charmed, and there were the stars and moon above them that night just as there are to-night, as clear and silent and solemn."

' There was again a pause, and he resumed—" One Sunday evening I went out to the Champ de Mars and saw a lamentable spectacle. The Champ was covered with people, its dusky half-grass, half-gravelled extent was almost hidden with the multitude. And what, thinkyou, had they to recreate themselves with that blessed Sabbath evening ? A balloon was to go up, and the men were there in great numbers holding it down by ropes during its inflation ; but before it was ready a sort of inflated semblance of a man was sent up. It was guided by ropes, I suppose, but the ropes were invisible from where I stood. I saw it go up, to the great delight of the Parisian populace. They shouted, yelled, clapped their hands, strained their necks, opened their eyes and mouths, and gave every evidence of intense satisfaction. It was pulled down afterwards somewhere, and by that time the balloon was ready. That was the amusement of the Parisian populace that blessed Sabbath evening. A spectacle to make one sad."

K.—" I doubt if you would find any other populace that would not be equally delighted with it. Sabbath or no Sabbath, the poor have not their books and thoughts to fall back upon. They want something to see, or hear, or taste—something palpable."

C.—" They do. But this open-mouthed levity and grimacing is a characteristic not of the poor only in France. Look at their writers. I opened Lamartine's *History of the Girondins*, and found it a foolish romance, yet professing to be a history. The man is a grimacing caricaturist, an empty windbag, and flatulent. History ! It's no history at all. And that's the man that thought he was to be the man of the age—the presiding genius of France. A genius worthy of the France of the present day, which is all talk, grimace, and insincerity."

K.—" Thiers is a profounder historian than Lamartine, but where the glory of France is concerned not over-scrupulous or accurate as to facts."

C.—" Thiers is a superior man to Lamartine, but, as an historian, he can take no rank. I expected great things from his *French Revolution*. It is a clever work, but eminently unfaithful. He is, as you say, an *unscrupulous* writer."

K.—" Guizot is altogether superior—more accurate and
more painstaking to arrive at facts."

C.—" Guizot is a cadaverous-looking man, who believes
in Louis Philippe. When I conversed with him long ago
about Cromwell, he thought Cromwell first an enthusiast
and afterwards a hypocrite. In his *English Revolution*
however, I find he has adopted my view of him, as far as it
was possible for him so to do. But he is an undecided man.
He believes in Louis Philippe and the Spanish marriage
still. Indeed, I don't know but he may be looking for the
resurrection of Louis Philippe and his Second Advent. The
second part of his work is a mere political essay on the
present state of France, or rather on its state when he wrote,
for its state changes every year now. A wretched country!
I once thought the Revolution was working itself out to a
higher, holier, and better state of things ; but I find my
mistake now. France, like England, will have to go through
the baptism of fire and blood that awaits us all, before anything better can come out of it. Look at its literature and
you will find it all lying and romance—the worst of both."

K.—" Your hopes for literature centre in Germany, I
suppose ; for I know you don't think much of our current
literature in England ? "

C.—" Our current literature is like our current life—
made up of shams, hypocrisies, counterfeits, deceits, lies.
I have a profound contempt for it. Lessing did a great deal
for Germany in showing them that their French models
were no models at all, but falsities, and in preaching up
Shakespeare to them ; and, since his time, Germany has
done more for literature than France and England—a
great deal more."

K.—" I have somewhere seen it remarked—in T. Jouffroy
I think—that Germany gives the raw material of thought ;
France puts it into shape and makes it clear ; whilst
England applies it practically."

C.—" Germany has given no raw material, then, for
some quarter of a century that I know anything of."

K.—" Are we making no progress, then, in Western
Europe ? Is there nothing great and good being done either
in Germany, France, or England at the present day ? "

C.—" Progress ! Our progress is in the wrong direction. We
move with accelerated velocity downwards. As to Germany,
the only thing they do there now is in a philological way ;
but they do that well. They are men of immense patience, of

wonderful plodding perseverance. They can clothe the dry bones of history and ancient literature for us in a perfectly marvellous way ; telling us of the pots and pans the Greeks and Romans used, how they walked and talked, and sat, and slept, and rose, and did other things less noble. Heyne did that in a wonderful way for Virgil, and that sort of thing has its use. Heeren told us much, too, of their commerce and politics that we knew not before ; but he is tedious, prolix, and dry. *In philology they still dig out new facts, and put them together for us, with wonderful labour ; but of anything better than that going on at the present day in Germany, I know nothing."*

K.—" You laugh at our progress. Is there no progress apparent in India and in British Colonisation—in the opening-up of new countries, peopling waste continents, and founding new empires ? "

C.—" A Gibeonitish sort of progress truly ; all hewing of wood and drawing of water ; nothing nobler or better that I can see. The United States were a greater and nobler people eighty years ago, when they were our colonies, than they are now, though they had only three millions of people then, and thirty now. The whole of the thirty put together wouldn't make one Franklin, or even a Washington."

K.—" Should we ever have heard of Washington had it not been for the circumstances in which he was placed ? "

C.—" Perhaps not ; but he would not have been the less a great man on that account. *I do not rate him very highly, however ; certainly not to compare with Franklin."*

K.—" And with the States, the Cape, Australia, New Zealand, India, as they are, you see no progress in the right direction ? "

C.—" *I see terrible calamities impending, a total severing of every tie and bond of the world as it exists—bloodshedding and destruction.* As to Australia, what is it doing but upsetting all our economic arrangements here by digging out gold that had much better be left where it was ? We didn't want it. The world didn't want it. There was enough before for all practical purposes. No nation ever became great by finding gold, though it were found in tons. Rome was pretty much as we are when it was congratulating itself on being the mistress of the world. Seneca was writing of her greatness, her prosperity, and her wonderful progress, and yet the northern barbarians were even then whetting their swords for slaughter. Death was nigh unto those luxurious Romans, steeped in refinement, and a career of ' progress ' that promised them, short-sighted as they were, wonderful things. And so with us."

K.—" Where are these modern barbarians to come from ? "

C.—" I don't know. *History does not exactly reproduce itself*,[1] but we want a superior race, to be got somewhere and somehow—a race of God-fearing, honest, sincere men. But it's no use cursing the world as it is. It remains the same after we have expended all the vials of our wrath upon it."

' Miss Jewsbury came in at this moment. She had been with Mrs. Carlyle. We walked home with her, and then C. walked home with me. He spoke of preaching and preachers as we went.

C.—" If I were a preacher I would tell them one Sunday what to do, and then, when they came back next Sunday, I would ask them, ' Well, have you done that ? How much have you done of it ? None ! Then go home and do it.' I would remind them once more, giving them a little at a time, but not a step faster than I thought right. A little at a time. What conceivable use is there in their going over a long rigmarole of the same thing, Sunday after Sunday, that they know well no one intends to practise, they themselves, perhaps, least of all. It is the silent, steady, persevering work that has been of use in all ages, not the windy clamorous work, that can't go on unless people talk about it."

' I told him of the Bishop of St. Asaph going into St. Mark's School, and asking one of the boys there, " Who am I ? " " A Bishop, my lord," said one youngster. They often see Bishops there. " Who made me a Bishop ? " asked his lordship solemnly. " Lord John Russell, my lord," said the urchin. The Bishop said no more to them that day !

' C. laughed heartily at the anecdote, and left me laughing, as we shook hands near my door. It was then half-past eleven, the river before us, and the moon shining brightly on it—a beautiful night, cold, bright, and frosty.'

---

[1] Italics generally added in this chapter.

VII

" WAGNER " AT WORK
(1857)

MEANWHILE Frederick Martin alias " Wagner " had been busy copying French and German, and earning his weekly wages of about £1 and expenses, and feeling, as he confided to the Missionary Mr. Wells,[1] that he was much underpaid, and fully entitled to take as much more as he could get anyhow. He made his wife fetch their baby for Mrs. Carlyle's inspection and so get many shillings from her, which were probably given as the best possible way of supplementing his wages, for it has to be told that Wells reported,[1]—" I saw much of Martin, but never once saw him quite sober."

The great hope of Martin was to make a gold mine of the MSS. of Carlyle which, he said to Mr. Wells, " my dear old master has given to me,—was it not good of him ? " Listening attentively to his tipsy confidences, Mr. Wells began at last reluctantly to suspect that Martin had been " stealing a lot," or at any rate " taking a great deal more than he had been meant to take." The method of Martin seemed to be to mislay papers, and find them if they were missed but keep them if not, while he contrived to escape suspicion of dishonesty by affecting to be more stupid and drunken than he really was,—a common Oriental trick.

Thus in the beginning of February, 1857, Carlyle was writing to Neuberg :—' Dear Neuberg, We are in utter despair here : " Book I " is lost (undiscoverable unless you happen to have it) : in the name of all the saints, help us to find it again ! *Lost* utterly it cannot at all be, without miracle ; but it was laid by in a certain drawer here,— then given out to you, and I *think* brot. back by you :— and neither high nor low is there now sight to be got of it. An awful tempest in a teapot ! If you know or can advise in any measure, do it by Note immediately.

[1] Statements of Mr. Wells to D. A. W.

'For the rest, I want you to come on Wedy. evening (*Wednesday*, day after to-morrow) at 5½ p.m., and eat a mutton chop with Lewes and me,—Lewes having volunteered It is to be hoped the MS. of Book I will have turned up in the interim !' And so it seems to have done, tho how it was found does not appear.

A few weeks later, when the copying of French and German had been finished, and " Wagner " was being tried and found incapable of making a fair copy of English MSS. there is a letter from Carlyle to Neuberg, undated, but pencil-marked by another hand as about 20th March.— ' Dear Neuberg,—You are evidently taking far too much pains with that imbroglio of Scrawlings. I merely wanted you to run over the masses with your fresh (undisgusted eye ; to judge what passages were worth the *chance* implied in having them copied by Wagner ; to mark with a pencil stroke on the margin what he was to copy,—and send him home to do it. With strict and strictest charge to bring every line of the original back to me.—He has not done that in the case of George II ; and I have sat, for three days over that Piece, in the uttermost wretchedness, not knowing what on Earth to do with it,—or where to begin upon it,— owing to that want ! But we will be patient : I do myself immeasurable mischief by the want of that virtue. No use asking Wagner what has become of the George II things he will " drop a tear over himself " (a very bad habit)— and that is all we shall get.'

Here it may be noted that about sixty years later a credible man reported[2] that he had been consulted by " a great American publisher " about a set of Carlyle MSS. on George II. It did not seem worth while to publish what appeared to be merely the rough draft of what is printed in the *Frederick*, and could be discovered there easily by anyone referring to the Index. The only interesting detail was that, altho there was no sufficient proof, the probabilities were that the original seller of the MSS. was Frederick Martin alias Wagner.

The letter quoted ran on—' Please do not meddle with *Soissons* at all : send that home by him tomorrow *straight hither ;*—and what of the *other* you have ready (not hurrying yourself) he is to commence copying (*sworn* to bring the original *all* back, and at least put it as he found it here.) '

Frederick Martin was discharged by Carlyle on 21.3.57 ;

[2] To D. A. W.

which suggests that when he came with the Soissons papers
that day, he brought a letter from Neuberg advising against
employing Martin farther. Carlyle assisted him to get other
work, and he was never in distress again, tho always " in
want." He preserved his plunder piously, looking hopefully
to a happy harvest when Carlyle died, which Martin then
expected would be soon, as Carlyle was over sixty and in
bad health and overworked. It seemed a reasonable hope,
but it was disappointed ; and after many years we may see
in 1877 what the sickness of hope deferred can make such a
fellow do.

In the meantime 1857 is the date for one of the stories he
told to Mr. Wells which Mr. Wells believed, and so may we.
On one occasion when he made his wife bring their baby to
the house for Mrs. Carlyle's inspection, Mrs. Carlyle began
patting the baby and talking to it, perhaps intending to
let Mrs. Martin and her husband see how much they had to
be thankful for, tho wages were not high. She said she loved
babies and could not help envying the Martins, for she would
have given all she had to have one of her own. Her tones
were growing more and more ' tearful,' according to Martin,
till Carlyle interposed and sent her off into a fit of laughing
by intimating, ' unscrupulously ' it seemed to Martin, that
this particular morsel of humanity was not a possession to
envy very much.[1]

After this let no man say that if Martin libelled his
employer he had no provocation. As a small seed may start
a forest, so this little thing along with the Ruskin divorce
case may have suggested to Martin the dirty theory that
Carlyle was like Ruskin, a rumour which began to delight
the Yahoos of literary London about this time.[3] What is
sure enough is only this, that Martin afterwards had dealings
with Mr. Froude, and having engaged Mr. Wells to make
many notes of the gossip of Ecclefechan, sold them to
Mr. Froude, who paid him, but of course Martin never paid
Mr. Wells what he had promised. Unless he lied, however,
he could not have said anything to Froude about Ecclefechan
gossips talking of Carlyle being like Ruskin, for Mr. Wells
was very explicit, that that was never heard of there till
Mr. Froude's book appeared, and then it was derided.

It was while all this was going on that Carlyle was
appointed a trustee of the National Portrait Gallery,
8.2.1857.

[1] Statements of David Masson to D. A. W.

VIII

MRS. CARLYLE DISCUSSES NERO, &c.
(1857)

MR. KNIGHTON occasionally went with his wife when she called on Mrs. Carlyle. He reports :—
'Thursday, 20th March, 1857.—Mrs. K. called on Mrs C. ; we found her invalided—furs and shawls and couch so arranged that the invalid looked quite cosy and comfortable. Carlyle was out. " You see I was right," said Mrs. C " Mr. K. thought I was only fancying when I said I should have a terrible time of it during the winter, but I was right Cannot sleep—read till two, then doze sometimes, sometimes not, till four, sometimes not at all ; reading Kingsley's last— a very poor thing." Talked of *Sartor Resartus*. " It was offered," said Mrs. C., " to nearly every publisher in London and refused. Keep it, I said to him ; it will come of us some day.—-At last published in *Fraser's Magazine*. I did my best to keep up his spirits that time ; they were sinking then." Talked of her little dog Nero. " He is extravagantly fond of me, but only very moderately of Carlyle. If I am away for a little, and come in, he bounds and frisks, and delighted. If C. is away, then he just yelps a little when he returns, that's all. But he cannot expect otherwise. C delights in torturing him, which he calls playing with him He snaps the tongs at him, and Nero does not like that. He once even tied an empty tin to his tail, and sent the poor dog scampering all over the house in great terror. It was cruel of him to do that—absolutely cruel—and I told him so I told him it was an amusement unfit for a philosopher—low degrading."
' " And what then ? " I asked.
' " Oh, he only laughed all the more at Nero and at me But he did not do it again," continued Mrs. C.
' It was on this occasion she gave us some interesting details of her early life.'—

" My father was very anxious for a boy. He was disappointed that I was born a girl. However, he brought me up as much as possible as a boy. I was taught as a boy. When my mother remonstrated he would say, ' At eighteen I will hand her over to you, and you can teach her all a girl ought to know.' But Carlyle came, and it was forgotten. *I did not know how to tack on a button when I got married, but I could write Latin.* When we got married he took me to a farmhouse, far from the busy haunts of men. A strapping red-armed wench waited on us. ' It is market day to-day,' said she to me one day, bobbing in an uncouth curtsy. ' I am going to market ; what meat shall I get ? ' I was reading at the time. ' Oh, anything you like,' was my reply. ' No, ma'am, not as I like, as you like.' Well, we decided on something. But the cooking was execrable. Day after day our dinner was uneatable. ' My dear,' said Carlyle gravely to me at length, ' I am a philosopher, but I must have butcher's meat properly cooked for dinner.' I had a good cry after that. Then getting a cookery book I shut myself up with my pots and pans, and soon mastered the details of practical cookery. In the same way with sewing. Carlyle was away from home, and I made him a waistcoat. It fitted him perfectly. I was very proud of it. ' You want praise for it,' said he, ' but this is only what every woman ought to be able to do. You do not want praise for doing your duty.' But I did, tho. Now, I am happy to say I can bake bread, cook a dinner, or make a shirt with any one,"—but she might have added, if she had not loved to parade herself as the working wife,—" I average less than an hour a day in my kitchen, even when I'm well."

IX

SCIENCE AND RELIGION AND "MODERN INSTANCES"
(1857)

THE last interview reported by William Knighton was on 25.3.1857.[1] Soon after then he returned to India and could report no more. The Indian Mutiny that summer gives significance to the first part of their talk. It was about a friend of Carlyle then serving in India, Brigadier MacKenzie, who had been unjustly censured by the Government for a serious disturbance there.

" His pamphlet," said Carlyle to Knighton, " gives what I have no doubt is a very correct account of the transaction. It appears that a Mohammedan procession, with drums playing and flags flying, was marching on the public road, past his encampment, consisting almost entirely of soldiers— some sort of irregular corps. They " (the procession) "had no right to be there, and he sent them away. They came again in greater force, with more drums, I suppose, and more flags, and he went out to them again, accompanied by another European. They attacked him mercilessly, cut and wounded him in many places, and, in fact, left him for dead. The real culprits were allowed by some incompetent magistrate to escape, and a native officer, a Havildar I believe, was about being punished for it—deprived of his office—who was really the only efficient and orderly officer in the regiment. Mackenzie interfered to prevent this injustice. He seems to me to have played quite a heroical part in the business. He appealed to the Governor-General against the decision of the incompetent magistrate, but I suppose the Governor-General wouldn't take the trouble to read his statement, and so he got no redress. The impression is strong in my mind that that man (MacKenzie) played quite a heroical part in the whole business, and I believe

[1] *Conversations with Carlyle*, by William Knighton, *Contemporary Review*, June, 1881.

what he says, because I respected him of old as a truth-telling, honest, sincere man. It is quite true, as the papers state, that he is a devout Christian ; but how that should be to any man's discredit in a Christian country is not easily explained, except in this way—that unbelief, and cant, and humbug, and insincerity are gaining the day."

Mr. Knighton seized the opening this gave him and succeeded in drawing Carlyle to speak upon religious topics.

'K.—" Is belief—such as belief was before geological and astronomical discoveries—possible nowadays ? "

'C.—" Only possible to those who are ignorant of such discoveries ; but when existing, it is a beautiful thing."

'K.—" And what is the position of the clergy in this matter ? "

'C.—" The position of the clergy is one of ignominy and deep degradation. The spectacle of a body of enlightened men solemnly, and in the face of God and man, professing their steadfast faith and belief in that which they know they do not steadfastly believe in, is enough to make any thinking man sick at heart. What enlightened man can conscientiously in these days tie up his reason by formulas and articles drawn up centuries ago, and say, 'I believe,' whilst the inner soul of him all the time is exclaiming, 'I do not believe—it is a lie'? "

'K.—" Some men, like Dr. Newman, for instance, first persuade themselves that there is an infallible church that cannot err, and then, taking refuge therein, are troubled no further about the matter—accepting all its *dicta* as heaven-descended truths, whatever their reason may whisper about the matter."

'C.—" And what is that but moral emasculation ? One of the most lamentable religious phases of our times. Even with respect to the clergy of the English Church, they doubtless have persuaded themselves, in most instances, that they did believe before they made their declaration to that effect. For the time being they do not believe, but—believe that they believe. There is little hope for a Church existing under such circumstances. No, no ; things cannot go on long in this way. Swift destruction is impending, not on the Church only—mother of dead dogs," '—a phrase for a stream which had become an open sewer, without any living fish in it and many dead dogs floating upon it. To such a stream, once familiar in London, the Church of England is here likened, and it is only fair to note the

T

" even " when it is mentioned, implying that it is better than Newman's " infallible church."

' K.—" The Buddhistic idea of the universe is that it goes on through certain cycles of existence, each cycle terminating in destruction, and reproduction again resulting from that destruction. This rule seems to hold to a certain extent in the moral world."

' C.—" Geology seems to favour this Buddhistic idea— there have undoubtedly been certain ages of animal and vegetable life separated from each other by vast changes and worldwide destruction."

' K.—" Humboldt has given a pleasant summary, succinct and agreeable, of these changes in his *Cosmos*."

' C.—" I read one volume of that book in German, but could never get further. What does he see in the universe ? Nothing but an old marine-store-shop collection of things putrefying and rotting, under certain forces and laws. A most melancholy picture of things ! The spiritual world, and all spiritual life, quite ignored. The higher and nobler side of man's existence not even hinted at—a lamentable picture, truly. Long ago I read his account of his travels in South America, and the same impression struck me ; but he was regarded by all men as one of the greatest of modern philosophers, and I did not then venture to say what I really thought. I was a young man then. Even this old marine-store-shop *Cosmos* of his was so highly praised by those whose opinions I revere, that I thought it my duty to read it ; but I never could get further than the end of the first volume. There is certainly something higher in Nature than rocks and laws, something nobler than mountains and fossils and forces, something more sublime than natural scenery, however grand." '

Which reminds one of the words of a Chinese classic paraphrased by Tennyson,—" The mountain is high and the stars are high, but the mind of man is higher." ' Carlyle continued :—" It is a very big Universe, Humboldt confesses, it is true—so big that it quite surprises him with its bigness, but nothing more. I saw him in Germany some years ago. He was talking all day about——" '

Miss Jewsbury came in at this point with a message from Mrs. Carlyle, and this led Carlyle to describe Frederick Martin to Knighton, concluding, " He has a wife and one or two children. If you can find any work for him, educational or other, I shall be obliged."

X

MRS. RUSKIN, SIR COLIN CAMPBELL, &c.
(1857)

ABOUT this time the artist Holman Hunt had another fine opportunity to Boswellize, and once more made a record as meritorious as the best of his pictures.[1]—

'At a dinner to which Lady Goodrich was kind enough to invite me, Mr. and Mrs. Carlyle were among the guests,' and the excellent Liberal M.P. 'Henry Bruce, afterwards Lord Aberdare, who had undertaken to draw (him) out,' and was very successful in doing it.

'There was a large company. Mrs. Carlyle was the lady allotted to me. She sat on my left, and Carlyle was exactly opposite. Mrs. Carlyle assailed me for my opinion anent the marriage of Millais with Mrs. Ruskin. I defended him strenuously, saying that the lady had ceased to be Mrs. Ruskin by the nullification of the marriage as declared by the Scotch Court. Millais had not run away with her, I said, but had waited to claim her in her father's house, a full year after the day she left Ruskin. " If because husband and wife are not in accord they should separate, many marriages would be annulled," she argued.'

According to Holman Hunt,[2] Ruskin had been the press champion of the Pre-Raphaelites, and got one of them, Millais, to paint his portrait. In the course of doing so, Millais discovered that the young and beautiful Mrs. Ruskin was feeling herself too like a flower that wastes its sweetness on the desert air. Nobody can ever know whether she was right, but Millais had no doubt about it, and it seemed a case for a knight-errant. So he became the lady's outspoken champion, remonstrating on her behalf with the husband who did not know how happy he should be. Millais ended

---

[1] *Pre-Raphaelitism and the Pre-Raphaelite Brotherhood*, by W. Holman Hunt, II, pp. 129–132. The date is fixed by a reference to the Indian Mutiny immediately following it. [2] *Ditto*, II, pp. 90–4.

by wedding the lady himself, when she had got rid of Ruskin by a nullity suit, one ideal conclusion of all such championships. Then they lived happy ever after, at least as happy as could be expected under the circumstances.

Of course, as Hunt says, ' No one could be cordially intimate with both Millais and Ruskin,' after this. ' Millais was my first and far greater friend. A bitter controversy arose in society about the case, and I always did battle ' for him against ' many misconstructions and falsehoods ' ; and that would be why Mrs. Carlyle on this occasion tackled Hunt with such pertinacity that, as he tells us, ' I had not been able to turn to the lady on my right, nor had I been able to listen to the torrent of talks on the opposite side of the table, which proceeded almost exclusively from ' Carlyle. It was very provoking for one of the best Boswells going, when Mr. Bruce was so assiduous and successful too in drawing Carlyle out.

' When the ladies rose from table and we were again seated, I found that the man on my right was rather short, with thick black hair growing up, in what, from French Revolutionary times, was called the Brutus fashion ; he sidled up to me, and in an undertone inquired if I knew the name of " the gentleman who talked so much." " Yes," I whispered, " he is Thomas Carlyle " ; then after a short pause he inquired, " What does he do ? " " He is the celebrated writer." At this my new friend muttered, " Ah, yes. He's the atheist ! " " No," I corrected him, with voice directed low, " you are thinking of another man of the same name who has been dead some years. He was a professed atheist. Thomas Carlyle says it is better to have Mumbo-Jumbo than no God at all." My interrogator then asked me to tell him what works Carlyle had written. I spoke of his translations from the German, of *The French Revolution*, of *The Life and Letters of Cromwell*, of *The Latter-day Pamphlets*. To satisfy his curiosity still further he drew himself up to scrutinise the object of his inquiry.

' At that moment Henry Bruce spoke across the table to my neighbour, " Sir Colin Campbell ! My friend Mr. Carlyle is at the present time engaged upon a history in which acquaintance with military life is much called for. I am quite sure that if you would be good enough to recount to us some of your own adventures in the field, it would be of value to Mr. Carlyle, and of not less interest to the rest of us." This appeal helped me to identify my quiet neighbour, and I looked at him with suspense ; his reply was curtly conclusive, " But I've nothing to tell."

' " Sir Colin," returned Mr. Bruce, " it is reported in the history of your campaign in the Peshawur district, that when in command of 700 men you had marched through a defile and had debouched into the plain, you were suddenly informed that a force of 30,000 native troops was only a couple of hours behind you, and that they were hastening to destroy your company. You then, it is said, immediately turned your troops about and made them scale the heights and march unseen until you were in the rear of your enemy, and then you, to their great dismay, appeared on the heights and surprised them by a bold descent on to their rear. The enemy, concluding that there must be a large army in front, were seized by sudden panic, became confused and dis-ordered, and were then quickly defeated by your small contingent. Now, may I ask whether this account of your action is correct ? "

' Sir Colin Campbell had no choice but to reply in some way. While all were intent on listening he simply said, " Well, there was nothing else to do."

' The persevering Mr. Bruce could make nothing more out of the taciturn hero. He then appealed to Carlyle to say what he thought of Froude's defence of Henry VIII, in his History of England.

' " For that matter," replied the Chelsea philosopher, " I cannot say much, for I have not yet read it, but I've always esteemed Henry to be a much maligned man. When I look into that broad yeoman-built face and see those brave blue eyes of his, as they are seen in the Holbein portrait, I must conclude that an honest soul resided within his sturdy body." Raising his voice then to a treble, he continued, " He certainly had much trouble with his wives. I won't pretend to decide anything for or against his divorce from Katherine, or the execution of the others ; whether or not they deserved it depends upon evidence that I have not seen : this is a personal matter ; but the great charge against the man is, that he had seventy thousand men hung for no ostensible crime whatever, merely because they were rogues and vagabonds. Now that seems like a serious incrimination, but then we have to consider the state of the country at the time. Until thirty years before the whole country had only a waste population, ready to be engaged on one side or the other of the York and Lancaster wars, to cut one another's throats. Such a national fury it is difficult to quench. Stalwart rascals were roving about, ready to do any unholy thing, and a good ruler was bound to eradicate marauders of all kinds. Henry would not tolerate them. He ordained that any man brought up who could not prove that he gained his living by useful work should be branded with a hot iron, and for a second offence ordered straight off to the gallows."

' Carlyle's emphasis had gradually subsided, but again he raised his voice, saying, " If any one here would like to come to me at Chelsea to-morrow morning, I would undertake to lead him to a spot, a hundred yards from my door, where we should find thirty vagabonds leaning against the rail which divides the river from the road, and although these men have never been, as far as I know, convicted of any particular crime whatever, I will not hesitate to affirm that they would be all the better for hanging, both for their own sakes and for every one concerned. Now, if you'll consider with me that I am only pointing out the case of one particular parish in London, or a part of it, and if you will calculate the number of parishes there are in the metropolis alone, and then extend your view over the whole country, you will agree that seventy thousand men was not by any means an extravagant number of irredeemable ne'er-do-wells whose suppression was put down to poor Henry's evil account."

' The silent guest, the slayer of hundreds in open warfare, who had interrogated me, stared with wide eyes at the eloquent talker as he condemned this number of hapless men to death, while in fact he would never have killed a fly. Underlying all was his idea of justice, the law that if a man will not work neither shall he live. The judgment upon the negro question in Jamaica was actuated by this feeling, and he seemed more impelled to enforce the principle, because there were many doctrinaires prating that men should be encouraged to regard labour as a degrading affliction rather than an ennobling blessing.

' A few months later,' Sir Colin went out at short notice and finished the Indian mutiny. " There was nothing else to do." Perhaps neither he nor any of the others present on this occasion had realised that Carlyle was merely arguing the case of Henry VIII in talking of hanging thirty vagabond loafers on the Embankment. He was trying to show how Henry was placed when ' the whole country had only a waste population ready to cut one another's throats.' It was and remains as sure as that two and two make four that nowadays nothing is needed but the right organisation of labour, for which Carlyle had been pleading for many years. Not Charity but Justice is what working men require, and have never yet received,—it is so much easier for do-nothing politicians to humbug them and waste public money on demoralising "doles," and so avoid mending our English and Scottish land-laws, perhaps the worst in Europe.

XI

HUGH MILLER
(1857)

IN April Mrs. Hugh Miller sent Carlyle a copy of *The Testimony of the Rocks*, a newly published book which her husband had just completed when he committed suicide on 24.12.1856. His death was the most significant tragedy in that generation ; and to explain it the truth which could only be whispered at the time may now be plainly told,— Hugh Miller had been driven mad by the false position in which he found himself.

He had early shied at the Church, which had long appeared to the people of Scotland the natural career for a clever boy to take in order to " better himself." Like Carlyle and many another he had seen that the dogmas of the Protestant Churches had become as incredible to a man of sense as the hocus-pocus of the Papists. So Hugh Miller became a mason in preference, and working in a sandstone quarry he read the open secrets of the rocks far better than any man had ever done before. Then by his books and essays he became known as a discoverer in geology and the best exponent of it. He quitted the trade of stone-cutting because of the unhealthy conditions of the work, and became a bank accountant and ultimately a newspaper editor.

Unfortunately he was then entangled in the disputes that ended in the disruption of the Church. As an editor he championed his country's religious independence, and made his paper, the *Witness*, a great power in the land, but almost without realising what was happening he found himself committed to argue for the theologians. As editor of the *Witness* he was tied to orthodoxy as much as if he had been in a pulpit, and even less able than a clergyman to choose his topics. He struggled to convince himself that an honest man of sense and science could believe enough of the general principles of Christianity to be able to preach it, and he rashly undertook to do the impossible and reconcile Geology with the Bible. He did the best he could, explaining the " days " of Moses as ages, and so on, but as he completed his *Testimony of the Rocks*, his mind gave way and all was ended. Acknowledging the gift of that book, Carlyle wrote to Mrs. Miller on 15.4.1857.—

' MY DEAR MADAM,

' Last night I received a Gift of your sending, which is at once very precious and very mournful to me.

' There is for ever connected with the very title of this Book the fact that, in writing it, the cordage of a strong heart cracked in pieces ; that the ink of it is a brave man's life-blood ! The Book itself, I already see, is full of grave, manly talent, clearness, eloquence, faithful conviction, inquiry, knowledge ; and will teach me and others much in reading it : but that is already an extrinsic fact, which will give it a double significance to us all. For myself, a voice of friendly recognition from such a man, coming to me thus out of the still kingdoms, has something in it of religion ; and is strange and solemn in these profane, empty times.

' In common with everybody, I mourned over the late tragic catastrophe ; the world's great loss, especially your irreparable and ever-lamentable one : but as for *him*, I confess there was always present, after the first shock, the thought that at least he was out of bondage, into freedom and rest. I perceived that, for such a man, there was no rest appointed except in the countries where he now is !

' Dear Madam, what can we say ? The ways of God are high and dark, and yet there is mercy hidden in them. Surely, if we know anything, it is that " His *goodness* endureth for ever." I will not insult your grief by pretending to lighten it. You and your little ones, yes, you have cause, as few have had, to mourn ; but you have also such assuagements as not many have.

' With respectful sympathy, with many true thanks and regards, I remain,

' Sincerely yours,
' T. CARLYLE.'

XII

EXIT HARRIET, LADY ASHBURTON
(1857)

THE last letter Carlyle ever wrote to Lady Ashburton
was dated 7.4.1857 :—' Dear Lady, We hear cheering
accounts of you ; vague, but all favourable, and more or
less agreeing with Lord Ashburton's last note ; which '
(notes) ' are a great comfort, you may believe ! To-day
Miss Farrar ' brought good news in short,—' you are
perhaps on the road to Paris by this time. Would to Heaven
we could believe all that ! We can hope at any rate ; we
have always refused not to hope.

' The April weather is miraculously warm here ; much
rain, but a temperature equal to the end of May. . . .
Once at Paris, you will seem to us next door to home ;
within a day,—fully nearer for a letter than my Scotch border
is,—almost looking over into your old haunts here. Bath
House is vacant, but safe and ready ; how ready would it
and other objects be for you !——

' As for myself I am not prosperous ; less so than usual.
. . . A sad business that I ever undertook that *Fried*ʰ· :
what had I to do with it ? . . . I find there is only one
remedy—to get the thing *done*, were it only at the rate of
an inch a day !

' My wife continues rather improving ; but is still weak.
. . . I find I have ridden too diligently : one cannot force
back lost health by vigour in riding. I am now ordered to
take it more moderately. One doesn't know one's limits ;
and one should, and must !

' A daydream of mine is, to see you quiet, well and
solitary at the Grange once more,—all Highland wildernesses
and wild things and journeyings given up ; a "*practical
school*" for girls, do. for boys (difficult exceedingly, important
exceedingly) occupy the Lady and the Lord, supply them
with a generous interest ; this and other things for genuine

human employ^{t.} and interest ever-new : No travelling, not even for health ;—in the whole World, where will you find a " better climate " (really *better*) than you have in your own England, in your own House and fields ? All is to be quiet, regular, wholesome, wise, beautiful. And I (this is always one item) am to have somewhere in a still glade of the Woods, a brick Cottage, two rooms and kitchen " with a deaf (or at least dumb) old woman," &c. &c., and to see you once every day, after my work is over ! Couldn't I tumble all my books into a cart ; send it forth in God's name—and follow !—This is a beautiful dream ! I am getting more and more passionate for the Country ; Country diet (of milk, &c.), Country air; innocent Country talk,— or else *silence,* and an end at least to so much of insane inanity ;—and in fact I must make a terrible trial for it, were this Book once done, if it ever be.

' Alas, yesterday at Charing Cross I passed while the Hanbury versus Chelsea Election was just ending. " Lord Chelsea nowhere," they told me, Brewer Hanbury preferred to him ; and at the top of the poll Ld. R. Grosvenor,— probably the greatest fool in England. Nobody seemed to be minding it, of the public. Hustings were about deserted, on the pavements in Cockspur Street stood parboiled groups of ugly people (Committee-men, presumably), looking out gloomily with bloodshot eyes :—I was near bursting into laughter in their faces,—poor devils, after all !—Adieu, dear Lady : I pray only these good accounts be confirmed. Good be with you evermore.

' T. C.'

It was not to be—she took a turn for the worse. The sunshine of the Riviera is often like the brightness of a whitewashed hospital, to which one goes to die. It could not cure Lady Ashburton. A London Medico brought to advise, " Sir A.B." is the name he got from handsome Venables, who was with the Ashburtons there, could only confirm the worst forebodings of the local doctors,—internal disease and death at hand.

About April Venables was at Cheyne Row and telling the news to Carlyle, and amazed to find him incredulous and cursing " Sir A.B." as " the most incapable member of his profession. He had mistaken the nature of Lady C.'s illness. Lady D. recovered after he had declared her case to be hopeless. His improper treatment, nothing else, killed Mrs.

E." And so on. Even handsome Venables was touched, and sent ' an accurate report of the conversation ' to the Ashburtons, and Lord Ashburton wrote to him in reply,—" She was delighted with Carlyle's new proof of affection, and laughed with all her former heartiness at the form which his feelings assumed."[1]

Returning home they arrived at Paris and there she died, 4.5.57, and Richard Milnes, ' our good Richard,'[2] as Carlyle used to call him, brought the news to Cheyne Row next day, and on hearing it Carlyle walked through the moonlit streets to ask for ' the weak, devoted, agëd mother,' Lady Sandwich. On 6.5.57 Lord Ashburton wrote to him :—" She has left me an inheritance of great price, the love of those who loved her. I claim that of you, in her name ; and I am sure it will be rendered to me."

On 11.5.57 Carlyle confided to his sister Jean, Mrs. Aitken, that the death of Lady Ashburton had been " altogether unlooked for " by him, and that it seemed " a lesson sent me, and truly a sad one ; and a loss in several respects such as I need not hope to replace. Since our dear Mother's death there has nothing like it come. ' God *sanctify* it to those concerned ! ' as my Mother would have prayed,— the one wise prayer."

The funeral was at the Grange on Tuesday, 12.5.57, and among the relatives and intimates at the grave stood Carlyle and Brookfield together, and Thackeray, Henry Taylor and Venables and many more.[2] Mrs. Carlyle reported to Mrs. Russell,—" All the men, who used to compose a sort of *Court* for her, were there, in *tears !* I never heard of a gloomier funeral."

To Neuberg Carlyle lamented that such an affliction had come upon him " in this delirious, disgusting element, too " (meaning the *Frederick* work), " which I must not quit under pain of worse." The printing of *Frederick* commenced on 14.5.57, the second day after the funeral, and the steady work upon it must have lessened his pain, tho he did not think of that at the time. As he wrote to his brother John on 22.5.57 :—" I got a great blow by that death you alluded to, which was totally unexpected to me ; and the thought of it widening evermore as I think further of it, is likely to be a heaviness of heart to me for a long time coming. I

---

[1] *Fortnightly Review*, May, 1883, p. 636.
[2] *Mrs. Brookfield and Her Circle*, by C. & F. Brookfield, II, pp. 520 and 456–7.

have indeed lost such a friend as I never had, nor am again in the least likelihood to have, in this *stranger* world ; a magnanimous and beautiful soul which had furnished the English earth and made it homelike to me in many ways is not now here."

Long afterwards he called Lady Ashburton " the most Queen-like woman I have ever known or seen. The honour of her constant regard had for ten years back been among my proudest and most valued possessions—lost now ; gone —for ever gone ! In no society had I seen the equal or the second " of her. At another time he praised another lady's description of her, and added :—" A *tragic* Lady Harriet, deeply tho she veiled herself in smiles, in light, gay humour and drawing-room wit, which she had much at command. Essentially a most veracious soul too. Noble and gifted by Nature, had Fortune but granted any real career. She was the greatest lady of rank I ever saw, with the soul of a princess and captainess had there been any career possible to her but that fashionable one."

This seems an echo of some of the lady's own remarks, and is very Carlylean, poetic rather than logical. In the common meaning of the word *tragic*, it is absurd, for hardly any woman then alive had less excuse to complain of her lot than Harriet Lady Ashburton. And yet—there is always something,—man can never be quite satisfied, " nor woman neither." Lady Ashburton " had ever the sorrow of her own life before her : she lost her only child while he was still an infant," and had no other.[3] The con- viction that what must be should be, " Islam," was the core of Carlyle's religion, controlling his conduct at every turn ; but whereas both saints and sinners in general apply it cheerily to others and forget it for themselves, the right sort of man, who never forgets it for himself, is prone as Carlyle was to forget it for anyone he loves or admires.

Meanwhile it was now noticed that in his afternoon rides Carlyle was often accompanied by Lord Ashburton.

[3] *Ditto*, p. 404.

XIII

LEWIS PELLY AND CARLYLE

I T may have been about 1857 that Lewis Pelly had an
interview of which he has made a fine record.[1] He was
still ' young ' in a sense,—32 in 1857, but he had been in
the Bombay army since he was sixteen, and he had had
much experience both of war and of civil administration on
the staff of General John Jacob and in other posts. Thus
he had been assistant resident at Baroda at the age of 26,
and so on.

' In early life,' he has written, ' I was lying idle on the
deck of a P. & O. steamer, wondering whether life was
worth living, when my hand happened to light on a tattered
volume of Carlyle's *Miscellanies*, in which I found his essay
on Burns and his second essay on Goethe. These papers
read to me almost like a new revelation of life, and seemed
to show that when earnestly regarded, the future, even of
a lieutenant in the East India Company's service, was sus-
ceptible of development. On reaching England I fell in
with *Sartor Resartus* and *Past and Present*, which yet further
attracted me.

' Shortly afterwards Mr. Carlyle invited me to his house,
but on presenting myself at the door an elderly Scotch
female intimated that her master was engaged and did not
see people. I said that I had come by appointment, upon
which I was conducted to the top of the house, a sort of
prophet's chamber, where I found Mr. Carlyle seated at a
small table.

' He welcomed me very kindly, and began talking on the
North-West Frontier of India. He seemed much interested
about General John Jacob and his work with the Scinde
Horse in the Bolan desert. I explained that my old chief,

[1] *Glimpses of Carlyle*, by Sir Lewis Pelly, *Fortnightly Review*, May,
1892, pp. 723–8.

tho employed in the command of cavalry, was yet a man of original thought and of an organising and constructive mind. Mr. Carlyle had evidently been reading some of the general's diatribes against the foolishness of governments and religious cant. He objected that Jacob was too profuse of the superlative degree ; and I remarked that I had often brought this characteristic under the notice of the general, suggesting that if he would begin with the positive he could hold the comparative and superlative in reserve, while by commencing with the superlative there was nothing left but to expand into big print and underlinings.

' " And what did Jacob say ? " asked Carlyle.

' " He said that what he wrote was God's truth, and it could not be printed too large."

' Mr. Carlyle then launched out upon the advantages of a life of action and military discipline ; he advised me utterly to avoid that great froth ocean called literature, and especially the thing called poetry. I submitted that he himself had mainly attracted me to letters, and that I understood his life had been passed in writing his genius upon the age.

' " Yes," he said, " I am a writer of books ; and once in a century a man may write a book worth reading. But the truth is, in early life I could not make anything of it, when someone told me that I should find what I wanted among the Germans, and thus I came upon Goethe. But for all that, life is an action and not a thought, and you had better stick to your work on the frontier and life will open round you."

' He finished by asking me to come to him again ; and a day or two afterwards wrote me a note in a very small hand, inviting me to accompany him to a dinner at Lord Ashburton's. I went accordingly, and sat next to a gentleman who proved to be Mr. Nassau Senior, and who soon engaged me in a conversation on political economy. I ventured to differ from him, and he was explaining to me that I knew very little of the subject, when Mr. Carlyle, from the other side of the table, burst in, saying that I was quite right, and telling Mr. Senior that he had driven God out of the universe, and would soon not let them have even the poor old Devil. I need not add that I was greatly relieved by this interruption, and left the two giants to fight the battle out.

' On leaving, Mr. Carlyle called a four-wheeler, and said

he would drive me as far as Hyde Park Corner, where our ways parted. No sooner had we started than he fired up on the politics of the day, and was anything but complimentary to Parliament and the Foreign Office ; he became so excited that he stood up and swayed his arms about, quite astonishing me by the fact that a man of genius who largely dominated the thought of his time should so agitate himself with matters which I, *at that time*, regarded as of little real importance. But he thundered on, and I did not attempt to get a word in even edgeways. At length the cab drew up, and we found ourselves at his door, whence I walked home to the other side of Hyde Park.'

Then Pelly came to tea, and ' Mrs. Carlyle received me,' he says. Carlyle ' soon worried me into an argument and upset everything I ventured to advance. Tea over, he went to the mantelpiece and filled his pipe, which he smoked often, and which I suspect affected his digestion, for he complained more than once of dyspepsia, and I ventured to suggest that his smoking might perhaps injure and depress him.

' " Yes," he said, " and the doctors told me the same thing. I left off smoking and was very miserable ; so I took to it again, and was very miserable still ; but I thought it better to smoke and be miserable than to go without."

' His pipe being filled, he descended to the small garden in rear of the house, but just as he was closing the door Mrs. Carlyle called out,—" Why, when Mazzini was here the other night, you took the side of the argument that Mr. Pelly did this evening."

' Carlyle, putting his head round the door merely said, *"And what's the use of a man if he cannot take two sides of an argument ? "*

' Sometime afterwards I was sitting in his room when the conversation turned upon Goethe. I remarked that I had been much puzzled, when reading *Wilhelm Meister*, by a diagram representing something between a key and a cross, and that I could not make out what it meant ; he looked at me intently from under his beetling brows and said, " No *more* can I." But perceiving that I was a little disappointed, he continued :—

" Well, you know, Goethe used to keep several works on hand, and hang his manuscript up in bags ; and I suppose that one day he must have pulled *Wilhelm Meister* down and scratched this cross while thinking of what he should say next." He then explained that Goethe was the many-sided liberator of the thought of Germany, and the germ of most that had come out since, whether in action or science.

'Miss Martineau had been extremely kind to me.' Upon my 'asking his estimate of her genius, and alluding in particular to her able summary of the Positive Philosophy, he paused for a moment, and then said slowly, " Well, she is the sort of woman that would have made a good matron in an hospital." I did not continue the subject ' . . . and may not have realised that this was praise.

'He was then writing *Frederick*. He explained that his view of Frederick was that he found himself set to govern a country with a simply insufferable frontier, and had there-fore by the only possible means, namely, drilled force, resolved to render his frontier tolerable and moderately secure. I asked him what he thought of Frederick's cavalry generals, Seidlitz and Ziethen. " Well," he said, " they were just famous gallopers." Now this was, perhaps, the only subject upon which my philosopher and guide could have roused me into contradiction. But fresh from my cavalry general, and imbued with all his lessons concerning the cavalry genius of Hannibal, Cromwell, Hyder Ali, and others, I rejoined somewhat sharply : " And do you not think, Mr. Carlyle, that as much genius can be shown in the handling of cavalry as in the writing of books ? "

' " Well," he said, " there is something in that."

' So I went on to expound to him what General Jacob had taught me about the fifteen campaigns of Hannibal, the battle of Dunbar, where the Lord delivered the enemy into the hand of Cromwell, and the letter of Hyder Ali to the English general. I concluded by referring to the battle of Rossbach, where Seidlitz, in command of the cavalry, repeatedly refused to obey the order of the king to charge until the right moment arrived, when he forthwith swept the foe from the field. Mr. Carlyle looked interested, but said nothing. When the *History of Frederick* appeared, I was amused to find that Seidlitz and Ziethen had become great cavalry commanders, and that no mention was made of " famous gallopers." '

Indeed there is more room for amusement here than the reporter suspected. Carlyle appreciated Seidlitz and Ziethen and had been merely drawing Pelly out ; but he had done it neatly, and like Dean Swift looked very grave on such

U

occasions, and so did not hurt anybody's feelings. The report continues.—

' I find it difficult to recall many of his serious sallies, for what chiefly rested in my mind were his quaint sayings uttered with a half-humorous expression of face. His language in conversation, as in his writings, was often in sledge-hammer fashion, and yet it did not sound so, for his manner was kindly, natural, and at intervals almost tender.'

No doubt Carlyle was one of those who encouraged Pelly to complete, as he was now doing, his book on the *Views and Opinions of General John Jacob*, the same man after whom Jacobabad was named, and one of the best generals we ever had. Pelly's book well deserves to be read again to-day. It shows the Indian Mutiny to have been foreseen and expected by men of sense,—the natural and inevitable result of wholesale stupidity at headquarters.

Pelly himself returned to his work in the East and did not fail to distinguish himself,—we will see him again by-and-by.[2]

[2] Book XXIV, Chapter XVI.

XIV

AN INTERIOR AT CHELSEA
(1857)

IN the spring of 1857 the artist Robert Tait, " a Dumfriesshire man from near Moffat and now living in London "[1] and " frequenting the Carlyles,"[2] had an inspiration, and declared that " a picture of their sitting room would be amazingly interesting to Posterity a hundred years hence." Mrs. Carlyle consented to let him paint such a picture, and told Mrs. Russell he " came and painted twice a week for three months " before she went to Scotland that summer, four times a week while she was away, and " every day for six weeks " after she came home, " except when, please God, the fog is so black that he cannot see."

His picture of their " little parlour," showing Carlyle in his dressing-gown, standing leaning against the mantelpiece and filling his pipe, while Mrs. Carlyle is sitting in her armchair on the opposite side of the fire, was accepted and hung at the next Royal Academy Exhibition, and was bought by Lord Ashburton for £500. When Tait reported that to Carlyle he was told,—" Well, in my opinion, £500 was just £495 too much ! "

Tait laughed and went about telling the saying at his own expense. He continued to thrive and to " frequent the Carlyles " as long as he lived, for about twenty years to come, and was occasionally seen walking in Carlyle's company, guiding him to historical pictures once. Many a time he would say to others that his " Interior at Chelsea " would keep him in the minds of men when better painters were forgotten. Which has come true,—it has been much reproduced.

It has also been much criticised. " I wish," said Mrs. Carlyle, " Tait had not painted Nero as big as a sheep.

---

[1] *Literary Recollections* of F. Espinasse, p. 102.
[2] Told D. A. W. by Miss Carlyle Aiken of Dumfries, a niece of T. C.

That provokes me more than being transmitted to ' Posterity ' in ' wrong perspective ' and with a ' frightful table-cover.' "[3] The enlargement of Nero was due to the lens for Tait was diligent in taking many photos,[4] and these photos let us see more than the picture. They let us look inside the attic workshop where Carlyle was doing the proofs of *Frederick* this year.

There were three bookcases, the bottom shelves of each made deep enough to carry folios. There were ninety-seven volumes of Voltaire and many hundreds of others, mainly about Frederick. Books in use were on a side-table or on the floor. The maps and loose papers were mostly kept in a cupboard. On the walls were maps and plans, and many pictures of Frederick and his men, and a few photographs of Carlyle's own relatives. On the mantelpiece there were a bronze statuette of Napoleon and china candlesticks while on a big screen were nearly a hundred portraits of Frederick,—enough to show that Carlyle was speaking from experience when he advised every student of history to seek for all the reasonable portraits he could get, because the portrait was often like " a small lighted *candle*, by which the biographies could for the first time be read " with " some human interpretation."

There were a couch and a chair or two, but the chief item of the furniture was the writing table, once Dr. Welsh's, and a mahogany chair beside it with plain wooden arms. In one of Tait's photos[4] we can see Carlyle at work there, correcting the proofs of the first two volumes of *Frederick* in 1857. His waistcoat had been taken off and hung on the arm of the chair. His left elbow was on the desk over which he was bending, the left hand supporting his head, while his right hand was fingering the papers. His feet were under the chair, one tucked over the other, while the projecting underlip and chin are conspicuous, illustrating what Tait afterwards told a lady[5] :—" In 1857 Carlyle's beard was in a transition stage,—it had not yet been allowed to grow much, and I afterwards had to paint in the beard in the picture purchased by Lord Ashburton."

[3] *Letters, &c., of Thomas Woolner*, p. 150.
[4] *The Carlyles' Chelsea Home*, by Reginald Blunt, pp. 8, 22, 28, &c. and the same author's *By Chelsea Reach*, p. 221, &c.
[5] Mrs. Strong, the first caretaker of the Carlyle's house.

AN INTERIOR AT CHELSEA. 1857

(*From the painting by R. Tait, exhibited at the Royal Academy, 1858.*)

[*face p. 292*

XV

MAPS AND BATTLE-PLANS, &c.
(1857)

IT was mainly in the evenings that Carlyle could be seen in the parlour pictured by Tait. He took no day of rest, and seldom more than a short walk in the mornings, which were mostly spent in the Attic workshop. In the afternoons now he used to go riding, sometimes with a companion, more often alone. Thus about June, 1857, he rode to Henry Taylor's house at Richmond to enquire for him, " sorry to see him looking so ill," and saying he had " brought down a bottle of medicine for him " which Mrs. Carlyle had found serviceable.[1]

His wife went to Scotland in July, to stay till September, but he remained continuously busy with his *Frederick* proofs, and stayed at home this year. The pleasantest event of the summer was Henry Larkin's relieving him of the labour of making maps and battle-plans. ' One day,' Larkin tells us,[2] ' I found Carlyle in great tribulation of spirit about maps and battle-plans, which had become necessary to illustrate the *Frederick*, and which he had found himself unable to arrange. He appealed to me to say " whether amongst your many faculties[3] of help, even map-making may not possibly be one ? " ' Larkin was at first dismayed, for he ' had had long and very bitter experience, not of map-making and battle-plans, but of very kindred employment. But what was I to do ? Was I to refuse him ? I promised to try what I could do. But from that time my labours with him were almost as weary a struggle as his own. My only satisfaction now is that notwithstanding repugnances I did succeed ; and gave him almost perfect satisfaction. So irksome was the misery that

---

[1] *Guests and Memories,* by Una Taylor, p. 208.
[2] *Carlyle and Mrs. Carlyle,* by Henry Larkin, *The British Quarterly Review,* 1881, No. 147, pp. 28–84, and p. 41, &c., for quotations here.
[3] Misprinted ' facilities,' here corrected ' faculties.'

in after years I could never hear him refer to them, as he
often gratefully did, as the one thing in which I had really
helped him, without a twinge of pain ; partly disappointment that it should be what I cared for least that he valued
and remembered best.

' The method was, I took the proofs or copy, and read
with the German map to verify every step taken and every
place described or mentioned ; and then select ' what was
necessary.

' The battle-plans ' were ' more abstruse. I had to gather
from the description a picture of the battle, and of the
arrangement of the opposing forces, at the moment of
attack ; and then, with a few strokes and dots ' show ' their
several positions. If any one should think this an easy
task, with an eye like Carlyle's to scan it when done, I
would like to see him try to do it.

' I had battle-plans in confusing abundance to help me ;
one large book, or perhaps two books, some two feet square,
expressly, and in strictest confidence, lent him by the
Prussian Government. But those were not of much real
help. Either they were vaguely inaccurate, or they gave
the positions of the forces at a different moment from that
which the description required. I was generally thrown
back on Carlyle's own words ' and the general map.

" To be shut up alone " with Carlyle when he was writing,
Larkin declared to be " misery," and his heart went out in
sympathy to Mrs. Carlyle when she described " with absolute shuddering " what she had endured at Craigenputtock.

Once the simple Larkin, feeling but not saying she needed
occupation, referred to Sterling's admiration of her writing,
and said,—" I wonder you do not try to find a little amusement in that way."

" Oh, Mr. Larkin," she exclaimed, " one writer is quite
enough in a house."

Nevertheless, Mr. Larkin admits with surprise,—" I ought
to say I never heard an angry word pass between themselves."

When Neuberg was translating the book and considering
Larkin's work from the point of view of a German reader,
he enquired of Carlyle and was told :—" As to the Battle
Plans, they came from a great variety of sources (Tempelhof,
or French Piracies of Tempelhof ; Kausler, which I had
from the Earl de Grey ; Tielcke the Saxon now in London

Library ; and occasionally perhaps one Müller, still in Cheyne Row, recommended in Preuss,—with various Jominis, &c. &c.) which I advise you *not* to get into, or meddle with at all !—"

In July William Allingham was in London on holiday and often walked with Carlyle. Once he suggested ' that Carlyle should write his autobiography,' and was answered :[4] —" I would as soon think of cutting my throat with my penknife when I get back home !—The biographers, too ! If those gentlemen would let me alone, I should be much obliged to them. I would say, as Shakespeare would say to Peter Cunningham, ' Sweet friend, for Jesus' sake for- bear ! ' " ' This was a slip of memory for ' Good friend,' of course, but tho Allingham told him so, and once even made him admit it by producing a photo of the tomb-stone at Stratford, he soon forgot the correction and was again ' using his beloved old formula, " Sweet Friend," as if nothing had happened.'

[4] *William Allingham, A Diary*, pp. 75–6, and 225.

XVI

AT HOME ALONE
(1857)

CONTINUING at his desk, while his wife was visiting friends in Scotland, Carlyle reported to her in full detail the news of Cheyne Row, and how he was ministering as bidden to her canaries and her dog Nero. He wrote on 26.7.57.—' To confess truth, I have had for about a week past a fit of villainous headaches, feverishness, &c., which I discover to be cold caught sitting in the sweep of the wind under the awning. I have been at proofs again all day. I am getting on slow, like an old spavined horse, but never giving in. One hope remains—that of working out of this sad element, getting my book done, and quitting London, I often think, or as good as quitting it, for the sake of fresh air and dairy produce in abundance.'

A few days later, ' I am glad,' he wrote, ' you make your bits of complaints freely to me ; if not to me, to whom else now alive on the earth ? Oh ! Never distrust me, as the Devil sometimes tempts your poor heart to do. I know you for an honest soul, far too sharp-tempered, but *true* to the bone ; and if I ever am or was unkind to you, God knows it was very far against my purpose. Do not distrust me. Tell me everything, and do not mind how weak you are before me. I know your strength and your weakness pretty well by this time. Poor little Goody ! Sha'n't I be glad to see you back again ? Yes ; for a considerable number of reasons.'

Writing to her on 5.8.57, he described the preceding Sunday morning, 2.8.57.—' Sunday I started broad awake at 3 a.m., went downstairs, out, smoked a cigar on a stool ; have not seen so lovely, sad, and grand a summer weather scene for twenty years back. Trees stood all as if cast in bronze, not an aspen leaf stirring ; sky was a silver mirror, getting yellowish to the north-east ; and only one big star, star of the morning, visible in the increasing light. This is a very grand place, this world, too. It did me no ill. Enough ! '

Thomas Woolner had done a good bust of Tennyson this year, and sent Mrs. Tennyson a report of Carlyle's talk at home this month.[1]—He ' spoke with profound contempt of Ruskin because the little Art Deity called " Aurora Leigh " the finest poem by far of the present age and gave him a copy to read.'

At the end of 1856 the English had made a shameless attack upon Canton ; and in 1857 they were continuing their iniquities in China. 1857 was also the year of the mutiny of the Indian army, and Woolner's report of the talk of Carlyle reveals how well he divined what is now known to be the truth.[1]—' I never heard Carlyle talk more solemnly than he did about the conditions which our statesmen are bringing our country to. He did not at all run into fierce declamation and denunciation, but talked calmly and keenly for fully an hour on India, China and the causes of the outbreaks in a style quite different to Parliamentary debates.' Of actual words we hear only,[2] " It's a sad thing when a man cannot respect the Government of his country."

But what Carlyle remembered best of this summer's events was his wife's appreciation of the book he was completing, on sight of the proof-sheets he had sent her. As he said himself, her letter was " the one bit of pure sunshine that visited my dark and lonesome . . . enterprise of *Frederick*."

' CRAIGENVILLA, EDINBURGH :
' *Monday, Aug.* 24, 1857.

' Oh, my dear ! What a magnificent book this is going to be ! The best of all your books. I say so, who never flatter, as you are too well aware ; and who am " the only person I know that is always in the right," '—a humorous quotation of an expression of Madame Lafayette.

' So far as it is here before me, I find it forcible and vivid, and sparkling as *The French Revolution*, with the geniality and composure and finish of *Cromwell*—a wonderful combination of merits ! And how you have contrived to fit together all those different sorts of pictures, belonging to different sorts of times, as compactly and smoothly as a bit of the finest mosaic ! Really one may say, of these first two books at least, what Helen ' (the maid) ' said of the letters of her sister

---

[1] *Thomas Woolner*, by Amy Woolner, pp. 136 and 144.
[2] Date uncertain.

who died—you remember!—"So splendidly put together, one would have thought that hand could not have written them!"

' It was the sheets that hindered me from writing yesterday; tho I doubt if a letter posted yesterday would have reached you sooner. . . . Certainly it is a devil of a place for keeping the Sunday, this! Such preaching and fasting, and " touting and praying," as I was never before concerned in! But one never knows whence deliverance is to come any more than misfortune. I was cut out of all, or nearly all, my difficulties yesterday by the simple providential means of—a bowel complaint! It was reason enough for staying away from church; excuse enough for declining to be read to; and the loss of my dinner was entirely made up for by the loss of my appetite! Nothing could have happened more opportunely! Left at home with Pen (the cat), when they had gone every one to her different " Place of Worship," I opened my desk to write you a letter. But I would just take a look at the sheets first. . . . Well, I took up the sheets and read " here a little and there a little," and then I began at the beginning and never could stop till I had read to the end, and pretty well learnt it by heart. I was still reading when Church came out, and so my letter got nipt in the bud. If it is so interesting for me, who have read and heard so many of the stories in it before, what must it be to others to whom it is all new? the matter as well as the manner of the narrative! Yes, you shall see, it will be the best of all your books—and small thanks to it! It has taken a doing!'

Writing on 7.9.1857 to one of Mrs. Strachey's sons, Sir John Strachey, Carlyle referred to the Indian Mutiny which had been the event of this summer, and to what Sir John had been telling him in the spring.[3]—'The East is not a pleasant place at present. . . . I have often thought how fatally soon your worst prognostications of it, that evening, have verified themselves! . . . People only weary me assigning " causes,"—I seek, at present, no further than the *uppermost* cause: an army commanded for fifty years by imaginary captains; . . . and capable of fermenting into results of any required degree of hideousness. . . . England thinks herself the " wisest nation of the world " quite as a settled truism, not worth asserting: England will, before long, become less conspicuously the most blockhead Nation in the world, or India will not be the last ill-news she hears! In fact, I am grieved and miserable about these things.'

---

[3] *Reminiscences of Carlyle with some Unpublished Letters*, by G. Strachey, *New Review*, July, 1893, pp. 17–33, and for quotation, p. 25.

XVII

LARKIN AND ROBSON AND MRS. CARLYLE
(1857)

THE maps and plans for the *Frederick* were only an intermittent affliction to Larkin. He was joyfully seeing through the press a new edition of Carlyle's works, not only correcting proofs but providing summaries and indexes wherever needful. On 18.10.57 he was made happy by this letter from Carlyle.[1]—

'It would have taken a round sum of money to pay anybody for what you are now doing ; and no amount of money (with me to lay it out here and now) could have got it done *so*, or at all like so. Robson appealed to me, the other day, whether I did not think those Summaries well done,—as well as any person could have done them ? To which my answer was decidedly affirmative.'

The printer Robson quoted here continued to be Carlyle's printer through changes of publishers ; and Larkin was ' astonished at the amount of vexatious and really editorial work which he cheerfully took upon himself whenever necessary.'[1] He charged a little more than other printers, but deserved the difference. As yet the Summaries had all gone to press without being seen by Carlyle ; but Larkin let his pen run free upon *Sartor*, and what he wrote was not only far beyond the space available, it was not a Summary at all but a prose-poetic interpretation. So whether Robson gave him a hint or not, he laid the manuscript before Carlyle and begged him to read it before it went to press.

Carlyle excused himself :—" It is quite unnecessary. I have no time for it—and must just leave it to your wise discretion." At last he was induced to look at the proof, and said at once it would never do—a commonplace Invoice of Contents was all that was needed, and there was no room

---

[1] *Carlyle and Mrs. Carlyle*, by Henry Larkin, *British Quarterly Review*, 1881, No. 147, pp. 35-54.

for more.—" I grieve much for the immense trouble you
have taken," he wrote, and Mrs. Carlyle comforted Larkin
by saying " You really ought to publish your little poem "
separately, which in due time he did ; but this freak of his
explains some other things.

He was much more at home with Mrs. Carlyle than with
her husband. The forenoon was the time he found most
convenient for going to their house. ' My practice,' he says,
' was to go straight up to Carlyle in his study and arrange
whatever I had to consult him about ; and then, as I passed
down, have half-an-hour's chat with Mrs. Carlyle in the
drawing-room, generally very pleasant half hours.

' I never knew anyone who could deal out little flatteries so
pleasantly and judiciously. I have seen it laid on copiously,
as with a trowel,' (Disraeli's way with Royalty, he said) ;
' but she knew better. She knew the sensitive points
exactly ; and if she chose, could touch them so delicately,
that it almost seemed like a happy inadvertence ; and she
could also prick them with the deftest of needles, if she saw
fit.'

She used to warn him he would never gain from Carlyle
the recognition he was looking for. Perhaps she was
trying to make him wince, as when she mocked his " youthful
enthusiasms " and said,—" It is mostly mad people who
come running after Carlyle," or with an expressive look,—
" What a comfort it is sometimes to have stupid people
about you,—it saves so much trouble ! " So in spite of
what Larkin admits, Carlyle's own ' very kind and hearty
appreciation of my poor services,' the good Christian clerk
began to feel that only the mistress of the household quite
understood him. He was always eager to do commissions
for her or advise about mechanical difficulties, fitting mirrors
into her walls, and so on. ' Even Carlyle's praise,' he says,
' always frankly conscientious, was far too serious and
admonitory ever to be lightly accepted, like Mrs. Carlyle's
playful flatteries.' Carlyle ' always seemed to imply—
" This is my clear and emphatic approval so far. Take
heed that you continue to deserve it."

' Once he was giving me some little bit of copying or
map-making to do, and was elaborately impressing on me
the importance of dispatch, but at the same time, of there
being no actual hurry about it ; which was a way he
had, like touching-up with the whip, and holding-in with
the bridle at the same moment. I intimated perfect

understanding and quoted Goethe's words " like a star, un-hasting and unresting." " Ah ! " interposed Mrs. Carlyle, " Carlyle is always hasting and *never* resting."

' She was once very severe upon Goethe's hard heart. " No one," said she, " but a hard-hearted man could have treated a pathetic character like poor little Mignon as *he* has treated her. If for his story he was bound to kill her, at least he was not bound to make stuffy speeches about it, and—embalm her." Meanwhile Carlyle looked on benignly as if listening to some pretty innocent prattle, but said nothing.' Which was the only prudent course for a man whose wife was capable of ' a bantering allusion to " Carlyle's friends the immortal Gods." '[1]

So far as concerned the current conventions of super-stition, the husband and wife were at one,—they tabooed pretence, as Larkin early found, when he ' ventured to send ' them a magazine article of his on ' The Poetry of Life,' upholding his ' Christian Ideal.' He reports the result :—' The next time I went—it was a passing call in the early part of the day—after we had transacted our business and I was about to leave, he returned me my little paper with a serious, almost a grieved look, but without a word of comment.' Downstairs, ' Mrs. Carlyle was equally silent, and I had to go my way pondering. They must have looked on me as a kind of feeble Irving. I have no doubt they were sincerely grieved.' This much was to be inferred from Mrs. Carlyle's subsequent attempts to open his eyes to the futility of the old beliefs, whereas ' Carlyle seemed to content himself with absolute silence on such topics.'[1]

XVIII

THE WINTER OF 1857-8, &c.

ALL this winter and for many months before and after it,—till the beginning of June, in fact,—Carlyle was reading the proofs of the first two volumes of his *Frederick*, (Books I to X). In December George Eliot (Miss Evans) was writing to a friend :[1]—' Dear Carlyle writes,—" I have had such a fourteen months as was never appointed me before—sorrow, darkness, and disgust my daily companions ; and no outlook visible, except getting a detestable business turned off, or else being driven mad by it." '

There was a financial crisis in America this Winter and many English investments were lost. Some of Carlyle's small savings were there, and Mrs. Carlyle's report about them to a Haddington lady is worth reading.—' I should like ill to be the Wife of a speculator just now ! Mr. C. has or *had* some money in America. He *doesn't recollect how much !* and doesn't feel even a natural *curiosity* what is become of it ! !—I have never heard a word out of his head about it, except to say *once*, " I suppose *my* money will have gone in the crash, and poor Butler " (the gentleman who invested it for him) " will be very sorry ! "—Being a Philosopher's Wife has some advantages !—I never think about money myself ; beyond what serves my daily needs ; but if *he* weren't of the same mind, I might be made sufficiently uncomfortable about it.'

In 1840 Carlyle had been consulted by James Hutchison Stirling, a young medical student in Glasgow, who was impatient of the trade he was set to learn, and hankering after literature, but who was persuaded by Carlyle's advice to stick to medicine. So Hutchison Stirling had practised in South Wales till in 1851 his father died, and he inherited money enough to be able to desist from doctoring. By that time he was preferring Emerson to Carlyle, and on

[1] *Life of George Eliot*, by J. W. Cross, p. 234.

going to the continent to study, he happened to be at Heidelberg when Hegel was resurrecting Christianity there. The cobwebs of Hegel captivated Hutchison Stirling, who devoted his time to disentangling the *Secret of Hegel,* which lasted in his pages some years longer than elsewhere.

In 1857 he had returned and was living in London ; and coming to tea one evening at Cheyne Row, made interesting notes which seem to fall about this December.[2] They had met before,—he was not quite a stranger, this handsome big man now in the prime of life, resembling Bismarck, and who was now taking snap-shots on the retina of his mind of the two Carlyles, a ' pair of good simple human beings,' with whom he was taking tea. He could not tell his wife, when he went home, what Mrs. Carlyle was wearing, but told her :— ' no head-dress, I think : middle-size, pale, with pleasant quiet voice, pleasant smiling eyes, a good face, hair apparently still black—spoke but seldom.' Carlyle appeared a tall, lank figure, hand an extraordinary bunch of fingers, decidedly long-fingered, ' moustache half grown, black still ' or dark-brown, ' whisker round chin grizzled at upper edge, cheek ruddy—a general *raised* look, as of a man with his nervous system in unnatural tension—kind of intellectual animal magnetism, every pore an eye—his hair grey now, still down on brow.'

They spoke of the weather and of Stirling's new home at Kensington and his life abroad.

" Do you *speak* German anything fluently ? " he was asked. The talk turned on Merthyr Tydvil, where he used to be, and people there. What Carlyle may have said we learn from a letter. It seemed to him when he saw it " a place never to be forgotten when once seen. The bleakest place *above* ground . . . *non-plus-ultra* of Industrialism, wholly Mammonish, given up to shopkeeper supply and demand ;—presided over by sooty Darkness, physical and spiritual, by Beer, Methodism, and the Devil, to a lamentable and supreme extent."

Homeopathy and daily three hour rides in cure of dyspepsia were mentioned ; and as a Glasgow man, the visitor could compare notes about Dixon's Blazes, the iron-works that illuminated the nights, and Glasgow Banks and ' money and titles ' with ' anecdotes of merchants.' " The

---

[2] See this work, Book XII, Chapter V. C. on *Cromwell and Others,* pp. 115-7 ; and *Life of James Hutchison Stirling,* by Amelia H. S., pp. 112-13, 138-144, 262-3.

British nation is going to Hell," said Carlyle, according to this reporter.

They spoke of Carpenter (probably the scientific professor of Forensic Medicine) and Sir J. Clark; but Hutchison Stirling had now taken leave of medicine and science. Mill's Logic was more his way, and he tried Spinoza and Kant and even the holy Hegel, but found Carlyle cold about them. Heidelberg, where he had been living, would lead to mention of the Bunsens, but the Bunsens did not dabble in Hegel, apparently. The talk fell on Dumfriesshire places and on literature; but the only words of Carlyle surviving in the notes are " useless epigrammatists " and " Classical marine stores."

Of modern men of letters, Douglas Jerrold was named, who had died last summer,—" an honest creature," Carlyle thought him, and both Carlyle and his wife, in one breath as it were, enquired,—" Which do you like best, Dickens or Thackeray ? "

" I answered, ' Dickens,' " said Hutchison Stirling,[3] " and pleased them both. Indeed the pair of them always seemed to me to have a joint opinion on most things."

On this occasion, Carlyle rejoined :—" Yes, he's a good little fellow, Dickens ; but he has no knowledge, he has no knowledge," speaking slowly and as if reluctantly, and pronouncing knowledge with a long o, in the old-fashioned way.[3]

On 28.12.57 Carlyle was writing a letter worth quoting.— " All mortals are tumbling about in a state of drunken Saturnalia, delirium or quasi-delirium, according to their several sorts ; a very strange method of thanking God for sending them a Redeemer ; a set singularly worth " redeeming," too, you would say. I spent Christmas and the two days following in grim contention all day each time with the most refractory set of proof-sheets I expect in this work ; the sternly sad remembrance of another Christmas, (when his mother died), ' present to me also at all moments which made a strange combination, peculiarly tragic when I had time to see it from the distance, like a man set to whittle cherry-stones and toy-boxes in the Valley of the Shadow of Death.'

Even three days at the Grange in January, and again in the spring, did not stop the proof-correcting,—he did his daily task there too ; and for the rest of the time at home

[3] Verbal report to D. A. W., by Dr. Hutchison Stirling, on 2.10.1896

it was the same. Tho shy of confessing it, he was enjoying his job.

About February Mrs. Carlyle was writing to her friend Mrs. Russell of Thornhill, describing her sittings to an artist friend, Mrs. Hawkes, who was painting her portrait.— ' And so, for the last fortnight, she has been coming every morning at eleven, and staying till two ;—just the time I used to have all by myself to write in, or to do what other thing needed privacy,—darn Mr. C.'s socks, perhaps. I dine between two and three ; and from three till six I am seldom without callers. Then comes Mr. C.'s dinner, at which I look on, and tell him the news of the day ; and thus the only time I have had to write letters in is at night, with Mr. C. sitting opposite me at the same table (as at this moment), an arrangement which feels to rather tie my *moral legs* together ! Accordingly, I have waited for a morning all to myself.'

Then followed much about a servant Ann who was leaving her, concluding with a reference to Geraldine Jewsbury, now a woman of 46 :—' Geraldine comes every day for longer or shorter time ; but she is no use to me in this matter or any other. She is so unsettled—" carried " as we call it. I *won't* hear a word about Mr. X. out of her head ; and there is nothing else she has care to talk about or think about.' Poor Geraldine !—There is something infinitely touching in a last-chance affection.

Writing to his brother Dr. John in March, Carlyle remarked,—' I refuse all invitations, and, except meeting people in the street, have next to no communication with my external fellow-creatures.' He did not like the new metal pens that were coming into fashion instead of quills, and wrote this spring :—' Nothing will ever reconcile me to these miserable iron pens. Often in writing the beautiful book now on hand I remind myself of the old Spaniard who had to do his on leather with a dagger ; and, in fact, I detest writing more and more, and expect fairly to end it if I can ever finish this—but all friends be soft with me, for I declare myself hard bested in the present season.'

X

XIX

" INFANT PRAYERS " AND SEXUAL TALK
(1858)

THO Carlyle was ' overwhelmingly busy ' this spring, the same W. Lattimer, a cork-cutter in Carlisle, who in 1853 had got advice from him about reading, succeeded in drawing from him advice about teaching children which many may wish to see again. His letter to Mr. Lattimer of 3.3.1858 has been often reprinted. It referred to translations of Jean Paul's *Levana* and Goethe's *Travels of Wilhelm Meister*, and contained some sentences which illuminate the ' Silence ' which Carlyle preached and practised.—

' 1. Forms of devotion, " Infant Prayers " and other, might have a very good effect, on one proviso (but this a rigorous one), That the father himself completely *believed* in them. If the father do not entirely believe, if he even unconsciously doubts, still more if he do not even know what belief is, the child will at once more or less clearly feel this ; and the effects will be *bad*, and that only,—perhaps to a degree little suspected at present.

' 2. That we are all " bound to speak the truth " to our fellow creatures ; and the divine importance of doing that is plain enough by this time, or ought to be. But the faithful man here too will keep his eye upon the concrete fact as well as upon the rubric, or *letter* of the law ; and will know that it is with the *fact* that he has got to deal. To set up " cases of conscience," and puzzle over them will not much help him. The permitted limits of simulation, who could undertake to define them ? We do not *inform* the *fox*, enquiring of us, where our poultry lodges. *All men are entitled at least to keep their thoughts dumb when they please.*[1] Answers that have that effect are a refuge possible in most cases.—And for the rest there is a far deeper *veracity* than that of the tongue ; which it is infinitely important

---

[1] Italics added.

to acquire, and which I have often noticed superstitious professors of tongue-truth to be greatly destitute of.

' 3. All nations that have risen beyond the rank of Samoyedes have had laws, which they kept as sacred, in reference to matters sexual : and generally the higher they have risen in the scale of nations, the nobler and more imperative have such laws been. *Continence* (in this and in all things) is the perpetual duty of all men and of all women. Chastity, in the true form of it, is probably the most beautiful of virtues,—essential to all noble creatures. A lewd being has fatally lost the *aroma* of his existence ; and become *caput mortuum* in regard to the higher functions of intelligence and morality. No frightfuller feature of these ruined generations presents itself than that of their utter corruption in this respect.—Alas, what can a parent do in such times ? He will need all his wisdom to do even a little for his child in that important particular. For injudicious meddling is capable, I believe, of frightfully *worsening* the affair.'

What Carlyle meant by " Continence " and the " true form of Chastity " was of course as far from celibacy as from vice,—he meant the healthy harmony of mind and body which makes a family the unit of society.

Indeed it is ludicrous to talk of women as only equal to men—they are infinitely better. We wild men of the west, as the civilised Chinese and Muslims think us European males, exaggerate the importance of the fighting sex. The evolution upward of our primitive ancestors in the last million years is mostly the work of the women. In short, the unit of society is, was and evermore shall be no person but a family ; and if ever we reach a stable civilisation, no man shall ever be trusted in any position of social responsibility without a wife to take charge of him.

XX

OUR POLITICIANS
(1858)

SPENDING an evening at Cheyne Row in March, 1858
the sculptor Woolner found all well there and cheerful,
and reports :[1]—Carlyle 'was talking chiefly upon the
barbaric ignorance of the English in matters historical, and
retailed an anecdote almost incredible, only as it happened
to himself he could manage to believe it. He was at a
nobleman's house where were collected some of the chief
lawyers and statesmen of the land, and happening to
mention the battle of Cheshme[2] in 1770 (the great naval
victory of the Russians, assisted by the English, where the
fleet of the Turks was annihilated and Constantinople
itself laid bare), 'he said not one of these distinguished
persons had ever heard of it.'

This revealed the mental nakedness of our ruling gentry,
ignorant and heedless, " drifting into war " with Russia to
deliver Turkey, without enquiring into recent history, so
that their Crimean War was a blunder as well as a crime.
As one of them said afterwards,—" They put their money
on the wrong horse." Unfortunately it was not their own
money they were risking, but the wealth of the nation, and
the lives of better men.

In the following June, Woolner was surprised when he
called to find neither Mrs. Carlyle nor her husband at
home ; and when he saw her afterwards she told him,—
" My husband was suddenly struck with my ' thinness '
and ' paleness,' and decided on taking me a few miles on a
railway to try if that would put any life into me." She added
that she might accept Mrs. Tennyson's invitation to stay
with them, but not until Mr. Carlyle had gone to Scotland.'

---

[1] *Thomas Woolner*, by Amy Woolner, pp. 145 and 150.
[2] A port west of Smyrna, opposite the island of Scio.

XXI

THE FIRST TWO VOLUMES
(1858)

BY the middle of June Carlyle had finished his work on the first two volumes of *Frederick*, which were then ready for publication in the autumn. The title-page said the work was to be in four volumes, and the author's private hope was that he would be done with it in two years more. But he was mistaken. Even as Homer's history of the quarrel between Achilles and Agamemnon grew into the *Iliad*, so the history of *Frederick* became a living picture of the world in the Eighteenth Century, surpassing anything of the sort on record in any language.

In these two volumes, which come down to the death of Frederick William, 1740, Carlyle holds the mirror up to Nature and reveals the Royalties and rulers of Europe with an insight like that attributed to the Recording Angel, insisting on righteousness and common sense with the earnestness of a Chinese or Jewish sage. This history is as clear and palpable as anything in the daily press, as wise as any scriptures, yet often as delightfully humorous as *Punch* at its best, and occasionally better, as the fun of reality is better than any make-believe.

Reality was sacred to him, a sacred *science*. As good doctors of medicine advise about diseases, so, in politics and history, Carlyle used theories to connect his facts, but never shaped his facts to support his theories. That was how he stumbled on the strangest discovery in these two volumes, that the Father of the freethinker Frederick, Frederick William, altho a hereditary king, was in thought, word and action a Christian man of the best conscientious type, and by that means prospered well. On the details of such a life it was natural for Carlyle to dwell so lovingly that what might have been told in a few chapters, so far as it concerned

Frederick only, grew into two big volumes, which vindicate the ways of God to man and show the justice of living Nature and the futility of human trickery. " He that was honest with his existence," says the historian, " has always meaning for us, be he king or peasant."

XXII

PRIVATE OPINIONS OF EMERSON, &c.
(1858)

NONE of the critics thought so little of these first two
volumes as the writer of them. In a letter to Emerson
on 2.6.1858 he frankly remarked :—' That book on Friedrich
of Prussia—first half of it, two swoln unlovely volumes,
which treat mainly of his Father, &c., and leave him at his
accession—is just getting out of my hands. One packet
more of Proofs, and I have done with it,—thanks to all the
gods ! No job approaching in ugliness to it was ever cut out
for me ; nor had I any motive to go on, except the sad
negative one, " Shall we be beaten in our old days, then ? "
—But it has thoroughly humbled me,—trampled me down
into the *mud*, there to wrestle with the accumulated stupidi-
ties of Mankind, German, English, French, and other, for
all have borne a hand in these sad centuries ;—and here
I emerge at last, not *killed*, but almost as good. Seek not
to look at the Book,—nay in fact it is " not to be *published*
till September," (so the man of affairs settles with me
yesterday, " owing to the political, &c., to the season,"
&c.) ; my only stipulation was that in ten days I should
be utterly out of it,—not to hear of it again till the Day of
Judgment, and if possible not even then ! In fact it is a
bad book, poor, misshapen, feeble, *nearly* worthless (thanks
to *past* generations and to me) ; and my one excuse is,
I could not make it better, all the world having played such
a game with it. Well, well !—How true is that that you say
about the skater (and the rider too) depending on his
vehicles, on his roads, on his et ceteras ! Dismally true
have I a thousand times felt it, in these late operations ;
never in any so much. And in short the business of writing
has altogether become contemptible to me ; and I am become
confirmed in the notion that nobody ought to write,—unless
sheer Fate force him to do it ;—and then he ought (if *not* of

the mountebank genus) to beg to be shot rather. That is deliberately my opinion,—or far nearer it than you will believe.

' Once or twice I caught some tone of you in some American Magazine ; utterances highly noteworthy to me ; in a sense, the only thing that is *speech* at all among my fellow-creatures in this time. For the years that remain, I suppose we must continue to grumble out some occasional utterance of that kind : what can we do at this late stage ? But in the *real* " Model Republic," it would have been different with two good boys of this kind !—

' Though shattered and trampled down to an immense degree, I do not think any bones are broken yet,—though age truly *is* here, and you may engage your berth in the steamer whenever you like. In a few months I expect to be sensibly improved ; but my poor Wife suffers sadly the last two winters ; and I am much distressed by that item of our affairs. Adieu, dear Emerson : I have lost many things ; let me not lose you till I must in some way !

' Yours ever,
' T. CARLYLE.'

' P.S. If you read the Newspapers (which I carefully abstain from doing) they will babble to you about Dickens's " Separation from Wife," &c. &c. ; fact of Separation I believe is true ; but all the rest is mere lies and nonsense. No crime or misdemeanor specifiable on either side ; *unhappy* together, these good many years past, and they at length end it.—Sulzer said, " Men are by nature *good*." " Ach, mein lieber Sulzer, Er kennt nicht diese verdammte Race," (Oh, my dear Sulzer, you don't know that damned Race !), ejaculated Fritz, at hearing such an axiom.'

Emerson's reply came many months afterwards, and a few sentences may be quoted here.—

'. . . The book (the first volume of the *Life of Friedrich*) came, with its irresistible inscription, so that I am all tenderness and all but tears. The book, too, is sovereignly written. I think you the true inventor of the stereoscope, as having exhibited that art in style long before we had yet heard of it in drawing. The letter came also. Every child of mine knows from far that hand-writing, and brings it home with speed. . . .'

After he had read the first two volumes, Emerson wrote in his diary.—

' Meantime here has come into the country three months ago a book of Carlyle, *History of Frederick*, infinitely the wittiest book that ever was written, a book that one would think the English people would rise up in mass to thank him for, by cordial acclamation, and congratulate themselves that such a head existed among them, and much-sympathizing, and on-its-own-account-reading America would make a new treaty extraordinary of joyful, grateful delight with England, in acknowledgment of such a donation,—a book with so many memorable and heroic facts, working directly, too, to practice ; with new heroes, things unvoiced before ; with a range of thought and wisdom the largest and the most colloquially elastic that ever was, not so much applying as inosculating to every need and sensibility of a man, so that I do not so much read a stereotype page, as I see the eyes of the writer looking into my eyes, with winks and long-commanding glances, and stereoscoping every figure that passes, and every hill, river, wood, hummock, and pebble in the long perspective ; and withal a book that is a Judgment Day, for its moral verdict on the men and nations and manners of modern times. With its wonderful new system of mnemonics, whereby great and insignificant men are ineffaceably ticketed and marked in the memory by what they were, had, and did. And this book makes no noise ; I have hardly seen a notice of it in any newspaper or journal, and you would think there was no such book ; but the secret interior wits and hearts of men take note of it, not the less surely. They have said nothing lately in praise of the air, or of fire, or of the blessing of love, and yet, I suppose, they are sensible of these, and not less of this book, which is like these. . . .

' Glad of Ellery Channing's cordial praise of Carlyle's *History* which he thinks well entitled to be called a " Work," and far superior to his early books. Wonders at his imagination which can invest with such interest to himself these (one would think) hopeless details of German story. He is the only man who knows.—What a reader ! How competent to give light now on the politics of Europe ! To-day this *History* appears the best of all histories. . . . Carlyle's *Friedrich* is a great book ; opens new extension to history. How much event, personality, nationality, is there disclosed or hinted at, and will draw multitudes of scholars to its exploring and illustration ! '

XXIII

ON SOLWAY SIDE
(1858)

HAVING finished his work on the first two volumes,
Books I to X, Carlyle went north in the last week of
June to his sister's farm of ' the Gill ' on Solway side ; and,
as he wrote to his brother Alick in Canada, ' continued
about two months there, as *idle* as a dry bone ; sauntering
about in silence, riding a little, reading a little,—peaceable
but . . . sad. . . . A man of 63 has a strange feeling when
visiting his native country,—as of a *ghost* coming back to
the Earth ! I rode one day, market day, thro Annan ; did
not see one soul whose face was known to me ; only the
old stone walls were familiar ; and strangers gazed at my
" wideawake hat " and old grey beard,—asking " who's
that ? " '

He received a letter from somebody at Oxford begging
" information about India," and sent on the letter to Mill
" after long years of abeyance." Mill was good enough to
give the young man an interview.

Scotsbrig and Craigenputtock were both within reach.
After visiting Craigenputtock he wrote to his wife :—' I
looked with emotion upon my old *library closet,* and wished
I could get thither again, to finish my *Frederick* under fair
chances.' Of course she ignored the hint ; but the fact
that he was capable of even hinting such a wish explains
why Larkin used often to hear her, especially when her
husband was listening, one may guess, " speak of their life
at Craigenputtock with absolute shuddering."[1] Indeed it
is worth remembering, and hard to realise, how great a sacrifice to his wife's wishes Carlyle was making by continuing
to live in London against his will, and when he had such a
job on hand as this *Frederick*. Sir James Crichton-Browne

---

[1] Larkin's *Carlyle and Mrs. Carlyle, British Quarterly Review,* July,
1881, No. 147, p. 51.

has well reminded us[2] of how he always hankered after Craigenputtock, esteeming their time there their happiest days, and confessing ' that, for living and thinking in, I have never since found a place in the world so favourable. . . . I found I could do fully *twice* as much work in a given time there as, with my best effort, was possible in London.'

' My best time is usually the evening,' he now wrote to her. ' Never saw such evenings for freshness, brightness— the west one champaign of polished silver, or silvergilt, as the sun goes down, and I get upon the wastes of the Priest- side ' (Bank,—a sandbank opposite the shore nearest to the Gill, between Ruthwell and Cummertrees),—' with no sound audible but that of tired geese extensively getting home to their quarters, and here and there a contemplative cuddy, giving utterance to the obscure feeling he has about this Universe. I go five or six miles, striding along under the western twilight, and return home only because porridge ought not to be belated overmuch. I read considerably here, sit all day sometimes under the shelter of a comfort- able hedge, pipe not far distant, and read Arrian.'

Arrian was the ancient Greek author whose *Enchiridion of Epictetus* had helped to make Carlyle a Stoic long ago. But Arrian was also the historian of Alexander the Great, and it is likely that what Carlyle was reading now was a translation in the London Library of the history of Alex- ander's campaigns. Like Goethe and Emerson, and Max Müller and many another man of sense, Carlyle would not waste time in reading Greek when there was a good transla- tion, any more than he would swim or ford a river after a bridge had been built.

Thinking of the work he had in hand, he now wrote to Neuberg who was in Germany.—' There is to be a visiting of Frederick's Battlefields after all ! The enterprise, I con- fess, seems horrible to me : but a certain uneasy feeling,— something connected with literary *conscience* among more questionable elements,—urges me forward and it must be done. . . . Foxton is to start with me, . . . a social intelli- gent fellow, thorough gentleman in habits and character. . . . I am to go round by Rügen, first after Hamburg ; and commence my special pilgrimage from Usedom's house ' there. . . . ' I wanted to see it ' (Rügen) ' at any rate. . . .

[2] *Stray Leaves from a Physician's Portfolio*, by Sir James Crichton Browne, pp. 334 and 340.

I regret to go so far round. . . . I have really nothing else to do but " see these Battlefields " : however, it was only by Usedom's help (directions, introductions, &c.), that I could fairly see a possibility of in actual fact (and not in sad semblance only) *doing* the small problem ; wherefore I was very glad of the offer made me.

' Come if you can. I count on your coming. . . .'

Among the books he enjoyed at the Gill this summer, and recommended to Lady Sandwich, were French translations of Turgenev's *Scenes of Russian Life* and *A Sportsman's Sketches*, and Béranger's *Autobiography*.

As for his business arrangements with his publisher, Chapman, his friend John Forster took charge of all that. As Carlyle had told him this June,[3] " You cannot go against my judgment in it while you follow your own."   On the day he left by the train for Carlisle, 23.6.1858, he wrote to him.[3]—

" DEAR FORSTER,

" Amid the agonies of packing, I write a word of thanks to you.   I am heartily your debtor for settling . . . as you have done ; the blessing of one altogether wearied out of his life be upon you ! . . . I accept however it may be what you have done and dismiss it from my mind, and till October arrive, shall, instead of an arithmetical-commercial intanglio " (which probably means entanglement), " retain merely a pleasant thought of Forster and human help in that corner of my memory.   More is the praise to Forster ; may his shadow never be less. . . Yours ever, T. CARLYLE."

[3] Copied 23.9.1902 and days following from the original papers in the Museum, South Kensington.

XXIV

TO GERMANY AGAIN
(1858)

WHEN Carlyle had decided to go to Germany again for a look at the Battlefields, he wrote to Lord Ashburton enquiring whether he could find him " a man with a yacht " who could land him in the Baltic. On Tuesday, 27.7.1858, Ashburton called at Cheyne Row and had a long talk with Mrs. Carlyle. He promised to see " all the yachtsmen today and find out something " ; but as yet he could only offer an invitation to " go with Lord Dufferin up the Mediterranean " and be landed at Trieste. Mrs. Carlyle was quite persuaded this offer should be accepted, and wrote to her husband,—" I vote for the Mediterranean too. It is the only chance you will have of seeing what everybody has seen." On his way to the Highlands Ashburton went round by Dumfries, and spent a day with Carlyle there, but could not persuade him to go by Trieste. He was too much concentrated on his business, which was to look at the battlefields.

Carlyle arranged to go with Foxton by the steamer leaving Leith for Hamburg on Saturday, 21.8.58. As usual, it was late of starting, and they might have been seen together " sprawling on the grass of the Calton Hill," and watching the evening shadows falling on land and sea. They were safe on board the *Dunedin* when she went out into the dark to go pitching and rolling on her watery way. " What care these roarers for philosophers ? " A man must take what weather comes. Monday was not so rough as Sunday, and as they were moving up the Elbe on Tuesday, 24.8.58, it was ' a bright, sunny, beautiful morning.' A friend of Neuberg was waiting to meet them, with a letter to say he was ready at Berlin. There was a pleasant " storm of wind-music spreading over the city . . . excellently sweet," as Carlyle sat writing to his wife at 11 p.m., and hoping for a better night's sleep than he had had at sea.

XXV

RÜGEN AND BERLIN
(1858)

EVEN three nights at sea with little sleep did not enable Carlyle to sleep at Hamburg. On Wednesday, 25.8.58, their first morning there, he dictated and Foxton wrote a letter to Neuberg, and at noon they departed together.

Next morning they were hastening from Rostock railway station to get a place in the diligence for Stralsund, ' with no prospect but eight hours of suffocation and a night to follow without sleep,' when a lady attended by a maid addressed Carlyle ' with sunny voice and look,'—" Are not you Mr. Carlyle ? " " Yes ! " " I am the Frau von Usedom, here to seek you, sixty-four miles from home, and you must go with me henceforth."

Which made him feel as if a ministering angel had reached down a helping hand from Heaven. He found a use for Foxton as they posted along,—he ' put him inside to do the talking,' while he sat on the box outside and smoked and looked about. By six o'clock they had come 45 miles and reached Stralsund, where Foxton left them, to go to Berlin, while Carlyle and his hostess, in the bright autumn evening, crossed in a steamer the ' little bit of sea ' which made Rügen an island.

A carriage was awaiting them, and four swift horses to take it twenty miles farther, over bare flat sandy ground, with plentiful tracks and paths but never a metalled road. As they went spanking along, he noted the abundant cultivation and ' brick-red beehives of cottages,' and felt ' strange,' as if ' in a *mährchen* ' or fairy tale, with a ' voluble, incessantly explosive, demonstrative, but thoroughly good Madame von Usedom ' beside him, telling the wonderful arrangements her man had made, has even ' spoken of it to the Prince of Prussia,' and is to be here to-morrow night himself. Between nine and ten they reached the house,

which was 'like nothing you ever saw,' Carlyle told his
wife, ' mediæval, semi-patriarchal, half a farm-house, half a
palace,'—something like the dwellings of the Kings in
Homer, if he had thought of it. A good night's sleep completed his comfort, so that he reported to Neuberg that he
was in ' the best quarters in the world,' and wrote to his
wife,—' If I but knew you were well, I think I could be
almost happy here today, in the silent sunshine, on these
remote Scandinavian shores. The wind is singing and the
Sun sporting in the lindens, and I hear doves cooing.
Windows up ! Two rooms all to myself. Coo ! Coo ! '

' Almost happy ! ' We have to remember the pious
upbringing of Carlyle to understand such a phrase. The
Christian conviction that we all are ' miserable sinners ' is
what would keep us all safe against the Devil himself, altho
we had bargained with him as Faust did,—

> " If e'er you find me quite content,
> And bidding Time stand still,
> To Death you then can have me sent
> And bind me as you will."

If Carlyle had been under any such bond, he would now
have been in danger, but not for long. He was so happy
that he *bathed* in the Baltic, and caught a chill. So he felt
feverish and took physic, and had to lie horizontal several
days.

Usedom arrived as his wife had foretold, and Carlyle and
he ' did beautifully together,' tho the substantial and sensible Usedom bored Carlyle with the current cant about the
picturesque. Whereby he meant only to ' do the honours '
of the place and be agreeable,—he did not realise that his
guest was suffering from the effects of a recent blue pill.

By Tuesday, 31.8.58, all was well again. Usedom and
Carlyle rode about together exploring Rügen, ' the German
Isle of Wight,' and crossed an arm of the sea on horseback.
" Insignificant sea ! " wrote Carlyle to his wife,—" Not
rightly salt at all ! "—as if resenting like a boy the chill it
had given him. On Friday, 3.9.58, the hospitable Usedom
convoyed him to Berlin, where on the Saturday Neuberg
and Foxton were ready waiting him.

There was not much time for calls, only Sunday ; and
Varnhagen von Ense wrote in his diary :[1]—' Sunday, 5th
September, 1858.—Visit from Carlyle and Neuberg ;—

---

[1] *Tagebücher von K. A. Varnhagen von Ense*, XIV, pp. 369–70 : quoted
here from R. H. Shepherd's *Thomas Carlyle*, II, pp. 168–9.

yesterday the former' (Carlyle), 'arrived here, accompanied by Herr von Usedom; and tomorrow early they will again set out for Zorndorf, Kunersdorf, Leuthen, Liegnitz, Sorr, Mollwitz, Prague, Kolin! Carlyle says that his book on Frederick the Great is the poorest, most troublesome and arduous piece of work he has ever undertaken : no satisfaction in it at all, only labour and sorrow. " What the Devil had I to do with your Friedrich ? " His complaints are very droll. He says that in England they know nothing of him, nothing of Prussia, and little even of Germany. All these transactions are quite unknown there, altho at the time they must have known something of them. He complimented Ludmilla on her book, and said she should write more of the same kind.

' " It has never happened before," exclaimed Neuberg, " that Carlyle has urged a woman to write. Up to this time he has always dissuaded every woman." Carlyle,' concluded von Ense, ' seems to be more healthy and livelier than when he was here before, and also more resolute.' Which is easily explained. His previous visit to Berlin was made after several weeks of broken sleep in German inns, whereas on this occasion he was fresh from pleasant Rügen and the kind Usedoms.

' When Carlyle visited Berlin,' reports Moncure Conway, speaking of this visit,[2] ' he went to a Museum there. " The keeper of it," he told me, " insisted on showing me everything in the place ; but what I went to see was Friedrich's clothes. It was as if one should go into an inn to take a chop, and they insisted he must eat everything in their store. Finally, after some contention, I looked upon Friedrich's military old clothes. And I saw that I really had properly nothing to do with those clothes. Considerations of self-respect, chiefly, made me undertake the *Life of Friedrich*, but it has been all toil and pain." '

" Considerations of self-respect " may not be literally accurate. He may have said something to that effect, meaning that he had to be doing something, and it was the best job that he could get, and he felt bound to finish what he had begun. Conway's report corroborates von Ense's,—about the ejaculation,—" What the Devil had I to do with your Friedrich ? "

[2] *Thomas Carlyle*, by Moncure D. Conway, pp. 63–4.

XXVI

SEEING BATTLE-FIELDS
(1858)

ON Monday, 6.9.58, Carlyle left Berlin for Cüstrin to look at Zorndorf. He was now accompanied by both Neuberg and Foxton, and fortified, by the favour of Usedom, with ' a general letter from the Prince's aide-de-camp to all Prussian officers whatsoever.' Which availed them well at Zorndorf, where a ' benevolent major ' who saw it showed them ' everything,' but it was of no use anywhere else. At Liegnitz, their next stage, a royal review was impending, which preoccupied the military men, and Carlyle passed unobserved and without looking,—he was not interested in such reviews. Breslau was their next headquarters, and from there they did Leuthen on 9.9.58 and Mollwitz the next day, climbing church steeples, and ' in barbarous jargon, questioning ignorant mankind.'

Almost miraculously perfect as his descriptions are, and short as his survey was, Carlyle was looking with more than a soldier's eye at the places he was visiting and the people there. His letters to his wife show him very wide-awake, and in no way narrowed by his concentration on the business in hand. Thus from Brieg, near Mollwitz, he was writing to her on 10.9.58 :—' The people are a good, honest, modest set of beings ; poorer classes, especially in the country, much happier than with us. Every kind of industry is on the improving hand ; the land, mainly sandy, is far better tilled than I expected.'

Writing from Breslau next day (11.9.58), he described it as,—' a queer old city. . . . High as Edinburgh. . . . Streets very strait ' (narrow) ' and winding. The people are not beautiful, but they seem innocent and obliging, brown-skinned, scrubby bodies, many of Polack or Slavic breed. You never saw such churches, Rath-houses, &c., old as the hills, and huge. An island in the Oder here is completely

covered with cathedrals and appendages. Brown women
with cock noses, snubby in character, have all got straw
hats, umbrellas, crinolines, &c., as fashion orders, and are
no doubt charming to the brown man.'

Leaving Breslau on Saturday (11.9.58), they reached
Landshut on the edge of the mountains, and crossing into
Bohemia next day Carlyle reported,—' Our drive was as
beautiful as any I ever had.' Taking train for Pardubitz,
they found themselves among a crowd of ' dirty, smoking,
Sunday gents, as ugly on the Elbe as on the Thames ';
and as the ' big noisy inn, full of evil smells,'—' the *oldest*
smells ' they had ever met,'[1]—did not tempt them to linger,
they began at 4 a.m. their next day's work, 13.9.58, and
finished Chotusitz and Kolin and reached Prague that
night.

' This is a grand picturesque town, this Prag,' he wrote
to his wife, 14.9.58, enclosing a ' wild pink plucked from
the battlefield. Give it to some young lady who practises
the " Battle of Prague " on her piano to your satisfaction.'

Neuberg was plainly ' the mainstay of every enterprise,'
—Carlyle ' could not do without him.' But Neuberg was
far from well, and took a day in bed at Prague, where
Foxton was equal to what little sightseeing was needed
there, the Ziscaberg, &c. The whole trip was a picnic to
Foxton. He had enjoyed the village inns, especially when
sitting with Carlyle in the sunshine at their doors under
' curling wreathes of tobacco smoke '; and even the
crowded trains were pleasant to him in memory as he recalled
that ' grim, bearded, Saracenic visage in the corner of the
railway carriage,' watching their fellow-passengers.[2]

They went to Dresden next, 15.9.58, the confusion of the
journey being compensated by the sight of ' the beautifullest
country ever seen, and the beautifullest weather.' A letter
from Mrs. Carlyle was awaiting them there, and her man
read it ' sitting on the Elbe Bridge in the sunshine.'

From Dresden they went to Hochkirch, where Marshal
Keith had died in rallying his men. He is a leading hero of
the bloody history. To Carlyle as well as to Frederick he
seemed one of ' the most deserving,' for many reasons, the
best of which is more likely to be appreciated in Asia, or
some future Europe, than among the money-grabbers of
to-day. Keith's brother reported when he died,—He ' leave

[1] *Frederick*, Book XIII, Chapter XIII.
[2] Letter of Mr. Foxton preserved by Neuberg.

ne a noble legacy. Last year he had Bohemia under ransom ; and his personal estate is 70 ducats ' (£25).

They had a toilsome day at Torgau next, and from there went to Leipzig and Weissenfels, to see Rossbach,—the last they had to look at of Frederick's battlefields. Then they took train to Weimar, where Secretary Marshall was expecting them, and had a quiet bedroom ready. From Weimar to Aix-la-Chapelle was a tiresome day, ' oftenest in slow trains, through broiling sun, sand clouds, and manu- facturing smoke,' but happily the bed in the hotel was as comfortable as at Weimar, long enough to stretch himself in, which he had seldom found in the hotels in Germany. In the morning he went to the Cathedral, and as he wrote to his wife, ' stood upon the *lid* of Charlemagne—abominable monks roaring out their idolatrous grand music within sight.' The three pilgrims came home by Ostend and Dover, ' Foxton branching off at Redhill, and taking leave almost with tears ' (22.9.58).

Meanwhile Mrs. Carlyle had gone about the end of July to Bay House, Alverstoke, and was there the guest of Lord Ashburton's sisters, the Misses Baring, till 24.8.58 ; but coming home before the end of August, she had gone to Scotland and greatly enjoyed some weeks at the house of her friend Mrs. Pringle, Lann Hall, Dumfriesshire. On 10.9.58 she wrote from there to her husband in Germany. ' . . . One's life here is remarkably cheerful. It is the very loveliest glen I ever saw, endeared to me by old associations ' (Glen Shinnel). ' The people in it . . . farmers or little lairds . . . were always hospitable. They are glad to see me again, and I am glad to see them. . . . (There) has been a perfect explosion of lunches to my honour and glory, all over Glen Shinnel and Glencairn. . . . It is so much heartier a sort of hospitality than one finds in the south! It makes me feel younger by twenty years! I catch myself laughing sometimes with a voice that startles myself as being not like my own but my mother's, who was always so much gayer than I. Indeed, it is good for me to be here. . . .'

So Carlyle would not be surprised to find he had reached home before her. He would only be amused to see what she had written to Larkin, bidding him in that event, " Go and see after him, poor Babe of Genius, till I come . . . in the beginning of next week." Which meant no more than to let Charlotte the maid know to be ready.

XXVII

THANKING LARKIN
(1858)

ON 23.9.1858, the day after arriving at home, Carlyl
resumed his work, and on 30.9.58 made Henry Larki
happy by giving him a copy of the first two volumes an
saying what Larkin has thus reported.[1]—' When he hande
me the volumes, Carlyle solemnly and impressively thanke
me for the great and unexpected help I had given him i
his heavy labour, without which he shuddered to thin
where he might then have been. I cannot recall all that h
said ; but the words, " with a luminous silence, and a stead
fidelity of effort, beyond all his experience or imagination
if it would be any satisfaction to me to know it,"—have re
mained with me, as if spoken but yesterday. He then kindl
insisted on my acceptance of a cheque (£100), and accom
panied it with many earnest wishes for my future welfare.

Soon afterwards he sent Larkin a life-ticket for th
London Library, writing,—' It is the best Lending-Librar
I know of in London or anywhere else ; I believe, som
100,000 volumes in it. . . . If I had been King Friedrich,
would have given you a pretty little Mansion and ground
for your merits to me ; but that not being so, I have o
cheap terms procured you a small *spiritual freehold*, whic
you are to occupy wisely, for my sake and your own, durin
the many years which I hope are still ahead for you. . .
' I am deep in Chapter I ' (Book XI of the *History
' Phenomena of Friedrich's Accession '), ' which has been
terrible quagmire first and last !—

' Yours very truly,

' T. CARLYLE.'

---

[1] *Carlyle and Mrs. Carlyle*, by Henry Larkin, *British Quarterly Review
July, 1881, pp. 28–84, and especially, 61–2 and 75. See also *Carlyle an
the Open Secret of his Life*, by H. Larkin, 1886, published by Kegan Pau
Trench & Co.

They had six years more to work together, and ' after his,' says Larkin, ' there were several presents of £50, handed or posted to me, as occasion served, in a spirit of no less friendliness '[1] ; and in short, like everyone who had to do with Carlyle except only the thief Martin, he makes no complaint about money matters.

" A helper sent me by favour of Heaven," Carlyle often felt and called him, a man " of clear, swift discernment, delicate sense of humour," able to work well without fuss, and in short my " factotum till *Frederick* ended." Joseph Neuberg was a much older man, and rich, retired from business ; but he and Larkin had the same motive, an eagerness to be useful to Carlyle in his work, and it is remarkably plain from the letters they both received and preserved how well any waste of effort was avoided. The work of each was kept separate. Neuberg was helping Carlyle in the writing of the history, corresponding for him, finding books, verifying references, and so on, while Larkin was helping to put what was written into perfect print, equipped with all essentials, notes and summaries, maps and battle-plans and indexes. Each was superlative in his way, and money could not have procured the equal of either.

They understood each other as if by instinct, and the absence of friction was beautiful. While Neuberg was now busy translating the first two volumes into German, Larkin relieved him as well as he could of the copying and Museum work, till the translation was finished, which was not till next summer, 1859.

XXVIII

RAJA BROOKE, ALLINGHAM, &c.
(1858–59)

ONE Saturday, 16.10.58, Thomas Woolner the sculpto
was at Cheyne Row, and when he had no more to say
about his hopes of getting a commission for a statue o
Cromwell, " We talked a great deal of the Raja Brooke '
(of Sarawak), said Woolner.[1] " Carlyle has the greates
admiration for him, which I am pleased to say is mutual.'
" It will be good fun to see them together," said he to
Mrs. Tennyson, and he decided to contrive a meeting when
the Raja came to town. As both were willing, that seemed
easy, but Raja Brooke fell ill. So Carlyle never saw him
He was told that a letter of sympathy from himself would
have " a cheering effect upon the Raja," and it seems likel
he wrote such a letter, but it has not been discovered any
where in print.

William Allingham came to London in October[2] and
found Carlyle ' brown, almost ruddy, and in the best humour
after two delightful months of solitude in Scotland, and on
disgustful month of travel in Germany. His experience
and mine agreed upon the difficulty of sleeping out of one'
own bed.'

Said Allingham :—" There are bonfires in all the review
for *Frederick*."

T. C. :—" I care nothing about it."   After a pause h
added :—" I have passed through two generations o
execration, and suppose there is a new set of men coming
forward now."

' In fact,' wrote Allingham to the Brownings, ' th
critics are simply huzzaïng after him . . . the scoffers hav
disappeared. Most warmly C. spoke of Robert Browning

---

[1] *Thomas Woolner*, by Amy Woolner, pp. 153, 167, 197.
[2] *Letters from William Allingham to Mr. & Mrs. Browning*, privatel
printed in 1914 by Mrs. Allingham.

Also said he had attentively read *Men and Women*, and understood it all at last but one thing . . . you'll remember, perhaps, how I used to stare at the same. . . .

' He rides a-horseback most days. He was sorry for Landor, whose courtesy when C. visited him at Bath had a smack of nobleness in it, and thinks him not to be noted as impure and wicked but as violently self-willed,' and in short misunderstood.

' Poor Mrs. Carlyle has suffered much from pulmonary disease during the past year, and looks greatly the worse. She cannot move for the winter . . . and must keep as warm as she can at Chelsea.'

Referring to the newly published volumes of his history, ' Carlyle is very vexed by the engraving of the children in *Frederick*, saying with entire truth that " the engraver is a mere mechanic, and has changed Freddy from a pretty boy of nine into a dwarf of fifteen." '

His labour on *Frederick* continued unabated. The book was growing like a tree. It was not to be a history of Frederick of Prussia only, but a mirror of the politics of Europe throughout the eighteenth century, revealing what other historians had tried to hide,—how natural was the rise to independence of the United States of America, and the explosion of the French Revolution. But as the work grew, it was not becoming easier ! Thus on 4.12.1858 he was writing to Neuberg :—

' Come to-morrow evening if you can, and bring Preuss. . . . I am extremely miserable, in the agonies of getting into work again, and so weak, so bothered, and my hand so out, that I absolutely cannot ! There was never any task half as damnable as this I have now on my hands, or so like breaking my heart if I ever do get done with it ! But I was a fool ; and a man must drink as he has brewed.

' Yours always truly,

' T. CARLYLE.'

It is a sure sign of a man of sense to be awake to his mistakes and quick to feel himself a fool. Carlyle was merely more outspoken than usual in these democratic days when speaking of other people. He was as sedulous as any saint in watching against " vanity,"—a beautiful habit bringing peace on earth, and too little seen to-day, whereby perhaps it happens that we are too ready to be gulled by self-assertion and self-advertisement.

From an entry in his journal of 28.12.58, it appears that the first two volumes of *Frederick* were selling well,—already in the fifth thousand,—so that he noted :—' I am fairly richer at this time than I ever was, in the money sense —rich enough for all practical purposes,' and what he was now ' haggling and struggling ' to do was to finish the *Frederick*, which he still believed possible in two more volumes.

Another thing of the same date is worth quoting.— ' Lord Ashburton has wedded again—a Miss Stuart Mackenzie—and they are off to Egypt a fortnight ago. " The changes of this age," as minstrel Burns has it, " which fleeting Time procureth ! " Ah me ! ah me ! '

A few days later Neuberg sent him the *Hanover Review*, to give him the pleasure of reading its praise of his history ; but he returned it at once on 7.1.59, without even waiting for the next Sunday when Neuberg was to be with them, and wrote :—' I re-inclose the *Hanover Review*, partly lest it be lost ; partly that I may *not* be tempted to read it ! I find it convenient to avoid all rubbish of that kind ; laudatory or other, it only creates a sordid sorrowful feeling and puts me out in what remains of my Egyptian Brick-making, with the thoṭ of what a crew they are that I am doing it for. I got Chapman's *Westminster* the other day, but sent it off uncut. My one wish is to have the Tale of Bricks (finding my own straw) *completed* in some honest way, and my hands washed to all Eternity of by far the abominablest job ever laid upon me,—much worthier of Förster, or of the Herren Preuss, Dryasdust, Ranke and Co. than of me ! '

Neuberg had given " the Master," as he liked to call Carlyle, in talking to Larkin and others, a meerschaum pipe to smoke while riding ; and many a time had Carlyle been seen knocking the ashes out of it over his whip ; but at last he had to write, (19.1.59) : '. . . The head dropped off, fell red into the dark night, and left me solitary. Bring another, please,— . . . I mean to *pay* for this one.'

One Sunday in the next month, February, Neuberg met at Cheyne Row one Alan Ker, " Scott's nephew," and able to answer all sorts of questions about the West Indies. The same month is as likely a date as any other for an excellent story of which nothing but the exact date is uncertain.[3]—

Charlotte Southam was at present Mrs. Carlyle's maid of all work, a bright girl still in her teens, and standing very high in her mistress's favour. She came into the drawing-room one evening and saw both master and mistress there as usual, just as in Tait's picture. He was at one side of the fire-place, smoking, but sending the smoke up the chimney. Mrs. Carlyle was sitting at the other side, but she had been looking out into the street a few minutes before, and seen Charlotte talking there to the next-door neighbour's maid. So now she asked,—" I saw you leave her suddenly with your head in the air. What had she been saying ? " " She was asking me, mum, if I was still with these daft people, and I said Yes, and walked away." Carlyle laughed loud and long, with his deep booming " Ho, ho, ho !," puffing away, and " Ho, ho, ho ! " Mrs. Carlyle was smiling and asked, " Do you know the meaning of daft, Charlotte ? " " Yes, it means clever," she answered, which made Carlyle laugh again and cry, " Oh Charlotte, Charlotte, worse and worse ! " He laughed so much that he omitted to send all his smoke up the chimney, and Mrs. Carlyle had to put her hands on her breast while she laughed and coughed by turns. In short, the room had to be aired before Charlotte could be told that daft was a Scotch word for silly.

The next-door neighbour was " something in the city," said Charlotte, and his household had for years shown all the stolid stiffness of the city snobs, and ignored the Carlyles as insignificant. By this time they had discovered the importance of some of the callers and decided the Carlyles were worth knowing, but " there was nothing doing," according to Charlotte. Mrs. Southam, her mother, was now in charge of the house while they were all in Fife, and one day about two weeks after they had come there, Mrs. Carlyle was laughing when giving Charlotte a letter to post in the village, and told her what was in it, saying, " I don't

[3] For Charlotte Southam, afterwards Mrs. Mills, see *New Letters and Memorials of J. W. Carlyle*, 1903, edited by A. Carlyle, II, pp. 189–190. In 1897 and later years, she was a widow, keeping lodgers in Upper Cheyne Row, and used to tell what is here given to William Cook, an engineer who lodged for more than three years in her house, and who used to spend his Sunday evenings in her parlour, listening to her talk, and particularly enjoying her reminiscences of the Carlyles, which he jotted down. He has for many years been living in retirement in Ayr, and been a friend of D. A. W.

know how I am ever to face the people next door again. Mr."—Robinson, let us call him, the next-door neighbour, —" sent a letter Mr. Carlyle received this morning. It stated that while walking in his garden, he had noticed that the windows in each room of our house were opened each day, but for some days lately one of the windows had not been opened, and he thought it was his duty to let Mr. Carlyle know. And can you guess, Charlotte, what Mr. C. has written in this letter to him ? " Charlotte replied, " No, mum." " Well, Mr. C. has written,—' I received your letter. I left one old woman in charge of the house. I did not know that I had left two. Yours truly, THOMAS CARLYLE.' "

The 25th January this year was the centenary of the birth of Robert Burns. Carlyle received so many and so pressing invitations to banquets then that his wife declared she was glad when it was over, telling Col. Davidson,[4] " If he had cut himself up into square inches, he could not have been present at all the ' occasions ' where he was summoned. He is as busy as ever tearing away at his new volume."

[4] *Memories of a Long Life*, by Col. Davidson, C.B., p. 323.

XXIX

CHARLOTTE SOUTHAM'S REPORT

WILLIAM COOK'S notes of the talk of Mrs. Mills from 1897 to 1900 have other passages well worth quoting. She had not been long at Cheyne Row when Tait was painting his successful picture, ' An Interior at Chelsea,' and in 1858, when it was on exhibition, " one afternoon," said Charlotte, " Mrs. Carlyle took me for a drive in the Park, and then we went to the Royal Academy. She sat down in one of the rooms and said to me,—' Walk round and look at the pictures for yourself.' " So Charlotte walked away, but soon she came back crying, " Oh mum, Mr. Carlyle and you and Nero are all in the other room. Come and see them." In telling this, Mrs. Carlyle used to say,—" Charlotte was so excited that her eyes were just like two saucers." What tickled Carlyle was her using the word—" them." Charlotte could not see what he saw to laugh at in that, remarking, " He had to have his joke."

As Charlotte explained to Mr. Cook, it was her duty to take to Mr. Carlyle every morning a hot cup of mixed coffee and castor oil, and he notes that ' it was amusing to hear her imitating Mr. Carlyle's voice and his " Ho, ho, ho ! " as she screwed up her face, shaking her head and saying like him, " Ay, ay,—it's gey wersh." '

One morning she noticed him to be unusually tired and haggard, and asked him, " are you not well ? " " I'm weel enough, Charlotte," he replied, " but I have not slept all night. There was a dog barking outside. It was not merely the barking once, but I lay awake to hear it barking again,— that's the annoying thing." So this morning after coffee Wright the dairyman brought round his horse from Church Street and he went for a morning ride. Charlotte had instructions from Mrs. Carlyle to make sure he had his hat on before going out, for once she had had to run after him down Cheyne Row and along the Embankment with his hat,—he had gone out without it.

At home among themselves they talked Scotch, which was apt to puzzle Charlotte. What was even more puzzling at first was that sometimes Carlyle would come down from the study for dinner, and take it and go away again back to the study, without saying a word. Mrs. Carlyle was never surprised and would say to Charlotte, " He'll make up for that yet." And sure enough he always did, remaining downstairs after tea without returning to the study, producing his long pipe and tobacco, sitting down on the floor alongside the fire-place and smoking up the chimney, and talking and joking with Mrs. Carlyle or Charlotte. Thus on one such night he started to explain to Charlotte how the world went round. He told her the courses of the Sun and of the Moon and the planets, and how far beyond these were the fixed stars, coming and going in their seasons though unseen by the naked eye. " As far as I or anyone else can know," he told her, " they may be inhabited by people even mair sensible than we are oorsels." Then Mrs. Carlyle interrupted him, saying,—" Dear me, what does the child know about these things ? " " A'm no saying she kens, only I'm just telling her," he answered serenely, and went on with his lesson, to the great satisfaction of Charlotte.

Charlotte declared she knew when Mr. Carlyle was angry before he spoke, because " a red spot burned upon each cheek and his eyes flashed behind his glasses. I often saw that when he was busy upstairs and unwelcome visitors called." She only once saw him angry with her, and never forgot it.

It was her work every day, when he was at dinner and Mrs. Carlyle kept him company downstairs, to clean the study,—see to the fire and the tobacco, and dust the table, always replacing anything she moved on the exact spot of the table where he had left it. One day after dinner, when Mr. Carlyle had just returned to his study, he shouted in a very loud voice,—" Charlotte, Charlotte, come up here at once." Mrs. Carlyle was alarmed and Charlotte rushed upstairs. " Whaur's ma glesses ? " he asked her, and she noticed the red spots on his cheeks. She answered quietly,— " I lifted the glasses, dusted the table, and replaced the glasses on the same spot." Mr. Carlyle said louder than ever,—" If ye did that, they would be there yet." " Perhaps they've fallen under the table," she answered, and went down on her hands and knees and searched in vain. On rising up she noticed that the glasses were on Carlyle's brow, and told him. He took off the glasses and looked at them, and then said to her in a different tone,—" I'm sorry, Charlotte " ; and after a pause he added,—" Nearly a' ma life I've been ca'ing other folk fools, but I think I'm yin ma'sel. Whit do you think, Charlotte ? " She said nothing, but went downstairs where Mrs. Carlyle was anxiously awaiting her.

Charlotte told the whole story and dwelt on how angry Mr. Carlyle had looked, but she laughed and said :—" Never mind, Charlotte. He'll soon forget all about it. Men are all alike,—they get angry at trifles,—they get angry at trifles,— you'll know that as you get older." Mr. Cook enquired of Mrs. Mills, then in her fifties, whether she had got to know that, and she replied she was not a year married when she learned that Mrs. Carlyle had been speaking the truth.

About this time Lord Ashburton gave Mrs. Carlyle a copy of Pesne's famous picture, ' The Little Drummer,' a portrait of Frederick the Great as a little boy with a drum, and his sister beside him. It seems likely that the copy had been made at Ashburton's expense to provide a good illustration for Carlyle's history ; and in the middle of February Mrs. Carlyle was writing to Col. Davidson, the Haddington friend of her childhood.[1] Mr. Carlyle ' is as busy as ever. . . . Meanwhile I am spending my life with the two royal children, as large as life ! Lord Ashburton having made me a present of the picture from which the engraving was made. It quite makes the fortune of my drawing-room. For one thing it serves the end pretty little *Shandy* used to serve at Haddington, and is something for the stupid *callers* to chatter about.'

[1] *Memories of a Long Life*, by Col. Davidson, c.b., p. 323.

XXX

THE IDEAL FOR DOCTORS
(1859)

IN acknowledging on 25.2.59 the receipt of a book from an anonymous doctor, Carlyle let himself go on the ideals of that profession.[1]

'. . . I beg to return you thanks. It is a book (unlike many that come to me here) of a serious nature, the fruit of long study, meditation, inquiry, and evidently of perfect conviction on your part.

' I have long believed the essential idea it sets forth to be not only true, but of the very highest importance to mankind, namely, that the physician must first of all be a priest (that is to say, a man of pious nobleness, devoted to the service of the Highest, and prepared to endure and endeavour for that same, taking no counsel of flesh and blood, as the theory of Priests is),—first of all, a real Priest, and then that the whole world should take supreme counsel of him, as it does of its real or imaginary Priests or Pontiffs this long while back, and follow said counsel as the actual will of God,—which it would be were the physician what I say.

' It is curious to remark that Heilig in our old Teutonic speech is both Holy and also Healthy ; that the words Holy and Healthy, as our antique fathers understood them, are one and the same. We have contrived to divorce holiness (as we call it) from health, and have been reaping the fruits very plentifully during these fifteen hundred years.

' The notion of bringing our present distracted anomaly of a Physician into union with our ditto ditto of a Priest, and making them identical, is of course chimerical ; nor

---

[1] Transcribed from a newspaper cutting on a file dated only 1894, C. O. Gridley's collection.

can one easily say what ought to be the first step towards
bringing each of them nearer to veracity, and the possibility
of coalescing. But I am very glad to see the idea started in
any form, and wish you success in bringing it home to
men's minds.

'I remain,

'Yours truly,

'T. CARLYLE.'

XXXI

THE HOGARTH CLUB
(1859)

IN 1856 some pushing young artists in London had formed a Hogarth Club, with Carlyle, Tennyson & Co. as "Honorary Members." On 2.3.1859 Carlyle went to Woolner's studio, and finding him out, wrote to him next day :—" I want you to persuade the Secretary of the *Hogarth Club* (in some friendly way, for I would not hurt his feelings on any account) to cease altogether sending me the *business* letters, &c. of that Institution,—to which I wish honestly well ; hoping always I may look at your exhibited works, or the like, one day ; but do not take hold farther, nor ever intend to do, least of all in present circumstances. Such letters are not only a waste of trouble and postage stamps to your society, but there is implied a kind of untruth in the affair, and I beg you, in a cunning silent way, stop them ! When anything that can interest a general member of the Community is afoot I shall be happy to hear tell of it. Excuse, etc."[1]

To the average modern Englishman, who feels he is doing a work of merit whenever he is pretending anything, it is difficult to explain this. But let him not call it an " eccentricity of Carlyle." The most of us, perhaps even in Europe, and certainly in the world as a whole, despise all false pretences. The respectability of these in England, attributed by Napoleon to our shopkeeping habits, is sure to diminish in the course of time.

---

[1] *Thomas Woolner*, by Amy Woolner, p. 164.

XXXII

" ADAM BEDE "
(1859)

ON 21.3.1859 Miss Thackeray and her sister Amy called
on Mrs. Carlyle and found Lady Stanley already there,
' looking very jolly,' and expatiating on ' mutton and rice.'
When she and her Maude departed, according to Miss
Thackeray, our recording angel,[1] ' Mrs. Carlyle was speaking
enthusiastically of *Adam Bede*. She had written some of
her enthusiasm off to George Eliot and had grateful messages
in reply. Mr. Carlyle quite declines reading the book, and
when Mrs. Carlyle hoped it might be sent to her, he said
" What should George Eliot send it to you for ? "

' " Why shouldn't he, as he sent me his first book ? " said
she.

' " You are just like all ' weemen ' "—for women, one of
the few Scotticisms in his familiar talk.—" You are always
forming unreasonable expectations," growls he,' according
to his wife, ' and at that moment ' (there is a) ' ring at the
bell, and in comes the maid with a brown paper parcel containing the book . . . Three orange volumes, with the author's
compliments.'

Carlyle must have left the room but noticed the arrival
of the parcel. He followed the maid coming in with it, and
sitting on the sofa he witnessed the triumph of his wife.
Nay, he must have listened while she read it aloud to him
as she used sometimes to do in the evenings, making him
listen to novels,[2] for soon after this he was heard explaining
how he was sure, from the contents of *Adam Bede*, that
" George Eliot " the author was a woman.

---

[1] *Letters of Anne Thackeray Ritchie*, edited by her daughter, p. 110,
and also her chapters from some *Memoirs*, p. 138.
[2] See *Carlyle at his Zenith*, p. 14, &c.

z

337

XXXIII

FORD MADOX BROWN
(1859)

IN the spring of 1859, Carlyle replied to an application from Ford Madox Brown to sit for a photo to be used in painting him in the picture ' Work,' commissioned the year before :—

' DEAR SIR,

' I think it a pity you had not put (or should not still put) some other man than me into your great Picture. It is certain you could hardly have found among the sons of Adam, at present, any individual who is less in a condition to help you forward with it, or take interest in it, active or passive. I was never in my days so overwhelmed and buried miles deep in the belly of an ugly Enterprise ; *too* heavy in sad truth for the strength I have left, as, even now, Jonah in the Whale's Belly is but a type of me in these sad months and years.

' I very well remember your amiable request, and the promise I made you to " sit for some photographs." That promise I will keep, and to that we must restrict ourselves, hand of Necessity compelling. Any afternoon I will attend here, at your studio, or where you appoint me, and give your man one hour to get what photographs he will or can of me. If here, the hour must be 3½ p.m. (my usual hour of quitting work, or, to speak justly, the chamber of work) : if at any other place attainable on horseback, it will be altogether equally convenient to me, and the hour may be such as enables me to arrive (at a rate of 5 miles *per* hour we will say !).

' Yours in great haste,
' T. CARLYLE.'[1]

---

[1] Printed without date in *Ford Madox Brown*, by F. M. Hueffer, pp. 163–4. The context fixes 1859 and some time well before 22.6.1859.

There were many other men in the picture, F. D. Maurice alongside Carlyle, for one, but the artist and his patron both thought Carlyle indispensable.[2] Madox Brown's copy of *Past and Present* bore signs of frequent perusal, and passages on Bobus and on the Gospel of Work were pencil-marked. Indeed it is impossible to read the artist's note upon the picture and doubt who inspired his crowded canvas.[3] In vain did Holman Hunt object that his portrait of Carlyle smiling broadly was a caricature. The artist believed in reality and painted what he had seen, and was rewarded by hearing (that) others too had seen the same expression,[4]—which gives him a special claim to our gratitude. He was a grandson of the great medical pioneer Dr. Brown, whose "Brunonian ideas," against bleeding and so on, made his professional brethren in Edinburgh persecute him, but ended by changing the fashion of their art.

[2] *Ford Madox Brown*, by F. M. Hueffer, p. 112.
[3] *Ditto*, pp. 189–196. The picture is now in Manchester Fine Art Gallery.
[4] *Ditto*, p. 165, &c.

XXXIV

MILL'S "LIBERTY"
(1859)

IT is said that when Mill's *Liberty* was published in 1859, Charles Kingsley noticed the new book in the publisher's shop, sat down and read it through, and said,—It has made me a clearer-headed braver-minded man on the spot,"[1] —which was a natural effect of it upon a modern Christian, "cabined, cribbed, confined" by professional shibboleths. Much of its argument for freedom of speech seems commonplace and superfluous to those familiar with Milton's magnificent *Areopagitica*; and even its more questionable plea for liberty of conduct was almost pathetic, when considered as an Apology for the twenty years' flirtation with Mrs. Mill while she was Mrs. Taylor. She had died in 1858; and Mill, who had avoided his best friends throughout the seven years of his wedded life, began to return to them when left alone.

Carlyle was one of those who had been "strictly silent" about what the Chinese call "inner matters"; and if only Mill had begun by renewing their acquaintance quietly, they might have had many another walk and talk together. But unfortunately, what he did was to send his new book on *Liberty* and challenge an opinion upon it. Whereupon he was plainly told, with a candour which he should have welcomed according to his own theories,[2] " I don't agree with a single word of it from beginning to end."

The Christian Henry Larkin was of the same opinion when he read the book, but what a time it gave him on arrival! " One morning," he says, " when I entered " (Carlyle's) " study, I found him as usual sitting at his table, but evidently in a condition of great suppressed irritability;

---

[1] A. Bain's *J. S. Mill*, p. 112, and *Life of J. S. Mill*, by W. L. Courtney, p. 125.
[2] See *J. S. Mill*, by A. Bain, p. 162, &c.

with Mill's *Liberty* lying before him. Until then I had never seen or heard of it. After I had discharged my trifling business, he rose angrily from the table with the book in his hand, and gave vent to such a torrent of anathema, glancing at Christianity itself, as filled me with pain and amazement. He addressed himself directly to me, almost as if *I* had written the book, or had sent it to him, or was in some way mixed up with it. I felt terribly hurt ; but what could I say ? I did not know how far I might agree. Neither did he expressly charge me with any complicity with its ideas. But he did, in his haste, say things which he ought not to have said "—about my creed, so to speak ; " and he was tragically sorry almost " at once. Larkin made no direct response, but " parted soon after in perfect friendliness " ; and assures us :—" I know the book well enough now with its balancing of enlightened self-interests, and its deification of every man's own heart ; and putting myself honestly in Carlyle's place, I do not wonder that his indignation was beyond endurance." In this connection, Larkin gladly recalled Carlyle's " abhorrence of the crowing, God-denying, death-stricken, fashionable life-philosophies"; but however much Carlyle may have regretted the incidental and almost accidental repudiation of Christianity, he never recanted it ; and Larkin adjusting himself to it has sorrowfully to admit,—" too palpably, another shadow had fallen between us."[3]

Theoretically it should have been different with Mill,—he should have been charmed with the contradiction ; but in fact he was offended and never came back, and when invited by letter, he never answered.[4] This was the saddest separation Carlyle ever suffered. Of all his disciples none was worthier than Mill,—" the saint of Rationalism ! " as Gladstone called him,[5]—none surer never to abuse the liberty he claimed for all, none likelier to go beyond his master in disinterestedness and superiority to all that savoured of self.

In his distress poor Larkin leaves us guessing what the professional Christians may have had in common with Mill,

[3] Henry Larkin's *Carlyle and Mrs. Carlyle*, *British Quarterly Review*, No. 147, pp. 73–74 (July, 1881).
[4] Told by T. C. to Dr. J. Beattie Crozier about 1873, and by Dr. J. B. C. to D. A. W.
[5] Gladstone's name for Mill in the Commons. See Gladstone's letter to Mr. Courtney, *Westminster Review*, January, 1905, p. 30, article on J. S. Mill, by S. Wellington.

that they should all be confounded together. Maybe their
common sin was ignoring reality and imagining they were
free to be freaks, because " whosoever will " can believe
any bosh he likes. So they were ever ready to debate ding-
dong, as if debating were the only road to truth, whereas in
fact artificial belief is sham belief and nothing but details
can be settled by debate. The right sort of belief is what
naturally grows from feeling and thinking, speaking and
acting, according to what one sees to be true.

Carlyle himself said to his brother John :—

' In my life I never read a serious, ingenious, clear, logical
Essay with more perfect and profound dissent from the basis
it rests upon, and most of the conclusions it arrives at.
Very strange to me indeed ; a curious monition to me what
a world we are in ! As if it were a sin to control, or coerce
into better methods, human swine in any way ;—as if the
greater and the more universal the " liberty " of human
creatures of the *swine* genus, the more fatal all-destructive
and intolerable were not the " slavery " the few human
creatures of the *Man* genus are thereby thrown into, and
kept groaning powerless under. *Ach Gott im Himmel !* '[6]

The free-lance William Maccall did not restrict himself
as Carlyle did to private criticism ; and his aggressive
individuality appears at its best in assailing Mill.[7]—

' Mr. Mill has the student's worst prejudices. He views
Society as a kind of debating club for the reception or
rejection of new ideas after boundless babblement. The
two primordial facts in the past are for him, the Platonic
Dialectics and the Dialectics of the Schoolmen ; for the
Almighty created the Universe not as a theatre of life, but
for the sake of fair discussion, and you are fulfilling your
mission as a Divine soul, not by achieving Divine victories,
but by studying your neighbour's side of the question as
well as your own.

' Verily, my brothers and sisters, crushed by tragic sin,
crucified by tragic sorrow, yearning for regeneration, for
consolation, and for effulgent valiant martyr deeds, after
the sharp hour of tribulation,—this is rather a shabby
outlook. If ye cannot take your turn at dialectical fencing,
ye had better bundle out of existence with convenient
promptitude, seeing that earth has no existence, except as

---

[6] O God in Heaven !
[7] *Literary Recollections*, by F. Espinasse, pp. 253–4.

a dialectical fencing academy. We now know well what we were made for, and that is something—if, indeed, Mr. Mill, as a fanatical Malthusian, will allow that we ought to have been made at all. That little babies are a nuisance, and that big babies should spend all their time in what the Scotch call arglebargling, seems to be Mr. Mill's compendious creed. To be choked in your infancy, if some one has committed the crime of being your father, or if Rhadamanthine Malthusianism permits you to live, to chatter evermore about progress and liberty—such is the pleasant alternative offered you.'

' This is one-sided but clever,' comments Espinasse, who quotes it, ' and there is a grain of truth in it.'

XXXV

CURRENT POLITICS
(1859)

THE English were afraid of an invasion by the French this summer, and Tennyson sent his ' Riflemen, Form,' to the *Times* in May :—

> ' True we have got—*such* a faithful ally
> That only the Devil can tell what he means.'

Carlyle agreed with his countrymen in disesteem for the ' Copper Captain,' as he called Napoleon, and described him in a letter to Neuberg, on 10.6.59, as ' the Ugliest of Emperors, and most mendacious ... the Galgen-Aas ' or Gallows-carrion, ' if ever there was one ! ' But he did not share the fears of his countrymen, and was heedless of their politics. As he wrote to Neuberg, 10.6.59,—' Dizzy *versus* Palmy is to be settled tonight, they say ; I care not a whit how it goes.' To him the difference between Derby's Tories and Palmerston's Liberals seemed negligible, like tweedledum and tweedledee. Which was an odd opinion then, tho it was true.

To the publisher Alexander MacMillan, Carlyle was ' an immortal,' and his ' message to mankind a revelation of permanent interest,' while the revered and reverend ' Broad Church ' leader, the great Maurice himself, seemed merely a ' prophet with a mission to expound Carlyle.' The world has come round to MacMillan's estimate today, but he was laughed at in 1859. Here is some chaff his biographer dates then.[1]—

' " Matt," stammered Charles Kingsley to Matthew Arnold, at one of the Thursday evening gatherings at Bedford Street, " Alec strongly suspects Tommy Carlyle of being a deeper humourist than Dante." Arnold snorted and smiled grimly.'

[1] *Life and Letters of Alex. MacMillan*, by C. L. Graves, pp. 95 and 102–3.

Our English volunteers got nothing to do but drill. It was with sympathy from the English and in support of Italian patriots that Napoleon was to fight, successfully, Marshal MacMahon commanding and defeating the Austrians twice in June this year, so that Cavour was able to bring Italian Unity into sight by expanding the kingdom of Sardinia.

XXXVI

SIR GEORGE GREY
(1859)

WHILE the peddling politicians in London were as heedless of Carlyle as their horses were, George Grey was one of several men who were practising in public business what he preached. Already Grey had governed well South Australia and New Zealand, and at the Cape had not only been a great peacemaker, but even deserved to be called one of the " Saviours of India," by sending troops to it in the crisis of the mutiny, and boldly assuming the great responsibility of diverting to Calcutta the army going to China. He was now endeavouring to set the copestone to the conglomerate structure of Cape Colony by a federation, which would have saved the foolish wasteful wars that followed afterwards. But the noble noodles at Downing Street did not want federation,—it meant less patronage and intrigue. And Grey had even appointed local judges without a thought of the disappointed place-hunters in London ! He had to be recalled and admonished that federation was not to be allowed. So 1859 found him in London, and gives us the likeliest date for his reminiscences of Carlyle.[1]

' The three men who exercised most influence on me,' said Grey, ' were Archbishop Whately, Sir James Stephen, and Thomas Carlyle. Carlyle I can only describe as . . . profoundly great.

' Being once introduced to Carlyle, I think by Sir Richard Owen, it was my delight, during any spell in London, to visit him at Chelsea. No want of harmony was apparent, in the relations between Carlyle and his wife. You were not conscious of any element of that description ; assuredly I was not. Carlyle would sit at the right side of the fire,

---

[1] Sir George Grey, *The Romance of a Proconsul*, by J. Milne, pp. 11, 40–42, 161.

through an evening, I on his left, and we would talk on all
manner of topics. I should most accurately describe our
talk by saying that we philosophised. Or, we might read
a little ; he was a loving reader.

' Carlyle believed, with truth, that I had been influenced
by his teachings, and if only for that reason he may have
been rather fond of me. . . . I had a regard for him as a
man, I gladly looked up to him, though that did not block
out differences of opinion ; and altogether we got on
admirably. During one of those fireside talks, he detailed
to me an incident which quite hurt his feelings.

' He had a horse then, and was in the habit of riding
out for exercise, almost every afternoon. He was never
very artistic in his manner of dressing, and for horseback
he had a long and singular fur coat, which enfolded his
legs. Between Chelsea and Maida Vale, some boys were
attracted by this quaint figure astride a horse. Not knowing
in the least who it was they shouted at Carlyle ; he spoke
something to them in reproof and passed on.

' But next day, at the same place, there were the boys
again, and not content with mocking Carlyle, they threw
pebbles at him. He did not sustain any injury, but he
mentioned the matter to me with a sore heart, as indicative
of the condition of the youth of the country, for want of the
better educational opportunities of which he was so earnest
an advocate.'

Sir George mentioned also that once, as they walked up
and down in the open air together, Carlyle stopped and laid
his hand on his companion's shoulder, and, looking him in
the face, exclaimed, " Oh, that I could believe like you."

The general impression of their personal intercourse was
summed up in what Grey said by-and-by, when Mr. Froude
visited him at Kawau off the New Zealand coast. ' He
wanted to ask me, if I approved the manner in which he
had written Carlyle's life. . . . My reply was that " I believed
Carlyle would have wished to be presented just as he was :
not a half picture, but complete. That would ultimately
make him appear all the greater." ' Which was the politest
reply possible, avoiding pain to a well-meaning Boswell,
who had not been successful.

XXXVII

AWAY TO FIFE
(1859)

IN the early summer of 1859, Thomas Woolner reported to Mrs. Tennyson 'a long evening with Carlyle,'[1] who was far from well, and had to confess,—" I have not done so much in three months as I am accustomed to do in as many weeks when I am in a higher tone of health." Mrs. Carlyle was also ailing, and Woolner concluded Carlyle would soon " cease working for awhile," and so he did.

On 22.6.59 Carlyle went with "clever little Charlotte" and Nero and his horse Fritz by steamer to Granton, and thence across to Humbie, a farm near Aberdour in Fife. Mrs. Carlyle followed by train to Haddington, and rested there till they were ready for her, and then came on to Humbie. On the first day there that happened to be fine, she mounted the horse on a side-saddle, and Carlyle led her at a walk through the wood and the village and along the shore,—' a good ride which quite reassured her.'[2] . . . Her own weak ankles made her ' indisposed to locomotion,' but she did not want to stay indoors. . . . So she made her husband get a donkey for her from Dumfriesshire, and escorted by Nero and Charlotte, she went riding about in all directions. On the day after its arrival, 9.7.59, she was called by her husband ' the envy of surrounding females with weak legs,' for the bather ladies crowded about her eagerly enquiring, " Is that a hired donkey ? " " Oh, no, ma'am, it is my own," was the reply.

As for the horse, " Fritz," said Carlyle, " is in a perfect ecstasy at his plenty of grass and new hay, tho unable to recover from his astonishment at the badness of the Fife roads."

[1] *Thomas Woolner*, by Amy Woolner, pp. 183 and 203.
[2] *Carlyle and Mrs. Carlyle, a Ten Years' Reminiscence*, by Henry Larkin, *British Quarterly Review*, July, 1881, pp. 28–84, and especially 62–8.

XXXVIII

IN FIFE
(1859)

O N 2.7.59 they received a call from the widow of Hugh
Miller.[1] She had come over from Edinburgh house-
hunting for summer quarters, accompanied by her eldest
daughter Harriet and a son, and on 2.7.59 was writing home
to her mother in Edinburgh.—

' Harriet heard that Thomas Carlyle and his wife were at
a farmhouse a bit above Aberdour, so I thought (of) paying
them a visit. So after breakfast I drove up to Humbie.
We were shown up into a little plain farmhouse parlour,
where Mrs. Carlyle . . . came forward to meet me with the
greatest simplicity, cordiality and kindness. Poor thing,
she looks very ill, worn, and exhausted. . . .

' At length he came in—not at all the man I looked for—
much younger and less reverend in appearance—a long and
somewhat slovenly beard and moustache. But he, too, was
very kind. Conversed first upon ordinary things—then got
on Louis Napoleon and the Austrians—abused the Italians,
said that really the Austrians were the only power in Italy
which had any obedience in it to the eternal laws. As for
Louis Napoleon, his (Carlyle's) light blue eye dilated with
scorn and rage when he talked against him. If he came his
way and offered to black his boots, he would tell him to
stand back—it was occupation much too good for him. . . .'

Then the talk turned to St. Columba, and ' there was like
never to be an end to the stream of talk till I said I *must*
catch the one o'clock boat. He then gave me his arm downstairs (and) saw me most politely and attentively into the
carriage. . . . It was a lovely day, and I enjoyed the sail
meditating not on Carlyle's faculty of silence but his marvellous faculty of speech. There was very much about him
that reminded me of him who is gone '—her own Hugh

---

[1] Printed in the *Glasgow Herald*, Saturday, 2nd February, 1929.

Miller—' the same simplicity superior to all affectation—
the same carelessness as to the outward man, and a certain
kindliness, too, in the eye when it softened—the same prejudice, too, on subjects on which he had made up his mind,
and a something in look, voice, and manner which was more
than actual likeness. But as far as I could judge, Mr. Miller's
powers of conversation were vastly more clear and rational,
and his ability of conveying information interestingly much
greater. But Mr. Miller always spoke of *things*, Carlyle
always of *persons*. . . .'

To John Forster, Carlyle was writing the next day, conscientious exceedingly.—' We are greatly shocked and surprised to hear of the bad turn of health you have had ; and
proportionately thankful that it is over again ! I had
intended, every day, for about a week before leaving Town,
to call at Montague Square,—and there is a mad feeling in
me (always till I reflect again) as if that omission had been
the guilty cause of what followed ! For the human conscience is sensitive, on some points, beyond what you
perhaps suppose.

' It seems to me, dear Forster, you ought to be out of
London altogether, in this hot season, while the country is
in all its glory and the town in all its noise and smoulder.
Nay why not fling up your Office altogether, if it tie you in
any measure in respect of what is so all-important as the
concern of Health ? To you no Office is of the least practical
moment. . . . I am seriously minded, if I ever live to get done
with this undoable Book, to *be* actually off, and quit the
horrors of Babel and *its* ugly Nebuchadnezzars for a place
of God Almighty's making ! Besides, one might have two
places, and alternate,—change sides, like a fish getting fried,
for the remainder of one's time.

' It is very clear to me if I had you *here* just now, to
ride two hours a-day with me among the silent Hills and
Valleys, by the shore of the beautifullest sea in the world ;
bathing daily, living on country messes, you would feel
yourself gathering strength again before a week were past.
Tell Mrs. Forster of all this. . . . On the whole, practically,
write a word to us, dear Forster, and say exactly *how you
are*, to ears interested.

' Yours ever,
' T. CARLYLE.'

He was not altogether resting. Besides riding hard he

ras ' reading and re-reading several Seven-Years War Affairs,' and hoped at first to be able to send Larkin material or maps ; but at last he ' shoved the whole matter off ' ill his return, so far as writing went. He continued to ead about it. . . .

The violent exercise his wife vituperated, ' more like a nan of sixteen than of sixty-four,' enabled him nevertheless o enjoy ' bathing, sauntering, walking, galloping ; lazily lreaming in the lullaby of the woods and breezes,' admiring he ' seas, mountains, cities, woods, (and) fruitful cornfields ' around.[2] A girl in the farm-house[3] watched him smoking nis long clay pipe in the woods, and always leaving it there or ' on the dyke-tops ' or some similar place, where the first poor passer-by would know it was meant to be taken. He did not seem a mirthful man,' but was noticed giving sixpences. As for his wife, once mounted on her donkey, she rode about without him in all directions escorted by Nero and Charlotte, but was little in the village.

Carlyle went over to Edinburgh once or twice to see his brother John, and wrote to Neuberg on 21.7.59.—

' I bathe, walk, loiter in woods ; ride, too, with my horse in a flourishing state, horse astonished beyond measure at the new phenomena of nature here, the sea waves, the precipitous stony paths, the *cows* almost most of all. It is one of the finest *scenes* I ever saw in the world : woody airy Hills (mostly made of trap rock, & very well cultivated) ; ours is a Farm House mounted on a Knoll of its own, and looking far over the Forth and its Islands (Inch-*Colm* has a monastery on it) and its steamers and ships special and miscellaneous, with Edinʰ 10 miles off on the other side, and mountains and green pleasant countries lying more directly across (for illustrious Edinʰ is somewhat to leftward) : " like a scene in a theatre," varying in aspect from hour to hour ; truly I question if the Bay of Naples itself is prettier on a fine day. The Forth in fact is a " Firth " ; or Norway Fiord ; only in a fruitfuller country, with gentlemen's Parks in it and the like. I try to be perfectly solitary ; and am so for most part, silence being much better than speech there is chance of. But the ground itself is eloquent

[2] *Carlyle and Mrs. Carlyle : a Ten Years' Reminiscence*, by Henry Larkin, *British Quarterly Review*, July, 1811, pp. 28–84, and especially 52–8.
[3] Reported by Kelso Kelly, F.S.A., in the *Weekly Scotsman*, 15.7.1916.

to me, with memories of 40 years back and more ;—I find old friendly faces still extant too, tho in small number.—

'I have been at Preuss, as you will see ; poring and wriggling once again among these hideous Blockheadisms that have swallowed a Heroism nearly out of sight : what on earth I *am* to make of it ? This question strikes into me, like a knife, the first thing, almost every morning. God help me with it !

'Of the so-called French Emperor, &c., I have been taking the minimum of note. Among human mountebanks of a sanguinary and atrocious nature I have seen none more disgusting,—none surer of a bad end, if I have any weather wisdom !

'Yours ever,

'T. CARLYLE.'

About the same time Mrs. Carlyle was writing from Aberdour to Mrs. Gilchrist, their neighbour in Cheyne Row.[4] —' Mr. Carlyle is much pleased with the place and the " soft food " it yields for himself—and horse—and, as he hardly *works* at all, he would be much better—*if* he didn't, as he always does in the country, take health *by the throat* (as it were). *Bathing* as if he were a little boy in the Serpentine, *walking* as if he had seven-league Boots, and riding like the Wild Huntsman !—the consequence of all which is that he keeps up in him a continual fever of biliousness.—

'Charlotte (the housemaid) is the happiest of created girls—everything so *new* to her, everything delightful ! especially the open admiration of Aberdour Lads ; who call her " *Bonnie wee Lassie* " in the public highway ! " So kind of them ! " she says " when they never saw her before and don't so much as know her name ! ! " Mr. Carlyle remarked justly that " the compliments to *herself*, were the only words of Scotch she could manage to understand ! and these she understood at once, by instinct ! "

'Nero is a much improved dog, by sea-bathing with his master, he snores less, scratches less, and is less selfish. And " *the* Horse "—Oh, Mr. Carlyle declares " It is in *perfect raptures* over its *soft food*—but incapable of recovering from its astonishment at the badness of the Fife roads ! "

'So we shall do very well at the Farm House till the 6th of August.'

[4] *Mrs. Gilchrist, Her Life and Writings*, by H. H. Gilchrist, pp. 70–1.

XXXIX

"FINAL FIFE"
(1859)

O N 6.8.59 they had to vacate their rooms near Aberdour, and moved into a house lent to them by a Mr. Liddell, near Kirkcaldy and within a quarter of an hour's walk of the house of the Rev. Walter Welsh, a cousin of Mrs. Carlyle and parish minister there.

Carlyle wrote to Neuberg that he had caught a bilious cold in the course of removing; but Mrs. Carlyle blamed his " bilious crisis " as she preferred to call it on the violent exercise he had been taking, walking, riding and bathing. In one of her witty letters to London she said that for a fortnight she felt ' like being keeper in a madhouse '; but in reality she was most of the time riding about cheerily on her donkey, and confessed she felt the better of it.

She quoted her husband as saying of a Mr. Mantell, who was Geraldine Jewsbury's latest hope, that he was ' far too clever and *substantial* a man to be flung away on a *flimsy tatter* of a creature like Geraldine Jewsbury.' Anything like this, repeated or invented foolishly, however blameless in confidential chat between husband and wife, would embitter poor Geraldine, and explain why she always delighted to think the worst of him, and also what she may have meant when she said to Espinasse,—Mrs. Carlyle " pours oil into your wounds, but it is oil of vitriol."[1]

' Final Fife had a certain gloomy beauty to me,' Carlyle wrote afterwards, ' strange, grand, sad as the grave ! ' No wonder ! The shadows were lengthening around him, and many a reminder he was receiving that the night was near. His first talk at Granton with Dr. John had been about the death of Isabella at Scotsbrig, his youngest brother's wife ; and on 28th August died Leigh Hunt at Putney.

One day he rode up the street in Kirkcaldy where his

[1] F. Espinasse's *Literary Recollections*, p. 134.

brother Alexander had lodged with him, and wrote to that
brother, now in Canada :—' I saw the old room where we
two lodged together long ago,—the staircase, window, etc.,
seemed all *younger* rather than otherwise, in their bright new
colouring of lime and paint, but the Two Lodgers had not been
growing younger the while ! Peter Swan (whom you may
remember as a little black-eyed boy), now an old bachelor,
inclined to corpulency, is the chief man of the place.'

In those days too—14th September—died Sir James
Stephen, better known till lately as " Mother-Country " or
" Over-Secretary Stephen " of the Colonial Office.

It may be true, as it has been told, that in the Rev.
Walter Welsh's house about this time, Carlyle at table was
sitting next another clergyman, described to him in advance
as " garrulous."   The then conspicuous and once friendly
Rev. George Gilfillan of Dundee was now vituperating Carlyle
because of his disrespect to " the cloth " in *Sterling*, and
the stranger, itching for a debate, addressed him suddenly,
—" Sir, I am the Rev. Mr. Grant of " So and so.

" One of the ' Trough '-Grants " ? he enquired.

The stranger was covered with confusion and soon departed, with a new experience to be garrulous about, and
happily without wasting the time of Carlyle.   " Was it not
cruel ? " he could ask, and men would agree who knew that,
tho the Grants were as proud as any other Highlanders,
the ' Trough '-Grants were the least respected of them
among themselves.   If the man had had more sense, he
need not have departed sulky.   Carlyle no more respected
—or despised—a clergyman because he was a clergyman or
a " Trough-Grant " because he was a " Trough-Grant," than
a Lord because he was a Lord, or a Prince because he was
a Prince.   Self-assertion of either self or clothes was always
apt to be snubbed.   So much was this a matter of course
that he probably forgot the Rev. Grant at once, but the
Rev. Grant could never forget him.[2]

Some farmer folk around were able to corroborate Grant
in his grievance and voted Carlyle " morose," because he
walked rapidly about and never dropped into a saunter to
chat with accidental strangers, in rustic fashion.   " They
have said,—what say they,—let them say."[2]

[2] At a meeting of the Glasgow Archæological Society in February,
1917, a trustworthy fellow-member stated all this and told privately of
his local enquiries at Auchtertool, and convinced D. A. W. that the direct
evidence of Mr. Grant's affliction and the country gossip were credible.
His name is suppressed by request. D. A. W.

XL

HOME AGAIN
(1859)

BEFORE September was out, Mrs. Carlyle went home as she had come, by railway, pausing for a night's rest at York, while her husband went round by Scotsbrig, to spend some days with his brother James there, whose wife had just died. To their brother Alexander in Canada Carlyle wrote.—

'You know what sad change has occurred in the first days of June ; poor Isabella carried to her last home. . . .
'Poor Jamie : we went to the Ecclefechan Kirkyard together, one day, and spent a few silent minutes, which could not be other than solemn. There they all lay, so still and dumb those that were once so blithe and quick at sight of us : gathered to their sleep under the long grass :—I could not forbear a kind of sob, like a child's out of my old worn heart, at first sight of all this.
'Dear brother, I must close almost without a word addressed from *my*self to *your*self ! You know all that I could say. . . . We have been young and now are old ; and surely it is a blessing to us that we are *thus* still together ! If I live to get done with my Book, I will write to you *then ;* I mean to work no more in this world then ! '

Returning south, with a short pause at Alderley, to please his wife by visiting her friends the Stanleys there, he was home by 1st October.

BOOK XXIV

THE PASSING SHOW
1859-62

I

STARTING AFRESH
(1859)

A PHRASE of Carlyle in writing to Neuberg when busy on the *Frederick* describes his concentration.—" I *see* half a million persons daily ; but communicate with absolutely nobody but my Horse, and that in a very limited style of communication as you may suppose."

When he was going to Germany last year and the first two volumes were about to appear, he was then hoping that two more volumes would complete the work. One of these he had already done in 1858, and he calculated that two years more would finish the *Frederick* altogether. So now after coming home in October he flung himself into the work, and tried to drive to an end " by sheer force " ; but on trial he found that that would not do.

William Allingham was on holiday at the time, and having called at Cheyne Row on his way to Germany, gives a glimpse of the Carlyles in a letter to the Brownings.[1]—' I saw Carlyle just from Scotland, sitting on the hearthrug by a hot fire with back against the mantelpiece, in a rich dressing-gown and smoking cap, smoking—face rustic brown, eyes flaming—vigorous altogether, but still refusing comfort as usual, grumbling about Frederick the Great, &c. &c. Mrs. Carlyle was much better than when I saw her a year before,—in fact as well as ever I saw her, apparently. He gave me an introduction to Hofrath Marshall in Weimar, a Scotchman there who is somehow Private Secretary to the Grand Duchess, and who proved very kind, gave me two whole days, and got me into Goethe's house (then strictly closed). . . .'

[1] W. Allingham's *Letters to the Brownings.* See also W. Allingham, *A Diary*, pp. 78–9.

359

On 11.10.59 Alexander Gilchrist, a young neighbour, looked in, and made notes which have been printed.[2]— 'Called on Carlyle about half past eight p.m. Found him in the dining-room, sitting at the table, looking over and marking a book catalogue. Mrs. Carlyle with a number of *All the Year Round* before her, and knitting.

'Carlyle very genial.' Referring to his own boyhood, 'he alluded to a cheap copy of a monthly magazine, which in an unbound state had fallen in his way—a companion had rummaged it out of a cupboard.—" Doesn't remember any earthly pleasure equal to what he had over that." Remembers in particular one sentimental story in imitation of Sterne, *The Sentinel*. A wife had lost her husband in battle, and wished to see his dead body ; the sentinel harshly refused ; the indignation of the bystanders and relater.—In the last degree vapid and watery, doubtless. " But I (Carlyle) went altogether along with it. Think it was the *Lady's Magazine*. But I remember no plates."

'Recollects afterwards reading *Roderick Random* with utmost delight. Remembers the day and hour ; the mossy bank on which he sat ; the golden rays of the setting sun ; and an old Irishman he met on his way home, who had been a soldier. A remarkable man, who lived despised by his fellow-creatures, as a Papist and Irishman : recalls his appearance that day. Only an odd volume, the first : when he returned to the shop, the man was obliged to confess he had not the other ; but (Carlyle) never rested till he got it.

'Remembers a year later first reading Robertson's *Preliminary Dissertation to Charles V.*, with the utmost delight and wonder. Opened to him new worlds of knowledge to be attained ; vistas in all directions. Never seen it since : doubtless weak enough ; the first book (was the only one that) he got any good out of ; did not get any good out of the others.

'Carlyle possessed an extraordinary appetite for, love (of) and delight in books during the first part of his life. This lasted for clever books till middle life. Then his appetite began to get ticklish, and now no book at all can give him delight. " Hard work the reading a book now. Much power in the hands of those who have the giving of books to young persons. Deserves thinking of."

'Carlyle praised *All the Year Round ;* worth reading. Dickens seemed to get hold of sensible, brief accounts of

---

[2] *Anne Gilchrist, Her Life and Writings*, by H. H. Gilchrist, pp. 62–6.

men's experiences out in the East Indies. Wondered where he got hold of such. I mentioned my wife's article on the Gorilla. Carlyle had read it. "A strange, horrible beast that gorilla, clutching hold of men out of trees, and killing for mere malice."

' (*Our Poor Relation* was the essay referred to. The article pleased Dickens, who showed it to the Carlyles. A trifle that drew forth the remark from Jane Carlyle, " and you know, my dear, you write very nicely ! ")

' Carlyle mentioned seeing Madame Vestris with Mathews some years ago, in a burlesque of Planché's, after Lewes's play ; declared there was " real genius " in her, which made its impression on him despite adverse preposses- sions. . . .'

About the same time, during one of their midnight walks together, Carlyle told Gilchrist of " the curious persons who came to London in Hogarth's time " ; William Emerson for one, who wrote books on mathematics still valuable, some of which Carlyle has. " A strange character ; living in the country on £70 a year ; his wife spinning with her distaff while her husband wrote : and his treatise written, he would come up to London to sell it. Got bald ; could not bear the idea of wearing other people's hair, so made a wig of flax and clapped it on his head.—Burnt his shins with sitting close to the fire " (as Carlyle remembers " seeing many old people's shins marbled ") : " contrived some kind of shield, which he called *shin-covers !* The Duke of Man- chester took Emerson up ; got him to come and live with him ;—offered him a seat in his carriage. Emerson asked, ' what did the Duke want with that whim-wham ? He could walk.' The country people thought him a sooth- sayer. An old woman came to ask what had become of her husband (long gone away), she wishful perhaps to be free. " He has been in Hell these three years past," said Emerson.

' " Emerson was a free-thinker, who looked on his neigh- bour the parson as a humbug. He seemed to have defended himself in silence the best way he could against the noisy clamour and unreal stuff going on around ; retreating to his mechanics and fluxions, which he knew to be real."

' Carlyle spoke of Arkwright as worthy a biography or essay. " None good hitherto. A wonderful man—rather of wonderful results to England. A poor barber, who bethought himself of the loom, the threads then shifted by

hand. This great invention so simple, a wonder no one had
thought of it before." Carlyle minutely described the loom,
using his hands freely to do so. He also told how the
weavers set upon Arkwright, " You son of Belial ! will you
not let us live ? " and drove him out of the village :—how
his wife destroyed his model one night when he was asleep,
thinking he ought to attend to his razors and suds, as the
more profitable ; how he told her to be off and sent her
adrift out of his house, for fear of a worse thing ; probably
giving her a licking first.

' " Strutt,—a neighbouring yeoman, found money for the
first weaving mill : he was grandfather of the present Lord
Belper." Carlyle had seen the mill—deserted and not at
work then. " Strutt showed the ability of a Frederick in
ordering his men and economising their labour ; his descen-
dants immensely wealthy, worth millions." '

It was in this year (1859) that George Meredith, a reader
to Carlyle's publishers, Chapman and Hall, published
Feverel and sent a copy to Carlyle. As he afterwards told
his friend Edward Clodd,[3] ' *Feverel* was written at Chelsea.
. . . In my walks I often came across Carlyle, and longed
to speak to him. One day my publishers received a letter
from Mr. Carlyle asking about me. Then I called on them.
Carlyle told me that his wife disliked *Feverel* at first, and
had flung it on the floor, but that on her reading some of
it to him he said,—" The man's no fool " ; so they per-
severed to the end. He said that I had the making of a
historian in me ; but I answered that so much fiction must
always enter into history that I must stick to novel-
writing.'

[3] *Memories*, by Edward Clodd, p. 148.

II

THACKERAY AND *CORNHILL*, &c.
(1859)

ONE evening, 14.10.59, Thomas Woolner came to tea,[1] and found Carlyle ' unusually well and so pleasant and entertaining' that Woolner did not leave till nearly midnight. After ' a great deal' of talk about snakes, they discussed ' at some length' what was alarming all England then,—the ' stupendous naval preparations being carried on' at Cherbourg and elsewhere in France ' with such astounding rapidity.' Woolner was anxious to hear what he was thinking of them, and wrote next day to Mrs. Tennyson, —" He does not like them at all and thinks it means mischief."

The letter to Mrs. Tennyson ran on :[1]—' Mrs. Carlyle is much better than when she left London' in the summer. ' She looks better than I have seen her look for fully twelve months : she had been in a great way for some time in consequence of a cart having passed over the neck of her " Nero " ; but after a few days he recovered and her grief assuaged.'

Thackeray was now preparing to launch the *Cornhill Magazine*, which was to start in January, and wanted a contribution from Carlyle,[2] who replied on 20.10.59.— ' Dear Thackeray,—Right gladly I would if only I could, but I can yet bethink me of nothing in the least likely. Indeed I am so crushed to death amid Prussian rubbish these long years past, I have nearly lost the power of thinking in any form, and am possessed by one sad futile ghost of a thought—How am I to get out of this cursed thing alive ? If ever I do live to get out of it and find the Thackeray magazine and editor still lively, then !

---

[1] *Thomas Woolner, His Life in Letters*, by Amy Woolner, pp. 175–6.
[2] Biographical Edition of *Thackeray*, Vol. XI, pp. XX and XXI. The second letter here quoted is not dated there.

‘ Meanwhile I do not quite give the matter up—your matter I mean—as desperate. And if any possibility do offer, be sure I will lay hold of it. With prayers for the new periodical and you,

‘ Yours ever,

‘ T. CARLYLE.’

Another letter refers to Carlyle's intention to tell for the *Cornhill* the story of the Fontenoy anecdote, which can now be read in *Frederick*.[3] The witty and well-known story was that about Lord Charles Hay, who was leading the English column which, with unexpected endurance of the French batteries, had got into the French centre. The French said he shouted to one of their officers, “ Bid your people fire, sir,” and was answered, “ No, sir, we never fire first.” ‘ After you, Sirs!’ being clearly implied, and Carlyle calls it ‘ a supreme politeness in that sniffing pococurante kind ’ ; but he reveals the vulgar truth that there was merely ‘ some slight preliminary talk and gesticulation, but in the Homeric style,’ without French polish, ‘ mere rough banter and “ chaffing,” ’ and then the usual murdering.

As Carlyle explained to Thackeray now, the truth had come to light in a ‘ letter from Lord Charles Hay, main actor in the business. It was sent me last year by Lord Gifford,’ Carlyle wrote. ‘ But on applying to Lord Gifford he—what he is himself, I believe, truly sorry for—cannot now give me permission, so the poor little enterprise falls to nothing again. . . . If I ever see the end of this book and have life left you shall have plenty of things. Fair wind and full sea to you.’

The *Frederick* work lasted longer than expected. Thackeray was dead before it was finished. So Carlyle never wrote anything for *Cornhill*.

---

[3] *Frederick*, Book XV, Chapter. VIII.

III

JOHN FORSTER AND OTHERS
(1859)

JOHN FORSTER had been away from London when the Carlyles came home. Carlyle was writing to him about the 26th October.—'My wife decidedly gained strength, one is thankful for never so little. As to me I did no farther good after quitting my friend the sea : but I went dreaming about, doing nothing, at least ; in that way my heart-breaking Prussian Concern (comparable to poor Christian's "Burden" in the *Pilgrim's Progress*) lay in abeyance ; so that I could, in some slight degree, better *see* it, and judge a little where (if anywhere) the true handles of it might be groped for. In fine, I too feel slightly better and am at work again daily on that thrice-disgusting Business,—much wishing I were either dead or else had done with it ! In which humble alternative I hope to be indulged, one way or the other, by the Upper Powers and the Under ! I have a kind of hope to begin printing about New Year's Day.

'Poor Hunt, poor Stephen ! The ranks are getting thin to one's right and to one's left :—it is an evident suggestion, "Close then ; rank closer, and stick to one another, ye that still stand ! "

'We are delighted to hear of Macready's Cheltenham purpose : my wife says it will lift a choking incubus, and shadow of death, from himself and his. *Ut Fiat.* (So let it be done !)—Poor Landor, with his white beard, with his strong old heart ! If you ever write to him, say I am still true (backed by my Wife) ; and know *better* than the rumouring Newspapers and barking Doggery of this world ! —I wish Craik were in his principalship ; I too can be of little help. When you go to Dickens, our best regards. *Tale of Two Cities* is wonderful ! Adieu, dear F. ; our duty to the Lady. Come and see me whenever you return.—'

IV

CHAT ABOUT WOMEN, &c.
(1859)

THE Gilchrists were still neighbours at Cheyne Row, and Alexander Gilchrist soon had more notes worth reading.[1] About the end of October, apparently, he tells us :—' Talking of the first volume of the *French Revolution*, Jane Carlyle thought that " the MS. was not lost in Mill's, but in Mrs. Taylor's house, whom Mill was then much with, and afterwards married ; and much more likely to have happened in a wholesale druggist's house, as her husband's was, than in a literary man's. The name kept secret for a long while ; but ultimately the Mills themselves let it out. Very uncomfortable affair for Mill before the name was known. Mrs. Austin, for instance, said in his presence there seemed to her only one plan open to the man—to have gone home and shot himself. Carlyle almost wild at the time : with great difficulty re-wrote it. It never seemed to him as good as the first copy ; and yet he could not remember what that first was."

' Carlyle asked me, " how long I had been at work to-day ? " " From the time I got up till tea-time." " How many hours ? " " Eight clear." " Too long." He never got more than six at the best of times. " Only three or four clear now. Over the *French Revolution*, six hours a day. Used to go out about two or three in the afternoon ; read in the evening." Carlyle said that " people in England had an interest in the *Cromwell ;* in the *Frederick*, he had to create it all ; do everything for his readers."

' Carlyle spoke of a small French volume (1685) on *Ziska* he had had from Palmer, and returned. Two things in it new to him and amused him. One, in besieging a town, Tabor, which the Hussites built for themselves, which Frederick once took and was often in, the other side threw over into the town waggon-loads of carrion. The other incident, how Ziska in a battle, when he was sore beset, got the women of his side to strew their veils, laces and other light garments ; he then provoked the

---

[1] *Anne Gilchrist, Her Life and Writings*, by H. H. Gilchrist, pp. 71-4.

opposite cavalry to advance into them. They got entangled —their spurs and so forth, in these things. Then Ziska attacked and cut them up. Carlyle laughed much at this. . . .

' Talking of the *Leader* to George Henry Lewes, Carlyle asked, " When will those papers on Positivism come to an end ? "

' " I can assure you they are making a great impression at Oxford," says Lewes.

' " Ah ! I never look at them, it's so much blank paper to me. I looked into Comte once ; found him to be one of those men who go up in a balloon, and take a lighted candle to look at the stars."

' Lewes mentioned that he had given up literature for Natural Science.

' Carlyle likes Lewes, and was so pleased with him that in the evening he said to his wife, " Well, I don't know why you shouldn't call on Miss Evans." '

It seems likely that Carlyle was not in the room when his wife said, according to Gilchrist :—" At a party at which that brute, the Duke of Malakoff, was present, conversation turned on our regrets for the past. Lady Jersey foolishly boasted she did not understand them ; she had no regrets. Then Malakoff said to her :—' Ce n'est pas vrai, Madame. You regret your youth, and you regret the fading beauty of your daughter.' " '

This Duke of Malakoff was the same Pélissier who lives in history for suffocating more than 500 Arabs when they had taken refuge in caves. As one of the bullies of Napoleon the Little, he had now got the job of Ambassador at London. According to Gilchrist's report, Mrs. Carlyle went on.—' " He affects the brutal and brusque in his style. The Duke of Malakoff and Skittles " (the courtesan), " a lady I hope you do not know, Mr. Gilchrist ? "

' I had heard of her.

' " A very pretty and very wicked lady who rides about the Park——"

' Here Carlyle entered at last,' which ' stopped the anecdote about " Skittles " to my regret.'

' 26 *November,* 1859.

' Mrs. Carlyle gave a curious account of Dr. Gilchrist who lived in Edinburgh. When an old man, (he) married a beautiful young girl. " Madly jealous of her ; suspecting every man about her : once picked up a card in her drawing-room, of a gentleman ; taxed her with it. She knew nothing about it. Dr. Gilchrist challenged the man ; who denied all knowledge of Mrs. Gilchrist. It turned out he had left a card of his in a circulating library book, which had passed on to Mrs. Gilchrist. The friends on both sides interfered and would not allow the duel ! " '

Mrs. Carlyle had taken warmly to the second Lady Ashburton, Miss Mackenzie ; and was writing to her in a letter dated only ' Tuesday.'

' Come at last ! Oh dearest of created *Ladies ;* past, present and to come ! I wonder if you have any adequate conception how your coming has been watched and waited for, by the person now addressing you, and that person's better half ? From day to day, since this day week, expectation and disappointment alternating ! Every day the one or the other of us has ridden or driven up to Bath House, to examine the windows and the gate ; sometimes even to cross-question Hannah, who had never more positive information to give, than that you " might arrive any day." " Every day " till yesterday ; just the day when ones perquisition would have had happy results ! for yesterday I had to stay at home to nurse " a chill,"—and Mr. C. was made too late out, by an *inburst* of Mrs. Cameron and Mr. Watts (the Artist), the former hardly to be restrained from forcing her way into Mr. C.'s bedroom while he was changing his trousers ! ! ! I told *her* as Baillie told *me ;* when I was pursuing Mr. Heath " to the Back " with your message : " It is a dangerous affair rather, that you are there entering on, Mam ! " So when your note arrived this morning it was *news* that it told ! Oh my Darling, my Darling, how I love you ! how glad I am—nay it is but just towards *him* to say how glad *we* are at the prospect of having you here to-morrow night ! *Will* you really come ? Bless you for even *intending* it ! But at all events you will arrange for my seeing you, one way or another, with the least possible delay ? And Mr. C. is *really impatient* to see you, also. If you heard how eloquently he was talking of your " exquisite kindness and *loveableness,* and *beautiful transparency of Soul,*" on the way home that evening, and on several occasions since, you would know whether he had the " eyes to see, and heart to understand," which a certain young Lady would have persuaded you he had *not.*

' Oh my Darling ! my Darling ! who that comes near to

you, and is cared for by you can help loving you with a whole heartful of love ? I am almost frightened at myself when I feel how dear, how indispensable you are become to me. I had fancied myself too calmed down with years and other things, ever to have bother with my *heart* any more. Yes, I was henceforth to take just such tepid pleasure of friendship as the Gods provided me ; leaving aside all strong feelings that can tend to pain and anxiety. If you were to tire of me now—if you were to die before me, if you were anyhow taken away out of my life, why, I should fall into as great trouble as ever I was in when young and excitable about a " lost love."

' Meanwhile, I shall see you to-morrow evening.

'Yours devotedly,

'JANE CARLYLE.'

Here is another letter uncertain as to date. Mrs. Carlyle had been helping Lady Ashburton to get a good Lady's maid, and wrote to her about it.—

' I am so glad dearest Lady that you have told Mr. Badger to come down to you. *Your own instinct* is the only safe thing to go by, in choosing a Servant to be about your own person—especially in the present state of things with you ; when to be loved, and cared for, and *humanly* waited on, is so much more important than to be " turned out " the pink of fashion and adornment. I defy any Lady's maid to make you look other than well dressed, but any Lady's Maid wanting in tact and human feelings *may* make you feel uncomfortable ;—in these anxious times, when, even had your nature been less *real* than it is, the stern realities of your life must have swallowed up vain shows.

' Pray let me know your decision about her, as if she does not please you I would ask Elise,'—a fashionable dress-maker who was also a friend.

' I thank God for Lord A's. amendment. Decidedly Quain is very clever—very prompt and dexterous also— he writes remarkably pretty and ingenious notes. The one he sent me about the Books was as good as a Poem. When I was calling for Lady William Russell yesterday, who is too poorly to move to Walmer Castle as she had intended, she talked of Dr. Quain as " the most rising medical Man in London." She was always, she said, hearing of cases " where he had at once hit the nail on the head, when other Drs. were puzzling to find it." It always does one good to visit

2 B

Lady William. She has such an unsurpassable gift of flattery. However *Cinderellaish* may be my opinion of myself in entering her room, I always come away thinking myself " one and somewhat." Yesterday, for example, I found a Colonel Percy with her, whom she " begged to introduce to Mrs. Carlyle, the Wife of Mr. Carlyle the *distinguished Philosopher*, and *herself a very distinguished Woman ; altho' she was not aware of it*." What more delicate compliment could be devised ? the " *altho' she was not aware of it* " at once investing me with an *admirable modesty* to my own eyes, and anticipating any doubts I might naturally feel as to the fact. She must have made a first-rate Ambassadress in her time. . . . Lady William asked me to tell " dear Lord Ashburton that she had been very glad to hear of his recovery."—That " sufferers like herself could best sympathize with others in suffering." Poor Soul, she has a dreadful time and endures so bravely. . . .

' JANE CARLYLE.'

On 30.11.1859 Carlyle was writing to the Edward Fitz-gerald of Omar Khayyam.—'Dear Fitzgerald, I have not for many a day had a welcomer bit of writing handed in to me than your friendly hurried Note the other morning. My Letters here,—" impacts from the owls of the Parish on the poor old Horn-lantern with a candle-end lighted in it," are not oftenest (meaning oftenest not) of an exhilarating character.' (Gives his news,—) '3 or 4 weeks in Annandale, almost 3 months in Scotland—wife, self and horse, all the better for the long rustication.' Now, he is riding diligently every day from half-past three 'till deep in the dusk. . . .

'I live in nearly perfect loneliness here : speak to no person (wife does all the society there is) ; and stand with my whole remaining strength to the task' of *Frederick* in short. Were I once out of this, it is my fixed purpose to rest for the remainder of my life, and after that we may look with some confidence to *rest* of a good *eternal* sort ; welcome to the wearied who can go no farther !

'Thackeray *fell* lately in a dark fog and lamed a leg, I am told, which still keeps him prisoner : (is) busy with his magazines . . . I cannot get to see him yet. Spedding is gone to Cumberland : you, when you are tired of Lowestoft, come to us, and smoke a pipe again in peace ! Good be with you, dear F. Yours ever. T. Carlyle.'

V

ABOUT BURNS AND MANY OTHERS
(1859)

MEANWHILE Alexander Gilchrist had been writing a *Life of Blake*, and was being helped by Carlyle to get a publisher,—which explains the beginning of his next report.[1]

'28 December, 1859.—Carlyle again asked me about the *Blake*; what I was doing with it. I stated that I had delivered his letter to Chapman, but was giving my MS. a last revisal before sending it in. He talked of the difficulties of a book, of getting it done, of reducing chaos to order. The whole world seems against you; but it is not so. Other men knock against you who are simply thinking of themselves, not of you at all. Carlyle's difficulties lately as to maps,—sent for some to Germany; certain towns, battle-fields of Frederick's he wanted; reads maps very ill now to what he used to; obliged to use spectacles for them, though then cannot see quickly.

'I mentioned Bradbury and Evans having given a hundred guineas for Tennyson's poem—a guinea a line.

'"Ah! they won't go on paying Alfred at that rate; just to say he wrote for it." Like Barnum's story (as Barnum told Carlyle) of a Yankee newspaper at a low ebb, bribing Everett, a man much respected in the States, with a fabulous sum of dollars, first offering 100, then 200, at last 2000; he in an evil moment consenting; and then their advertising throughout the length and breadth of the Union that the great Everett had been paid 2000 dollars to write an article in it; and the newspaper went up to a great circulation.

'Carlyle took his seat on the footstool by the fire as usual to smoke. Talk fell on the dog Nero, now very ailing. Mrs. Carlyle has had it ten and a half years; six months old when Nero was brought to her. Carlyle said, "Never dog had given trouble more disproportionate to its use and worth than Nero had to him." (Mrs. Carlyle said.—) "It had been worth it all." He denied it, and reiterated the absurdity of its existence. It would be a kindness to kill it.

'(Mrs. Carlyle.—) "If he is to be believed, he shouldn't make affectionate speeches to Nero in the garden when he thought no one heard."

[1] *Anne Gilchrist, Her Life and Writings*, by H. H. Gilchrist, pp. 74–7.

'Carlyle regretted not to have been taught music or at least singing.

'When a boy at school, the class was singing once, the master remarked on the beautiful voice of that boy (Carlyle), which boy was destined never to turn his voice to any account. Liked Scotch tunes much : " Robin Adair," " Gilderoy," very plaintive and melodious. Carlyle was also fond of Irish airs,' and said :—

'"*Gilderoy* showed a soul bathed in melancholy. Rude music, probably first performed, as Burns said, on cow-horns, these old Scottish airs ; but came from the heart. That old tune to which Bruce led his men at Bannockburn, for instance."

'Carlyle recited " Scots wha hae wi' Wallace bled " ; the whole poem, with measured emphasis, the right stress on each word. Recited it with great fervour, repeated some passages, in particular the

> " Lay the proud usurpers low ! "

and

> " Liberty's in every blow !
> Forward !—let us do or die ! "

'Remarked on the practical character of the song " Burns hit the nail on the head at each blow ; not a blow lost. Rude, but not a word too much or too little, or to be altered.

'" Burns sat down and strummed the air for an hour, and then, possessed of the spirit of it, wrote, ' Scots wha hae wi' Wallace bled.' No such song-writer as Burns. Some of the songs in Shakespeare alone equal to them. Béranger not to be compared. Whatever theme Burns took, the same qualities shown."

'Carlyle recited :—

> " Had we never lov'd sae kindly,
> Had we never lov'd sae blindly,
> Never met and never parted,
> We had ne'er been broken-hearted."

'(Then he said.—) " This Jessie, a very nice girl, (was) the daughter of a neighbouring exciseman : Burns (was) married at the time. No princess had ever had such a song written of her." Some of the Jacobite songs fine, about a dozen genuine. " Bonnie Prince Charlie " the finest, breathing devotion and love. Carlyle recited this also :—" Quite carries you along with it into readiness for the time to join the cause "; expatiated on the swing and lilt and picturesqueness of it. Another humorous one, " *There was a German laddie*," breathing entire contempt of the German laddie, but hoping the world would have justice on him yet, "through the sow's tail he had caught hold of," meaning fat Kilmansegge his mistress. . . . One of the coarsest of songs.'

This may refer to one of the early coarse versions of an old Jacobite song, which Allan Cunningham transformed into the delightful ditty called " The Wee, Wee German Lairdie." The report concludes.—

' At parting Carlyle again kindly asked about the book, and wished me a happy deliverance of it. Manner kind throughout, and his face looked kind.'

It is a pity that Gilchrist was not able to correct the mistake of memory that Carlyle had made, for Carlyle might have been glad to be reminded how sincere was the song he liked. The Jessie he spoke about was Jessie Lewars, who helped her friend, the wife of Burns, to nurse the poet in his last illness. She was rewarded poetically by various nice things he wrote for her, but of course there never was any serious suggestion of love between her and him; whereas the four lines quoted by Carlyle, and by Byron before him, and by Walter Scott, who declared them " worth a thousand romances," were part of a *parting* love-song as sincere as any could be.

It was addressed to " Nancy" or Agnes Craig, Mrs. Maclehose alias Clarinda—a grass-widow whose husband in the West Indies was little but a *legal* husband. She and Burns were exactly of the same age, and they had met and loved each other on his first visit to Edinburgh. Fain would she have prolonged indefinitely the sentimental connection; but Burns was wiser and went back to his Jean, tho taking leave of " Nancy" cost an effort, and inspired some lines as good as any he ever wrote :

> "Ae fond kiss, and then we sever !
> Ae fareweel, and then for ever ! . . .
>
> I'll ne'er blame my partial fancy,
> Naething could resist my Nancy :
> But to see her was to love her;
> Love but her, and love for ever.
>
> Had we never loved sae kindly,
> Had we never loved sae blindly !
> Never met or never parted,
> We had ne'er been broken-hearted."

Mrs. Maclehose lived to be an old woman and was piously proud of the admiration of Burns all her life, and well she might be.

VI

SIDNEY HERBERT, JEROME NAPOLEON, &c.
(1860)

ON 5.1.60 the Carlyles went to the Grange for a week,
and that may have been the date of something
Mr. Venables has reported.[1] Apropos the current politics,
Carlyle was telling about 1759, when Pitt had become the
real ' King of England.'[2] His War Offices and Admiralties
' were not of themselves quick-going entities ; but Pitt
made them go. Slow-paced Lords in Office have remonstrated, on more than one occasion : " Impossible, Sir ;
these things cannot be got ready at the time you order ! "
" My Lord, they indispensably must," Pitt would answer,
(a man always reverent of coming facts, knowing how
inexorable they are), and if the Negative continued obstinate
in argument, he has been known to add : " My Lord, to
the King's service, it is a fixed necessity of time. Unless
the time is kept, I will impeach your Lordship ! " Your
Lordship's head will come to lie at your Lordship's feet !
Figure a poor Duke of Newcastle listening to such a thing ;
—and knowing that Pitt will do it ; and that he can, such
is his favour with universal England ;—and trembling and
obeying.'

' " That," continued Carlyle in a tone of eloquent indigna-
nation, ' according to Venables,' " is the way to speak to
an incompetent minister." At this point he remembered
that he was thundering in the face of Mr. Sidney Herbert,'
(then the War Secretary), ' and his ready apology ended in
a good -humoured laugh, in which they both heartily joined.'

At this time, tho Cobden was diligent in promoting what
turned out to be a successful commercial treaty between
France and England, there was a great deal of uneasy
apprehension in England of a possible French attack, and

---

[1] *Fortnightly Review*, May, 1883, pp. 629–30.
[2] *Frederick*, Book XIX, Chapter VI.

that is the key to ' a still more untoward mistake of the same nature,' which Venables heard Carlyle confess.   He was expatiating to Prince Jerome Napoleon about ' the miraculous effects of discipline in a 74-gun ship, manned by a rabble swept together in the old times by crimps and press-gangs.   " In a few months," said he, " the ship has become a perfect machine, worked with undeviating regularity, and if she meets a Frenchman of her own size, she blows her into atoms." '

On this visit the women had something more important than politics to heed.   Among the twenty-four guests, there were no less than four newly-married women, eagerly competing in finery, so that according to the older women, the blaze of diamonds round the dinner-table " quite took the shine out of the chandeliers."   The second Lady Ashburton presided prettily.   She had been a MacKenzie, and in years she might have been a daughter of Mrs. Carlyle ; and soon after this visit Alexander Gilchrist reports :[3]— ' I asked Mrs. Carlyle about Lady Ashburton ?   " Oh, I have been completely vanquished."   Resolved not to like her, but had been obliged to.   " Stood out five days."   It was not her fascinations in the drawing-room, but when on " the fifth day she came up into my room, and spoke like an unaffected Highland girl, Lady Ashburton won my heart. She spoke so freely and unguardedly about persons and things,—most people in that station (are) so guarded and careful " '

To amuse the idle men there was a slaughter of pheasants on this occasion, " from 700 to 1000 shot in one day."   The brutality made Mrs. Carlyle " perfectly sick " ;   but she must have accepted some of the birds when she went home, on 13.1.60, for she had some to give away.

Perhaps it was the sight of the newly-married women " taking the shine out of the chandeliers" that suggested to Venables a truly English remark :—[4] " I cannot understand what the Millennium means unless it means that every man will then possess a thousand a year."

[3] *Anne Gilchrist, Her Life and Writings*, by H. H. Gilchrist, pp. 82–3.
[4] *Mrs. Brookfield and Her Circle*, by C. & F. Brookfield, p. 487.

VII

BACK TO WORK
(1860)

RETURNING from the Grange before the middle of January, Carlyle started the printers on Volume III, having decided to " see the whole book in slips " before he corrected more (16.1.60). But in two weeks he stopped the printing and began reshaping his MSS., which kept him busy most of the year.

The riding he did for health had generally to be done alone. The weather seldom stopped him. Thus we accidentally see him this winter concluding a letter to Neuberg,—' Yours always (just going out to ride in the rain, wh— wh—!) T. Carlyle.'

As the days grew longer, he occasionally had company. Tho rather ashamed of liking Bishop Wilberforce in spite of the Bishop's wiliness, he was not ashamed to ride with him in town, and sometimes Neuberg himself, who seems to deserve the credit of convincing Carlyle that horse exercise could be got at an easy rate in London, came riding up at the appointed hour.

' We saw a good deal of the Carlyles,' wrote young Lady Strachey afterwards,[1] referring to about this time. ' They were both very kind and friendly. Mrs. Carlyle was one of the cleverest women I have ever met, full of wit and humour. I never saw anything that made me suppose the Carlyles were not on good terms.

' One day Mrs. Carlyle was speaking derisively of the wife of some illustrious man, declaring that she set her husband on a pedestal, and remained on her knees before him. She went on :—" If I had treated Carlyle like that, he'd have been in an asylum by now."

' Carlyle burst into one of his Homeric shouts of laughter ; then broke off, and said demurely :—" I've been mercifully dealt with in that respect." '

[1] *Some Recollections of a Long Life,* by Lady Strachey, printed serially in the *Nation,* 12.7.1924, p. 473.

VIII

THE DEATH OF NERO
(1860)

MRS. CARLYLE was very fond of her lap-dog Nero. In recent years, according to Larkin,[1] 'Carlyle used to take Nero out with him for a run every night when he went for his eleven o'clock walk ; and I often noticed, when I have walked with him, how carefully he looked after his little charge ; occasionally whistling to him with a small pocket whistle lest he should come to grief.' To Carlyle the little dog appeared, as he said by-and-by, a ' little white speck of Life, of Love, Fidelity and Feeling, girdled by the Darkness as of Night Eternal.'

Larkin continued :[1]—' This little dog at last grew old and asthmatic, until it was a misery to look at his sufferings.' He had seemed at first to recover from his recent accident, being run over by a butcher's cart when in Charlotte's company, and for a month or two his mistress had ceased to worry ; but in January, 1860, he was ill again, and Carlyle more than once advised " a little Prussic acid " ; tho Mrs. Carlyle overheard him saying to the dog when they were in the backyard together,—" Poor little fellow ! I declare I am heartily sorry for you ! If I *could* make you young again, upon my soul I would ! "

The end came on 31.1.60, when he died painlessly by the hands of Mrs. Carlyle's doctor, Dr. Barnes, King's Road, Chelsea, to whom she was writing next day :—' Oh don't think me absurd, you, for caring so much about a dog. Nobody but myself can have any idea what that little creature has been in my life. My inseparable companion during eleven years, ever doing his little best to keep me from feeling sad and lonely. Docile, affectionate, loyal up to his last hour. When weak and full of pain, he offered

---

[1] Larkin's Article, " Carlyle and Mrs. Carlyle," *British Quarterly Review*, Vol. 74, p. 55.

himself to go out with me, seeing my bonnet on, and came panting to welcome me on my return, and the reward I gave him—the only reward I could or ought to give him, to such a pass had things come—was, ten minutes after, to give him up to be poisoned. . . .'

By 12.2.1860 she had sufficiently recovered from her distress to describe the event to Lady Ashburton.—

' MY DEAR LADY,

'Have you ever noticed how long—preternaturally long—the time looks, when one has been thinking and feeling more than usual in it, even without changing of place or interrupting of one's outward routine ?

' I have just been making an experience of this. . . . It wasn't much " to speak of." A small tragedy—very small—and yet, more heart-rending than some grander ones.

' My little dog had become rapidly worse, till " common humanity required that he should be made away with," I was told. " My Dear " (urged Mr. C.) " it is an Act of Roman Virtue that is demanded of you ; *and so* (!) you surely will not shrink from it ! "—as if Acts of Roman Virtue were among the simplest ordinary obligations on a nine-teenth Century Scotchwoman !—and I who have no taste at all for Roman Virtue—oh, *any* other sort of virtue rather than that ! Indeed I have never been able to understand what these old Romans could be made of, or to altogether believe in them. The appeal to any latent Roman Virtue in *me* found nothing to act upon. But the intervention of my Doctor, who happened to call, was more effective. He told me the little creature was suffering dreadfully, and would suffer still worse if he lived ;—that keeping him going on so was " a bit of selfishness " he wouldn't have given me credit for. And then he asked, suppose he himself should come some day when I was out—in a week or so—and give the poor dog something to put him out of pain *in one moment*, " without hurting him the least ; " would I be very angry ? Of course I burst out crying which meant consent. He had said " in a week or so," but *that*, I knew, was merely to put off apprehension, and accordingly, the very next day, the Dr. in driving past our house, seeing the Drawing room windows open, supposed me gone out ; and was half way up stairs, when we met each other face to face. He was for retreating, good kind man ; but I felt, " *the sooner the better*," the sight of my little dog following one about, trying to discharge his bits of duties the same as ever, in spite of his agony of breathlessness ; with my knowledge that he was about to *die*—to be *poisoned ;* that the *reward* about to be given him for his lifelong devotion—the *only* reward that *could* and *ought* to be given him, was—prussic acid ! Oh it was too horrible, could not be ended too soon. So I called him (the Dr.) back, and said *now* was no worse than any other time would be, and bade Charlotte take my little dog away. I *could* not lift him to put him into her arms, but I kissed his poor little head. And *He licked my cheek.*

' Then I ran and shut myself into my bedroom, and flung myself down and cried—as I hadn't cried since I was a girl.

' My Dr. kept his promise, the little creature died in *one moment* (Charlotte said) without a struggle. Fortunately Mr. Carlyle was himself entirely upset by little Nero's death ; so that he could not *lecture me* on my " excessive grief," his " own heart being " (as he expressed it) " quite *unexpectedly* and *distractedly* torn to pieces by the misery of the thing."—His lyrical recognition of " the poor little creature's docility, and loyalty, and sense of duty, and *manifold undeniable* merits," interrupted more than once by downright human *tears*, might have seemed to some people a fall from his (Mr. C.'s) philosophic heights. But for me, I liked him for it more than for all the philosophy that ever came out of his head.

' Now, however, already, he speaks of " poor Nero " very composedly. And Charlotte, who went about, the first two days, with her face swollen and red with weeping, on the third day recovered her prettiness and cheeriness. Only myself whom the little creature belonged to, and whom he loved before everybody and everything else, only *I* am still horribly sad and *perplexed*. For, what *is* become of that beautiful, engaging little *life*, with its " *manifold undeniable virtues* " (as Mr. C. said) ? Could these be extinguished, abolished, annihilated by some drops of Prussic Acid ? Is *that* credible ? Is Prussic Acid more powerful than qualities which, found in a *Human Being*, the self same qualities—we call *divine, immortal ?* " I cannot make myself believe that," I said the other day to Lady William Russell ; and *she* whom people call " so

Worldly," (I could never see why), answered—" But why *should* you make yourself believe it, my good Lady ? Who does believe it ? *I* don't." And then she gave me her ideas about the *Future* of dogs, which, if not particularly well founded, were so poetical and so sympathetic to me, that I was tempted to jump up and kiss her. Luckily I didn't ; for it would have given her a dreadful fright.

' All my other visitors have spoken odiously on what they call my " little bereavement." They don't conceive what pain they give me. Three several men, the only men I am intimate with here, offered one after another to " give me *another little dog*." And two women, of the sort called " *full of sensibility*," inquired if I had " had him *stuffed ?* " " I wonder you didn't " said one of them plaintively, " he would have looked *so* pretty in a glass case in your room, and still been quite a companion to you." Merciful Heavens ! If one lived in what Mr. Carlyle calls " a sincere age of the world," wouldn't one take such a Comforter as *that* by the neck and pitch her out at the window ? '

According to Larkin,[1] Mrs. Carlyle had indignantly cried, " Stuffed ! would you stuff your Baby ? " ' She was always very tender-hearted with her pets,' adds Larkin, historic- ally, ' and especially with her servants, whom she tried in every way to attach to her ; sometimes, but not always, with perfect success.' In her letter she went on :—

' The frank indifference of one's fellow-creatures, that is a common complaint. But it is not *that* one suffers most from ; their so called sympathy is often far worse to bear.

' But why, you think, in the name of wonder, do I write always to *you*, my Lady ? I know well enough why. It is because the Heavenly kindness in your eyes and voice, when we talked about my little dog at the Grange, has come back to me many times since, and *magnetises* me into these strange confidences. But understand, I have no expectation that you should *answer* such a letter as this. If you read it to an end without protest it is as much as could be asked. Someday however when you have much leisure perhaps you will write me two or three lines, just to say how you feel, and when you come to Town, and how the dear wee Baby is.

' I heard from " St. Thomas " a few days since. His letter was mostly about *you*—all the better for that.

' I have so many things to thank you for, my Lady, that I really don't know where to begin—or end. All that game,

that unfailing Addiscombe hamper. " My Heavens ! " (as
Lord Ashburton used to say, as often as Mr. Carlyle says
" Ah me ! ") what *am* I to do with it all ?

> ' Ever yours,
> J. W. CARLYLE.'

Lady Ashburton being perhaps unable to reply, this
may be the likeliest date for a letter of sympathy from Lord
Ashburton, for which Mrs. Carlyle was very grateful. In
responding Mrs. Carlyle had some unusual news for him.—

> ' 5 CHEYNE ROW,
> ' *Thursday.*

' DEAR LORD ASHBURTON,

' In the first place, *thanks from the heart*, for the kind
little letter you wrote about me to Mr. C. The sympathy
shown me on this *melancholy occasion* has been of much the
same benefit to me, as the *quinine* Dr. Quain advised for
my neuralgia ;—it has not lessened the positive pain, but
it has made me stronger to bear it.

' I am—*we* are—sincerely glad to hear the capital account
of you, given in Miss Anstruther's letter of this morning.
I have news of Baby too this morning, from Mrs. Mackenzie,
which removes one's anxieties on *her* dear little account.

' So I am in good spirits this morning ; having nobody
to feel anxious about, and my own pains being *rather
bearable.*

' In proof thereof I send you a printed document which
arrived for Mr. C. last evening. And if it only amuse you
half as much as it seemed to amuse *him*, especially the
writer's solemn prayer for Mr. C's. *death* gave him (Mr. C.)
the highest gratification.—The thing is rather too inflated
for *my* taste, but Mr. C. declares " No—there is a great
deal of a very high sort of Talent in it, and a profound
sincerity." It is to be hoped, not of a practical sort, for
if *that* " profound sincerity " felt a need of putting itself
into action, Mr. C.'s assassination would be inevitable.

' My kind regards, and thanks, and *good intentions* to
Miss Anstruther, please.

> ' Yours affectionately,
> ' JANE W. CARLYLE.'

To her aunt Grace Welsh in Edinburgh, who was addicted
to divinity, Mrs. Carlyle passionately wrote :—" What *is*

become of that little, beautiful, graceful *Life*, so full of love and loyalty and sense of duty up to the last moment ? Is *it* to be extinguished, abolished, annihilated in an instant '' while every brutalized good-for-nothing lives for ever ?' She ' expected a terrible lecture ' for such heterodoxy ; but Grace had loved little Nero too, and instead of scolding her, referred her to " certain verses in Romans which seem to warrant your belief in the immortality of animal life as well as human ! ! ! "

Meanwhile Nero had been interred in a corner of their back yard below a marble slab, and when writing to Neuberg on 3.2.60 about the *Frederick* work and saying, " I expect you on Sunday evening," Carlyle added,—" The poor little dog has got his quietus ; do not mention or allude to him ! "

The back yard of the house at Cheyne Row at the time when Nero was buried there was thus described by poet Allingham.[2]—' Some twenty yards by six ; ivy at the end. Three or four lilac bushes ; an ash stands on your left ; a little copper beech on your right gives just an umbrella to sit under when the sun is hot ; a vine or two on one wall, neighboured by a jasmine—one pear tree.'

In the heat of summer Carlyle occasionally worked there many hours, with his books and papers under an awning but in colder weather he went into it mainly to smoke. As Allingham and he were sitting smoking together near Nero's new-made grave, they were not discussing the dog at all. What Allingham was curious to know was whether the London rumour was right, that on looking closer at *Frederick*, Carlyle was finding his hero unsatisfactory. The answer was,—not so at all. The simple fact was,— " I am twenty years too old for writing *Frederick ;* but must go on."[3]

[2] *William Allingham, A Diary,* p. 79.
[3] 23.6.1860. *William Allingham's Letters to the Brownings,* privately printed, 1914.

IX

CHRIST IN THE TEMPLE
(1860)

AFTER the death of Lady Ashburton, Carlyle did his best to comfort her mother, Lady Sandwich. Thus on 19.4.1860 when she had entered on her eightieth year, he was writing to her a letter,[1] containing commonplace matter enough, about the weather and so on, and then some sentences still worth reading.—

' I went one day, somebody dragging me, to see a new Picture (Christ disputing in the Temple, Father and Mother finding him there) by Hunt the Preraphaelite ; upon which he had been working for 3 years, (7 in all, for he spent 4 years in Palestine as preliminary) : a worse job for him than even Fritz, I think ! ' (meaning—than even writing the history of Frederick was to me).

' But the Picture, and the Painter, did seem to me to have extraordinary merits. The Christ is an exquisite mixture of a God and a peasant lad. His mother too is very fine ; but I thot. she sh'd. have been a little angry withal (at having got such a fright from her careless son) instead of merely rapturous over him, as she might be over a baby saved from the wolf. There were other criticisms :—but I have not seen such a Picture, for fidelity of execution, for exquisite finish, and limner and other talent, by any modern man.—It had turned out worth my while to go ! '

---

[1] From the original letter now in the National Library of Scotland, Edinburgh.

X

TALKS WITH MILBURN, THE BLIND PREACHER
(1860)

APPARENTLY it was this summer that one of the most welcome callers from America, Milburn the blind preacher, came many times to " tea at six o'clock."[1] By-and-by he dictated to a faithful scribe what he remembered. " Never," said he, " had I any idea of what eloquent talk meant until I listened to Carlyle."

' At their first interview,' as soon as tea was done, Carlyle said :—

" I hope, sir, that, unlike many of your countrymen, you sometimes indulge in the solace of a pipe ? "

Milburn declared he did and Carlyle led him into the garden, where there were seats under an awning, a table with a canister of tobacco and new clay pipes. As they lit up he said :—

" People in moderate circumstances in this country can not afford to offer their friends a good cigar, and I suppose only what you would consider very middling tobacco. The Government finds it needful to have such a revenue that it must needs lay a tax of some hundreds per cent. upon the poor man's pipe, while the rich man's glass of wine pays scarcely one-tenth of this impost. But I learn that there is as much tobacco smuggled into England as pays the duty. Thus, as you see, it is as it ever will be when the laws are unjust and onerous ; for the smuggler is the Lord Almighty of the Chancellor of the Exchequer, saying to him, ' Thus far shalt thou go, and no farther, and here shall thy proud waves be stayed.' "

The development of steamers and railways has hampered the smugglers since then, and something better than smuggling is needed now.

[1] *Thomas Carlyle*, by Alfred H. Guernsey, pp. 12–18, 21, 26–8, 86–9.

Plate VI

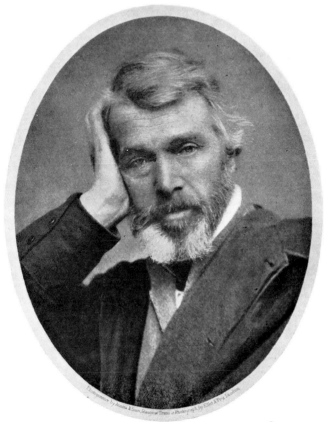

THOMAS CARLYLE
(*From a photograph by Elliott & Fry*)

[*face p. 384*

The talks reported by Milburn would mostly be under the awning, and he did not distinguish day from day, nor endeavour to reproduce all he said himself. Here is what he recalled as said by Carlyle in several dialogues on different days, most likely about June.

"Well, Sir, this part of the town, I think, should have an interest for people from your side of the water, for it has associations connected with a certain countryman of yours named Benjamin Franklin. When he was toiling as a journeyman printer in the metropolis, more than a century ago, he was accustomed to stroll upon the Sunday afternoon along the banks of Father Thames, and this end of this Cheyne Row was usually his goal. One day, as he walked discoursing with a friend, he declared himself able to swim from here to London Bridge, distant about five miles. His friend offered a wager that it was impossible ; and he, upon the instant stripping, plunged boldly in, and started for his mark, while his friend, bearing the clothes, strode down the bank ; and a great multitude of spectators, growing ever greater as he proceeded, followed to see the feat.

"He, with brave stroke and lusty sinew buffeting the tide, gained the bridge and the wager. Whereupon, amidst great acclamations, the people suggested that he should start a swimming-school. But God had other work for him to do : for in later years he was to teach the people of your continent how, by Frugality and Labor, and Patience and Courage, any man might buffet the waves of Fortune, and swim straight on to prosperity and success. And that was the swimming-school which he was to establish."

"Did you ever happen to see Louis Napoleon while he lived in London ? " Milburn asked, and was told.—

"Oh, yes, I chanced to meet him a few times at the houses of people who were accustomed to give dinners here ; and I thought even then that there was something lurking in him of the blood of the old Napoleon, who was, as I read it, the great Highwayman of history ; his habit being to clutch King or Kaiser by the throat, and swear by the Eternal, ' If you don't stand and deliver instantly, I'll blow your brains out.' A profitable trade he did at this sort of thing, until another man—Arthur Duke of Wellington by name—succeeded in clutching *him* and there was an end of him.

"This Louis Napoleon, as he is called, used to talk to

2 C

me about the Spirit of the Age, the Democratic Spirit, and the Progress of the Species ; but, for my own part, it seemed that the only Progress the Species was making was backward, and that the Spirit of the Age was leading the people downward ; and we discovered that we didn't understand each other's language ; that we had no key in common for our dialects. And we parted asunder—as mayhap did Abraham and Lot—each going his several ways. It looks to me very much as if *his* way led him to Sodom.

" After that I used to see him in this neighbourhood (I think he had lodgings in this part of the town), with his hands folded across his breast, and his eyes fixed with a melancholy stare upon the ground, and he looked to me like a poor opera-singer in search of an engagement. God knows he has suceeded in finding an engagement upon a stage sufficiently vast, before an audience ample enough for any man, and the whole thing got up regardless of expense. But I certainly expect that the day will come when the blue sulphurous flames will dart from behind the scenes and consume the pile with all that are in it ; or that the edifice will give way in a crash of ruin, and the whole—singer, audience, and all—sink into the nethermost depths of uttermost perdition, where, it seems to me, they certainly belong.' One cannot read this and not think of the war of 1870–71.

Another man in whom the preacher was naturally interested was Edward Irving, and he tells us Carlyle said :—

" I had gone through the University of Edinburgh and had . . . become associated with . . . an old friend " as a teacher at Kirkcaldy, in short. " It was Edward Irving— my old friend Edward Irving. Together we talked, and wrought, and thought ; together we strove by virtue of birch and book to initiate the urchins into what is called the rudiments of learning ; until, at length, the hand of the Lord was laid upon him, and the voice of his God spake to him, saying, ' Arise, and get thee hence, for this is not thy rest.' And he arose and girded up his loins, and putting the trumpet of the Almighty to his lips, he blew such a blast as that men started up with surprise, and said that the like of it had not been seen since the days of the Covenant itself.

" And from Scotland he came to this great Babel ; and he stood up in the pulpit of the Hatton Garden Chapel, the eyes of him blazing and the Herculean form of him erect. And the great and the learned, the high and the titled, the gifted and the beautiful, came round about him, and sat mute and spell-bound listening to his wonderful words. And they thought—for fools will ever think according to their folly, which is the law of their being—they thought that, because they were looking at him, he was looking at them. He was not looking at them at all. He was trying to do what no man can do and live—trying to see God face to face.

" I have heard that the eagle's eye suffers eclipse ; that the curtain of darkness falls over the pupil of his eye by the steadfast gazing at the brightness of the sun. It was thus with my poor friend Irving. The fools said—let the fools have their own way ; they know no better—the fools said that Irving was *daft*—that his head was turned with the popular applause. He was not *daft :* he was *dazed*. The curtain of darkness fell over the pupil of the eagle's eye by too steadfast gazing at the sun. In blindness and loneliness he sobbed the great heart of him to sleep."

There is little new in what Milburn heard. He was told about the loss of the MS. of the first part of the *French Revolution* without Mill being named ; and when he described himself as a Methodist, the American equivalent, he explained, of English Wesleyan, Carlyle frankly told how he had been disgusted by English lay preachers among the Wesleyans in Derbyshire Peaks.—Their religious fervour was a mere fear of Hell which " made cowards."[2]

In reply to Milburn he described his father and his father's pastor,—" the first person that ever taught me Latin, and I am not sure but that he laid a very great curse upon me in so doing. I think it is likely I should have been a wiser man, and certainly a godlier one, if I had followed in my father's steps, and left Greek and Latin to the fools that wanted them."

" You seem to be the victim of dyspepsia—I had almost said a martyr," said Milburn once. " How does it come ? Did you inherit it, or have you acquired it ? "

" I am sure I can hardly tell, sir," was the reply. " I only know that for one or two or three and twenty years of my mortal existence I was not conscious of the ownership of that diabolical arrangement called a stomach. I had grown up the healthy and hardy son of a hardy and healthy Scotch dalesman ; and he was the descendant of a long line of such : men that had tilled their paternal

[2] See *Carlyle on Cromwell and Others*, pp. 389, 390.

acres, and gained their threescore years and ten—or even mayhap, by reason of strength, their fourscore years—and had gone down to their graves, never a man of them the wiser for the possession of this infernal apparatus.

"And the voice came to me, saying, 'Arise and settle the problem of thy life!' And so I entered into my chamber and closed the door, and around me there came a trooping throng of phantasms dire from the abysmal depths of nethermost perdition. Doubt, Fear, Unbelief, Mockery and Scorn were there ; and I arose and wrestled with them in travail and agony of spirit. Whether I ate I knew not ; whether I slept I knew not ; I only know that when I came forth again it was with the direful persuasion that I was the miserable owner of a diabolical arrangement called a stomach ; and I have never been free from that knowledge from that hour to this, and I suppose that I never shall be until I am laid away in my grave."

About his father he spoke to Milburn with delightful candour and simplicity, declaring,—" Of all the men I have ever known, I think my father was quite the remarkablest. Quite a farmer sort of person, using vigilant thrift and careful industry ; abiding by veracity and faith, and with an extraordinary insight into the very heart of things and men. I can remember that from my childhood I was surprised at his using many words of which I knew not the meaning ; and even as I grew to manhood I was not a little puzzled by them, and supposed they must be of his own coinage. But later, in my black-letter reading, I discovered that every one of them I could recall was of the sound Saxon stock which had lain buried, yet fruitful withal, in the quick memory of the humbler sort of folk.

" The last time I ever saw my father was on my journey from Craigenputtock to London. I was on my way to this modern Babylon, with a manuscript in my hand, *Sartor Resartus* by name, which I wished to get into print. I came upon my fool's errand, and I saw my father no more, for I had not been in town many days when tidings came that he was dead. He had gone to bed at night as well as usual, it seemed ; but they found in the morning that he had passed from the realm of Sleep to that of Day. It was a fit end for such a life as his had been. He was a man into the four corners of whose house there had shined through the years of his pilgrimage, by day and by night, the light of the glory of God. Like Enoch of old, he had walked with God; and at the last he was not, for God took him.

" If I could only see such men now as were my father and his minister—men of such fearless and simple faith, with such firmness in holding on to the things that they believed, in saying and doing only what they thought was right, in seeing and hating the thing that they felt to be wrong—I should have far more hope for this British nation, and indeed for the world at large."

Then in continuation of this or as a reply to more questions, he went on :—

" Alas ! Sir, the days in which our lot is cast are sad and evil. All Virtue and Belief and Courage seem to have run to Tongue ; and he is the wisest man, and the most valiant, who is the greatest Talker. The world has transformed itself into a Parliament, an assemblage whose prime and almost only business is to talk, talk, talk, until the very heavens themselves must have become deaf with the ceaseless vociferation. Our British nation occupies a sad pre-eminence in this matter. Demagogy, blustering, vainglorious, hollow, far-sounding, unmeaning Talk, seems to me to be its great distinction. On earth I think is not its fellow to be found, except, Sir, in your own demagogic and oratorical nation. I am certainly afraid that modern Popular Oratory will be the ruin of the race ; and that the verdict of the jury that shall sit upon the corpse of our Civilization will be, ' Suicide by an over-dose of Oratory.' "

Professional Christians of the Palaver-Provider type might have taken offence at this ; but not so the good blind Milburn. He treasured all he heard for many years in an unusual memory, and delighted to repeat it whenever wanted, like an ancient rhapsodist reciting Homer.

XI

WILLIAM HEPWORTH DIXON
(1860)

IN July, 1860, William Hepworth Dixon, a man of 39, had been editing the *Athenæum* successfully for seven years, and was himself already a distinguished man of letters. His *Personal History of Lord Bacon* too came out this year. So it was natural for a contemporary novelist, Miss Mulock, the 'creator' of *John Halifax, Gentleman,* to feel afflicted by censure from such a quarter, and complain to Alexander MacMillan, the publisher, whose partner Craik she married by-and-by. And here is how MacMillan comforted her.[1]

"What does it matter what the *Athenæum* says ? " asked he. "Let them go to Jericho and fall among thieves. Words have no relation to fact or thought in such minds." To help her to feel as he did about that, he described how at a dinner-table Carlyle had been denouncing the irreverence of the newspapers, which babbled about anyone and everyone, so that one might wish for some paralysis of the general gabbling faculty. "I don't agree with you, Mr. Carlyle," cried Hepworth Dixon, "I should like to know everything and to talk about everything." A little later, Carlyle finished something he was saying, as if clenching an argument with a well-known fact,—"And there's Dixon there,—he's sore distressed because his tongue is not long enough to do all the gabbling he wants to do."

---

[1] *Letters of Alexander MacMillan*, by G. A. MacMillan, 1818–96, p. 57.

XII

FROM LONDON TO THURSO
(1860)

IN June this year Carlyle had gone off his sleep. On 6.6.60 Mrs. Carlyle had been writing to Mrs. Russell at Thornhill :—' My husband is working himself to death ; has no thought of going north this year ! And I shall not dare to leave him in his present way. I cannot make him take care of himself : but I can put all sorts of hindrances in the way of his absolutely killing himself.'

In July she took a lodging at Brighton ; but three days' trial of it were enough for him. He hurried home, and was little better there. He lay ' whole nights awake.' Once he was sitting smoking ' up the chimney ' in the middle of the night, ' huddled in rugs, dressing-gown and cape.' A dark terror crossed his mind, that he would *never* finish *Frederick*, the book would finish him. The facts which made this likely seemed ' undeniable,' and saddened him the whole of the next day. But on the day following, he thought it was like Luther's temptings by the Devil, and to be answered in his dialect,—" Well, well, Herr Teufel (Devil), we will just go on as long as we are alive ; and keep working all the same till thou do get us killed." This ended the fright, but did not bring back sleep.

Several mornings he rose at six and rode to Hammersmith region or Clapham Common ; but a morning ride could not do for him what sleep would have done. He ' had an unpleasant cloudy feeling ' in his head, and consulted his brother Dr. John, who was lodging in Brompton, and advised him to take a sea voyage. Sir George Sinclair was then, for the third or fourth time, inviting him eagerly to pay a long visit to Thurso Castle, near John o' Groat's house in the farthest north ; which coincided with his wife's advice and the prescription of the doctor, who offered to convoy him as far as Wick.

Sir George was a fine old man of seventy, familiar in London, where he had been a Member of Parliament at 19, they say, and tho now retired from politics he often came to town. Lunching at Cheyne Row, he was pronounced "amusing" by such critics as Mrs. Carlyle and her friend Mrs. Twisleton, the Bostonian, who were not prejudiced in his favour by his open piety. Carlyle did not join in such banquets, glued to his desk till three ; but had been seen walking and talking with the handsome old Laird, and it was noticed that they seemed to part reluctantly. We are left guessing what they talked about. Sinclair was a worthy son of his father, Sir John, of ' The Statistical Account of Scotland.' He had recoiled from the " reforming " Whigs, because of their jobbery and seeking of spoils. Unlike them, he sympathised with the working-classes. He admired Thomas Chalmers, sincerest of the divines. He had worked hard tho in vain to prevent the " Disruption " of the church, but when it took place he followed Chalmers into the new " Free Church."[1]

In spite of the pleasantest personal relations with royalties, he loathed Napoleon the Little as much as Carlyle did, and spoke of him as " The Man of December."

On 24.7.60 Carlyle was writing to him,—' There is something so truly hospitable in the tone of your letter, something so human-looking and salutary in the adventure proposed to me, that I decide on accepting it.' In reply to the ' beneficent lady ' who was to be his hostess, he tells her that ' good cream ' was the luxury he most esteemed, ' rustic farm produce ' his favourite diet, with ' milk and meal,' ' eggs, chickens, moor-mutton,' and ' bread-pudding ' ; and in conclusion, ' I am accustomed to say, " The Cow is the friend of man, and the French Cook his enemy,"—and not one day in ten drink beyond a single glass of wine.' And therefore, altho quite gay with the hope of being like a ' King in Thule,' he could not promise to match ' the bibacities of that old gentleman ' in his ' Castle on the Sea.'

His sleep was coming back before he left London with his brother John, in the Aberdeen steamer on Wednesday, 1st August ; and on the first night at sea he slept soundly six or seven hours in ' an overcrowded piggery of a place,' and the night that followed was equally good. On Friday

---

[1] James Grant's *Memoirs of Sir George Sinclair*, pp. 24, 39, 40, 122–8, 271, 289, 422–9, 433.

night they reached Aberdeen,[2] and left the steamer. After dinner at the hotel, he went out for a walk in the streets.

" Passing a little shop," he afterwards said to Masson, an Aberdonian, " I heard a drunken row and a woman's voice screaming, ' You're a damned, eternal leear ' ; and I couldn't help thinking,—' You're probably quite right.' "

Masson felt he was being chaffed, and could only say he could recognise the street from the description as one of the lowest in the town. Carlyle :—" Some very strong language was used in Aberdeen."

In the morning he saw Marischal College, and then went on, and reached Thurso on the Saturday.

[2] What follows is from his talk to Prof. David Masson on his return, told to D. A. W. by David Masson 16.12.1896.

XIII

NAPOLEON AND FREDERICK
(1860)

THE sea voyage and the five weeks at Thurso enabled Carlyle to sleep all right, and he had no more trouble on that account for a long time to come. One of his bedroom windows there looked out on ' the great ocean,' where he bathed every day. ' The sea is pure as crystal,' he reported, ' and rages oftenest among the wild rocks at a loud rate.'[1]

He contrived without offence to evade the family ' prayers' by breakfasting an hour earlier ; and on Sundays he was excused the Church performances. His work never stopped. He was allowed to be as ' invisible ' as he liked till three o'clock, and was able here to finish as far as the books with him allowed the Second Silesian War, which carried him beyond the end of Volume III, and fairly start what came after it, the " Ten Years of Peace " (Book XVI). He wrote to Neuberg,—' I have (in hoping moments !) a notion to resume *printing*, directly on my return.'

In a fine old-fashioned style, Sir George reported to Mrs. Carlyle :—

' He has rendered himself a universal favourite with all the inmates of this house, young and old, male and female, high and low. For *all* he had a kind word, and a willing ear, and could accommodate his conversation with equal capacity and cheerfulness, to the habits, occupations and predilections of auditors the most widely differing from each other in all their elements of thought, action and experience. His absence will leave a blank in my daily arrangements and pursuits, which cannot be supplied, or cease to be felt and lamented. There never passed between us the most transient feeling of discord or impatience ; and much as I

---

[1] See Note [1], Chapter XII.

admired his genius, I was even more fascinated by the strong undercurrent of tenderness and sympathy, which a superficial or commonplace observer might be unable to discover.'

Which reads like a certificate, but was sincere. ' Sir George was abundantly conversible,' Carlyle wrote, ' anecdotic, far-read, far-experienced, indeed a quite learned man (would read me lyrics, &c., straight from the Greek, any evening, nothing pleased him better), and full of piety, veracity and good-nature,' not amusing indeed, to a man weary and sleepy, but something better ;—' his constant perfect goodness, and the pleasure he always expressed over me, were really welcome, wholesome, and received with gratitude.'

Sinclair excelled at anecdotes, and had rare experiences to tell. He had been a classmate of the poet Byron, who declared him " the prodigy of our schooldays," and in 1806, when he was sixteen, his father sent him to Göttingen to complete his education, and master French and German as he had mastered Latin and Greek. Going from Gotha to Leipzig with a friend a few days before the battle of Jena, he was taken prisoner by the French, and closely questioned by Murat, who sent him to Napoleon.

As soon as the boy looked at Napoleon, after bowing low, he saw ' a little figure in white nightcap and dressing gown.' Napoleon had his arms crossed and a cup of coffee in his right hand. Marshal Berthier was standing beside him and there was a map on the table.

Young Sinclair was bidden trace his route ; and tho he felt strongly prejudiced against ' the implacable enemy of my country,' who sat down to listen, with his right elbow on the table, leaning his face on his thumb and forefinger, yet in a few minutes the boy felt that he was in front of ' the greatest man of the age,' and declares he never forgot ' the expression of his countenance.' It was ' thin and sallow, but every feature beamed with intelligence. The penetrating glance of his eye seemed to anticipate the answer to every question, by reading it intuitively in the soul. His manner was abrupt, but became gradually softer,' and ' relaxed into a smile ' on hearing read some letters from the boy's father, proud of his prodigy. Sinclair said he could never forget the kindness with which Napoleon eyed him, as he asked what authors he had read at school,

—' I could not quit his presence without admiring the acuteness of his intellect, and feeling the fascination of his smile.'

In later days Sinclair had been behind the scenes in Courts and Parliaments, and watched the play-actors there performing, which makes it easy to understand why he and Carlyle used to meet often when he was in town, and how on this visit of five weeks " the hours and minutes hand in hand " went lightly by.

One of Sinclair's best stories, probably told then, is embalmed in *Frederick* (Book XXI & Ch. VIII).—A Countess of Findlater he knew had been Maid-of-Honour to the Duchess of Brunswick, Frederick's sister, and heard her tell something about her brother which Carlyle believed, upon such corroboration of the anecdote-books.—

' You go on Wednesday, then ?

' Loss of time was one of the losses Friedrich could least stand. In visits even from his Brothers and Sisters, which were always by his own express invitation, he would say some morning (call it Tuesday morning) : " You are going on Wednesday, I am sorry to hear ! " (what *you* never heard before).—

" Alas, your Majesty, we must ! "

" Well, I am sorry : but I will lay no constraint on you, pleasant moments cannot last for ever ! "

' And sometimes, after this had been agreed to, he would say : " But cannot you stay till Thursday, then ? Come, one other day of it ! "

" Well, since your Majesty does graciously press ! "

And on Thursday, not Wednesday, on these curious terms, the visit would terminate.'

One Thursday (23.8.60) ' the womenkind ' took Carlyle in their carriage and pair to see John o' Groat's house and Duncansbay Head—a twenty miles' drive and a mile or two to walk at the end. He admired the pretty shore, ' trim grass or fine corn to the very brow of the sea.' Between the farmfields and the shore, where the sand was ' white as meal,' was a steep slope of grass, that was fragrant with meadow-sweet,—Queen of the Meadow. Three ships were passing westward ; and bits of an old wreck were sticking in the sands. The little isle of Stroma seemed close at hand, about two miles away, and farther off, the

' precipitous, picturesque Orkneys,' (Seal-Islands), ' looking over on one,' lay ' dim' and ' dreamlike, with a beauty as of sorrow ' in the dim gray light.   John o' Groat's house was ' terribly like some extinct farmer's lime-kiln,' but the site was beautiful, at the bottom of a kind of scoop rising slowly, towards high ground that protected it, on many sides.   The only living things in sight were sheep.

" From Maidenkirk " in the Mull of Galloway, the extreme south, " to John o' Groat's," near Duncansbay Head and in the extreme north, used to mean " the whole of Scotland," just as " From Dan " in the north " to Beer-sheba " in the south implied " the whole of Palestine."

The country there in the north seemed on the whole ' equal to Craigenputtock for picturesque effects, plus the sea, which is always one's friend. . . . Much of it is *well* fenced ; a good Country, only hardly a tree to be seen in it ; tempest ruling everywhere, no shelter except under walls.'

He had settled to sail south on Friday, 7.9.60, but unfortunately his wife mistook some intimation about that for news that he was returning straight to London, and hurried home from Cheshire, where she had been visiting Lady Stanley, instead of going on to Dumfriesshire.   She was also cherishing a grievance, imputing delays in letters to his negligence instead of the slowness of the northern posts.   Not even Neuberg whom he invoked could prevail on her to return to the country.   Apparently she preferred to stay at home, but wished to appear a martyr.   Her husband wrote to his brother on Thursday 6.9.60.—

' Jane has at last written : nothing the matter, after all my alarms ; considers herself the aggrieved party,—good soul, obstinately ignoring the inexorable regulations of mail time in this country ! I cannot tell you how much I was relieved.   She has put away her old woman servant ; has got, what I have been advising these seven years, *two* effective servants (as we hope they are) ; which may be a great improvement.'

Next morning he departed as arranged, leaving Sir George delighted with the assurance that their best hopes had been fulfilled.   Tho " wearisome nights had been appointed him " in London, he had had nothing but sound sleep since the day he " laid his head upon the pillow " in Thurso Castle.

XIV

THEOLOGY AT TABLE, &c.
(1860)

LEAVING Thurso on 7.9.1860, Carlyle went to stay with Thomas Erskine at Linlathen, near Dundee ; and there, as he told Sinclair,[1]—" We had plenty of pious discourse for the two days I stayed." He can still be seen by us enduring it, through the eyes of Alexander Muir, a young footman diligently waiting table and devoted to divinity.[2]

The sister of Erskine, Mrs. Stirling, was at the head of the table, and Erskine at the other end. Alexander Scott was staying in the house, " a big man," according to Muir, " full-bearded, heavy-browed," profuse in utterance, a University Principal from Manchester. He once had been assistant to Edward Irving, and it is interesting to read in a letter Erskine wrote a few weeks after this[3] to Maurice, who seems to have applied to him, on behalf of Mrs. Oliphant, for help towards knowledge of Edward Irving :—' I knew Irving, but not enough to be able to give much help. . . . Carlyle and Scott knew him well, and have very living portraits of him in their own hearts. Scott cannot speak of him without becoming Irving in voice and manner, even in countenance.'

Scott was lecturing in Edinburgh this year,[3] and he and Erskine were continually swimming in deep discourse on the eternal conundrums of theology. Muir did his best to absorb the wisdom going without omitting his proper duties ; and was clearly of the opinion that Scott was not so deferential as he should have been to Mr. Erskine. All

[1] *Memoirs of Sir George Sinclair*, by James Grant, p. 427.
[2] Alexander Muir was minutely questioned by D. A. W. on 7.8.1918. Thanks are due to Dr. G. Douglas Mc.Rae, of Glengall, Ayrshire, who made known to D. A. W. that Muir had something worth hearing to tell.
[3] *Letters of Thomas Erskine of Linlathen*, by W. Hanna, II, pp. 134-5, 384-6.

the more did Muir admire the perfection of Carlyle's politeness. " Mr. Carlyle never spoke a word about religion. When they talked about it at table, he sat silent, resting his head on his hands, his elbows on the table, attentive, missing nothing, listening to and looking at one after the other."—" Bum ! . . . Bum ! . . . ! ! ! " One can picture the scene. Mrs. Stirling herself perhaps was bored, but she was as patient as Carlyle, according to Alexander Muir.

" I heard Carlyle conversing about other things," said Muir, " but he said nothing about Theology," which was the main thing in which Muir was interested. All the rest he could tell about Carlyle was this :—" He was a man of six feet, and extremely strong ; moustache and beard growing gray, and cheeks more than red,—purple in colour ! He seemed thoughtful, never spoke a word I remember to me, but he gave me half a crown, which was more than I expected, both then and another time he stayed at Linlathen. I brushed his boots and clothes. Both Mr. Erskine and also his sister Mrs. Stirling were *very* fond of Carlyle."

XV

CARLYLE MAKES A VOW
(1860)

FROM Dundee Carlyle came to Scotsbrig for a few days, and then to his sister's farm of the Gill, a few miles west of Annan. He enjoyed the bathing and liked the place and was loath to depart. About the middle of September it would be that he went ; for returning south, with a short pause at Alderley, to please his wife by visiting her friends the Stanleys there, he was home about 22.9.60.

Whatever the exact date, on his last morning at the Gill he made a resolution, which he confided to Emerson on 14.6.65, on the occasion of his *next* visit to Scotland, and after the longest absence he had ever had from it.—' My work was getting desperate at that time ; and I silently said to myself, " We won't return till *it* is done, or *you* are done, my man ! " '

This was as close an approach to an old-fashioned " solemn vow " as is possible to a clear-headed man to-day,—closer perhaps than any such person would come who had not a private tenderness for pious old habits, and a moral tendency upwards, like that of the flowers in spring. The essence of a vow was to be a " good resolution." But Carlyle reserved to himself alone, and did not leave to any Bishop or Pope, the power of dispensation. In other words this was a *conditional* vow,—to be kept if there was no sufficient cause to the contrary. It was not a promise to a God nor to a Church. It was a promise to nobody at all but himself. In short, it was a truly *Protestant* vow. It differed from religious " solemn vows " in general in many respects, and particularly in this, that it was performed to perfection.

XVI

THE ROBE OF CAMEL'S HAIR
(1860)

IT may have been about now that Carlyle received a gift
from Lewis Pelly, who had become acquainted with
him some years ago.[1] As Pelly himself has explained,[2]
he had returned to duty in the East, and in 1860, when he
was secretary to the British legation at Teheran, the capital
of Persia, he had been ' ordered to ride ' from there ' to
the Indian frontier, to report on the political condition of
the intervening territories.' His modesty may be mis-
leading. His lonely ride was a great achievement, and the
' order ' is likely to have been really a permission, for what
he did required the sort of courage equal to a Forlorn Hope.
The ' Ride to Khiva ' of Colonel Burnaby in 1875 and
Burton's pilgrimage to Mecca in 1853 were similar feats,
perhaps less useful, and certainly not more bold or difficult.
' I was at Herat in 1860,' he continues, ' when the Persian
army, beaten by the Turcomans, was retreating along the
line of the Murghab ; and when on this and other public
accounts one's head at times felt a little loose on one's
shoulders. I was lying one evening outside the walls of the
Herat Fort, under the starlight and near the singularly
beautiful mausoleum of the Timur family, when it occurred
to me that I was unaccountably calm and happy for an
ordinary man who found himself a thousand miles away from
any other European, and surrounded by excitable Asiatics,
some of whom had old blood feuds with the Indian Government. On reflection I attributed my mental condition to
the influence of Carlyle, and I remember repeating to myself
the lines which he had translated from Goethe, and which
in that, as in many other crises, have shot strength and
solace into my heart : '—

[1] Book XXIII and Chapter XIII.
[2] *Glimpses of Carlyle*, by Sir Lewis Pelly, *Fortnightly Review*, May,
1892, pp. 723–8.

" The Future hides in it
Gladness and sorrow :
We press still thorow,
Naught that abides in it
Daunting us—onward.

" And solemn before us
Veiled the dark Portal,
Goal of all Mortal.
Stars silent rest o'er us,
Graves under us silent.

" Whilst earnest thou gazest
Comes boding of terror,
Comes phantasm and error :
Perplexes the bravest
With doubt and misgiving.

" But heard are the Voices,
Heard are the Sages,
The Worlds and the Ages :
' Choose well ; your choice is
Brief and yet endless.

" ' Here eyes do regard you,
In Eternity's stillness ;
Here is all fullness,
Ye brave, to reward you ;
Work, and despair not.' "

' The next morning I went into the bazaar and selected a finely-woven camel's-hair robe, and a small Persian prayer-carpet of exquisite colour and texture, and resolved to carry both of them with me through Afghanistan and Beluchistan for transmission to Cheyne Row. These articles in fact formed my only luggage, besides what was contained in my saddle-bags. The robe and rug reached Mr. Carlyle in due course, and many years afterwards my friend Miss F. told me that the little carpet had been taken by Carlyle to his wife's dressing-table. Soon afterwards she gave it to the second Lady Ashburton, declaring the " lovely Persian Rug " to be " quite out of place in our small rooms, and out of harmony with our plain furniture." '[3]

The camel's-hair robe, " delightfully soft and warm and light,"[4] was worn by Carlyle as a dressing-gown to the end of his life ; and in the fine portrait statue by Sir Edgar Boehm, the sitting figure of Carlyle can still be seen enveloped in the robe of camel's hair.

[3] Undated letter of Mrs. C., which seems to be about 1861 or 1862.
[4] Words used of it by Miss M. C. Aitken, a niece of Carlyle, talking to D. A. W., and corroborated by Alexander Carlyle, a nephew, who added,—" I wore it 24 years after 1881, and then it succumbed to moths."

XVII

A DIVINITY STUDENT IN DOUBT
(1860)

IN 1860 there was a divinity student in Scotland called
David Macrae, who felt half-distracted by religious
doubts, for he was simple enough to suppose he could make
the ' Exodus from Houndsditch '[1] and also carry on his
hereditary trade of professional Christian. His father was
a parson, and he may have been afraid to break his father's
heart by quitting the church. So he wrote to Carlyle, and
received in reply a letter which he printed about half a
century afterwards,[2] at the close of a scintillating career as
a free-thinking preacher. The Gilfillan Memorial Church
at Dundee was built for David Macrae, by the congregation
to which Gilfillan used to preach, and which had chosen
Macrae as his successor,—to the huge disgust of Mrs.
Gilfillan, who had held her husband in leading strings,
editing his sermons.[3] By that time, in the seventies, Macrae
had been expelled from the United Presbyterian Church,
for expressing a doubt about the eternity of Hell. At
present he was only a student, when he appealed to Carlyle
for guidance and received this reply.—

' CHELSEA,
23rd October, 1860.

' I have read your letter with real sympathy. I can but
too well conceive the sorrow and uncertainty in which you
have to struggle till these vital matters be settled. My
wish to help you need not be doubted ; but, alas ! there is

[1] See *Carlyle on Cromwell and Others*, pp. 236–7 and 409, and *Carlyle at His Zenith*, pp. 368–370.
[2] Appendix to No. VIII of David Macrae's Sunday Lectures, *Thomas Carlyle and His Gospel*.
[3] D. A. W. knew David Macrae slightly, and had relatives and friends intimate with Mr. and Mrs. Gilfillan and the father of Macrae.

literally as good as nothing to be done. This is one of the numerous cases in which the patient must be his own physician. To no other of mortals is the case wholly known (even if this were all) except to him.

'Luther said long ago—"It is neither safe nor prudent to do aught against Conscience"—a motto you abundantly recognise as valid everywhere, especially where things sacred are the question. Of this I need not remind my present correspondent. On the other hand, may not I perhaps say withal that there is a morbid punctiliousness of conscience, which should not be indulged upon details, the heart of the matter being once settled and out of peril. Strict silence will remedy many details ; and for silence there is no end of demand upon us in any kind of life which we will lead wisely ! I cannot advise as to your Divinity studies and profession ; indeed I cannot ; no man can understand another in regard to such a thing ; no man's practice can be a rule to another.

'Something—by no means the whole, yet something, and that very considerable—will depend on the question, "What other outlooks of a life have you, should you quit theology ? " If there lay open to you an honest unspeaking profession, or course of commended industry, I should almost say at once, "Quit this speaking one." Speech is wholesome to very few in these times, to perhaps fewer than ever before ! If on the contrary you have nothing at all of definite elsewhere ? The prospect of drifting into " literature " and living by " the Press " ought to be very horrible to you, and, I can well assert, is apt to be more perilous to moral well-being than any Church that is not wholly a false one !

'You will, of course, do nothing rashly ; take long, earnest, frequent, and oftenest silent counsel with your own mind—perhaps still for months and years to come. Be valiant to adopt the wise course, whether flesh or blood repugn or not ; in the end, if you be faithful, I can promise you a good deliverance.'

A senior student and old family friend of David Macrae has remarked about this letter,[a]—"How well Carlyle took the measure of David ! " His friends and relatives could be grateful at once, so far as their knowledge of it went ; and he must have had some such feeling himself, or he would not have published it after many years. Its reticence is

[a] To D. A. W. verbally.

remarkable and typical. Carlyle appeared to feel that directing a man to this or that job is as delicate as advising about taking a wife. The only thing certain is that whatever a man does, he is sure to repent it sooner or later.

XVIII

CHEERING RUSKIN
(1860)

IN 1859 some strikes in the London building trade had
turned the attention of John Ruskin to economics. In
the summer of 1860 he finished the writing of *Modern
Painters*, and at once went on to write the four essays *Unto
This Last*.'[1] Thackeray published them in his magazine,
the *Cornhill*, in August, September, October and November,
but in October he had had to write to say that the first
three ' were so unanimously condemned and disliked that,
with all apologies, he could only admit one more.' Ruskin
sent Carlyle an advance copy of the fourth and last, and
received this letter[2] in reply.—

'CHELSEA,
29th Oct., 1860.

'DEAR RUSKIN,
'You go down through these unfortunate Dismal-
Science people like a treble-X of Senna, Glauber and Aloes ;
like a fit of British cholera, threatening to be fatal ! I have
read your paper with exhilaration, exultation, often with
laughter, with bravissimo ! Such a thing flung suddenly
into half a million dull British heads on the same day, will
do a great deal of good. I marvel in parts at the lynx-eyed
sharpness of your logic, at the pincer-grip (red-hot pincers)
you take of certain bloated cheeks and blown-up bellies.
More power to your elbow, (tho it is cruel in the extreme).
If you dispose, stand to that kind of work for the next seven
years, and work out there a result like what you have done in
painting. Yes, there were " a something to do "—not easily
measurable in importance to these sunk ages. Meanwhile

---

[1] *John Ruskin*, by W. G. Collingwood, II, pp. 3–12.
[2] *Collected Works of John Ruskin*, Vol. XVII, Introduction, pp.
XXXII–III, &c.

my joy is great to find myself henceforth in a minority of two, at any rate. The Dismal-Science people will object that their science expressly abstracts itself from moralities, from &c. &c. ; but what you say and show is incontrovertibly true ; that no " science," worthy of men (and not worthier of dogs or of devils), has a right to call itself " political economy," or can exist at all, except mainly as a fetid nuisance and public poison, on other terms than those you shadow out to it for the first time. On third last page and never till then, I pause slightly, not too sorrowfully, and appeal to the times coming (Noble is the spirit there, too, my friend ; but alas, it is not Philanthropismus that will do these ; it is Rhadamanthismus I sorrowfully see) which are yet at a very great distance ! Go on and prosper.

'I am yours always (sleeping a little better and hoping an evening soon),

'T. Carlyle.'

XIX

GERALD BLUNT, RECTOR OF CHELSEA
(1860)

IN 1860 Gerald Blunt, a man of 33, came to Chelsea as Rector, with a pleasant wife and family. He was an ex-pupil and disciple of Maurice and recently acquainted with Macready, but it was not by a letter of introduction from either that he made himself known to Carlyle. " A library and scientific institution " had been planned for Chelsea, and he and another parson were deputed " to ask Carlyle if he would become one of the Vice-Presidents." He afterwards told what happened :—" With trembling and misgiving, we went to No. 5 Cheyne Row, one very dark and wet afternoon. We were both dripping and wet, and perhaps not very presentable. I sent up my card, and we were shown up to Mrs. Carlyle. She received us very ungraciously. She held my card in her hand, while I explained to her the object of our visit. She told us that Mr. Carlyle was very much engaged, that there was no use her asking him to undertake more, and, in fact, we were bowed out without having been asked to sit down. But, about half an hour afterwards, a note came from Carlyle himself, saying that his ' good wife ' as he called her, had not read their card, being half blind and the room being dark, and adding that he would be glad to help anything good at Chelsea. So he became one of the Vice-Presidents. Never again was there any occasion to complain of want of courtesy."[1]

Mrs. Carlyle was soon familiar with Mrs. Blunt, and when the Blunts were at Mrs. Carlyle's " five o'clock tea " and Carlyle looked in, he used to enter in his dressing-gown, and sit down beside the fire to send up the chimney the smoke from his churchwarden. His talk seemed like his books to Blunt, ' depressing. He seemed to feel that we

[1] *Memoirs of Gerald Blunt,* by Reginald Blunt, pp. 95 and 96.

408

were living in a fool's paradise, going straight to destruction ' ; but he ' often ended with a hearty laugh.' And
in the course of years Blunt learned to laugh with him and
shared his point of view much better than the American
theologian, Henry James, who had been inspired to revolu-
tionize theology by interpreting Genesis as allegory.[2] One
of the best things that James ever wrote, however, was his
report of Carlyle's account of an early encounter with
Blunt.—

' He spoke of a call he had just received from the new
rector of the parish. He had some previous intimation of
the rector's design, so met him at the door, hat on head and
cane in hand, ready for a walk. He apologized for not asking
him in, but the fact was that his health was so poor that a
walk in the afternoon had become a necessity for him.
" Would (he) be going towards the city, perhaps ? Yes ?
Ah, then we can confer as we walk." '

So as soon as they started, he said.—" I have heard of
your settlement in the parish with great pleasure, and my
friends give me great hope that you have a clear outlook
on the very serious work that lies before you here. The
butcher up there at the corner of Sloane St. was a great
thorn, I am told, in the side of your predecessor, and is
prepared, no doubt, to give you as much trouble as he can
consistently with the constitution of the vestry and his own
evangelical principles ; and the dissenters are notoriously
a forward, lively folk in the parish. But it is my firm
belief that if these turbulent people could once be brought
to know some one who really believed for himself the
eternal veracities, and didn't merely tell them of some one
else who in old time was *thought* to have believed them, they
would all be reduced to speedy silence. Our sanguinary
evangelical friend at the corner, yonder, would betake
himself hopelessly to his muttons, and dissent have no leg
left to run upon. It is much, no doubt, to have a decent
ceremonial of worship, and an educated, polite sort of person
to administer it. But the main want of the world, as I
gather, just now, and of this parish especially, which is
that part of the world with which I am altogether best
acquainted, is to discover someone who really knows God
otherwise than by hearsay, and to tell us what divine work
is actually to be done here and now in London streets, and

[2] *Literary Remains of Henry James*, by William James, pp. 58, 434-6
and 460 : reprinted from the *Atlantic Monthly*, May, 1881.

not of a totally different work which behooved to be done two thousand years ago in old Judæa. I have much hope that you are just the man we look for, and I give you my word that you will strike dissent dumb if such really be the case. What ? Your road carries you now in another direction ? Farewell, then ! I am glad to find that we are capable of so good an understanding with each other." '

Gerald Blunt was quickly able to understand what Henry James has told us that Carlyle was ' always ' saying : —" That "—seeing what it is right to do here and now and doing it—" *That* is the one condition, in my poor opinion, of any much-talked-of millennial felicity for this poor planet, —the only thing which will ever rescue it from being the Devil's churchyard and miserable donkey pasture it now for the most part turns out to be."

XX

BLASPHEMING THE DEVIL, DAN O' CONNELL & Co.

1860 is as likely as any other date for the rest of the reports of the theologian Henry James.[1] One day he enquired, " What would be the most auspicious hour to bring a friend MacKay, who wants to thank you for the aid and comfort your books have given him years ago on the shores of Lake Erie ? "

" Ask Jane," was the reply. " What she appoints I will give my diligence to conform to."

Mrs. Carlyle was on the sofa beside them and told James to come " tomorrow after dinner, or between two and three, a very placid hour with the creature."

So next day at the appointed hour they arrived, and found Carlyle standing on a chair with his back to them repairing a window shutter, and calling out without looking round,— " Is that you, James, and have you brought your friend MacKay with you ? I don't know whether he is at all related to *my* friend Sandy MacKay of Glasgow. If he is, he can't be related to a worthier man."

In a little time Carlyle was seated beside them, and the stranger made an exaggerative speech of the sentimental sort which James admired. He never recovered from the horror that filled him when Carlyle replied :—" I don't believe a word of it ! I don't believe that I ever helped any man " (in the way you say). " I don't believe that any man ever helped another " (so). " It is indeed unspeakable folly to conceive such a thing.

" The only man I ever found—and him I didn't find— who seemed to be sincere in such a thought was a ship captain, some time ago, who wrote to me to say, without giving me name or address, that he had called his vessel the *Thomas Carlyle*, because he had got some good, he

---

[1] *Literary Remains of Henry James*, by William James, pp. 446–9, 441–4 453–6. He writes only McK. MacKay is conjecture.

fancied, from my books. I thought it behooved me to look
the man up " (were it only to make sure it was not a hoax).
" So I traversed the London Docks from end to end, asking
of the sailors ever and anon if they knew any vessel in those
parts bearing the portentous name of *Thomas Carlyle ;* but
it was all in vain, and I returned home persuaded that,
whatever else might betide me, I should probably never
see under this sun the extraordinary individual who had
named his vessel the *Thomas Carlyle.*"

One Sunday evening Henry James happened to be ' at
Mr. Carlyle's when a large company was present,' including
an American General he does not name and a man from
Massachusetts whom he calls Henry Woodman and describes.
Henry Woodman had begun by being a successful Unitarian
clergyman, but when he had made the ' discovery that
there is no personal Devil,' he gave up preaching and took
to agriculture. " He is so tickled," wrote James, " with the
discovery he has made of old Nick's long imposture, that he
never makes an acquaintance without instantly telling him
of it," and on this occasion had " saturated Carlyle's ear
with the intelligence."

Woodman was a favourite of Mrs. Carlyle, and was
talking to her at one end of the room, when he overheard
Carlyle and the General, at the other end, discussing
Jefferson Davis and the Mississippi State repudiating public
debt, and Carlyle remarking,—" You are all on your way to
the Devil in America." Now Woodman would have heard
the Devil's name even if it had been whispered, says James ;
and turning from Mrs. Carlyle he cried aloud, delighted :—
" What Devil do you speak of, Mr. Carlyle ? "

" What Devil, do you ask ? " Carlyle fairly roared back
in reply. " What Devil do you ask, Mr. Woodman ? The
Devil, Mr. Woodman, that has been known in these parts
from the beginning, and is not likely soon to become,
unknown,—the father of *all liars, swindlers and repudiators,*
Mr. Woodman ! The Devil that in this Old World boasts a
very numerous tho unconscious progeny, and in your
New World, Mr. Woodman, seems from all accounts to be
producing a still more numerous and still more unconscious
one ! That is just the Devil I mean, Mr. Woodman, and woe
be to you and yours the day you vote *him* lifeless ! "

The rest of the company were exhilarated by the breeze
and Woodman not distressed. He resumed his quiet talk
with Mrs. Carlyle, and the General tactfully said,—

" Speaking of the Evil One, I have been visiting to-day subterranean London, its sewers and so forth. . . ." and the conversation subsided again, while it dawned on Henry James that Carlyle disbelieved the Devil stories of the creeds so much as to ' disdain the trouble of denying ' them.

Perhaps the best way to explain the meaning of Carlyle may be to quote an anecdote told by Froude.—' One November day an apparently well-conditioned gentleman ' came to Carlyle with ' a request for help in some local Chelsea charity. A sovereign was at once forthcoming ' ; but ' ten minutes ' after he departed, Carlyle discovered that ' the plausible stranger was a ticket-of-leave man,' and a swindler. ' Too late he remembered an air of " varnished devilry " in the fellow. " Well ! well ! " he reflected, " you must just take your just wages whatever mortification there is." The handsome scandalous face came back to him at night in a half-waking dream. " Hah ! " he thought, " I had a personal visit of the *Devil* too, as poor St. Colm had many ; and slept off with something of real pity for this miserable Devil of mine." ' St. Colm was St. Columba.

Henry James reports a real squall on another Sunday evening. As Mrs. Carlyle told him afterwards, her husband had taken his Sunday dinner that day as he often did at the house of a favourite friend, who may be called Pious Peaceful, the name being suppressed. Replying to remonstrances, Carlyle had said,—Tho the Pious Peacefuls " have no acquaintance with books or literary people, I never pay them a Sunday visit without feeling myself renovated against all the soil of the week, and never come away without being baptized anew in unconsciousness." On this particular day, when he came home about three or four he said to his wife :—" Jane, I am henceforth a regenerate man, and eschew evil from this hour as a snake does its " (cast-off) " skin ! " He said this with earnest purpose, his wife told James, and yet—Here is James's report of what happened and made Mrs. Carlyle tell this good resolution at her husband's expense.

Besides James and Carlyle, there were present Mr. Woodman, and an ' Aide-de-camp ' fresh from India, who was ' entertaining Mrs. Carlyle with any amount of anecdotes.' Then came in Dr. Carlyle with a big and burly Englishman, nicknamed ' Mr. Bull.'

Mrs. Carlyle said in ' an aside ' to Henry James,—" He

has the faculty of always exciting Carlyle to frenzy by talk about O'Connell, of whom he is a thick-and-thin admirer." When the talk turned on politics, she nudged his elbow and whispered in a tone ' of dread ' (or what the reporter so supposed) :—" Now for the deluge ! "

It came, ' hot and heavy for an hour. At last tea was served to our relief. But No ! the conflict went on. Mrs. Carlyle had placed me at her left with bellowing Mr. Bull next to me. I felt her foot crossing mine to reach the feet of my neighbour and implore peace ! The ruffian no sooner felt the pressure than he turned from Carlyle to meet her with undisguised savagery.'

" Why don't you," he fiercely screamed, " why don't you, Mrs. Carlyle, touch your husband's toe ? I am sure he is greatly more to blame than I am ! " Whereat there was a general laugh in which Carlyle took the lead, and then there was peace till after Henry James departed.

He called next day and asked Mrs. Carlyle,—" Was there anything disagreeable after I left ? " To which she answered :—" Everything went on swimmingly till about eleven o'clock, when it pleased your unfortunate country- man, Mr. Woodman, to renew the war-whoop by saying,— ' Let us return a moment to O'Connell.' If the talk was frightful before you left, what did it now become ? Alto- gether unbearable, and when, about twelve o'clock, John Carlyle got up to go, taking Mr. Bull along with him, Carlyle, lighting his candle to see the company to the door, stretched out his hand to his late antagonist, with the frank remark, ' Let bygones be bygones ! ' Mr. Bull scorned to take it, saying, ' Never again shall I set foot in this house ! '

" I knew how cruelly Carlyle would feel this rebuff, and scarcely dared to glance at him as he came upstairs after lighting his guests out ; but when I did look, there he stood at the door of the room, holding the candle above his head, and laughing as he repeated the words of the morning : ' Jane, I am henceforth a regenerate man, and eschew evil from this hour as a snake does its ' cast-off ' skin ! ' "

And the best of the joke is that James did not see there was any fun at all, and talks of the final laughter as " bitter, remorseful," and so on. A sense of humour is the happiest gift of Heaven. Poor Henry James !

XXI

MRS. CARLYLE AND FRIENDS
(1860, &c.)

ABOUT 1860[1] Mrs. Oliphant who had undertaken a *Life of Edward Irving* went to see Dr. John Carlyle, and found him a ' spruce ' little man, ' surrounded with huge books, the *Acta Sanctorum* ' (*Acts of the Saints*) ' and the like, writing a *Life of Adamnan*, the successor of Columba.' Dr. John told her to go and see his brother, which she did as soon as she could go to London, feeling ' shy,' she tells us, but ' with the courage that comes to one when one is about one's lawful work. He (Carlyle) received me with that perfect courtesy and kindness which I always found in him. I never should have learned from any look or tone of his that I had run risk by thus intruding. I remember his tall, thin, stooping figure between the two rooms on the ground floor, in the pleasant shadow of the books, and subdued light and quiet, a very appropriate atmosphere.'

The little woman was ' fluttered,' she confessed. She could remember that he said,—" I can tell you little, myself, but the wife could tell you a great deal, if you saw her." She could never remember how he was to arrange for her to see " the wife," and departed disappointed. But ' a day of two after ' that, Mrs. Carlyle called where she was staying, and took her out for a drive " that we might talk about Irving," Mrs. Oliphant says she said.

' Her hair was black without a grey hair in it—mine at half the age already grey, her features and her aspect very keen, perhaps a little alarming. She began by asking me if I did not come from East Lothian. I had to answer that my mother had,' and we were ' friends on the moment. What

---

[1] 1860 or 1861. For this and what follows see *Autobiography and Letters of Mrs. Oliphant*, pp. 73–78, 343.

warmed my heart to her was that she was in many things like my mother ; not outwardly, for my mother was a fair, radiant woman with a beautiful complexion, and Mrs. Carlyle was very dark, but in her power of narration. She told me that day, while we drove round and round the Park, the story of her childhood and of her tutor.'

Mrs. Oliphant came to live at Ealing in 1861, and tells us,—' My friendship with Mrs. Carlyle was never broken. She came to see me frequently, and I spent some memorable evenings in her house, but at that time did not see her husband again.'

Much of the talk she reports falls vaguely between 1861 and 1866. Mrs. Carlyle used to say of Dr. John (Carlyle) that ' he was one of the people who seemed to have been born in creaking shoes.'

Mrs. Oliphant tells us, ' There is a phrase which shows Mr. Froude's methods. He says, " a ' good joy ', as Mrs. Carlyle used to say." Now Mrs. Carlyle did say it in her sarcastic way as an absurd expression used by Leigh Hunt's children, who lived near her, and who, when they were coming back from their walk, used to run in and tell her they had had such a good joy. She quoted it in illustration of the high-flown talk in which they were trained, and here it is put into her own mouth, as if she had ever spoken in that way.'

She never told Mrs. Oliphant whether she had ever really ' fancied ' Irving, but she showed a ' perfectly genuine feminine dislike ' of Mrs. Irving and all her kin,[2] which much amused the younger woman. She used to say of her husband that he would " spend an anxious week sometimes to make sure whether a certain incident happened on the 21 or 22 of a month in the Sixteen or Seventeen Hundreds."[2] But he seems to have believed whatever his wife said to him about other women—her lightest jest as strong as Holy Writ to a believer. So whether she was describing Mrs. Irving's character, or saying Mrs. Montagu's dress " must have required daily the fastening of sixty or eighty pins," he supposed it was as she said, and thought no more of the matter. " A fallible being will fail somewhere," as Dr. Johnson said, in excusing a prelate.[3]

[2] Article by Mrs. Oliphant on ' Thomas Carlyle,' in *MacMillan's Magazine*, April, 1881, pp. 487–495.
[3] Probably Dr. Robinson, Primate of Ireland, 1765–95. Printed by Boswell under 1770. Napier's Edition of *Boswell's Dr. Johnson*, II, p. 130.

Plate VII

CARLYLE ON FRITZ

(From a photograph, Hyde Park, 2/8/1861)

[face p. 416

Scheherazade of the Arabian Nights seemed to Mrs. Oliphant inferior as a story-teller to Mrs. Carlyle, for Mrs. Carlyle could dispense with wonderful incidents and make reality interesting.   She fully enjoyed watching to see what her husband—' the big blundering male creature—would do next,' as when ' in the valley of the Shadow of *Frederick* the results of a bad day's work would be a gloomy apparition, brow lowering, mouth shut tight, cramming down ' without a word spoiled sheets upon the fire.   The very servants' doings, most tiresome of all domestic topics, she made interesting, still more the neighbours' cocks and hens, pianos and other nuisances.   The best story about fowls is perhaps one told by Mrs. Oliphant.   The house next theirs was occupied once by ladies polyandrous by profession ; and when their fowls were too noisy, and they heard how much their neighbour Mr. Carlyle was distressed thereby, they nobly sent all the fowls away, ' all the inhabitants of Cheyne Row,' according to the story-teller, ' crowding to their windows ' to watch the ' cackling and frightened procession of fowls ' being ' driven, coaxed and carried ' into a cab.

What will Mrs. Carlyle do now ? the neighbours would ask each other.   Not speak to such women, at any rate,— was the common conclusion.   But Mrs. Carlyle ' had sufficient experience to be cynically indifferent to the more honest kind of impurity,' says Mrs. Oliphant.   She called upon the neighbour who had been so promptly obliging in removing the troublesome fowls.   She found ' a bright and capable creature with sleeves rolled up on her round arms, making a pie, who showed no alarm at the sight of her and accepted her thanks with simplicity.'

Mrs. Carlyle was as ready as others to talk scandal, which her husband tended to taboo.   Alone with her in the brougham, ' with the old horse and the steady old coachman ' jogging along, Mrs. Oliphant heard interesting details about contemporaries of every kind.   One day she tells us the topic ' might be called the " Loves of the Philosophers."   I interrupted her by a foolish remark that " Mr. Carlyle alone, of all his peers, seemed to have trodden the straight way."   She turned upon me.—" My dear," she said, " if Mr. Carlyle's digestion had been better, there is no telling what he might have done ! "   Thus she would take one's breath away,' and then go on with her stories. In short, ' she had so much to say and I was so eager to hear,' wrote good Mrs. Oliphant after many years, that ' we might

2 E

have been going on so until now for anything either of us cared.'

Nobody who has read the letters of Mrs. Carlyle can doubt that she deserved all Mrs. Oliphant's praise as a story-teller. Here is a letter of hers not yet published, and interesting in itself. It was one of the first she wrote to the second Lady Ashburton, whom she was very fond of, and tho dated only ' Saturday,' it seems to have been written about this time.

' Oh thank you, Lady dear. I am so glad, and obliged. I wasn't expecting any sign of remembrance ; had indeed no claim *to ;* but—I was *wishing* for one all the same ; my thought of you was feeling to need one, just as alum in solution (it may be said in highly figurative speech) feels to need a thread for crystallizing on ! !

' You think, why couldn't your last letter have sufficed for that purpose ? It was a dear lovely letter, and, truly it might have given the encouragement I required for writing, any time betwixt then and now—if betwixt then and now, things had been going on in a natural human way, but they haven't, that is the fact, the way they have been going on has been quite the contrary of natural and human. That unlaid and apparently *unlayable* Ghost of *Frederick* has broken all bounds latterly ; reminding me rather poignantly of old Dr. Ritchie the Edinr. Professor of Divinity's de-scription of a certain Personage, " *with the trumpet of Discord in his mouth,* and *the Torch of Dissension in his hand* (pray picture him to yourself), he goeth about as a *roaring Lion* seeking whom to devour. And when he hath set Son against Father and Husband against Wife, he returns to his Den, *with a horrible grin on his countenance,* rejoicing in the mischief he hath wrought " ! !

' Whereby I merely mean to say, in plain English—Mr. C. has been getting on dreadfully ill with that unlucky book—and his health and spirits, and especially his temper, have suffered in consequence, to a degree that has been making me not only very sorrowful, but very anxious. Indeed I never before in all my life have seen him so—what shall I say ?—" *put out* " (that is the strongest Cockney term for mental upset, from whatever cause. A Woman here, who had just seen a poor little boy's head split into two by a wheel of one of Pickford's Vans, and waited till the Mother was brought, answered my question " Oh what *did* become of her ? " with, " Oh well Mam, as you may think, she was

sadly *put out*.")— Now, besides the worry of seeing *him*
and *feeling* him in this state, I have been " *suffering Martyrs*"
(as a French friend of mine used to express it) from rheumatic
pains in my own head ; and all this together has produced
a solution of continuity in my small life ; turned up, as it
were, a furrow through it, which alters nothing of what
was a few weeks since, but alters my own firm hold of it
all—so that I need to take a new grasp over the interruption.
Do you understand what I mean ?   I should think not.
When one lives much alone, one feels so many things
one never puts into thought, not to say words.   No wonder
if one gets to express oneself obscurely and fancifully.

' When *will* that Baby take a notion of coming to light ?
I declare I never cared so much for any prospective Baby
in all my life before.   I actually *dreamt* about it the other
night ; dreamt that I was at the Grange, and heard it
crying, and felt it my duty to go and feed it ! ! and went
wandering about in the dark and could never find it.   And
still the crying became more and more plaintive till—it
awoke me.   Awoke me to the vexatious discovery that our
poor cat had been shut out from her week-old kittens, and
was mewing, like to break her heart, to get at them.   A
consummation only brought about thro' my getting out
of bed, and putting some clothes on, and going down stairs.'

XXII

BEGGARS AND OTHERS
(1861)

BOTH the Carlyles spent a few days at the Grange at the beginning of the New Year, 1861, and he reported, —'everybody as kind as possible. Nobody but ourselves and Venables, an honest old dish, and Kingsley, a new, of higher pretensions but inferior flavour.'

Returning to the *Frederick* work, he would sometimes have Froude for a companion in his afternoon walks, if Froude is accurate in his dates ; and so it may have been in January, 1861, in ' the first of these walks,' that Froude saw something which surprised him.—

' It was after nightfall. At Hyde Park Corner, we found a blind beggar anxious to cross over from Knightsbridge to Piccadilly, but afraid to trust his dog to lead him through the carts and carriages. Carlyle took the beggar's arm, led him gently over, and offered to help him further on his way. He declined gratefully ; we gave him some trifle, and followed him to see what he would do. His dog led him straight to a public-house in Park Lane. We both laughed, and I suppose I made some ill-natured remark. " Poor fellow," was all that Carlyle said ; " he perhaps needs warmth and shelter."

' This was the first instance that I observed of what I found to be a universal habit with him. Though still far from rich, he never met any poor creature, whose distress was evident, without speaking kindly to him and helping him more or less in one way or another. Archbishop Whately said that to relieve street beggars was a public crime. Carlyle thought only of their misery. " Modern life," he said, " doing its charity by institutions, is a sad hardener of our hearts. We should give for our own sakes. It is very low water with the wretched beings, one can easily see that."

' A small vagabond was at some indecency. Carlyle touched him gently on the back with his stick. " Do you not know that you are a little man," he said, " and not a whelp, that you behave in this way ? " There was no sixpence this time. Afterwards a lad of fourteen or so stopped us and begged. Carlyle lectured him for beginning so early at such a trade, told him how, if he worked, he might have a worthy and respectable life before him, and gave him sixpence. The boy shot off down the next alley. " There is a sermon fallen on stony ground," Carlyle said, " but we must do what we can."

XXIII

ABOUT DOGS AND OTHERS
(1861)

FROM this time on, for the last twenty years of Carlyle's life, Froude boasts that he was allowed to walk and talk with him two or three times a week, whenever they were both in town. He tells us about Carlyle some things worth repeating.—

' I noticed hatred of waste. If he saw a crust of bread on the roadway he would stop to pick it up and put it on a step or a railing. Some poor devil might be glad of it, or at worst a dog or a sparrow. To destroy wholesome food was a sin.

' I had not expected so much detailed compassion in little things. I found that personal sympathy with suffering lay at the root of all his thoughts ; and that attention to little things was as characteristic of his conduct as it was of his intellect.

' His conversation when we were alone together was even more surprising to me. I had been accustomed to hear him impatient of contradiction, extravagantly ex- aggerative, overbearing opposition with bursts of scornful humour. In private I found him impatient of nothing but of being bored ; gentle, quiet, tolerant, *sadly*-humoured, but never *ill*-humoured ; ironical, but without the savage- ness, and when speaking of persons, always scrupulously just. He saw through the " clothes " of a man into what he actually was. But the sharpest censure was always qualified. He would say,—" If we knew how he came to be what he is, poor fellow, we should not be hard with him."
. . . The crowds of children growing up in London affected him with real pain ; these small plants, each with its head just out of the ground, with a whole life ahead, and such a training ! '

He cursed both Dizzy and Gladstone, Tories and Whigs alike, as the Labour Party inspired by him are doing to-day, because they were neglecting the real interests of the Commonwealth. " There is anarchic Ireland to be brought to order," Froude reports he said, " There are the Colonies to be united with the Empire ; there is the huge, hungry, half-human population of our enormous towns to be drafted out over the infinite territories of Canada, Australia, and New Zealand, where, with land to cultivate and pure air to breathe, they might recover sanity of soul and limb."

' He used to speak with real anger of the argument that such poor wretches were wanted at home in their squalid alleys, that labour might continue cheap. *It was an argument worthy only of Carib cannibals.*

' He would point to rows of houses so slightly put together that they stood only by the support they gave to one another, intended only to last out a brief lease, with no purpose of continuance. " Human life," he said, " was not possible in such houses." All real worth in man came of stability. Character grew from roots like a tree. In healthy times the family home was constructed to last for ages ; sons to follow their fathers. Modern houses were not houses at all. They were tents of nomads. The modern artisan had no *home*, and did not know what home meant. Everything was now a makeshift. Men lived for the present. They had no future to look forward to. . . . . .

' He was very tender about animals, especially dogs, who were like horses, types of fidelity if well treated. I horrified him with a story of my Oxford days. The hounds had met at Woodstock. They had drawn the covers without finding a fox, and, not caring to have a blank day, one of the whips had caught a passing sheep-dog, rubbed its feet with aniseed, and set it to run. It made for Oxford in its terror, the hounds in full cry behind. They caught the wretched creature in a field outside the town, and tore it to pieces. I never saw Carlyle more affected. He said it was like a human soul flying for salvation before a legion of fiends.'

This is one of the best things told by Froude. It is a fair sample of the sort of brutality that, exemplified in many ways, makes it impossible for Asiatics, especially Buddhists and Hindus, to respect the Europeans.

XXIV

HOW " FREDERICK " WAS WRITTEN
(1861)

ON 22.2.1861 he was writing to Neuberg :—' I find I *must* get the 2nd Silesian war into this First Vol.,' meaning Vol. III of the *Frederick*, the next to appear ; ' and that you are the man to mainly do it,—by ruthlessly cutting down, and copying fair, the Papers we already have. It must be done ; and it can ! By art and vigour and rigour.'

Happily Neuberg had an eye for what was too good to cut out. The *History of Frederick* was growing wonderfully into a view of history as a whole during much of the eighteenth century, and showing how the domination both of North America and of India passed from France to England. We see Washington learning soldiering and discovering how English officers could be beaten. We see General Wolfe and his crowning victory and death, and the desperate struggles of poor Lally, who had " gained Fontenoy for us," as some of the French said, and tried to clear the English out of India for them, but could not,—we can see it all at least as well as we can see anything to-day in the recent Willy-and-Nicky war of 1914-18. We are also shown how Pitt made England great and Frederick Prussia. We can see Voltaire to be the spiritual father of Frederick, and continue to be so, tho he mocked too much at Maupertuis and left Berlin in a hurry.

It would be tedious even to try to name the men who seem to come to life again as we read. There are Carteret and Stair, Noodle of Newcastle and ' the Fat Boy too (Royal Highness of Cumberland, one should say),' who ' never could get experience, tho trying it for five-and-twenty years to come, under huge expense to this Nation ! '

Perhaps even more contemptible than the ' Austrian Tolpatcheries ' were some of the politicians resurrected by Carlyle, the Saxon Brühl or the magnificent humbug Kaunitz of Vienna, as mischievous an evil-doer as any

424

politician of to-day ; but others, again, like Belleisle and Pitt, were as clever as Frederick himself. There are great soldiers too, who could match him, or more,—the old Dessauer and Seidlitz, Fieldmarshal Keith and Winterfeld, Cunctator Daun and fiery Loudon, and many more, to say nothing of such smart blackguards as the Marshal de Saxe. What best distinguishes this from common histories is that he shows us the common people too, and enables us to " think in the skin " of the common men and officers. Nay, lower still, as if sending X-rays into the innermost depths, he lets us see our sailors carousing, and whores stripping the gold lace from the uniforms of dead officers on the battlefield of Fontenoy in 1745.

In short there is unrolled in *Frederick* a spiritual panorama never likely to be equalled in its line : for nowadays when chemicals and machinery have changed our style of whole- sale slaughter, the sort of fighting exhibited there is as extinct as the fashions of it prevailing in the time of Homer. Indeed it is true that a battlefield then was more like to one in Homer's time than to anything we shall ever see again. And there is a real use in holding the mirror up to nature's scenes of that sort. Whoever looks upon such sights and does not perceive the wickedness of war must be a fool indeed.

Perhaps the pleasantest part of the work are the domestic details that form a kind of background, about Frederick's sister Wilhelmina and his father and mother, and his grand- parents and forebears for many generations ; and still more profitable as well as pleasant is the wonderful summary of European history from A.D. 928 to 1713 in two of the opening Books (II and III). Our Georges, too, were cousins of Frederick's family, and nowhere else in history can they be seen so well, and not they alone, but also the shadow-hunting Kaiser and his daughter, Maria Theresa, Louis XV and his mistresses, August the Strong and his three hundred and fifty-four bastards, the Termagant Queen of Spain and the innumerable rabble of minor royalties,—a set of little earthly Gods as ridiculous as the holy crocodiles of ancient Egypt.

Such a crowd had come into the history before the end of the ' 2nd Silesian War ' that, in spite of compression long continued, it overflowed Vol. III by about 100 pages.

Now from 1858 till Frederick was done, Larkin copied Carlyle's manuscript, whenever it was too hard for the type-setters, and perfected the proofs. So behold a letter he shows us which a much-enduring man, Robson the printer, had to send to one of his best customers,—

' Thomas Carlyle, Esq.[1]

March 14, 1861.

' DEAR SIR,

' I send you the slips completing the chapter, but I have not been able to make out a great deal of it, though I have spent far more time over it than I can spare ; and the poor Compositors are at their wits' end. In fact, the whole of this part ought to be copied out. I never saw such imperfect copy before. Much of it is mere abbreviation, and referring backwards and forwards. I am quite out of heart with it ; and fear, if there be any more like this, I shall be obliged to send it to you as it comes from the hands of the Compositors, as I cannot find time, among my many calls upon it, for deciphering such copy. I am sorry to write this, and have deferred till I can no longer get on.

' Your obedient servant,

' CHARLES ROBSON.'

This was passed on to Larkin, endorsed.—

' DEAR LARKIN,

' Will you come to me to-morrow :—you see Robson is fallen nearly desperate ! Bring the book *Orlich* with you ; I sometimes need it here. *Fontenoy* I suppose is not ready yet ? In haste,

' Yours always,

' T. CARLYLE.

' CHELSEA,

' *Thursday*, 10 p.m.

'(14.3.1861.)'

Larkin thought the ' literary puzzle ' justified Robson, and did the needful. He assures us :—' I was always thoroughly interested in this kind of work, which had for me nothing of the intense dreariness of battle-plans and map-making. It was especially interesting to me to find how I could sometimes, as it were, meet his thought half-way, and see what he was trying to express, even before I had got all the words together. But I was not very ready at it either ; I seldom could do this sort of thing at a glance. I generally had to puzzle and brood over it, until the idea seemed almost to come of its own accord. Carlyle never

[1] *Carlyle and Mrs. Carlyle,* by Henry Larkin, *British Quarterly Review* (July, 1881), Vol. 74, pp. 68–69.

realized how much trouble these things sometimes cost me,
nor did I care to speak much of it. Talking to him about
trouble as a rule only made him disinclined to trouble you.'

Once he was visibly relieved when Larkin entered his
study. . . . ' He had been worrying himself almost beyond
endurance over some unusually refractory specimen, which
had stubbornly resisted every attempt to force it into
shape.' He at once handed Larkin ' the page of hieroglyphics
to take away and copy ; saying with a kind of self-mocking,
self-pitying laugh,—" I cannot make out the sense of it,
but I have no doubt *you* will be able ! " ' '

On another similar occasion he said,—" it's almost like
asking for the interpretation without even giving you the
dream ! "

.Perhaps nothing shows better the spirit in which
Carlyle was living and working than a casual letter[2] on
6.4.1861 to old Lady Sandwich, who had now passed her
eightieth year. He confessed to being ' not quite fifteen
years younger,' and said he hoped to finish the *Frederick*
' in 7 or 8 months more.' Then he went on to give
her some information she wanted about the introduction
of mulberries into England, and talk of other trifles, but
concluded :—' You are beautiful, quietly brave, bright
as the evening sun in your great age ; and age is itself
beautiful after a fine fashion, if we take it rightly. . . .
We know not " the day nor the hour " ; the youngest
child may go before either of us : we will wait in quiet
composure our appointed time ; and not doubt but it
will be in some way towards welcome rest ; *rest* growing
ever more welcome. And it is whither our loved ones
have all gone. Enough, enough ! '

[2] Letter in the National Library of Scotland, Edinburgh.

XXV

HEARING RUSKIN LECTURE
(1861)

JOHN RUSKIN was now doing as Carlyle had last year advised him,—he was trying to show that our orthodox Political Economy was 'a fetid nuisance and public poison.' So Carlyle went to hear him lecture at the Royal Institution on 19.4.1861, before what was called by the scribes "a most brilliant audience,"[1] and here is Carlyle's report to his brother John.[1]—

"Friday last I was persuaded—in fact had inwardly compelled myself, as it were—to a lecture of Ruskin's at the Institution, Albemarle Street. Lecture on Tree Leaves as physiological, pictorial, moral, symbolical objects. A crammed house, but tolerable even to me in the gallery. The lecture was thought to 'break down,' and indeed it quite did ' *as a lecture* '; but only did from *embarras de richesses*—a rare case. Ruskin did blow asunder as by gunpowder explosions his leaf notions, which were manifold, curious, genial; and in fact, I do not recollect to have heard in that place any neatest thing I liked so well as this chaotic one."

[1] *Life, &c., of John Ruskin*, by W. G. Collingwood, II, p. 14. See Chapter XVIII, pp. 406–7 here.

XXVI

A CLEANLY SMOKER
(1861)

I T was not till long after this time (1861) that any observer thought it worth while to mention that he had seen Carlyle on a rare occasion spitting.[1] It was a common custom. A popular story told of a fine lady entering a London bus and enquiring,—" Conductor, is spitting allowed here ? " and being answered,—" Yes, my Lady, spit where you please ! "

It was not till this century that the Speaker of the House of Representatives in the American Congress ventured the bold innovation of desisting from spitting at large, which etiquette had till then required him to do, in order to make members feel at home.[2]

The habit of chewing quids made Yankees so superior in volume that Carlyle once mentioned as a joke that two American callers had " spat his fire out." What has changed our habits recently was the discovery that spitting spread the seeds of disease. It seems likely that early reporters who spoke of Carlyle as a cleanly smoker were not thinking of spitting at all, but of his habit of sending his smoke up the chimney of a hall or drawing-room, and of beginning a new churchwarden every day, whereby, indeed, he seldom needed to spit at all.

He was merely old-fashioned in being faithful to his pipe. Cigars were little seen in London when he first went there, and cigarettes never seen at all. Nearly every smoker used a pipe.

---

[1] *Memoirs of Gerald Blunt,* by Reginald Blunt, p. 97.
[2] According to the American *Literary Digest,* a copy of which was used by D. A. W., sometime about the first decade of this century, to make peace in Burma. Some foolish persons had caused trouble by punishing spitting in Courts. D. A. W. sweetened the air by reminding the English that they had learned from the Indians to wash themselves, and that spitting on court floors could be prevented by providing spittoons.

THE HOUSE OF ROTHSCHILD
(1861)

THE big house Rothschild was building "next the Duke of Wellington's" caught the eye of Carlyle in his walks in June, 1861; and in the house of Charles Dickens soon afterwards he delighted Dickens by declaring at once what he often repeated in passing the same place in company[1] :—

" I do not mean that I want King John back again, but if you ask me which mode of treating these people I hold to have been the nearest to the will of the Almighty about them—to build them palaces like that, or to take the pincers for them, I declare for the pincers."

Then in the very style of Dickens he acted the up-to-date King John with " Baron " Rothschild before him, saying : —" Now, sir, the State requires some of those millions you have heaped together with your financing work. 'You won't ? ' Very well," and he gave a twist with his wrist. " Now will you ? " Then another twist, till the millions were yielded.

Sancho-Panza-Froude enquired once whether Rothschild was objectionable personally or as a Jew. The reply was reassuring,—it was neither the man nor the Jew, it was only the too profitable financeering that was loathsome.

Dickens was doing his " Great Expectations " serially this summer and specially valued the approval of Carlyle. Doubtless it was Mrs. Carlyle herself who told him how the book had at first been put aside, but soon when the night came on which a new number was due and the hour when she used to read to him, there was an outcry for " that Pip nonsense ! " and " roars of laughter " as she read it.[2]

[1] Dated from a letter sold at Sotheby's about 1.12.1891, according to newspapers of the day following. D. A. W. is obliged to Robert Cochrane once of *Chambers' Journal*, Edinburgh, for a sight of its contents.
[2] Life of Charles Dickens by John Forster, III, p. 335.

THE WORKSHOP AGAIN
(1861)

NOTHING is more remarkable in Carlyle's researches than his economy of time and absence of pedantry, combined with scrupulous accuracy. The best of stories had to be left untold unless they could be verified. Thus he wrote to Neuberg (6.6.1861) :—' I have spent 1½ hours in search of the *powder monkies,*—without result of any kind. We will now honestly let it go to the ——, being able to get thro' without it.'

In the same letter were details to help Tauchnitz reprinting *Cromwell,* concluding :—' You might mention also my astonishment at the sublime sum of money he pays me for this *Cromwell,*—no less than £15 per large 8vo Volume. . . . I feel the price to be scandalous ; and would have the fat blockhead apprised that I do,—in case of future applications on his part.'

The weather was sunny and sultry. Mrs. Carlyle went to Ramsgate with Miss Jewsbury ; but the only change her husband made was to write under an awning in his backyard instead of in the Sound-proof Study at the top of the house.

He was writing steadily, whenever not engaged with proofs. By midsummer, 1861, Volume III was completed, and 100 pages more. On 9.7.1861 he was noting, " Vol. III now entirely off my hands," and in short all ready for publication, which was fixed for 1862.

On ' 24 July, 1861,' Carlyle was writing,—[1]

' Dear Lady Sandwich,

' I was very sorry for myself I could not get out yesterday to lunch with the Infants and you : as was too evident, had I thought of it, there is no lunching possible for me at all ; the rule being that I dine (what is called

---

[1] Letter now in the National Library of Scotland.

dining) here at 3 P.M.; then go to sleep (deliberately);
and am roused at 5 by the Horse stamping at the door,
"Come and ride me, you lazy fellow, till half-past 7,
when you shall have tea!" That is the fixed regulation,
at this season; Water-Butt and Horse alike inflexible
to their times. Nevertheless I hope to get out some
evening, and see a glimpse of you before your
dinner. . . .'

Meanwhile he was hoping that Volume IV would be the
last and easiest, and it was already well advanced; but
before the end of August, 1861, he was writing to Neuberg,
—"Vol. IV threatens to be more 'impossible' than any
part I have yet done: but indeed the whole has been a
work of sheer force, spasm after spasm,—and I am sick
of *dead-lifts* any farther."

His strength was failing, sleep threatening to depart. In
the middle of September he was persuaded to spend twelve
days with his wife in a lodge in Windsor Forest, where
they were the guests of Lady Sandwich, the bright old Irish
mother of the late Harriet Baring, Lady Ashburton. All
other invitations to the country were beckoned away.

On 22.10.1861, 'at the end of a Chapter of King
Friedrich, when there is "holiday" for half an hour if
we be in luck!' He was about to write to Lady
Sandwich to beg news of her when a letter came to
announce her speedy return.

After a while he ran on:—[1] 'Your little ladies' (her
grandchildren) 'were a comfort to me to think of as
beside you,—the "morning rays" are so bright and
beautiful, and gild, in that loving relation especially, all
the other parts of life. Courage, courage! The Sun
always shines, whether *we* are in the morning of it or the
uncertain afternoon!'

XXIX

THE REV. HATELY WADDELL COMES TO TOWN
(1861)

IT may have been this year, 1861, that Mrs. Carlyle received a call from a then-famous divine, the Rev. Hately Waddell of Girvan, near Ayr. He had gone to Girvan in 1844, the year after the " Disruption " of the Church, but when he was being ordained a " Free Church " minister there, he wished to sign the Confession with sundry reservations about the powers of the Civil Magistrate, and the Presbytery refused to agree. So he and his congregation, in bookmakers' slang, " stood up for themselves."

He plumped for a " Church of the Good, a Christian Communion emancipated from all shackles of outward opinion, and held together solely by faith in God, and charity to one's fellowmen," which had been the ideal of Voltaire. His congregation built a church for him and maintained him on frugal terms. They were commonly called " The Waddellites."

" I could make very little of his preaching," reports the local historian.[1] " It was neither doctrinal nor practical ; which were the only kinds of preaching I was then accustomed to. It was what *he* called *vital*, and based not on Scripture so much as on his own spiritual experience. He gave out texts," but in short did not preach upon them, and " spoke as a man who saw the truth, without reasoning about it."

In 1859 the annual " Burns' Night " was a centenary of the birth of Burns ; and the Alloway Club, designing something unusually good, were inspired to call on the new prophet in adjacent Girvan. Hately Waddell rose to the occasion. His speech in toasting " the immortal memory " was widely reported and so loudly applauded that he soon got a call to a bigger congregation in Glasgow, which he

---

[1] *Places of Interest about Girvan,* by the Rev. R. Lawson, pp. 28 to 33.

illumined handsomely for many years. But what con-
cerns us now is that it brought him to lecture in London
about this time, with a letter of introduction to the Carlyles
in his pocket from the Rev. William Carson of Girvan,—
the same William Carson who had been " the minister of
their parish " when the Carlyles lived at Craigenputtock.

When Mr. Waddell called, it appears that Mrs. Carlyle
invited him to come and spend an evening and make the
acquaintance of Carlyle himself, in hours of leisure. Carlyle
was never visible to callers in his working hours, and was
usually out walking in the afternoons.

So on the appointed evening when Waddell entered, a
slim active figure of a man in his forties, dressed punctil-
iously in black, he saw Carlyle ' leaning against one end of
the mantel-piece, while Mrs. Carlyle sat at the other ' end,
in a chair,—as we see them in Tait's picture of 1857.

Carlyle turned to him and said :—" You're a minister ? "
Waddell bowed. " What Kirk do you belong to ? " This
was an awkward question to answer, so Waddell, like Brer
Rabbit, lay low and said nothing, a futile device when
cornered by Carlyle, who pressed the point.—

" Ye'll belong to the Auld Kirk ? "

" No."

" Then ye'll belong to that compendium of all righteousness, the Free Kirk ? "

" No."

" Then ye'll be a dissenter ? "

" No."

" Then what in the name of goodness are ye ? "

At this point there is a palpable gap in the report. We
are left to imagine the questions and answers whereby
Carlyle was told about the Waddellites, and may suppose
them sitting, and Mrs. Carlyle assisting to put the caller at
his ease. He turned to Carlyle at some point and said,—
" My views on religious subjects, Mr. Carlyle, are, I pre-
sume, much the same as your own."

" The same as mine ! " said Carlyle looking up. " And
who told you what mine were ? " This was too much.
' Stiffening his back a little ' and presumably rising, ' Mr.
Waddell said,—" I came here at your invitation, Mr. Carlyle, but seeing my company does not seem agreeable to
you, I shall withdraw." But Carlyle said, " Tut, tut, man,
never mind. Sit down, and my wife will give us some tea,
and we'll have a crack." ' So says the reporter, and it is

possible that in talking to a man from Girvan who was disposed to be huffy, the familiar Scotch word " crack," which
means a chat, may have been used.

So Waddell sat down again, and he must have enjoyed
his visit, for he stayed till midnight ; but we are left guessing
what the talk was. Maybe it was too free for publication.

Not long after then, it was reported to Carlyle that the
Rev. Hately Waddell insisted on quitting a company of
literary men with whom he was supping because obscenity
began, and we are told and can believe that Carlyle praised
him, saying, " That was right, now. There's more stuff in
that fellow than I thought." And so honourably exit
Hately Waddell, to go and shine in Glasgow.

XXX

HENRY PARKES AT CHEYNE ROW
(1861)

IN 1861 New South Wales sent Henry Parkes and another man to England to " make known the advantages " which Australia offered to immigrants. They could hardly have made a better choice.[1] Parkes had been born in 1815 and learned to be an ivory-turner at Birmingham. He married young, in 1836, at 21,—often the wisest thing a first-rate young fellow can do, and so he found it, in the end. His wife's father disowned her for taking him, and in 1839 his wife and he went together to Australia, two " bounty immigrants " and without a single letter of introduction, yet worth more to the country than all the gold in it. After working on the fields for awhile, and then in an iron-monger's store and in a foundry, he became a tide-waiter in the Customs, and then opened a shop as an ivory and bone turner. Soon he was writing for the *Atlas*, edited by Robert Lowe, and when Lowe was elected to Parliament, Parkes was a " powerful working-class agitator," and a leader of the anti-transportation movement, which stopped the dumping of criminals, and got Home Rule for Australia. From 1849 to 1857 he was an editor of a newspaper, and when responsible government was won, he was elected for East Sydney, and recognised as the leader of the democratic party. Thus it happened that he was sent to England in 1861 to stimulate emigration.

It never was more needed for England's sake, as well as Australia's. The American War was dislocating English manufactures, and hosts of working-men were starving for want of work. Yet the money-men in power " felt no call " to help any of the wretches to escape to where such labour

[1] See the *Dictionary of National Biography*, and *Fifty Years in the Making of Australian History*, by Sir Henry Parkes, pp. 157–167, &c. Also Froude's *Oceana*, p. 195.

as theirs was in demand. To do so, or to do anything else in the way of organising labour, would have required more sense and energy than was yet available in what Dickens was calling our " Circumlocution Offices."   Besides, it was not wanted.

In 1847 even John Bright opposed the Factory Act, which limited the labour of women and children to ten hours a day. He informed the gentlemen from Australia wanting immigrants that " in this country there has been great difficulty of late in keeping machinery at work owing to the scarcity of labour."   So he bluntly said he would not promote emigration, and in saying so he was not worse than the other money-men, merely more honest and more plain-dealing. Thus Parkes had to report,—" Tho thousands of families were destitute, I found little sympathy among large employers or the middle class generally. A few noblemen and philosophical reformers, and men connected with the colonies, were the principal promoters." To which historians now cynically add that some of the gentry helped emigration for the same reason that they favoured the Factory Acts, in order to spite the manufacturers who helped to repeal the Corn Laws. " Tit for Tat."

There were thousands of would-be emigrants, but who was to pay the fares ? Not England then. Carlyle's suggestion, to use the idle navy, was ignored because it was too practical, and sure to succeed. The very " Boards of Guardians " wanted none but " the unthrifty and troublesome " to be let go. Cobden was friendly. He had a brother at " the diggings " in Australia ; and wished well to New South Wales, and did it a great service when in private talk he proved to Parkes the folly of Protection on pretence of fostering infant industries ; but of all the new acquaintances made in twelve months here, the one of whom Parkes has most to say is Carlyle.

A letter of introduction from Gavan Duffy procured him a prompt invitation to tea in the evening about 8 p.m., and so, in October, 1861, he tells us, ' with a strange feeling of mingled curiosity and reverence, I knocked at the famous door from which celebrities were often turned away. My knock was answered by a demure young person who at once ushered me into the presence of the grim philosopher and his gentle wife.

' The evening meal was thin cakes of oatmeal, and a cup of richly-made tea. After tea my host sat down on the floor with his back straight up against the wall and his legs stretched out at full length, and, charging and lighting a long white clay pipe, he happily puffed away, stopping at short intervals to talk on all manner of things in the style of one of his later books.

' He spoke unreservedly of great men whom he had known, and he asked many curious questions about Australia, which showed the original light in which he viewed some well-threshed-out subjects. . . . If governing men could only free themselves from the trammels of custom and be truly wise, they would remove the Sovereign and the Court and all the machinery of Government to Australia, where the field for national life was so wide, attractive and unencumbered, and so leave the contracted spaces and the murky atmosphere of England behind them,'—to say nothing of the sordid intrigues of European diplomacy, its Turks and Anti-Turks, and the little Willy-and-Nicky puppets of 1914, playing with the fates of nations, like monkeys with bombs.

Of modern statesmen he spoke most approvingly of Peel, and in bitterest terms of Lord Melbourne. Alluding to the alleged compact between the Melbourne ministry and O'Connell, he said that a British statesman, inspired by true ' patriotism, would have ' said to O'Connell, " What ! I rule England with your aid ? No, I'll hang you as a public enemy ! "

' He spoke of America and of the Civil War then raging. He said he had met Daniel Webster when in England, and regarded him as a great man.' Note this : Americans agree with Carlyle's esteem for Daniel Webster. They should recall it when raging against him for styling their Civil War a Nigger-Agony. He shared with Webster the opinion that whatever emancipation was right could have been done by degrees, without a war at all.

' Nothing could excel,' in Parkes's eyes, ' the charming manner of Mrs. C., whose conversation sparkled with quaint humour and womanly sympathy with noble effort.'

The greatest pleasure in ambition is to be great where once you were small. Parkes returned to his native Warwickshire, and, in sending something from there, and writing to Mrs. Carlyle, he suggested that her husband might spend a day or two with him at Shakespeare's Stratford, as a rest from *Frederick*. Her reply was (22.10.61):

—" My husband, who is up to the roots of his hair in work, has bade me thank you in his name for your kind invitation, which ' would be a fine thing to accept,' he says, ' if *he were situated like other men.*'   And I was to explain how it was ' impossible.' . . .

" Also I was to tell you that he found the Almanac a great curiosity, and that you were ' not to suppose that he wished any foul play to the wretched scoundrels of criminals, only he could not approve of wild attempts to *wash* black men white—the thing being hopeless.' "

XXXI

A LETTER TO GAVAN DUFFY
(1861)

WRITING about 1892, to introduce a letter from Carlyle to himself dated 10.11.1861, Gavan Duffy explains[1] that Parkes was then 'Emigration Agent' for New South Wales in England, and that his colleague was W. B. Dalley, to whom there is 'a memorial tablet in St. Paul's for his share in the Australian expedition to the Soudan.'—

> 'CHELSEA,
> 'November 10, 1861.

'DEAR DUFFY,

'Your friend Parkes, who did not present himself till quite lately, "hearing I was so busy," came the other evening, and gave us a few pleasant hours. We find him a robust, effective, intelligent and sincere kind of man, extremely loyal to C.G.D.; which is not one of his smallest merits here. He gave me several more precise notions about Australian life; seemed to be thoroughly at home in the anarchic democratic Universal-Palaver element, and to swim about in it, with a candid joy, like a fish in water; and indeed, I could not but own that in comparison with the old Colonial Office and Parliamentary-Fogie methods of administration, it might be a real improvement; tho, in short, Yankeeland and England and "all countries with National-Palaver and Penny Newspapers in them . . . will have to abolish or tightly chain up all that," if they are to continue to prosper.

'The worst news Parkes gave us was, that you did not seem to be in good health.' . . . Now that you are out of office, why not come home again ?—' You promised to come home at any rate, and see us again. If you delay

---

[1] *Conversations with Carlyle*, by Sir C. Gavan Duffy, pp. 210–214.

too long, some of us will not be discoverable here, when you land expectant. I write to try for a letter. . . . Many people have criticised you to me ; I answer always, " Yes, yes, and of all the men I saw in Ireland, the two *best*, so far as I could judge, were Lord George Hill and Charles Duffy."

' By the *lex talionis*,' the rule of making the punishment like the crime, ' I have not the least right to a letter, but if you knew the case here, you would drop that plea. I have not, for years past, any leisure at all ; but have had to withdraw out of all society, and employ every available minute of my day. . . . I ride daily, have ridden on a horse, which I call " Fritz " (an amiable, swift, loyal creature, now falling old), for eight years past : I think about 24,000 miles or so in quest " of health to go on with," and do not write the smallest note if it can possibly be helped ! This is true, and I will say no more of it ; only let it serve you for an explanation, and in the course of next summer or autumn, I do now hope I shall be out of this unutterable quagmire, and shall then have leisure, leisure to the end of the chapter, as I intend ! For I have for once got a complete bellyful of " work "—curiously enough reserved for me to finish off with. In my young time I had no work that was not a mere flea-bite to this which lay appointed for my old days.

' It is only by accident I have found time and spirit to write you so much. My intention was only to send you the enclosed bad *photograph* accompanied by a word or two, which might stand as an apology for a letter. . . .[2] There is a strange worth in *indisputable* certainty however limited. I wish you would send me such a *sun-picture* from Melbourne ; it would be very welcome here. . . .

' Yours, ever truly,

' T. CARLYLE.'

---

[1] See Illustration, Carlyle on Fritz, in this book.

XXXII

MORE REPORTS FROM HENRY PARKES
(1862)

THE acquaintance with Duffy's friend Henry Parkes, auspiciously begun in 1861, continued pleasantly during the first nine months of 1862. As long as Parkes was in England, he ' often spent part of an evening with Mr. and Mrs. Carlyle,' and occasionally by special invitation a Sunday morning. ' One Sunday morning I was called upstairs to a room at the top of the house ' by Carlyle himself, and found him there ' engaged upon the proof sheets of *Frederick* ' in a room without other furnishing than ' portraits and plans and books relating to the subject.

' One Sunday afternoon,' walking together to Grosvenor Square, ' I was accosted by a little begging girl ' and ' gave the child a sixpence,' and was told by Carlyle :—" The other day I was asked for alms in one of these squares by a poor little weeping girl. I had a profound conviction that no gift from me could benefit her, but, nevertheless, I gave her some loose pence. After walking a short distance, I turned round to see what she " did with herself," and " saw another beggar girl taking the pence from her, and beating her to make her cry for more. It is of no use —it is worse ; it is supporting their tyrants to give to these children."

In the evening talks, ' I seldom did more than listen,' says Parkes, as he ' resumed his place on the floor with his long pipe. Speaking of the American war between the North and South, he exclaimed, " Let them blaze away— it is the dirtiest chimney that has been on fire for many a long day ! "

' On one occasion I was rather incautiously led into speaking of the equality enjoyed in Australia.'

Here may be intercalated what Parkes told in an Australian Parliament in 1891,[1] but expressly assigned to this visit.—

'Thomas Carlyle told me that in youth he had been charmed by Burns's *The man's the gowd for a' that*. But had since found out how completely hollow is the dictum in Burns's verse. The man is not the gold ; but is often very base metal, indeed, and one man is so far from being equal to another as not to be a thousandth part equal to another.'

Recalled in the heat of debate, from memory after 28 years, this cannot be expected to be literally accurate, and certainly it was not. Carlyle was merely correcting a mistake which was less common in Scotland than abroad. What he said is likely to have been to this effect :—" I soon found out how absurd it was to suppose that all are gold, and the song does not mean that. Men are often very base metal." He was referring to his boyhood—only very simple persons needed to be told such a thing in Calvinist Scotland, where the very freethinkers had the stamp of Geneva.

An essay of his never reprinted was an anonymous review in the *Examiner*[2] of Heintze's German translation of selected poems of Burns. He sarcastically noted the absence from it of *A Man's a Man for a' that*, " which would not be acceptable to certain persons in Berlin."

But it is not from such stray allusions that his opinion is to be gathered. There is really no room for doubt. *Sartor* itself meant the same thing as this song, that native quality is what makes the value of men as of things. As the stamp could not make the copper guinea into gold, so the clothes of rank and wealth cannot make a common man venerable to anyone with an eye for reality.

To resume the direct report of the evening talks :— speaking of Australian equality, Parkes ' used some such language as this,—" *There* every man can stand erect and look his fellow in the face." Carlyle looked at me with a half-pitying, half-ironical gleam in his eyes :—" Did you see the Lord Mayor's Show ? " he asked. " Yes." " Well," said he, " there were a hundred men in that crowd who would stand erect, and look you in the face, and knock

---

[1] *Fifty Years in the Making of Australian History*, by Sir Henry Parkes, II, p. 315.

[2] 27.9.1840. F. Espinasse's *Literary Recollections*, p. 117.

your hat over your eyes into the bargain." ' But ' on my next visit he said : " I have been thinking over your praise of your responsible governing machine out there, which you have set up in place of the Old Fogies of the nominee days ; on the whole, I think it is better—if you must have one or other—than the Old Fogies." '

It may have been in the early sixties that Milnes, Lord Houghton, heard Carlyle mention[3]—" Palmerston, the chief Anarch of England at this given time," and thenabout is the only date to be gathered from G. S. Venables for one of the best things he has told us.[4]— ' Lord Palmerston, during his last administration, was placed at a dinner-party at Bath House on the opposite side from Carlyle of a large round table. While Carlyle was engaged in animated talk, Lord Palmerston leant forward and listened, and, as if unwilling to be interrupted, he gave a short negative answer to his neighbour's inquiry whether he had ever met Mr. Carlyle before. Before the party had been five minutes in the drawing-room, Lord Palmerston and Carlyle were in close conversation, and it might be inferred from Carlyle's repeated bursts of laughter, that Lord Palmerston's conversation was highly amusing.'

In telling this Mr. Venables is sure that Carlyle was more polite to Palmerston after it, and declares that Carlyle's appreciation of Sir Robert Peel was also due to acquaintance with him at the Ashburtons' houses, Bath House and the Grange. "I often heard," says he, "from both of them," the Ashburtons, "and their accounts were confirmed by Carlyle, of (Peel's) pleasantness, his gaiety, and his amusing stories."

[3] *R. Monckton Milnes, Lord Houghton,* by T. Wemyss Reid, II, p. 477.
[4] *Carlyle in Society,* &c., by G. S. Venables, *Fortnightly Review,* May, 1883, pp. 634–5.

XXXIII

A LIST OF BOOKS FOR HENRY PARKES, &c.

(1862)

THO Henry Parkes had been 'compelled to earn his own living as a child of eight,' it was remarked of him in later life that he was one of the most widely read of public men, and a 'devoted lover' of good literature. Which makes it seem worth while to mention a list of books he got from Carlyle. On one of his many evenings at Cheyne Row he was happily inspired to make a modest suggestion.—' I said to Mr. Carlyle,' he tells us,—' " I have sometimes thought that it would be a good thing for a man like me,—imperfectly educated and with many things always pressing upon his time,—to put aside all books, save ten or twelve authors, and thoroughly master them. In such case, what authors would you suggest ? "

' He made some curt observation which I interpreted as unfavourable, and I felt half-ashamed of what I had said. When I called again he said,—" I have jotted down some books for you, if you carry out your plan of studying a few authors," and he fetched me the list written in pencil,' whereof a facsimile is printed.—

The list was specially suited for Parkes, who docketed it :—' List of books given to me by Thomas Carlyle, which he recommended me to buy. H. P.'

Pope's Works.
Swift's Works (*Gulliver, Battle of Books*).
Ld. Hailes's *Annals of Scotland*.
Camden's *Britannia* (Philemon Holland's translation, I vol. 4to. Costs abt. 12/-, date abt. 1620–30).
Heimskringla (or *History of the Norse Sea-Kings*, Laing's Translatn. 3 vols. 8vo.).
Anson's *Voyage* (excellt.) ; Byron's *Narrative* (good).

445

Goldsmith's *Vicar of Wakefield* ⎱ (Richardson, Fielding,
Smollett's *Humphrey Clinker* ⎰ &c. if you like such
things).

Arabn. Tales (meaning *Arabian Nights*) ; *Don Quixote.*
Franklin's *Essays and Autobiography.*
Shenstone's Works.
Boswell's *Life of Johnson.*
—— *Journey to Western Isles*
Plutarch's *Lives* (Editn. revised by Clough, Boston,
America, 7 or 8 years ago, is far the best).
Fuller's *Worthies of Engld.* (i.e. *Notabilia of Engld. ;*
tolerably good).
Chaucer (& make the young ones learn to read him) is
excellt.

' Another book,' says Parkes, ' which Carlyle frequently
urged upon my notice '—properly enough as he was a
politician in a country likely to have ' family men ' for
' Governors ' awhile—' was Collins's Peerage,—I think the
fourth edition ' . . . not ' the costly edition by Sir Egerton
Bridges.'

As the day for the departure of Parkes came near, he
tells us,—' I called on the Carlyles to say farewell. We
recalled much of our conversations during the year that
had passed. . . . Again I sat down at the simple tea table.
Mrs. Carlyle unbent to a little innocent gossip. A gentleman of rising reputation, who had lately returned from the
colonies, and had established himself in London society,
felt himself under an obligation to entertain an old colonial
acquaintance just arrived ; " but," said he to Mrs. Carlyle,
" I don't know who to ask to meet him—will you come ? " '

The name is not given. It may have been Robert Lowe,[1]
who had been a popular leader in Sydney, and was supported
there by Parkes in his public-spirited wrestle with the
powers of darkness, embodied in Squatters and Investors
and ' the men in office in England,' who ' regard the colonies
as places where relatives could be provided with light
berths at heavy salaries.'[1]

Lowe's biographer mentions his attentions to Parkes in
England.

' As I was on the point of leaving, never to see them
again,' says Parkes, ' Mrs. Carlyle gave me a photograph

[1] Robert Lowe . . . *Viscount Sherbrooke,* by A. P. Martin, I, p. 389 ;
also 357, 384, &c.

of her husband, with his name written underneath it ; and that photograph is still (1892) among the most precious things in my quiet home in Sydney. The memory of those days will never leave me ; and I trust I have not altogether failed to profit by the lessons I received from the great Professor of heroic wisdom.'

The photo was probably the same as that sent to Gavan Duffy, showing Carlyle on " Fritz " and dated Hyde Park, 2.8.1861.[2] In the fulness of time Henry Parkes became Prime Minister of New South Wales, a post he filled five times. He was the champion of Free Trade there, and not for goods alone. He faced and overcame the Roman Catholics opposing education. He was also a pioneer and principal advocate of the Federation now happily grown into the Commonwealth of Australia. He died as he had lived, a poor man, and all the more respected for that, for long before he died he was seen to be and was called " the grand old man " of Australian politics. Woolner made a bust of him ; and Australia may proudly remember him for many generations.

[2] See Chapter XXXI. Also *Conversations with Carlyle*, by Sir C. Gavan Duffy, p. 210–214.

XXXIV

A WEDDING AND A CHRISTENING
(1862)

IN January, 1862, while Henry Parkes was frequenting Cheyne Row, the daughter of Dr. Barnes, Mrs. Carlyle's doctor, was about to get married, and Mrs. Carlyle meant to be present, but on 24.1.1862 she wrote to Miss Barnes[1] to beg her not to ask Mr. Carlyle to the wedding, as he has said " it would be a real vexation to me to refuse that bonnie wee lassie what she asked, and to her marriage *I could not go !* It would be the ruin of me for three weeks." And that,' adds his wife, ' is no exaggeration, *I* can say, who knows his ways better than anybody else.' He added that ' the rational thing to be done ' was, that you should ' bring your husband, when you had married him, to spend an evening with him (T.C.) in his own house, among quiet things.' Meaning ' me and the cat,' suggested Mrs. C.

She was herself afraid of a chill, and so she decided to avoid the ceremony and be at the breakfast party only. But when the Rev. Gerald Blunt heard that from his wife, he had the fires in the church kept up from Sunday to Tuesday morning, so that Mrs. Carlyle was able to come and see the show.

" Isn't the English way of marrying better than the Scotch ? " asked Blunt. " How did you like it ? "

" My feelings are very mixed," replied Mrs. Carlyle.

" Mixed of what ? "

" Well," she said, " It looked to me something betwixt a religious ceremony and a—pantomime ! "

And if a wedding, why not see a christening too ? The Rector's house was near, and in May she was easily persuaded to come and see his baby christened ; and so she made her husband write ' by way of kindly benison some slips of favourite sayings.' One of these was remembered, —" Be thankful you are not in Purgatory."

[1] *By Chelsea Reach*, by Reginald Blunt, pp. 158–164, and of course the L. & M. of J. W. C., and the *Memoirs of Gerald Blunt*, by Reginald Blunt, pp. 78–9.

XXXV

A RUMOUR ABOUT MARTIN TUPPER
(1862)

A JOURNALIST recording-angel who remains *anon* has told of a rumour worth repeating,—the thing seems likely.[1]—' One summer night in the study of a well-known literary man Martin Tupper found himself sitting amidst wild young wits, and with his white hair and beaming face (he) looked like Father Christmas. The fun was fast and furious. To draw Martin, one of the wags mentioned Carlyle's name disparagingly.

' " Sir," exclaimed Martin Tupper, with an angry nod of the head, " Mr. Carlyle was my friend. He paid me once a very high compliment. When my *Proverbial Philosophy* came out," and sold with amazing success, he implied but did not need to say, " Thackeray mentioned to somebody that, were he not himself, he would like to be Martin Tupper. I repeated this to Carlyle. He evidently thought Thackeray presumptuous in hinting at such a thing, for he at once exclaimed,—' Save us frae a guid conceit of ourselves ! ' " Whereupon ' the young bloods dissolved in inextinguishable laughter,' adds the reporter, and Tupper laughed along with them, supposing it was Thackeray who was conceited.

---

[1] From a cutting in a scrap book belonging to C. Oscar Gridley, a trustee of the Carlyle House Trust. It is undated, but placed between a cutting dated January, 1890, and another dated February, 1890 ; and it resembles other cuttings marked as from the *Star*.

XXXVI

"ESSAYS AND REVIEWS," &c.
(1862)

TOWARDS the end of January Carlyle spent a few days at the Grange with the Ashburtons. Both Milnes and Venables were among the guests, and the Kingsleys and Soapy Sam (Bishop Wilberforce), and many others including the Duke and Duchess of Argyll, who were the more remarked as unusual there. They seem to have liked and been liked by Carlyle, who told his wife,—" The most agreeable man among us is the Duke ; really a good, solid, Scotch product."

The American Civil War supplied topics for talk, as well as the eternal conundrums of theology, whereof the " Essays and Reviews " were then the topmost bubble.

On 28.1.1862 Soapy Sam was writing in his diary :—
' After luncheon, rode with Carlyle to Cheriton on the way to the Beacon, Carlyle against the essayists, on dishonesty grounds and atheistic.'[1]

Elsewhere[2] it is reported that what Carlyle said was,—" The sentinel who deserts should be shot." But what Carlyle wrote to his wife on the day after that ride has little about theology.—' The Bishop is gone to see some little ape called Keble, of *The Christian Year*. He (the Bishop) is very perceptibly older in the face, but (there is) no change in the shifty, cunning, thoroughgoing ways of him. He took me riding yesterday, galloping to see something which he called the Beacon Hill, which we never saw, daylight failing us, tho we had a gallop of some sixteen miles.'

In quoting this Mr. Froude has told that Carlyle—presumably bored by theology,—once said to him, " Cardinal Newman has not the intellect of a moderate-sized rabbit,"—a common opinion then among men of sense. One has to

[1] *Life of . . . Samuel Wilberforce, Bishop, &c.*, by R. G. Wilberforce, III, p. 8.
[2] *Life and Letters of Ben Jowett*, by Messrs. Abbott and Campbell, I, p. 294.

remember that for several generations that would have been the general opinion in Scotland about any educated man supposed to be sincere in believing what Newman professed to believe. If Carlyle erred, it was on the side of charity. Prof. Francis William Newman, the brother of the pervert, appeared to him much the better man, " an excellent Classicist," he called him, in answer to Allingham.[3]

Writing to old Lady Sandwich on 1.2.1862, Carlyle told her,[4] ' I have been here since Monday, I return to-morrow.'. . . . After giving the news about the guests and about Lord Ashburton, reported as ' cheery but gouty and weak,' he went on to mention a visit to her daughter's grave.

' One of my pilgrimages was to the *Church of Northington*. I walked silently round that building ; visited the inside, and read a little tablet, " 4 May 1857 ", which will be memorable to me all the days of my life. Weak sorrow does not beseem one, dear Lady, as *you* well know ; but there is no forgetting possible in certain cases ; and if I mention this one to *you*, it is sacred and silent from all other mortals.'

On 27.3.62 Mrs. Carlyle was writing to the sculptor, Thomas Woolner,[5] to ' come to tea on Friday (29.3.62). . . . . It would be a charity towards my husband ' who needed ' efficient help,' inasmuch as a bride was bringing a Husband to make acquaintance with Mr. C. (Mrs. Simmonds, ex-Miss Barnes, it may be guessed.) ' He has been doing what he could about ' a statue Woolner wanted to be employed to make.

[3] *Letters to William Allingham*, p. 133.
[4] Original Letter now among the MSS. in the National Library of Scotland.
[5] *Thomas Woolner, Letters*, pp. 216–17.

XXXVII

CHARLES BONER'S NOTES
(1862)

IN April 1862 Charles Boner spent an evening at Cheyne
Row, and was happily inspired to make notes. Himself
the writer of much printed matter interpreting to English
readers "the Continent," he was then a man of forty-
seven, and naturally expected to survive Carlyle, who was
twenty years his senior ; and so the notes which were meant
for reference would minimize his own share of the talk,
which memory could more easily supply. But Death was
awaiting him at a few years' distance—we must be content
with his notes.[1]

As tutor and journalist, he had dwelt for many years in
the Danube countries, living in a German atmosphere which
was spoiling his command of English, as his friend Miss
Mitford warned him. He was settled in Munich now, and
merely on a visit to England. He shared the prejudices of
those around him—" There's only one Imperial town,
There's only one Vienna "—and thought Carlyle was
prejudiced in favour of Prussia.—

' April, 1862.—Found Carlyle sitting in dressing-gown
and slippers, looking over the proofs of his *Frederick*. . . .
Mrs. Carlyle sitting on the sofa by the fire. After a while
the conversation fell upon Prussia. Carlyle said the
Prussians were full of energy and activity. There was
energy and perseverance in their character—there was
much resemblance to the English. If *they* did not do something there was little hope for Germany. Elsewhere in
Germany he could see little else than talk and noise, and
wretched Radicalism. The king, he thought, was right, if,
as he believed, he meant to have no one but himself meddling
in the affairs of the army, for that was and ever had been in

---

[1] *Memoirs and Letters of Charles Boner*, by R. M. Kettle, II, pp. 5-12 ;
also pp. 32, &c.

Prussia the reliable, honourable body, which had done everything for Prussia. If its affairs were to be talked over and
speechified about by a parliament, there would soon be an
end of this. The army would soon be as inefficient as the
English army with its Balaclava and its General Burgoyne.
He had seen nothing elsewhere that had impressed him so
much as conversation with one or two (not more) Prussian
officers had done. From these two he judged all the army,'
according to Charles Boner. 'From what he saw in a week
or two, while travelling, of the common soldiers, he judged
of all the men,' a sneer, which gives us the measure of the
reporter.

'He said there was, he believed, no other army like it;
neither English, nor French, nor any other. The officers
were well educated, and with a high sense of honour; the
men filled with a sense of duty. Ours, with our newspaper
rant about British pluck, was nothing to it. Our officers
knew nothing—absolutely nothing. Some few might, by a
common-sense view of things, get a sort of routine of their
business, but there was, and had been, for the last hundred
and fifty years, wretched ignorance and inefficiency.
Wellington came at last. He had no genius, but he was one
of the not more than two or three men,' meaning military
men, 'in all Britain who seemed to understand that from
certain facts certain circumstances are sure to arise. Therefore, he made himself master of the least trifles, attended to
them, and looked for the inevitable results. There was no
hurry about him: he went on step by step: he was content
to wait. There was veracity in the man and in all he did.
He was thoroughly honest—and it is the want of honesty
which is so deplorably felt in the public men of the present
day. There was no more veracious man in Britain than he.
'Wellington took the materials given him, Carlyle said,
and made the best of them; he knew the officers were
ignoramuses, blockheads;—he saw the shortcomings of
others, but he said, " If I cannot get better materials, I
must take them, and make the most of them."
'Talking of General Burgoyne (in the American war), he
said it was impossible a general in Frederick's army would
have acted so. A Prussian army would have cut its way
through the enemy rather than surrender.
'He abused Parliaments, and the talk and rant and
speechifying, and the publication of the same in the newspapers; laughing at what the press and the public had said

about the soldier's dress. They abused the stock. " Why, a stock was most comfortable ; the best neck-covering a soldier could wear. He always wore a stock." He, on his part, did not see why the soldiers were not to wear stocks. He resented indignantly the interference of the press in such matters. . . .

' Parliament, the press, the English army, he abused royally, but in language so quaint, so droll, so unlike anything I ever heard before, that once or twice I burst out laughing, though it was evident he saw nothing humorous or out of the way in his expressions. One thing was evident, his detestation of anything approaching dishonesty or inconsistency. Another was his utter appreciation of conscientious work ; not work slurred over.

' He is full of humour, but he does not seem to know it is humour, for he goes on gravely as though the humorous thoughts were merely strict reasoning. F. (Froude) told me going home that another time he might quite probably take the opposite side, and abuse uncontrolled authority as much as he had done constitutional government. Asked if he had heard (someone) read, Carlyle said,—" No, he did not care to hear anyone read aloud. He did not like it. He had only heard one person read to please him, that was Mrs. Fry, in Newgate. He was a boy then." '

He must have said young, or a young man. The reporter runs on.—' " There were the poor unfortunate outcasts opposite to her, looking and laughing as tho they were the world, and all the rest nothing ; and there she, the wonderful creature, calmly and quietly took out the Bible, and began reading to them the history of Martha, and she read in a way that showed she understood it, had thought it over, and knew perfectly well all about it.[2] She made you understand it *all*:—all the meanings and all the bearings. She had a good voice, but it was not that so much as the earnestness of the creature, and her sincerity.

" And it had its effect, for the women were quiet and listened. There Mrs. Fry stood among them in her Quaker dress, clean and neat, and calm and strong in her own persuasion of the righteousness of the work. And there were some other cleanly dressed creatures about her— Quakers they were too, I believe ; and altogether it was a wonderful sight. I have never seen the like of it. But " as to so-and-so, " I don't want to hear him ; I had much

2 Luke, x, 38–42.

rather not. With my own two eyes I can follow the line of a book much faster than he can read, and it is *that* I want to do to get through a book."

'Leigh Hunt's reading he liked. He was once obliged to hear him read something—for what he read had not been printed—a play of his, and that too he liked.

'He said that when a young man he had great hopes for German literature, but they had been deceived,' or rather disappointed. 'All was going and had gone downwards. There was a sort of Socialism rampant everywhere. All had degenerated into newspapers and parliaments. The aristocratic spirit which showed so prominently in Goethe was no longer to be found. Spoke of Heine. One thing he thought he discovered in him,'—humour,—'a stern, grim sort of humour, but still, more than he had generally seen in Germans. "A Jew," he said, "never laughed a hearty out-bursting laugh." I told him Mrs. Austin once met Heine at Boulogne when she was a child, and he said, "Now you can say you have seen Heinrich Heine." She said, "Who is Heinrich Heine?" which seemed to amuse him greatly, for he burst into a hearty laugh, showing that, at all events, he was no Jew,'—showing a Jew could laugh out—to be exact. Carlyle continued.—

'He should not go to Germany again. As long as he was there he could get nothing fit for a Christian man to eat— no bed big enough to sleep in. The bedsteads were always too short, and like a trough. Once, to his surprise, the mattress was too long for the bed, so he lay all night with it arched like a saddle in the middle. There were no curtains, and in the hotels people stamped overhead, and tramped past his door all night. He had not slept' (well) 'all the seven weeks he was in Germany, and felt the worse for it, he verily believed, up to the present day.

'Talked of soldiers marching. Of course, he asserted that the Prussians marched best of any troops. I told him the Spaniards were good marchers, and spoke of their foot covering. When I told him of the value of good shoes, roomy and strong, and of their being well greased to make the leather supple, he seemed to enter into the matter with zest. He evidently knew the value of a greased shoe. "Well rubbed in," he said, "till the leather is soft and proof against water. That is the thing." I said much of the success of an army depended, more than was generally thought, on their foot covering. He said it was very probable.

'Carlyle's long, wild, grey hair hangs over his forehead. His eye is light and lively, his complexion healthy, and his look generally betokens a man who leads a *calm* life, not mixing in the struggle and rush going on around him. His wife told me she took in the *Daily Telegraph* in order to know what was going on in the world. Her husband never reads the papers. He speaks slowly, and as if what he says were well weighed beforehand, as if all had been thoroughly thought over long ago. His way of stating his opinions shows that there is not a shadow of doubt in his mind as to their correctness. He makes you feel, too, he had no thought of changing his views, or of allowing himself to be influenced by aught another may say. His mind is made up, once and for ever.

'Nothing here written conveys any idea of his conversation, for the words he used were so strange, and the flow of his conversation so copious, that it is impossible to remember all. This account bears as much resemblance to the reality as a cake of colour does to the painting produced by it,'—a sensible and maybe too modest remark of Charles Boner.

XXXVIII

EDWARD IRVING AND OTHERS
(1862)

ABOUT May this year the third volume of Carlyle's *Frederick* was published ; and also a *Life of Edward Irving* by Mrs. Oliphant. It was by far the best of all the ' 250 volumes ' Mrs. Oliphant was to write ; and tho the ' Irvingites ' were sad to see she cared a great deal for her hero and little for them, she was comforted abundantly by the praise of better judges, and of Carlyle in particular.[1]

She had not yet seen him a second time, but had been much in the company of Mrs. Carlyle, who told her :—" I never heard him praise a woman's book, hardly any man's, as cordially as he praises this of yours. You are ' worth whole cartloads of Mulocks and Brontës and *things* of that sort,' " meaning mere fictioneers, Miss Mulock being the author of *John Halifax, Gentleman*, and the Brontë ladies of *Jane Eyre* & Co. " You are ' full of geniality and genius even ! Nothing has so taken him by the heart for years as this biography ! ' You are really ' a fine clear, loyal, sympa-thetic female being.' The only fault he finds in you is a *certain dimness about dates and arrangements of time !* . . . I never heard so much praise out of his head at one rush ! And I am so glad ! Mr. C. got to the end last night, and says,—' The last part was the best of all,' and he is ' very glad,—very glad indeed that such a biography of Edward Irving exists.' "

Soon afterwards Mrs. Carlyle went to see Mrs. Oliphant at Ealing, and spoke to her at large and brought her to spend an evening at Cheyne Row, where she heard what Carlyle thought about her from himself. Whereupon Mrs. Oliphant had to confess to posterity that she was so delighted by his praise that ' for the space of a night and a day I *was* uplifted and lost my head.' But the permanent result was to make her ' like ' him ' heartily and more than ever,' and feel ' ready to stand up for all those peculiarities which other people think defects, and to do battle for him whenever I hear him assailed.'

---

[1] *Autobiography and Letters of Mrs. Oliphant*, pp. 76–80, 186–8, &c.

Thursday 22.5.1862 may have been the day Mrs. Oliphant was thinking of. At any rate she came to Carlyle's that day accompanied by the Rev. R. H. Story of Roseneath, a Broad Church leader, who noted only that he heard much talk from Carlyle, " most affable and brilliant."[2]

A few days later, maybe in less than a week, the Rev. F. D. Maurice overcame, he said, the " reluctance and fear " which had been keeping him away from Cheyne Row, and came to learn what to think of Mrs. Oliphant's *Edward Irving*. People were enquiring of him. Carlyle soon put him at his ease, and satisfied him, as he said, that Irving was ' the man who felt most deeply and inwardly the truth of the old Puritan Theocracy.' So Maurice was able to report to his enquiring friend :[3]—' Carlyle knew Irving well, and likes the book on the whole very much, saying it is the most loyal biography he has read for a long time.'

" After a long conversation " with Carlyle, Maurice wrote to a friend about this interview,—" I came away with a strong conviction " of various things and mainly this, that " the terrible contradictions " in the thought of Carlyle " belong to the time : we may find them in ourselves. And they cannot be resolved, as you fancy they may, into the mere worship of Might. That comes uppermost at times ; often he recoils from it with the intensest horror, and affirms and feels Justice to be the one ruler in heaven and earth."

In fairness to Mrs. Oliphant it should be added that in the published diary of Bishop Wilberforce[4] there is a curious mistake. " Mrs. Oliphant " appears by mistake for " Mrs. Irving." What the Bishop should have written, and maybe meant, was this.—The place was the Grange, the topic a talk with Mrs. Carlyle.—' Mrs. Carlyle—account of E. Irving. Mrs. Irving did not understand him at all ; his variety ; so kind—never depreciated a living creature ; his love and lovableness the point of his character ; fond of creature comforts. Mrs. Irving narrow and jealous, and greatly the cause of submitting him to his foes,'—she meant by her silly credulity,—it was tenderness for his silly wife that made poor Irving too tolerant of the new-fangled nonsense that was the ruin of him.

[2] *R. H. Story*, by his daughters, p. 54.
[3] *Life of F. D. Maurice*, by his son, F. Maurice, II, pp. 403–5.
[4] *Life of . . . Samuel Wilberforce, Bishop, &c.*, by R. G. Wilberforce, III, p. 64.

BOOK XXV

FINISHING THE "FREDERICK"
1862–65

I

HENRY LARKIN ON CREEDS AND GHOSTS
(1862, &c.)

HENRY LARKIN was coming to the house ' three or four times a week ' at present, and says,[1]—' I occasionally spent the evening there, in which case I always joined Carlyle in his eleven o'clock walk. I had all along been tacitly and uncomfortably conscious that both he and Mrs. Carlyle were greatly concerned about me, lest I should persist in wasting my life. On one occasion I suppose he felt constrained to clear his own conscience towards me, as he has told us he once did towards Irving. I well recollect his speaking to me of Irving—his great gifts ; his truthful, affectionate, and courageous heart ; and how it was all wasted and wrecked on the maddest of futilities ; ending only in a heart-broken half-consciousness that his life had been a disastrous mistake. In no spirit of boasting, or self-sufficiency, but in the deepest sorrow and pity,' Carlyle ended by saying :—

" I have been credibly informed that towards the end he has been heard to lament ' how different it might all have been if he had kept nearer to myself ' ; or at least that was the conclusion I drew from what I was told."

The humour of reality surpasses Puck's. Larkin listened all agog,—' knew, from the time Carlyle began to speak, that he was trying to teach me by a parable. I knew nothing of Irving at that time, and my chief wonder was how Carlyle could place me in any similar category. He could hardly have cautioned me against a too unshaken faith in the love and truth of Jesus Christ ; nor could I for a moment suppose so. In truth, I can most positively assert ' the contrary. Which is an unconscious tribute to the perfection

---

[1] Henry Larkin's *Carlyle and Mrs. Carlyle, British Quarterly Review,* No. 147, pp. 70–72 (July, 1881.) Also see *Carlyle and the Open Secret of his Life,* by Henry Larkin, 1886.

of Carlyle's tact and talent for silence on some topics. By-and-by the excited Larkin read Mrs. Oliphant's book, and reasonably inferred that the publication of it was what ' set Carlyle speaking ' about Irving ; but even then he continued to be sure that when Carlyle was talking of him, he was thinking of Henry Larkin.

There was one of the common revivals of necromancy or ghost-religion then in fashion ; and ' on another occasion,' says Larkin, ' he referred in utter condemnation to so-called " spiritualism " ; evidently wishful to know how I regarded it.'

Said Larkin :—" the basest thing about it is its miserable attempt to turn the awful *stillness* of Eternity into a penny peep-show," which was *well* said.

Carlyle, he reports, ' entirely agreed,' but seemed to ' want me to declare my total disbelief in the whole thing. But this, with the Bible before me, I was not prepared to do. We had many little tentative encounters of this kind,' Carlyle being as scrupulous to taboo humbug as rudeness ; ' but never got to any actual disputation. Once he spoke in strong disparagement of the pitiful inconsistency of someone, I forget now who it was, professing to believe in his teaching, and *also* in the nonsense taught in the name of religion. But this again was far too widely aimed to touch me, and I let it pass.'

' We were both reaching out to each other in the dark ; ineffectually and to our mutual disappointment,' is how Larkin finishes the talk about Irving ; and this may have been true of other topics too. ' The fact is,' he continued later, ' it was enough for me in perplexity and doubt, to fall back on his own wise words,—" Do with all thy might what thy hand findeth to do : speak of the same only to the infinitesimal few,—nay, oftenest to nobody, not even to thyself." These words, when I first read them, sank very deeply into my heart.'

He confesses indeed that he felt ' somewhat hurt ' at the time,—' Here was I, striving to live according to his teaching, and, because I was not, what he had warned me against, a glib talker, he was dissatisfied with me.' But Larkin held his tongue, and made no complaint, and in time the sore feeling passed away.

II

" NO, THANK YOU "
(1862)

ON Friday night, 30.5.1862, Carlyle and his wife were at a dinner-party in Upper Brook Street, at the house of " Dicky " Milnes, with Venables and Kinglake and others.[1] Next Carlyle sat W. F. Pollock, a barrister who was the son of a Judge and had got a job in the Exchequer Court, an old acquaintance of Carlyle and a friend of Macready. Opposite them sat a famous Frenchman in exile, Louis Blanc, the pioneer of the " Organization of Labour," and the champion of common honesty in politics, who had made old Louis-Philippe, the son of the first Egalité, skedaddle in 1848, but had had to come over to London for safety himself soon afterwards. According to Pollock, Carlyle spoke of Louis Blanc as " looking as neat as if he had just come out of a bandbox." He mentioned his histories and concluded,— " Would you like to be introduced to him after dinner ? "

Pollock :—" No, thank you." He said himself he spoke emphatically, and Carlyle was tickled.

Then it happened that several dishes and sundry wines were offered to Pollock, and he said to each in turn,—" No, thank you."

" So it's always ' No, thank you,' " said Carlyle to him at last, breaking into ' an uncontrollable and boisterous fit of merriment,' according to Pollock, laughing at every fresh " No, thank you," while Pollock (and doubtless others near) joined in the laughing, as laughter is contagious, till Milnes himself from the head of the table called out to them, and begged to be allowed to share the joke, which was not possible till Louis Blanc was out of hearing.

[1] Sir W. F. Pollock's *Personal Remembrances*, II, pp. 106–7.

III

WHEN FINISHING THE FOURTH VOLUME
(BOOK XVII)
(1862)

FOR a long time Carlyle had been hoping to see *Frederick* completed within a year, and he felt so again in 1862, but he was growing desperate. It seemed to be lengthening out. 'At times,' he confessed to himself, 'I am quite downcast on my lonesome, long, interminable journey, through the not Mount Horeb[1] Wilderness, but the beggarly " Creca Moss "[2] one. Then at other times I think with myself,—" Creca and the Infinite of barren, brambly moor is under Heaven too. What if thou couldst show the blockhead populations *that* withal, and get honourably out of this heart-breaking affair, pitied by the Eternal Powers ! If I can hold out another year ! Surely before this time twelvemonth we shall have done." '

The date of this does not appear ; but it was near another entry of similar tone, dated July 2, 1862. ' Silence, even of the saddest, sadder than death, is often preferable,' i.e. preferable to speech, ' to shake the nonsense out of one. Last night, in getting to bed, I said to myself at last,— " Impossible, sir, that you have no friend in the big Eternities and Immensities, or none but Death, as you whimper to yourself. You have had friends who, before the birth of you even, were good to you, and did give you several things. Know that you have friends, unspeakably important, it appears, and let not their aweful looks or doings quite terrify you. You require to have a heart like theirs in some sort. Who knows ? And fall asleep upon that honourable pillow of whinstone." '

At this time, 2.7.1862, Mrs. Carlyle was spending a few

---

[1] Exodus, iii, 1, ' The mount of God, Horeb' (Sinai).
[2] Between the River Annan and Kirtle Water, to the east of Annan town.

days at Folkestone with the Ashburtons. Lord Ashburton
had been ill, but was now ' able to move about,' and to-day
Lady Ashburton was writing to persuade Carlyle to give
them his company also for a week-end. Mrs. Carlyle wrote
at the same time to reinforce the invitation in her own
way.—' Lady A. says she can give you " a perfectly quiet
room " :—indeed mine is quiet as the grave. . . . And the
cookery would suit you . . . roast mutton and boiled
chickens ! Now pray take no counsel with flesh and blood
but come straight off on Saturday morning, according to the
invitation that will reach you (I expect) along with this.
And in all likelihood we will go home together on Monday.
If you don't come, I will stay away as long as ever they
will keep me, just to spite you ! ' There was no resisting
this, and he went accordingly.

By 20.7.62 they were home again, and here is a letter
from Mrs. Carlyle to Lady Ashburton which may have been
written not long after their return.

' 5 CHEYNE ROW,
' *Saturday*.

' DEAREST LADY ASHBURTON,

' Most sincerely do I thank you for writing to me
just now, for remembering me at all with so much else to
think of. What between the kindness and the sadness of
your little note, I fairly fell to crying over it. We had been
wishing so much for a word of news about Lord Ashburton,
and I did not like to write to ask, for fear of bothering you.
When Mr. C. saw me crying, he fancied Lord Ashburton
must be worse, and showed so much emotion, that you would
have loved him for it, had you seen, and pardoned him all
his " *rongs* " (as my old Nurse would say). His eloquent
praises of your dear Husband, his declaration emphatically
repeated twice over " he is the only Man in the World that
I care for, that I have still any pleasure in meeting, the
only *friend* I have left in the World,—God help me ! I
wish he were well again ! " All that, and still more his look
and tone in saying it would have gone to your heart.

' I don't believe Lord Ashburton suspects how much true
love is felt for him, beyond his own immediate circle.
*He is without exception the most unselfish Man I ever saw in
my life.*[3]

' Mr. C. thought he looked " so much better " that

---

[3] Italics added.

2 H

evening we were at Bath House, he had been quite in good spirits about him since, and said :—" If he would only stay quietly at home in his own comfortable house there, and take care of himself, it would be all right."

' You will write us two lines soon again ? I wish to God that I could do any earthly thing for your or his good. But the good-doing between us has always been, alas, " with the reciprocity all on one side," and I see no help for that unless I can find some in the Precedent of *The Lion* and the *Mouse*. Ach !

' I was very disappointed at not seeing you again, but did not at all wonder. I knew how occupied you must be, both heart and hands.

' You will not forget my likeness of Baby ? I have *my heart set on it*, to an extent almost sinful. *The coming Man*, who will go on his knees for her grown up miniature, I defy to desire it more than I desire her baby-photograph.

' God be with you dear, dear Lady Ashburton.

'   Yours loyally,

'   JANE CARLYLE.

' Since I began writing there has come game from you. How many times I have to return you *thanks*.'

Writing to Mrs. Russell at Thornhill, Mrs. Carlyle now enquired,—' Are you well enough to feel any pleasure in—in—in seeing me if I should come ? ' She then went on to explain.—

' Look here ! I am not sure about it ! But Mr. C. said something this morning that I am determined to view as permission for me to go away by myself—where I please and when I please for a very little while. We had got into words about an invitation to the Marquis of Lothian's, in Norfolk. I had written a refusal by his (Mr. C.'s) desire, and Lady Lothian had written to me a second letter, holding out as inducement for altering his mind that there was a wonderfully fine library at Blickling Park, and that Lord Lothian's health prevented company ; and Mr. C., tempted a little by the library and the no company, had suggested I might write that if the weather got unbearable ! and if he got to a place in his work where he could gather up some papers and take them with him ! and if—if—if ever so many things, he might perhaps—that is, we might perhaps—come " by and by "!!! I had said " By no means. I have written a refusal by your desire ; I shall gladly now write an acceptance by your desire ; but neither yes nor no, or yes and no both in one, I can't and won't write ; you must do that sort of thing yourself." And then he told me, " since I was so impatient about it," I had better go by myself. To which I answered that it wouldn't be there that I would go by myself, nor to the Trevelyans, nor to the Davenport Bromleys ; but to Scotland to Mrs. Russell. " Then go to Mrs. Russell—pack yourself up and be off as soon as you like."

' Now it wasn't a very gracious permission, still it was a permission—at least I choose to regard it as such,' and, in short, I'll come when convenient to you. Which in due course she did, and was there the whole of August, writing to her husband every day. And here is how she was writing about him to Thomas Woolner :⁴—' Go and see my unfortunate Husband. . . . And go often, if you please, till I come back. . . .

' Affectionately yours,

' JANE W. CARLYLE.'

---

⁴ Thomas Woolner, *Letters*, p. 226.

IV

"UNTO THIS LAST," &c.
(1862)

IN 1862 John Ruskin was republishing in a little book, *Unto This Last*, the essays which appeared in *Cornhill* two years before, and adding to them now those afterwards reprinted as *Munera Pulveris*. Both were being cordially cursed by the critics in periodicals, because they discredited the accepted Cash-Gospel of ' Supply and Demand,' and other such commonplaces, supposed till then to be laws of politics, tho long ago derided as the ' dismal science ' by Carlyle in *Past and Present*, and many other places. Accordingly Carlyle was now comforting Ruskin and Ruskin's old father, disturbed by the critics.[1] Carlyle declared these essays were ' rising into the sphere of Plato, salutary and pressingly needed. . . . There is a felicity of utterance here and there, such as I remember in no other writer, living or dead, and it's all as true as gospel.'

In comforting the Ruskins, Carlyle was fond of telling a favourite parable.[1]—" When Solomon's Temple was a-building, it was credibly reported that at least 10,000 sparrows, sitting on the trees around, declared that it was entirely wrong, quite contrary to received opinion, hopelessly condemned by public opinion, &c. &c. Nevertheless it got finished, and the sparrows flew away, and began to chirp in the same note about something else."

On 4.8.1862 Carlyle was sending *Unto This Last* to Erskine of Linlathen.—' Here is a very bright little book of Ruskin's . . . extremely well worth reading. Two years ago, when the Essays came out, there rose a shriek of anathema from all newspaper and publishing persons. But I am happy to say that the subject is to be taken up

---

[1] Besides Collingwood's *John Ruskin*, II, pp. 16–26, see the Library Edn. of the *Works of John Ruskin*, Vol. XVII, pp. XXXIII, &c., and LXIX, &c.

again and heartily gone into by the valiant Ruskin, who, I
hope will reduce it to a *dog's likeness*—' (which seems hard
on dogs, but Carlyle continued), ' its real physiognomy for
a long time past to the unenchanted eye, and peremptorily
bid it prepare to quit this afflicted earth, as R. has done to
several things before now. He seems to me to have the
best talent for *preaching* of all men now alive. He has
entirely blown up the world that used to call itself " Art,"
and left it in an *impossible* posture, uncertain whether on
its feet at all or on its head, and conscious that there will
be no continuing on the bygone terms. If he could do as
much for Political Economy (as I hope), it would be the
greatest benefit achieved by preaching for generations past ;
the chasing off of one of the brutallest nightmares that ever
sate on the bosom of slumbrous mankind, kept the *soul* of
them squeezed down into an invisible state, as if they had
no soul, but only a belly and a beaver faculty in these last
sad ages, and were about *arriving* we know where in
consequence. I have read nothing that pleased me better
for many a year than these new *Ruskiniana*.

' I am sitting here in the open air under an awning with
materials by me for writing, being burnt out of my garret
at last by the heat of the sun. *I hope by this time twelvemonth I may be at Linlathen again ;*[2] . . . There is a long
stiff hill to get over first, but this is now really the last ;
fifth and final volume actually in hand, and surely, with
such health as I still have, it may be possible. I must
stand to it or do worse. . . . London has not been so
noisy and ugly for ten years, but this too is ending.' (Which
refers to the second great International Exhibition held in
1862. The letter concludes ' Adieu, dear friend.

' Yours ever,
' T. CARLYLE.'

Erskine had heard Ruskin lecturing in London many
years before and liked him, ' in his measure.'[3] But Ruskin
had now to be tried by a new scale of inches. He had dropped
the art-dilettante, and was translating the Political Economy
of Past and Present and Latter-day Pamphlets into current
biblical English.

[2] Italics added.
[3] *Letters of T. Erskine*, II, 82.

V

A NATURAL HISTORY MUSEUM
(1862)

M RS. CARLYLE had stayed with Mrs. Russell all through August. She went to Edinburgh on Monday, 1.9.62, pausing on the way at Crawford, where she wept at her mother's grave. She spent about a week in Edinburgh with her maiden aunts, the Misses Welsh, and a day or two at Auchtertool in Fife, with her cousin, the Rev. Walter Welsh, a son of her uncle in Liverpool. She came home about the middle of September.

By that time her husband had made such progress in his work that he had been able to write to Neuberg on 4.9.1862,—' Come on Sunday evening. You will find me just finishing Vol. IV ;—Very weak and weary ; but in prospect of running off to the Grange for a week of holiday.'

Thus another milestone was passed, and he was expecting that Volume V would be the last, and would be finished in a year more, just as in 1861 also he had expected Volume IV would be the last and would be finished in a year. So now he gladly decided to take a week at the Grange for a rest ; and while awaiting his wife's convenience, he found time to oblige his friend Richard Owen with a letter Owen wanted.

At that time the Natural History Museum, which is now conspicuous in the map of London, existed only in the minds of Richard Owen and a few others, mainly men of science and British Museum officials. Owen had put his proposals into a book, and now persuaded Carlyle to read it and write him a useful letter, dated 15.9.1862.[1]

' DEAR OWEN,

' I hope you will get your Museum. The nation really might take counsel of its chief naturalist, and build such a museum as will satisfy him.' (He cited for admiration

---

[1] *Life of Richard Owen*, by the Rev. R. Owen, II, pp. 55–6.

some details of Australasian birds and the British jackdaw in Owen's book, and made a friendly private suggestion to Owen.) 'My opinion is, if the Professor would gather himself steadily about such a thing, and devote his whole soul to it for a few years, he might write—say in two vols. with portraits, for it ought to be very brief and distilled to the utmost,—such a book of Natural History as was never written before! which would far outshine the biggest museum even the British nation could build, and might a long time outlive such—done by one's own right hand and head, independent of committees! I am quite serious; more so than you think.

'Yours always,

'T. CARLYLE.'

This lets us see inside, so to speak. His own *Frederick* was the same sort of outlet for his energies that he was advising Owen to find in a book on Natural History. The only difference was that Owen took all living beings for his province, while Carlyle restricted himself to ascertainable facts in the adventures of some typical samples of the commonest species of the order Primates. We are indeed such stuff as dreams are made of, but we remain first cousins to the monkeys all the same.

VI

IN THE FALL OF THE LEAF
(1862)

CARLYLE had been ready for the Grange in September, but October was well advanced before his wife was ready. She needed a rest after her recent wanderings, and first she spent a week-end at Dover with Miss Davenport Bromley, and then she had to stay some days more in London to see her friend, the American actress Charlotte Cushman, passing through. When at last she did go to the Grange with her husband, she found herself, if possible, happier there than ever before. She and the second Lady Ashburton were growing fonder of each other every time they met.

By 21.10.1862 the Carlyles were home again, and Mrs. Carlyle was writing from Chelsea to her best friend, Mrs. Russell, at Thornhill.—

'DEAREST MARY,

'I am not doing "what England expects of me," my duty! I *ought* to begin writing at least half a dozen Letters that are troubling my conscience; and here I am writing to *you*, from no sense of duty at all, but because I like it.

'Well, my wanderings for this year are over; and it must be owned they have been far and wide! The Grange visit was very successful. Every time I come away from there with increased affection for the Lady, and in a sort of amazement at her excessive kindness to me. That she is naturally a very kind woman, and also a very demonstrative woman, is not enough to account for the sort of passion she puts into her expressions of fondness and unwearied attention to me! I always wonder will it last? But it has lasted a good while now; and I begin to feel ashamed of myself for not accepting it all with absolute faith.

'Mrs. Anstruther came for two days, and pressed me to spend my Christmas with *her ;* as Lady A. would be away at Nice all the Winter. But the answer to that was simply, "impossible!" I told her about meeting Mr. S. at your house, and she said in her soft, silky, rather drawly voice, "Oh, dear Mrs. Carlyle, did you ever in your life see so ugly a man?"—The Bishop of Oxford was there too,' (Wilberforce) 'and Mr. C. set him right in *two* Scripture quotations ! ! ! But the most interesting visitor was Mr. Storey, the American Sculptor, who sang like an angel ! There was a Photographer down for three days, taking views of the place at the easy rate of five guineas a day ! And Lady A. made him photograph me sitting, with herself standing beside me ; and he did another of Lord A. and Mr. C. sitting on the same bench, under the portico ; and another of a whole party of us sitting about on the steps of one of the porticos. That one was half good, and the other half spoiled. Lord A., one of his Sisters, and Mrs. Anstruther "had moved" ; Mr. C. and Lady A., and myself, came out perfect ; and so we "perfect ones" were all *together*, and were to be "cut out" from the failed ones. I have not seen the Photographs on *paper* yet ; but hope to have them in a few days ; and if they are worth anything, I will send you them—to look at, at least.

'But the rose-coloured petticoat, Oh my Dear ! I must tell you about the first appearance of *that !* I put it on the second day, and the black silk tunic trimmed with half-a-yard-wide lace (imitation), with long falling sleeves lined with rose-colour ; and a great bunch of rose-coloured ribbon on my breast, and smaller bows at the wrists of my white under-sleeves. It was really, as Miss Baring said, "Quite a costume !" And in spite of its prettiness, I couldn't help feeling nervous about appearing, for the first time, in a guise which would make me remarked by all the *women*, at least ! So I dressed in good time, that I mightn't have to walk into the drawing-room when many people were down. There had been some uncertainty about the dinner hour that day, as people were coming from London by a late train. At all events, I should hear the gong sound for dressing, I thought, half an hour before dinner ; and in the mean time I sat down, all ready, to read a novel. How long I had sat without hearing either bell or gong I can't say ; but I was startled from my reading by a sharp knock at my bedroom door, and the voice of one of the manservants informing me " everybody was gone in to dinner ! " Upon my honour, I can believe some hardened wretches have gone out to be hanged with less emotion than I had in hurrying along the corridor and down the great staircase, to have the two leaves of the dining-room door flung wide open before me by two footmen ! and then to walk up the great room to my seat at the dinner-table, everybody's head turned to see *who* was so late ! To put the finishing stroke to my agony, the rose-coloured petticoat was a trifle too long in front for the stooping way in which I walked, and was like to trip me at every step !—But bad moments and good moments and all moments pass over ! I got into my seat, Lord knows how, and any one who had heard me complaining aloud to Lady A. up the table, that the gong had never been sounded, would have fancied me endowed with all the self-possession I could have wished.

' Another ordeal was in store for me and my " costume " later. Being Sunday night, the Bishop was to read a Chapter and say Prayers in that same dining-room before all the servants, and such of the visitors as would attend. Eight-and-thirty servants were seated along two sides of the room ; the men all in a line, and the women all in a line ; and with these thirty-eight pairs of eyes on me (six pairs of them belonging to Ladies' maids !) I had to sail up, in all that rose-colour, to the top of the room, on the opposite side, *first !* The other Ladies being members of the family pushed me into that horrid dignity. And the same in going out ; I had to walk the length of the room, like to trip myself at every step, with the petticoat and the embarrassment ! before one of that frightful line of servants budged. It took all the compliments paid me on the costume to give me courage to put it on a second time ! As an old Aunt of Mr. C.'s said, when she had become somehow possessed of a one-pound note and didn't know where on earth to hide it for safety, " They're troubled that hae the worl', and troubled that want it."

' And now my Letter is long enough, and it is bedtime.

' I was so glad of your dear Letter yesterday ! If you were my Sister, I couldn't have you nearer my heart, or more in my thoughts.

' Love to the Doctor ' (Mrs. Russell's husband), ' and a kiss to Nipp, whose likeness I have opposite my bed.

' Your loving friend,
' JANE W. CARLYLE,'

The Carlyles were not long home when Ashburton was brought to town for two days, " very ill," and his wife seems to have written[1] to Mrs. Carlyle to say he would like " Mr. C. to sit with him tomorrow evening." Apparently that note was only received on the morrow, which had been assigned to Neuberg, for as Carlyle was going out to be with Ashburton, he called out to his wife to " send Neuberg a line to say how I am situated," which she did, and the sick man had the company he wanted.

---

[1] Writing to Neuberg Mrs. Carlyle quotes the writer without saying exactly who the writer was.

VII

IN THE NATIONAL PORTRAIT GALLERY
(1862, &c.)

CARLYLE had been appointed a Trustee of the National Portrait Gallery when it was started in 1857, and did what he could for it till 1868.[1]

He was looking at the pictures one day in the company of Mr. Brookfield, and " after contemplating for a time Wilkie's very repulsive portrait of George IV . . . as a tall Highlander in full costume,[2] he said nothing, but quoted Milton's description of the Devil as he reviewed his soldiers in Hell :—

> " He, above the rest,
> In shape and gesture proudly eminent,
> Stood like a tower : his form had yet not lost
> All her original brightness, nor appeared
> Less than archangel ruined . . ."[3]

In 1862 the Trustees were inclined to accept a portrait of Lord Brougham. Their rule was to let in no likeness of anyone still living ; but Brougham was then eighty-four, and sooner or later a portrait of him would be wanted. Tho all felt that the acceptance of it would be a bad precedent, there was silence till Carlyle rose and said that " since the rest hesitated, he begged leave to move that the Brougham picture be for the present rejected."[4] He added,—" Brougham is still living, and when he does die, he'll be speedily forgotten." Lord Stanhope, the Chairman, politely ejaculated,—" Oh, a very remarkable man, surely,— great statesman, great orator ! " " No," replied Carlyle. " Brougham has done nothing worth remembering particularly ; and at all events the rules of the Gallery . . ." and so on, and gained his point.

[1] Letter to D. A. W. from the Secretary, 10.9.1914.
[2] *Random Reminiscences*, by Charles H. E. Brookfield, son of Carlyle's friend, Rev. W. H. Brookfield. Chapter I, p. 20, popular edn.
[3] *Paradise Lost*, I, l. 589–593.
[4] *Thomas Carlyle*, by Moncure D. Conway, pp. 113–14.

Carlyle told Allingham afterwards that on this occasion he noticed that Disraeli, another Trustee who was present but silent, was looking at him " with a face of brotherly recognition—a wholly sympathetic expression. I found this look in his face altho I had more than once said hard things of him publicly. I saw he entirely agreed with me as to Brougham."[5]

[5] From *William Allingham, A Diary*, pp. 80–81.

VIII

BOOKS WORTH READING, &c.
(1862)

LORD ASHBURTON being ill was about to go to Nice for the winter. He offered Carlyle a horse and was answered (2.11.1862).—

'Dear Lord Ashburton,

'On at last fairly considering the Horse question, "Fritz" (my own poor old quadruped) *versus* your noble Grey (whh. might be mine), I have to admit.—

'1st. That poor old Fritz is adequate apparently to carry me thro his Namesake's sad business (*more* adequate, at least, than I am to be carried).

'2nd. That *he* is my old friend (almost the one friend I am to have in these dark winter months) ; whom it were a sin, and a remorse, to desert in his decay.

'3rd. That *change* of any kind will be attended with trouble, with uncertainty, better to be avoided in this my nearly extinct conditn.

'And, in fine, that I am not permitted to accept your flattering offer ; but only to regard it (whh. I always will and must) as a beautiful bit of friendly munificence,—and in that way, retain the *Soul* of it, as a lasting possession. This is the real truth of the affair. . . .

'I mean to call again *quam primum*' (as soon as possible). 'My Proofsheets, my &c. in the muddy dark weather, drive me delirious.

'Yours ever faithfully,

'T. Carlyle.'

Perhaps when he made the promised call, the Ashburtons begged a list of books worth reading, to kill time at Nice. At any rate here is a list he made out for them three days later. To explain the first note on the first item it should

be remembered that the second Lady Ashburton was a
Highlander, a Mackenzie.

' BOOKS WORTH READING

Boswell's *Tour to the Western Isles* $\left\{\begin{array}{l}\text{Along with Johnson ;}\\ \text{very entertaining}\\ \text{(\textit{to a Highlander}).}\end{array}\right.$

—— *Life of Johnson.*

Hawkin's *Life of Johnson ;* Mrs. *Piozzi's Anecdotes ;* &c.
(All lives of Johnson deserve reading.)

Swift's Works. (*Gulliver, Battle of the Books,* &c., are still
popular. He is far the greatest of his age. *Life* of
him by Sir Walter Scott ; &c.)

Anson's *Voyage.* (Capital little Book.)

Voltaire's *Tragedies ;* *Racine's ;* *Corneille's* (all worth a
serious re-perusal, after one has come to the years of
discretion).

Mémoires sur la Revolution (Michaud's Collection, about
100 volumes, entertaining, every one of them.)
Petitot's Collection (*earlier* French).

French *Mémoires,* (also about 100 volumes, do. in some
degree : A good deal of good French reading, in that
and the cognate kinds).

Campbell's (late Thomas) *Specimens of British Poets.*
(Good, both *criticisms* and *pieces.*)

Pope's *Correspondence ;* Marion's *Life of Gray* (Gray's
letters excellent) ; Shenstone's *Poems,* his *Letters*
too ; a great deal of good English reading in that
kind. *Horace Walpole's Letters* (lately edited by
Cunningham) is the best of its sort in the world.

Don Quixote ; *Arabian Nights ;* *Homer* (by Pope, by
Cowper), *Virgil* (by Dryden),—French Translations
of *Classic Ancients,* no end.

My paper is ended, and your patience !

T. C.

(5th Novr. 1862).'

On 11.11.1862 Carlyle was writing to the good wine-
merchant, C. A. Ward.[1]—

' DEAR SIR,
' Thanks to you for the Gift of Fruits in their Season ;
which brings you pleasantly to memory in this gloomy exit

---

[1] See Book XXI, Chapter XXXIV. The letter is from the *Daily
Mail, Over-Seas Edition,* 4.7.1914, p. 400.

of the year. Spanish onions do credit to their country ; the
plums are so beautifully packed ; they ought to stand
untasted, merely admired as a bit of Fine Art, till perhaps
Christmas comes.

'I am very busy constantly (tho making poorish progress) ; and see with patience and in silence " the fall of
sceptres and of crowns," and look with a pity and awe,
which also are silent, on the consummation of Constitutional
Palaver and Universal Suffrage, and our poor Yankee
Brothers tearing one another in pieces about Nothing at all,
and, in fact, " the earth opening," and *Hell* and its fires
bursting out on them as visibly, or more so, than on Sodom
and Gomorrah long ago ! Silence ! Silence !—

'I remain yours, with thanks, and regards,

'T. CARLYLE.'

IX

ILLNESS OF LORD ASHBURTON, &c.
(1862)

ON the way to Nice, Lord Ashburton fell ill with inflammation of the lungs, and was being nursed through that in Paris for several weeks, and more than once seemed likely to die. Lady Ashburton had her sister beside her; but the sister's husband fell ill in London so that she had to hurry home, and told Mrs. Carlyle,—" *You* are the only other person Lady Ashburton would like to have beside her. Write and ask if you may come." Which of course she did at once, and as she reported to another, soon received a reply,—' No—I was not to come, " it could do her no good and would knock me up "; for the rest, she was " past all human help," she said, " and past all sympathy." And the poor dear soul had drawn her pen through the last words. So like her, that she might not seem unkind, even in her agony of grief and dread she thought of that.

' Their doctor's last two letters to me were very despondent, and neither to-day nor yesterday has there been any word from him, as there would have surely been, could he have imparted a grain of hope. We dread now that the next post will bring the news of our dear Lord Ashburton's death. Carlyle will lose in him the only friend he has left in the world, and the world will lose in him one of the purest-hearted, most chivalrous men that it contained.'

On 21.11.1862 Mrs. Carlyle was sending four letters received from Paris about Lord Ashburton to her friend Mrs. Russell, and described how the latest was received.—
' We were talking very sadly of Lord Ashburton, already almost in the past tense; Mr. C. saying, " God help me! since I am to lose him, the kindest, gentlest, friendliest man in my life here! I may say the one friend I have in the

world ! " and I, walking up and down the room, as my way is when troubled in mind,'—a characteristic worth remembering,—' had just answered, " It's no use going to bed and trying to sleep, in this suspense ! " when the door opened and a letter was handed me. It was from Paris, a second letter that day ! I dursn't open it. Mr. C. impatiently took it from me but was himself so agitated that he couldn't read it, when he had it.' (Something was amiss with the spectacles, it is easy to guess.) ' At last he exclaimed, " ' Better ! ' I see the one word ' better,' nothing else ! Look there, is not that ' better ' ? " To be sure it was ! and you may imagine our relief ! and our thankfulness to Lady A. and Mrs. Anstruther for not losing a moment in telling us ! The letters go on more and more favourable.' . . .

In another letter vaguely dated " November," but following a letter dated 21.11.62, Mrs. Carlyle shows herself doing what she was very fond of doing,—*mothering* her husband, so to speak,—a thing worth looking at.—

' I have a new woman coming as cook next Tuesday, and intense as has been Mr. Carlyle's abhorrence of the present " mooncalf," " cow," " brute-beast," I look forward with trepidation to having to teach the newcomer all Mr. C.'s things, which every woman who comes has to be taught, whether she can cook in a general way or not.' . . . (As Alexander Carlyle says and others[1] can corroborate, it was only Mrs. C. who gave trouble to the servants, Mr. C.'s tastes being simple and easily satisfied. Mrs. Carlyle's letter goes on.)—
' There is the anxiety about dear Lord Ashburton too. . . . I have a note in my pocket at this moment which Mr. C. does not know of, leaving scarce a hope of his recovery. As it was not from the doctor, but from Lady A.'s niece, who expresses herself very confusedly, and might have made the case worse than it is, I decided not to unsettle Mr. C. at his writing with a sight of it ; and it has felt burning in my pocket all day ; and every knock at the door makes my heart jump into my throat, for it may be news of his death.' . . .

[1] D. A. W. having also questioned the servants, including one who was a remarkably intelligent woman, Mrs. Broadfoot, for many years a successful manageress of a hotel at Thornhill, can only corroborate what Alexander Carlyle has written in the footnote, *New Letters and Memorials of Jane Welsh Carlyle*, II, pp. 276-7.

(Next day she added.)—' A note has just come from Lady Ashburton's sister in London, forwarding a telegram just received :—" My Lord has passed a better night. Dr. Quain thinks him no worse." ' And the recovery continued and the anxiety abated.

ILLNESS OF LORD ASHBURTON, &c.   483

Next day she confided :—'A more hurt [it come from Lady
Ashburton's illness] to which I have made a mistake feel.
never feels . . . if I had had a head a little right, Dr.
Quain thinks she won't die . . . but that her nerves correlated
and the finish' &c.&c.

X

WIFE-WORSHIPPING EXTRAORDINARY
(1862)

WRITING to Mrs. Russell on 15.12.1862, Mrs. Carlyle
had said :—' I should not be at all afraid that after
a few weeks my new maid would do well enough if it weren't
for Mr. C.'s frightful impatience with any new servant
untrained to his ways, which would drive a woman out of
the house with her hair on end if allowed to act directly
upon her ! So that I have to stand between them, and
imitate in a small, humble way the Roman soldier who
gathered his arms full of the enemy's spears, and received
them all into his own breast.' . . . Whereto Carlyle
added a footnote by-and-by,—' Oh heavens, the comparison ! it was too true ' ; but the maids themselves
declared it the reverse of the truth.

The simple truth is what has just been written in the last
chapter and the foot-note to it. The servants all seem to
have agreed that he was easy to serve and she very difficult
to endure. Another thing they agreed about,—that he was
always ready to " pet and spoil her," fool her to the top of
her bent, in short, as if they had been young people in love
and newly wed, and as one expressed it, " he never thought
of disputing anything she said or did."

It is written in the Chinese scriptures[1] that Confucius
himself confessed : " Of all people, young married women
and servants are the most difficult to behave to. If you are
familiar with them, they lose their humility. If you main-
tain a reserve towards them, they are discontented."

The lesson to be learned from Carlyle's behaviour seems
the commonplace one,—to put the wife on a pedestal and
leave her to rule the other women. Which is often the
easiest thing to do, and sometimes sensible. You never
can tell,—it depends on circumstances.

[1] *Confucian Analects*, Book XVII, Chapter XXV, and the Note in
Legge's edition.

XI

THE TAIPINGS
(1862)

IT is common knowledge now that the Taipings were Chinese patriots. Their leaders were good men, and the Europeans who throve on the slaughter of them by the help of better weapons were mercenaries at least as mean as the concession-hunters. St. Augustine's description of the Empire he knew,—" organised rascality,"—was true of the Chinese empire then ; and the English waging war to make the Chinese let opium into China were "plain-dealing villains," of the same beautiful type as those who take advantage of a conflagration to do a little stealing.

Here is a hurried note of 30.11.1862 to Woolner, who had invited Carlyle to meet Gladstone and two experts on China, a Captain Osborn and another.[1]—' Dear Woolner, If I could but get myself under way, on such a voyage at night ! But alas, I fear that will be impossible on Tuesday.

' Pirates are fair game on all waters, on the part of all men. But does Captn. Osborn know for certain that the Taipings require to be shot ? One Mr. Meadows, a very ingenious man, who had been twelve years in China, and is gone back, had, when I saw him, the idea that the Taipings were intrinsically in the *right ;* and that it was the unworthy Phantasm of an " Emperor " and his yellow Cousins who got hopelessly out of square !

' Yours always truly,

' T. CARLYLE.'

Unluckily " Chinese Gordon " heeded no such adviser as Mr. Meadows, and entering the service of the yellow

[1] *Thomas Woolner, Letters,* pp. 228–9.

" Emperor " he was to slaughter as if for the pleasure of it, for he would not even pocket the fee that was offered him. Poor Chinese Gordon ! But after all it is an unheroic business to be a mercenary murderer.

XII

ENGLISH GARROTTING, &c.
(1862)

GARROTTING used to mean strangling a man by twisting a stick (in Spanish ' *garrotte* ') so as to make tighter and tighter a cord round his neck. It was used for executions in some countries, like the Turkish bow-string, and either of these ways of killing was quicker and surer than our hanging ; but the " garrotting " that came into fashion among English thieves in 1862 was to grip a victim from behind and *half*-strangle him, and then rob him. As the nights grew longer in winter, the new fashion spread, till at last a thief handled roughly a legislator between Parliament and his club, and alarmed both Lords and Commons. But they did not affect the night walks of Carlyle.

His brother Dr. John remonstrated with him, and at 11 o'clock on Thursday night, 4.12.1862, he was writing a reply :—' The garrotting is more a terror and a rumour than anything very practical. But I do generally leave my watch ; carry a thick stick, and keep a sharp eye in these night walks.' And even as he was writing, ' Jane ' was giving order,—" Out ! "

His letter was about a Christmas gift to a lady, whose address John had given him, and he requested his brother to call upon her ' for your sake and mine. There is something strange and pathetically pleasant to me in the recollection of that little Bonnet at " Tom Donaldson's " (school), in the " Brick House," at the distance of 60 years ! You can tell her they asked me, when I came home, the first day,— " Who was the nicest lassie ? " To which I answered without hesitation, " Jean Johnston,"—but had a great deal of quizzing to stand, which I had not the least expected. This day is my sixty-seventh birthday. Time, Death, Eternity : what an element this is that all of us have ! " We are such

stuff as dreams are made of ; and our little life is rounded
with a sleep ! "   In my utter solitude I live much in these
contemplations ; which are not joyous, but perhaps better,
and have a grandly quieting character, and lift one above
the world and its beggarhoods.   If I were only done with
my book !   But really now it is getting to be high time.
My weariness of it, occasionally, no tongue can tell ;   at
other times I am rather pleased to feel myself shaping,
according to ability, so long as I live, something cosmic
and true out of the chaotic, mendacious and unknown.   Oh
that I had done with it, *done !* '

He had been more than ten years steadily at it, now.
Impatience to have done with it was so natural that the
satisfaction he was still feeling in doing it was remarkable.

XIII

DR. QUAIN BRINGS NEWS, &c.
(1862)

ON ' Christmas Day, 1862,' Mrs. Carlyle was writing to
Mrs. Braid, who had been a servant in her mother's
house in Haddington long ago, and a girl along with her.—

' We have been in great anxiety about Lord Ashburton.
It is six weeks past on Monday that he has been hanging
betwixt life and death, at an hotel in Paris, where he was
taken ill of inflammation of the lungs, on his way to Nice ;
and all the time I have been receiving a letter from Lady
A.'s sister by her directions, or from their travelling physician, Dr. Christison (son of that Robert Christison, who
used to visit at my uncle Benjamin's in your time), every
day almost, sometimes two letters in one day ; such constant changes there have been in the aspect of his illness !
The morning letter would declare him " past all human
help," and in the evening would come news of decided
" improvement," so that we couldn't have been kept in
greater suspense if we had been in the same house with
him. The last three days there has been again talk of " a
faint hope," " a bare possibility of recovery." And Dr.
Quain, ' who has been five times telegraphed for to Paris,
called here to-day immediately on his return, directed by
Lady A. to go and tell us of his new hopes. When I was
told Dr. Quain was in the drawing-room, I went in to him
with my heart in my mouth, persuaded he had been sent
to break the news of Lord A.'s death. My first words to
him (he had never been in the house before) were, " Oh,
Dr. Quain, what has brought you here ? "—a reception so
extraordinary that he stood struck speechless, which confirmed me in my idea, and I said, violently, " Tell me at
once ! You are come to tell me he is dead ? " " My dear
lady, I am come to tell you no such thing, but quite the
contrary ! I am come by Lady Ashburton's desire to

489

explain to you the changes which again have raised us into hope that he may recover." Then, in the reaction of my fright, I began to cry. What a fool that man must have thought me ! Poor Lady A., who is devotedly attached to her husband, has nursed him day and night, till she is so worn out that one could hardly recognise her (her sister writes). Next to her and their child, it is to us, I believe, that he would be the greatest loss. He is the only intimate friend that my husband has left in the world—his dearest, most intimate friend through twenty years now.'

A week or two later, on a ' bitter, frosty January morning ' early in 1863, a man of ' extreme youth ' and ' ill-concealed timidity,' natural under the circumstances, contrived ' to introduce himself to Carlyle, on one of' his ' morning rambles.' [1]   It was Richard Herne Shepherd, who published a biography of Carlyle in 1881, wherein he tells how he was ' received kindly and graciously,' and questioned about ' his occupation, what he was *doing* in the world,' and then ' the talk must have run mainly on schoolmastering.' . . . No doubt Carlyle discovered the timid youth was the same who had in 1862 sent him ' a little list of errata discovered in the first edition ' of *Frederick*. ' Then there came parting at his door—a shake of the hand—and an expression of his readiness to render any service to his young disciple that might be practicable, should need for such arise.'

Later in the same year, 1863, young Shepherd had the luck to be a fellow-passenger with Carlyle in a bus from Piccadilly, and he and Carlyle left it together. Carlyle had noticed him in the bus taking snuff, and advised him to stop the snuffing and ' try smoking as a substitute,' which he says he did ' with the most beneficial results.'

' Then came an outburst of enthusiasm ' about Emerson, and if Shepherd's memory served him aright, there was a contradiction he could not understand. Carlyle paid what is called a ' warm and glowing tribute ' to the ' beautiful soul,' and said—or maybe Shepherd's memory is at fault, and it was himself who said,—' Is it not wonderful that in a country in such an anarchic condition as the United States at this time, such a master-mind as Emerson's should not share in the practical conduct and control of affairs ? ' Happily there seems no room for mistake about the rejoinder to this being Carlyle's :—" God forbid that I should ever be governed by Emerson ! We should have Chaos come again ! "

[1] *Life of Thomas Carlyle*, by R. H. Shepherd, II, pp. 263-7.

XIV

HENRY LARKIN AND HIS WIFE
(1862, &c.)

HENRY LARKIN was about to marry, and Mrs. Carlyle approved of his choice. She had known the young woman for a year and a half, and welcomed her as a neighbour with emphasis when the Larkins took the house No. 6 Cheyne Row, next door to their own, No. 5.[1]

" She was always the kindest of friends to me," said Mrs. Larkin, speaking of the next three years, and saying she " was frequently in and out " of their house, and " used to write letters " for her, and Mrs. Carlyle " used often to look in upon me."

" I cannot imagine how Mrs. Carlyle could be called a jealous neurotic. She was anything but that. When I knew her, of course, she was rather an old lady. *She was tall and held her head up very erect.* She was very chatty, knowing both how to talk and what to talk about. As a housewife, she was very clever, but not having been brought up to be the housekeeper herself, she thought it something of a bother, and preferred that it should be done by servants. She was a very good manager, and Carlyle never found fault with her in the slightest respect. He was entirely ignorant of these matters, and as long as all went smoothly, and he got his meals regularly and exactly as they were required to be, he took no further notice. His meals had to be studied carefully owing to dyspepsia. Mrs. Carlyle knew how everything should be done, and would sooner do things herself at any time than that they should not be exactly right.

[1] Credible report of interview with Mrs. Larkin in 1903, at Christchurch, New Zealand. She had been in that colony for 13 years. The interview with her was reproduced in Scotland and elsewhere from the New Zealand press, in January, 1904, and cuttings sent to D. A. W. by G. McRobert, Missionary, Edinburgh. She was described as a " well-educated, refined lady, the widow of the late Mr. Henry Larkin," author, &c.

" She was not bad tempered, but she had a sharp tongue, and when she wanted to snub anyone she could do so (and even) say cutting things at times, but did not mean them as such."

As for the stories about Carlyle giving sweets to children, Mrs. Larkin said he " took very little notice of them " and " she did not suppose he ever saw the children whom he passed," which would be natural in those busy years.

It was untrue that " either of the Carlyles was jealous or had the slightest cause to be. The first Lady Ashburton had a great admiration for Carlyle, and *was disposed rather to ignore his wife in comparison (with him)*, (which) Mrs. Carlyle resented. With the second Lady Ashburton Mrs. Carlyle was on terms of the very warmest friendship." Mrs. Larkin of course would only know what Mrs. Carlyle told her about the first Lady Ashburton.

" The fact was that Carlyle's seeming harshness and his wife's cutting remarks were really only mannerisms, and each understood perfectly how little such displays actually meant from the other. Certainly *Froude* was not in the best position to judge, because *until after Mrs. Carlyle's death he was only a very rare visitor at their house.* Mrs. Carlyle herself always had the greatest horror at the idea of having her private affairs forced into any kind of publicity. It was easy to misinterpret. Some people might call Carlyle's behaviour ' violent temper ' when I would be disposed to call it ' tantrums.'

" Carlyle and his wife were not unhappy by any means. It never entered the minds of any of their friends to think they were."

Mr. Larkin did not enjoy the close neighbourhood of the Carlyles so much as his wife did, and is frank about it, saying[2] :—' I soon found that it was a mistake, so far as I was concerned. Carlyle had become so accustomed to apply to me in every little difficulty, that, now that it could be done so conveniently, it grew to be a very serious tax upon my time. Mrs. Carlyle continued as affectionate as ever ; but his spirit of irritability and impatience became more frequent, and more unconscious on his part, the more familiar we became ; and I often had painful misgivings as to how far I was justified in thus giving way to him. But

[2] Henry Larkin's *Carlyle and Mrs. Carlyle : a Ten Years' Reminiscence, British Quarterly Review* (1881), Vol. 74, pp. 75-76, 74, and 51-54.

there was really no help for it, except by weakly leaving him in the lurch, and deserting him in the midst of his difficulties,' which Larkin would not do, were it only for the sake of Mrs. Carlyle. He proceeds.—

'One consequence of my living so handy was that letters dwindled into :—" Please come."

" Come for a moment."

" Will you come to me to-morrow Morning as you pass."

" Dear Larkin, Will you call this Evening as you go home ; there is some MS. to copy (very cramp in parts). T. C."

" Dear Larkin,—Could you copy me the Inclosed (readable to *you*) before, or by, 10 o'clock to-night ? Yours always, T. C." '

Once he handed Larkin a London Library circular requiring the return of Strauss's *Life of Jesus*, which had been put down to him by mistake, as Larkin was to explain. Upon the circular a note was written in blue pencil which greatly delighted the Christian soul of Larkin :—" Please don't trouble me about this book any more ! I never had it, never saw it (nor wished to see it, nor shall wish), your Copy or another.—T. C."

The long-continued strain of *Frederick* was getting on his nerves, which illuminates Larkin's single sensation.—' It was in the drawing-room,' says Larkin, ' and Mrs. Carlyle was present. He was asking me to do some trifling mechanical service for him, similar to what I had done once before, and lest I should have forgotten, proceeded to give me altogether wrong instructions. Of course I corrected his mistake and explained to him how the thing had really been done ; but I could see that he was not altogether himself, and spoke as tenderly as I could. Perhaps even this gave offence. He grew more and more irritable, as I tried to convince him that it could not possibly be done in the way he said. He stormily insisted that he was right, and that *he surely* ought to know. We were both standing looking at each other. I sorrowfully knowing that mechanism would not alter its conditions to please either of us ; and he, in his loose-fitting coat, and with his long sceptre-like pipe admonitorily sweeping the air, angrily and utterly refusing to be convinced,' concluding ' in strangely measured sarcastic cadences,—" It may—be perfectly—credible—to *you*—that I am entirely—devoid of sense," and then impatiently left the room. Mrs. Carlyle and I looked at each other in despair. He had betaken himself to the garden. I have seldom been more reverently affected and even humbled, than when, in about five or ten minutes, he again entered the room, frankly admitting his error, and expressing his great regret that he should have allowed himself to be so carried away.

' I never knew a man more free from all personal vulgarities of any kind, or one whose presence carried with it such clear unassuming dignity of manhood ; which I can only describe as a certain royal graciousness of manner, as different from a spirit of condescension as wisdom is different from personal pretentiousness. He had a graphic discernment of all the facts he knew, and such a world-wide wealth of knowledge to liberally dispense, that few " kingdoms " have been more grandly real or more honestly won. His very failings compelled respect by their absolute and evident sincerity. Of his mocking Berserkir hilarity, and overwhelming power of speech when roused by worthy opposition, we have often been told ; but, for my own part, I greatly preferred his half-silences, when one seemed to commune with his heart rather than with his head. At such times of quiet converse I have sometimes known him as simple, as gentle, and as open to conviction as any child. The recollection of such moments keeps his memory dear.'

Both Carlyle and his wife ' had singularly expressive voices, and yet singularly different, like a powerful organ and a mellow flute. They both spoke heartily, with their genuine native accents, but with the easy grace of cultivated sincerity, and with no other rusticity of manner than daring to be true to the soil from which they sprang. They simply brought with them, into the midst of the French-polished upholstery of London conventional life, the fresh breezes ' of their native hills. But Carlyle was never playful as his wife ' often was. Laughter he had of many kinds ; scornful, genial, triumphant ; and even a strangely sympathetic laugh of reproving pity ; but I should say, never the clear ring of overflowing heartfelt joy. Even his humour, richly abundant as it was, was never playful, like Shakespeare's, or like Thackeray's at his best ; but always either grim, or sadly pitiful, or else merely grotesquely admonitory.' In short, as Larkin read him, he was always ' grimly earnest, fearfully self-conscious, almost from the cradle to the grave.' Yet he ' defined the only healthy self-consciousness to be—" When Know thyself has been wisely translated into—Know what thou canst work at."

' With all this grim earnestness I do not suppose Mrs. Carlyle ever had any deep or real sympathy. She may once have greatly overestimated her ability to rally him out of it. Perhaps she never altogether gave up the attempt. She was always very ready with playful surprises,' says Larkin, recalling what seemed to him at the time a great event. One morning, after he had finished his business upstairs, he looked in at the drawing-room as usual, and was asked :—" Has Carlyle mentioned that little paper he is to speak to you about ? "

Larkin :—" No, but I suppose he has forgotten it. I will go back to enquire."

Back he went ; but Carlyle who was ' busily writing ' knew no more about the paper than he did ; and came downstairs with Larkin at his heels to ask her what it was. She did not look at them when they entered, but let them come ' close up to her table, where she was writing ; and then held up before them a slip of paper bearing,—" The 1st of April ! " ' '

Carlyle and Larkin looked at each other in momentary bewilderment and burst out laughing, Carlyle striding off to his study, while Mrs. Carlyle cock-a-doodled,—telling Larkin,—" I am proud to have brought down *two* such philosophers with one shot ! "[3]

---

[3] As Larkin puts it, p. 54,—". . . was highly triumphant at having, as she said, brought down," &c. See also, *passim,* the book by Henry Larkin, *Carlyle and the Open Secret of his Life,* Publishers, Kegan Paul, Trench & Co., 1886.

XV

FRITZ AND NOGGS
(1863, &c.)

OUR dogs and horses have even shorter lives than ourselves, their hurried human fellow-mortals. Fritz was ceasing to be equal to the long rides required of him. He never had excelled at the high trot ; and when he was trying it in Regent's Park one Friday (6.2.1863, it seems), he came down. He righted himself and rose, and trotted half a mile as if unhurt ; but then Carlyle, 'looking over his shoulder, saw the blood streaming over his hoof,' drew bridle and dismounted, and saw that both the knees were ' quite smashed,' and came slowly home. In the weeks that followed he was looking round for a new owner likely to be good to the horse, and discovered an apothecary willing to undertake to use him for riding only. So the " beautiful Fritz " became the apothecary's cheap, for £9 ; and Fritz's master took to walking and going in buses, declaring he liked the change,—" I now find human beings to speak to." So at least his wife reported to his relatives, adding, " How long he will be able to enjoy his walking I cannot predict."

Here is what she was writing to Lady Ashburton soon afterwards.—

'I wonder if you are returned to Paris ? I wonder if you are better ? I wonder if the wee Darling *knew* you ? Oh I wonder so many things ! It wouldn't surprise me to find that you hadn't been able to let the little " *lump of delight* " out of your arms, after having again got her into them ; and so that she had accompanied you back to Paris. Oh what a pleasure it will be to think of you all under one roof again, and a roof of your own ! The Grange—oh to be going to see you—to be with you all at the Grange again—after all these troubles and terrors. I think you scarcely *take in* the deep, glad interest with which your

496

return is looked forward to. " People are so illnatured ! "
Aye that they are—illnatured and disloyal—most of them,
but People are *human* ; are capable of being touched by
noble patience, and warm-hearted devotion. *I* know not
the Man or the Woman who speaks of Lord Ashburton and
you, in these sad times, otherwise than sympathizingly and
reverently. Even Women, whom envy and jealousy made
spiteful towards you before, have quite changed their
tone, and speak of you now as fellow-women not as rivals.

' I dare not ask Dr. Christison to " predict " any more,
but surely when Lord Ashburton is got the length of cutting
up the leaves of books again, *predicting* must be beginning
to assume less unfeasibility even for Men " only educated
at the Edinr. College of Medicine " as he said.

' Mr. C. is *really* thriving for the time being, on his horse-
lessness, finds it " an unspeakable deliverance " he says,
" to be no longer strapped to the back of that miserable
quadruped, as he had been for the last eight years, but
at liberty to walk out into the streets and speak to human
beings ! " So he has taken no steps towards replacing
" Fritz," nor will, so long as the novelty of *walking* pleases
him. " It will be time enough to return to his *dreary
isolation,*" he says, when his health seems to require horse-
exercise again. So you see—Most generous of created
Women.

' Poor Fritz was sold to a neighbouring Apothecary for
nine pounds ! Mr. C. rode him *once* before he was sold
" just to *soothe the poor quadruped's feelings,* by showing him
he was forgiven." I wonder what *Biped* he would have
done as much for ? The town has been much enlivened by
the " Convicted Felon " at the Drawingroom. I was told
that it was the Chief Baron who sentenced him & who
recognised him there. *Dramatic* if true.

' I have a photograph of you, but I don't think it half
so good as the one on the hearthrug.

' Yours devotedly,
' J. W. CARLYLE.'

But in writing to her aunts in Edinburgh, advising them
to take a *very nourishing* diet, as she herself was doing,
Mrs. Carlyle remarked : " I don't believe Mr. C. could have
lived thro' this *Book* if it hadn't been for his horse exercise
and his almost daily breakfast-cupful of clear essence of
beef," or rather as he called it, " strong gravy soup." She

2 K

quoted him as admitting that he had " been kept so long alive, by that one article of food."

Lady Ashburton agreed with Mrs. Carlyle that a horse was equally needful, and soon presented to him a young Arab, superlative at the gallop, the favourite pace of Arabs, and of the rider too in this instance. " Noggs," he named him, after Newman Noggs, the gentleman by nature in Dickens's *Nicholas Nickleby ;* and tho Noggs seemed inferior to Fritz in " moral qualities " and " sense," he soon was on good terms with his rider, and became his principal " companion " as long as *Frederick* lasted.

XVI

A WOOLLEN SHAWL
(1863)

ON Tuesday, 10.2.63, Mrs. Carlyle received a shawl and a letter worth reading yet.

> ' Mrs. Thomas Carlyle.

' MADAM,

' Unwilling to interrupt your husband in his stern task, I take the liberty of addressing you, and hope you will accept from me a woollen long shawl, which I have sent by the Parcel Delivery Co., carriage paid, to your address. If it does not reach you, please let me know, and I shall make inquiries here, so that it be traced and delivered. I hope the pattern will please you, and also that it may be of use to you in a cold day.

' I will also name to you my reason for sending you such a thing. My obligations to your husband are many and unnameably great, and I just wish to acknowledge them. All men will come to acknowledge this, when your husband's power and purpose shall become visible to them.

' If high respect, love, and good wishes could comfort him and you, none living command more or deserve more.

' You can take a fit moment to communicate to your husband my humble admiration of his goodness, attainments, and great gifts to the world ; which I wish much he may be spared to see the world begin to appreciate.

> ' I remain, &c.,
>
> ' J. T.'

She replied next day, 11.2.63.

> ' 5 CHEYNE ROW, CHELSEA.
>
> ' *Feb.* 11, 1863.

' I wish, dear sir, you could have seen how your letter brightened up the breakfast-time for my husband and me yesterday morning, scattering the misanthropy we are both given to at the beginning of the day like other nervous people who have " bad nights." I wish you could have heard our lyrical recognition of your letter—its " beautiful modesty," its " gentleness," and " genuineness ; " above all I wish you could have heard the tone of real feeling in which my husband said, at last, " I do think, my dear, that is the very nicest little bit of good cheer that has come our way for seven years ! " It might have been thought Mr. C. was quite unused to expressions of appreciation from strangers, instead of (as is the fact) receiving such almost every day in the year—except Sundays, when there is no post.   But, oh, the difference between that gracious, graceful little act of faith of yours, and the intrusive, impertinent, presumptuous letters my husband is continually receiving, demanding, in return for so much " admiration," an autograph perhaps ! or to read and give an opinion on some long, cramped MS. of the writer's ; or to—find a publisher for it even ! or to read some idiotic new book of the writer's (that is a very common form of letter from lady admirers)—say a translation from the German (!) and " write a review of it in one of the quarterlies ! " " It would be a favour never to be forgotten ! " I should think so indeed.

'Were I to show you the " tributes of admiration " to Mr. C.'s genius, received through the post during one month, you, who have consideration for the time of a man struggling, as for life, with a gigantic task—you, who, as my husband says, are " beautifully modest," would feel your hair rise on end at such assaults on a man under pretence of admiring him ; and would be enabled perhaps, better than I can express it in words, to imagine the pleasure it must have been to us when an approving reader of my husband's books came softly in, and wrapped his wife in a warm, beautiful shawl, saying simply—" There ! I don't want to interrupt you, but I want to show you my good-will ; and that is how I show it."

'We are both equally gratified, and thank you heartily. When the shawl came, as it did at night, Mr. C. himself wrapped it about me, and walked round me admiring it. And what think you he said ? He said, " I am very glad of that for you, my dear. I think it is the only bit of real good my celebrity ever brought you ! "

' Yours truly,

' JANE W. CARLYLE.'

XVII

TYNDALL ON THE METHODS OF CARLYLE

PROF. JOHN TYNDALL was about twenty-five years younger than Carlyle, and a spiritual son of his. He was now a leading champion of the Darwinian theory to explain evolution in general and human origins in particular by the Struggle for Life and Natural Selection. "They had become acquainted at the Grange, and Tyndall tells us,[1] 'as time went on I drew more closely to Carlyle, seeking, among other things, to remove all prejudice by making clear to him the spirit in which the highest scientific minds pursued their work,' thinking little of profit and applause and practising self-denial. 'He was surprised to find me fairly well acquainted with *Wilhelm Meister's Travels*, declaring that, as far as his knowledge went, the persons were few and far between who showed the least acquaintance with Goethe's "Three reverences"—reverence for what is above us, reverence for what is around us, reverence for what is beneath us. To this picture of Goethe's ethics Carlyle always attached great importance. . . . .

'He was intimately acquainted with every nook and corner of Gothe's work. . . . I once had occasion to quote the poem "Mason Lodge," translated in *Past and Present*. The article in which it was quoted was afterwards translated into German; the original poem, therefore, required hunting up. None of my friends in Berlin knew anything about it. On learning this I went down to Chelsea, where, in answer to my inquiry, Carlyle promptly crossed his sitting-room and took from a shelf the required volume. . . . .

'Carlyle's respect for conscientiousness and earnestness extended to all things. "We once went together to an exhibition of portraits at South Kensington. Pausing

[1] *Personal Recollections of Thomas Carlyle*, by John Tyndall, in his *New Fragments*, pp. 347–357.

before the portrait of Queen Mary (Bloody Mary, as we had
been taught to call her), he musingly said, " A well-abused
woman, but by no means a bad woman—rather, I should
say, a good woman—acting according to her lights. . . ."

' The facts of history were as sacred in his eyes as the
" constants " of gravitation in the eyes of Newton ; hence
the severity of his work. The *Life of Frederick*, moreover,
worried him ; it was not a labour into which he could throw
his whole soul. He was continually pulled up by sayings
and doings on the part of his hero which took all enthusiasm
out of him. " Frederick was the greatest administrator
this world has seen, but I could never really love the man."
Such were his words.'

It is plain that he was wearying to see the *Frederick*
finished. On 15.4.63 he confided his hopes to his friend Sir
George Sinclair :[2]—' In some six or eight months—surely
not longer than eight—I hope to have at last done : it
will be the gladdest day I have seen for ten years back,
pretty much the one glad day ! I have still half a volume to
do ; still a furious struggle, and tour-de-force, as there have
been many, to wind matters up reasonably in half a volume.
But this is the last.'

About this very time, according to Tyndall,[1] ' he was invited to stand for the Rectorship of Edinburgh University.
For the moment he declined, promising, however, to consider the proposal when his labours on *Frederick* were
ended.' So when the time came ' by-and-by, he accepted
the invitation.'

[2] *Memoirs of Sir George Sinclair*, by James Grant, p. 428.

XVIII

MRS. CARLYLE'S STORY ABOUT A PRIEST, &c.

HERE is Tyndall's report on Mrs. Carlyle.[1]—There was in her, he tells us, ' a fund of tenderness and liberality ; but her sarcasm could, on occasion, bite like nitric acid. Like her husband, she could hit off a character or peculiarity with a simple stroke of the tongue. Her stories sparkled with wit and humour. She caused me to shake with laughter by her inimitable way of telling the story of an old French priest, who discoursed to his peasant congregation on Samson's feat of tying the foxes' tails together, and sending them with burning brands through the standing corn. The ruin to agricultural produce was described so vividly, and with such local and domestic applications, that the people burst into weeping. Their sobs and tears reacted on the old priest himself. He also fell to weeping, but tried to assuage the general grief by calling out,—" Ne pleurez pas, mes enfants. Ne pleurez pas ; ce n'est pas vrai ! " " Don't weep, my children. Don't weep,—it isn't true ! "

[1] *New Fragments*, by John Tyndall, p. 370, footnote.

XIX

AT A READING BY DICKENS
(1863)

ON the afternoon of 28.4.63,[1] Mrs. Carlyle went to Woolner's, and persuaded him to come to tea at her house, and go with her husband to hear a reading by Dickens. " Dickens has sent him two tickets," she said,[2] " and told him it would do him good to hear a little reading. I am not strong enough to go, and he won't go himself, and stipulated for your company."

So Woolner came to tea, and then he and Carlyle took a cab to Hanover Square, and were in time for one of the readings. Dickens " was the best reader I ever heard," declared Woolner, " and the changes of voice and manner suitable to the various characters were so easy and natural (that) they appeared before the audience like veritable human beings."

At the ten minutes' interval, Dickens came and took Carlyle away to an inner room. In a minute or two Carlyle returned to fetch Woolner,—" to have some brandy and water." Woolner did not want any, but Carlyle insisting, he went with him. Each poured out what he wanted of the brandy. Carlyle took his glass and nodding to Dickens said,—" Charlie, you carry a whole company of actors under your own hat."

The second part of the reading was equally well done, and Carlyle had nothing but praise for it ; but Woolner confessed to " doleful forebodings. The performance was a terrible strain " (upon Dickens) " as it was clear that his whole mind was concentrated upon the long continuous effort. He must be using up his splendid faculties too rapidly," thought Woolner !

[1] *Letters of Thomas Carlyle to his Youngest Sister*, by C. T. Copeland, pp. 228–9.
[2] *Thomas Woolner*, by Amy Woolner, pp. 232–3.

What Carlyle was writing the next day[1] was more cheerful.—'Dickens does do it capitally, such as *it* is; acts better than any Macready in the world; a whole tragic, comic, heroic *theatre* visible, performing under one *hat*, and keeping us laughing—in a sorry way, some of us thought— the whole night. He is a good creature, too, and makes fifty or sixty pounds by each of these readings.'

'Of Dickens's readings,' says Moncure Conway,[3] 'no description can convey any adequate impression. He was in himself a whole stock company. He seemed to be physically transformed as he passed from one character to another; he had as many distinct voices as his books had characters; he held at command the fountains of laughter and tears. Dickens's voice in its every disguise was of such quality that it reached all of those thousands in St. James's Hall, and he stood before us a magician. When he sat down it was not mere applause that followed, but a passionate outburst of love for the man. Dickens was a unique man, and his writings insinuated themselves equally into the hearts of rich and poor, learned and illiterate.'

What Conway heard Carlyle saying was,[4]—"I had no conception, before hearing Dickens read, of what capacities lie in the human face and voice. No theatre-stage could have had more players than seemed to flit about his face, and all tones were present. There was no need of any orchestra."

[3] *Autobiography of Moncure D. Conway*, II, p. 7.
[4] *Thomas Carlyle*, by Moncure D. Conway, pp. 120–1.

XX

THE WAYS OF WOMEN, &c.
(1863)

THROUGH 1863 Carlyle's concentration on *Frederick* was greater than ever, if possible. As he said afterwards, he was feeling like the " migratory swallows," which his friend Owen had described as continuing to fly after their " strength was done and coma or dream had supervened, till the Mediterranean Sea was crossed." To suit the weather in summer he was dining at half-past three instead of his usual hour a little later, and after dinner he used to take a rest and then go riding in the cool of the evening. His sleeplessness, according to the doctors most likely to be right, was the natural result of sitting up late and reading till long after midnight. This habit had prevailed among students in Scotland for centuries, and was the natural result of a cold climate, which makes dwellings too cold in the early morning to sit and study in. Its bad effects were made worse when one took a nap after dinner in the afternoon, as Carlyle often did.

Mrs. Carlyle was now taking a drive in a brougham every afternoon, and he was advising her to buy a brougham and keep one of her own ; but, as one of her candid friends said afterwards,[1] " she behaved about that like the petted baby she was,—tho it would have been quite easy for her to do it, far easier than it was for him. She objected to the expense, and said in effect, ' if a brougham is to be bought for me, you must do it yourself.' "

About the beginning of May this year Moncure Daniel Conway came from Massachusetts to England, a bright Unitarian divine not long turned 30. His errand was to lecture on the American Civil War, and show us that for England to take sides with the Southern states would be supporting slavery. He succeeded well. An introduction

---

[1] To D. A. W. . . . She was an intimate lady friend of Mrs. C. . . .

from Emerson made him welcome at Cheyne Row, and he tells us[2] that Carlyle ' met me, pipe in mouth, cordially. For a few moments I was left alone with Mrs. Carlyle, who was too thin and pale to preserve traces of beauty, but had a look of refinement and dignity.' Among the solemn portraits on the wall were two modern miniatures of beautiful ladies nude to the waist.

" You may be surprised," she said, " at seeing such portraits in a grave house like this.   They were found in the tent of a Russian officer during the Crimean war, and presented to Carlyle."   Cheerful, kindly, witty and frank, she conversed pleasantly of the habits and labours of Carlyle. She thought the *Life of Frederick* a terrible piece of work, and wished that Frederick had died when a baby.   " The book is like one of those plants that grow up smoothly and then (it) forms a knot, smoothly again and then forms another knot, and so on ; what Carlyle is when one of those knots is being passed must be left to the imagination." Carlyle was a picture of meekness when his wife said this.

On 17.6.63 the Rev. William H. Brookfield was writing in his diary.[3]—' Sat an hour with Carlyle, who was very good.   Speaking of Ruskin, he said that the last lecture was a sort of set-off against the breakdown which he had achieved in consequence of Mrs. M. going with a termagant of a woman called Lady E. to a former lecture on purpose to disconcert him.'

" Mrs. M." would be Mrs. Millais, a woman of Perth, who in 1855 had annulled her marriage with Ruskin and married Millais.   Whoever she was, the breakdown of the lecture must have been more than compensated to the gossiping crowd by the way the two impudent women effected it.

One day this summer Mrs. Carlyle went to Ealing to spend the afternoon with Mrs. Oliphant, and found her ' sitting before the fire ' and nursing her two-and-a-half-year-old baby, which had had convulsions.   Mrs. Oliphant had had a great fright, and remembered and described long afterwards[4] what happened.—" Mrs. Carlyle sat by me, kind and tender and full of encouragement, as if she had known all about babies, telling me all kinds of comforting things."   She departed when she could be of no more use, but " by the first possible post that same evening I got a

[2] *Autobiography of Moncure D. Conway*, I, pp. 251–2.
[3] *Mrs. Brookfield and Her Circle*, by C. & F. Brookfield, II, p. 500.
[4] *Autobiography and Letters of Mrs. Oliphant*, p 81.

letter from her, telling me that Mr. Carlyle had made her
sit down at once and write to tell me that a sister of his
had once had just such an attack, which never was repeated.
God bless them, that much maligned, much misunderstood
pair!"

Apparently a few weeks afterwards, Mrs. Carlyle received
the present of a basket of mulberries, brought to her from
the Rectory by little Reginald Blunt, 'about eight,' the
son of the Rector. "I can well remember," he testified
by-and-by,[5] when a grown man and an author, how Mrs.
Carlyle "looking very worn and white and delicate, called
her husband down from the garret room, to present me, in
return for my mulberries, with an apple-covered inkstand
of china, which I now prize mightily."

[5] *Memoirs of Gerald Blunt*, by Reginald Blunt, p. 80. The only clue
to the year is that he was 'about eight,' and he was eight on 17.9.63, as
may be seen at p. 57. In 1864 Mrs. Carlyle was ill and in Scotland at
the season indicated. So 1863 is the likeliest.

XXI

MONCURE CONWAY'S DESCRIPTION
(1863)

MONCURE CONWAY was one of the best of Carlyle's Boswells. Describing his first evening at Cheyne Row,[1] in the early summer of 1863, he goes on to say.— 'An American politician,' probably 'our minister at the Hague,'[2] came in just as we were at nine o'clock tea, and soon got Carlyle into a stormy denunciation of "ballot-boxing." But the American was ignorant, and while Carlyle was firing cannon on a sparrow, I silently observed him. Tall, and almost slender, with a longish head, bent forward from slightly stooping shoulders, with a magnificent brow overhanging a tender blue eye that sometimes flashed, a short beard and moustache, a ruddy colour at times overspreading the whole face with flushes, a voice that began gently but could rise to a tornado which usually burst in laughter that ended in a fit of coughing, nervous movements of fingers and shoulders telling of overstudy, an undertone of grief, even in his laughter—these characteristics together wove a charm in notable contrast with that of Emerson. In his presence I recalled the sublimity mingled of beauty and awe which impressed me in the Mammoth Cave ' (in Kentucky).

' He was interested to know all I could tell him about Emerson, and brought out a photograph he had recently obtained, desiring to know if he looked just like that now. I was able to show him a much better one. All that he said about Emerson indicated the strongest personal attachment.

' My second interview with him,'[1]—which would be not long afterwards—' was during a walk which he invited me

---

[1] *Autobiography of Moncure D. Conway*, I, pp. 352–361.
[2] Letter of Moncure D. Conway to the *Boston Commonwealth* about this date, read by D. A. W. in one of Mr. Gridley's cuttings.

to take with him.' On arriving 'I was shown into the
room at the top of the house where he was writing his
History of Frederick. There were about a thousand books,
every one as he told me bearing upon the history he was
writing, the regular library being downstairs. On the walls
were a score of pictures, all either portraits of Frederick or
engravings related to his life. " I have found it," he said,
" of the utmost importance to surround myself with the
images and illustrations of the man whose history I am
writing."

'When we started on our walk he began at once upon
America, the ballot-box, and negro emancipation,' and
quoted Anthony Trollope, the then popular novelist and
civil servant, who seems to have visited Carlyle, and once
said, tho Carlyle would not know that, that he " ever
revered " him, and learned more from him than from any
other English writer. What Trollope had amused Carlyle
by quoting was Emerson's saying,—" The American Eagle
is a mighty bird ; but what is he to the American Peacock ? "[3]

According to Conway, Carlyle thought there was more in
that than in most books about America ; and he went on
to say.[1]—" A lie can never be uttered in this world but
those who utter it will be paid for it what they deserve.
Nothing I have ever witnessed so fills me with astonishment and sorrow as the present condition of things in
America. I see it all as fire rained out of the heavens."
Conway said he ' quite agreed, but should probably differ
from him as to the evil the fire was raining on.' " Ah, I
was once an emancipator, too," replied Carlyle, " and used
to spout whole chapters of Martyn, but I came to see that
I was following a delusion."

' Just then we passed along Church Lane, where Swift
used to live, and Carlyle began to talk about him with much
feeling. He declared Swift a man of the finest force of every
kind, and spoke bitterly of the way in which he had been
swamped under " the pressure of an evil time " ; then added
with a sigh, " but his case is not that of one alone."

' It was impossible not to love this man, however much
I might deplore his opinions about slavery, so entirely was
he speaking what he regarded as truth, and so guileless was
his whole expression. The humility that is characteristic

[3] Told D. A. W. by F. M. Spencer, Bournemouth, and see the book on
Trollope, by Michael Sadler. For Trollope's report of Emerson, see the
Correspondence of *Carlyle and Emerson,* by C. E. Norton, II, pp. 292–3.

of all real genius was very striking in Carlyle. In his talk the personal reference was rarely made unless it was to mention, as in the above remark, some error into which he had fallen.

'Although brought up with a holy horror of profanity, I found a certain satisfaction in Carlyle's occasional " damnable." . . . There was a kind of authenticity in his " damnable " or in the less frequent " damned." The invocation " damn " he never used, his brands never being affixed to persons, but to evil systems and falsities.

'It was impossible with this frank, outspoken man not to enter at once upon the great social problems of the hour. All was going wrong ; our ballot-boxings, our negro emancipations, our cries for liberty, all showed nothing but that the nations were given over to believe a lie and be damned. Possibly, indeed, the only way to Paradise lay thus through Hell ; but what the people were seeking thus they would never obtain. Not New Jerusalem but New Gehenna they would find it.—

' " Ballot-boxing ! Why, we have *tried* that *vox populi* (popular cry) in England." ' He described Hudson and another, and concluded—' " As soon as your ballot-box is opened, out springs the most whippable rascal that can be found. *You know well that in America, for years, you have had your meanest men in the White House.* But so they all go—pell-mell. There is no real king that will be " ' (or wants to be) ' " sought for ; though I *do* know some men who are kings—loyal men in their workshops, discerning the laws of this universe and obeying them. Ah, a king is a rare gift ! "

' But how little can anyone report the charm of Carlyle's conversation ! Of the wealth showered on the visitor intent on getting near the man's heart ! I soon perceived that the vehemence of Carlyle in discussing public affairs was due to the torture he suffered in seeing the errors and agonies of mankind. I resolved not to put him on that rack,' and avoided events in America as much as possible.

' Nothing was too small for his study and interest. He would pass in a moment from talk about Frederick or Bonaparte to tell the story of some poor little lady unknown to fame, so sweetly that the mist gathered to one's eyes.

' Emerson (had) told me that when he was in England (1848) some young men had asked him to introduce them to Carlyle, and he had said, " Why do you wish to have vitriol thrown upon you ? " I was prepared by this for sharpness and severity, but I found tenderness and sympathy. Personally, that is to say ; but I had discovered the vitriol, too,—the man's relentless confrontation of optimistic visions and " reforms " with an insight that pierced their bias. One after another the believers in one or another national or humanitarian ideal had ceased to visit him, finding his ideas too depressing.

' One evening, when Froude and I had gone together to Carlyle's, and had listened to a particularly vigorous arraignment of the movements supposed to be progressive, we walked away in silence. Then I remarked, " All that is a dreary enough outlook." Froude answered, " Yes, and the worst of what he says is, that it is true." '

' Occasionally American writers in London asked me to introduce them to Carlyle. I invariably warned these visitors that if they desired useful visits they had best leave the initiative of talk entirely with Carlyle. David A. Wasson, John Burroughs, and some others whom I took to Carlyle's house, observed my advice and had successful visits. My friend Samuel Longfellow, who came over with his nephew Ernest (son of the poet), was cordially received. Carlyle had pleasant feelings towards the poet Longfellow, and there was an unworldliness and modesty about our beloved Samuel ' which shielded him. ' When Carlyle said something against universal suffrage, Samuel's conscience overbore my warning, and he made some mild plea for democracy. Carlyle after a moment's silence said smilingly and in a meditative tone,—" Then in Jerusalem you would have given Jesus and Judas the same vote ? " Samuel's utter inability to answer was amusing. Charles G. Leland, whom I took there, also grappled with Carlyle, and got the worst of it.

' The position taken up by Carlyle on that matter impressed a great many more Americans than ever ventured to admit their misgivings in public. Carlyle told me that after his unintended offence to Americans in speaking of their millions as " bores," '[4] in 1850, ' he had been visited by a considerable number of their influential men who entirely sympathised with his feelings about popular suffrage.—" I have nothing but the kindest feelings towards

---

[4] See *Carlyle at His Zenith*, Book XVIII, Chapter XI, p. 242 ; and *Latter-day Pamphlets*, No. 1, p. 19 of the Ashburton Edition.

the Americans," he said. " Personally, I have indeed the best reasons for gratitude to them ; there was something maternal in the way in which my works were taken up there at a time when they were neglected in this country. The first money I ever received for any book of mine was brought into my house from Boston. So far as this democratic tendency is concerned, I have rather envied America ; we in this country are in the same train on the same track ; we are linked on just behind the American compartment ; they will be smashed first, but we just after them, by dashing against the law of the universe that wisdom in government cannot be obtained from the collective ignorance and folly of swarms of men. If that delusion is ever recovered from, it will probably be soonest in America. But, alas ! the dreadful war going on there renders all calculations vain."

' Once when his brother, Dr. John Carlyle, was present, we two and Mrs. Carlyle being the only listeners, Carlyle referred to slavery,' saying.—' " I have no dislike of the negroes. By wise and kindly treatment they might have been made into a happy and contented labouring population. I do not wish for them any condition which I would not under like circumstances wish for myself. No man can have anything better than the protection and guidance of one wiser and better than himself, who would feed him and clothe him and heal him if he were sick, and get out of him the exact kind of work that he is competent to achieve. Many a man is driven by a cruel mastery of circumstance and want to do whatever will yield him a crust of bread, and others never master what they have ability to achieve in these days of emancipation. There is my brother John sitting there ; the world will never get out of him the best that is in him."

' Here the rest of us began to laugh, the doctor being amused and giving a gesture of assent. Mrs. Carlyle said, " And what about Mr. Thomas Carlyle ? "

' " Ah, well," the answer came with a sigh, " Thomas Carlyle tried in every way possible to him to get some practical work for which he believed that he had some competency ; was baffled at every attempt ; and he has been compelled to travel on the only path open to him." '

On another occasion, ' Thomas Appleton, brother of the poet Longfellow's wife, told me that one evening when he was conversing with Carlyle, he mentioned some favourite

2 L

writer of his, and Carlyle called the said writer a " phrase-monger." " I was vexed," said Appleton, " and retorted on him by saying, ' Well, Mr. Carlyle, what are the best of us but phrase-mongers ? ' ' Very true, sir—very true,' said Carlyle, breaking into a laugh. And the evening passed off more pleasantly than ever." '

On another evening when Conway was there and nobody else present but the Carlyles, Mrs. Carlyle interrupted her husband in a pretty way when he was storming against emancipation. She remembered that Conway tho a slave-owner's son had taken up the anti-slavery cause as a religion, and she said,—" Carlyle, you ought not to talk so about his cause to a man who has suffered and made sacrifices for it."

' Carlyle, who always took his wife's reproof meekly, turned to me and said softly,—" You will be patient with me. All the worth you have put into your cause will be returned to you personally ; but the America for which you are hoping you will never see ; and never see the whites and the blacks in the South dwelling together as equals in peace." '

Writing many years afterwards, poor Conway added,— ' How often in these last years have I reason to remember that prophecy ! ' Then he added some reflections worth quoting.—

' Carlyle I have found curiously misunderstood in England and America, even by his admirers. He is supposed to be a worshipper of force, and of military leaders. But it was because the European masses resorted to violence in 1848 that he lost all faith in the people ; it was because Louis Napoleon reached power by massacre that Carlyle pro-claimed him a " swindler " ; he opposed every war waged during his time.'

The massacres doubtless made Carlyle abhor Napoleon III, but it was for his lies and tricks that the fellow was called a " swindler." Conway continued.—' The thing that especially amazed me about Carlyle was the extent of his intellectual pilgrimage. From the spring of 1863 until shortly before his death in 1881 I saw him often. During that eighteen years after my thirty-first birthday I had studied scientific problems under great scientific men and revised my religious and political philosophy ; I had entered new phases of thought and belief ; but there was never one in which Carlyle had not been there before me. He had studied closely every philosophy, generalisation, and theology. He knew every direction where an impenetrable wall would be found, and every deep and byway of speculation.

'Another erroneous impression about Carlyle is that he was stationary in his ideas. But Carlyle, even within my memory, grew in a way rare (even) among literary men in advanced years. I remarked this especially in regard to the discovery of Evolution,' which, in short, he ended by cordially accepting as proved.[1]

'Ah, what a heart was in him! When our child Emerson died, Carlyle, who rarely made calls, travelled across the seven or more miles to visit us in our sorrow. His sympathetic talk, his narrative concerning his mother, his appeal that we should bear up under our distress and find consolation in what remained to us, were to us the voice of the great love that while dealing with the history of empires marked the sparrow's fall.'

As Conway was a Unitarian preacher, he may here have been thinking of Matthew, x, 29-30,—'Are not two sparrows sold for a farthing? And not one of them shall fall on the ground without your Father.' But he did not refer to that passage, and merely said[5]:—'A characteristic of Carlyle was his sympathetic interest in all animal life. Often when walking in the park he would pause to observe the sparrows which, hardly getting out of his way, would pertly turn their heads and look at him as landlords might observe a suspicious character trespassing upon their estate. This seemed to amuse him much. He had always a severe anathema for vivisection, and all cruelty to animals,' saying once :—' "Never can I forget the horror with which I once saw a living mouse put into the cage of a rattlesnake in the Zoological Gardens, to be luncheon for that reptile. The serpent fixed upon it his hard glittering eyes, and the poor little creature stood paralysed, trembling with terror. It seemed to me a cruelty utterly unjustifiable, and one to be unceasingly protested against." '

On another occasion Conway describes,[6] 'when John Burroughs went with me one evening to Chelsea, Carlyle astonished us by his knowledge of birds and love of them. The mavis he thought next to the nightingale in song, and then came the blackbird. The lark, tho monotonous, is

[5] *Thomas Carlyle*, by Moncure D. Conway, pp. 80-85.
[6] *Autobiography of Moncure D. Conway*, II, pp. 101-2.

always pleasing,—he found it a kind of welcomer wherever he went. The linnet was a pleasant bird. The London house-sparrow was (as) impudent as could be, and would hardly get out of one's path. He imitated its pert look and (the) popping up of its head quaintly. He remembered the dignified unconcern of a cat passing close by about five hundred of them chattering away about their affairs, and bethought him of the Arabian legend that Solomon's temple was erected under the chirping of 30,000 sparrows, " all met to give a joint disapproval of the project."

' Leigh Hunt used to send him here and there to listen to the singing of the nightingale. But he could not hear one until there came a song which he recognised by Goethe's description ; he compared the poet to it—" a voice sounding amid the din like a nightingale—touching and strong." These words told the whole thing. It was not sad, yet pathetic, and somewhat piercing. It is incomparable. He listened to it fifteen minutes, but never heard the nightingale again. It is passing away from about London. He heard of one lately singing in Green Park. It doesn't go further north than the bottom of Yorkshire. It is said it cannot find farther up what it requires to eat.'

On another day Conway was reminded of the description of the swallows in *Sartor* when Carlyle was speaking to him[5] of ' an experience of the philosopher Kant, when he was walking in a wood, near the wall of a ruin. He heard a clamour among the swallows, high up on the wall, so loud that it made him pause. The birds were in shrill debate about something. Presently there was a pause, then a long, low, plaintive note from one of them ; and immediately thereafter a nestling, not yet able to fly, fell to the ground. Kant concluded that the debate was that of a council which decreed that there was not nest-room or food enough for all the little ones ; one must be sacrificed ; and the one low, plaintive note was that of the mother submitting to the fatal conclusion. Kant picked up the fallen swallow, which was not yet dead, and looked into its eye. How deep it was ! As he gazed into it, he seemed to be looking into an infinite depth, a mystical vista.

' " This struggle for existence," said Carlyle, " of which our scientific men say so much, is infinitely sad. We see it all around us. Our human reptiles are outcomes of it. Somebody told me of a subtle fellow, a small lad, who heard a poor rustic, warned to take care of his money in the crowd, say he had only a pound and meant to keep it in his mouth. Soon after the street-boy crosses the poor man's path, and sets up a cry, " You give me my money ! " A crowd having gathered, the boy explains that he had been sent by his poor mother with a sovereign to buy something, had fallen, and as the money rolled away the man had picked it up and put it in his mouth. The crowd cried ' Shame ! ' and he from the country had to disgorge and get home as he could. The story is credible of a boy struggling for existence in this vast abyss of greed and want.

' " Survival of the fittest ! Much that they write about it appears to me anything but desirable. I was reading lately some speculations which seemed to be fine white flour, but I presently found it was pulverized glass I had got into my mouth—no nourishment in it at all, but the reverse. What they call Evolution is no new doctrine. I can remember when Erasmus Darwin's *Zoonomia* was still supplying subjects for discussion, and there was a debate among the students whether men were descended from an oyster or a cabbage. I believe the oyster carried the day.

" That the weak and incompetent pass away, while the strong and adequate prevail and continue, appears true enough in animal and human history ; but there are mysteries in life, and in the universe, not explained by that discovery. They should be approached with reverence. An irreverent mind is really a senseless mind. I have always said that I would rather have written those pages in Goethe's *Wilhelm Meister* about the ' Three Reverences ' than all the novels which have appeared in my day."

' It was in speaking of our grief and that of others (when our child Emerson died),' says Conway, ' that he said :— " I still find more in Goethe about all high things than in any other. His gleams come now from a line, or even a word, or next a scrap of poetry. He did not believe in a gray-haired Sovereign seated in the Heavens, but in the Supreme Laws. A loyal soul ! Concerning things unknown he has spoken the best word—*Entsagung.*[7] In thinking about immortality, we jump to selfish conclusions, and support them as if they were piety : even if we sanctify our conclusion by associating with it our departed friends and clinging affections, it is *something you want.* But nothing can be known. Goethe says—*Entsagung.* Submission !

[7] In Dictionary, =renouncing, renunciation.

Renunciation! That is near to it. I studied the word long before I knew what he meant by it; but I know there is such a thing as rising to that state of mind, and that it is the best. Shall it be as I wish? It shall be as it *is*. So, and not otherwise. To any and every conceivable result the loyal man can and will adapt himself; face that possibility until he becomes its equal; and when any clear idea is reached, bend to that till it becomes ideal. *Entsagung* shall then mean, 'tis best even so!" '

XXII

HOW BROWNING HAD WON HIS WIFE
(1863)

ONE evening about this time the pleasant story of
Browning's courtship and marriage was told in Cheyne
Row, and Moncure Conway recorded ' the same night ' his
recollections of the talk.[1] At that time ' Robert Browning
was by no means famous. Tennyson, to whom Browning
introduced me,' says Moncure Conway, ' told me he thought
his poems powerful, but too " rough." Anthony Froude
had a similar feeling. William Henry Channing and I had
an enthusiasm then shared only by Dante Rossetti. Channing told me that the obscurity of *Sordello* lay in the fact
that in the original edition there was no punctuation at
all ; he had taken his pencil and punctuated the book, and
it was comprehensible enough.' Here now is Conway's
record.—

Carlyle.—" I remember Browning as a fine young man,
living in the neighbourhood of Croydon. I liked him better
than any young man about here. He had simple speech
and manners and ideas of his own. A good talk I recall
with him, when I walked with him to the top of a hill,
which had a fine prospect. When he published *Paracelsus*
I did not make much out of it, but his works proved a
strong man.
" Miss Barrett (had) sent me some of her first verses in
manuscript. I wrote back that I thought she could do
better than write verses. She wrote me then saying, ' What
else can I do ? Here I am held hopelessly on a sofa by
spinal disease.' I wrote taking back all I had said. Her
father was a doctor late from India—harsh and impracticable ; his lightest utterances must stand out hard as the
laws of the Medes and Persians. He saw her a moment

[1] *Autobiography of Moncure D. Conway*, II, pp. 19–21.

519

every day as a physician : then she was left alone. Then she read some compliments of Browning's to her poetry."

Mrs. Carlyle, interposing.—" Oh, no, Mr. Browning never wrote a word about her."

Carlyle.—"Ah, well, you shall tell it all revised and corrected when I get through.—Then she wrote something about him, comparing him to a nectarine."

Mrs. Carlyle.—" Oh ! "

Mr. Ballantyne.—" A pomegranate."

Mr. Conway.—" And from Browning some pomegranate, which if cut deep down the middle, shows a heart within blood-tinctured of a veined humanity."

Carlyle.—" I stand corrected. Well : Browning becomes interested in that and other poems, and resolves to find her out. He has no clue to her except an acquaintance with her wealthy uncle, John Kenyon. He writes to John Kenyon, asking for an introduction. How was it then, madam ? "

Mrs. Carlyle.—" Mr. Kenyon was absent. As soon as he returned he wrote a note to Mr. Browning saying that his niece was a confirmed invalid—never saw anyone, nor left her couch—and that an introduction was impossible."

Carlyle.—" Ah yes—meanwhile Browning, hearing nothing from Kenyon, determined not to stop on ceremony, and went to Dr. Barrett's house. The servant man had been taking too much beer ; thought Browning a doctor, and admitted him. He went into the study where Miss Elizabeth was reclining. They had a conversation ; liked each other ; and she made arrangements for him to call again. He did so, and the spinal disease passed away ; the spell-bound princess was reached by her knight ; took up her bed and walked ; one day went all the way to Marylebone Church, where they were married. They could not face the angry father, and went to Italy. Kenyon supplied the money ; and when he died left them more. She was never suffered by her father to see him again—not even when he was dying. She caught sight of him through an open door. Now, madam, you may give the history in chronological order."

Whereupon Mrs. Carlyle did " dress up a few points," says Conway, and in the talk that followed declared she had tried to read *Sordello*, but could not tell whether Sordello was " a book, a city, or a man." Which might have reminded Conway of what he had heard ten years before from Lowell :—" I own a copy of *Sordello*, and anybody may have it who will lay his hand upon his heart and says he understands it."

Conway confesses he then said to Lowell,—" I have not read it, but what is it about ? "

Lowell answered, ' placing his hand over his heart,' " I don't know."

So Conway presently read *Sordello*, but he did not win Lowell's copy, he had to confess he ' found it obscure,' but he modestly attributed his failure to his ' ignorance of Italian history.'

XXIII

MILNES BECOMES A LORD
(1863)

THE 'republicanism' of 'Dicky' Milnes did not hinder him from accepting a peerage this summer. He did not buy it in the usual way, and confessed he took it as the token of " a half-success in life,—a second class in politics. . . . In this lord-loving country, one ought not to decline anything that helps to make other people listen to one."[1]

The day after the news came out, an old friend met him walking in Piccadilly and enquired,—" What does it feel like to be a lord ? "

" I never knew until to-day," replied the new peer, with twinkling eyes, " how immeasurable is the gulf which divides the humblest member of the peerage from the most exalted commoner in England."

" If you tell that story," said Tennyson afterwards to T. W. Reid, the recording angel of ' Dicky,' " every fool will think that Milnes meant it."

Carlyle called to congratulate him on it as " a thing we are all glad of and wish well to " ; but missing him when he called, he sent him a letter to that effect, which said,— " May the noble British peerage find you an honour and possession to it, and you *it* a ditto, ditto, to you ! "[1]

Which was very polite indeed, and not misunderstood by poor Monckton Milnes, who needed all the comfort he could get from his friends on the occasion. It clearly appears from a confidential letter of his in 1856,[2] when his father refused a peerage, that he now took one ' more for my wife and children's sake than for my own.' It was like taking a back seat for life in politics, and he had only turned fifty-four ; but it would rather help than hinder his philanthropic doings, promoting reformatories and so on, and the genial " Dicky " Milnes was always more of a philanthropist than a politician. There was another thing it is difficult to explain. The sale of peerages in England had for centuries

[1] *R. M. Milnes, Lord Houghton*, by T. Wemyss Reid, II, pp. 89–113.
[2] Ditto, p. 3.

past been one of the worst political scandals in Europe, and the acceptance of a peerage by the like of Milnes restored a little respectability to the " Upper House." It was a patriotic action. One of the best things told of him in his House of Commons days now ending was that the " Whip" of his party, Sir Thomas Freemantle, went up to him in the House of Commons and whispered, " Now, do try for once in your life, to make a speech in which you are not going to be candid."

Just before he changed his name, his biographer has something to report which gives us a glimpse into the house in Cheyne Row.[1]—' It had been his wish to entertain the Carlyles, Thackeray, and Spedding at Fryston during the Easter recess. The two latter came. But Carlyle was deep in his *Frederick* and sternly withstood the temptation.

'*Mrs. Carlyle to R.M.M.*

'CHEYNE ROW, *March* 19*th* (1863).

' MY DEAR MR. MILNES,
'It is no go! I was a fool to hope that anything so pleasant could get carried out, and the ghost of that old Prussian despot still unlaid. I have introduced the subject at every least inauspicious moment presenting itself since the night you were here, but every time with more determined ill-success.

' " It is such a distance !" " Well, what of an hour or two longer on the road when we are once started ? " " Oh ! Very easy for *you* to say that, who rather like railway travelling ; but for me, who hate it, a-bo-minate it, am driven *perfectly mad* by it, etc., etc., etc." And, in short, he thinks to give a week of his time at Easter, for the good of his health and the assuagement of his soul, would be a sort of schoolboy truant-playing unworthy of a historian ! And so may God help him ! And God particularly help *me !* For (in the words of an Annandale poet not sufficiently known to fame)

> " I'm a poor luckless cretur ;
> And if I were ded,
> And a stone at my hed,
> I think it would be beter."

' Yours affectionately anyhow,
' JANE W. CARLYLE.'

XXIV

AN AMERICAN ILIAD IN A NUTSHELL
(1863)

IN *Macmillan's Magazine* for August this year appeared a small parable signed T. C., and quickly reproduced in hundreds of newspapers.[1]

'ILIAS (AMERICANA) IN NUCE

'Peter of the North (to Paul of the South).—" Paul, you unaccountable scoundrel, I find you hire your servants for life, not by the month or year as I do ! You are going straight to Hell, you ——— ! "

'Paul.—" Good words, Peter ! The risk is my own ; I am willing to take the risk. Hire you your servants by the month or the day, and get straight to Heaven ; leave me to my own method."

'Peter.—" No, I won't. I will beat your brains out first ! " (*And is trying dreadfully ever since, but cannot yet manage it.*)—

'T. C.

'*3d May* 1863.'

To Emerson this seemed "unfortunate, but no more than could be expected." He said so afterwards to "an English literary gentleman,"[2] and explained that Carlyle "purposely made exaggerated statements, merely to astonish his listeners,"—which may be a mistake of Emerson's, due to his lack of a sense of humour.

According to the same reporter, Emerson went on to tell how Carlyle spoke of "a distinguished English poet" of the "fleshly school" in a way which seemed to the reporter "too hideous and scathing to be given in print." Decency of expression is often a screen for putrid thoughts and

---

[1] Printed in the Essays of Carlyle as a footnote to *Shooting Niagara : and After?*

[2] Ireland's *Emerson*, p. 293.

feelings. The reference may have been to the same unclean creature, not worth naming, who was sunk himself in vice, and set London laughing by criticising the *Frederick* of Carlyle as coarse and immoral!

The ' Iliad in a Nut-shell ' had unexpected consequences better known in America than in Europe. It concentrated attention on the slavery question as the real cause of the war. It was plainly intended to have the effect it certainly had of diminishing the danger of the war spreading. England would never think of making war in support of slavery.

XXV

SUMMER QUARTERS IN 1863

IN August, 1863, Mrs. Carlyle was writing to Lady Ashburton, dating merely ' Wednesday.'—

' You have seen children building card-houses, as eagerly as if it were houses to live in, and you have seen, at some push against the table, the *Houses* become a shower of cards. With just such an absurd suddenness and completeness, did your letter yesterday morning sweep down the schemes of travel, which Mr. C. and his Doctor-Brother had been building up, and hithering and thithering amongst, for the two preceding days—to say nothing of my own separate schemes (the fullest liberty to dispose of myself in Mr. C.'s projected absence, having been accorded me in the offer of " a draft to any amount you choose to specify ").

' We were sitting at breakfast, which, to judge from the look of the table, consisted mainly of pocket Maps and Bradshaws, with a supply of which my Brother in law *always* surrounds himself ; and for the twentieth time Dr. C. had just urged on Mr. C. that " say what he liked, to sail to *Jersey* would be the most feasable thing, *or* to *Denmark*." And Mr. C. had just detailed the superior advantages of " taking a look at Orkney and Shetland," or " perhaps better, after all, sail to Plymouth, and go on by land to Froude's ; tho' it *would* be a nicer thing a cruise round— the Western Isles ! ! ! " The only point of agreement between them being that they should start for *somewhere* tomorrow,—when your letter was brought in, which, when I had read it in silence, I handed to Mr. C. who, having read the first page, said quite simply—" Oh ! that is all right, we are going to the Grange, Sir." " And you won't sail anywhere ? " " Certainly not ! I tell you we are going to the Grange." I could hardly help laughing as the Dr. swept together, in an indignant manner, his aids to locomotion.

' " And will you afterwards go to Blickling on the 10th ? '
I asked. " Certainly not ! how am I to leave my work
again on the tenth ? " " Then what am I to say to Lady
Lothian ? You *promised* you know, and I must answer her
letter today." " Say ?—oh ! just say anything that is most
courteous ; only make it perfectly clear that we are not
coming." A pretty difficult problem, that combination.
And I had to *tell* we were going to the Grange. And the
Lady had politely written to me that if the tenth did not
suit us we might choose our own time earlier. I spent a
whole hour in poising and wriggling over the note to her,
and felt ashamed of it when written.

' For the rest, the important rest ; we will come on
Monday, if we hear nothing to the contrary. And I am
sure Mr. C. *means* to be very *good*, and not excite Lord
Ashburton with too much or too loud talk, or in any other
way. And if he *do*, in spite of his intentions, I will take
him away on the instant ; and I will take your orders in
every particular.

' Oh dear ! how glad I am to be going to the Grange
again after all. At one time I felt to hate the dear old place
in spite of all the good days I had spent at it, and all the kindness I had received there. You know when that time was.

' My fond remembrace to Baby. I wonder will she know
us again ?

' Yours loyally,

' JANE CARLYLE.'

So they went to the Grange for " three weeks of beautiful
green solitude," as Carlyle announced to Neuberg ; and
once there, he declared the silence " quasi-divine after such
a den of uproars " (as London), and said he had " a great
deal of brisk riding " in spite of rainy, thundery weather,
and " almost daily " work. The queries he sent to Neuberg
on 10.9.63 relate to matters now in the last book of the
Frederick, concluding volume VI as published ; but he was
still hoping to get everything into volume V.—" This last
portion of my Task, with Larkin and everybody falling
away, and my own poor strength on the edge of doing the
like, is generally horrible and frightful to me ;—and I very
much need a shove from one who has never yet wearied of
helping me."

XXVI

A STREET ACCIDENT TO MRS. CARLYLE
(1863)

ON Tuesday, 22nd September,[1] Mrs. Carlyle went to
have tea at the General Post Office with a widowed
cousin, who was a " matron " there. When she was departing and in the act of stepping from the pavement to
enter a bus which had stopped for her, a cab dashed between
her and the bus, and in avoiding it she fell heavily on the
left side, her weak arm being useless to break her fall. She
was lifted into a cab which took her home.

Aware that Carlyle would have returned from his ride
and be awaiting her upstairs, she sent her maid for Larkin
who was luckily at home next door. He found her on a
chair in the backroom on the ground floor, and plainly in
great pain. She said to him,—" Oh, Mr. Larkin, do get
me up into my own room before Mr. Carlyle knows anything
about it. He'll drive me mad if he comes in now." Easier
said than done ! Carlyle had heard the cab stop, and rung
to find out what was wrong. Getting " no clear answer,"
he rushed down, " looking terribly shocked," says Larkin.[2]
Together they carried her to her room, and in a few minutes
Dr. Barnes was beside her, doing all he could. The agony
of a sprained thigh was made worse by her all-round weakness and the pain all over, which doctors called neuralgia.
Carlyle seems to have supposed afterwards that the sinews
of the thigh had been torn, and that was possible. The
worst of her illness was her weakness. Her life was like a
fire whose fuel was nearly finished.

Next morning Larkin called in passing and was brought
to her bedside and found her ' full of thanks,' he tells us,
and saying,—" It'll be a great comfort to me if you'll come

[1] Exactly dated from an unpublished letter from T. C. on 27.9.1863
to J. Neuberg.
[2] H. Larkin's *Carlyle and Mrs. Carlyle, British Quarterly Review* (1881),
Vol. 74, pp. 76–77.

up every morning for five minutes. I know I'll often be
wanting some little thing done. It'll be something to look
forward to."

Date-able by the post-marks that day, 23.9.1863, there is a
shop-keeper's note about books that had been ordered, to say
that those not sent had been ' all sold.' Carlyle wrote below,
in sending on the letter ' For the Lady Ashburton to *know*,'
that what they were sending would be ' the *worst* of the
" six," most likely ; tho' I know not what the name of it
is ! ' Then he ran on.—' My poor wife had an ugly accident
yesterday ; in some crowded place, while getting into a
street vehicle too rapidly, *fell* on the curb-stone ; hurt her
left leg and side, and was brought home to me quite lame.
No bones broken, hip-joint *not* injured (as I feared) ; but
very great misery of pain ever since ;—and in short a bad
job for us, wh^h. we had no need of as things were. In a
day or two (the Dr. promises) it will be easier to bear.
' Hoping there is nothing wrong at the Grange !

' Yours ever,

' T. C.'

As Mrs. Carlyle had requested, Larkin was calling every
day, and ' carrying into effect many little arrangements for
her comfort,' including ' cords and appliances ' to make the
most of the one hand she could use. But she lay in bed for
months, and Larkin said afterwards, " I suppose no one
who really watched her ever thought to see her leave that
bed alive."[2]

According to Froude, the doctor and Mrs. Carlyle agreed
to hide from Carlyle how seriously she had been hurt, which
may well be only a Froudified report of some of Mrs. Carlyle's later talk. Omitting invented matter, it seems likely
to be true that Carlyle had not been told that his wife was
for the time disabled from shutting her mouth by the fall.
And so ' one morning he came into her room, and stood
looking at her, leaning on the mantel-piece. " Jane," he
said presently, " ye had better shut your mouth." She
tried to tell him she could not. " Jane," he began again,
" ye'll find yourself in a more compact and pious frame of
mind, if ye shut your mouth." In old-fashioned phraseology
he told her that she ought to be thankful that the accident
was no worse. " Thankful ! " she said to him ; " thankful
for what ? For having been thrown down in the street
when I had gone on an errand of charity ? for being

2 M

disabled, crushed, made to suffer in this way ?   I am not
thankful, and I will not say that I am." He left her, saying
he was sorry to see her so rebellious.' He had to tell his
brother (Dr. John) she ' did not accept him as a sick nurse,'
and one of the best servants she ever had, and who came
to her in July next year, Jessie Hiddlestone,[3] said in effect[4]
that she was sure to bid him " shut up yourself," or say
something to that effect.   " She was a petted and spoiled
wife, if ever there was one," was the verdict of Jessie.[4]

" Oh, what a sea of agony my Darling was immersed in,'
wrote he in the *Reminiscences*, ' and had to plunge and toss
and desperately struggle in, month after month ! Sleep
had fled.   A hideous pain of which she used to say that
" common honest pain, were it cutting of one's flesh or
sawing of one's bones, would be a luxury in comparison,"—
seemed to have begirdled her, at all moments and on every
side.   Her intellect was clear as starlight, and continued
so ; the clearest *intellect* among us all ; but she dreaded
that this too must give way.   " Dear," she said to me, on
two occasions, with such a look and tone as I shall never
forget, " *promise* me that you will not put me into a madhouse, however this go.   Do you *promise* me, now ? "   I
solemnly did.   " Not if I do quite lose my wits ? "   " Never,
my Darling ; oh compose thy poor terrified heart ! "
' Another time, she punctually directed me about her
burial ; how her poor bits of possessions were to be distributed, this to one friend, that to another (in help of their
necessities, for it was the *poor* sort she had chosen, old
indigent Haddington figures),—what employment in the
solitary night watches, on her bed of pain : ah me, ah
me ! '

[3] Jessie Hiddlestone, afterwards Mrs. Broadfoot of Thornhill.   See
New Letters and Memorials of Jane Welsh Carlyle, edited by Alexander
Carlyle and Sir James Crichton-Browne, II, pp. 276–7, and footnote.
Also see *Mrs. Carlyle and Her Housemaid*, by Reginald Blunt, *Cornhill
Magazine*, October, 1901, pp. 456–467.
[4] To D. A. W.

XXVII

" FREDERICK " GROWING
(1863)

I NSTEAD of being "huddled up at the end," as some have
said, *Frederick* was growing and growing far beyond what
was intended. Writing it was like climbing mountains,—
"hills peep o'er hills and Alps on Alps arise." In October,
1863, the help of Neuberg was needed most in preparing
Volume IV for the printer. The man employed to copy
(a young Mr. Bishop) was willing and docile, but had to
be told not to copy where he could not see the meaning.
Till Neuberg took him in hand, he was an affliction. Carlyle
was cautious not " to affront " him, and bade Neuberg pay
him well :—" Compute liberally what he can expect of pay
(the worth of him to me is not the question)." . . . When
that part was done, Carlyle wrote to Neuberg (12.11.63) :—

' I have at length got through that frightful mass of
" copy." . . . Your hand was very visible. . . . The poor
lad too had done his best :—on the whole, he teaches me
what use I had of old in *your* " copying " services (which
were a partial *editing* withal), and how *un*replaceable these
are. Which, I think, will lead me to *avoid copying* altogether
for the future !—
' I begin to have a frightful suspicion, almost conviction,
that the *7-Years-War* being done, there will be a *Volume VI*
needed, instead of a Book 20 (i.e. instead of concluding with
Book XX and Vol. V, we'll need a Book XXI and Volume
VI). Horrible is the thought to me. But I fear there is no
help.—Come on Sunday.'
The Book XXI thus reluctantly undertaken, 1763–1786,
is perhaps the most instructive part of the history, and to-
day the most interesting part of that book may be the
account of Miller Arnold's Lawsuit. What that lawsuit
teaches us is the need for the Executive Government,
whatever its shape or name, to keep the law-courts efficient.
Our present English arrangement gives us, in the House of
Lords or Privy Council Court, the most expensive and least
efficient Court of Appeal in the whole world.

XXVIII

LAST GLIMPSE OF THACKERAY
(1863)

IN the gray dusk of a winter afternoon, a few days before
Christmas, 1863, Thackeray was driving with his daughter
in Hyde Park, and saw Carlyle riding along by the Serpentine, and " threw him a shower of salutations." Carlyle
looked up and recognised them, and returned the greetings.[1]
Thackeray had recovered from a serious illness and was
feeling well again. He was doubtless " cheerful and bright,"
as Dickens saw him to be soon afterwards, when they passed
each other on the steps of the Athenæum Club. They
passed in silence, having had a row some years before which
terminated conversation. But on this occasion, Thackeray
turned and held out his hand to Dickens, saying he could
no longer bear to be on any but the old terms of friendship,
and they shook hands and were friends again, to the delight
of Theodore Martin looking on.[2]

A few days later, on Christmas Eve, 24.12.1863, Thackeray
was found in the morning dead in his bed, and on 29.12.63
Carlyle was writing to Milnes, and telling of his last sight
of Thackeray, adding,—" He had many fine qualities, no
guile or malice against any mortal ; a big mass of a soul,
but not strong in proportion ; a beautiful vein of genius
lay struggling about in him. Nobody in our day wrote, I
should say, with such perfection of style. Poor Thackeray !
—adieu ! adieu ! "

Moncure Conway was surprised to hear that Thackeray
was only fifty-two,—' his hair was so white that I supposed
him old ' ; and he tells us that Carlyle described to him now
how Thackeray with " urgent work on hand, escaped from

---

[1] *R. M. Milnes, Lord Houghton*, by T. Wemyss Reid, II, p. 113.
[2] *W. M. Thackeray*, by L. Melville, II, pp. 64–68.

invitations, callers and letters, and went off from his house
without leaving any address.   One night a messenger came
to me," added Carlyle, " from a public-house near by with
a request from Thackeray for the loan of a Bible."[3]—

[3] *Autobiography of Moncure D. Conway*, II, pp. 4 and 5.

XXIX

STRANGERS ONE REMEMBERS
(1863)

ON 28.12.1863 Carlyle was writing to Neuberg and
mentioning a passing German gentleman who had
sent him a long letter in ' cursiv-schrift ' or running hand,
which ' I cannot read,' he said, ' not in less than two hours
which I have not to spare for it.' He must have looked
into it, however, for in sending it to Neuberg for disposal
he enclosed a note for the Director of the National Portrait
Gallery, which was all the stranger needed, and in the note
to Neuberg are some words which may keep his memory
green.—' I do not know Otto ' . . . (the rest of the name is
not readable). ' I know only the face of him—which is the
image of a cock's, and quite unlovely to me.'

One seems to know that man, tho his name is indecipher-
able.

In the meanwhile the invalid, Mrs. Carlyle, was having
a little excitement to beguile the time in bed. What her
husband wrote about it is still worth reading.—' One scene
with a Catholic sick-nurse I also remember well. A year
or two before this time, she had gone with some acquaintance
who was in quest of sick-nurses to an establishment under
Catholic auspices, in Brompton somewhere (the acquaintance, a Protestant herself, expressing her " certain knowledge " that this Catholic was the one good kind) ;—where
accordingly the aspect of matters, and especially the manner
of the old French lady who was matron and manager, produced such a favourable impression, that I recollect my
little Woman saying, " If I need a sick-nurse, that is the
place I will apply at."

' Appliance was now made ; a nun duly sent, in consequence :—this was in the early weeks of the illness. The
nurse was a good-natured young Irish nun ; with a good

deal of brogue, a tolerable share of blarney too, all varnished
to the due extent ; and, for three nights or so, she answered
very well.

' On the fourth night, to our surprise, though we found
afterwards it was the common usage, there appeared a new
Nun ; new and very different,—an *elderly* French *young
lady*, with broken English enough for her occasions, and a
look of rigid earnestness, in fact, with the air of a life broken
down into settled despondency, and abandonment of all
hope that was not *ultra*-secular. An unfavourable change ;
—though the poor lady seemed intelligent, well-intentioned ;
and her heart-broken aspect inspired pity and good-wishes,
if no attraction. She commenced by rather ostentatious
performance of her nocturnal Prayers, " *Beata Maria*," or
I know not what other Latin stuff ; which her poor Patient
regarded with great vigilance, though still with what
charity and tolerance were possible. " You won't understand what I am saying or doing," said the Nun ; " Don't
mind me." " Perhaps I understand it better than yourself," said the other (who had *Latin* from of old), and did
" mind " more than was expected.

' The dreary hours, no sleep, as usual, went on ; and we
heard nothing,—till about three a.m. I was awakened (I,
what never happened before or after, though my door was
always left slightly ajar, and I was right above), (usually a
deep sleeper),—awakened by a vehement continuous ringing
of my poor Darling's bell. I flung on my dressing-gown,
awoke Maggie by a word, and hurried down. " Put away
that woman ! " cried my poor Jeannie vehemently ; " away,
not to come back ! " I opened the door into the drawing-
room ; pointed to the sofa there, which had wraps and
pillows plenty ; and the poor Nun at once withdrew, looking
and murmuring her regrets and apologies.

' " What was she doing to thee, my own poor little
Woman ? " No very distinct answer was to be had ; but
I learned in general, that during the heavy hours loaded,
every moment of them, with its misery, the Nun had
gradually come forward with ghostly consolations, ill
received, no doubt ; and at length, with something more
express, about " Blessed Virgin," " *Agnus Dei*," or whatever it might be ; to which the answer had been : " Hold
your tongue, I tell you : or I will ring the bell ! " Upon
which the Nun had rushed forward with her dreadfullest
supernal admonitions, " *im*penitent sinner," etc., and a

practical attempt to *prevent* the ringing.   Which only made it the more immediate and more decisive.

' The poor woman expressed to Miss Welsh much regret, disappointment, real vexation and self-blame ; lay silent, after that, amid her rugs ; and disappeared, next morning, in a polite and soft manner : never to reäppear, she or any consort of hers.   I was really sorry for this heavy-laden, pious or quasi-pious and almost broken-hearted French-woman,—though we could perceive she was under the foul tutelage and guidance, probably, of some dirty muddy-minded semi-*felonious* Proselytising Irish Priest :—but there was no help for her, in this instance ; probably, in all England, she could not have found an agonised human soul more nobly and hopelessly superior to her and her poisoned-ginger-bread " consolations."—This incident threw suddenly a glare of strange and far from pleasant light over the sublime Popish " Sisters of Charity " movement ;—and none of us had the least notion to apply there henceforth.'

Carlyle's letters to his sister Jean and to his brother Dr. John let us know that in December Dr. Quain and also Dr. Blakiston from Hastings and Dr. Barnes were all agreed that there was nothing the matter with Mrs. Carlyle except Neuralgia.   Old age was understood, and did not need to be mentioned.   She was weaker at 62 than many who are much older.

XXX

REPORTS OF THE REV. GAVIN CARLYLE, &c.
(1863–64)

IN newspaper articles the Rev. Gavin Carlyle gave a
credible report of some private talks, with no date
mentioned but the winter of 1863-4, tho part of what he
tells may have been before or after that.[1] He was himself
a namesake rather than a kinsman. None of Carlyle's near
relatives were professional Christians.[2]

In describing to the Rev. Gavin a theological professor,
whose " dryasdust " lectures had afflicted him in his student
days, Carlyle said,—" He had a face like the setting sun on
a misty day. Such a man speaking of the ethereal and the
heavenly ! " If the Rev. Gavin is not mistaken, Carlyle
' utterly abhorred the clergy who predominated before the
evangelical enthusiasm of Chalmers,' and said,—" Many of
them took no interest in religion. Many were almost sots."
They were " low and degraded, with some noble exceptions,
(such) as Duncan of Ruthwell." The Rev. Gavin may have
been showing his candour by admitting the sins of his pre-
decessors, and Carlyle mentioned Duncan. The once famous
' Jupiter ' Carlyle of Inveresk was expressly disesteemed.

Dr. Hodge of Richmond, America, came to visit England
this winter, while the civil war was going on ; and being
anxious for an interview, applied to the Rev. Gavin, who
took him down and introduced him. Carlyle ' became the
hearer, listened with intense interest, his eyes filled with
tears,' while Dr. Hodge ' described the scenes of the war
through which he had just passed, and told with great simplicity the influence of passages of scripture quoted to the
dying as they were passing away. When he finished,

---

[1] Newspaper articles, preserved in cuttings, and lent to D. A. W. by
Robert Cochrane, a retired editor of *Chambers' Journal*.

[2] In 1895 one of his sisters, Mrs. Hanning in Canada, said to D. A. W.
that the nearest such relative he ever had was one of her sons-in-law, a
clergyman.

Carlyle said,—" The sending of Bibles to these soldiers was the noblest work I have ever heard of the Bible society doing."

One night the Rev. Gavin was walking with Carlyle down Sloane Street from Dr. John Carlyle's lodgings to Cheyne Row, when Carlyle began to speak of Holman Hunt's picture of " Christ before the Doctors " (or the Finding of Christ in the Temple). ' He had just seen it and been much pleased with it, especially with the wonderful life-like feelings described in the faces of the doctors of the law,' but ' suddenly turned and said in effect,—" I dislike all pictures of Christ. You will find that men never thought of painting Christ till they had begun to lose the impression of Him in their hearts." ' He then appealed to history, and indeed it is now one of the settled points in the history of the Church that all the pictures of Christ are imaginary, and long subsequent to primitive times.

At the houses of the Ashburtons and Milnes, G. S. Venables had heard perhaps more of Carlyle's talk than almost any of his contemporaries. Here is something which he is credibly reported to have told.[3]—Carlyle ' had a stereoscopic imagination ; he put everything before you in a solid shape. . . . I was walking with him one day near Fryston (and he) said as a train rushed by, (the afternoon train taking the big business men of smoky Leeds to their homes in the country),—' " There is the great God of Leeds going home." '

[3] *Notes from a Diary*, by Sir M. E. Grant Duff, II, pp. 300–2.

XXXI

THE END IN SIGHT
(1864)

THROUGH 1864 the work was boiling, and coming to a conclusion. Volume IV came out soon after the year began. Volumes V and VI (the last) were nearly ready when it ended. He afterwards lamented he had been so engrossed when his wife was ill from the shock of her street accident, which kept her an invalid most of the year ; but at the time he felt differently, perhaps more wisely. On 9.1.1864 he was writing to Neuberg.—

' DEAR NEUBERG,
' There is still no visible improvement here ; and we are in great confusion and distress, the very sight of such misery a constant pain. My printers have begun again ; and will perhaps keep me closer at work ; which is the one consolation left to me,—could I get forward even with *it*. Vol. VI threatens to be as tough *a fight with chaos* as any. " To it ; get done with it ! " there is no other remedy.
' I have got your Mecklenburg-Strelitz Pamphlet ;— I have also got a pretty bit of *excerpting* &c. for you to do for me : plenty of that now and coming ! If you will stand true (as I know you will) to the end of this Vol. VI,—I promise you immunity for the rest of my life.
' Come on Sunday evening at any rate.
' Yours always truly,
' T. CARLYLE.'

A few days later he added to another *Frederick* letter to Neuberg.—

' We are in profound misery here ;—I cannot for my life *understand* in what degree of *danger* :—but the suffering itself is heartbreaking. The Fates are not kind to me in these months. Ah me ! '

The doctors were now advising a " change of scene " for
Mrs. Carlyle, and she decided to accept the invitation of
Mrs. Blakiston at St. Leonards. Mrs. Blakiston had been
" Bessy Barnet," her young servant at Cheyne Row thirty
years before, ' servant and friend both in one,' Carlyle said,
daughter of the Mrs. Barnet who had been housekeeper to
Badams, when Carlyle stayed long with Badams at Birmingham in 1824, in the desperate hope of being cured of
dyspepsia. Bessy was now the wife of Dr. Blakiston at
St. Leonards, and in his name and her own persuaded her
old friend and mistress to come and stay with them for
treatment.

So on a wet and windy day in the first week of March,
a new-fashioned railway " invalid-carriage " came to the
door. " This time," said Mrs. Carlyle to Larkin, " I have
insisted on Carlyle keeping out of the way till I am safe in
the carriage. I don't think you'll find me very heavy."[1]
Indeed he was " literally appalled " to feel how light she
had become, like " a child of twelve years old."[1] Carlyle
was at the room door as they ' glided past,' and by order
waited inside till sent for, and so was spared the ' stifled
shriek ' his wife gave when she saw herself about to be slid
into what looked like a hearse, feet first. Her cousin
Maggie Welsh was soon sitting beside her, and in a few
hours her husband was watching her being carried ' up
Blakiston's long stairs at St. Leonards. He came home by
the last train that night. Maggie Welsh remained to assist
Mrs. Blakiston in nursing, and when by-and-by she had to
go home, Mary Craik came from Belfast to do so in her
stead, and Carlyle came often from London to see them.

[1] H. Larkin's *Carlyle and Mrs. Carlyle, British Quarterly Review* (1881),
Vol. 74, pp. 77–8.

XXXII

LORD ASHBURTON'S LEGACY
(1864)

BEFORE the end of March, Lord Ashburton died, and Mrs. Carlyle wrote at once to his young widow from Dr. Blakiston's house,—' Oh my Darling, my Darling, I have only been told now—the Drs. ordered it should be kept from me till this morning. Oh God comfort you. If ever there was a Man ready to pass from this sorrowful Earth to be an Angel in Heaven, it was he.

' My spirit flies to your dear side, while my poor body is chained here with a cruel malady that *I* believe will prove fatal, tho' the Drs. hold out hopes still. Oh God ! it is among the few things for which I pray to be spared in life a little longer, this that I might prove to you my love and gratitude. Oh do not forget me and may your kindness to me help to warm your own sad heart.

' Ever your affectionate,
' JANE CARLYLE.'

Lord Ashburton had left Carlyle a legacy of two thousand pounds, to be paid free of legacy duty ; and he gave it all away, not loosely or at once, but in sums that varied from ten shillings to fifty pounds, to deserving persons who had no claim upon him but pity. As each payment was made, he noted it in an account book, and is occasionally reported to have said in giving the money,—" Here is something from a fund I am trustee for." After the last entry, he wrote,— " This is the end." The account was not meant to be kept ; but it came with other papers into the hands of his niece, and was preserved by her.[1] Carlyle was habitually careful to avoid mention of anything he gave in charity.

---

[1] Told to D. A. W. on 3.1.1917 by the niece's husband, Alexander Carlyle, who still had the book and was willing to show it, and allow the fact of its existence to be told.

XXXIII

AT ST. LEONARDS
(1864)

MRS. CARLYLE was prospering at St. Leonards under
the care of Dr. Blakiston, tho the doctor had
candidly remarked to Carlyle—" I can do nothing against
hysterical mania." But she was wearying for more of her
husband's company. Here are two of her letters to him.

19.4.64. ' It is no "morbid despondency"; it is a
positive physical torment day and night—a burning,
throbbing, maddening sensation in the most nervous part
of me ever and ever. How be in good spirits or have any
hope but to die! When I spoke of going home, it was to
die there; here were the place for *living*, if one could! It
was not my wish to leave here. It was the Blakistons' own
suggestion and wish that we should get a little house of our
own.

' Oh, have pity on me! I am worse than ever I was in
that terrible malady.
' I am,
' Yours as ever,
' JANE CARLYLE.'

25.4.64.—' Oh, my husband! I am suffering torments!
Each day I suffer more horribly. Oh, I would like you
beside me! I am terribly alone. But I don't want to
interrupt your work. I will wait till we are in our own
hired house; and then, if I am no better, you must come
for a day.
' Your own wretched J.W.C.'

As explained by the doctors, the malady was ' in her
womb, some nervous derangement,' attributed to the
street accident last September. A suitable house was now
rented for her, and she moved into it on 28.4.64, and bade

her husband prepare to come and occupy a room that would be ready for him there on Saturday, 14.5.64. On 9.5.64, the Monday before then, he was writing to Neuberg :

' I am packing up my *tools* (a thing I never *tried* before, and find to be like a *Friedrich Campaign*, in a sort), my tools and goods ; settling with laggard Printers, laggard etceteras of all kinds ; and very miserable in my weak flurry and want of skin. God help me to get through this Book *in opposition to the whole World and the Devil to back, as it often seems to me.*'

Details of *Frederick* work follow, concluding in terms which show how little this exclamation was literal.

' I wish much you would make a serious effort, and actually *get* me (without delay, or as fast as the *Post* can bring it) an *authentic* reasonable Book on (Kaiser) Joseph (references given, etc.). After the endless favours you have done my Task and me, this is one still possible ! Write to some intelligent man in Germany (explaining as *you* can) :—if you know none better, T. Wilson is back to Weimar again ; let him consult the scientific-historisch oracles at Weimar (in my name and Allah's), and dispatch by Post (if possible in a sewed condition) the *money*, for which shall be a small matter to me !

> ' Yours always,
> ' T. CARLYLE.'

Neuberg never failed. He was helping Carlyle this year more than ever, from making summaries about ' Miller Arnold's Lawsuit ' and the ' Second Prussian Law-Reform,"[1] down to bargaining for a brougham and a horse for Mrs. Carlyle. Four days after Carlyle was settled at St. Leonards, the book he begged Neuberg to get was with him (18.5.64), and Larkin was ready to send any book he found he needed but had left at home. Larkin also was doing his best, and tho about to shift his home to Camden Town, he seems to have been working now for Carlyle harder than ever. As a convenience to both, he had brought his family to live in the Carlyles' house while it was vacant.

So the work never stopped and the printers had never to wait for copy.

Indeed it appears possible that the change to St. Leonards rather helped than hindered Carlyle, for a morning walk

[1] T. C.'s *Frederick*, Book XXI, Chapter VII.

and a swim in the sea were better for his sleep than a walk
on Chelsea Embankment ; and he was enjoying the clear
sky he loved, ' every morning, miraculous to London eyes,'
and the long ' rides by shore and silent lanes white with
hawthorn, all beautiful.'[2]

He tried to persuade Neuberg to come there and join him
in the rides. His brother Dr. John came and joined in the
morning swims, and was at hand to be useful to Mrs.
Carlyle. After a talk with her and an early breakfast,
Carlyle was at his desk, with occasional short pauses for
refreshment, till four o'clock, when he was due to join his
wife in her last drive for the day (4 to 5.30). After which
he had Noggs for exercise, exploring all around from
Winchelsea to Beachy Head and far inland, remembering
whatever he could of the glimpses of the past in history
books. Did that old yew see Cæsar ? Hardly ! While now
sending Larkin material for battle-plans in the *Frederick*,
he was looking with a soldier's eye on the ground he was
riding over in all directions, and fancied he could spot the
strategy of ' the Harold-William duel at Hastings.' Why
has nobody yet taken the trouble to disentangle it ? he
asked himself,—needlessly. Battles cease to be interesting
soon after they finish ; and as Wellington tried in vain to
convince Walter Scott, the whole truth never is nor can be
told about any of them.

[2] *Thomas Woolner*, by Amy Woolner, pp. 247–8 (31.5.64).

XXXIV

WOOLNER'S WEDDING
(1864)

MANY young friends of Carlyle were well aware that he "approved of marriage." In one case at least, of which publication is not permissible,[1] he interceded successfully with two angry fathers on behalf of young people who had "married rashly." Here is a letter[2] which illustrates his way of feeling about that, and gives a glimpse of life at St. Leonards.

'117, MARINA,
 'ST. LEONARDS-ON-SEA,
   June 11, 1864.

'DEAR WOOLNER,

'Your letter from The Grange, last Sunday, was naturally very interesting to us ! My poor Wife is still too weak for writing, almost ever : but both she and I, and she bids me say so, are delighted to hear of your getting an eligible young Wife,—which we are aware is the crown and keystone of all comfortable *Housekeeping*, and expect will be a very great improvement to you, in that and all other respects. Solomon said long ago, " He that getteth a good wife, getteth a good thing " ; and I never heard anybody contradict him,—nor will I myself, by a long way !

'In early times I used to hear a great deal of your fair Bride's Grandfather ; " Dr. Waugh," oracle of all Scotchmen in that strange London, and much talked of at home among the Dissenting Religious Circles ;—an excellent reasonable solid kind of man, I do still understand. Whom if a certain Young Person resemble, it will be well with her and Another ! Very seriously we wish, to her and to you, all manner of prosperity, and a fortunate and useful life together.

[1] Told to D. A. W. by a prosperous old lady, who had been the bride concerned, but without express permission to publish details.
[2] *Thomas Woolner, R.A.*, by Amy Woolner, pp. 249–50.

' We still imagine there is improvement visible here from week to week,—at least I do, rather more and not *less* confidently as we go on ; and am for my own share at length got thoroughly busy again ; which is an immense point in my favour. Everything is lovely exceedingly in these green environs, in this bright sea and sky ;—and, till July unkennel London on it, the place is nearly empty of foreign guests. Except indeed a few Gipsies, squatted comfortably in some woody bank, on one's evening ride.

' Yours ever truly (tho' in haste),

' T. CARLYLE.'

The words of Solomon were in Proverbs, xviii, 22,— ' Whoso findeth a wife findeth a good thing,'—a much wider statement than Carlyle's. The variation may have been merely a slip of memory.

XXXV

MARY CRAIK AS THE PERFECT HOUSEKEEPER
(1864)

B Y Sunday evening, 3rd July, Carlyle was able to let Neuberg know his wife's chief ailment was only " that old cause," want of sleep.—" The Doctors happily have left us, however ; she herself quite sick of them : *there is now nothing but the disease to struggle with.* I still keep hoping, hoping." The disease he meant was sleeplessness.

Nine days later she took a sudden resolution to go north, and escorted by Dr. John Carlyle went first to London (12.7.64), and then to Carlisle and the Gill,[1] Dumfriesshire ; and thence to Thornhill, to stay at Dr. Russell's, with her friend Mrs. Russell. Carlyle returned home to Chelsea as soon as possible ; and in a very brotherly way tried to persuade Neuberg to use the house he was vacating, but had to pay for till the end of the month.—" Say Yes, if you will have a swish of sea-bathing, all of you, and do me a favour ! "

He hurried home to Chelsea himself, and from then the work went rushing forward, as if with the increasing speed of a falling stone.

In Mrs. Carlyle's absence the ministering angel in the house was Mary Craik, the daughter of their old friend, now Professor Craik at Belfast. She it was who had the home at Cheyne Row re-adjusted for Carlyle. " She has been perfect," he reported. On Monday evening, 25.7.64, as she was about to go home, she instructed him how much to pay the poulterer and others, and what to pay on future Mondays, and he gave her a cheque for herself. She was not hired, but ought to be paid, and was more than satisfied, " protesting it was too etc. etc. but all in a modest natural way."

Next morning at eight she " stole out softly as a dream." He heard her, being awake and smoking, but said nothing.

[1] A farm near Ruthwell, between Annan and Dumfries, where one of Carlyle's sisters lived.

XXXVI

A COUNTRY DOCTOR versus A GREAT CONSULTANT
(1864)

CARLYLE sent his wife details of household history to keep her mind at ease, and he confirmed her in her faith in Dr. Russell. Long after both had passed away, some of the words he wrote appeared in many newspapers, to the joy of common doctors and the dismay of fashionable consultants, tho one of the best of the consulting doctors then alive[1] declared he was right.—This did not hinder his colleagues being offended. The rascal judges who maintained that " the greater the truth is, the greater the libel," were like other rascals in holding that opinion. Carlyle wrote to his wife now, when she was in the house of her friend Mrs. Russell, the wife of Dr. Russell, Thornhill.—

' I think with you of Dr. Russell, that his advice is probably worth *more* than that of all the doctors you have yet had. A sound-headed, honest-hearted man, passing his life in silent company with *facts*, earnestly studying Disease at a thousand *bedsides*, with an eye only to knowing and helping it—what a different man from one, or from a thousand ones, who are always " on the stage," and have no time to think of anything except of claptrap, and how they shall get a reputation in a totally stupid world ! I beg him very much to survey and investigate your case, and throw what light on it he can. *Darkness* he will not throw on it ; I suppose there is but little " light " except what our own common sense might lead us to. " Time and the hours," which wear out the roughest day, are what I have looked to from the first.'

---

[1] 1890, Dr. Samson Gemmell, Professor, Glasgow University. It was he who in 1882 persuaded D. A. W. to read Carlyle's works at length.

XXXVII

THE SABBATH SUPERSTITION
(1864)

WORRIED by anxiety about his wife, Carlyle was irritated by the Sabbath interruption of letters, then more complete than now, and wrote to her :—' What a blessed course of religious industry is that of Scotland, to guard against letters coming or going so many days every month. The seventh day, fourth part of a lunation ; that is the real fact it all rests on ; and such a hubbub made of it by the vile flunkey souls who call themselves special worshippers of the Most High. Mumbo Jumbo on the coast of Guinea almost seems a shade more respectable.' Two years before a similar provocation had made him reflect :—' Truly that Phariseean Sabbath and mode of disarming Almighty wrath by something better than the *secret pour lui plaire* is getting quite odious to me, or inconvenient rather, for it has long been odious enough.'

In Scotland as elsewhere, orthodox Christianity was fossilising, and becoming an unpleasant sight to eyes that could see. But in general Carlyle kept his thoughts to himself, and seems never to have hurt anyone's feelings by betraying impatience with the Sabbath-keeping of others. He had no objection to the weekly holiday, but only, like Luther, disliked the superstition which made a fetish of it. Before the end of August, 1864, he was writing to his wife :— ' The blessed silence of Sabbath. Nobody loves his Sabbath as I do. There is something quite divine to me in that cessation of barrel organs, pianos, tumults and jumblings. I easily do a better day's work than on any other day of the seven ; and, if left alone, have a solemn kind of sadness, a gloom of mind which, though heavy to bear, is not unallied with sacredness and blessedness.'

This is the sort of thing that makes Carlyle perplexing to fanatics of every fashion. We love a genius like the one in the Arabian story, who could swell in smoke to the skies, and yet be corked in a bottle. Carlyle can never be corked into any formula.

552 FINISHING THE "FREDERICK"

so patient, 'too little,' said I. 'You are the right thing of the sort,' said he.

XXXVIII

IN THE CARE OF DR. RUSSELL, &c.
(1864)

THE most Carlyle could do for his wife was to humour
her and incite Dr. Russell and Dr. Carlyle to do likewise, suggesting to treat her " as a creature *without skin.*"
" It would not do," might be the verdict of a Female
Rhadamanthus, after perusing all the surviving letters,
" to say Carlyle was perfect, for no woman should flatter
men by allowing that any husband can be perfectly satisfactory. But he should be admired and imitated. He
humoured her every whim when she was ill, and let her be
as ill as she liked whenever she wanted. He believed or
at least accepted all she said, and allowed her to be dictator
inside their house, requiring no more than leave to live and
work, which is all a man should want. His patience was
greater than Job's; but needed no pity. He was quite
content with her, and it would be an impertinence to
discuss them if that fool of a Froude had not made a theory
in his head and buttressed it by snatching sentences that
seemed to fit in. Any jury of maids or matrons, any woman
of sense, can see Mrs. Carlyle was a petted wife. If Froude
had really read the letters candidly, he could not have failed
to see it himself."

As usual when they were not together, they were now
corresponding in great detail. Thus Carlyle was writing to
her, 25.8.64.—
' The girls are raging and scrubbing; the curtains all
on the ropes in the garden. Cat, with miniature black
likeness of herself, contemplatively wandering among the
skirts of them. Not a mouse stirring! Oh dear! I wish
my Goody was back, but I won't be impatient. Oh, no,
no; as long as I hear of her getting inch by inch into her
old self again.

' 29–30.8.64.—Poor little soul! You are the helm, intellect of the house. Nobody else has the least skill in steering. My poor scissors, for example, you would find them in perhaps five minutes. Nobody else I think will in five months. " Nowhere to be found, sir." " Can't find them," say they, as so many rabbits or blue-bottle flies might.

' 20.9.64.—You are evidently suffering much. I cannot help you at all. The only thing I can do is to wish for you here again, such as you are; quiet in your own chimney-nook where it would be new life to me to see you sitting, never so lame if not quite too miserable and not in pain *un*endurable. Endurable or not, we two, and not any other body, are the natural bearers of it. Of myself there is nothing to record, but a gallop of excellence yesterday, an evening to myself altogether, almost incapable, not quite, and a walk under the shining skies between twelve and one a.m. The weather is as beautiful as it can be. Silent strangely when the infernal cockneyisms sink away—so silent, brilliant, sad, that I was like to greet (shed tears) looking at it.

" 22.9.64.—I had the pain of *excluding* poor Farie last night. I knew his rap and indeed was peremptory before that. " Nobody ! " But Farie really wishes well to both of us. . . . And Farie's withdrawing footsteps had a kind of sadness.'

He would receive on 29.9.64 this letter from her.—

' HOLM HILL,
Wednesday, September 28, 1864.

' Again a night absolutely sleepless, except for a little dozing between six and seven. There were no shooting pains to keep me awake last night, although I felt terribly chill, in spite of a heap of blankets that kept me in a sweat ; but it was a cold sweat. I am very wretched to-day. Dr. Russell handed me the other night a medical book he was reading, open at the chapter on " Neuralgia " that I might read, for my practical information, a list of " counter-irritants."

' I read a sentence or two more than was meant, ending with " this lady was bent on self-destruction." You may think it a strange comfort, but it was a sort of comfort to me to find that my dreadful wretchedness was a not uncommon feature of my disease, and not merely an expression of individual cowardice.

' Another strange comfort I take to myself under the present pressure of horrible nights. If I had continued up to now to feel as much better as I did in the first weeks of my stay here, I should have dreaded the return to London as a sort of suicide. Now I again want a change—even that change ! There lies a possibility, at least, of benefit in it ; which I could not have admitted to myself had all gone on here as in the beginning.

' I am very sorry for Lady Ashburton, am afraid her health is irretrievably ruined. Pray do write her a few lines.

' It has been a chill mist from the water all the morning, but the sun is trying to break through.

' God send me safe back to you, such as I am.

' Ever yours,
' J. W. C.'

On 29.9.64 he was answering.—' Oh, my suffering little Jeannie ! Not a wink of real sleep again for you. . . . And yet, dearest, *there is something in your note which is welcomer to me than anything I have yet had—a sound of PIETY, of devout humiliation and gentle hope and submission to the Highest, which affects me much and has been a great comfort to me. Yes, poor darling ! This was wanted. Proud stoicism you never failed in, nor do I want you to abate of it. But there is something beyond of which I believe you to have had too little. It softens the angry heart and is far from weakening it —nay, is the final strength of it, the fountain and nourishment of all real strength.*[1] Come home to your own poor nest again. How to thank Dr. and Mrs. Russell for what they have done for you, much more how to repay them beats all my ingenuity.'

On Saturday, 1.10.64, Dr. John Carlyle brought her home, and as her husband afterwards remembered,—' A faint, kind timid smile was on her face, as if afraid to believe fully ; but the despair had vanished from her looks altogether,' and she ' continued to prosper ; and in spite of utter weakness, her life to the very end continued beautiful and hopeful to both of us—to me more beautiful than I had ever seen it in her best days. Strange and precious to look back upon ' were ' her last eighteen months, now beginning, as of a second youth (almost a second

[1]   Italics added.

childhood with the wisdom and graces of old age), which by Heaven's great mercy were conceded her and me.   In essentials never had she been so beautiful to me ; never in my time been so happy.'

In England then people were addicted to kissing, or as we called it in Scotland, slobbering, and a letter Mrs. Carlyle sent on 9.10.64 to Mrs. Austin, her husband's sister, living at the Gill,—the same to whom she had hurried in July,— described the English fashion as a kind of joke.—' I arrived quite safe, and the dreaded moment of re-entering a house, which I had left in a sort of hearse, with a firm conviction of returning no more, was tumbled head over heels by Mr. C. rushing out into the street to meet me, in his dressing-gown and in violent agitation.—John had given him reason to expect us an hour and half earlier.   He had been momentarily expecting a telegram to say I had died on the road.

' I got a heavenly sleep the first night after my return. I have slept every night since, rather better than I was doing at Holm Hill (Dr. Russell's).   For the rest I have been wonderfully well.   Everybody is astonished at me, and so glad and kind,—especially the men.   I remarked to Mr. C. that *women* were always considered to have the tenderest hearts ; but George Cooke and Lord Houghton had em- braced and kissed me with far more enthusiasm !   He answered, " There was nothing very wonderful in that ; men have been understood to have more notion than women of kissing *women* ever since the world began ! " '

About the same time she was writing to Mrs. Russell, whose house at Thornhill was called Holm Hill.—' At Holm Hill, at this hour, I should have just drunk my glass of wine, and been sitting down at the dining-room table to write the daily letter to Mr. C.   The likest thing I can do here is to sit down at the drawing-room table and write to you.   I feel the same sort of responsibility for myself to you, as to him, and to you only, of all people alive ! and feel, too, the same certainty of being read with anxious interest.   Oh, my dear Mary, it is an unspeakable blessing to have such a friend as you are to me !   Often, when I have felt unusually free from my misery of late, it has seemed to me that I could not be grateful enough to God . . . ; and just so I feel as if I needed God's help to make me humanly capable of the sort of sacred thankfulness I ought to feel for such a friend as yourself ! '

XXXIX

THE CIVIL WAR IN AMERICA, &c.
(1864)

AS long as it lasted, the Civil War in America was worse
than a nightmare to Carlyle, perhaps the most dis-
tressing of all the contemporary events in his long life.
But whereas in England " Society " sympathised with the
South and Democracy with the North, Carlyle appears to
have been impartially sorry for both, and especially for the
men sent to the slaughter and their relatives. ' The efforts
made by the Confederates in England,' says Moncure
Conway,[1] ' were desperate. They derived help from several
London journals, which printed every American item that
might irritate English pride.

' The Southerners quite misunderstood Carlyle. One
evening Mrs. Carlyle mentioned that after Carlyle had written
on the negro question ' (his ' Occasional Discourse on the
Nigger Question,' in 1849,)[2] ' he received from eminent
Southerners letters suggesting that England should restore
slavery in her West Indian possessions, in which case the
slave States would unite with them, and a great British
empire be formed in the New World. Mrs. Carlyle mentioned
no names, and I asked no questions. Carlyle spoke of the
scheme as wild, one he could have no sympathy with at all,
but said to his wife mildly,—" It might have been as well
not to trouble Mr. Conway with that ; I can conceive that
it might become his duty to report it to America."

' It did startle me that eminent Southerners, some ten
years before the war, should have wished to throw their
States and slavery under the protection of the British flag,
but they must have known little of Carlyle to suppose he
had any wish to see Great Britain expanding. Abhorring
the condition of the mass of labourers around him, Carlyle

---

[1] *Autobiography of Moncure D. Conway*, I, pp. 348 and 365–6.
[2] *Carlyle at his Zenith*, Book XVIII, Chapters II and III, pp. 215–221.

idealised the condition of the negroes in the Southern States ; that was all.'

Conway's composure was completely justified ; but when he found among those received familiarly as friends at Cheyne Row an old acquaintance he describes, John R. Thompson, one of the best Confederate advocates then in England, he was glad to be there to answer him, so that ' there was now a Virginian at each ear, not only of Carlyle, but of some other literary men whose silence about America distressed me.'

He tells us that Thompson had for many years been editor of the *Southern Literary Messenger*, at Richmond, and ' an important literary figure in Virginia.' When sent to England by the Confederate Government in 1864, Thompson's ' gentlemanly presence, pleasant manners, and intimacy with the Confederate leaders secured him entrance in both aristocratic and literary society.'[1]

Carlyle told Moncure Conway[1] that Thompson had called on him with an autograph letter from General Stonewall Jackson recommending the bearer to Carlyle ; and tho Carlyle never knew Stonewall Jackson, he soon was friendly with Thompson and used to ' pour out statements ' of his to Conway, to hear the other side. The *Diary* of Thompson was not published for many years to come, but seems authentic and interesting.[3]

' October 14, 1864.—Drank tea and spent the evening with Thomas Carlyle. Mrs. Carlyle has for some time been an invalid, but made her appearance. Lady Ashburton and Miss Baring came in after tea. Mr. Carlyle said it was his habit to drink five cups of tea. He ran off into table-talk about tea and coffee, pipes and tobacco, and then enquired about the Confederacy, its resources, army, its supplies of food and powder. He read a letter from Emerson ' declaring ' that the struggle now going on was the battle of humanity. He had received us in dressing gown and slippers. When we rose to say good-night, he called for his coat and boots, and walked with us (to) within a stonethrow of Grosvenor Hotel, two miles, at half past eleven !

' On the way, passing Chelsea Hospital, he burst into a tribute to Wren, the architect, of whom he said " there was a rare harmony, a sweet veracity, in all his work." We

---

[3] Quoted here from cuttings collected by Mr. Gridley, from the *Pall Mall Gazette*, without date, and from *Lippincott's Magazine*, November, year uncertain.

mentioned Tennyson, and he spoke with great affection of him, but,' presumably in reply to questions, ' thought him inferior to Burns : he had known " Alfred " for years : said he used to come in hob-nailed shoes and rough coat to blow a cloud with him. Carlyle thought Mill's book *On Liberty* " the greatest nonsense he ever read," and spoke despairingly of the future of Great Britain,—" *too much money would be the ruin of the land.*" '

When Thompson called again a few weeks later, Carlyle ' made many enquiries about Lee, whom he greatly admires. He talked brilliantly ; spoke disparagingly of Napier and other English historians,—said they knew nothing of war as an art.'

This General Lee whom Carlyle praised had in 1862 become the Commander-in-Chief of the Confederate armies in the Civil War, and after it was over he became the President of Washington College, Lexington, Virginia, now called the ' Washington and Lee University.' He was one of the best men and best soldiers conspicuous in the war.

Once this October, when John Thompson was not present to be hurt by it, Carlyle showed Conway a long letter dated 26.9.64 which he had just received from Emerson.[4] It was a hearty defence of the war and called it a Poem, ' which will, in the next age, inspire a genius like your own. I hate to write you a newspaper, but in these times, 'tis wonderful what sublime lessons I have once and again read on the Bulletin-boards in the streets. Everybody has been wrong in his guess, except good women, who never despair of an Ideal right. . . . Forgive this long writing, and keep the old kindness which I prize above words.'

" No danger but that will be kept," said Carlyle to Conway,[4] and added :—" For the rest, this letter, the first I have received from Emerson this long time, fills me with astonishment. That the clearest mind now living—for I don't know Emerson's equal on earth for perception— should write so is quasi-miraculous. I have tried to look into the middle of things in America, and I have seen a people cutting throats indefinitely to put the negro into a position for which all experience shows him unfit."

Carlyle was sorry for both sides, and impartially lamented the bloodshed.

[4] *Thomas Carlyle*, by Moncure D. Conway, pp. 95–7 ; and for the letter see the *Correspondence of Carlyle and Emerson*, II, pp. 283–8.

XL

WHEN 'WORKING DAY AND NIGHT'
(1864)

THE *Frederick* was not to be completed to the last scrap of proof till 6th February, 1865,—it had taken him about thirteen years,—' a desperate dead-lift pull, my whole strength devoted to it,' and often ' desperate of ever getting through.' When afterwards recalling his long labour upon it, what he loved to dwell upon ' with loving admiration ' was his wife's behaviour.—

' She was habitually in the feeblest health ; often, for long whiles, grievously ill. Yet by an alchemy all her own, she had extracted grains of gold out of every day, and seldom or never failed to have something bright and pleasant to tell me, when I reached home after my evening ride. In all, I rode, during that book, some 30,000 miles, much of it (all the winter part of it) under cloud of night, sun just setting when I mounted. All the rest of the day, I sat silent aloft ; insisting upon work, and *such* work, *invitissima Minerva* ' (much against the grain) ' for that matter. Home between five and six, with mud mackintoshes off, and, the nightmares locked up for a while, I tried for an hour's sleep before my bit of dinner ; but first *always*, came up for half an hour to the drawing-room and Her ; where a bright kindly fire was sure to be burning (candles hardly lit, all in trustful chiaroscuro), and a spoonful of brandy in water, with a pipe of tobacco (which I had learned to take sitting on the rug, with my back to the jamb, and door never so little *open*, so that all the smoke, if I was careful, went up the chimney) : this was the one bright portion of my black day. Oh those blessed half-hours, how beautiful and blessed they were !* She was oftenest reclining on the sofa ; wearied enough, she too, with her day's doings and endurings. But her history, even of what was bad, had such grace and truth, and spontaneous tinkling melody of a naturally cheerful and loving heart, I never anywhere enjoyed the like.'

It seems to have been about this time, the later months of 1864, that she told him how he had bored her eight years before by telling all about the battle of Mollwitz, ' night after night,' and she had endured it all, tho ' at that time, privately convinced she was dying. . . . Which how could I listen to without shame and abasement ? Never in my pretended-superior kind of life, have I done, for love of any creature, so supreme a kind of thing. It touches me at this moment with penitence and humiliation, yet with a kind of soft *religious* blessedness too.—She *read* the first two volumes of *Friedrich*, much of it in printer's sheets,' and told him it was the best thing he had ever written ; and he declared,—' Her applause was beautiful and as sunlight to me,—for I knew it was sincere withal, and unerringly straight upon the blot, however exaggerated by her great love of me. The other volumes (hardly even the third, I think) she never read. . . . Too weak, too weak by far, for a dismal enterprise of that kind, as I knew too well.'

About this time Carlyle gave his wife a brougham, to her great delight, and when writing to Neuberg on 13.10.64 for a ' reference to that passage of Nicolai about the " weeping Virgin " who depended upon a Brew-house,' he concluded : —' My Mrs. keeps wonderfully hearty ; I tremble every morning lest I find it all altered. Not only a Brougham but Brougham and Horse are wanted. (Horse that will *both* draw and ride, and that is equal to a Brougham, which my present little sparrow, it seems, is not.) Help if you can !

'In haste, Yours Always,
'T. CARLYLE.'

From which it is plain that his faithful friend Neuberg was delivering him from all the worry of bargaining about the brougham and the new horse he needed.

On 3.11.64 Woolner wrote in a letter to Mrs. Tennyson :— ' I have seen Mrs. Carlyle since I wrote and was charmed to see how well she was looking : she is too weak to do much more than stand upright ; but her spirits are good, and her state may almost be called a resurrection from the dead.'

Six days later, 9.11.64, Carlyle was writing to Neuberg, and puts some personal news between notes on the Boston Tea business and another matter and the letters of Field-marshal Conway, of which Neuberg was making the summary printed in Ch. V, Book XXI :—

' My poor Jane has fairly caught a cold last week ;— which has brought her a good way down from her former high stage ; and indeed fills me with anxiety privately. Meanwhile I am working day and night, as for *life*, with the little strength left, and the unabating obstinacy.'

On 7.12.64 he had occasion to write to an Edinburgh lawyer, an old friend, Henry Inglis,[1] to beg a job as factor or manager of landed property for a nephew, and added :—

' In January or soon after I hope to have *done* with a certain Book, which has almost literally killed me—at least it has kept me buried alive for 12 years past, *killt* as the Irish say. . . . My poor wife (who is greatly recovered from a sad fit of illness which was very threatening last year) joins in kind regards.'

---

[1] *Glasgow Herald*, 16.2.82, the name supplied to D. A. W. by the widow of Henry Inglis.

XLI

THE PENITENTIAL CANDLES
(1865)

DURING this winter, maybe about January, 1865, Mrs.
Carlyle said a curious thing to Mrs. Warren, one of her
servants.—" When I am dead, go upstairs into the closet
of the spare room. There you'll find two wax candles
wrapped in paper. I want you to light and burn them beside
me. When once I was giving a party after I came to live
in London, my mother who was here and wanted everything to be very nice went out and bought candles and con-
fectionery. She set out a table and lighted the room
splendidly, and then called me to come and see. I was angry,
saying people would say I was extravagant and would ruin
my husband, and I took away two of the candles and some
of the cakes. My mother was hurt and began to cry ; and
that hurt me and I repented and tried to comfort her and
was dreadfully sorry. The two candles I had taken away
are those you'll find—I have put them where they can be
easily found."

XLII

THE CONCLUSION OF THE " FREDERICK " AND
OF NOGGS
(1865)

ON the evening of Monday, 9.1.65, when Noggs and
Carlyle were returning together from a gallop, Noggs
bucked with vigour, as lively Arabs sometimes do,[1] and
here is what Carlyle had to write to Neuberg a week later[2] :
—' My little villain of a horse exploded under me, like a
powder magazine, suddenly, in the dark, out of " joy at being
done," not with *Friedrich*,—flung me over his ears, and
kicked my ankle rather badly while I was in the air : dextrous Horse ! I can now cripple about again.'

Mrs. Carlyle's remarks can be imagined. The only comfort to her was that no great harm was done, and that the
accident showed how completely she had been right in
objecting to his galloping about in his seventieth year.

On Sunday, 15.1.65, he sent the last scrap of copy to the
press, and the last proof was handed in on the evening of
Saturday, 4.2.65, and sent back finished next Monday. So
that very night, 6.2.65, as the first important business to
follow, Carlyle went to the Rectory adjoining and offered
Noggs to the Rev. Gerald Blunt on easy terms unknown
now. He said he had ridden as far as would have taken
him round the globe, and was now to ride no more. After
a few trials, Noggs was taken to the Rectory stables for
farther probation.[3]

In the weeks following the Rev. Gerald Blunt was assisted
by the Rector of Holborn in examining Noggs, who failed
to give satisfaction and was sent home again. Neuberg had
refused him as a present.[4] So Noggs had to be retired to

---

[1] Discovered by D. A. W. by experience in 1887.
[2] Unpublished letter of 16.1.65.
[3] *Memoirs of Gerald Blunt*, by Reginald Blunt, pp. 87–97.
[4] Unpublished letters, and see *MacMillan's Magazine*, 1884, Vol. L,
p. 295, article ' Carlyle and Neuberg.'

a country life. In Scotland he was ridden again by his old master, who had not been making a vow when he said he would ride no more, and had only meant that he would not buy another riding-horse. He continued riding Noggs in London through the spring, apparently, till the time came for going north.

As usual when anyone fails to enter the church, there are various explanations of undisputed facts. Mr. Blunt said,[3]—" The horse had exceedingly bad manners. There was no riding him. Carlyle used to ride him out to Wandsworth Common and to Clapham Common, and would begin to think about *Frederick*, so that the horse had his own way, and frequently people would see the horse grazing at the side of the road, and a tall figure sitting all unconscious on his back, thinking about Frederick the Great. When I tried to get the animal past some places, nothing would induce him to move, and I gave him up altogether. He had been entirely spoiled by Carlyle's habits."

Noggs was an Arab, it is said. If so, he may have been like many another of that breed, a glorious mount for ambling, galloping, or even walking, but unable to do any ecclesiastical trot. It is pleasant to see with the mind's eye Carlyle on the back of his horse, as it quietly grazed on the Common ; and nothing was more natural than the good Rector's guess ; for in those years, when he said to Carlyle " How d'ye do ? " and stayed for an answer, he was occasionally told,—" As well as can be expected, barring the shadow of Frederick the Great."[3] Yet it is as certain as any such thing can be that Carlyle was not thinking of *Frederick* when sitting there. He was not absent-minded, and least of all in the saddle. He rode hard, allowing his horse to enjoy itself. He needed no whip for galloping gently. Between one gallop and another, a man who could feel in the skin of a horse would naturally let the beast pause and graze if it liked, till it recovered its wind and wanted to toss its heels again. But it must be confessed that such a life was not the best training for a parson's cob.

XLIII

THE GOSPEL OF SILENCE IN PRACTICE
(1865)

WITH *Frederick* finished and its indexes, in February, 1865, Henry Larkin could, as he said,[1] " consider my long apprenticeship to Carlyle fairly and honourably ended." The more is the pity that a few months before then he and his family had " removed to Camden Town," which made co-operation more difficult than it had been before.

He tells us that all along he had made every index " a complete key " instead of a mere " verbal reference, which was all Carlyle asked for or expected."[2] His elaborate work was worth its extra space, and he was allowed to go his own way. The indexes were nothing but a joy to him. But now for *Frederick* the separate indexes for the first four volumes previously published had " to be taken to pieces," he tells us,[1] and along with " the manuscript index to the fifth and sixth volumes rearranged into one making 73 pages." Everything was now ready for publication but this ; and Carlyle had not the slightest idea of the amount of actual labour it involved. On 9th February he mentioned to Larkin that the 20th had been appointed as publication day, saying,—" I depend on you for exactitude and despatch," which appeared to Larkin a needless reminder ; and at the same time, Carlyle unfortunately said something about the maps that had been the source of so much sorrow :

" Kausler or big Atlas of Plans belonging to Lord de Grey : *clean* them as much as you can, and tie them together for delivery (cannot be too *soon*, after so many years' exile !) "

Larkin resolved to be faultless. " My wife and I," he

---

[1] *Carlyle and Mrs. Carlyle*, by Henry Larkin, *British Quarterly Review*, 1881, No. 147, pp. 79–81.
[2] *Ditto*, pp. 38–9.

says,[1] " worked at it together, night after night, till one and two in the morning, as we never worked before or since ; and yet he got more impatient with me about it than he had ever been before. I kept close to the essential work, thinking Lord de Grey could well afford to wait till I was out of the wood. Great then was my surprise and annoyance, when Mrs. Carlyle one day drove up in her brougham, wearied and vexed, and informed me that he had been imagining all sorts of disasters about those large Atlases belonging to Lord de Grey ; and that, if they were not already returned, she was to bring them away with her, and return them herself.

" I had got more than I could well bear with. When I announced to him that the last stroke was faithfully completed, I gave vent to my pent-up feelings. I have no recollection of the actual words. It was rather a longish letter.[1] I first expressed my regret for the absolutely unavoidable delay ; and then reminded him how I had originally volunteered to do the summaries and indexes, in which work I had been thoroughly interested, and always found my own profit ; how my work had gradually extended to difficult copying, in which I was also interested ; and how finally it had drawn me into maps and battle-plans, so utterly irksome and abhorrent to me that I had only compelled myself to it out of personal loyalty to himself ; and I wound up by saying that nothing short of ' Dr. Francia's Gallows ' could ever induce me to go through the like again ! It was a foolish sort of triumph at the best, telling ' a bit of one's mind ' ; and if I had been only a little stronger I should never have indulged in it. I recollect the relief with which I grimly posted that letter. I took the earliest opportunity of calling on him again in the usual way, to let him see that I was as loyal at heart as ever, notwithstanding my fine spirit of independence !

" When I entered the study, he met me very much as usual, but I could both see and feel that he was greatly hurt ; and when I looked in at the drawing-room, Mrs. Carlyle received me with wide-open eyes of astonishment ; which might have meant " various things. " Whatever it may have really included,—what she meant to *express* was, simple astonishment ; and she perfectly succeeded."

Here is a likely key to the miniature mystery. Some of the many papers stolen by Frederick Martin had been missed, and a man deserving credit[3] had indicated Larkin as having taken them, presumably as unconsidered trifles of value to him, but not to the owner. Carlyle gave no sign of belief or disbelief, excelling as usual in really reserving judgment ; but when he remembered the valuable atlases lent to him long ago, became suddenly uneasy till they were safely returned to their owner.

Larkin's explosion might go to show his innocence, but nothing was ever said by Carlyle on the subject, and the only reply to Larkin's ' rather longish letter ' was praise of the work he had done on the *Frederick*. Any explanation would have hurt him cruelly. So he was left supposing Carlyle had been in fault and unreasonable ; and was able to tell[1] how pleasantly they continued to meet and talk together, saying :—" Perhaps," tho living now in Camden Town, " I was there," at Cheyne Row, " almost as frequently as before. There were many friendly little services which I still continued to render. And certainly we never afterwards met in any other spirit than that of the friendliest cordiality."

This Lord de Grey, accidentally visible lending Carlyle Atlases, seems to have been the same Radical Lord who had been called " Goderich " and by-and-by was " Ripon," and who in 1863 succeeded Sir G. C. Lewis as Secretary for War, and became a Cabinet colleague of Palmerston. Carlyle and he must occasionally have been fellow-guests.

On 6.2.65, when the proofs were finished, Carlyle was sending to John Forster, his volunteer but efficient business adviser, the papers about his bargain with Chapman the publisher, and saying,—" *You*, like the Champion of Christendom you have always been, will pin down these financial Dragons to the place that belongs to them, and save an afflicted worn-out man from such cattle."[4] John Forster's help in this left Carlyle free to turn his mind to science, as the best sort of rest after history, so that on 22.2.65 he was able to write to John Ruskin,[5] offering ' to come out actually some day soon ; and take a serious Lecture from you on what you really know about the Rocks, —bones of our poor old Mother ' Earth.

---

[3] He is not mentioned in this book, and died before Carlyle. His sister, a very shrewd woman, knew all about the matter at the time, and made it known to D. A. W. in confidence and on a promise of secrecy as to names.

[4] From the MS. in South Kensington Museum.

[5] *Life of John Ruskin*, by W. G. Collingwood, II, p. 35.

XLIV

BUST OF SHAKESPEARE, &c.
(1865)

BEFORE the end of February Carlyle had returned the books that had been lent to him for use in the history he had just finished. On Saturday, 25.2.65, Mrs. Carlyle was writing to their old friend, the Rev. William Brookfield[1] :—' You must not come *to-night!* You must come to-morrow night or Monday night, because, you see, there are two " terrible blockheads " coming to-night by their own appointment, and Mr. C. says he " wouldn't for any consideration have Brookfield there along with such a pair of Jackasses ! " I suggested that the very Jackassness of the people might amuse you. But he declared, " No ! No ! such a combination is not to be thought of ! "

' You *will* come to-morrow evening ? Or Monday ? We shall be going away presently to Seaton now the weather is auspicious. But Lady Ashburton was to fix the day.'

On 1.3.65 Carlyle was writing to his brother Dr. John, who was then in Dumfries :—' I don't feel as if there were much of *ruined* in me ; but everything is in such a smashed and completely tired out condition as never before. In particular this right hand (the left *not* yet) has for about two years back taken to *shaking* at a new and unpleasant rate ; especially shakes if I have been muscularly working at any thing. It must take its own way !— . . . I feel as if I had not only got done with *Frederick*, but with all the work I had to do in this planet. . . . I am determined to see the Spring skies somewhere *without* London defilement.'

So on Wednesday, 8.3.65, Carlyle and his wife went to Lady Ashburton's house near Seaton, on the Devonshire coast, and stayed nearly four weeks. On 12.3.65 Mrs. Carlyle was

---

[1] *Mrs. Brookfield, &c.*, by C. & F. Brookfield, II, p. 512.

writing to ' My own darling Betty,' meaning Mrs. Braid in
Edinburgh, who had been a young servant in her mother's
house a few years older than herself.   They had grown from
girlhood to womanhood alongside each other, and become
friends for life.   She was now writing to sympathise with
Mrs. Braid for the death of her son George,—' In my life I
never heard anything so sad !   And yet how merciful ! '
And passing on to news about herself she remarked :—' I
am just as much at home with Lady Ashburton as with
Mrs. Russell : they are the two kindest hostesses on earth.
So I doubt not but I shall improve here.'   And so she did,
and her husband also.

Sir Walter and Lady Trevelyan were neighbours at
Seaton, often fellow-guests.   They were also old acquaintances of Dr. Carlyle and Thomas Erskine ; and nearly
every day Sir Walter was riding at large with Carlyle, who
found him a ' silent, placidly solemn old gentleman,' with
' lengthy block wig ' and quasi-scientific talk.

They had Woolner's company for a couple of weeks,[2] and
it may have been on this occasion that Woolner heard
Carlyle say,—" Sir Francis Chantrey expressed an opinion
that the Stratford bust of Shakespeare was taken from a
cast after death."   Whereupon Woolner went and studied
it and found many reasons for agreeing with that opinion.
For one thing, the long upper lip seemed to be due to the
shrinking of the nostrils and dropping of the lips after
death, " chapfallen " was the old word.   The poet had an
upper lip like that of other men as long as he lived, and the
sculptor of the monument caricatured the upper lip without
intending to do so because he copied the death-mask.
Perhaps the Chandos portrait is the best likeness.

As for Mrs. Carlyle at Seaton, she was delighted by the
sea and the cliffs and said, " My head was quite turned at
first."   So she tried to persuade her husband to buy what
she called " a Devonshire Craigenputtock," which was then
for sale and seemed cheap,—a fine house and a hundred
acres of bog being offered for £2000.   Perhaps she did not
know he was giving away by degrees the £2000 Lord Ashburton had left him.   It is less likely that she knew what
he had recently noticed, that his accumulated savings
waiting investment came to £2000.   Doubtless she recalled
how many a time he had craved to quit London for
Craigenputtock or some other place in the country, and

---

[2] *Thomas Woolner*, by Amy Woolner, pp. 314, 238 and 258-9.

she would not agree. She was disposed to indulge him now. " There's the place,—buy that ! "

Lady Ashburton blithely abetting arranged a picnic,— " luncheon in the open air " for the whole house-party on the terrace of the desirable house.

Carlyle to his wife.—" I fear you would die of the solitude in six months." " Oh, no ! " she answered, " for I will keep constant company." This " wrecked the speculation," she wrote to Mrs. Oliphant, confirmed by Woolner, who wrote to Mrs. Tennyson that Carlyle had given up the notion of buying it. Perhaps he never had any. What Woolner heard him say was,—" If I were ten years younger and able to enter a new kind of life, I could not wish a happier looking spot."

Then Lady Ashburton pressed Woolner to buy, and offered to lend him as much of the money as he liked ; but he wisely said,—" No," and explained to Mrs. Tennyson,— " A big house to me would be like buying a pack of hounds."

On Monday, April 3, the Carlyles and Lady Ashburton came back to London together.

XLV

WOOLNER, LARKIN AND OTHERS
(1865)

THE news that met the Carlyles when they came back to town was the death of Richard Cobden, and Gavan Duffy calling a few days later lamented it as everybody was doing.[1] Carlyle did not join the Chorus, but articulated the other side of the matter.—" Yes," he said, " a pack of idle shrieking creatures are going about crying out that the great Richard is dead, as if the world were coming to an end, which it is not at all."

About John Bright he spoke plainly :—" I consider him one of the foolishest creatures I have ever heard of, clamouring about America and universal suffrage, as if there is any sensible man anywhere in the world who puts the smallest confidence in that sort of thing now-a-days. Their free trade is the most intense nonsense that ever provoked human patience. The people of Australia are quite right to protect their industries and teach their young men trades in complete disregard of Parliamentary and platform palaver. No nation ever got manufactures in any other way."

Gavan Duffy.—" It is not desirable to have a permanent population of diggers ready to fly from ' rush ' to ' rush,' as new discoveries are made, but, if possible, a settled population engaged in all the ordinary pursuits of life ; and Australians are willing to make a sacrifice to secure this end."

Carlyle.—" They do right, and you may lay this to heart, that of all the mad pursuits any people ever took up, gold digging is the maddest and stupidest. If you got as much gold as would make a bridge from Australia to Europe, it would not be worth a mealy potato to mankind."

The first thing Carlyle had to do at home this April was to examine the *History of Frederick the Great* which was

---

[1] *Conversations with Carlyle*, by Sir C. Gavan Duffy, pp. 218–19.

now completely printed, and to send copies to friends. Here is the letter to Larkin, the most interesting of all the forwarding letters.[2]—

> ' CHELSEA,
> ' 13 *April*, 1865.

' DEAR LARKIN,

' We are got home from the Country ; and I have at length got sight of the Book in its complete state, and have been looking over it hither and thither—*your* part of it as well, tho not yet with critical eye. The Plans &c. are very neat and pretty, so much I can testify ; nor do I hitherto see above one or two even slight points on which I could have advised alteration, had there been the freëst chance for it.

' I am very sensible of the great pains you took, the true wish you have had all along (even in your own confusions and distresses) to be helpful to me ; and your loyalty in this sore Enterprise from first to last is a thing I shall always remember. Let us be thankful we have seen the *end* of it ; which, at one time, and indeed more times than one, seemed almost desperate !—

' I enclose you a cheque,—*crossed* so that nobody can steal it ; and need not add that if I can ever help you in any honest purpose I gladly will. And so, with my best wishes to Mrs. Larkin and you, and the kindest auguries I can form, I remain,

> ' Yours sincerely always,
> ' T. CARLYLE.'

On 14.4.65 President Lincoln was murdered, and the Vice-President, Mr. Johnson, reigned in his stead. Conway described him as " a tipsy tailor from Tennessee," and Mr. Thompson calling on Carlyle had the pleasure of hearing Carlyle say he was " a sanguinary tailor seated on Olympus." What most consumed the time of Carlyle this April was the sittings (or standings they might be called) he had to give to Woolner for a marble bust of himself which Lady Ashburton had commissioned. By 26.4.65 he was able to announce to his brother Dr. John in Dumfries that there remained only two more sittings, and that he hoped to be off for Dumfries by 10.5.65.

[2] *Carlyle and Mrs. Carlyle*, by Henry Larkin, *British Quarterly Review*, 1881, No. 147, p. 81.

Five days before then, however, Mrs. Carlyle was confiding to her friend Mrs. Russell :—' Mr. C. has been sitting
to Woolner for his bust ; and it seems he " is as difficult to
catch a likeness of as a flash of lightning " is, so that it is
a trying business for both sitter and sculptor. I have had
to drive up to Woolner's every two or three days to tell
what faults I see. And in connection with this bust, there
has been such a sitting to photographers as never was heard
of ! Woolner wants a variety of photographs to work from,
and the photographer wants a variety to sell ! And Mr.
Carlyle yields to their mutual entreaties. And then, when
they have had their will of him, they insist on doing me
(for my name's sake). And Mr. C. insists too, thinking
always the new one may be more successful than former
ones ' as a likeness. Which had in short delayed her writing
a letter. But now she would soon see him off to the country
and have the house to herself, and be able to do what she
liked. Which all duly happened. He went to Dumfries
before the end of May and stayed a long time in the country.
But before he went there was an event quite rare in their
household,—he was insubordinate to his wife ! It was all
about George Eliot and George Henry Lewes, the biographer
of Goethe. Carlyle's excuse was that he was constrained by
conscience ; and it has to be admitted that he was a disciple
of Jesus Christ and of Martin Luther, and in the habit of
cultivating his conscience.

XLVI

GEORGE ELIOT AND MR. LEWES
(1865)

MARIAN EVANS, whose pen-name was George Eliot, had taken Mr. Lewes, another woman's husband, without the sanction of the law. When Carlyle was asked who this George Eliot was and this man Lewes, he answered[1] :—" George Eliot is a female writer of books, like myself and himself. I got one of her books and tried to read it, but it would not do. Poor Lewes ! Poor fellow ! "

Gavan Duffy was in London this May and tells us[2] he asked one evening at Cheyne Row :—" Will you follow *Frederick* by any other historical study ? "

" No," replied Carlyle. " I will probably write no more books. Writing books is a task without proper encouragement in these times. Modern literature is all purposeless and distracted, and leads I know not whither. Its professors are on the wrong path just now, and I believe the world will soon discover that some practical work done is worth innumerable ' Oliver Twists ' and ' Harry Lorrequers,' and any amount of other ingenious dancing on the slack rope. The journalism which calls itself critical has grown altogether Gallic, and exults over the windy platitudes of Lamartine and the erotics of George Sand."

Mrs. Carlyle.—" We have small right to throw the first stone at George Sand, tho she has been caught in the same predicament as the woman of old, if we consider what sort of literary ladies may be found in London at present. When one was first told that the strong woman of the *Westminster Review* had gone off with a man whom we all knew, it was as startling an announcement as if one heard that a woman of your acquaintance had gone off with the strong man at Astley's ; but that the partners in this adventure had set

[1] W. B. Scott's *Autobiographical Notes*, II, p. 249.
[2] *Conversations with Carlyle*, by Sir Charles Gavan Duffy, pp. 221-3.

up as moralists is a graver surprise. To renounce George
Sand as a teacher of morals is right enough, but it is scarcely
consistent with making so much of our own George in that
capacity. A marvellous teacher of morals, surely, and still
more marvellous in the other character, for which nature
has not provided her with the outfit supposed to be essential."

This outburst was like her. She was far from pleased at
her husband's toleration of George Eliot. Gavan Duffy
played up to her promptly, adding,—" The gallant is as
badly equipped for an Adonis and conqueror of hearts," and
Mrs. Carlyle coincided, as may be imagined.

" Yes," Carlyle replied. " He is certainly the ugliest little
fellow you could anywhere meet, but he is lively and pleasant. In this final adventure it must be admitted he has
escaped from worse, and may even be said to have ranged
himself. He originally married a bright little woman,
daughter of Swinfin Jervis, a disreputable Welsh member ;
but everybody knows how that has turned out. Miss Evans
advised him to quit a household which had broken bounds
in every direction. His proceeding is not to be applauded,
but it can scarcely be said that he has gone from bad to
worse."

Then Mrs. Carlyle talked of something else, as she usually
did when Carlyle would not say what she wanted.[3]

According to Espinasse,[4] Lewes himself was a favourite
of Mrs. Carlyle, who called him " Poor dear Lewes," and
her husband, who was pleased by his book on Goethe and
his progressive ideas, declared him " the Prince of Journa-
lists," and accepted as true his statements on domestic
affairs. In spite of the misgivings of Espinasse and Mrs.
Lynn Linton, and Mrs. Carlyle and the suburban ladies who
refused to call on the second Mrs. Lewes, the world in the
end did as Carlyle and some others did at once, and decided
that Lewes and George Eliot were not to be outlawed
because they lived together openly, altho the law-courts
prevented Lewes from marrying her. Our bad English law
was the only sinner in the case. " The letter killeth ! "

In Asia the Muslims and the Buddhists are more moral
than the Europeans ; and both law and custom would have
led them to take the same view of the union of Lewes and
Miss Evans as was taken here by Carlyle.

A London legend that Carlyle " prohibited " his wife

---

[3] Sir C. Gavan Duffy to D. A. W. verbally.
[4] *Literary Recollections*, by F. Espinasse, pp. 282 and 290–300.

from calling on George Eliot seems untrue. The latest expounder of it[5] wants the public to disbelieve Gavan Duffy because Mrs. Carlyle afterwards asked whether her husband would " let " her take young Lady Lothian to call on George Eliot.[6] When it was a question of Mrs. Carlyle calling herself, she would never think of asking her husband. Whether to take a young married woman from the country on such a call would depend on many things.

[5] An anon. contributor of the George Eliot centenary article to *Truth*, 1919.

[6] *Letters and Memorials*, III, p. 329.

XLVII

CONCLUSIONS
(1865)

IN June, when Carlyle had gone to the country, his wife began refitting the dining-room on the ground floor so as to make it a Study. The " Sound-proof Study," where *Frederick* had been written, became the servants' bed-room, and so it continued while the house was used in the ordinary way ; but now, of course, when the whole house is sacred to his memory, we can see it again if we will, with the mind's eye, by means of the Illustrated Catalogue and the writings of Reginald Blunt and others and the photographs of Mr. Tait.

Mrs. Carlyle had made enough progress to be able to set the painters to work when she went on a long visit to Mrs. Russell at Thornhill, within easy reach of her husband, who was living at " the Gill," a farmhouse which was the home of his sister's family. Occasionally they met at Dumfries. More often he came to Dr. Russell's to see her. One day when he had done so, perhaps the first time, she was coming with him to Thornhill Railway Station about 7 p.m. as he was returning, and told him on the way that the Confederate advocate John Thompson had said to her,—" There is little doubt they will *hang* President Davis." By this summer the Northern States were victorious in the American Civil War, and the Confederate President Davis was a prisoner.

Carlyle was deeply moved, and, as he noted in the *Reminiscences* next year, ' almost resolved to write a Pamphlet upon it ' ; but ' in a day or two I found I could not enter upon that thrice-abject Nigger-delirium (viler to me than old witchcraft, or the ravings of John of Münster, considerably viler) ; and that probably I should do poor Davis nothing but harm.'

This ' John of Münster ' alias ' John of Leyden ' was the German Communist prophet of the fifteen hundreds. As for Jefferson Davis, he was only confined in a fortress for a couple of years and then set free. He lived to over eighty.

XLVIII

JOHN BURROUGHS ON " FREDERICK," &c.

IT is often said that distance in place has the same effect
as in time, and that the opinions of foreigners about our
books may be like those of posterity at home. While Latin
races think the Teutonic partial to Carlyle, the Teutonic
races think the Latin prejudiced against him. So perhaps
America is the country whose critics are likeliest to be right ;
and if so admirers of Carlyle may rejoice indeed, for it would
be easy to show by a cento of the best of their critics that
they count his *History of Frederick* one of the best histories
in English. Instead of a shower of snippets by many
authors, here at length is the criticism of John Burroughs,[1]
a downright man and trustworthy.—

He tells us that Carlyle ' did not merely preach the
gospel of work ; he was it,—a worker from first to last.
Each of his review articles cost him a month or more of
serious work. *Sartor* cost him nine months, the *French
Revolution* three years, *Cromwell* four years, *Frederick*
thirteen. No surer does the Auldgirth Bridge carry the
traveller over the water beneath it, than these books convey
the reader over chasms and confusions.
' Carlyle never wrote a book except to clear some gulf or
quagmire, to span and conquer some chaos. No architect
or engineer ever had purpose more tangible and definite.
To further the reader on his way, not to beguile or amuse
him, was always his purpose. He had that contempt for
all dallying and toying and lightness and frivolousness that
hard serious workers always have. He was impatient of
poetry and art ; they savoured too much of play and
levity.' . . . In short John Burroughs maintains that the
famous description of *The Gifted* in *Past and Present* (IV
and VII) was an unconscious painting of Carlyle himself :—

[1] *Fresh Fields*, by John Burroughs, pp. 79–81, &c.

" Not a May-game is this man's life ; but a battle and a march, a warfare with principalities and powers," &c.

John Burroughs went on.—' Those who seek to explain Carlyle on the ground of his humble origin shoot wide of the mark.

' It seems to me Carlyle was as little of a peasant as any man of his time,—a man without one peasant trait, or proclivity, a regal and dominating man, " looking king and beggar in the face with an indifference of brotherhood and an indifference of contempt." The two marks of the peasant are stolidity and abjectness ; he is dull and heavy, and he dare not say his soul is his own. No man ever so hustled and jostled titled dignitaries, and made them toe the mark, as did Carlyle. It was not merely that his intellect was towering ; it was also his character, his will, his standard of manhood that was towering. He bowed to the hero, to valour and personal worth, never to titles or conventions. The virtues and qualities of his yeoman ancestry were in him without doubt ; his power of application, the spirit of toil that possessed him, his frugal, self-denying habits, came from his family and race, but these were not peasant traits, but heroic traits. A certain coarseness of fibre he had also, together with great delicacy and sensibility, but these again he shares with all strong first-class men. You cannot get such histories as *Cromwell* and *Frederick* out of polished littérateurs ; you must have a man of the same heroic fibre ; of the same inexpugnableness of mind and purpose. Not even was Emerson adequate to such a task : he was fine enough and high enough, but he was not coarse enough and broad enough.

' The scholarly part of Carlyle's work is nearly always thrown in the shade by the manly part, the original raciness and personal intensity of the writer. He is not in the least veiled or hidden by his literary vestments. He is rather hampered by them, and his sturdy Annandale character often breaks through them in the most surprising manner. His contemporaries soon discovered that if here was a great writer, here was also a great man, come not merely to paint their pictures, but to judge them, to weigh them in the balance. He is eminently an artist, and yet it is not the artistic or literary impulse that lies at the bottom of his works, but a moral, human, emotional impulse, and attraction,—the impulse of justice, of veracity, or of sympathy and love.

'What love of work well done, what love of genuine leadership, of devotion to duty, of mastery of affairs, in fact, what love of man pure and simple, lies at the bottom of *Frederick*. Of all histories that have fallen into my hands, *Frederick* is the most vital and real. If the current novels were half so entertaining I fear I should read little else. The portrait-painting is like that of Rembrandt ; the eye for battles and battle-fields is like that of Napoleon, or Frederick himself ; the sifting of events, and the separating of the false from the true, is that of the most patient and laborious science ; the descriptive passages are equalled by those of no other man ; while the work as a whole, as Emerson says, " is a Judgment Day, for its moral verdict, on the men and nations and manners of modern times." It is to be read for its honest history ; it is to be read for its inexhaustible wit and humour ; it is to be read for its poetic fire, for its felicities of style, for its burden of human sympathy and effort, its heroic attractions and stimulating moral judgments. All Carlyle's histories have the quick, penetrating glance, that stroke of the eye, as the French say, that lays the matter open to the heart.

'He did not write in the old way of a topographical survey of the surface ; his *French Revolution* is more like a transverse section ; more like a geologist's map than like a geographer's ; the depths are laid open ; the abyss yawns ; the cosmic forces and fires stalk forth and become visible and real. . . . His pages are unique and matchless, of their kind, in literature. He may be deficient in the historical sense, the sense of development, and of compensation in history ; but in vividness of apprehension of men and events, and power of portraiture, he is undoubtedly without a rival. " Those devouring eyes and that portraying hand," says Emerson.

'Those who contract their view of Carlyle till they see only his faults, do a very unwise thing. Nearly all his great traits have their shadows. His power of characterisation sometimes breaks away into caricature ; his command of the picturesque leads him into the grotesque ; his eloquent denunciation at times becomes vituperation ; his marvellous power to name things degenerates into outrageous nick-naming ; his streaming humour, which, as Emerson said, floats every object he looks upon, is not free from streaks of the most crabbed, hide-bound ill-humour. Nearly every page has a fringe of these things, and sometimes a pretty broad one, but they are by no means the main matter, and often lend an additional interest. The great personages, the great events, are never caricatured, though painted with a bold, free hand, but there is in the border of the picture all manner of impish and grotesque strokes.

' In *Frederick* there is a whole series of secondary men and incidents that are touched off with the hand of a master caricaturist. We are never suffered to forget George the Second's fish eyes and gartered leg, nor the lean May-pole mistress of George the First, nor the Czarina's big fat cheek, nor poor Bruhl, " vainest of human clothes-horses," with his twelve tailors and his three hundred and sixty-five suits of clothes, nor Augustus, " the dilapidated strong," with his three hundred and fifty-four bastards. Nor can any reader of that work ever forget " Jenkins' Ear,"—the ear of an English sailor snipped off by the Spaniards, and here made to stand for a whole series of historical events. Indeed, this severed ear looms up till it becomes like a sign in the zodiac of those times.

' His portrait of the French army, which he calls the Dauphiness, is unforgettable, and is in the best style of his historical caricature. It makes its exit over the Rhine before Duke Ferdinand, "much in rags, much in disorder, in terror, and here and there almost in despair, winging their way like clouds of draggled poultry caught by a mastiff in the corn. Across Weser, across Ems, finally across the Rhine itself, every feather of them,—their long-drawn cackle, of a shrieky type, filling all nature in these months."

' A good sample of the grotesque in Carlyle is in this picture of the Czarina (Elizabeth) of Russia, stirred up to declare war against Frederick by his Austrian enemies. " Bombarded with cunningly-devised fabrications, every wind freighted for her with phantasmal rumours, no ray of direct daylight visiting the poor Sovereign Woman ; who is lazy, not malignant, if she could avoid it ; mainly a mass of esurient oil, with alkali on the back of alkali poured-in, at this rate for ten years past, till by pouring and by stirring they get her to the state of soap and froth."

' Carlyle was, indeed, in certain moods *a kind of divine blackguard,—a purged and pious Rabelais*, who could be-spatter the devil with more telling epithets than any other man who ever lived. What a tongue, what a vocabulary ! He fairly oxidises, burns up the object of his opprobrium, in the stream of caustic epithets he turns upon it. He had a low opinion of the contemporaries of Frederick and Voltaire ; they were " mere ephemera ; contemporary eaters, scramblers for provender, talkers of acceptable hearsay ; and related merely to the butteries and wiggeries of their time, and not related to the Perennialities at all, as these two were." *He did not have to go very far from home for some of the lineaments of Voltaire's portrait.* " He had, if no big gloomy devil in him among the bright angels that were there, a multitude of ravening, tumultuary imps, or little devils, very ill-chained, and was lodged, he and his restless little devils, in a skin far too thin for him and them ! "

' Of Frederick's cynicism he says there was " always a kind of vinegar cleanness in it, except in theory." Equally original and felicitous is the " albuminous simplicity " which he ascribes to the Welfs. Newspaper men (are) the " gazetteer owls of Minerva " ; and the " consolations " the nuns deal out to the sick (are) " poisoned gingerbread." In *Frederick*, one comes upon such phrases as " milk-faced," " beadroll histories," " heavy pipe-clay natures," a " stiff-jointed, algebraic kind of piety," etc.

' Those who persist in trying Carlyle as a philosopher and man of ideas miss his purport. He had no philosophy. He was a preacher of righteousness to his generation, and a rebuker of its shams and irreverences. . . .

' Carlyle made no terms with himself nor with others. He would not agree to keep the peace ; he would be the voice of absolute conscience, of absolute justice, come what might. " Woe to them that are at ease in Zion," he once said to John Sterling. The stern, uncompromising front which he first turned to the world he never relaxed for a moment. Conscience had its way with him at all times in his relations with mankind. He made no selfish demands, but ideal demands. It was not mere obstinacy ; it was not the pride of opinion : it was the thunders of conscience, the awful voice of Sinai, within him ; he dared not do otherwise.

' A selfish or self-seeking man Carlyle in no sense was, though it has so often been charged upon him. His own genius came nearer the demon of Socrates than that of any modern man. The watchword of his life was " *Entsagung*," renunciation, self-denial, which he learned from Goethe. His demon did not possess him lightly, but dominated and drove him. One would as soon accuse St. Simeon Stylites, thirty years at the top of his penitential pillar, of selfishness.

' For the making of good Democrats, there are no books

like Carlyle's, and we in America need especially to cherish him, and to lay his lesson to heart.

' It is his supreme merit that he spoke with absolute sincerity ; not according to the beliefs, traditions, conventionalities of his times, for they were mostly against him ; but according to his private and solemn conviction of what the will of his Maker with reference to himself was. The reason why so much writing and preaching sounds hollow and insincere compared with his is that the writers and speakers are mostly under the influence of current beliefs or received traditions ; they deliver themselves of what they have been taught, or what is fashionable and pleasant.' In reading other histories ' we drink from a cistern, and not from a fountain-head. Carlyle always takes us to the source of intense personal and original conviction.'

On 29.7.1865 William Allingham went for a week-end on a visit to Alfred Tennyson at Farringford. He was a poet himself, and naturally curious to know what the other poet thought of the latest great addition to history in English, but had to write in his note-book :[2]—" Tennyson said he had read part of Carlyle's *Frederick* till he came to, ' *they* did not strive to build the lofty rhyme,' and then flung the book into a corner."

[2] *William Allingham, A Diary*, by H. Allingham and D. Radford, p. 119.

XLIX

"THE HISTORY OF FREDERICK THE GREAT"
(1865)

CARLYLE'S great *History of Frederick* is like a movie-picture of eighteenth-century life, and may be called the best epic in the world, if epic be taken in its widest meaning of a history of events. It is as vivid as Homer and as wise as Tacitus, and while it is as readable as Voltaire's histories, it is as accurate as anything written in any language. Its characters seem as transparent to the reader as those of Shakespeare's plays.

" Everything has its day," wrote Dr. Johnson in his *Life of Prior.* " Through the reigns of William and Anne no prosperous event passed undignified by poetry. In the last war, when France was disgraced and overpowered in every quarter of the globe, when Spain, coming to her assistance, only shared her calamities, and the name of an Englishman was reverenced through Europe, no poet was heard amidst the general acclamation ; the fame of our counsellors and heroes was entrusted to the Gazetteer." The Gazetteers appear in the history, but sometimes in a way to raise a smile. The narrative is utterly matter-of-fact. Occasionally one cannot help feeling, like Emerson and Burroughs, as if familiar with all that can be known to a Spiritual Secretariat, arranging in advance the business of the Day of Judgment.

When this history was finished, the work of Carlyle's life was mainly done. For the rest of his time he was merely making remarks as he looked around and enjoyed himself, better than most of us can at his age, while old habit kept him trying to feel miserable as often as it occurred to him that he should be so. He was to be seventy this year and live to complete eighty-five ; and it was only in the later years of his life, apparently, that inability to assimilate food caused physical depression.

The history which had occupied him about thirteen years
continuously is not so thrilling to read as his early masterpiece, the *French Revolution ;* but it is more pleasant and
profitable. It mirrors public events in Europe, especially
for much of the seventeen-hundreds, and so prepares the
reader to be patient with the Revolution which was the
sequel. There is no doubt that Wellington was right in
what he is reported to have said to Scott,—it is impossible
to describe a battle perfectly. One can only be sure of
the result of it. But of all the descriptions of battles, the
critics seem to agree that those in the *Frederick* are the
best,—which gives the book a kind of antiquarian interest
nowadays, when the wager of battle is mere machinery
murder, and the leading practitioners of war are ugly poisoners,
a horror to humanity. Nobody can continue to respect a
man who lives by such a trade. It may in time become
impossible for a good man to be nothing but a soldier, and
the business is too dangerous to be left haphazard to ignorant
hands. The little killing really needed can be done by
respectable executioners, doctors or policemen.

The business of bloodshed was not yet shabby in the
seventeen-hundreds. But even in the *Frederick*, the battles
cannot be made pleasant to behold, however vivid or even
occasionally picturesque. The book is full of better stuff,—
sound knowledge, mellow wisdom and kind humour,—so
that we may all agree with Dr. Garnett who called it " the
book for the man of one book." A man of sense who has
read it well is better grounded in history than he would have
been if he had omitted to read it, but spent many years
attending lectures and cramming for degrees.

Here is one of many anecdotes that might be told to
show this. In the summer of 1913 one who had protracted
business in the London Parliament and law-courts[1] was
assured by many politicians, including highly educated men
of all parties, that they believed the statements of the
tennis-champion Grey who was Foreign Secretary,—they
were sure he would never entangle us in the intrigues of
France or Russia so as to drag us into their wars.

The only man he met who knew better was the late James
Keir Hardie, who said to him frankly,—" Grey is endangering

---

[1] D. A. W., recently retired from the I.C.S., but in London seeking,
with success in the long run, thanks mainly to Sir Robert, now Viscount
Finlay, ex-Lord Chancellor, redress for a Rangoon editor, who had been
victimised by sundry evil-doers.

peace by keeping the country in the dark, while making us the playthings of rascals in Paris and Russia. He and Asquith are playing the game of the Tories." Walking in the Embankment Gardens between Westminster and Charing Cross,[2] Keir Hardie paused to watch a passing column of " scouts." He sighed and said, " Poor children, poor children! The politicians want to cultivate the military temper in England. That is why they are itching for a war. It is to make the working-men more manageable." There was a Christ-like tenderness in his face as he stood quietly watching the boys go by, and then as he looked after them he murmured softly, " Poor children, poor children! "

Towards the end of 1914, and after the business of bloodshed had fairly begun, Keir Hardie was asked at his own fireside in Cumnock,[3]—" Had you any special information last year which made you more knowing than the rest ? " He answered,—" None whatever. The palpable facts were enough to let me see the games of diplomacy were going on, and I had learned from that book how to think about it," and he pointed to Carlyle's *Frederick*.

It had to be admitted that diplomacy was now, as much as two hundred years ago, mere organised rascality. The conclusion of Carlyle is continually being confirmed by current events.—' Modern diplomacy is nothing. Mind well your own affairs, leave those of your neighbour well alone.'

This is one of the best practical lessons in politics to be learned from Carlyle. The political insight which seemed to Lucian indispensable to the " perfect historian " abounds in the *Frederick*,—there should be a copy of it in every public library, and suitable extracts from it should be in our schoolbooks. If only Grey & Co. had assimilated the *Frederick* as well as Keir Hardie, the English Commonwealth might have been spared the war of 1914-18.

But for this book it is likely that no Englishman would ever have been able to understand the German kings we have afforded ourselves for the last century or two. In *Frederick* we not only see them as they were, we can also see the species they belong to, and make allowances that even such a genius as Thackeray could not easily make.

The best of the German kings, the Frederick of this history, is far from being the best man we see in it,—he was not even the best soldier on his own side. But he was

[2] With D. A. W.   [3] By D. A. W.

good enough to pass for the place he gets under the circumstances. As the judicious Plutarch wrote of Cleopatra's
Anthony, in words that Shakespeare might have copied,—
" It was in the nature of Anthony to show his best qualities
in difficulties, and in misfortune he was as like as may be
to a good man." The same is true of many another besides
Frederick. It is a commonplace as old as Æsop that adver-
sity is easier to bear than prosperity.

   Mr. W. H. White (Mark Rutherford),[4] has explained one
thing that makes a book like this interesting :—it is ' the
biography of a hero reduced more than once to such extremities that apparently nothing but some miraculous
intervention could save him, and who did not yield, but
struggled on and finally emerged victorious. When we
consider Frederick's position during the last part of the
Seven Years' War, we must admit that no man ever was
in such desperate circumstances or showed such uncrush-
able determination. Over and over again Frederick would
have been justified in acknowledging defeat, and we should
have said that he had done all that could have been expected.
If the struggle of the will with the encompassing world is
the stuff of which epics are made, then no greater epic than
that of Frederick has been written, and it has the important
advantage of being true. . . . . It (Frederick's perseverance)
was due to no religious motive ; it was bare, pure humanity.
Carlyle loves it all the more on that account. It is strange
that an example so salutary and stimulating to the meanest
of us should be set by an unbelieving king, and that my
humdrum existence should be secretly supported by
" Frederick II, roi de Prusse." '

   In a letter of 27.6.1894 he added :[5]—' The *Frederick* is to
me the great modern epic, the Iliad of a man who was
driven into the most desperate extremities ; so desperate
that destruction seemed absolutely certain, but who did not
yield and was finally victorious. That unquenchableness is
what has drawn Carlyle to him ; and what more precious
doctrine is there, even for us poor work-a-day creatures ? '

   It is nonsense to suppose as some have done that Frederick
is held up as a model and all his deeds approved. In seizing
Silesia he was acting as naturally as a cat that kills a mouse
when it sees a chance ; but he was doing wrong in going to

   [4] *Pages from a Journal*, by Mark Rutherford, pp. 10–11.
   [5] *Letters to Three Friends*, by W. Hale White, pp. 66–7.

war and had to suffer for that,—the pleasant genial life he had hoped to lead became impossible.

The great novelty in Carlyle's philosophy of history is a feeling he shared with Confucius, that what the Chinese call Heaven, and we God or living Nature, makes no mistake and is always just. This is one of the bed-rock truths that underlie sound science and philosophy. Consider Poland, for example, as it appears in this history. Frederick and the rest who partitioned it were like vultures tearing a carcase ; but Poland had become a nuisance in the world. The Poles were sunk in superstition, persecuting Protestants and prolonging the anarchy of the middle ages, like drunken rowdies who have been making a night of it and want to keep on brawling through the day. What happened was what should have happened,—and the same is true of what has happened since then.

Such glimpses into the causes of things are often possible, and Carlyle is always eager, too eager sometimes, to help us in guessing ; but it must be confessed, and he helps us to see it, that we remain a great deal in the dark. Nature is not so plain as melodrama ! The web of our life is a mingled yarn of good and ill together. It is not by groping among the details of other people's lives, but by cultivating the conscience and making the best of our own, that we can arrive at confidence in Nature and ourselves. The man who lies and sins sinks into more stupidity, and all the learning in the world cannot deliver him,—he can at best become " a bookful blockhead, ignorantly read, with loads of learned lumber in his head."

There is an old saw endorsed by Voltaire,—" The unexpected generally happens." We can foresee a little the movements of the stars ; but only in a much less degree the changes of living Nature, whereof we are a part. Which at least keeps history interesting,—it is never monotonous altogether ; and when we have learned aright to have confidence in Nature, there is something supremely satisfactory in the sight of things as they are. Many a time the Christian or Muslim reader of *Frederick* may feel as if he were reading what had been written by the Recording Angel. While its merit is that it teaches faith in reality, the righteousness of Nature, its method is narrative and not argument. It differs from most of our other good books in only one thing,—it is as true as it can be made, as far superior to common histories as they are to common fictions.

While character as well as rank make Frederick odd, the rest of the royalties are amusing by their commonness and the self-indulgence and swagger that go with their trade. The sight of them makes one thankful to have escaped temptation. In addition all the world and his wife appear to be at home in these lively pages, and undisguised, that is the best of it. Even the " military cattle " had once been men and one is often sorry for them. And look at their camp-followers, " English females of the lowest degree " ! Two of them were seen on the battle-field of Fontenoy, " one of whom was busy slitting the gold lace from a dead officer, when a cannon-ball came whistling, and shore her head away. Upon which, without sound uttered, her neighbour snatched the scissors, and deliberately proceeded." Could Cæsar himself have been more cool ?

Unlike other historians, Carlyle gave women the same place that they have in real life ; and many of the best pages in the history are provided by them, from the females of Fontenoy to the mistresses of royalty and Queens and Empresses.

It is indeed an old, old story that " what devilry soever Kings may do, the peoples have to pay,"—but the peculiarity of the *Frederick* is that we *see* the people paying, namely, many of them suffering and dying in sore affliction, and all in a sense kept poor by " national debts," because they left their politics to be the amusement of a pack of common creatures. We are never allowed to forget the people in this history,—they figure in it more than a Chorus in a play of Æschylus or Sophocles ; and all sorts of spokesmen emerge to enlighten us, from a humble " Thuringian Dominie Sampson," alias Candidatus Linsenbarth, up to Voltaire himself, the uncrowned Pope of Europe.

' Such episodes as that of Voltaire,' wrote Lowell,[6] ' would make the fortune of any other writer. . . . There is nothing superior in imaginative literature. It is delicious in humour, masterly in minute characterisation. We feel as if the principal victim,' meaning Voltaire, ' had been put upon the theatre before us by some perfect mimic. It is in such things that Mr. Carlyle is beyond all rivalry, and that we must go back to Shakespeare for a comparison. . . . The figures of most historians seem like dolls stuffed with bran,

[6] *My Study Windows*, by J. R. Lowell, pp. 99, 179, 190.

whose whole substance runs out through any hole that criticism may tear in them ; but Carlyle's are so real in comparison, that if you prick them, they bleed.'

Voltaire, however, is more than an " episode." He gives the key-note of much in the *Frederick* and many other writings of Carlyle. It should be remembered also that the favourite maxim of Carlyle, that most men are fools, was not only familiar in free-thinking circles in Scotland when he was young, but had been plainly articulated by Voltaire, in the first chapter of his History of the Parliament of Paris. There we may read how ' most of the towns and all the villages of France were in a state of slavery.

' The whole of Europe except the Greek Empire had long been ruled in that way. If it be asked how it was possible that so many people differing in other things agreed to live in that humiliating condition, under sixty or eighty tyrants who had other tyrants under them, and who all together made life in Europe abominable anarchy, I cannot think of any other answer than that *most men are fools* (*imbéciles*), and that it was easy for the successors of the conquerors, Lombards, Vandals, Francs, Huns and Burgundians, being armed and mounted on iron-clad horses and in possession of the castles, to keep under their yoke the unarmed townsmen and countryfolk, who had to work for their living and naturally supposed they were born to be servants.'

The sparkling passages that mirror the life of Voltaire in this history of Frederick reveal him, as if in spite of the author, to be the leading character then alive, the intellectual leader of the age in general, and of Frederick in particular. Perhaps Carlyle himself might never have been able to give us so good a bird's-eye view of European affairs, if Voltaire had not preceded him. Assuredly he benefited in many ways by the work of Voltaire, and the upshot is a permanent addition to the literature of the world. This history of Europe in the seventeen-hundreds, and of Frederick its fighting man and Voltaire its prophet, is likely to be alive and read millenniums hence, as Tacitus and Herodotus are to-day. Books also, like the men that make them, fulfil their fates.

Already Carlyle's writings as a whole have brought English Literature up to the moral level of the wisest anywhere, a level reached centuries ago by many good men, articulated by Jesus Christ himself indeed, but by no means such a literary commonplace among us as it is in the east. That righteousness is the road to liberty and prosperity is as sure as that two and two make four; but some of our best literary critics are not always aware of it. They suppose it a defect in Carlyle that he makes veracity the supreme virtue, and as they say, subordinates æsthetics to ethics. In time men will wonder that anybody ever differed from him about that; and men of sense in every country and creed will agree to a Chinese maxim already millenniums old:

> When you've to do with wrong and right,
> Then *never* think the question slight:
> For what is wrong you're like to do
>   If once you think it small;
> And if what's right seems small to you
>   It won't be done at all.

INDEX

591

2 Q